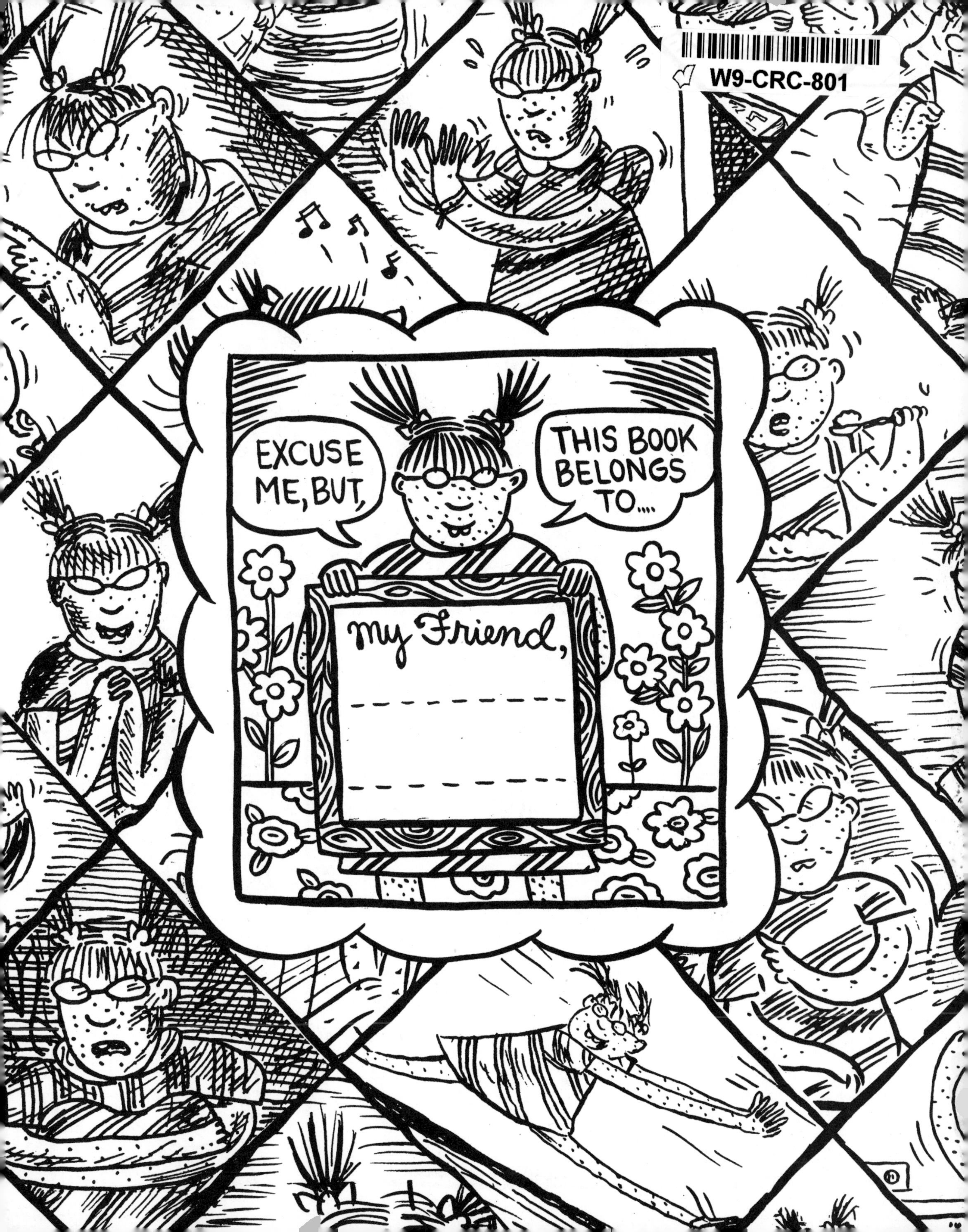
EXCUSE ME, BUT,
THIS BOOK BELONGS TO....
my Friend,

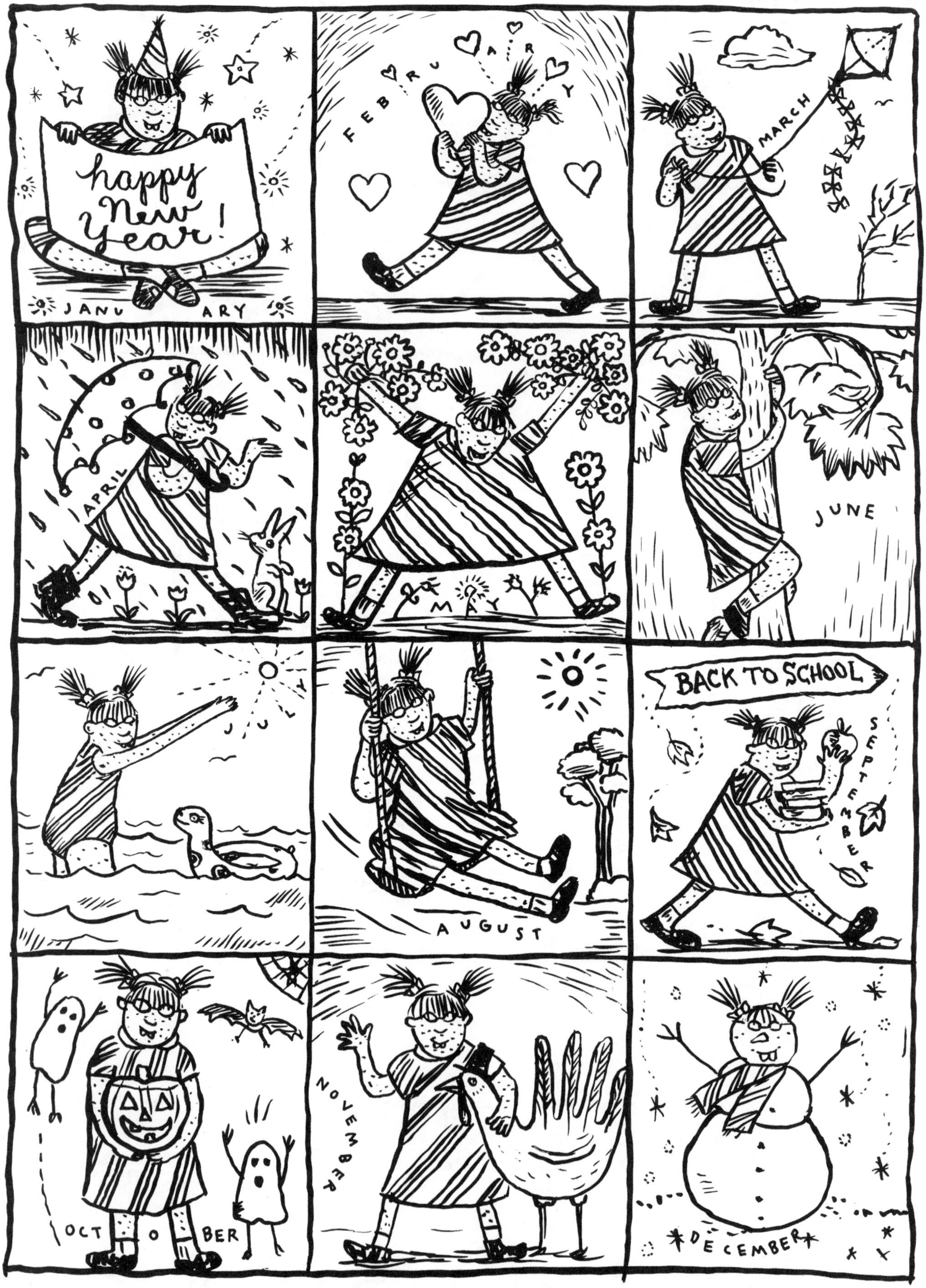

happy New Year!
JANU ARY
FEBRUARY
MARCH
APRIL
MAY
JUNE
JULY
AUGUST
BACK TO SCHOOL
SEPTEMBER
OCT O BER
NOVEMBER
DECEMBER

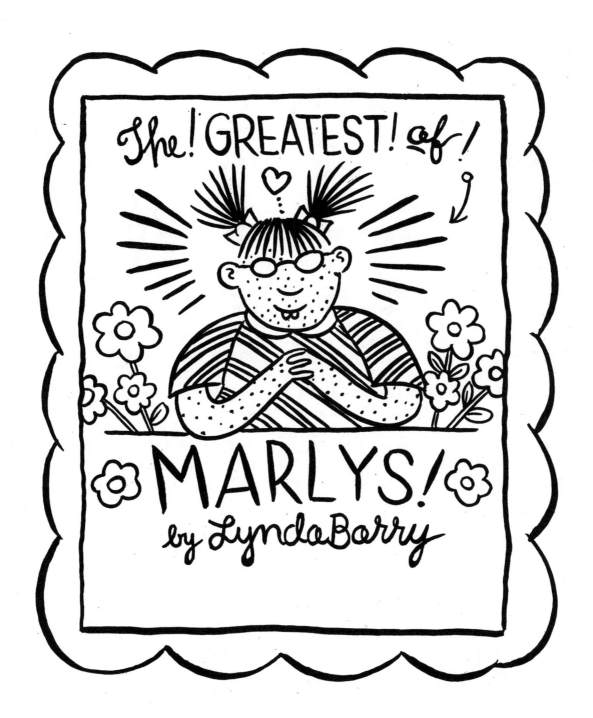

The! GREATEST! of! MARLYS!
by Lynda Barry

SASQUATCH BOOKS
SEATTLE

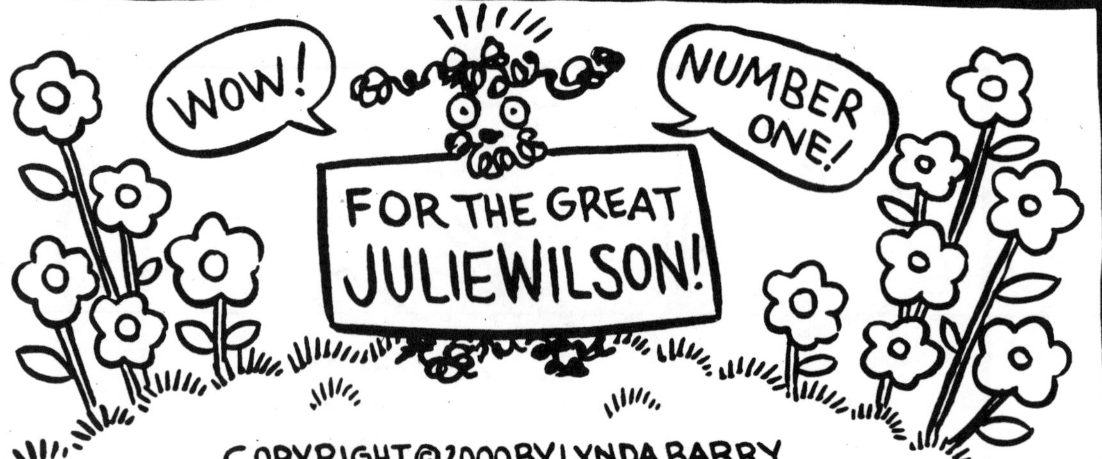
WOW!
FOR THE GREAT JULIEWILSON!
NUMBER ONE!

Printed IN THE UNITED STATES OF AMERICA · DISTRIBUTED IN CANADA BY RAINCOAST BOOKS LTD.

03 02 01 00 5 4 3 2

LIBRARY OF CONGRESS CATALOGING IN PUBLICATION DATA
BARRY, LYNDA 1956- THE! GREATEST! OF! MARLYS! / LYNDA BARRY
P.cm. ISBN 1-570610260-9 I. TITLE. PN6727.B36G742000
741.5973-dc21 99-086069

SASQUATCH BOOKS
615 SECOND AVENUE
SEATTLE, WA 98104
206·467·4300
www.SasquatchBooks.com
books@SasquatchBooks.com

Special Thanks to
GARY LUKE, KATE BASART, LIZ DARHANSOFF, KEVIN KAWULA, MIKE "SCROUNGE" ROCHELEAU AND ESPECIALLY Fred Milton!

AND IN MEMORY OF
Ario Ieoli ♡

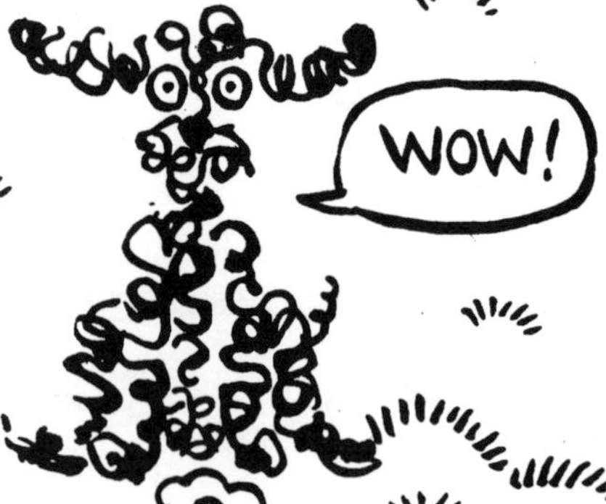
WOW!

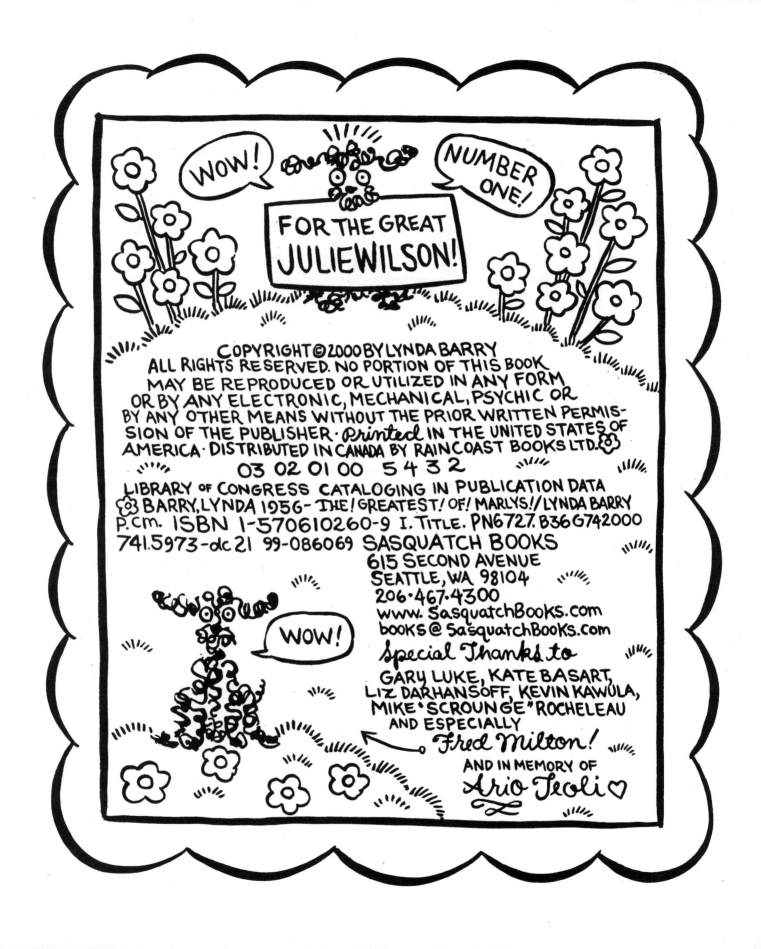

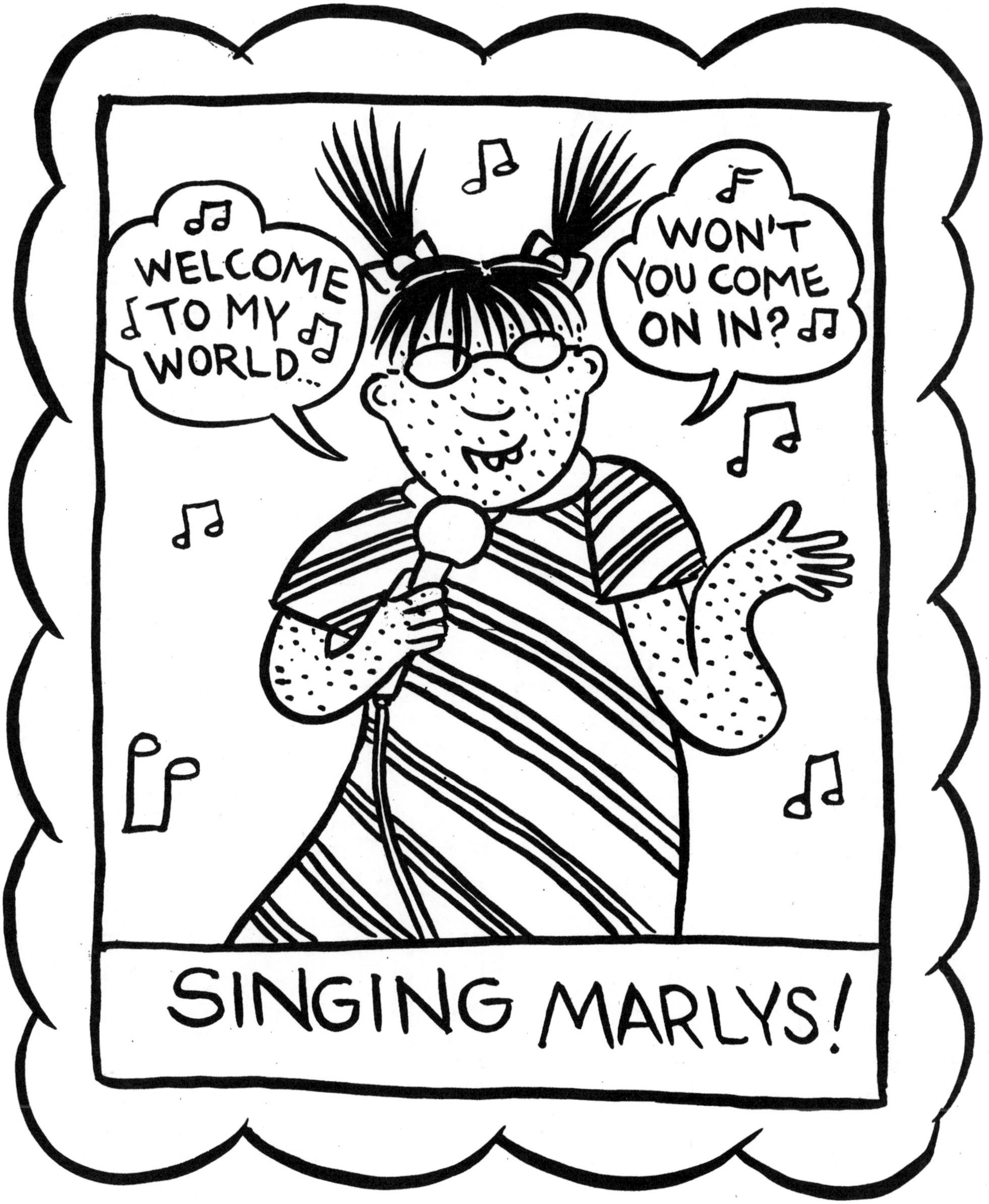
WELCOME TO MY WORLD...
WON'T YOU COME ON IN?
SINGING MARLYS!

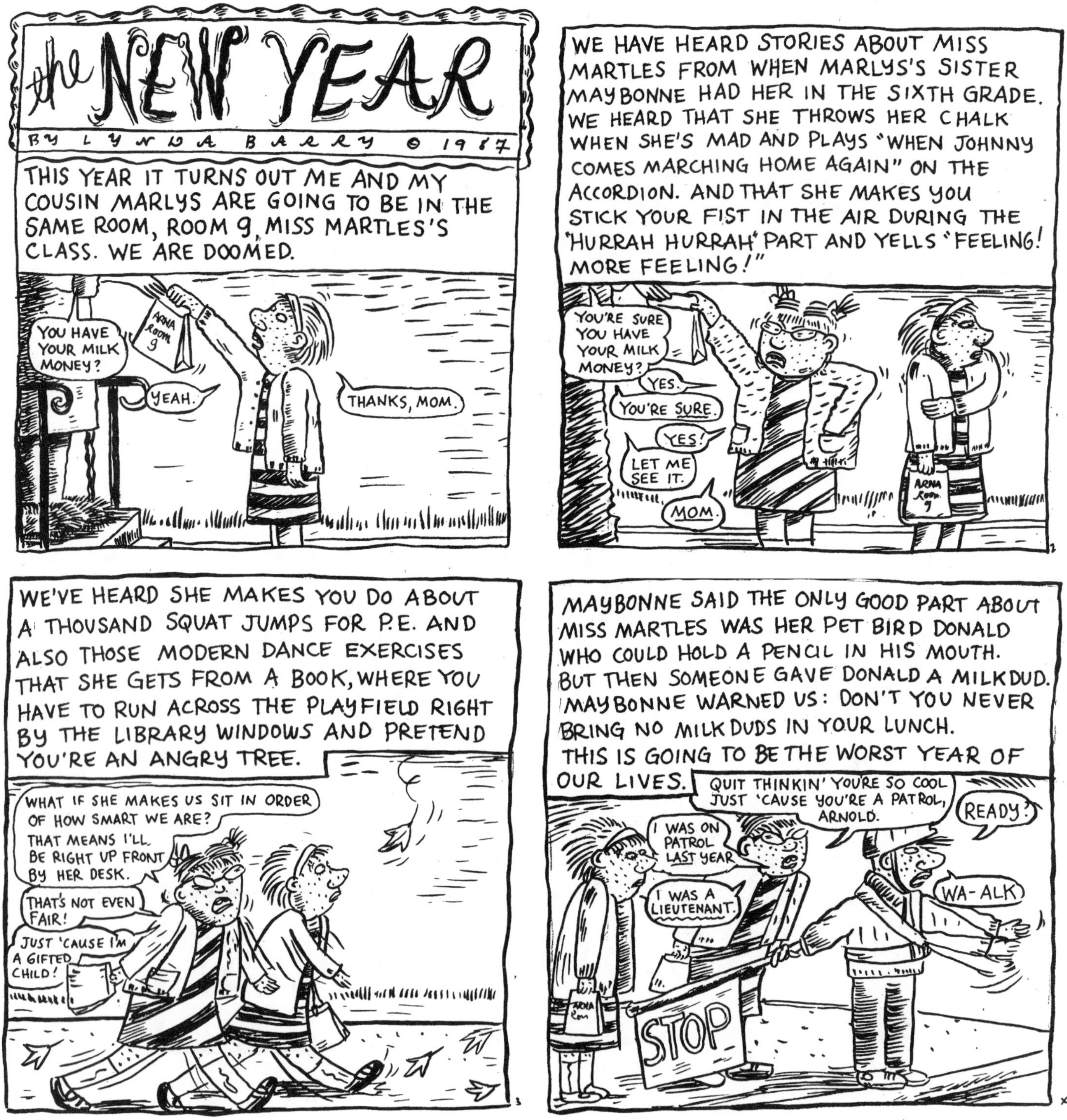
the NEW YEAR
BY LYNDA BARRY © 1987
THIS YEAR IT TURNS OUT ME AND MY COUSIN MARLYS ARE GOING TO BE IN THE SAME ROOM, ROOM 9, MISS MARTLES'S CLASS. WE ARE DOOMED.
YOU HAVE YOUR MILK MONEY?
ARNA ROOM 9
YEAH.
THANKS, MOM.
WE HAVE HEARD STORIES ABOUT MISS MARTLES FROM WHEN MARLYS'S SISTER MAYBONNE HAD HER IN THE SIXTH GRADE. WE HEARD THAT SHE THROWS HER CHALK WHEN SHE'S MAD AND PLAYS "WHEN JOHNNY COMES MARCHING HOME AGAIN" ON THE ACCORDION. AND THAT SHE MAKES YOU STICK YOUR FIST IN THE AIR DURING THE "HURRAH HURRAH" PART AND YELLS "FEELING! MORE FEELING!"
YOU'RE SURE YOU HAVE YOUR MILK MONEY?
YES.
YOU'RE SURE.
YES!
LET ME SEE IT.
MOM.
ARNA ROOM 9
WE'VE HEARD SHE MAKES YOU DO ABOUT A THOUSAND SQUAT JUMPS FOR P.E. AND ALSO THOSE MODERN DANCE EXERCISES THAT SHE GETS FROM A BOOK, WHERE YOU HAVE TO RUN ACROSS THE PLAYFIELD RIGHT BY THE LIBRARY WINDOWS AND PRETEND YOU'RE AN ANGRY TREE.
WHAT IF SHE MAKES US SIT IN ORDER OF HOW SMART WE ARE?
THAT MEANS I'LL BE RIGHT UP FRONT BY HER DESK.
THAT'S NOT EVEN FAIR!
JUST 'CAUSE I'M A GIFTED CHILD!
MAYBONNE SAID THE ONLY GOOD PART ABOUT MISS MARTLES WAS HER PET BIRD DONALD WHO COULD HOLD A PENCIL IN HIS MOUTH. BUT THEN SOMEONE GAVE DONALD A MILKDUD. MAYBONNE WARNED US: DON'T YOU NEVER BRING NO MILK DUDS IN YOUR LUNCH. THIS IS GOING TO BE THE WORST YEAR OF OUR LIVES.
QUIT THINKIN' YOU'RE SO COOL JUST 'CAUSE YOU'RE A PATROL, ARNOLD.
READY?
I WAS ON PATROL LAST YEAR.
I WAS A LIEUTENANT.
WA-ALK
STOP

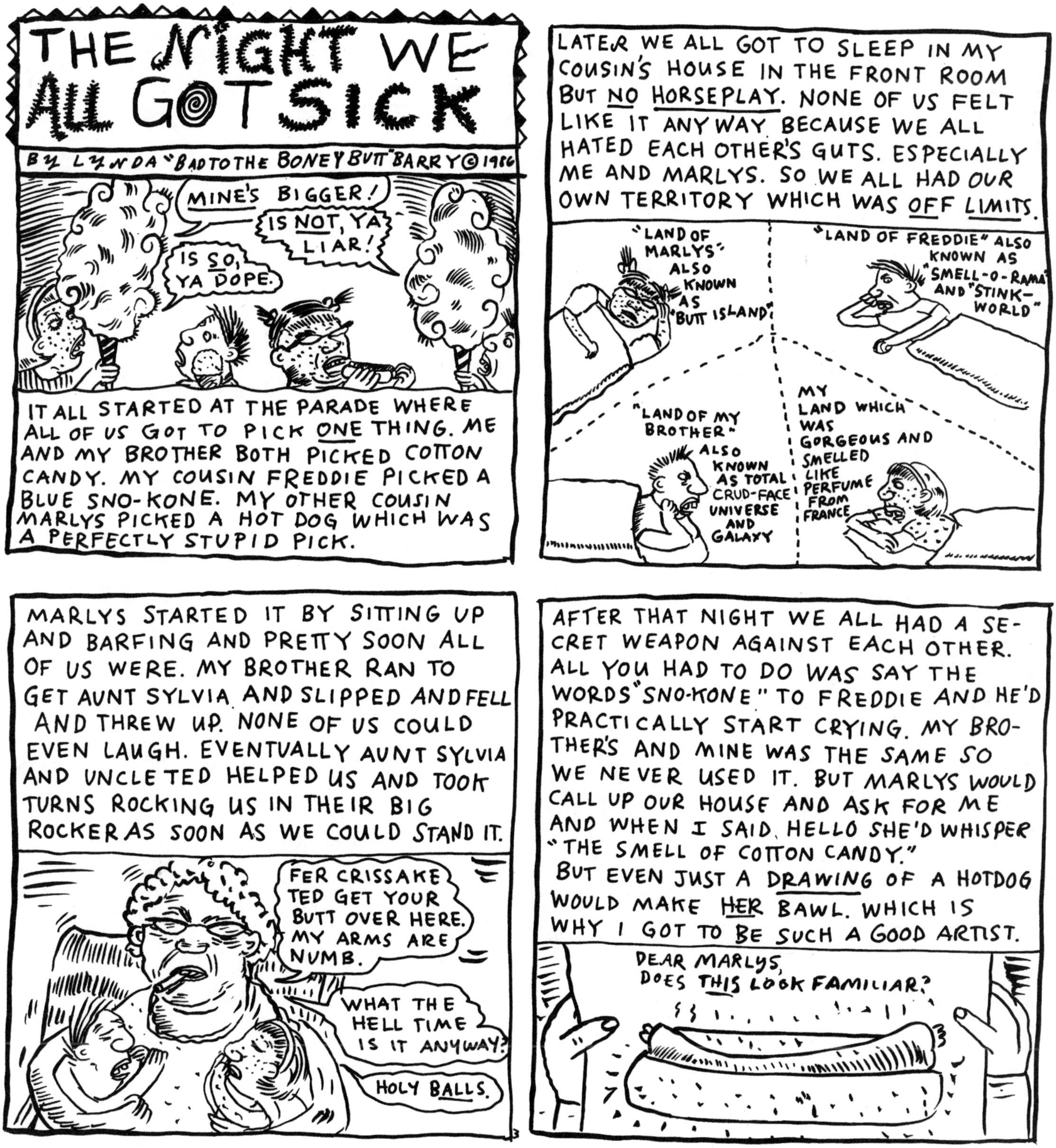
THE NIGHT WE ALL GOT SICK
BY LYNDA "BAD TO THE BONEY BUTT" BARRY © 1986
MINE'S BIGGER!
IS NOT, YA LIAR!
IS SO, YA DOPE.
IT ALL STARTED AT THE PARADE WHERE ALL OF US GOT TO PICK ONE THING. ME AND MY BROTHER BOTH PICKED COTTON CANDY. MY COUSIN FREDDIE PICKED A BLUE SNO-KONE. MY OTHER COUSIN MARLYS PICKED A HOT DOG WHICH WAS A PERFECTLY STUPID PICK.
LATER WE ALL GOT TO SLEEP IN MY COUSIN'S HOUSE IN THE FRONT ROOM BUT NO HORSEPLAY. NONE OF US FELT LIKE IT ANYWAY BECAUSE WE ALL HATED EACH OTHER'S GUTS. ESPECIALLY ME AND MARLYS. SO WE ALL HAD OUR OWN TERRITORY WHICH WAS OFF LIMITS.
"LAND OF MARLYS" ALSO KNOWN AS "BUTT ISLAND"
"LAND OF FREDDIE" ALSO KNOWN AS "SMELL-O-RAMA" AND "STINK-WORLD"
"LAND OF MY BROTHER" ALSO KNOWN AS TOTAL CRUD-FACE UNIVERSE AND GALAXY
MY LAND WHICH WAS GORGEOUS AND SMELLED LIKE PERFUME FROM FRANCE
MARLYS STARTED IT BY SITTING UP AND BARFING AND PRETTY SOON ALL OF US WERE. MY BROTHER RAN TO GET AUNT SYLVIA AND SLIPPED AND FELL AND THREW UP. NONE OF US COULD EVEN LAUGH. EVENTUALLY AUNT SYLVIA AND UNCLE TED HELPED US AND TOOK TURNS ROCKING US IN THEIR BIG ROCKER AS SOON AS WE COULD STAND IT.
FER CRISSAKE TED GET YOUR BUTT OVER HERE. MY ARMS ARE NUMB.
WHAT THE HELL TIME IS IT ANYWAY?
HOLY BALLS.
AFTER THAT NIGHT WE ALL HAD A SECRET WEAPON AGAINST EACH OTHER. ALL YOU HAD TO DO WAS SAY THE WORDS "SNO-KONE" TO FREDDIE AND HE'D PRACTICALLY START CRYING. MY BROTHER'S AND MINE WAS THE SAME SO WE NEVER USED IT. BUT MARLYS WOULD CALL UP OUR HOUSE AND ASK FOR ME AND WHEN I SAID HELLO SHE'D WHISPER "THE SMELL OF COTTON CANDY."
BUT EVEN JUST A DRAWING OF A HOTDOG WOULD MAKE HER BAWL. WHICH IS WHY I GOT TO BE SUCH A GOOD ARTIST.
DEAR MARLYS, DOES THIS LOOK FAMILIAR?
3

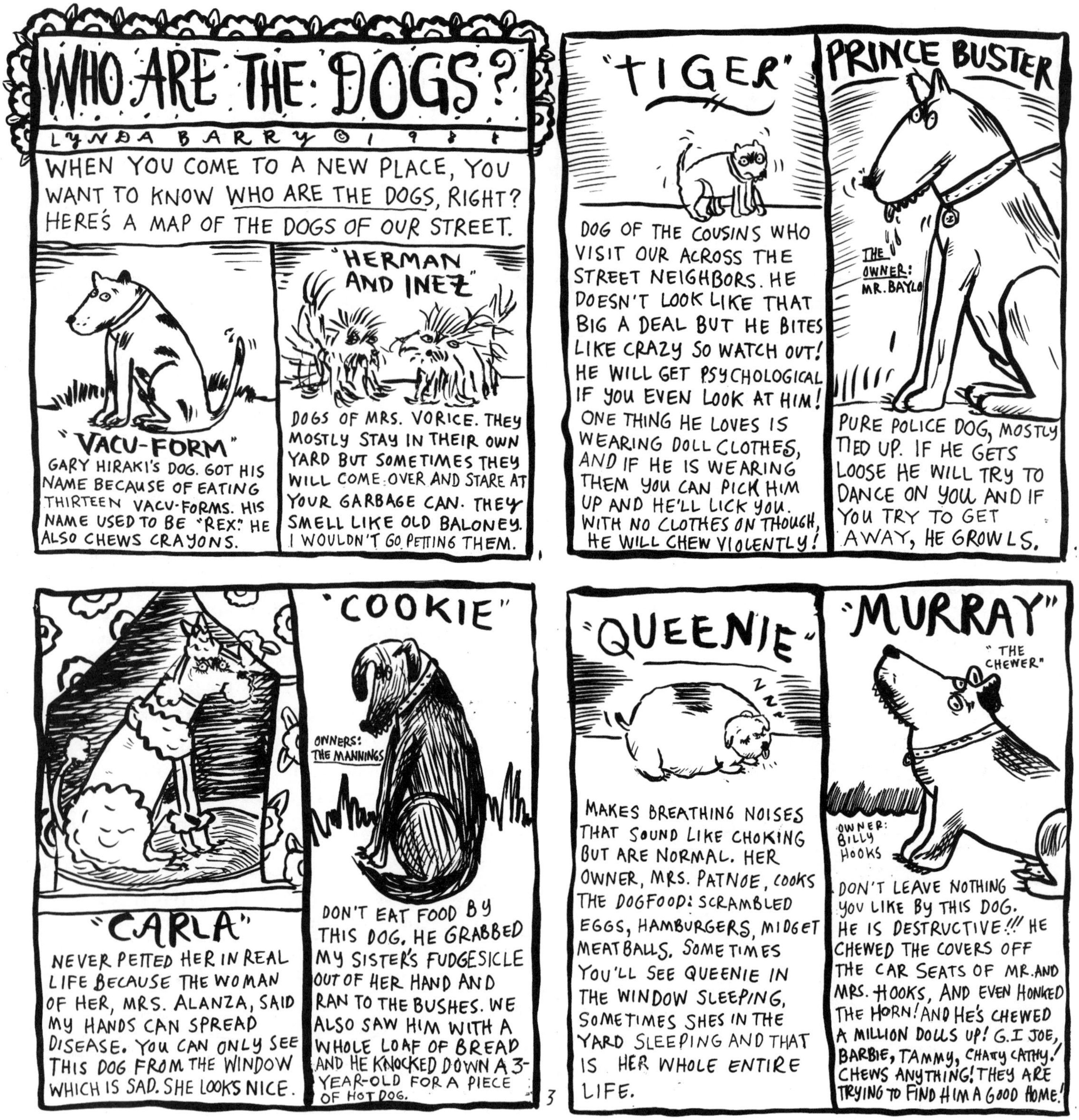
WHO ARE THE DOGS?
LYNDA BARRY ©1988
WHEN YOU COME TO A NEW PLACE, YOU WANT TO KNOW WHO ARE THE DOGS, RIGHT? HERE'S A MAP OF THE DOGS OF OUR STREET.
"VACU-FORM"
GARY HIRAKI'S DOG. GOT HIS NAME BECAUSE OF EATING THIRTEEN VACU-FORMS. HIS NAME USED TO BE "REX." HE ALSO CHEWS CRAYONS.
"HERMAN AND INEZ"
DOGS OF MRS. VORICE. THEY MOSTLY STAY IN THEIR OWN YARD BUT SOMETIMES THEY WILL COME OVER AND STARE AT YOUR GARBAGE CAN. THEY SMELL LIKE OLD BALONEY. I WOULDN'T GO PETTING THEM.
"TIGER"
DOG OF THE COUSINS WHO VISIT OUR ACROSS THE STREET NEIGHBORS. HE DOESN'T LOOK LIKE THAT BIG A DEAL BUT HE BITES LIKE CRAZY SO WATCH OUT! HE WILL GET PSYCHOLOGICAL IF YOU EVEN LOOK AT HIM! ONE THING HE LOVES IS WEARING DOLL CLOTHES, AND IF HE IS WEARING THEM YOU CAN PICK HIM UP AND HE'LL LICK YOU. WITH NO CLOTHES ON THOUGH, HE WILL CHEW VIOLENTLY!
PRINCE BUSTER
THE OWNER: MR. BAYLO
PURE POLICE DOG, MOSTLY TIED UP. IF HE GETS LOOSE HE WILL TRY TO DANCE ON YOU AND IF YOU TRY TO GET AWAY, HE GROWLS.
"CARLA"
NEVER PETTED HER IN REAL LIFE BECAUSE THE WOMAN OF HER, MRS. ALANZA, SAID MY HANDS CAN SPREAD DISEASE. YOU CAN ONLY SEE THIS DOG FROM THE WINDOW WHICH IS SAD. SHE LOOKS NICE.
"COOKIE"
OWNERS: THE MANNINGS
DON'T EAT FOOD BY THIS DOG. HE GRABBED MY SISTER'S FUDGESICLE OUT OF HER HAND AND RAN TO THE BUSHES. WE ALSO SAW HIM WITH A WHOLE LOAF OF BREAD AND HE KNOCKED DOWN A 3-YEAR-OLD FOR A PIECE OF HOT DOG.
"QUEENIE"
Z Z
MAKES BREATHING NOISES THAT SOUND LIKE CHOKING BUT ARE NORMAL. HER OWNER, MRS. PATNOE, COOKS THE DOGFOOD: SCRAMBLED EGGS, HAMBURGERS, MIDGET MEATBALLS. SOMETIMES YOU'LL SEE QUEENIE IN THE WINDOW SLEEPING, SOMETIMES SHES IN THE YARD SLEEPING AND THAT IS HER WHOLE ENTIRE LIFE.
"MURRAY"
"THE CHEWER"
OWNER: BILLY HOOKS
DON'T LEAVE NOTHING YOU LIKE BY THIS DOG. HE IS DESTRUCTIVE!!! HE CHEWED THE COVERS OFF THE CAR SEATS OF MR. AND MRS. HOOKS, AND EVEN HONKED THE HORN! AND HE'S CHEWED A MILLION DOLLS UP! G.I. JOE, BARBIE, TAMMY, CHATTY CATHY! CHEWS ANYTHING! THEY ARE TRYING TO FIND HIM A GOOD HOME!

Fine Dining

BY chef LYNDA LA BARREE © 1 9 8 6

ALTHOUGH HARDLY ANYBODY HAD EVER GONE TO A GREAT RESTAURANT, ALL OF US HAD OPINIONS ON WHAT WAS A EXCELLENT MEAL. FOR MY BROTHER IT WAS 2 CHICKEN POT PIES WITH COLD SPAGHETTI-O'S RIGHT OUT OF THE CAN. I PREFERRED THE DELICATE TASTE OF FRIED BALONEY AND MAYONAISE ON SUNBEAM BREAD.

LEAVE IT IN THE CAN PLEASE

MILK GLASS MUST HAVE HANDLE

ETTI-O'S

INITIALS CARVED ON PIE

SOLE UTENSIL

T.V. TRAY: "A MUST"

FRY BALONEY UNTIL IT HUMPS UP. BURN EDGES. HIDE FRYING PAN UNDER BED SO MOM WON'T CREAM YOU FOR THE BLACK MARKS THAT YOU CAN'T SCRUB OUT.

AT EVERYONE'S HOUSE THEIR FAMILY ATE AT LEAST ONE THING THAT WAS SCARY.

DEENA'S — MUSTARD AND ONION AND RELISH SANDWICHES

THE TWINS — JELLY ON SPAGHETTI

OUR HOUSE — "DINOU-GOUAAN" (A.K.A. "MIDNIGHT MEAT" and "BLACK OUT")

MARLYS — "BAGOUNG" (SCARY PINK FISH CONDIMENT THAT THE SMELL WOULD MAKE YOU START RUNNING)

WALTER'S — SARDINES AND COOL WHIP (HE ATE THIS FOR SHOW OFF ONLY)

DICKY'S — FRIED PIG GUTS

2

OUR MAIN OPINIONS, HOWEVER, REGARDED THE WORLD OF DESSERTS. FOR EXAMPLE EVERYONE AGREED ANYTHING TASTED THE BEST WHEN YOU ATE IT IN YOUR CLASSROOM DURING A HALLOWEEN OR VALENTINES PARTY. EVEN THE WORST KOOL-AID WAS SIMPLY DELICIOUS IF IT WAS IN A PAPER CUP ON YOUR DESK WITH A CUPCAKE. (ESPECIALLY IF THE CUPCAKE WAS IN A BLUE PAPER HOLDER. THE WORST CUPCAKE HOLDER WAS THE YELLOW.) (YELLOW WAS ALWAYS BAD DUE TO P.)

REGARDING CANDY NATURALLY EVERYONE HAD ONE FAVORITE. BUT THERE WERE TWO THINGS WE ALL AGREED ON.

① CHUNKYS WERE A TOTAL RIP OFF

② THE WORST CANDY KNOWN TO THE ENTIRE UNIVERSE IS THOSE ORANGE MARSHMALLOW "PEANUTS" ESPECIALLY WHEN THEY HAVE BEEN SITTING IN A BOWL SO LONG THEY HAVE DUST ON THEM BUT YOUR MOM FORCES YOU TO EAT IT BECAUSE IT WAS A OLD PERSON WHO GAVE IT TO YOU.

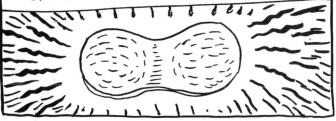

4

THE CARNIVAL
BY LYNDA SWANGTHANG BARRY ©1986
WE DECIDED TO HAVE A CARNIVAL SHOW AND WE DECIDED TO HAVE IT ON A DAY WHEN NO ONE'S PARENTS WOULD BE ANYWHERE EXCEPT AT WORK. OUR MAIN ATTRACTION WAS GOING TO BE: "THINGS LIGHTED ON FIRE." OUR MAIN PROBLEM WAS GOING TO BE: "MARLYS TELLING".
YOU THINK YOU'RE SO BIG.
YOU'RE NOT THE BOSS OF US MARLYS.
I'M GONNA WRITE DOWN EVERYTHING YOU DO.
WHY DON'T YOU GO BACK INSIDE AND WATCH YOURSELF IN THE MIRROR SOME MORE?
THEN I'M GOING TO HAVE YOU PUT IN JAIL.
1
MY SISTER AND DEENA WERE GOING TO DO A SPECIAL TUMBLING SHOW TO THE SONG "LOVE IS BLUE." TO GET THE MUSIC THEY HAD TO PUT IT ON FULL BLAST AND PUSH THE RECORD PLAYER OVER BY THE WINDOW. MARLYS WAS GOING TO TELL ON THEM FOR THAT TOO.
CAN YOU HEAR IT GOOD?!
LOUDER!
IT CAN'T GO NO LOUDER!
PUSH IT MORE BY THE WINDOW!
THERE'S NO MORE PLUG!
YOUR MOM SAID NEVER TOUCH HER RECORD PLAYER BUT YOU HAD TO DO IT, DIDN'T YOU?
I'M WRITING YOU A TICKET.
2
MARLYS WAS MAKING A HARD TIME FOR EVERYBODY TO THINK UP THINGS TO DO BECAUSE NO MATTER WHAT YOU THOUGHT OF, SHE SAID SHE'D TELL ON YOU FOR IT. AND SHE WOULD TOO. FINALLY SOMEONE HAD THE GENIUS TO ASK MARLYS TO BE THE STAR OF THE SHOW.
YEAH MARLYS! YOU CAN BE THE MAIN QUEEN!
YOU CAN HOLD THE MATCHES!
YOU CAN ANNOUNCE EVERYBODY!
YOU CAN WEAR MY MAMA'S HIGH HEELS!
WE'LL EVEN LISTEN TO YOU SINGING!
COME ON MARLYS!
YEAH! COME ON MARLYS!
3
FOR ABOUT ONE SECOND MARLYS STOOD THERE LOOKING AT US LIKE SHE NEVER EVEN MET US BEFORE. THEN SHE WENT OUT OF HER MIND AND YELLED "I HATE YOU, I HATE YOU ALL" ABOUT 600 TIMES UNTIL SHE WAS PRACTICALLY DROOLING. IT SCARED US AND DEENA AND MY SISTER STARTED CRYING ALONG WITH MARLYS WHO WOULDN'T EVEN LET US COME NEAR HER. AFTER THAT WE REALIZED IT WAS A LOT BETTER FOR MARLYS IF YOU JUST KEPT TREATING HER LIKE YOU HATED HER GUTS.
X

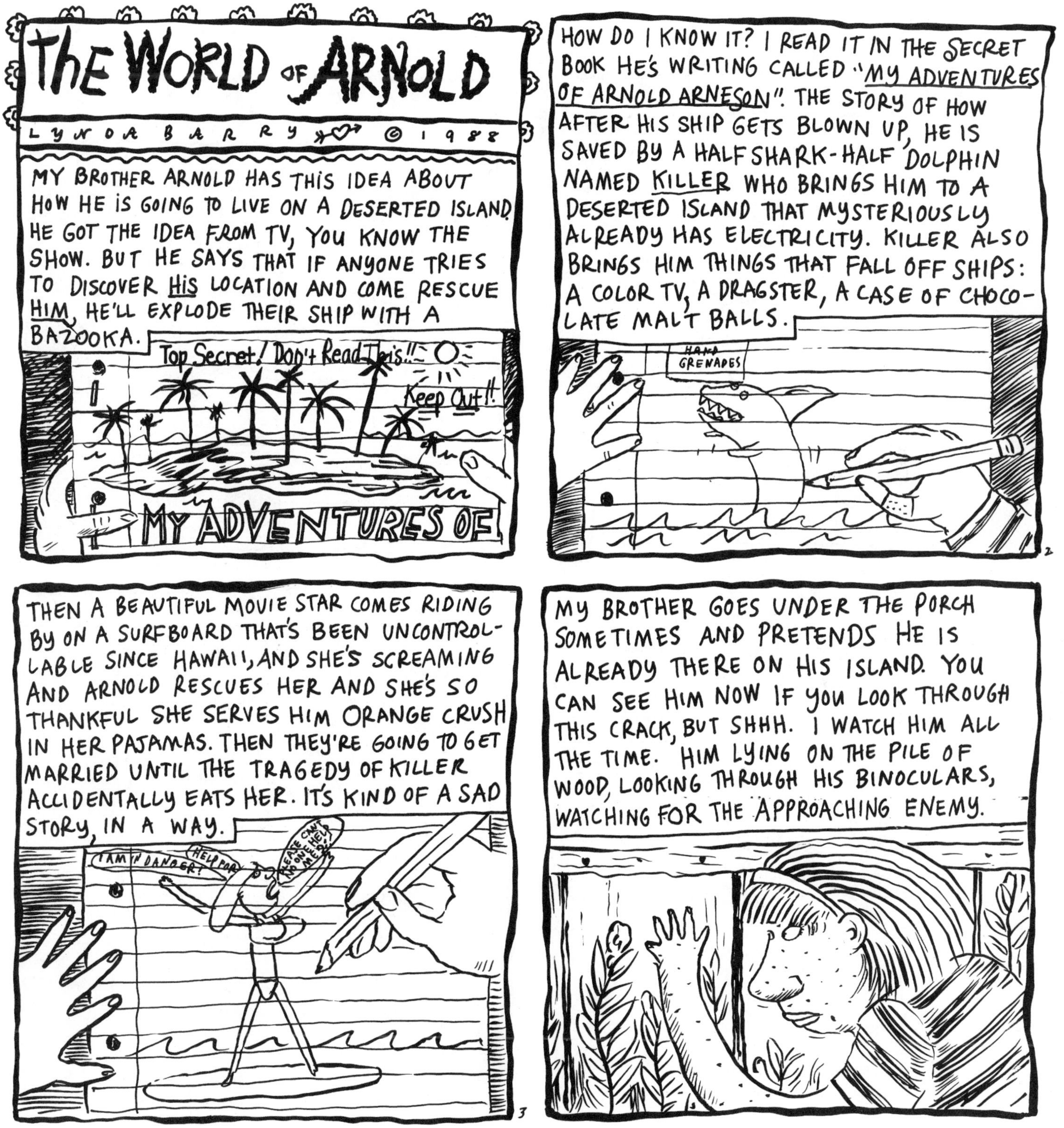
THE WORLD OF ARNOLD
LYNDA BARRY © 1988
MY BROTHER ARNOLD HAS THIS IDEA ABOUT HOW HE IS GOING TO LIVE ON A DESERTED ISLAND. HE GOT THE IDEA FROM TV, YOU KNOW THE SHOW. BUT HE SAYS THAT IF ANYONE TRIES TO DISCOVER HIS LOCATION AND COME RESCUE HIM, HE'LL EXPLODE THEIR SHIP WITH A BAZOOKA.
Top Secret! Don't Read This!!
Keep Out!!
MY ADVENTURES OF
HOW DO I KNOW IT? I READ IT IN THE SECRET BOOK HE'S WRITING CALLED "MY ADVENTURES OF ARNOLD ARNESON". THE STORY OF HOW AFTER HIS SHIP GETS BLOWN UP, HE IS SAVED BY A HALF SHARK-HALF DOLPHIN NAMED KILLER WHO BRINGS HIM TO A DESERTED ISLAND THAT MYSTERIOUSLY ALREADY HAS ELECTRICITY. KILLER ALSO BRINGS HIM THINGS THAT FALL OFF SHIPS: A COLOR TV, A DRAGSTER, A CASE OF CHOCOLATE MALT BALLS.
HAND GRENADES
THEN A BEAUTIFUL MOVIE STAR COMES RIDING BY ON A SURFBOARD THAT'S BEEN UNCONTROLLABLE SINCE HAWAII, AND SHE'S SCREAMING AND ARNOLD RESCUES HER AND SHE'S SO THANKFUL SHE SERVES HIM ORANGE CRUSH IN HER PAJAMAS. THEN THEY'RE GOING TO GET MARRIED UNTIL THE TRAGEDY OF KILLER ACCIDENTALLY EATS HER. IT'S KIND OF A SAD STORY, IN A WAY.
I AM IN DANGER!
HELP POR
PLEASE CAN'T NO ONE HELP ME?
MY BROTHER GOES UNDER THE PORCH SOMETIMES AND PRETENDS HE IS ALREADY THERE ON HIS ISLAND. YOU CAN SEE HIM NOW IF YOU LOOK THROUGH THIS CRACK, BUT SHHH. I WATCH HIM ALL THE TIME. HIM LYING ON THE PILE OF WOOD, LOOKING THROUGH HIS BINOCULARS, WATCHING FOR THE APPROACHING ENEMY.

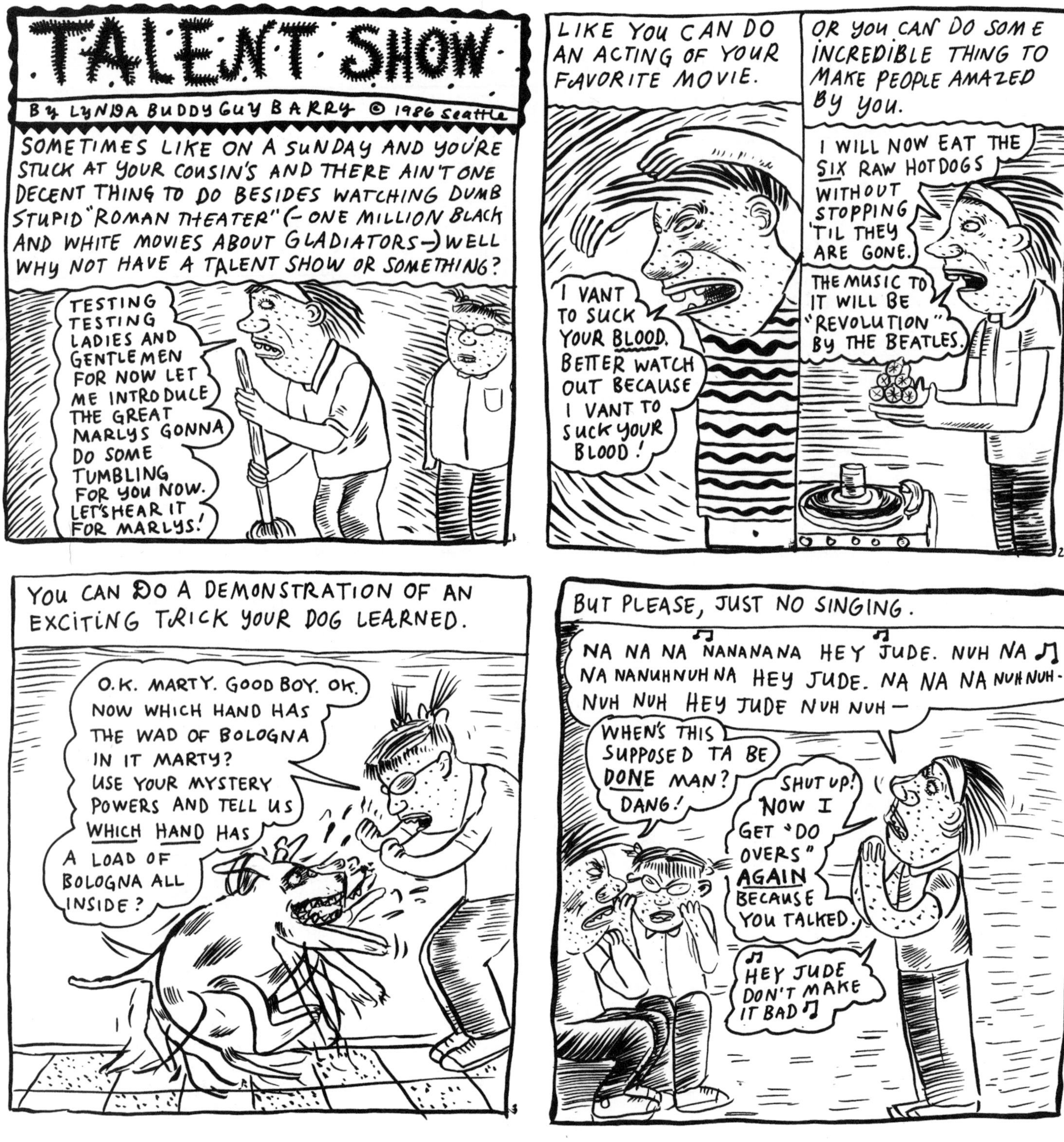
TALENT SHOW
BY LYNDA BUDDY GUY BARRY © 1986 SEATTLE
SOMETIMES LIKE ON A SUNDAY AND YOU'RE STUCK AT YOUR COUSIN'S AND THERE AIN'T ONE DECENT THING TO DO BESIDES WATCHING DUMB STUPID "ROMAN THEATER" (- ONE MILLION BLACK AND WHITE MOVIES ABOUT GLADIATORS -) WELL WHY NOT HAVE A TALENT SHOW OR SOMETHING?
TESTING TESTING LADIES AND GENTLEMEN FOR NOW LET ME INTRODUCE THE GREAT MARLYS GONNA DO SOME TUMBLING FOR YOU NOW. LET'S HEAR IT FOR MARLYS!
LIKE YOU CAN DO AN ACTING OF YOUR FAVORITE MOVIE.
I VANT TO SUCK YOUR BLOOD. BETTER WATCH OUT BECAUSE I VANT TO SUCK YOUR BLOOD!
OR YOU CAN DO SOME INCREDIBLE THING TO MAKE PEOPLE AMAZED BY YOU.
I WILL NOW EAT THE SIX RAW HOT DOGS WITHOUT STOPPING 'TIL THEY ARE GONE.
THE MUSIC TO IT WILL BE "REVOLUTION" BY THE BEATLES.
YOU CAN DO A DEMONSTRATION OF AN EXCITING TRICK YOUR DOG LEARNED.
O.K. MARTY. GOOD BOY. OK. NOW WHICH HAND HAS THE WAD OF BOLOGNA IN IT MARTY? USE YOUR MYSTERY POWERS AND TELL US WHICH HAND HAS A LOAD OF BOLOGNA ALL INSIDE?
BUT PLEASE, JUST NO SINGING.
NA NA NA NANANANA HEY JUDE. NUH NA NA NANUHNUHNA HEY JUDE. NA NA NA NUHNUH-NUH NUH HEY JUDE NUH NUH —
WHEN'S THIS SUPPOSED TA BE DONE MAN? DANG!
SHUT UP! NOW I GET "DO OVERS" AGAIN BECAUSE YOU TALKED.
HEY JUDE DON'T MAKE IT BAD

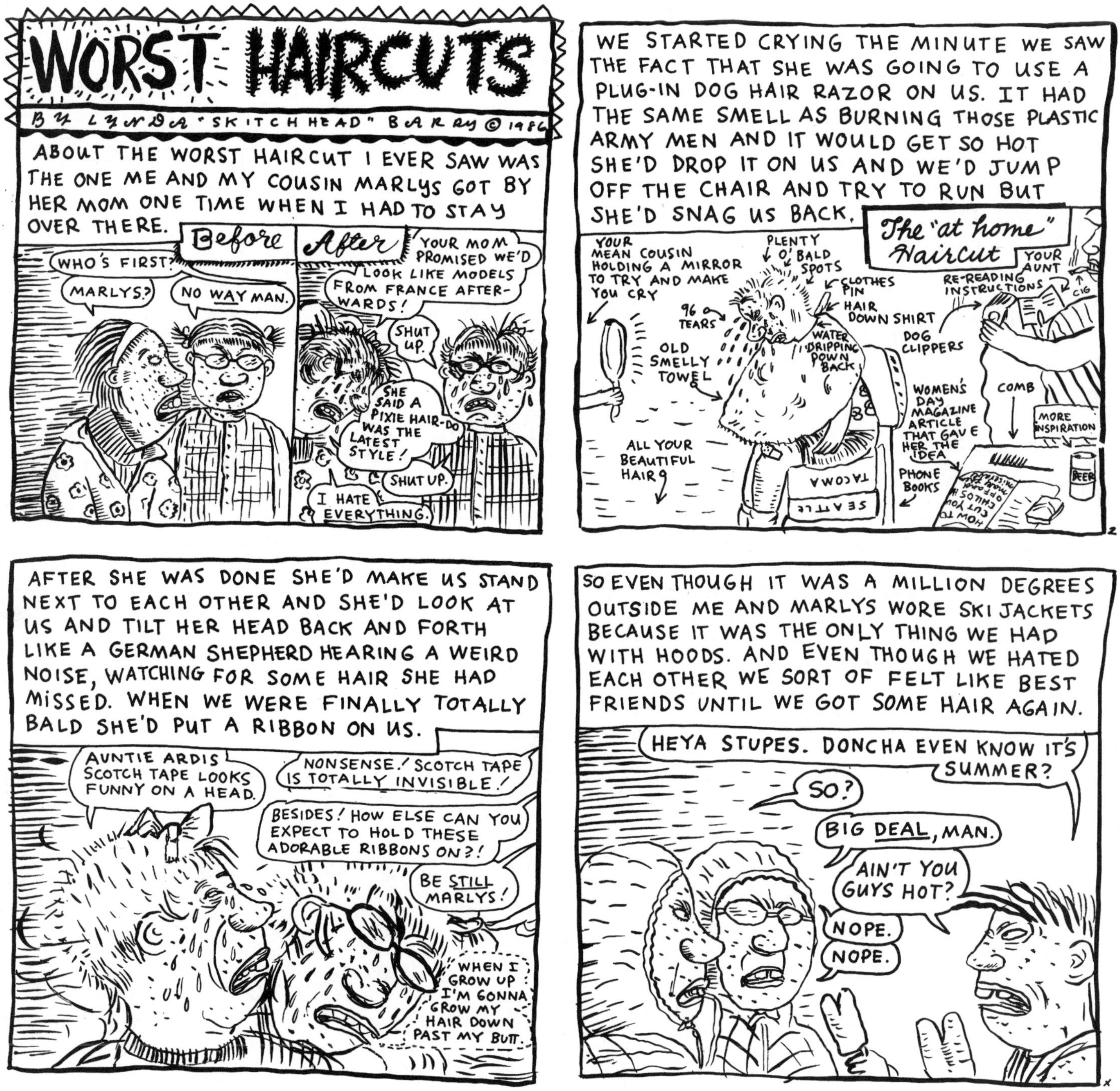
WORST HAIRCUTS
BY LYNDA "SKITCHHEAD" BARRY © 1986
ABOUT THE WORST HAIRCUT I EVER SAW WAS THE ONE ME AND MY COUSIN MARLYS GOT BY HER MOM ONE TIME WHEN I HAD TO STAY OVER THERE.
Before
WHO'S FIRST?
MARLYS?
NO WAY MAN.
After
YOUR MOM PROMISED WE'D LOOK LIKE MODELS FROM FRANCE AFTERWARDS!
SHUT UP.
SHE SAID A PIXIE HAIR-DO WAS THE LATEST STYLE!
SHUT UP.
I HATE EVERYTHING.
WE STARTED CRYING THE MINUTE WE SAW THE FACT THAT SHE WAS GOING TO USE A PLUG-IN DOG HAIR RAZOR ON US. IT HAD THE SAME SMELL AS BURNING THOSE PLASTIC ARMY MEN AND IT WOULD GET SO HOT SHE'D DROP IT ON US AND WE'D JUMP OFF THE CHAIR AND TRY TO RUN BUT SHE'D SNAG US BACK.
The "at home" Haircut
YOUR MEAN COUSIN HOLDING A MIRROR TO TRY AND MAKE YOU CRY
PLENTY O' BALD SPOTS
CLOTHES PIN
HAIR DOWN SHIRT
YOUR AUNT RE-READING INSTRUCTIONS
CIG
96 TEARS
WATER DRIPPING DOWN BACK
DOG CLIPPERS
OLD SMELLY TOWEL
WOMEN'S DAY MAGAZINE ARTICLE THAT GAVE HER THE IDEA
COMB
MORE INSPIRATION
BEER
ALL YOUR BEAUTIFUL HAIR
TACOMA
SEATTLE
PHONE BOOKS
HOW TO CUT YOUR CHILD'S HAIR
AFTER SHE WAS DONE SHE'D MAKE US STAND NEXT TO EACH OTHER AND SHE'D LOOK AT US AND TILT HER HEAD BACK AND FORTH LIKE A GERMAN SHEPHERD HEARING A WEIRD NOISE, WATCHING FOR SOME HAIR SHE HAD MISSED. WHEN WE WERE FINALLY TOTALLY BALD SHE'D PUT A RIBBON ON US.
AUNTIE ARDIS SCOTCH TAPE LOOKS FUNNY ON A HEAD.
NONSENSE! SCOTCH TAPE IS TOTALLY INVISIBLE!
BESIDES! HOW ELSE CAN YOU EXPECT TO HOLD THESE ADORABLE RIBBONS ON?!
BE STILL MARLYS!
WHEN I GROW UP I'M GONNA GROW MY HAIR DOWN PAST MY BUTT.
SO EVEN THOUGH IT WAS A MILLION DEGREES OUTSIDE ME AND MARLYS WORE SKI JACKETS BECAUSE IT WAS THE ONLY THING WE HAD WITH HOODS. AND EVEN THOUGH WE HATED EACH OTHER WE SORT OF FELT LIKE BEST FRIENDS UNTIL WE GOT SOME HAIR AGAIN.
HEYA STUPES. DONCHA EVEN KNOW IT'S SUMMER?
SO?
BIG DEAL, MAN.
AIN'T YOU GUYS HOT?
NOPE.
NOPE.

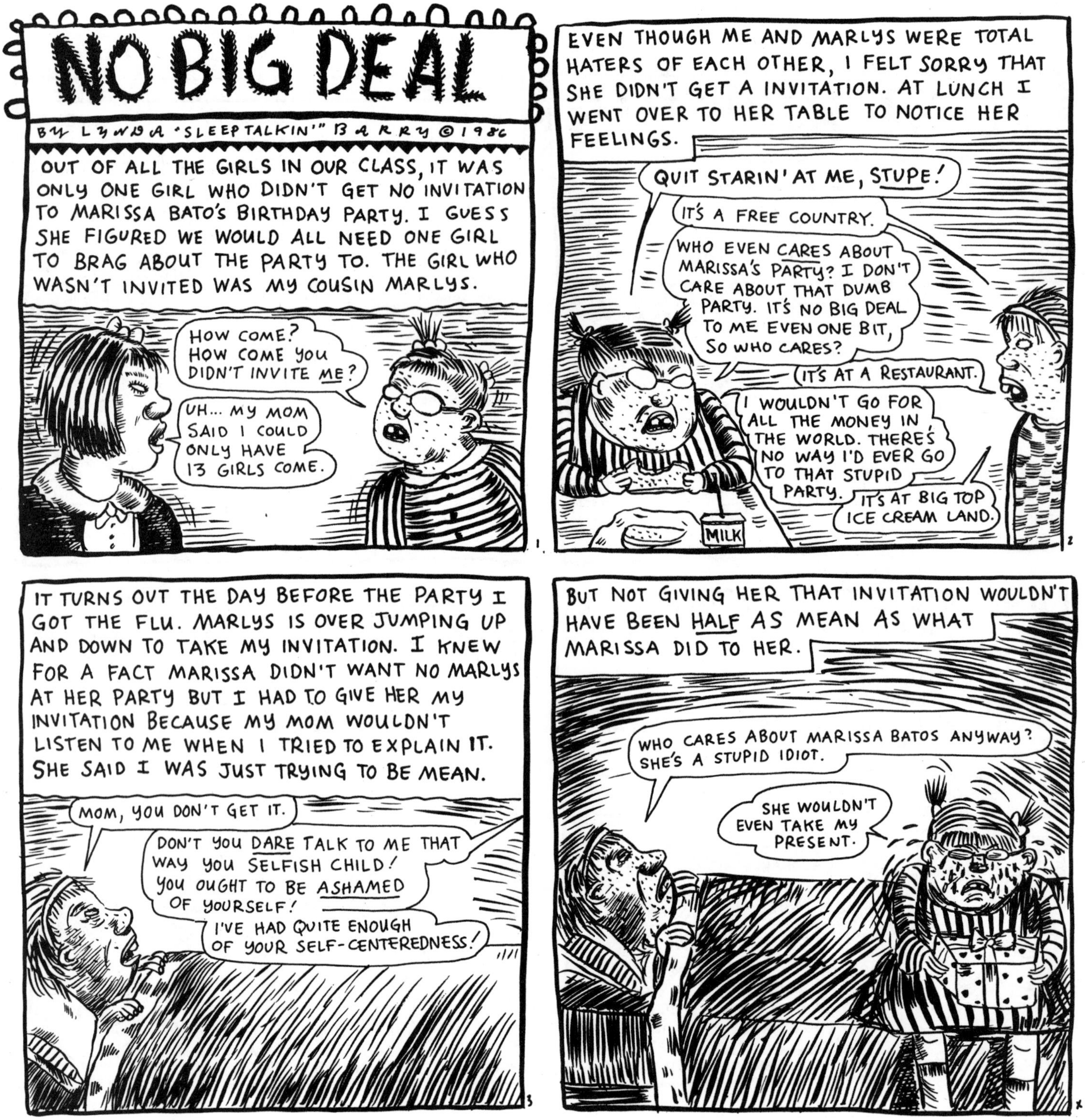
NO BIG DEAL
BY LYNDA "SLEEPTALKIN'" BARRY ©1986
OUT OF ALL THE GIRLS IN OUR CLASS, IT WAS ONLY ONE GIRL WHO DIDN'T GET NO INVITATION TO MARISSA BATO'S BIRTHDAY PARTY. I GUESS SHE FIGURED WE WOULD ALL NEED ONE GIRL TO BRAG ABOUT THE PARTY TO. THE GIRL WHO WASN'T INVITED WAS MY COUSIN MARLYS.
HOW COME? HOW COME YOU DIDN'T INVITE ME?
UH... MY MOM SAID I COULD ONLY HAVE 13 GIRLS COME.
1.
EVEN THOUGH ME AND MARLYS WERE TOTAL HATERS OF EACH OTHER, I FELT SORRY THAT SHE DIDN'T GET A INVITATION. AT LUNCH I WENT OVER TO HER TABLE TO NOTICE HER FEELINGS.
QUIT STARIN' AT ME, STUPE!
IT'S A FREE COUNTRY.
WHO EVEN CARES ABOUT MARISSA'S PARTY? I DON'T CARE ABOUT THAT DUMB PARTY. IT'S NO BIG DEAL TO ME EVEN ONE BIT, SO WHO CARES?
IT'S AT A RESTAURANT.
I WOULDN'T GO FOR ALL THE MONEY IN THE WORLD. THERE'S NO WAY I'D EVER GO TO THAT STUPID PARTY.
IT'S AT BIG TOP ICE CREAM LAND.
MILK
2
IT TURNS OUT THE DAY BEFORE THE PARTY I GOT THE FLU. MARLYS IS OVER JUMPING UP AND DOWN TO TAKE MY INVITATION. I KNEW FOR A FACT MARISSA DIDN'T WANT NO MARLYS AT HER PARTY BUT I HAD TO GIVE HER MY INVITATION BECAUSE MY MOM WOULDN'T LISTEN TO ME WHEN I TRIED TO EXPLAIN IT. SHE SAID I WAS JUST TRYING TO BE MEAN.
MOM, YOU DON'T GET IT.
DON'T YOU DARE TALK TO ME THAT WAY YOU SELFISH CHILD! YOU OUGHT TO BE ASHAMED OF YOURSELF!
I'VE HAD QUITE ENOUGH OF YOUR SELF-CENTEREDNESS!
3
BUT NOT GIVING HER THAT INVITATION WOULDN'T HAVE BEEN HALF AS MEAN AS WHAT MARISSA DID TO HER.
WHO CARES ABOUT MARISSA BATOS ANYWAY? SHE'S A STUPID IDIOT.
SHE WOULDN'T EVEN TAKE MY PRESENT.

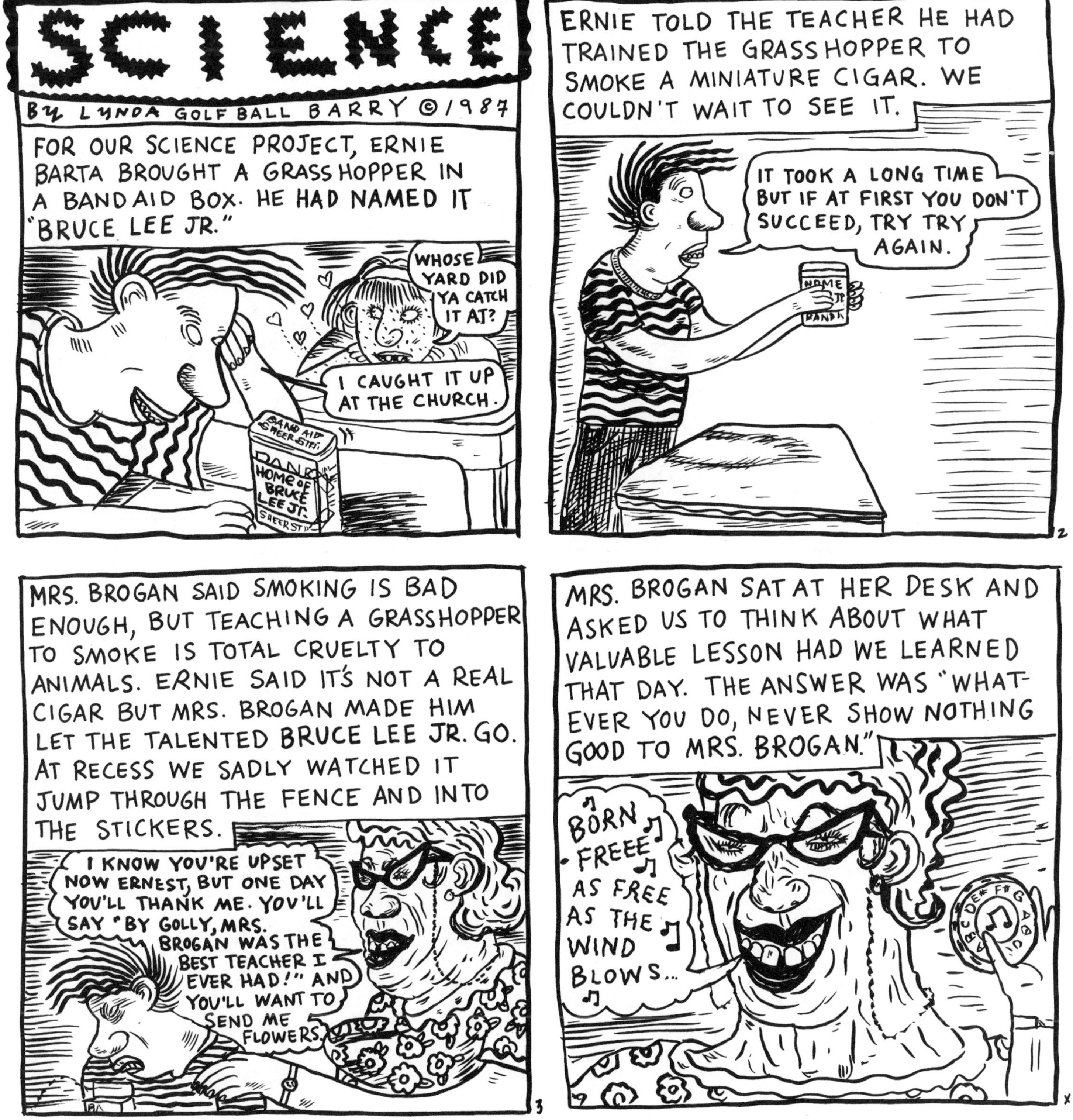
SCIENCE
BY LYNDA GOLF BALL BARRY ©1987
FOR OUR SCIENCE PROJECT, ERNIE BARTA BROUGHT A GRASSHOPPER IN A BANDAID BOX. HE HAD NAMED IT "BRUCE LEE JR."
WHOSE YARD DID YA CATCH IT AT?
I CAUGHT IT UP AT THE CHURCH.
HOME OF BRUKE LEE JR.
ERNIE TOLD THE TEACHER HE HAD TRAINED THE GRASSHOPPER TO SMOKE A MINIATURE CIGAR. WE COULDN'T WAIT TO SEE IT.
IT TOOK A LONG TIME BUT IF AT FIRST YOU DON'T SUCCEED, TRY TRY AGAIN.
MRS. BROGAN SAID SMOKING IS BAD ENOUGH, BUT TEACHING A GRASSHOPPER TO SMOKE IS TOTAL CRUELTY TO ANIMALS. ERNIE SAID IT'S NOT A REAL CIGAR BUT MRS. BROGAN MADE HIM LET THE TALENTED BRUCE LEE JR. GO. AT RECESS WE SADLY WATCHED IT JUMP THROUGH THE FENCE AND INTO THE STICKERS.
I KNOW YOU'RE UPSET NOW ERNEST, BUT ONE DAY YOU'LL THANK ME. YOU'LL SAY "BY GOLLY, MRS. BROGAN WAS THE BEST TEACHER I EVER HAD!" AND YOU'LL WANT TO SEND ME FLOWERS.
MRS. BROGAN SAT AT HER DESK AND ASKED US TO THINK ABOUT WHAT VALUABLE LESSON HAD WE LEARNED THAT DAY. THE ANSWER WAS "WHATEVER YOU DO, NEVER SHOW NOTHING GOOD TO MRS. BROGAN."
BORN FREEE AS FREE AS THE WIND BLOWS...

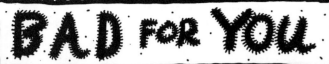

BAD FOR YOU

BY LYNDA ORSON WELLS BARRY © 1989

MRS. BROGAN TOLD THE LIGHT MONITOR TO TURN THE LIGHTS OFF, THEN SHE SWITCHED ON THE OVERHEAD PROJECTOR AND SHOWED US ABOUT 40 PICTURES OF ROTTEN TEETH AND SAID THE SUBJECT OF THE DAY WAS POP.

A LOT OF YOU WILL END UP WITH TEETH EXACTLY LIKE THIS.

SHE SAID OF ALL POP, COKE WAS THE WORST AND IF YOU HUNG A HUNK OF MEAT IN A CAN OF COKE IT WOULD ROT RIGHT OFF THE STRING IN ONE DAY. SO THINK OF WHAT IT DOES TO YOUR STOMACH.

HOW MANY OF YOU LIKE THE THOUGHT OF BIG HOLES IN YOUR STOMACH LINING?

WHEN ARNOLD ARNESEN SHOWED UP THE NEXT DAY WITH A THERMOS FULL OF COKE AND A HOT DOG FLOATING IN IT MRS. BROGAN SAID "O.K., WE SHALL SEE WHAT HAPPENS" AND PUT THE THERMOS ON A TABLE BY ITSELF WITH AN INDEX CARD TAPED TO IT THAT SAID "EXPERIMENT."

Experiment
THIS IS NOT A TOY

ALL DAY WE WONDERED ABOUT THE HOT DOG TRAPPED IN THE THERMOS WITH THE COKE. WHAT A HORRIBLE WAY TO GO.

AFTER 24 HOURS MRS. BROGAN TOOK US ALL OUT TO THE STORM DRAIN WHERE SHE WAS GOING TO POUR OUT THE COKE, AND SHE POURED IT AND THE HOT DOG FELL OUT IN PERFECT CONDITION.

FOR SOME REASON ALL OF US KNEW THIS WAS ABOUT THE SADDEST THING WE HAD EVER SEEN. ESPECIALLY MRS. BROGAN.

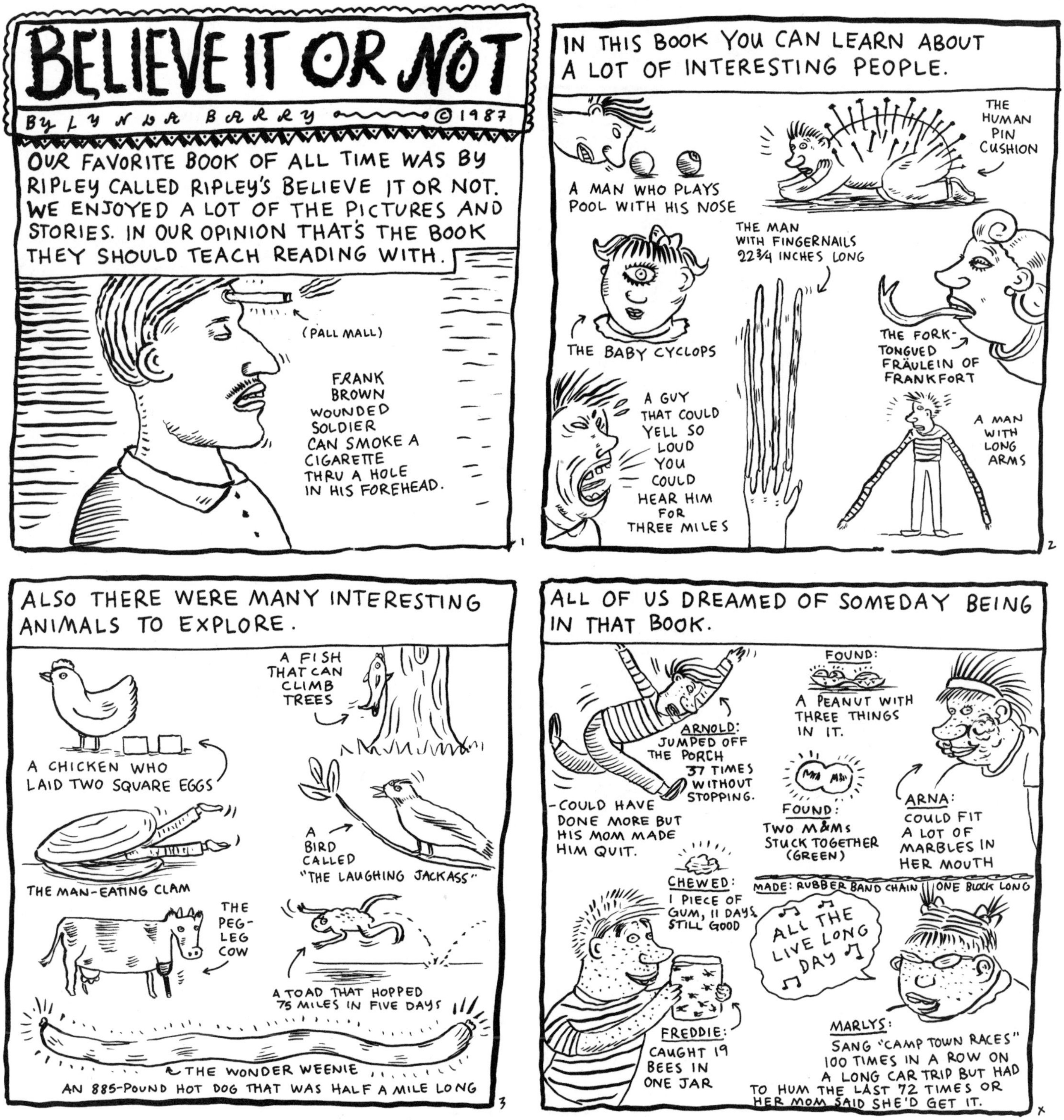
BELIEVE IT OR NOT
BY LYNDA BARRY ©1987
OUR FAVORITE BOOK OF ALL TIME WAS BY RIPLEY CALLED RIPLEY'S BELIEVE IT OR NOT. WE ENJOYED A LOT OF THE PICTURES AND STORIES. IN OUR OPINION THAT'S THE BOOK THEY SHOULD TEACH READING WITH.
(PALL MALL)
FRANK BROWN WOUNDED SOLDIER CAN SMOKE A CIGARETTE THRU A HOLE IN HIS FOREHEAD.
1
IN THIS BOOK YOU CAN LEARN ABOUT A LOT OF INTERESTING PEOPLE.
A MAN WHO PLAYS POOL WITH HIS NOSE
THE HUMAN PIN CUSHION
THE BABY CYCLOPS
THE MAN WITH FINGERNAILS 22¾ INCHES LONG
THE FORK-TONGUED FRÄULEIN OF FRANKFORT
A GUY THAT COULD YELL SO LOUD YOU COULD HEAR HIM FOR THREE MILES
A MAN WITH LONG ARMS
2
ALSO THERE WERE MANY INTERESTING ANIMALS TO EXPLORE.
A CHICKEN WHO LAID TWO SQUARE EGGS
A FISH THAT CAN CLIMB TREES
THE MAN-EATING CLAM
A BIRD CALLED "THE LAUGHING JACKASS"
THE PEG-LEG COW
A TOAD THAT HOPPED 75 MILES IN FIVE DAYS
THE WONDER WEENIE
AN 885-POUND HOT DOG THAT WAS HALF A MILE LONG
3
ALL OF US DREAMED OF SOMEDAY BEING IN THAT BOOK.
ARNOLD: JUMPED OFF THE PORCH 37 TIMES WITHOUT STOPPING.
-COULD HAVE DONE MORE BUT HIS MOM MADE HIM QUIT.
FOUND: A PEANUT WITH THREE THINGS IN IT.
FOUND: TWO M&Ms STUCK TOGETHER (GREEN)
ARNA: COULD FIT A LOT OF MARBLES IN HER MOUTH
CHEWED: 1 PIECE OF GUM, 11 DAYS STILL GOOD
MADE: RUBBER BAND CHAIN ONE BLOCK LONG
ALL THE LIVE LONG DAY
FREDDIE: CAUGHT 19 BEES IN ONE JAR
MARLYS: SANG "CAMP TOWN RACES" 100 TIMES IN A ROW ON A LONG CAR TRIP BUT HAD TO HUM THE LAST 72 TIMES OR HER MOM SAID SHE'D GET IT.
x

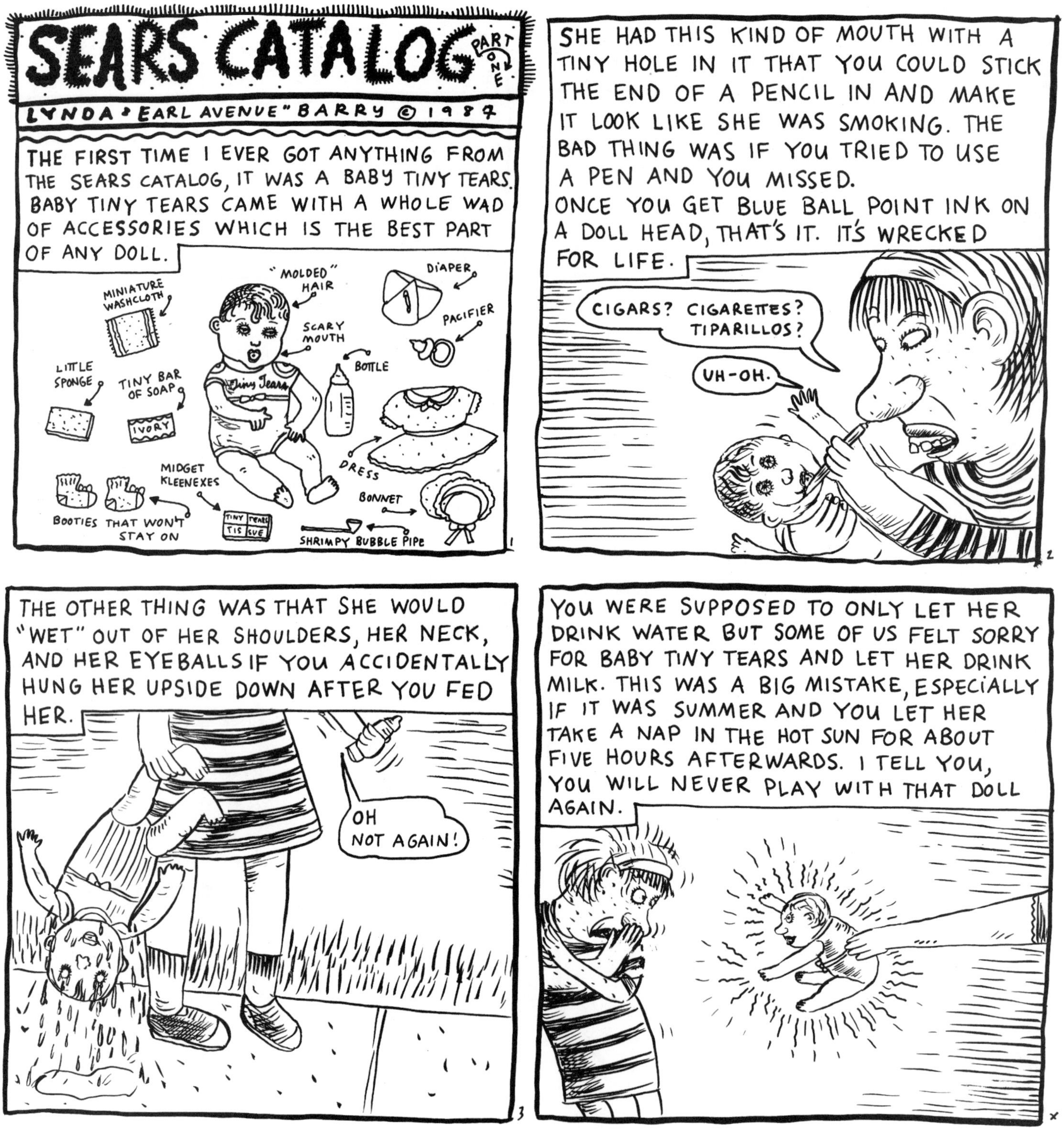
SEARS CATALOG PART ONE
LYNDA "EARL AVENUE" BARRY © 1987
THE FIRST TIME I EVER GOT ANYTHING FROM THE SEARS CATALOG, IT WAS A BABY TINY TEARS. BABY TINY TEARS CAME WITH A WHOLE WAD OF ACCESSORIES WHICH IS THE BEST PART OF ANY DOLL.
MINIATURE WASHCLOTH
"MOLDED" HAIR
DIAPER
PACIFIER
SCARY MOUTH
BOTTLE
LITTLE SPONGE
TINY BAR OF SOAP
IVORY
Tiny Tears
DRESS
MIDGET KLEENEXES
TINY TEARS TISSUE
BONNET
BOOTIES THAT WON'T STAY ON
SHRIMPY BUBBLE PIPE
SHE HAD THIS KIND OF MOUTH WITH A TINY HOLE IN IT THAT YOU COULD STICK THE END OF A PENCIL IN AND MAKE IT LOOK LIKE SHE WAS SMOKING. THE BAD THING WAS IF YOU TRIED TO USE A PEN AND YOU MISSED. ONCE YOU GET BLUE BALL POINT INK ON A DOLL HEAD, THAT'S IT. IT'S WRECKED FOR LIFE.
CIGARS? CIGARETTES? TIPARILLOS?
UH-OH.
THE OTHER THING WAS THAT SHE WOULD "WET" OUT OF HER SHOULDERS, HER NECK, AND HER EYEBALLS IF YOU ACCIDENTALLY HUNG HER UPSIDE DOWN AFTER YOU FED HER.
OH NOT AGAIN!
YOU WERE SUPPOSED TO ONLY LET HER DRINK WATER BUT SOME OF US FELT SORRY FOR BABY TINY TEARS AND LET HER DRINK MILK. THIS WAS A BIG MISTAKE, ESPECIALLY IF IT WAS SUMMER AND YOU LET HER TAKE A NAP IN THE HOT SUN FOR ABOUT FIVE HOURS AFTERWARDS. I TELL YOU, YOU WILL NEVER PLAY WITH THAT DOLL AGAIN.

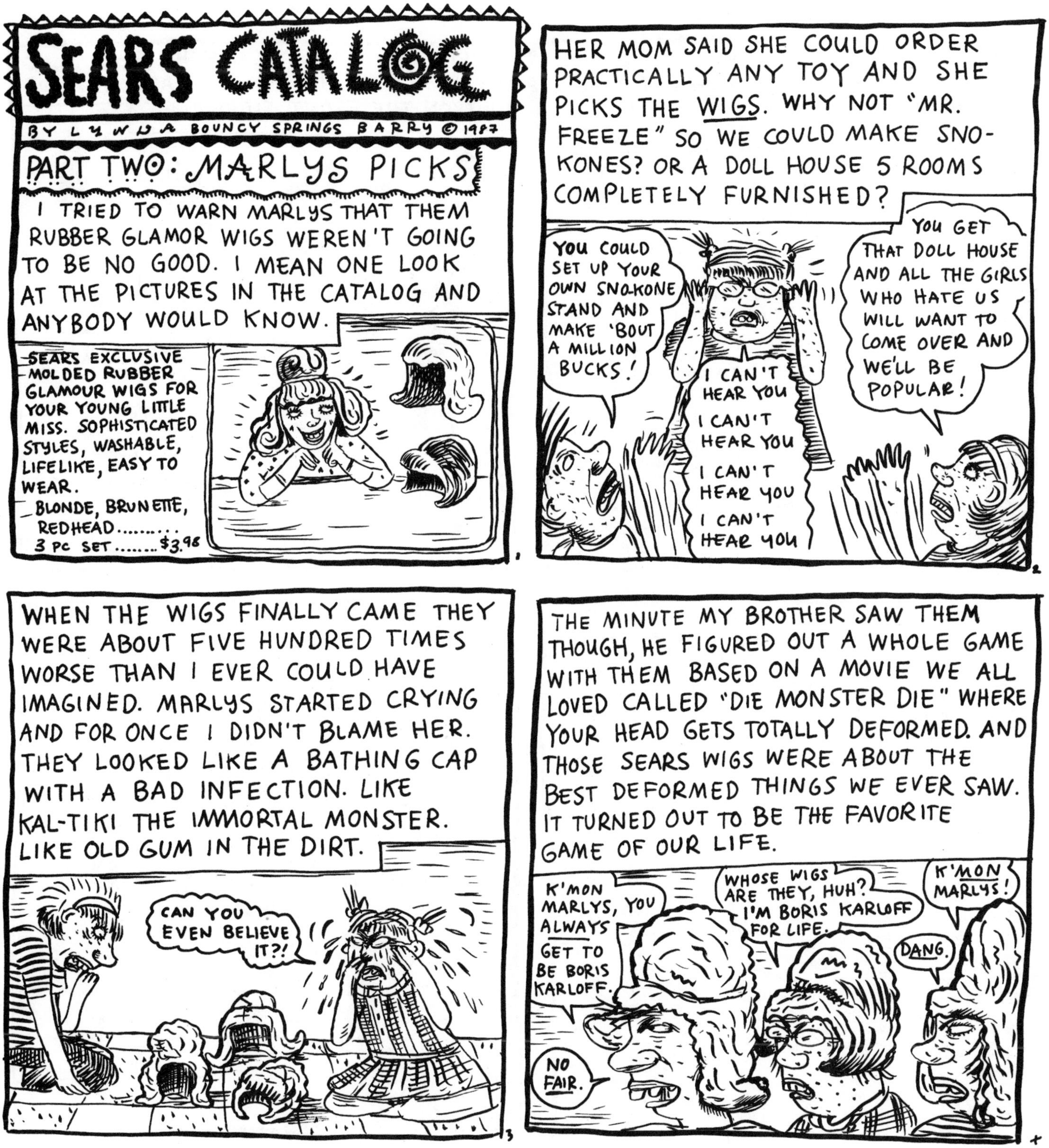
SEARS CATALOG
BY LYNDA BOUNCY SPRINGS BARRY © 1987
PART TWO: MARLYS PICKS
I TRIED TO WARN MARLYS THAT THEM RUBBER GLAMOR WIGS WEREN'T GOING TO BE NO GOOD. I MEAN ONE LOOK AT THE PICTURES IN THE CATALOG AND ANYBODY WOULD KNOW.
SEARS EXCLUSIVE MOLDED RUBBER GLAMOUR WIGS FOR YOUR YOUNG LITTLE MISS. SOPHISTICATED STYLES, WASHABLE, LIFELIKE, EASY TO WEAR.
BLONDE, BRUNETTE, REDHEAD..........
3 PC SET........$3.98
HER MOM SAID SHE COULD ORDER PRACTICALLY ANY TOY AND SHE PICKS THE WIGS. WHY NOT "MR. FREEZE" SO WE COULD MAKE SNO-KONES? OR A DOLL HOUSE 5 ROOMS COMPLETELY FURNISHED?
YOU COULD SET UP YOUR OWN SNO-KONE STAND AND MAKE 'BOUT A MILLION BUCKS!
I CAN'T HEAR YOU I CAN'T HEAR YOU I CAN'T HEAR YOU I CAN'T HEAR YOU
YOU GET THAT DOLL HOUSE AND ALL THE GIRLS WHO HATE US WILL WANT TO COME OVER AND WE'LL BE POPULAR!
WHEN THE WIGS FINALLY CAME THEY WERE ABOUT FIVE HUNDRED TIMES WORSE THAN I EVER COULD HAVE IMAGINED. MARLYS STARTED CRYING AND FOR ONCE I DIDN'T BLAME HER. THEY LOOKED LIKE A BATHING CAP WITH A BAD INFECTION. LIKE KAL-TIKI THE IMMORTAL MONSTER. LIKE OLD GUM IN THE DIRT.
CAN YOU EVEN BELIEVE IT?!
THE MINUTE MY BROTHER SAW THEM THOUGH, HE FIGURED OUT A WHOLE GAME WITH THEM BASED ON A MOVIE WE ALL LOVED CALLED "DIE MONSTER DIE" WHERE YOUR HEAD GETS TOTALLY DEFORMED. AND THOSE SEARS WIGS WERE ABOUT THE BEST DEFORMED THINGS WE EVER SAW. IT TURNED OUT TO BE THE FAVORITE GAME OF OUR LIFE.
K'MON MARLYS, YOU ALWAYS GET TO BE BORIS KARLOFF.
NO FAIR.
WHOSE WIGS ARE THEY, HUH? I'M BORIS KARLOFF FOR LIFE.
K'MON MARLYS!
DANG.

SEARS CATALOG

BY LYNDA BEEFARONI BARRY © 1987

PART THREE: ARMY MEN

MY BROTHER HAD $7.00 FROM COMBINATION CHRISTMAS AND BIRTHDAY MONEY SO HE HAD MOM ORDER HIM **TWO** SETS (75 PIECES EACH) OF "THE ARMY TRAINING CAMP." I SAID "WHY YOU GOTTA GET TWO OF THE SAME THING?" HE LOOK AT ME LIKE I WAS A TOTAL IDIOT.

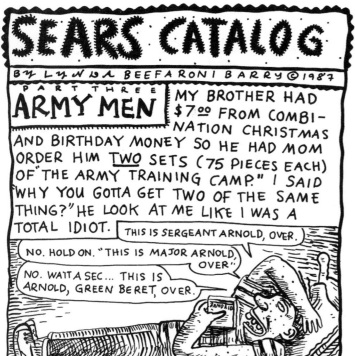

THIS IS SERGEANT ARNOLD, OVER.

NO. HOLD ON. "THIS IS MAJOR ARNOLD, OVER."

NO. WAIT A SEC... THIS IS ARNOLD, GREEN BERET, OVER.

WHEN THEY FINALLY CAME HE TOOK ABOUT TWO HOURS TO FIX IT ALL IN A LONG ROW OUT ON THE FRONT SIDEWALK.

GUYS MARCHING

ONE GUY SALUTING

GUYS SHOOTING

KNEELING GUYS WITH BAZOOKAS

LAYING DOWN GUYS WITH RIFLES

GUYS THROWING GRENADES

GUY WITH BAYONET

GUYS WITH BINOCULARS

TENTS THAT NONE OF THE GUYS COULD FIT INTO

FLAG POLE THAT WON'T STAND UP

FENCE THAT WON'T STAND UP

JEEP NONE OF THE GUYS CAN RIDE IN.

FREESTANDING GUNS THAT YOUR DOG CHEWS

LIGHTER FLUID

THE NEXT DAY HE SETS UP A WHOLE WAR OUT IN THE GARDEN. HE MADE A REALISTIC LAKE FROM A MIRROR PART BURIED IN THE DIRT. HE MADE A RIVER FROM THE GARDEN HOSE. HE MADE PARACHUTERS OUT OF HANDKERCHIEFS. HE HAD THE WHOLE THING SET UP PERFECTLY, THEN HE GOT A BOWL OF CEREAL AND ATE IT OUT ON THE GRASS AND JUST LOOKED AT IT ALL. THEN HE TOOK HIS BOWL IN THE HOUSE, CAME OUT AND BLEW THE WHOLE THING UP WITH DIRT BOMBS.

AAGGGH!

BLAM-BLAM-BLAM!

KA-BLOOEY!

NO! NO! NOOOOO!

RATA-TAT-TAT-TAT-TAT-TAT

I'LL GET YOU YOU DIRTY LITTLE

BLASH!

BLAM!

HELP! HAVE MERCY!

BLAM!

DUCK!

KER-PLUNK!

BLAMMO!

ON THE THIRD DAY I SMELL A TERRIBLE BURNING SMELL AND I CAN HEAR MY BROTHER UNDER THE PORCH WITH HIS MEN. I SNEAK AROUND AND SEE HIM WITH THE LIGHTER FLUID, MATCHES AND HE HOLDS UP THIS ONE GUY HE JUST LIT ON FIRE AND PART OF IT MELTS ON MY BROTHER'S HAND AND HE YELLS AND HE STILL HAS THE SCAR FROM THAT TOO.

YOUCH!

HEY MAN NO FAIR!

OW-OW OW-O-W OOOW!

CHHHHHH!

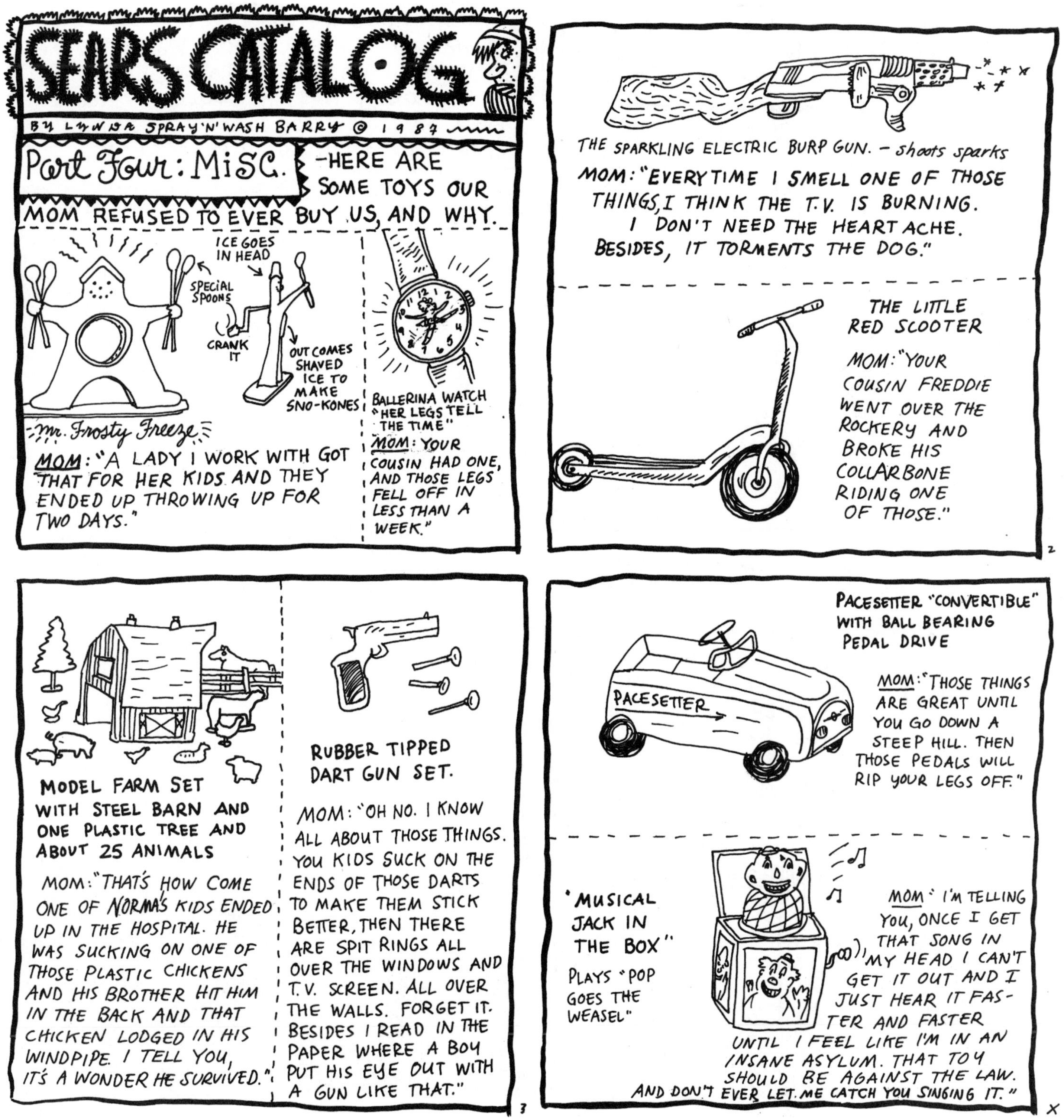
SEARS CATALOG
BY LYNDA SPRAY'N'WASH BARRY © 1987
Part Four: MiSC.
-HERE ARE SOME TOYS OUR MOM REFUSED TO EVER BUY US, AND WHY.
ICE GOES IN HEAD
SPECIAL SPOONS
CRANK IT
OUT COMES SHAVED ICE TO MAKE SNO-KONES
Mr. Frosty Freeze
MOM: "A LADY I WORK WITH GOT THAT FOR HER KIDS AND THEY ENDED UP THROWING UP FOR TWO DAYS."
BALLERINA WATCH "HER LEGS TELL THE TIME"
MOM: YOUR COUSIN HAD ONE, AND THOSE LEGS FELL OFF IN LESS THAN A WEEK."
THE SPARKLING ELECTRIC BURP GUN. - shoots sparks
MOM: "EVERYTIME I SMELL ONE OF THOSE THINGS, I THINK THE T.V. IS BURNING. I DON'T NEED THE HEARTACHE. BESIDES, IT TORMENTS THE DOG."
THE LITTLE RED SCOOTER
MOM: "YOUR COUSIN FREDDIE WENT OVER THE ROCKERY AND BROKE HIS COLLARBONE RIDING ONE OF THOSE."
2
MODEL FARM SET WITH STEEL BARN AND ONE PLASTIC TREE AND ABOUT 25 ANIMALS
MOM: "THAT'S HOW COME ONE OF NORMA'S KIDS ENDED UP IN THE HOSPITAL. HE WAS SUCKING ON ONE OF THOSE PLASTIC CHICKENS AND HIS BROTHER HIT HIM IN THE BACK AND THAT CHICKEN LODGED IN HIS WINDPIPE. I TELL YOU, IT'S A WONDER HE SURVIVED."
RUBBER TIPPED DART GUN SET.
MOM: "OH NO. I KNOW ALL ABOUT THOSE THINGS. YOU KIDS SUCK ON THE ENDS OF THOSE DARTS TO MAKE THEM STICK BETTER, THEN THERE ARE SPIT RINGS ALL OVER THE WINDOWS AND T.V. SCREEN. ALL OVER THE WALLS. FORGET IT. BESIDES I READ IN THE PAPER WHERE A BOY PUT HIS EYE OUT WITH A GUN LIKE THAT."
3
PACESETTER "CONVERTIBLE" WITH BALL BEARING PEDAL DRIVE
PACESETTER
MOM: "THOSE THINGS ARE GREAT UNTIL YOU GO DOWN A STEEP HILL. THEN THOSE PEDALS WILL RIP YOUR LEGS OFF."
"MUSICAL JACK IN THE BOX"
PLAYS "POP GOES THE WEASEL"
MOM: I'M TELLING YOU, ONCE I GET THAT SONG IN MY HEAD I CAN'T GET IT OUT AND I JUST HEAR IT FASTER AND FASTER UNTIL I FEEL LIKE I'M IN AN INSANE ASYLUM. THAT TOY SHOULD BE AGAINST THE LAW. AND DON'T EVER LET ME CATCH YOU SINGING IT."
x

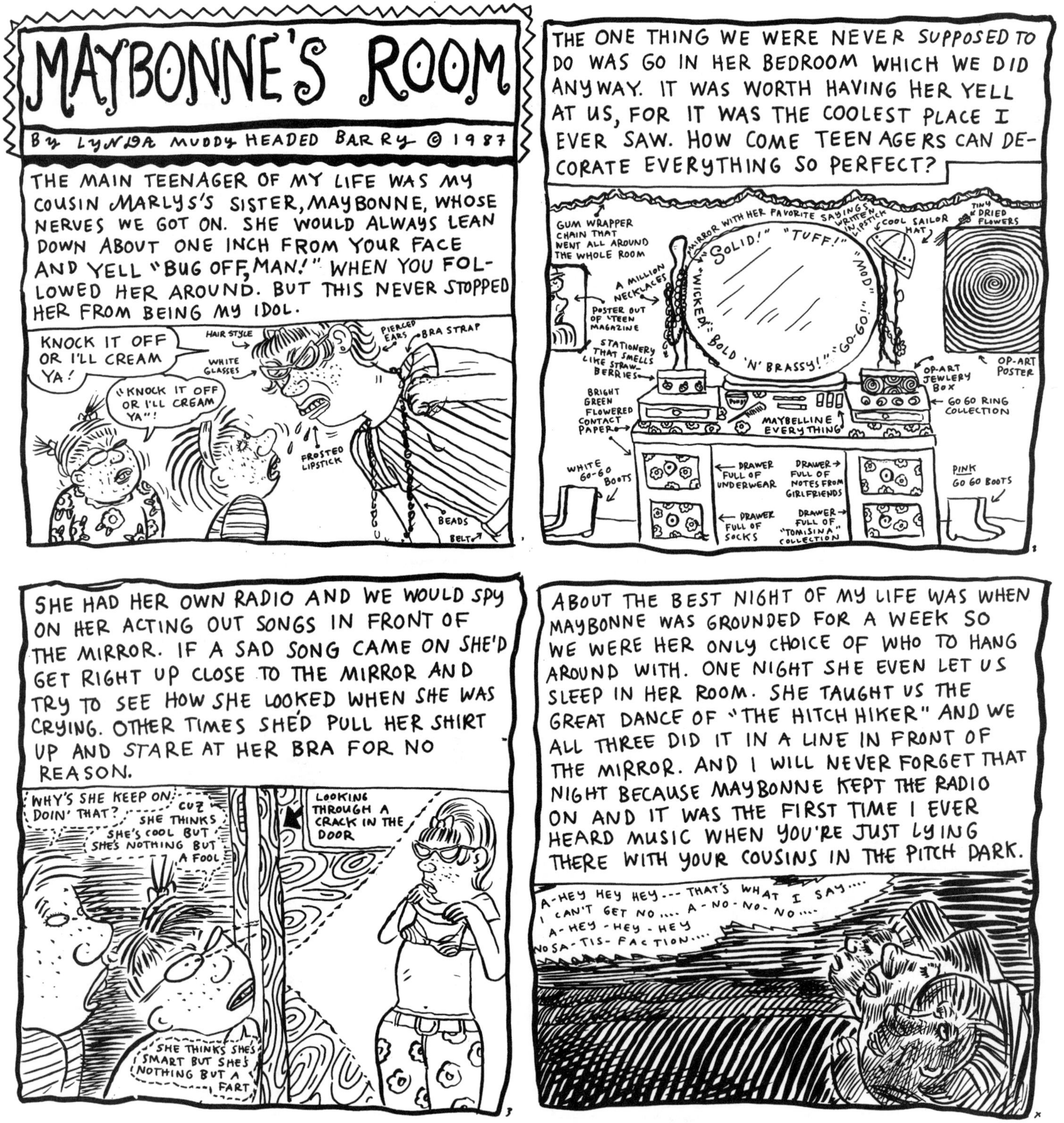
MAYBONNE'S ROOM
BY LYNDA MUDDY HEADED BARRY © 1987
THE MAIN TEENAGER OF MY LIFE WAS MY COUSIN MARLYS'S SISTER, MAYBONNE, WHOSE NERVES WE GOT ON. SHE WOULD ALWAYS LEAN DOWN ABOUT ONE INCH FROM YOUR FACE AND YELL "BUG OFF, MAN!" WHEN YOU FOLLOWED HER AROUND. BUT THIS NEVER STOPPED HER FROM BEING MY IDOL.
KNOCK IT OFF OR I'LL CREAM YA!
"KNOCK IT OFF OR I'LL CREAM YA"!
HAIR STYLE
WHITE GLASSES
PIERCED EARS
BRA STRAP
FROSTED LIPSTICK
BEADS
BELT
THE ONE THING WE WERE NEVER SUPPOSED TO DO WAS GO IN HER BEDROOM WHICH WE DID ANYWAY. IT WAS WORTH HAVING HER YELL AT US, FOR IT WAS THE COOLEST PLACE I EVER SAW. HOW COME TEENAGERS CAN DECORATE EVERYTHING SO PERFECT?
GUM WRAPPER CHAIN THAT WENT ALL AROUND THE WHOLE ROOM
MIRROR WITH HER FAVORITE SAYINGS WRITTEN IN LIPSTICK
"SOLID!" "TUFF!" "MOD" "GO-GO!" "BOLD 'N' BRASSY!" "WICKED!"
COOL SAILOR HAT
TINY DRIED FLOWERS
A MILLION NECKLACES
POSTER OUT OF 'TEEN MAGAZINE
STATIONERY THAT SMELLS LIKE STRAWBERRIES
BRIGHT GREEN FLOWERED CONTACT PAPER
MAYBELLINE EVERYTHING
OP-ART JEWLERY BOX
OP-ART POSTER
GO GO RING COLLECTION
WHITE GO-GO BOOTS
DRAWER FULL OF UNDERWEAR
DRAWER FULL OF NOTES FROM GIRLFRIENDS
DRAWER FULL OF SOCKS
DRAWER FULL OF "TOMISINA" COLLECTION
PINK GO GO BOOTS
SHE HAD HER OWN RADIO AND WE WOULD SPY ON HER ACTING OUT SONGS IN FRONT OF THE MIRROR. IF A SAD SONG CAME ON SHE'D GET RIGHT UP CLOSE TO THE MIRROR AND TRY TO SEE HOW SHE LOOKED WHEN SHE WAS CRYING. OTHER TIMES SHE'D PULL HER SHIRT UP AND STARE AT HER BRA FOR NO REASON.
WHY'S SHE KEEP ON DOIN' THAT?
CUZ SHE THINKS SHE'S COOL BUT SHE'S NOTHING BUT A FOOL
LOOKING THROUGH A CRACK IN THE DOOR
SHE THINKS SHE'S SMART BUT SHE'S NOTHING BUT A FART
ABOUT THE BEST NIGHT OF MY LIFE WAS WHEN MAYBONNE WAS GROUNDED FOR A WEEK SO WE WERE HER ONLY CHOICE OF WHO TO HANG AROUND WITH. ONE NIGHT SHE EVEN LET US SLEEP IN HER ROOM. SHE TAUGHT US THE GREAT DANCE OF "THE HITCH HIKER" AND WE ALL THREE DID IT IN A LINE IN FRONT OF THE MIRROR. AND I WILL NEVER FORGET THAT NIGHT BECAUSE MAYBONNE KEPT THE RADIO ON AND IT WAS THE FIRST TIME I EVER HEARD MUSIC WHEN YOU'RE JUST LYING THERE WITH YOUR COUSINS IN THE PITCH DARK.
A-HEY HEY HEY--- THAT'S WHAT I SAY....
I CAN'T GET NO.... A-NO-NO-NO....
A-HEY-HEY-HEY
NO SA-TIS-FACTION....

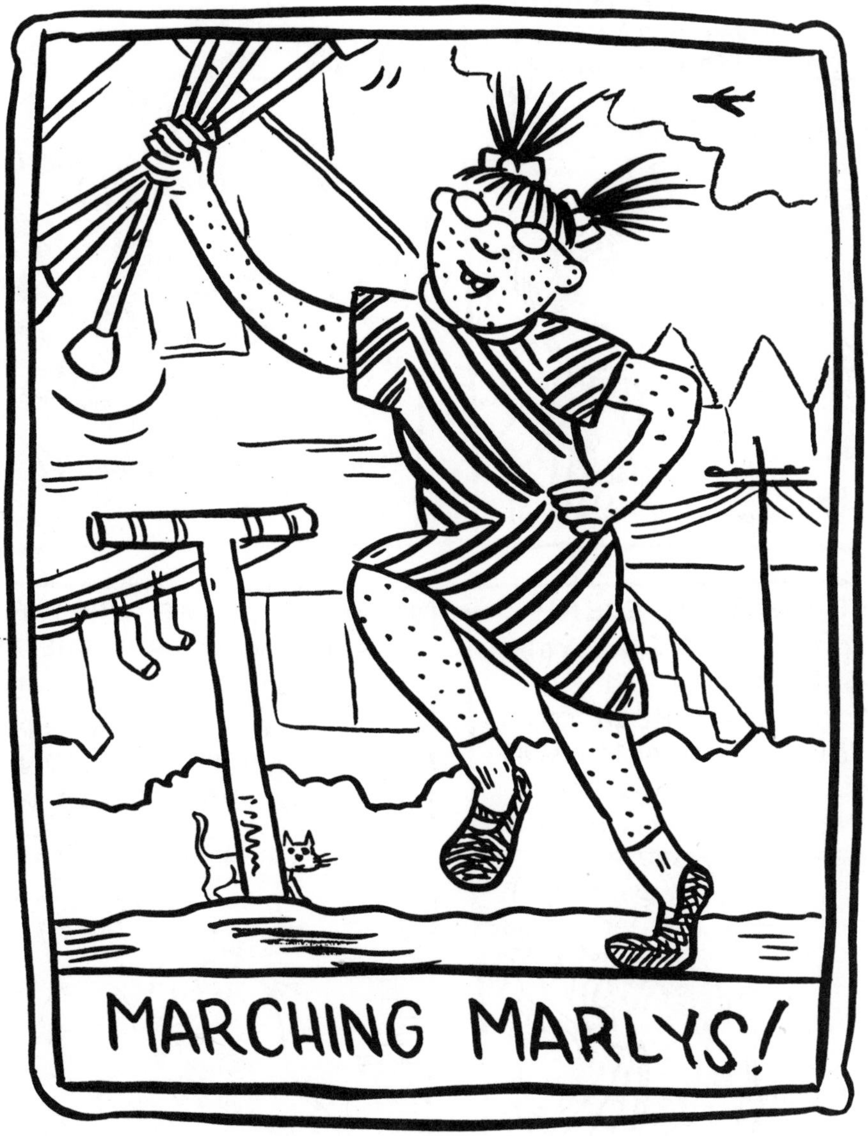
MARCHING MARLYS!

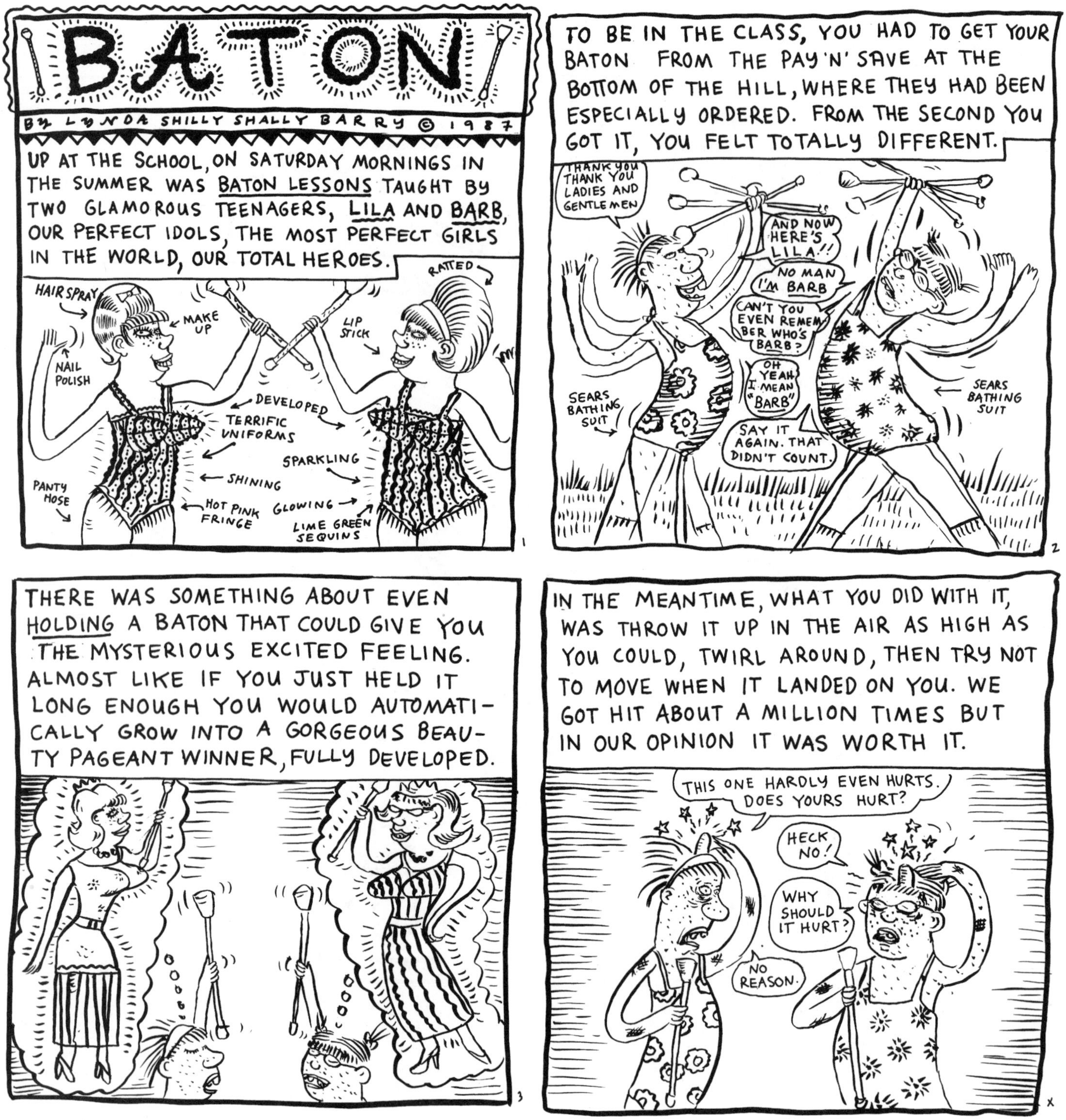
BATON
BY LYNDA SHILLY SHALLY BARRY © 1987
UP AT THE SCHOOL, ON SATURDAY MORNINGS IN THE SUMMER WAS BATON LESSONS TAUGHT BY TWO GLAMOROUS TEENAGERS, LILA AND BARB, OUR PERFECT IDOLS, THE MOST PERFECT GIRLS IN THE WORLD, OUR TOTAL HEROES.
HAIR SPRAY
MAKE UP
NAIL POLISH
RATTED
LIP STICK
DEVELOPED
TERRIFIC UNIFORMS
SPARKLING
SHINING
PANTY HOSE
HOT PINK FRINGE
GLOWING
LIME GREEN SEQUINS
TO BE IN THE CLASS, YOU HAD TO GET YOUR BATON FROM THE PAY 'N' SAVE AT THE BOTTOM OF THE HILL, WHERE THEY HAD BEEN ESPECIALLY ORDERED. FROM THE SECOND YOU GOT IT, YOU FELT TOTALLY DIFFERENT.
THANK YOU THANK YOU LADIES AND GENTLEMEN
AND NOW HERE'S LILA!!
NO MAN I'M BARB
CAN'T YOU EVEN REMEMBER WHO'S BARB?
OH YEAH. I MEAN "BARB"
SAY IT AGAIN. THAT DIDN'T COUNT.
SEARS BATHING SUIT
SEARS BATHING SUIT
THERE WAS SOMETHING ABOUT EVEN HOLDING A BATON THAT COULD GIVE YOU THE MYSTERIOUS EXCITED FEELING. ALMOST LIKE IF YOU JUST HELD IT LONG ENOUGH YOU WOULD AUTOMATICALLY GROW INTO A GORGEOUS BEAUTY PAGEANT WINNER, FULLY DEVELOPED.
IN THE MEANTIME, WHAT YOU DID WITH IT, WAS THROW IT UP IN THE AIR AS HIGH AS YOU COULD, TWIRL AROUND, THEN TRY NOT TO MOVE WHEN IT LANDED ON YOU. WE GOT HIT ABOUT A MILLION TIMES BUT IN OUR OPINION IT WAS WORTH IT.
THIS ONE HARDLY EVEN HURTS. DOES YOURS HURT?
HECK NO!
WHY SHOULD IT HURT?
NO REASON.

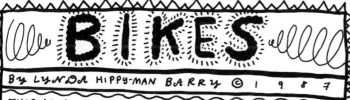

BIKES
BY LYNDA HIPPY-MAN BARRY © 1987
THIS IS A STORY ABOUT OUR BIKES. LIKE MY FIRST ONE, ASSEMBLY NOT INCLUDED, WITH TRAINING WHEELS, FROM SEARS. IF YOU HAVE TRAINING WHEELS EVERYONE WILL YELL "BABY" AT YOU, SO BETTER GO AHEAD AND TAKE THEM OFF AND JUST MAKE SURE YOU'RE BY SOME BUSHES WHEN YOU START TO WIPE OUT.
WHERE YOU ARE NOT SUPPOSED TO RIDE YOUR FRIENDS
HORN
STREAMERS
REFLECTOR
THIS MEANS IT'S A BOY'S BIKE
"BABY" WHEELS
THE "JR. ROADMASTER"
1
THE NEXT BIKE, ME AND MY BROTHER HAD TO SHARE. A SEARS STING RAY "SPYDER" ALL GOLD WITH BUTTERFLY HANDLE BARS, A LEOPARD SKIN BANANA SEAT AND A GIANT SISSY BAR. WE PUT TONY THE TIGER HANDLES ON IT AND ABOUT A HUNDRED CLOTHES PINS WITH PLAYING CARDS ON THE WHEELS TO MAKE IT SOUND LIKE A ACTUAL DRAGSTER. YOU COULD TELL IT WAS THE BEST BIKE IN THE WORLD JUST BY LOOKING AT IT.
HEY MAN, POP A WHEELIE!
NOW YOU CAN RIDE SOMEONE PERFECT
GEAR SHIFT KNOB
BIG DADDY ROTH STICKERS
KUSTOM FENDERS
TWO CURB JUMPER TIRES
GOLD REFLECTORS ON PEDALS
2
OUR THING TO DO WAS GO UP THIS ONE HILL AFTER DARK WITH OUR BIKES AND TWO POP CANS WHICH YOU STEPPED ON SIDEWAYS REALLY HARD SO THEY MOLDED TO THE BACK OF YOUR SHOES. THEN EVERYBODY GETS IN A LINE AND WHEN THE GUY AT THE BOTTOM YELLS "NO CARS!" YOU TAKE OFF DRAGGING THOSE CANS ON THE STREET AND IT MAKES TERRIFIC SPARKS FLYING ALL OVER. WE CALLED THIS "THE TORCH-LIGHT PARADE."
TIMES!! MY CAN IS COMING OFF. YELL FOR HIM TO HANG ON A SEC.
OK?! NO CARS!!
3
OF COURSE SOMETIMES YOU JUST DON'T LISTEN TO ADVICE ON GOOD BIKE SAFETY ABOUT "DON'T RIDE YOUR FRIENDS DOWN THAT ONE PERFECT HILL THAT GOES TO THE A+P WITH NO BRAKES." THE ONLY LAW WE HAD ABOUT WIPING OUT WAS AFTER YOU WIPED OUT, NO MATTER HOW MUCH IT HURT, YOU HAD TO YELL "RUPTURE!" FIRST, WHICH WOULD USUALLY MAKE YOU START LAUGHING AT THE SAME TIME YOU WERE CRYING BECAUSE YOU'RE BLEEDING AND MAN LOOK HOW WRECKED-UP YOUR BIKE IS.
BIKE UPSIDE DOWN WITH WHEEL STILL SPINNING
RUPTURE!
RUPTURE!
OW
DANG!
4

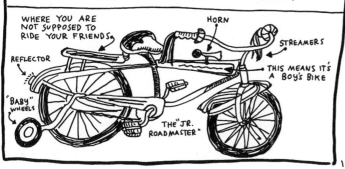

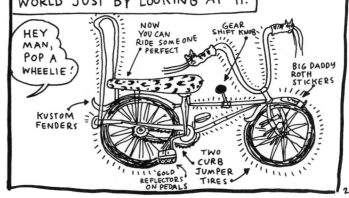

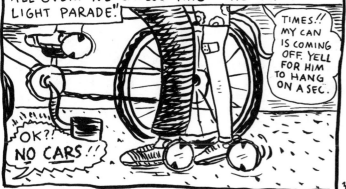

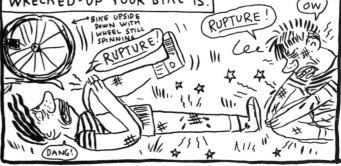

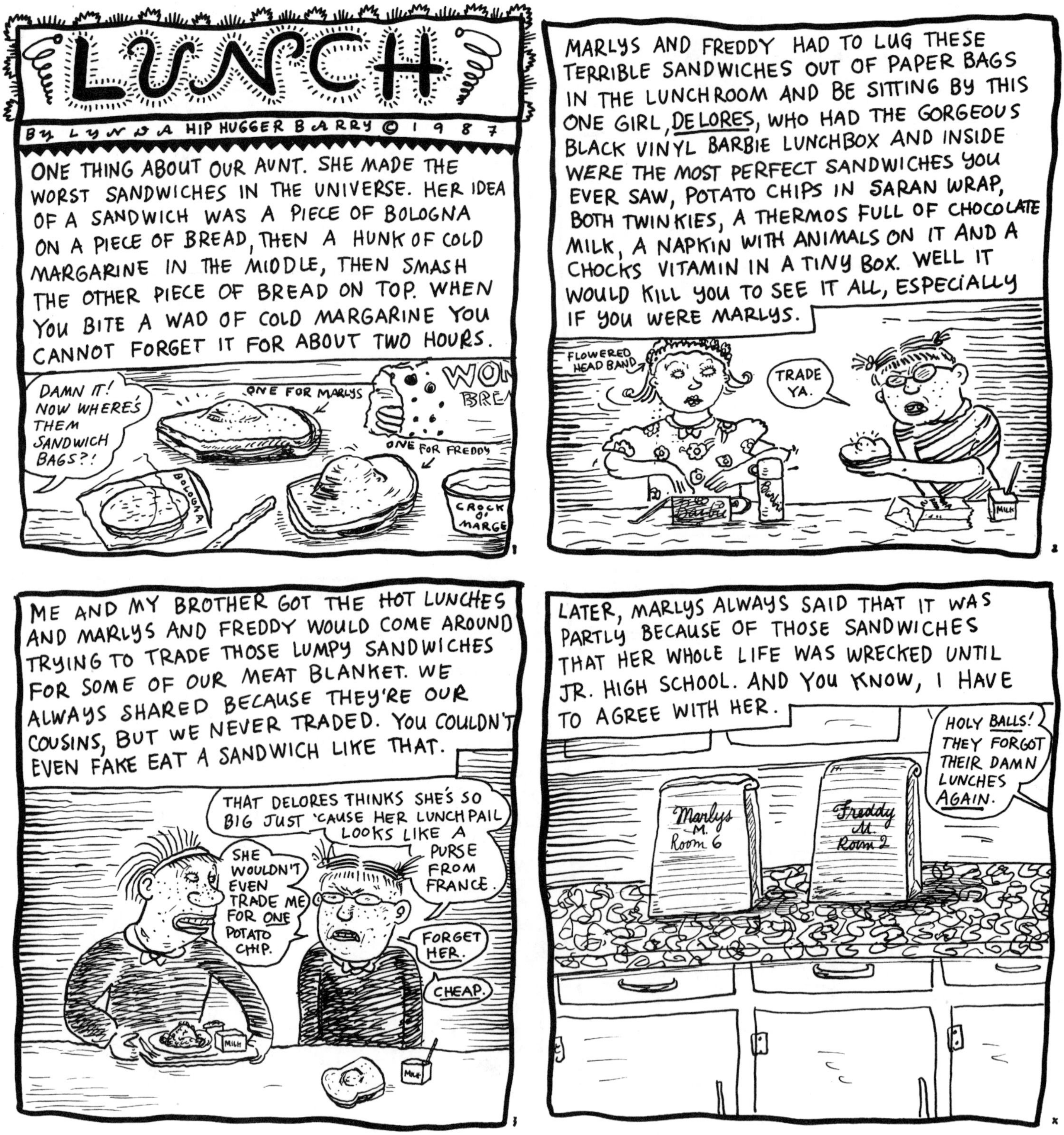
LUNCH
BY LYNDA HIP HUGGER BARRY © 1987
ONE THING ABOUT OUR AUNT. SHE MADE THE WORST SANDWICHES IN THE UNIVERSE. HER IDEA OF A SANDWICH WAS A PIECE OF BOLOGNA ON A PIECE OF BREAD, THEN A HUNK OF COLD MARGARINE IN THE MIDDLE, THEN SMASH THE OTHER PIECE OF BREAD ON TOP. WHEN YOU BITE A WAD OF COLD MARGARINE YOU CANNOT FORGET IT FOR ABOUT TWO HOURS.
DAMN IT! NOW WHERE'S THEM SANDWICH BAGS?!
ONE FOR MARLYS
ONE FOR FREDDY
BOLOGNA
CROCK O' MARGE
MARLYS AND FREDDY HAD TO LUG THESE TERRIBLE SANDWICHES OUT OF PAPER BAGS IN THE LUNCHROOM AND BE SITTING BY THIS ONE GIRL, DELORES, WHO HAD THE GORGEOUS BLACK VINYL BARBIE LUNCHBOX AND INSIDE WERE THE MOST PERFECT SANDWICHES YOU EVER SAW, POTATO CHIPS IN SARAN WRAP, BOTH TWINKIES, A THERMOS FULL OF CHOCOLATE MILK, A NAPKIN WITH ANIMALS ON IT AND A CHOCKS VITAMIN IN A TINY BOX. WELL IT WOULD KILL YOU TO SEE IT ALL, ESPECIALLY IF YOU WERE MARLYS.
FLOWERED HEAD BAND
TRADE YA.
Barbie
MILK
ME AND MY BROTHER GOT THE HOT LUNCHES AND MARLYS AND FREDDY WOULD COME AROUND TRYING TO TRADE THOSE LUMPY SANDWICHES FOR SOME OF OUR MEAT BLANKET. WE ALWAYS SHARED BECAUSE THEY'RE OUR COUSINS, BUT WE NEVER TRADED. YOU COULDN'T EVEN FAKE EAT A SANDWICH LIKE THAT.
THAT DELORES THINKS SHE'S SO BIG JUST 'CAUSE HER LUNCHPAIL LOOKS LIKE A PURSE FROM FRANCE.
SHE WOULDN'T EVEN TRADE ME FOR ONE POTATO CHIP.
FORGET HER.
CHEAP.
MILK
LATER, MARLYS ALWAYS SAID THAT IT WAS PARTLY BECAUSE OF THOSE SANDWICHES THAT HER WHOLE LIFE WAS WRECKED UNTIL JR. HIGH SCHOOL. AND YOU KNOW, I HAVE TO AGREE WITH HER.
HOLY BALLS! THEY FORGOT THEIR DAMN LUNCHES AGAIN.
Marlys M. Room 6
Freddy M. Room 2

THE SubStitute

BY LYNDA RINGA DING A DING DANG BARRY © 1987

OUR USUAL TEACHER HAD ACTUALLY QUIT BECAUSE OF US. BECAUSE OUR MOST ROTTENEST PERSON, NAME OF JOHN BAILEY, KICKED HER LEGS AND YELLED "YOU'RE NOT THE BOSS OF ME!" MISS ANASLY STARTED CRYING AND WALKED OUT. THEN WE HEARD SHE HAD TO MOVE TO NORTH DAKOTA WHERE CHILDREN HAVE BETTER RESPECT.

I AM MISS BEVENS,

YOUR SUBSTITUTE.

MISS BEVENS WAS OUR MAIN PUNISHMENT FOR BEING SUCH A AWFUL CLASS. SHE HAD THIS CRUSTY PITCH PIPE WHICH SHE WOULD BLOW, THEN MAKE US SING THE WORST SONGS YOU EVER HEARD IN YOUR LIFE. ALSO SHE HAD A BIG POINTY BOSOM AND FAKE TEETH THAT FLIPPED AROUND.

"SOMEONE" IS NOT PAYING AT-TEN-TION...

CLICK CLICK CLICK CLICK

SHE ALSO HAD A SPECIAL SMELL, A PERFUME SMELL THAT PRACTICALLY CHOKED YOUR HEAD OFF WHEN SHE WAS BY YOU. AND SHE DIDN'T EVEN CARE IF YOU SAW HER EAT. DURING A MATH TEST WE SAW HER TRY TO EAT A CHICKEN LEG. EVERYONE GOT AT LEAST MINUS 8 ON THAT MATH TEST.

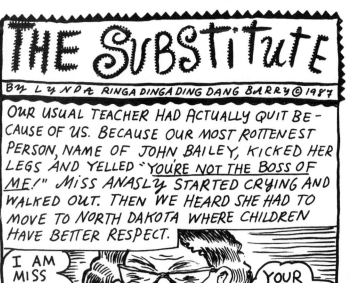

ON A FRIDAY MISS BEVENS TOLD US THE SCHOOL HAD GOT US A PERMANENT TEACHER, SO THIS WAS HER LAST DAY. SHE ASKED US FOR A SPECIAL FAVOR WHICH WAS TO SING HER HER FAVORITE SONG OF "JOHN BROWN'S BODY LIES A-MOLDERING IN THE GRAVE." WE STOOD UP AND SANG IT AND IF WE HATED HER SO MUCH HOW COME A LOT OF US STARTED CRYING?

READY? HERE'S OUR NOTE...

OTHER PLANETS
BY LYNDA BARRY ©1987
EVERYONE IN OUR CLASS LOVED the Solar System. ESPECIALLY DRAWING IT. IT WAS SO PERFECTLY GORGEOUS.
outer Space
mercury - year = 88 days
Venus - year = 225 days
the earth - year = 365 days
Mars - year = 1 year + 322 days
Jupiter = year = 11½ earth years
Saturn = year = 29½ earth years
Uranus year = 84 earth years
Neptune year = 165 earth years
Pluto year = 248 earth years
ONE OF THE MAIN OBJECTS WAS TO GET THE NUMBER OF MOONS RIGHT FOR EACH PLANET. WE COULDN'T HELP FEELING GYPPED BY HOW EARTH ONLY GETS ONE. JUPITER GETS SOMETHING LIKE ELEVEN MOONS AND NO ONE EVEN USES THEM.
Darla Martles
May 3
Extra Credit Report
The Moons of the Planets
1. Mercury (0) no moons
2. Venus (0) no moons
3. Earth (1) one moon
4. Mars (2) two moons
5. Jupeter (11) eleven moons
6. Saturn (9) nine moons
7. Uranus (4) four moons
8. Neptune (1) one moon
9. Pluto (0) no moons
Total of Moons = 28 moons
OF COURSE EVERYONE'S FAVORITE PLANET WAS SATURN BECAUSE IT TRULY LOOKED LIKE THE WORLD OF OUTER SPACE. IT WAS THE HARDEST PLANET TO DRAW ALTHOUGH A COUPLE PEOPLE WERE EXPERTS AT IT.
Darla Martles and Howard Grimes. The world's best drawers of Saturn
The Planet of SATURN
SATURN OUR 6TH PLANET
FOR THE ASSEMBLY OUR CLASS GOT TO ACT OUT THE SOLAR SYSTEM FOR THE REST OF THE SCHOOL. ONE GIRL CRIED BECAUSE ALL SHE GOT TO BE WAS A DISTANT STAR AND TWO BOYS GOT INTO A FIGHT OVER WHO GOT TO BE SATURN AND ONE GOT A BLOODY NOSE.
HEADS DOWN, CLASS. I'M ASHAMED OF YOUR BEHAVIOR THIS AFTERNOON.
IF OUR SOLAR SYSTEM BEHAVED THE WAY YOU DID TODAY WE'D ALL BE IN BIG TROUBLE.

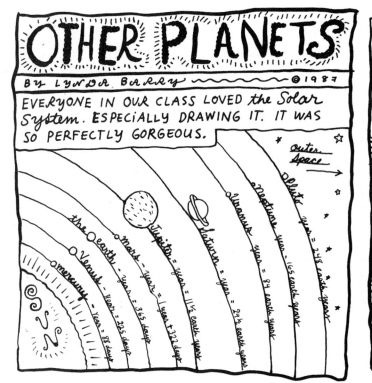

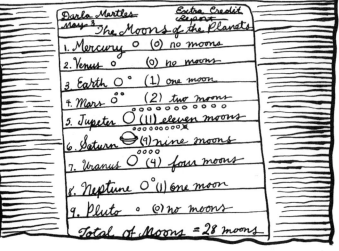

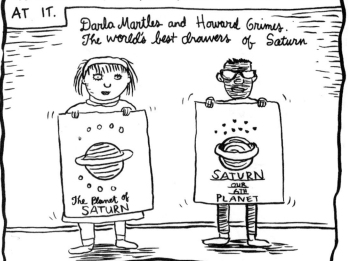

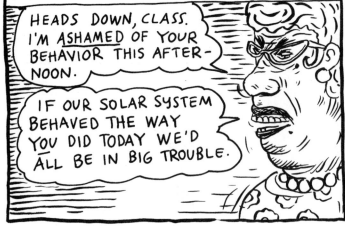

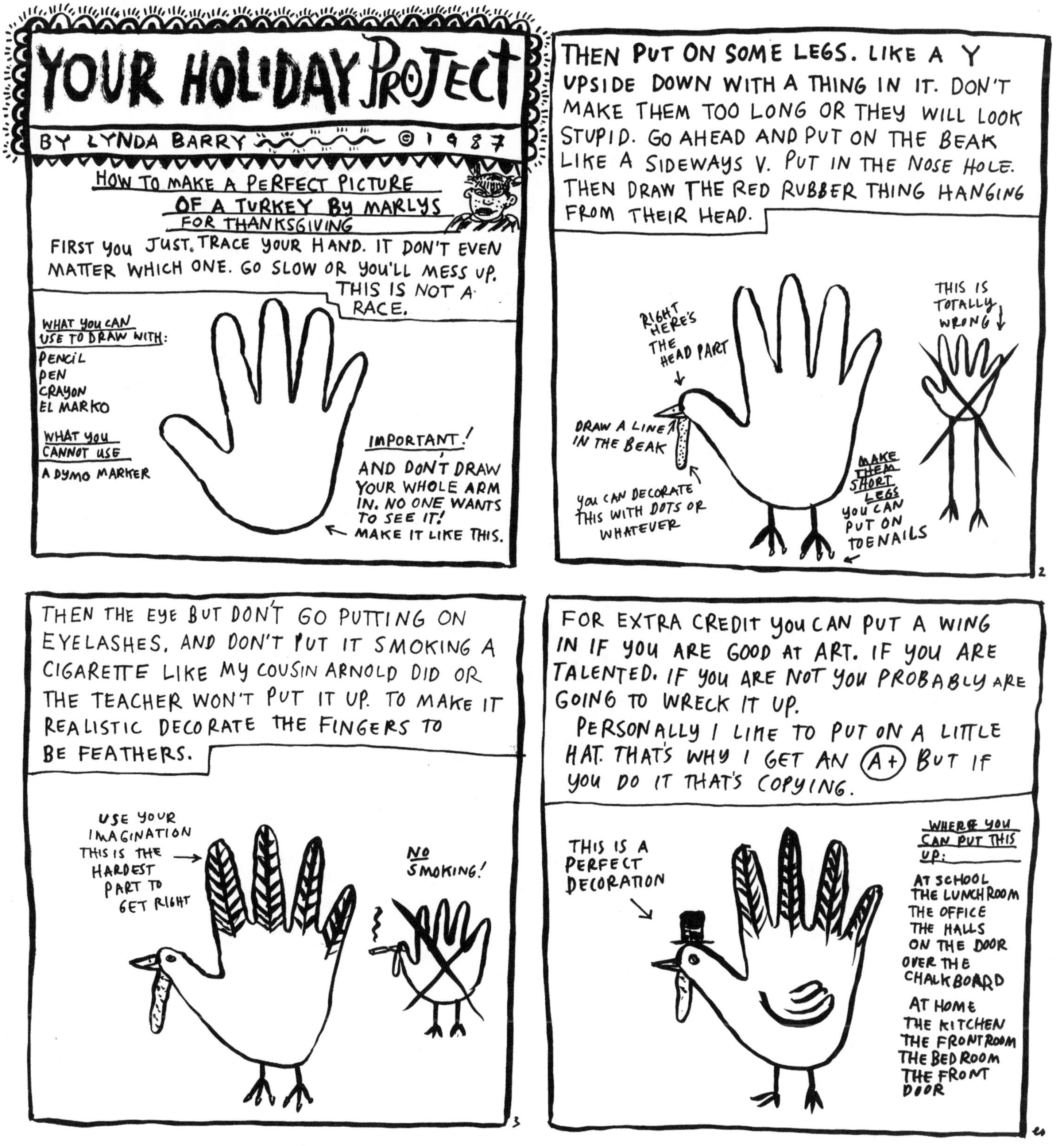
YOUR HOLIDAY PROJECT
BY LYNDA BARRY ©1987
HOW TO MAKE A PERFECT PICTURE OF A TURKEY BY MARLYS FOR THANKSGIVING
FIRST YOU JUST TRACE YOUR HAND. IT DON'T EVEN MATTER WHICH ONE. GO SLOW OR YOU'LL MESS UP. THIS IS NOT A RACE.
WHAT YOU CAN USE TO DRAW WITH:
PENCIL
PEN
CRAYON
EL MARKO
WHAT YOU CANNOT USE
A DYMO MARKER
IMPORTANT!
AND DON'T DRAW YOUR WHOLE ARM IN. NO ONE WANTS TO SEE IT! MAKE IT LIKE THIS.
THEN PUT ON SOME LEGS. LIKE A Y UPSIDE DOWN WITH A THING IN IT. DON'T MAKE THEM TOO LONG OR THEY WILL LOOK STUPID. GO AHEAD AND PUT ON THE BEAK LIKE A SIDEWAYS V. PUT IN THE NOSE HOLE. THEN DRAW THE RED RUBBER THING HANGING FROM THEIR HEAD.
RIGHT HERE'S THE HEAD PART
DRAW A LINE IN THE BEAK
YOU CAN DECORATE THIS WITH DOTS OR WHATEVER
MAKE THEM SHORT LEGS
YOU CAN PUT ON TOENAILS
THIS IS TOTALLY WRONG
2
THEN THE EYE BUT DON'T GO PUTTING ON EYELASHES. AND DON'T PUT IT SMOKING A CIGARETTE LIKE MY COUSIN ARNOLD DID OR THE TEACHER WON'T PUT IT UP. TO MAKE IT REALISTIC DECORATE THE FINGERS TO BE FEATHERS.
USE YOUR IMAGINATION THIS IS THE HARDEST PART TO GET RIGHT
NO SMOKING!
3
FOR EXTRA CREDIT YOU CAN PUT A WING IN IF YOU ARE GOOD AT ART. IF YOU ARE TALENTED. IF YOU ARE NOT YOU PROBABLY ARE GOING TO WRECK IT UP.
PERSONALLY I LIKE TO PUT ON A LITTLE HAT. THAT'S WHY I GET AN A+ BUT IF YOU DO IT THAT'S COPYING.
THIS IS A PERFECT DECORATION
WHERE YOU CAN PUT THIS UP:
AT SCHOOL
THE LUNCHROOM
THE OFFICE
THE HALLS
ON THE DOOR
OVER THE CHALKBOARD
AT HOME
THE KITCHEN
THE FRONT ROOM
THE BED ROOM
THE FRONT DOOR
4

WINTER MARLYS

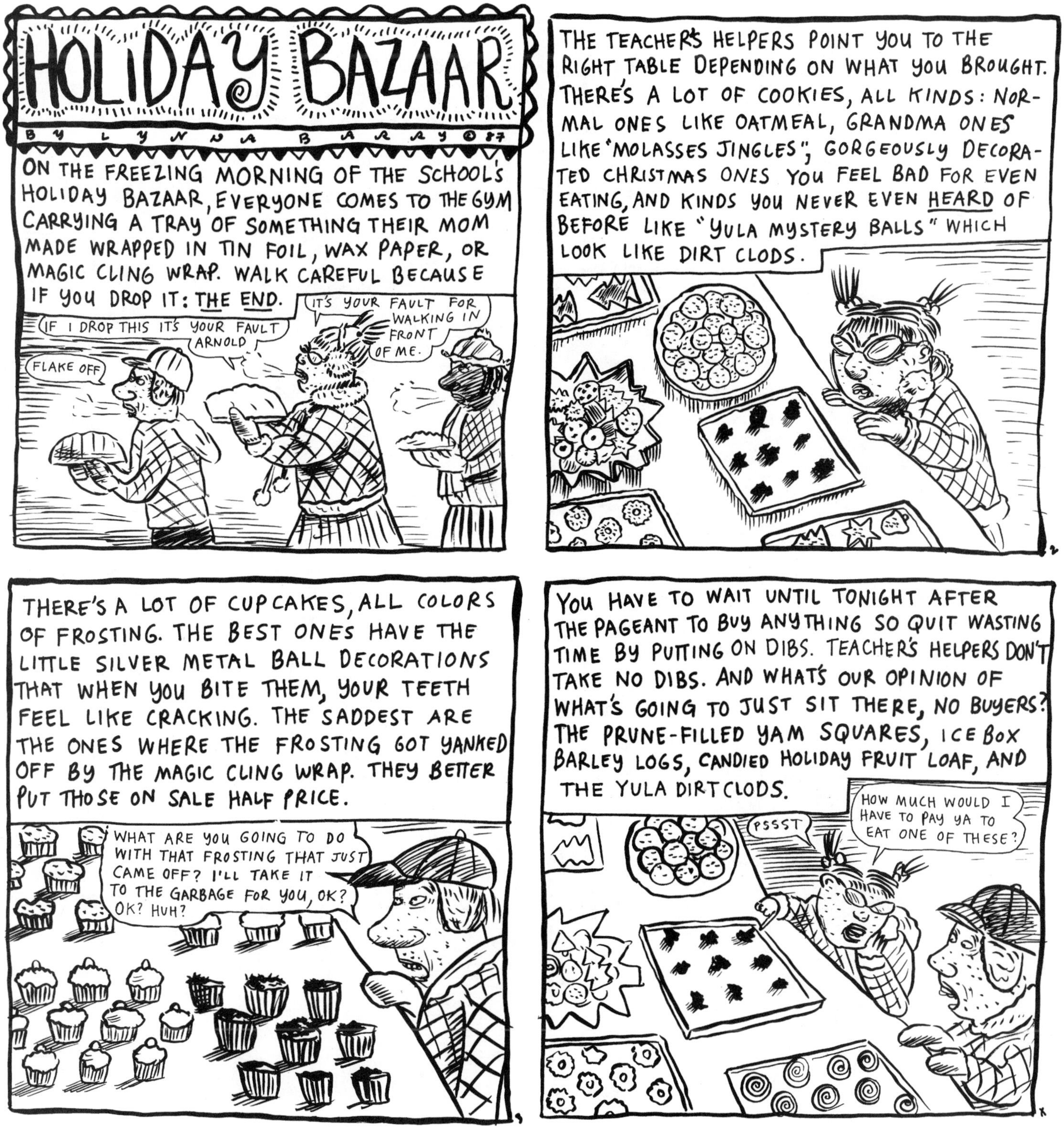
HOLIDAY BAZAAR
BY LYNDA BARRY ©87
ON THE FREEZING MORNING OF THE SCHOOL'S HOLIDAY BAZAAR, EVERYONE COMES TO THE GYM CARRYING A TRAY OF SOMETHING THEIR MOM MADE WRAPPED IN TIN FOIL, WAX PAPER, OR MAGIC CLING WRAP. WALK CAREFUL BECAUSE IF YOU DROP IT: THE END.
IF I DROP THIS IT'S YOUR FAULT ARNOLD
FLAKE OFF
IT'S YOUR FAULT FOR WALKING IN FRONT OF ME.
THE TEACHER'S HELPERS POINT YOU TO THE RIGHT TABLE DEPENDING ON WHAT YOU BROUGHT. THERE'S A LOT OF COOKIES, ALL KINDS: NORMAL ONES LIKE OATMEAL, GRANDMA ONES LIKE "MOLASSES JINGLES", GORGEOUSLY DECORATED CHRISTMAS ONES YOU FEEL BAD FOR EVEN EATING, AND KINDS YOU NEVER EVEN HEARD OF BEFORE LIKE "YULA MYSTERY BALLS" WHICH LOOK LIKE DIRT CLODS.
THERE'S A LOT OF CUPCAKES, ALL COLORS OF FROSTING. THE BEST ONES HAVE THE LITTLE SILVER METAL BALL DECORATIONS THAT WHEN YOU BITE THEM, YOUR TEETH FEEL LIKE CRACKING. THE SADDEST ARE THE ONES WHERE THE FROSTING GOT YANKED OFF BY THE MAGIC CLING WRAP. THEY BETTER PUT THOSE ON SALE HALF PRICE.
WHAT ARE YOU GOING TO DO WITH THAT FROSTING THAT JUST CAME OFF? I'LL TAKE IT TO THE GARBAGE FOR YOU, OK? OK? HUH?
YOU HAVE TO WAIT UNTIL TONIGHT AFTER THE PAGEANT TO BUY ANYTHING SO QUIT WASTING TIME BY PUTTING ON DIBS. TEACHER'S HELPERS DON'T TAKE NO DIBS. AND WHAT'S OUR OPINION OF WHAT'S GOING TO JUST SIT THERE, NO BUYERS? THE PRUNE-FILLED YAM SQUARES, ICE BOX BARLEY LOGS, CANDIED HOLIDAY FRUIT LOAF, AND THE YULA DIRT CLODS.
PSSST
HOW MUCH WOULD I HAVE TO PAY YA TO EAT ONE OF THESE?

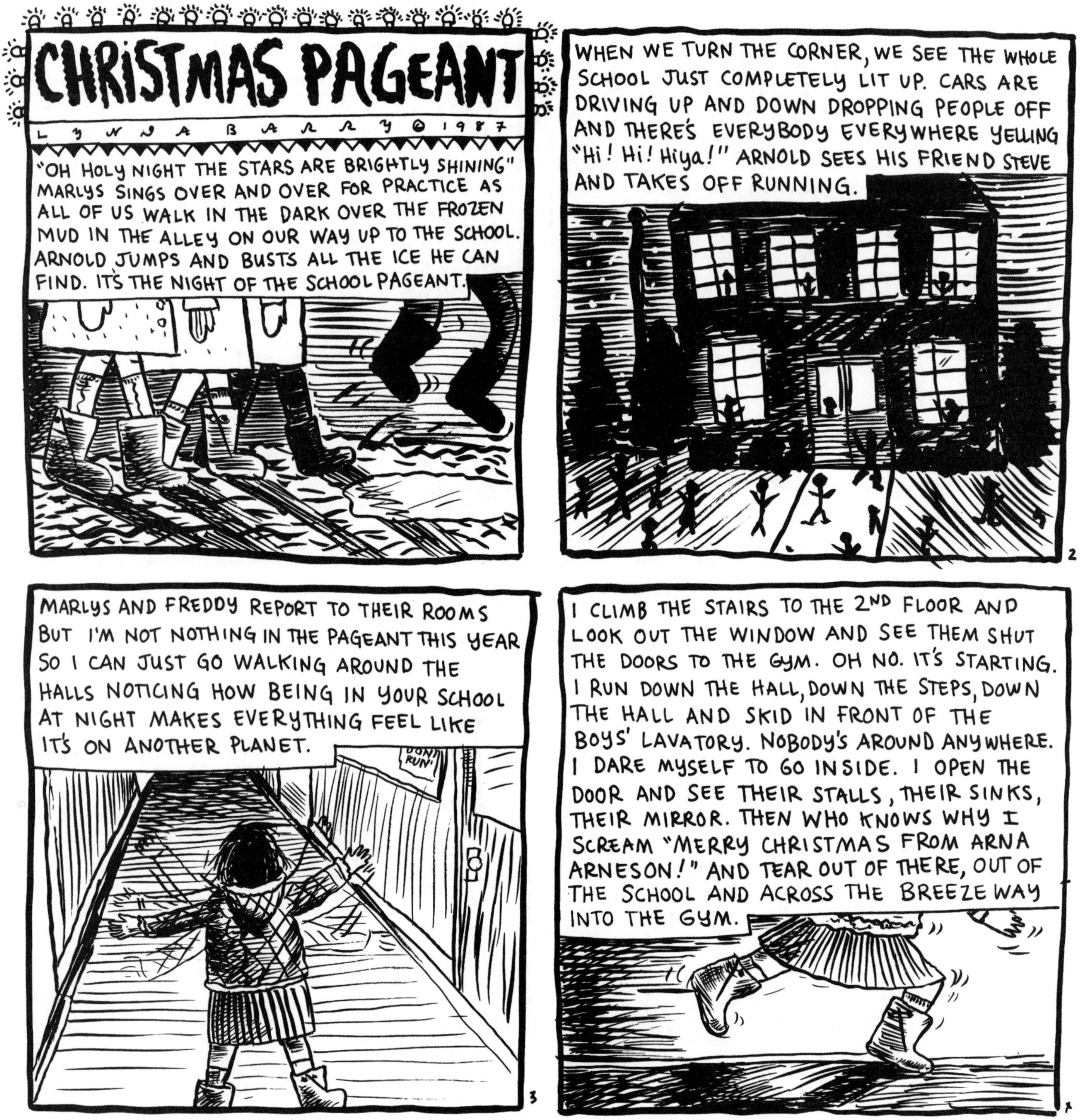
CHRISTMAS PAGEANT
LYNDA BARRY ©1987
"OH HOLY NIGHT THE STARS ARE BRIGHTLY SHINING" MARLYS SINGS OVER AND OVER FOR PRACTICE AS ALL OF US WALK IN THE DARK OVER THE FROZEN MUD IN THE ALLEY ON OUR WAY UP TO THE SCHOOL. ARNOLD JUMPS AND BUSTS ALL THE ICE HE CAN FIND. IT'S THE NIGHT OF THE SCHOOL PAGEANT.
WHEN WE TURN THE CORNER, WE SEE THE WHOLE SCHOOL JUST COMPLETELY LIT UP. CARS ARE DRIVING UP AND DOWN DROPPING PEOPLE OFF AND THERE'S EVERYBODY EVERYWHERE YELLING "Hi! Hi! Hiya!" ARNOLD SEES HIS FRIEND STEVE AND TAKES OFF RUNNING.
2
MARLYS AND FREDDY REPORT TO THEIR ROOMS BUT I'M NOT NOTHING IN THE PAGEANT THIS YEAR SO I CAN JUST GO WALKING AROUND THE HALLS NOTICING HOW BEING IN YOUR SCHOOL AT NIGHT MAKES EVERYTHING FEEL LIKE IT'S ON ANOTHER PLANET.
DON'T RUN
3
I CLIMB THE STAIRS TO THE 2ND FLOOR AND LOOK OUT THE WINDOW AND SEE THEM SHUT THE DOORS TO THE GYM. OH NO. IT'S STARTING. I RUN DOWN THE HALL, DOWN THE STEPS, DOWN THE HALL AND SKID IN FRONT OF THE BOYS' LAVATORY. NOBODY'S AROUND ANYWHERE. I DARE MYSELF TO GO INSIDE. I OPEN THE DOOR AND SEE THEIR STALLS, THEIR SINKS, THEIR MIRROR. THEN WHO KNOWS WHY I SCREAM "MERRY CHRISTMAS FROM ARNA ARNESON!" AND TEAR OUT OF THERE, OUT OF THE SCHOOL AND ACROSS THE BREEZE WAY INTO THE GYM.
4

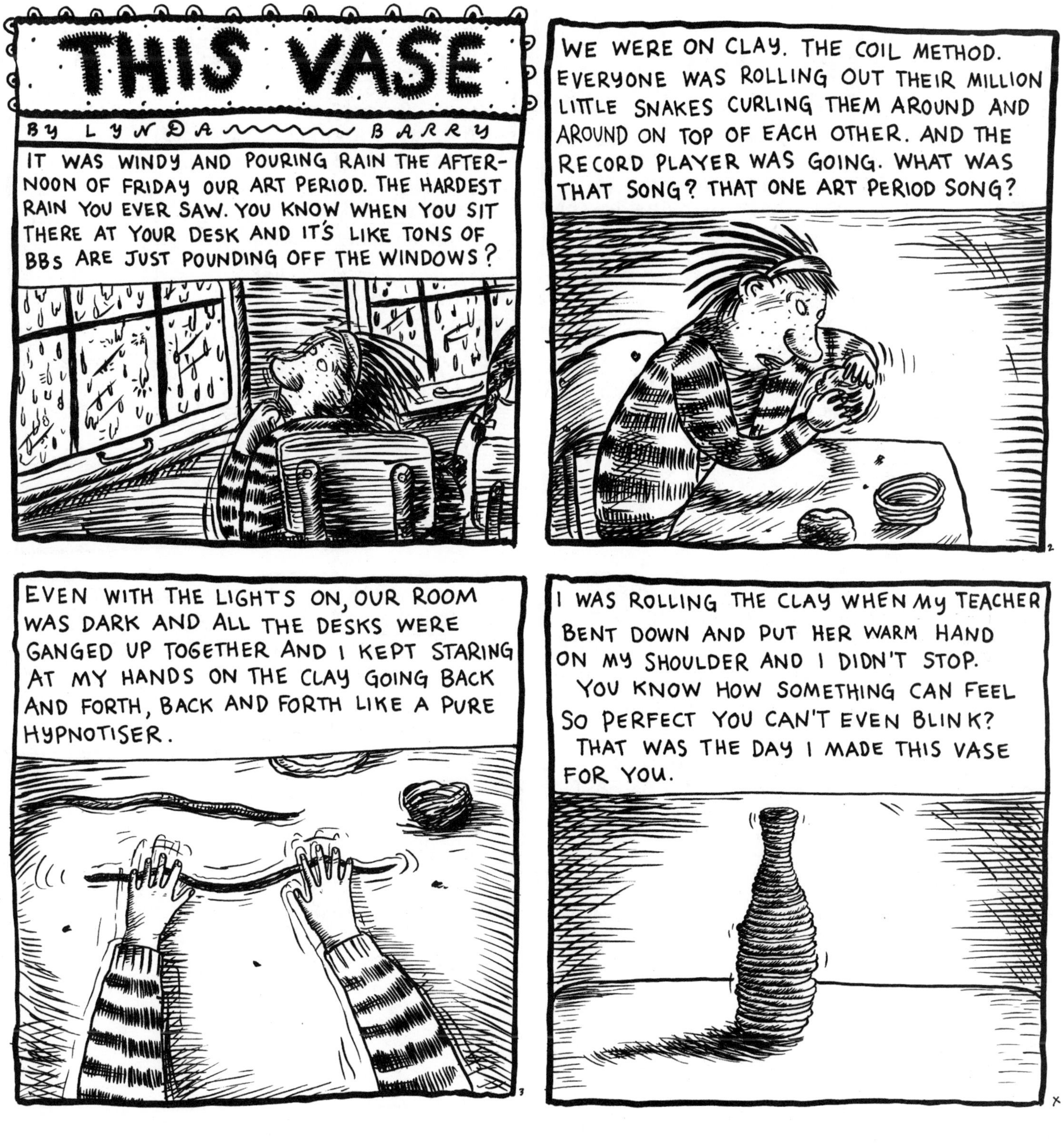
THIS VASE
BY LYNDA BARRY
IT WAS WINDY AND POURING RAIN THE AFTERNOON OF FRIDAY OUR ART PERIOD. THE HARDEST RAIN YOU EVER SAW. YOU KNOW WHEN YOU SIT THERE AT YOUR DESK AND IT'S LIKE TONS OF BBs ARE JUST POUNDING OFF THE WINDOWS?
WE WERE ON CLAY. THE COIL METHOD. EVERYONE WAS ROLLING OUT THEIR MILLION LITTLE SNAKES CURLING THEM AROUND AND AROUND ON TOP OF EACH OTHER. AND THE RECORD PLAYER WAS GOING. WHAT WAS THAT SONG? THAT ONE ART PERIOD SONG?
EVEN WITH THE LIGHTS ON, OUR ROOM WAS DARK AND ALL THE DESKS WERE GANGED UP TOGETHER AND I KEPT STARING AT MY HANDS ON THE CLAY GOING BACK AND FORTH, BACK AND FORTH LIKE A PURE HYPNOTISER.
I WAS ROLLING THE CLAY WHEN MY TEACHER BENT DOWN AND PUT HER WARM HAND ON MY SHOULDER AND I DIDN'T STOP. YOU KNOW HOW SOMETHING CAN FEEL SO PERFECT YOU CAN'T EVEN BLINK? THAT WAS THE DAY I MADE THIS VASE FOR YOU.

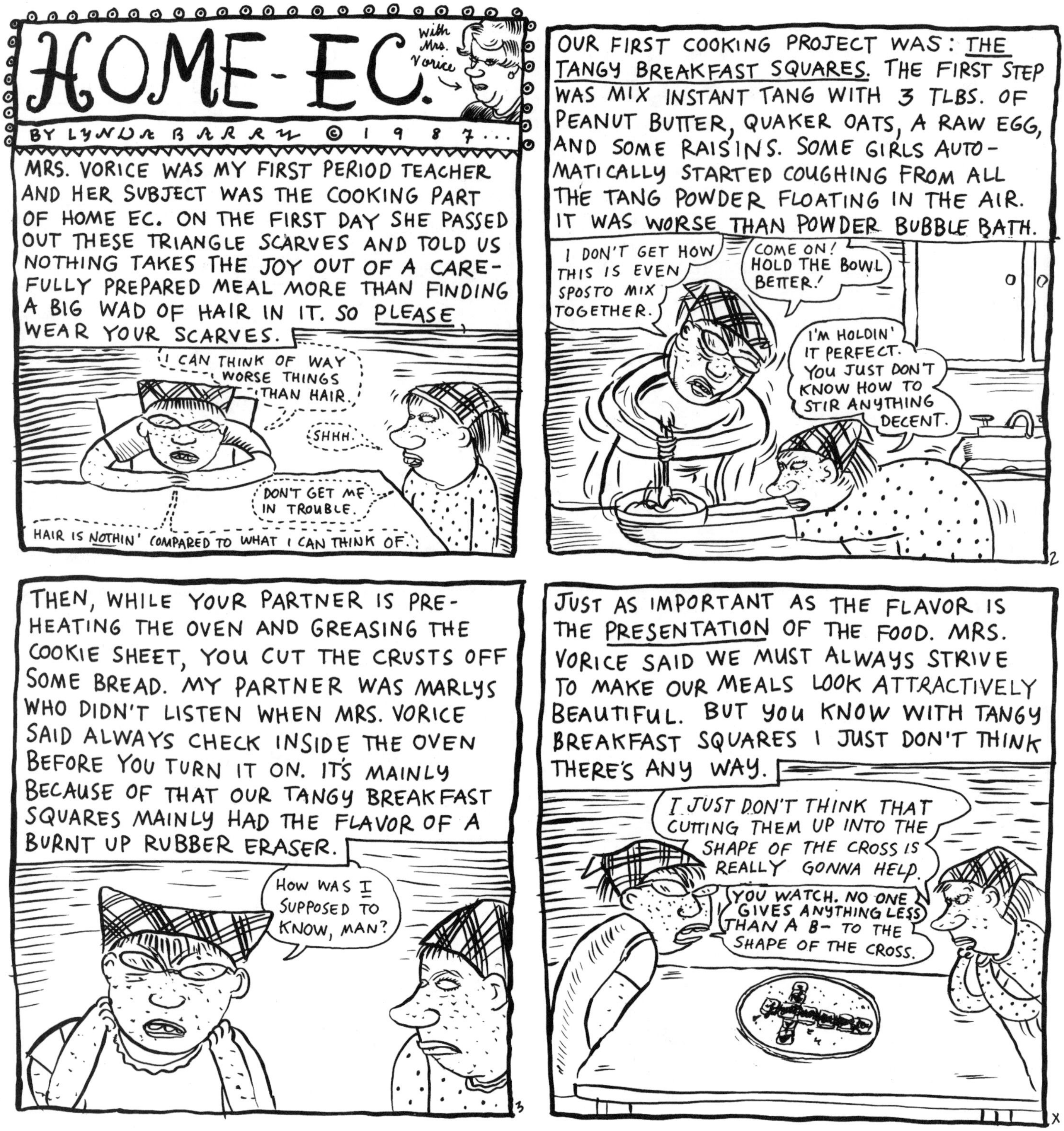
HOME-EC.
with Mrs. Vorice
BY LYNDA BARRY ©1987...
MRS. VORICE WAS MY FIRST PERIOD TEACHER AND HER SUBJECT WAS THE COOKING PART OF HOME EC. ON THE FIRST DAY SHE PASSED OUT THESE TRIANGLE SCARVES AND TOLD US NOTHING TAKES THE JOY OUT OF A CAREFULLY PREPARED MEAL MORE THAN FINDING A BIG WAD OF HAIR IN IT. SO PLEASE, WEAR YOUR SCARVES.
I CAN THINK OF WAY WORSE THINGS THAN HAIR.
SHHH.
DON'T GET ME IN TROUBLE.
HAIR IS NOTHIN' COMPARED TO WHAT I CAN THINK OF.
OUR FIRST COOKING PROJECT WAS: THE TANGY BREAKFAST SQUARES. THE FIRST STEP WAS MIX INSTANT TANG WITH 3 TLBS. OF PEANUT BUTTER, QUAKER OATS, A RAW EGG, AND SOME RAISINS. SOME GIRLS AUTOMATICALLY STARTED COUGHING FROM ALL THE TANG POWDER FLOATING IN THE AIR. IT WAS WORSE THAN POWDER BUBBLE BATH.
I DON'T GET HOW THIS IS EVEN SPOSTO MIX TOGETHER.
COME ON! HOLD THE BOWL BETTER!
I'M HOLDIN' IT PERFECT. YOU JUST DON'T KNOW HOW TO STIR ANYTHING DECENT.
THEN, WHILE YOUR PARTNER IS PRE-HEATING THE OVEN AND GREASING THE COOKIE SHEET, YOU CUT THE CRUSTS OFF SOME BREAD. MY PARTNER WAS MARLYS WHO DIDN'T LISTEN WHEN MRS. VORICE SAID ALWAYS CHECK INSIDE THE OVEN BEFORE YOU TURN IT ON. IT'S MAINLY BECAUSE OF THAT OUR TANGY BREAKFAST SQUARES MAINLY HAD THE FLAVOR OF A BURNT UP RUBBER ERASER.
HOW WAS I SUPPOSED TO KNOW, MAN?
JUST AS IMPORTANT AS THE FLAVOR IS THE PRESENTATION OF THE FOOD. MRS. VORICE SAID WE MUST ALWAYS STRIVE TO MAKE OUR MEALS LOOK ATTRACTIVELY BEAUTIFUL. BUT YOU KNOW WITH TANGY BREAKFAST SQUARES I JUST DON'T THINK THERE'S ANY WAY.
I JUST DON'T THINK THAT CUTTING THEM UP INTO THE SHAPE OF THE CROSS IS REALLY GONNA HELP.
YOU WATCH. NO ONE GIVES ANYTHING LESS THAN A B- TO THE SHAPE OF THE CROSS.

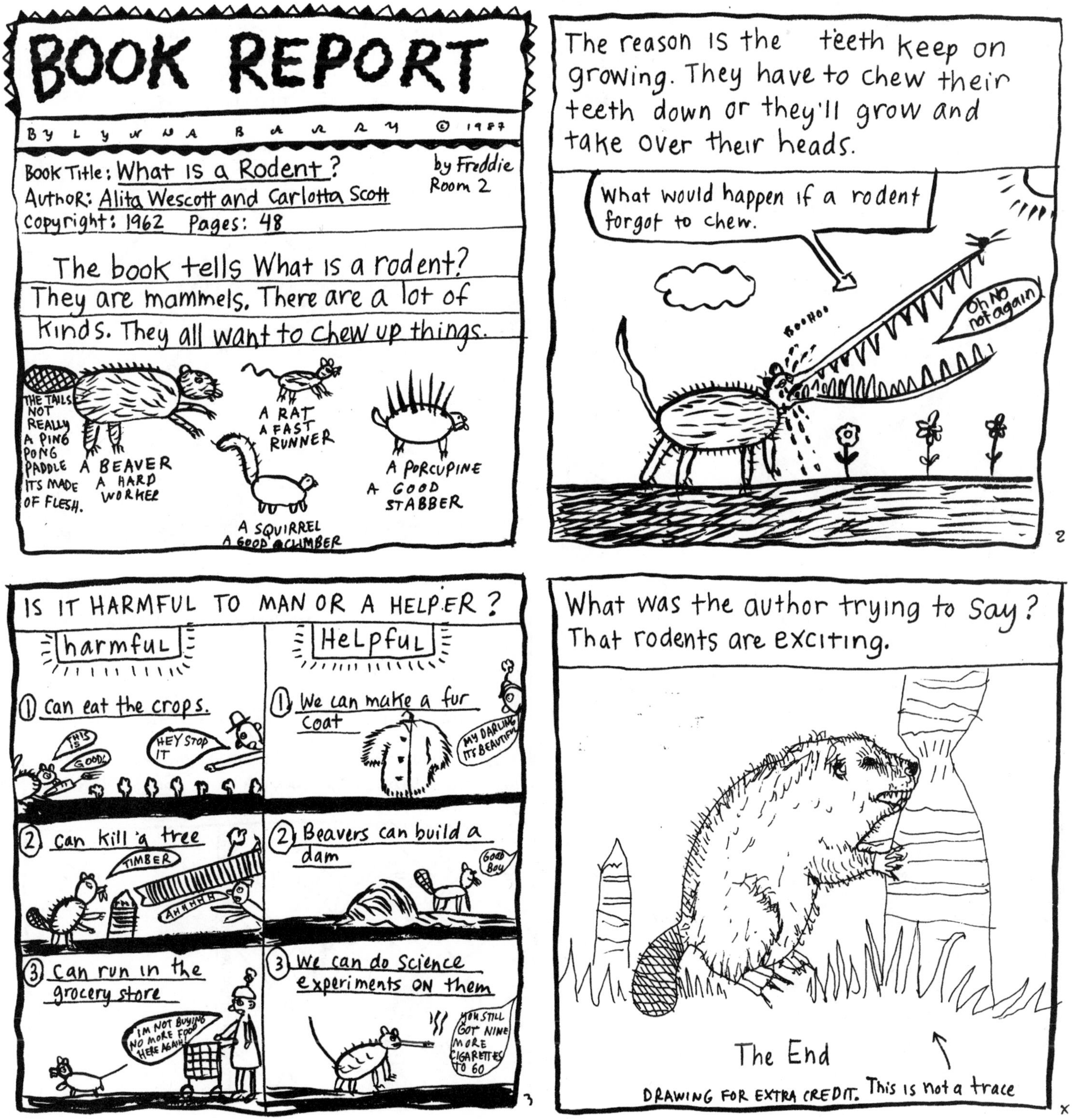

BOOK REPORT
BY LYNDA BARRY © 1987
Book Title: What is a Rodent?
by Freddie Room 2
Author: Alita Wescott and Carlotta Scott
Copyright: 1962 Pages: 48
The book tells What is a rodent? They are mammels. There are a lot of kinds. They all want to chew up things.
THE TAILS NOT REALLY A PING PONG PADDLE ITS MADE OF FLESH.
A BEAVER A HARD WORKER
A RAT A FAST RUNNER
A PORCUPINE A GOOD STABBER
A SQUIRREL A GOOD CLIMBER
The reason is the teeth keep on growing. They have to chew their teeth down or they'll grow and take over their heads.
What would happen if a rodent forgot to chew.
BOOHOO
Oh No not again
2
IS IT HARMFUL TO MAN OR A HELPER?
harmful
Helpful
1 can eat the crops.
THIS IS GOOD!
HEY STOP IT
1 We can make a fur coat
MY DARLING ITS BEAUTIFUL
2 can kill a tree
TIMBER
AHHHHH
2 Beavers can build a dam
Good Boy
3 Can run in the grocery store
IM NOT BUYING NO MORE FOOD HERE AGAIN!
3 We can do science experiments ON them
YOU STILL GOT NINE MORE CIGARETTES TO 60
3
What was the author trying to say? That rodents are exciting.
The End
DRAWING FOR EXTRA CREDIT.
This is not a trace
x

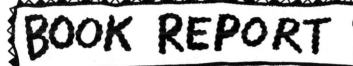

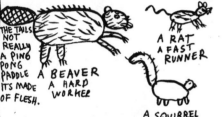

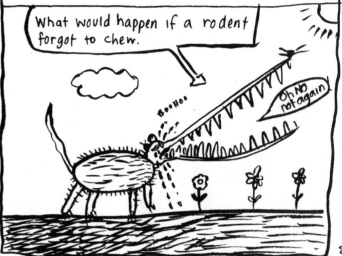

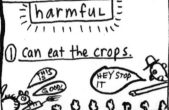

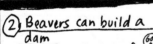

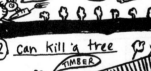

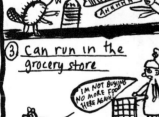

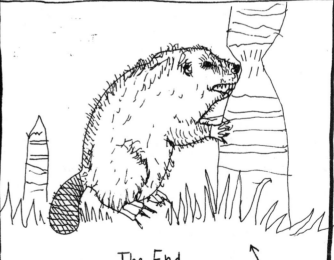

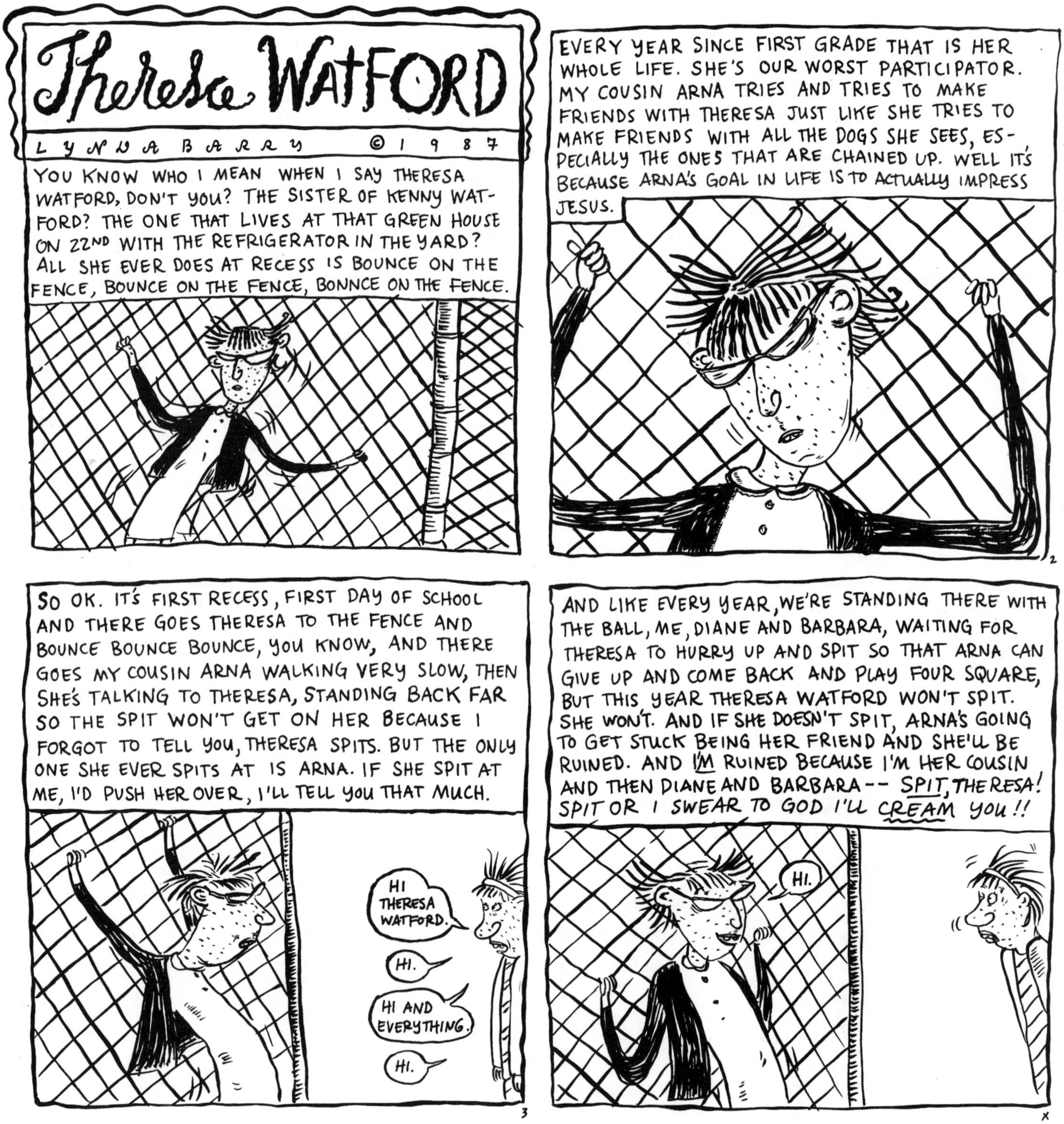
Theresa WATFORD
LYNDA BARRY ©1987
YOU KNOW WHO I MEAN WHEN I SAY THERESA WATFORD, DON'T YOU? THE SISTER OF KENNY WATFORD? THE ONE THAT LIVES AT THAT GREEN HOUSE ON 22ND WITH THE REFRIGERATOR IN THE YARD? ALL SHE EVER DOES AT RECESS IS BOUNCE ON THE FENCE, BOUNCE ON THE FENCE, BONNCE ON THE FENCE.
EVERY YEAR SINCE FIRST GRADE THAT IS HER WHOLE LIFE. SHE'S OUR WORST PARTICIPATOR. MY COUSIN ARNA TRIES AND TRIES TO MAKE FRIENDS WITH THERESA JUST LIKE SHE TRIES TO MAKE FRIENDS WITH ALL THE DOGS SHE SEES, ESPECIALLY THE ONES THAT ARE CHAINED UP. WELL IT'S BECAUSE ARNA'S GOAL IN LIFE IS TO ACTUALLY IMPRESS JESUS.
SO OK. IT'S FIRST RECESS, FIRST DAY OF SCHOOL AND THERE GOES THERESA TO THE FENCE AND BOUNCE BOUNCE BOUNCE, YOU KNOW, AND THERE GOES MY COUSIN ARNA WALKING VERY SLOW, THEN SHE'S TALKING TO THERESA, STANDING BACK FAR SO THE SPIT WON'T GET ON HER BECAUSE I FORGOT TO TELL YOU, THERESA SPITS. BUT THE ONLY ONE SHE EVER SPITS AT IS ARNA. IF SHE SPIT AT ME, I'D PUSH HER OVER, I'LL TELL YOU THAT MUCH.
HI THERESA WATFORD.
HI.
HI AND EVERYTHING.
HI.
AND LIKE EVERY YEAR, WE'RE STANDING THERE WITH THE BALL, ME, DIANE AND BARBARA, WAITING FOR THERESA TO HURRY UP AND SPIT SO THAT ARNA CAN GIVE UP AND COME BACK AND PLAY FOUR SQUARE, BUT THIS YEAR THERESA WATFORD WON'T SPIT. SHE WON'T. AND IF SHE DOESN'T SPIT, ARNA'S GOING TO GET STUCK BEING HER FRIEND AND SHE'LL BE RUINED. AND I'M RUINED BECAUSE I'M HER COUSIN AND THEN DIANE AND BARBARA-- SPIT, THERESA! SPIT OR I SWEAR TO GOD I'LL CREAM YOU!!
HI.

BEAN PLANTS

BY LYNDA BARRY ©1987

ALL YOU NEED FOR LEARNING ABOUT THE PLANT KINGDOM IS: YOUR MILK CARTON THAT YOU SAVED FROM LUNCH, SOME DIRT, SOME WATER, SOME BEANS, SOME SARAN WRAP, SOME RUBBER BANDS AND YOUR TEACHER MRS. BROGAN YELLING AT YOU TO NOT GOOF UP IN ANY WAY.

COVER IT WITH THE SARAN WRAP TO KEEP IT WARM AND THE WONDER OF EVAPORATION

REMEMBER. THESE ARE THE EARTH'S NATURAL RESOURCES SO BE RESPONSIBLE CITIZENS AND DON'T MAKE A MESS. MR. BEAN IS DEPENDING ON YOU TODAY FOR A GOOD HOME.

YOU WILL HAVE A GREAT FEELING WHEN YOUR BEAN STARTS TO GROW. YOU WILL HAVE TO SHARPEN YOUR PENCIL A LOT JUST FOR AN EXCUSE TO PASS BY IT.

ARNA! THE PENCIL SHARPENER IS NOT A TOY.

SOMEONE GOT THE IDEA TO NAME THEIR BEAN PLANT AND PRETTY SOON EVERY-ONE DID IT.

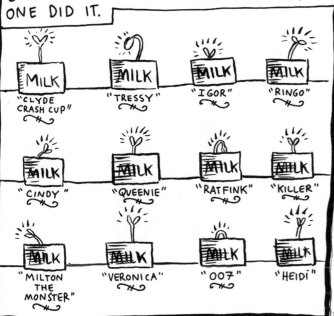

"CLYDE CRASH CUP"
"TRESSY"
"IGOR"
"RINGO"
"CINDY"
"QUEENIE"
"RATFINK"
"KILLER"
"MILTON THE MONSTER"
"VERONICA"
"007"
"HEIDI"

FINALLY ON THE LAST DAY OF SCHOOL YOU GET TO TAKE YOUR BEAN PLANT HOME. AFTER SHE GAVE US ALL OUR PLANTS, MRS. BROGAN STOOD AT THE FRONT OF THE ROOM TO SAY GOOD BYE. SHE TOLD US WE WERE A LOVELY CLASS AND SHE WILL MISS US VERY MUCH. AND SHE STARTED TO CRY WHEN SHE TOLD US TO BE SURE TO REMEMBER TO WATER OUR BEANS.

RRRIINNGGGGG

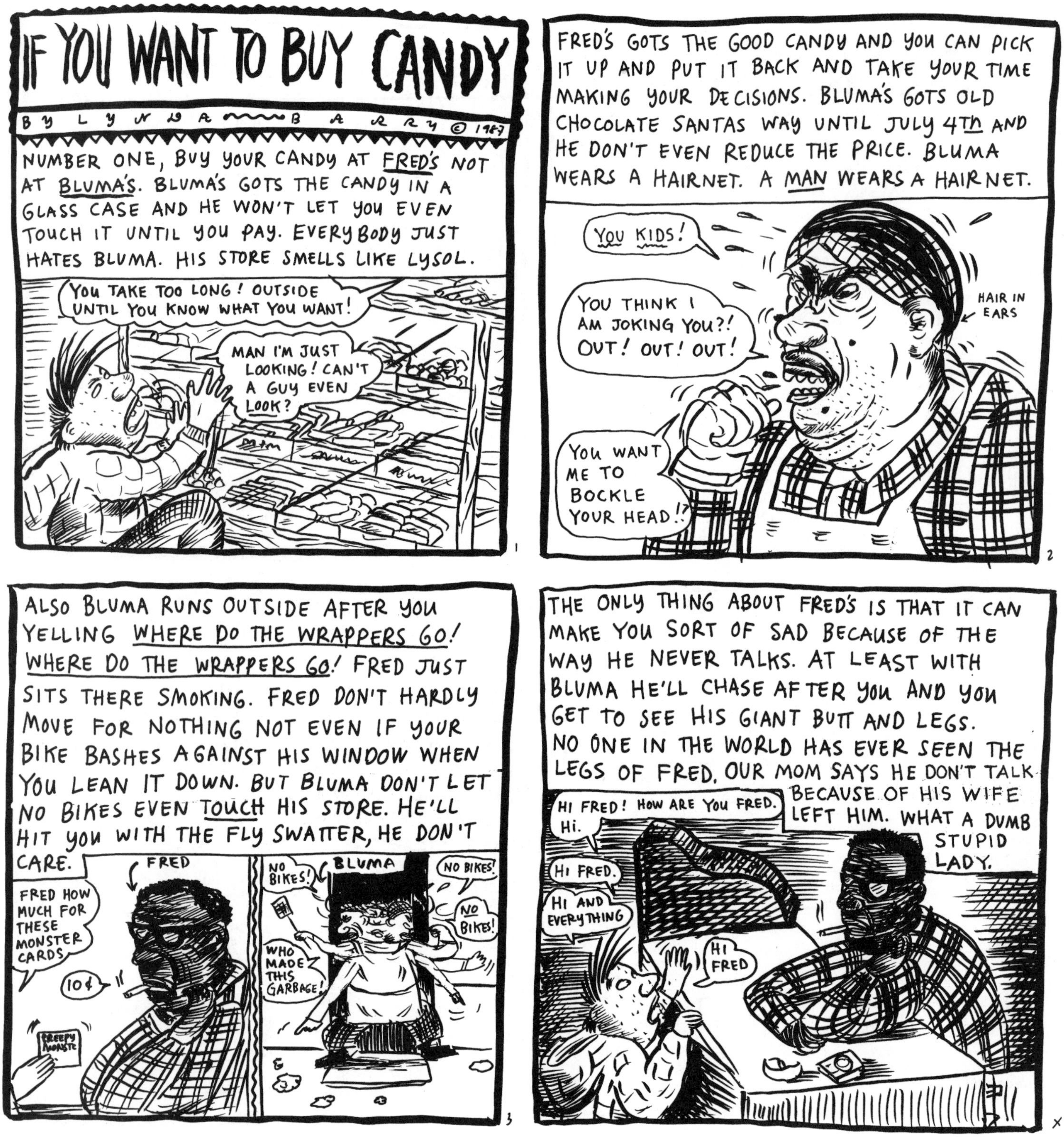
IF YOU WANT TO BUY CANDY
BY LYNDA BARRY © 1987
NUMBER ONE, BUY YOUR CANDY AT FRED'S NOT AT BLUMA'S. BLUMA'S GOTS THE CANDY IN A GLASS CASE AND HE WON'T LET YOU EVEN TOUCH IT UNTIL YOU PAY. EVERYBODY JUST HATES BLUMA. HIS STORE SMELLS LIKE LYSOL.
YOU TAKE TOO LONG! OUTSIDE UNTIL YOU KNOW WHAT YOU WANT!
MAN I'M JUST LOOKING! CAN'T A GUY EVEN LOOK?
1
FRED'S GOTS THE GOOD CANDY AND YOU CAN PICK IT UP AND PUT IT BACK AND TAKE YOUR TIME MAKING YOUR DECISIONS. BLUMA'S GOTS OLD CHOCOLATE SANTAS WAY UNTIL JULY 4TH AND HE DON'T EVEN REDUCE THE PRICE. BLUMA WEARS A HAIRNET. A MAN WEARS A HAIRNET.
YOU KIDS!
YOU THINK I AM JOKING YOU?! OUT! OUT! OUT!
HAIR IN EARS
YOU WANT ME TO BOCKLE YOUR HEAD!?
2
ALSO BLUMA RUNS OUTSIDE AFTER YOU YELLING WHERE DO THE WRAPPERS GO! WHERE DO THE WRAPPERS GO! FRED JUST SITS THERE SMOKING. FRED DON'T HARDLY MOVE FOR NOTHING NOT EVEN IF YOUR BIKE BASHES AGAINST HIS WINDOW WHEN YOU LEAN IT DOWN. BUT BLUMA DON'T LET NO BIKES EVEN TOUCH HIS STORE. HE'LL HIT YOU WITH THE FLY SWATTER, HE DON'T CARE.
FRED
FRED HOW MUCH FOR THESE MONSTER CARDS
10¢
CREEPY MONSTE
BLUMA
NO BIKES!
NO BIKES!
NO BIKES!
WHO MADE THIS GARBAGE!
3
THE ONLY THING ABOUT FRED'S IS THAT IT CAN MAKE YOU SORT OF SAD BECAUSE OF THE WAY HE NEVER TALKS. AT LEAST WITH BLUMA HE'LL CHASE AFTER YOU AND YOU GET TO SEE HIS GIANT BUTT AND LEGS. NO ONE IN THE WORLD HAS EVER SEEN THE LEGS OF FRED. OUR MOM SAYS HE DON'T TALK BECAUSE OF HIS WIFE LEFT HIM. WHAT A DUMB STUPID LADY.
HI FRED! HOW ARE YOU FRED. HI.
HI FRED.
HI AND EVERYTHING
HI FRED
X

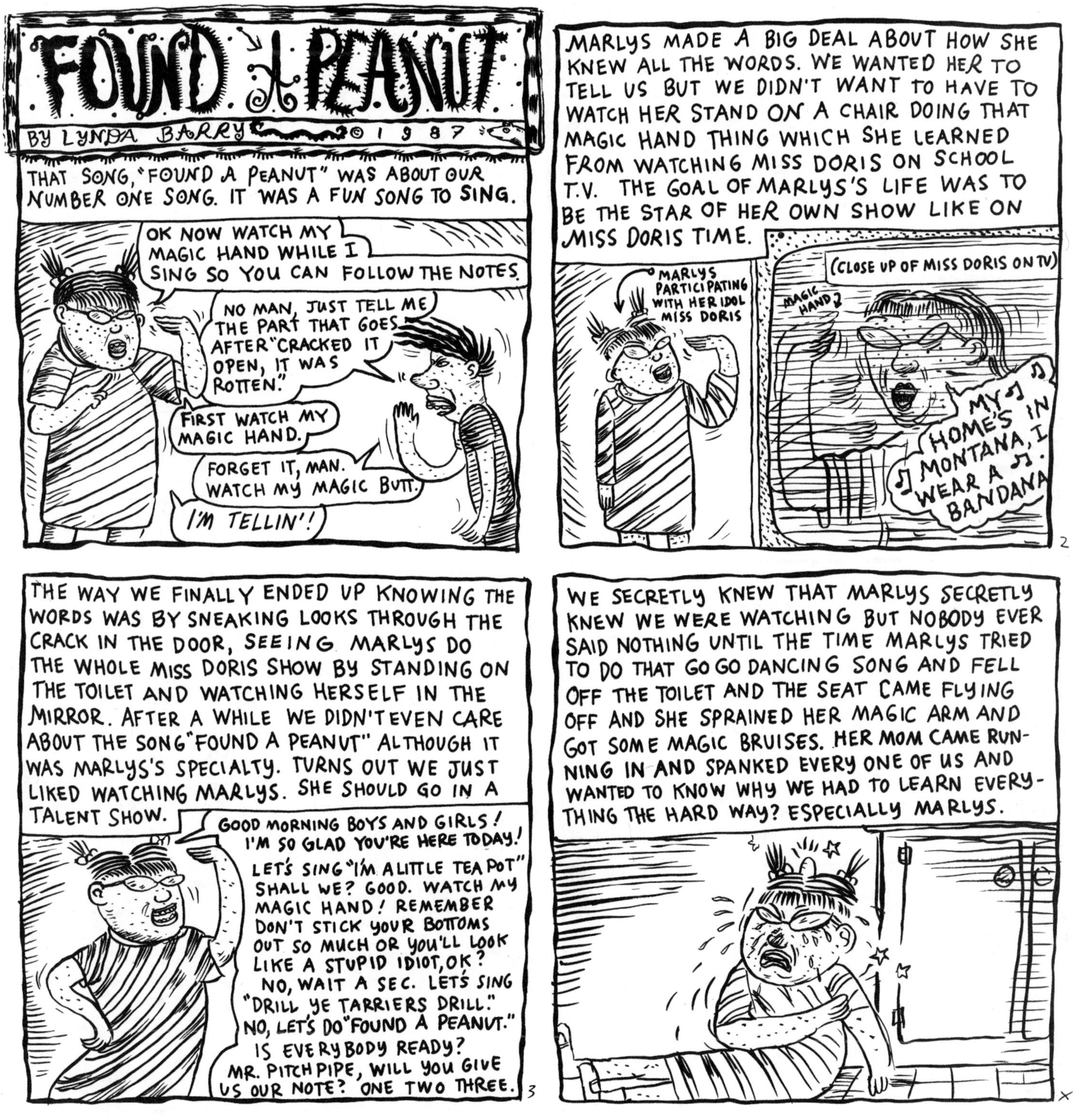
FOUND A PEANUT
BY LYNDA BARRY ©1987
THAT SONG, "FOUND A PEANUT" WAS ABOUT OUR NUMBER ONE SONG. IT WAS A FUN SONG TO SING.
OK NOW WATCH MY MAGIC HAND WHILE I SING SO YOU CAN FOLLOW THE NOTES.
NO MAN, JUST TELL ME THE PART THAT GOES AFTER "CRACKED IT OPEN, IT WAS ROTTEN."
FIRST WATCH MY MAGIC HAND.
FORGET IT, MAN. WATCH MY MAGIC BUTT.
I'M TELLIN'!
MARLYS MADE A BIG DEAL ABOUT HOW SHE KNEW ALL THE WORDS. WE WANTED HER TO TELL US BUT WE DIDN'T WANT TO HAVE TO WATCH HER STAND ON A CHAIR DOING THAT MAGIC HAND THING WHICH SHE LEARNED FROM WATCHING MISS DORIS ON SCHOOL T.V. THE GOAL OF MARLYS'S LIFE WAS TO BE THE STAR OF HER OWN SHOW LIKE ON MISS DORIS TIME.
MARLYS PARTICIPATING WITH HER IDOL MISS DORIS
(CLOSE UP OF MISS DORIS ON TV)
MAGIC HAND
MY HOME'S IN MONTANA, I WEAR A BANDANA
2
THE WAY WE FINALLY ENDED UP KNOWING THE WORDS WAS BY SNEAKING LOOKS THROUGH THE CRACK IN THE DOOR, SEEING MARLYS DO THE WHOLE MISS DORIS SHOW BY STANDING ON THE TOILET AND WATCHING HERSELF IN THE MIRROR. AFTER A WHILE WE DIDN'T EVEN CARE ABOUT THE SONG "FOUND A PEANUT" ALTHOUGH IT WAS MARLYS'S SPECIALTY. TURNS OUT WE JUST LIKED WATCHING MARLYS. SHE SHOULD GO IN A TALENT SHOW.
GOOD MORNING BOYS AND GIRLS! I'M SO GLAD YOU'RE HERE TODAY! LET'S SING "I'M A LITTLE TEA POT" SHALL WE? GOOD. WATCH MY MAGIC HAND! REMEMBER DON'T STICK YOUR BOTTOMS OUT SO MUCH OR YOU'LL LOOK LIKE A STUPID IDIOT, OK? NO, WAIT A SEC. LET'S SING "DRILL YE TARRIERS DRILL." NO, LET'S DO "FOUND A PEANUT." IS EVERYBODY READY? MR. PITCHPIPE, WILL YOU GIVE US OUR NOTE? ONE TWO THREE.
3
WE SECRETLY KNEW THAT MARLYS SECRETLY KNEW WE WERE WATCHING BUT NOBODY EVER SAID NOTHING UNTIL THE TIME MARLYS TRIED TO DO THAT GO GO DANCING SONG AND FELL OFF THE TOILET AND THE SEAT CAME FLYING OFF AND SHE SPRAINED HER MAGIC ARM AND GOT SOME MAGIC BRUISES. HER MOM CAME RUNNING IN AND SPANKED EVERY ONE OF US AND WANTED TO KNOW WHY WE HAD TO LEARN EVERYTHING THE HARD WAY? ESPECIALLY MARLYS.
X

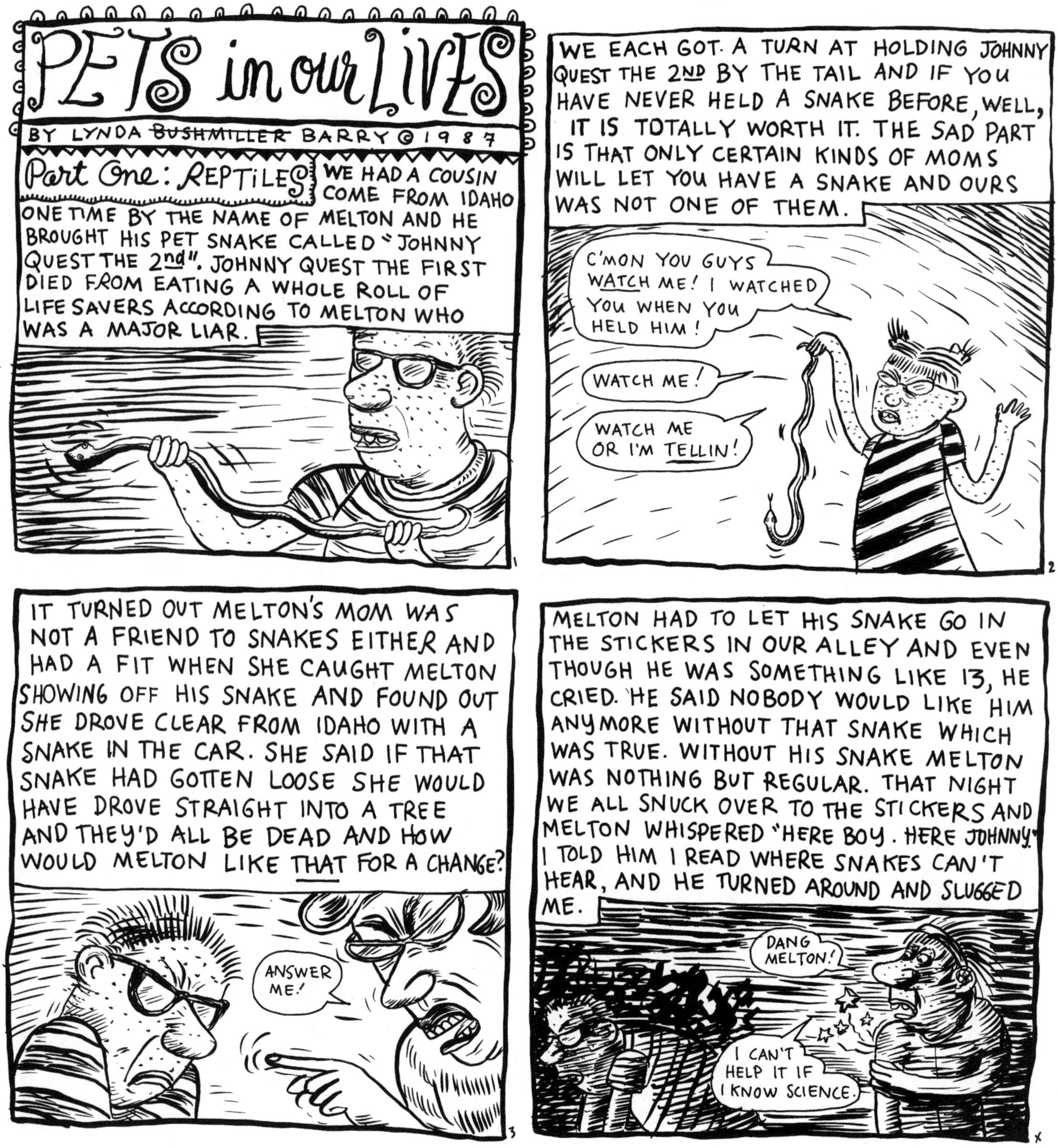
PETS in our LIVES
BY LYNDA ~~BUSHMILLER~~ BARRY © 1987
Part One: REPTILES
WE HAD A COUSIN COME FROM IDAHO ONE TIME BY THE NAME OF MELTON AND HE BROUGHT HIS PET SNAKE CALLED "JOHNNY QUEST THE 2nd". JOHNNY QUEST THE FIRST DIED FROM EATING A WHOLE ROLL OF LIFESAVERS ACCORDING TO MELTON WHO WAS A MAJOR LIAR.
WE EACH GOT A TURN AT HOLDING JOHNNY QUEST THE 2ND BY THE TAIL AND IF YOU HAVE NEVER HELD A SNAKE BEFORE, WELL, IT IS TOTALLY WORTH IT. THE SAD PART IS THAT ONLY CERTAIN KINDS OF MOMS WILL LET YOU HAVE A SNAKE AND OURS WAS NOT ONE OF THEM.
C'MON YOU GUYS WATCH ME! I WATCHED YOU WHEN YOU HELD HIM!
WATCH ME!
WATCH ME OR I'M TELLIN!
IT TURNED OUT MELTON'S MOM WAS NOT A FRIEND TO SNAKES EITHER AND HAD A FIT WHEN SHE CAUGHT MELTON SHOWING OFF HIS SNAKE AND FOUND OUT SHE DROVE CLEAR FROM IDAHO WITH A SNAKE IN THE CAR. SHE SAID IF THAT SNAKE HAD GOTTEN LOOSE SHE WOULD HAVE DROVE STRAIGHT INTO A TREE AND THEY'D ALL BE DEAD AND HOW WOULD MELTON LIKE THAT FOR A CHANGE?
ANSWER ME!
MELTON HAD TO LET HIS SNAKE GO IN THE STICKERS IN OUR ALLEY AND EVEN THOUGH HE WAS SOMETHING LIKE 13, HE CRIED. HE SAID NOBODY WOULD LIKE HIM ANYMORE WITHOUT THAT SNAKE WHICH WAS TRUE. WITHOUT HIS SNAKE MELTON WAS NOTHING BUT REGULAR. THAT NIGHT WE ALL SNUCK OVER TO THE STICKERS AND MELTON WHISPERED "HERE BOY. HERE JOHNNY." I TOLD HIM I READ WHERE SNAKES CAN'T HEAR, AND HE TURNED AROUND AND SLUGGED ME.
DANG MELTON!
I CAN'T HELP IT IF I KNOW SCIENCE.

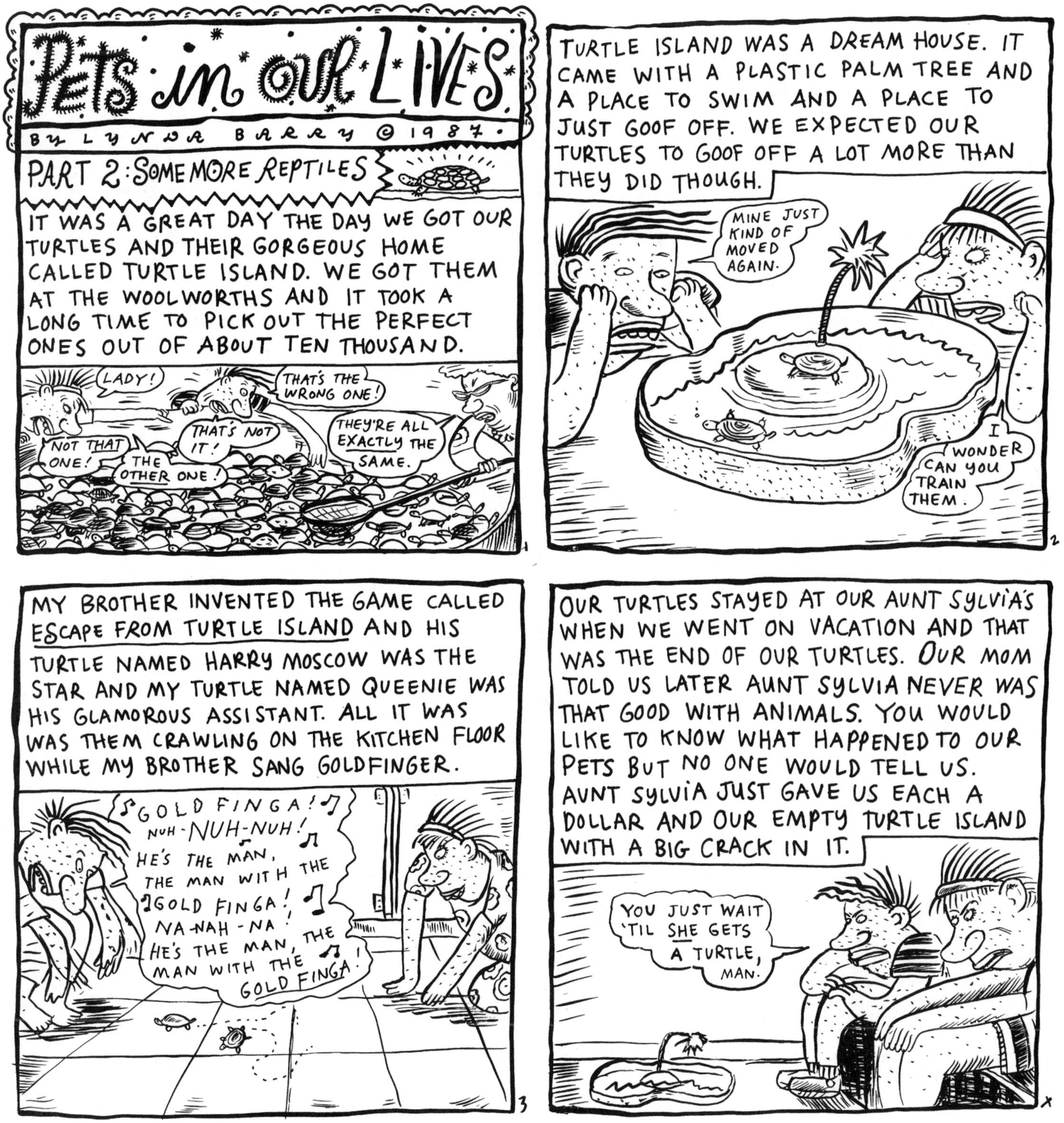
PETS IN OUR LIVES
BY LYNDA BARRY ©1987
PART 2: SOME MORE REPTILES
IT WAS A GREAT DAY THE DAY WE GOT OUR TURTLES AND THEIR GORGEOUS HOME CALLED TURTLE ISLAND. WE GOT THEM AT THE WOOLWORTHS AND IT TOOK A LONG TIME TO PICK OUT THE PERFECT ONES OUT OF ABOUT TEN THOUSAND.
LADY!
THAT'S THE WRONG ONE!
NOT THAT ONE!
THAT'S NOT IT!
THE OTHER ONE!
THEY'RE ALL EXACTLY THE SAME.
TURTLE ISLAND WAS A DREAM HOUSE. IT CAME WITH A PLASTIC PALM TREE AND A PLACE TO SWIM AND A PLACE TO JUST GOOF OFF. WE EXPECTED OUR TURTLES TO GOOF OFF A LOT MORE THAN THEY DID THOUGH.
MINE JUST KIND OF MOVED AGAIN.
I WONDER CAN YOU TRAIN THEM.
MY BROTHER INVENTED THE GAME CALLED ESCAPE FROM TURTLE ISLAND AND HIS TURTLE NAMED HARRY MOSCOW WAS THE STAR AND MY TURTLE NAMED QUEENIE WAS HIS GLAMOROUS ASSISTANT. ALL IT WAS WAS THEM CRAWLING ON THE KITCHEN FLOOR WHILE MY BROTHER SANG GOLDFINGER.
GOLD FINGA! NUH-NUH-NUH! HE'S THE MAN, THE MAN WITH THE GOLD FINGA! NA-NAH-NA! HE'S THE MAN, THE MAN WITH THE GOLD FINGA!
OUR TURTLES STAYED AT OUR AUNT SYLVIA'S WHEN WE WENT ON VACATION AND THAT WAS THE END OF OUR TURTLES. OUR MOM TOLD US LATER AUNT SYLVIA NEVER WAS THAT GOOD WITH ANIMALS. YOU WOULD LIKE TO KNOW WHAT HAPPENED TO OUR PETS BUT NO ONE WOULD TELL US. AUNT SYLVIA JUST GAVE US EACH A DOLLAR AND OUR EMPTY TURTLE ISLAND WITH A BIG CRACK IN IT.
YOU JUST WAIT 'TIL SHE GETS A TURTLE, MAN.

OUR MUSEUM
BY LYNDA BARRY ©1987
ONE TIME WE GOT THE INTERESTING IDEA OF STARTING AN ACTUAL MUSEUM DOWN IN THE GARAGE. MAINLY ALL YOU NEED TO DO THIS IS: TAPE AND FASCINATING THINGS.
This is the most chewn up pencil in the WORLD. IT WAS DONE BY ME THE GREAT ARNOLD! AND I am not even suppösed to be chewing no pencils! ARNOLD IS #1!
ARM OF THE CHATTY CATHY BROKE OFF BY MARLYS WHO TRIED TO BLAME IT ALL ON FREDDIE. BY ARNOLD #1
what a lie! By Marlys
PRACTICALLY ANYTHING CAN LOOK MORE INCREDIBLE IF YOU TAPE IT TO A WALL AND STICK UP A SIGN ABOUT IT.
CROSS I MADE OUT OF TWO POPSICLE STICKS. IT IS HARD TO FIT JESUS ON THERE WITHOUT MAKING A MISTAKE. THE DRAWING PARTS THE HARDEST. BY SIR Freddie
A bunch of my pictures. My Mom ordered extra ones for they were so great. For Sale $1.00 each one. By Marlys
THIS IS THE STRING OFF THE HOOD OF MY JACKET IT CAME OFF BY ACCIDENT. BY ARNA
BLOOD OF ARNOLD #1 FROM WHEN I BASHED MY FINGER IN. THE CUT LOOKED LIKE A SHARK MOUTH
EVERYBODY PUT SOMETHING UP THAT WAS SUPPOSED TO STIMULATE YOUR IMAGINATION.
ACE
A Messed up comb of my Dad's. by ~~Freddie~~ Sir Freddie.
Xx Xx Xx Xx
Yy Yy Yy Yy
Zz Zz Zz Zz Zz
Here is an example of another one of my perfect papers that I got another A on. By Marlys
Can you solve these problems?
242 + 167 + 98 = 507
361 + 33 + 209 = 541
981 + 429 + 763 = 2,173
123 + 991 + 198 = 1312
427 + 82 + 824 = 1333
Good work!
100
This is the best math paper of my whole life. 100%. No wrongs. by Arna
MARLYS
Marlys Marlys Marlys
Marlys Marlys Marlys
Marlys Marlys Marlys
Marlys Marlys Marlys
Marlys Marlys Marlys
Here is my name written a blunch of times. By Marlys
WE COULD HAVE KEPT GOING BUT WE RAN OUT OF TAPE. WE TRIED ELMER'S GLUE BUT IT TAKES TOO LONG TO JUST STAND THERE AND HOLD IT UNTIL IT STICKS, YOU KNOW?
THIS IS Marlys' DOLL
MARLYS
MARLYS
C'MON YOU GUYS! SOME ONE ELSE TAKE A TURN AT THIS! NO FAIR!
MY ARMS ARE GETTING DEAD!
YOU GUYS! WHERE YA GOIN'?!! I'M TELLIN'! MOM! MOM!

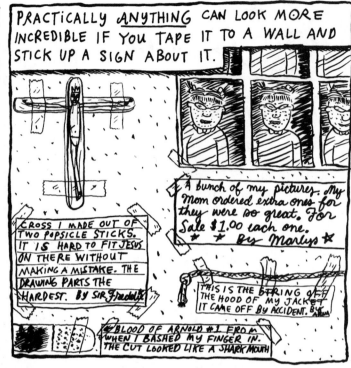

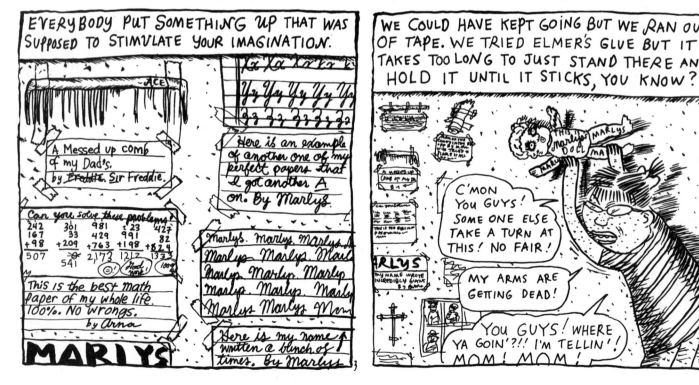

BEDROOMS OF OUR DREAMS
BY LYNDA BARRY ©1987
DREAM BEDROOM OF FREDDIE
BUILT IN GIANT ANT FARM
MICRO-SCOPE
MAGIC ROPE LIKE ON JOHNNY QUEST
BUILT IN T.V.
SNAKE
WHOLE WALL OF A REPTILE ZOO BUT THEY CAN ESCAPE ALL THEY WANT
TALKING BIRD NAMED ELVIN
LIVE TRAINED MONKEY I ORDERED FROM A COMIC BOOK
PYTHON
GEKKO
DOORS FOR ANIMALS TO COME ON IN
IN
OUT
HAMMOCK FOR A BED
GILA MONSTER
REAL GRASS FOR THE RUG
SPECIAL HATCH 2
UNDER HERE IS A FIRE POLE TO KITCHEN
P.S. SECRET COMPARTMENTS ARE EVERYWHERE!
DREAM BED ROOM OF ARNOLD
CUSTOM BLOODY EYEBALL WALL PAPER
POP MACHINE (FREE)
CANDY MACHINE (FREE)
GIANT BUILT-IN T.V. UP ON CEILING
ROPE LADDER TO ROOF
I-SPY T.V. SCREEN WHERE YOU CAN WATCH WHAT EVERYBODYS DOING EVERY WHERE
DRAWER FULL OF COMICS AND MADS.
DRAWERS FULL OF MONSTER CARD COLLECTIONS, ARMY MEN, WEAPONS, MATCHES, GOT A PLAYBOY IN THERE TOO IN CERTAIN ONE
CONTROL PANEL FOR WHOLE ROOM
CLIMB ROPE TO GET ALL THIS
PERISCOPE
WALKIE TALKIES
MY BED: LOOKS LIKE A DRAGSTER, CAN ACTUALLY TAKE OFF PLUS LAY A PATCH.
REAL SMOKE IS COMING OUT
DOOR WITH ELECTRIC SHOCKERS FOR IF PEOPLE COME IN WITHOUT ASKING
2 WAY MIRRORS
LIGHTS COME ON
DIRT CLODS
FLOOR IS OF REAL DIRT!
OPEN THIS HATCH AND RIDE GIANT SLIDE FOR ONE MILE.
IMPORTANT WARNING! THIS ROOM HAS A LOT OF BOOBY TRAPS!
TRAP DOOR
ESCAPE HATCH
2
DREAM BEDROOM OF ARNA
HIGH UP SECRET LIBRARY OF EVERY BOOK IN THE WORLD
TRAPEZE
HIGHEST BED ON EARTH. YOU HAVE TO CLIMB A LADDER TO GET TO IT
INVISABLE DOOR TO THE OUTSIDE
HANGING T.V. THAT GOES UP+DOWN
MOVIE SCREEN WHERE YOU CAN SEE ANY MOVIE JUST BY THINKING OF IT
STACK OF MAGAZINES YOU CAN CUT UP
DRAWERS OF SISSORS, GLUE, PAINTS, COLORS, SPARKLE PAINTS
CONSTRUCTION PAPER
SPECIAL PET ELEVATOR
TRAMPOLINE
BUILT IN RECORD PLAYER PLUS 1,001 RECORDS
REVOLVING DOOR
SWIMMING POOL
3
DREAM BED ROOM OF MARLYS
"MARLYS" WALL PAPER
WHOLE WALL OF BUILT IN "WORLD OF BARBI" AND ALSO: HER BEST FRIEND A NEW DOLL CALLED "MARLYS"
GOLD
DIAMONDS
marlys
SILVER
RUBIES
CLOSET FULL OF BALLERINA DRESSES
THRONE WHERE I SIT WHEN I FEEL LIKE IT
THIS WHOLE WALL IS A BIG MIRROR
BARBIS BEDROOM
BARBIS BALCONY
MARLYS BEDROOM
BARBIS DREAM KITCHEN
MARLYS DREAM GARAGE
BARBIS DREAM HALL
TOTAL STEPS MADE OF PEZ
MY PICTURES A PAINTING OF ME
BIG MIRROR
MICRO-PHONE
MARLYS PILLOWS
RECORD PLAYER RISES OUT OF HERE
T.V. RISES OUT OF HERE
PINK FUR BED IN THE SHAPE OF A HEART THAT SPINS AND PLAYS MUSIC. NO ONE EXCEPT ME IS ALLOWED ON IT!
A BUTLER HOLDING A BOWL OF M+MS CONSTANTLY FULL AND HE ANNOUNCES WHO CAN COME IN.
YES YOUR HIGNESS MARLYS
WHAT HE ALWAYS SAYS
RED VELVET COVERED STAGE FOR ME TO DO MY SINGING ON
PINK FUR RUG
THE SMELL OF PERFUME IS EVERYWHERE: OH! DE LONDON.

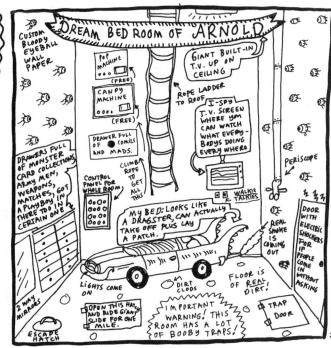

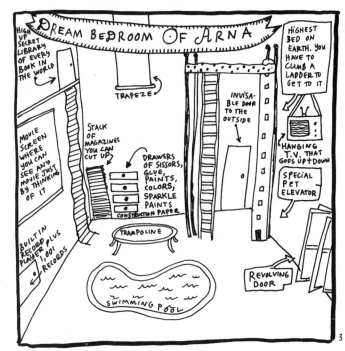

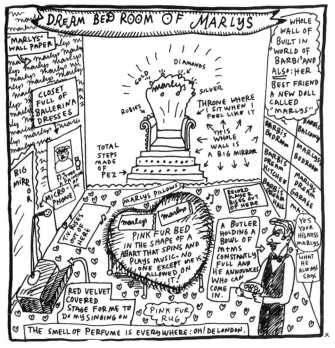

MOVING AWAY

BY LYNDA SLAMMER DOOR BARRY © 1987

UP THE STREET, ON THE DIRT PART OF THE ROAD, WAS THE HOUSE OF LOUIS CHEEK AND HIS SISTER SANDRA CHEEK. NONE OF US EVER LIKED THEM BECAUSE THEY HAD BAD TEMPERS, SO "BIG DEAL" IS ALL WE THOUGHT WHEN LOUIS TOLD US THEY WERE MOVING AWAY.

AND YOU GUYS WANNA KNOW WHERE WE'RE MOVIN' TO?

HUH?

WE'RE MOVIN' OVER TO DISNEYLAND.

HOW COME PAPER ALWAYS STICKS TO POPSICLES?

I'M GONNA LIVE AT DISNEYLAND YOU GUYS.

1

LOUIS YELLED AT US THAT WE WOULD NEVER EVER SEE HIM AGAIN FOR THE REST OF OUR LIVES. HE WAS STANDING ON HIS PORCH WHEN HE YELLED IT AND HE YELLED IT ABOUT NINE HUNDRED THOUSAND TIMES 'TIL HIS MOM'S ARM CAME OUT THE DOOR AND YANKED HIM INSIDE. WE WERE TOTALLY USED TO LOUIS'S YELLING ANYWAY.

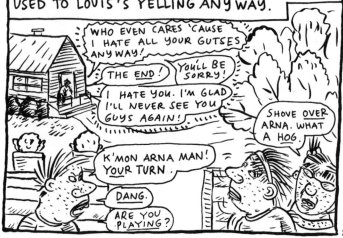

WHO EVEN CARES 'CAUSE I HATE ALL YOUR GUTSES ANYWAY!

THE END!

YOU'LL BE SORRY!

I HATE YOU. I'M GLAD I'LL NEVER SEE YOU GUYS AGAIN!

SHOVE OVER ARNA. WHAT A HOG.

K'MON ARNA MAN! YOUR TURN.

DANG.

ARE YOU PLAYING?

2

I WANT TO TELL YOU THAT NONE OF US EVEN KNEW WHAT MOVING AWAY WAS UNTIL WE ALL WALKED OVER TO LOUIS'S HOUSE AND SEEN IT WAS TOTALLY EMPTY. MY BROTHER AND MARLYS BOOSTED ME UP THROUGH THE WINDOW SO I COULD GO INSIDE AND OPEN THE DOOR. MAINLY I NOTICED A SMELL. THE SMELL OF LOUIS AND HIS SISTER. AND SEEING STUFF ON THE FLOOR, LIKE A BLUE CURLER AND SOME MATCHES. IT GAVE ME THE SHIVERS.

3

AND EVEN THOUGH WE NEVER LIKED LOUIS WE DIDN'T THINK IT WAS ANY FAIR THAT WE WOULD NEVER, FOR THE REST OF OUR WHOLE ENTIRE LIVE'S, GET TO SEE HIM AGAIN. MY BROTHER MADE US A BET WE WOULD SEE HIM SOMEWHERE IF WE KEPT LOOKING AROUND BUT YOU KNOW WE NEVER DID.

AND EVEN THOUGH A BUNCH OF DIFFERENT FAMILIES LIVED IN THAT HOUSE LATER ON WE STILL CALLED IT LOUIS CHEEK'S HOUSE. THAT WAS THE REAL NAME OF IT AND SINCE WE WERE THERE THE LONGEST, WE MADE THE RULES.

YOU'RE THE ONE WHO LIVES OVER AT LOUIS CHEEK'S HOUSE NOW, RIGHT?

IT AIN'T NO LOUIS CHEEK'S HOUSE, SO QUIT CALLIN' IT THAT. IT'S MY DADS HOUSE.

X

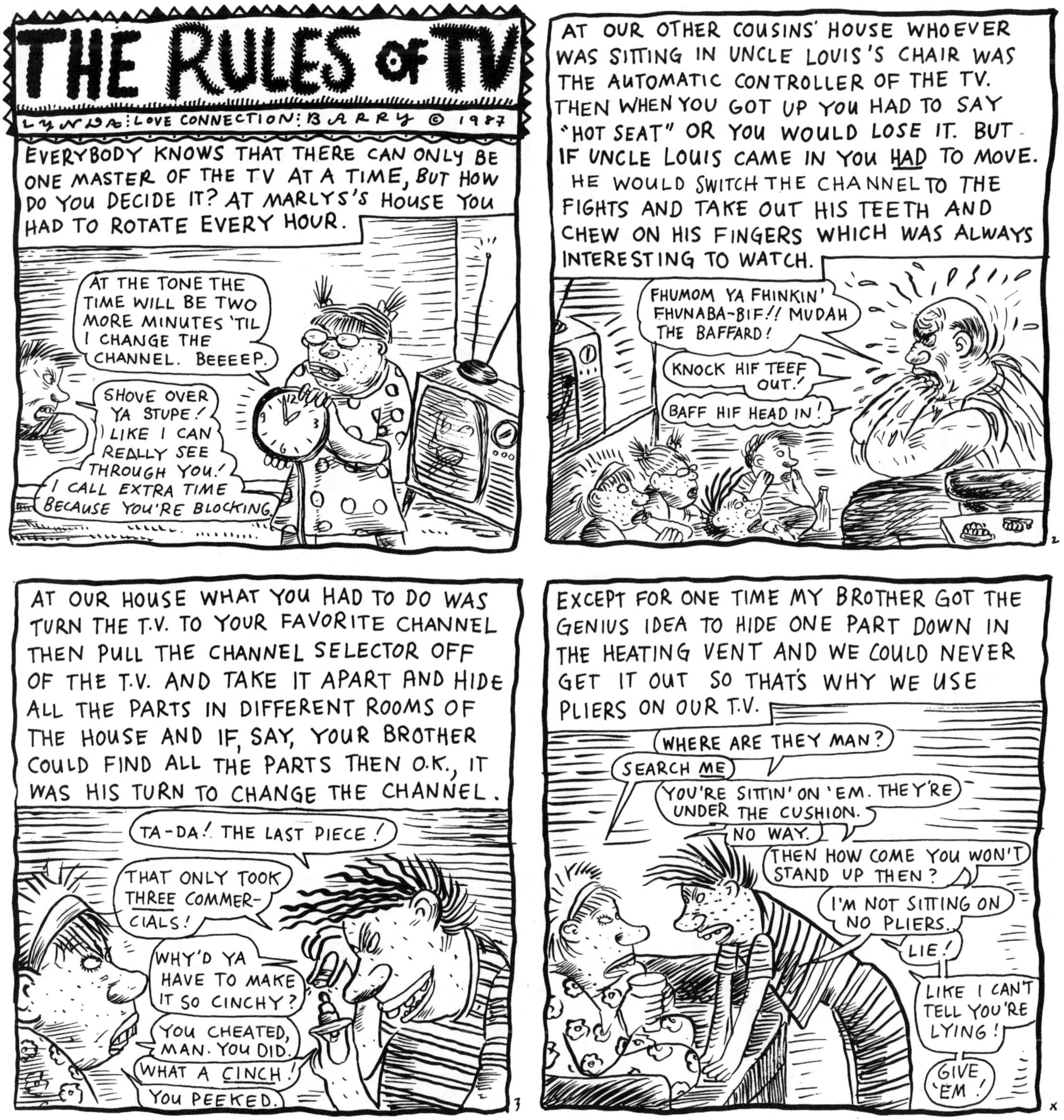
THE RULES OF TV
LYNDA: LOVE CONNECTION: BARRY © 1987
EVERYBODY KNOWS THAT THERE CAN ONLY BE ONE MASTER OF THE TV AT A TIME, BUT HOW DO YOU DECIDE IT? AT MARLYS'S HOUSE YOU HAD TO ROTATE EVERY HOUR.
AT THE TONE THE TIME WILL BE TWO MORE MINUTES 'TIL I CHANGE THE CHANNEL. BEEEEP.
SHOVE OVER YA STUPE! LIKE I CAN REALLY SEE THROUGH YOU!
I CALL EXTRA TIME BECAUSE YOU'RE BLOCKING.
AT OUR OTHER COUSINS' HOUSE WHOEVER WAS SITTING IN UNCLE LOUIS'S CHAIR WAS THE AUTOMATIC CONTROLLER OF THE TV. THEN WHEN YOU GOT UP YOU HAD TO SAY "HOT SEAT" OR YOU WOULD LOSE IT. BUT IF UNCLE LOUIS CAME IN YOU HAD TO MOVE. HE WOULD SWITCH THE CHANNEL TO THE FIGHTS AND TAKE OUT HIS TEETH AND CHEW ON HIS FINGERS WHICH WAS ALWAYS INTERESTING TO WATCH.
FHUMOM YA FHINKIN' FHUNABA-BIF!! MUDAH THE BAFFARD!
KNOCK HIF TEEF OUT!
BAFF HIF HEAD IN!
AT OUR HOUSE WHAT YOU HAD TO DO WAS TURN THE T.V. TO YOUR FAVORITE CHANNEL THEN PULL THE CHANNEL SELECTOR OFF OF THE T.V. AND TAKE IT APART AND HIDE ALL THE PARTS IN DIFFERENT ROOMS OF THE HOUSE AND IF, SAY, YOUR BROTHER COULD FIND ALL THE PARTS THEN O.K., IT WAS HIS TURN TO CHANGE THE CHANNEL.
TA-DA! THE LAST PIECE!
THAT ONLY TOOK THREE COMMERCIALS!
WHY'D YA HAVE TO MAKE IT SO CINCHY?
YOU CHEATED, MAN. YOU DID.
WHAT A CINCH!
YOU PEEKED.
EXCEPT FOR ONE TIME MY BROTHER GOT THE GENIUS IDEA TO HIDE ONE PART DOWN IN THE HEATING VENT AND WE COULD NEVER GET IT OUT SO THAT'S WHY WE USE PLIERS ON OUR T.V.
WHERE ARE THEY MAN?
SEARCH ME
YOU'RE SITTIN' ON 'EM. THEY'RE UNDER THE CUSHION.
NO WAY.
THEN HOW COME YOU WON'T STAND UP THEN?
I'M NOT SITTING ON NO PLIERS.
LIE!
LIKE I CAN'T TELL YOU'RE LYING!
GIVE 'EM!

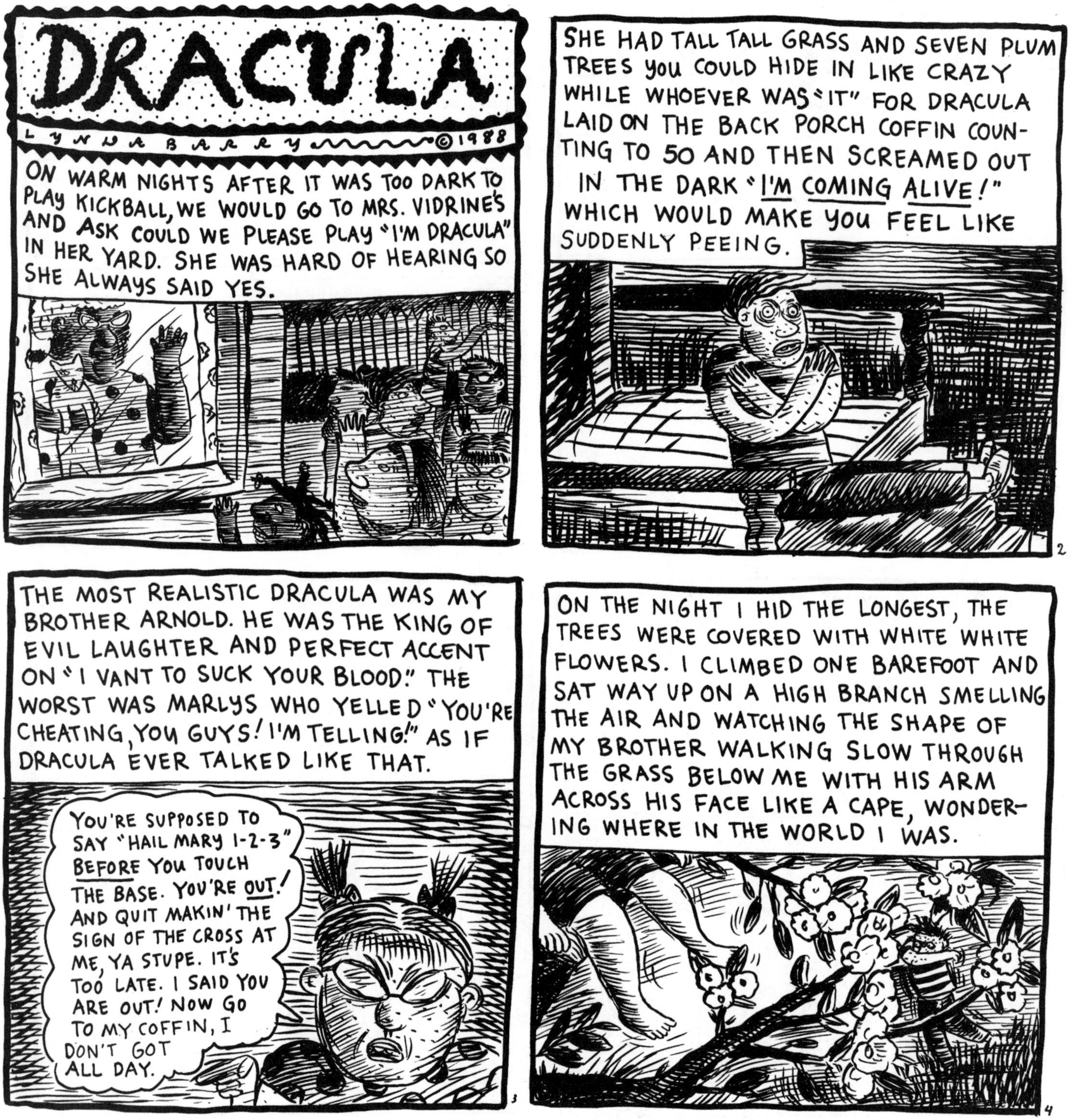
DRACULA
LYNDA BARRY ©1988
ON WARM NIGHTS AFTER IT WAS TOO DARK TO PLAY KICKBALL, WE WOULD GO TO MRS. VIDRINE'S AND ASK COULD WE PLEASE PLAY "I'M DRACULA" IN HER YARD. SHE WAS HARD OF HEARING SO SHE ALWAYS SAID YES.
SHE HAD TALL TALL GRASS AND SEVEN PLUM TREES YOU COULD HIDE IN LIKE CRAZY WHILE WHOEVER WAS "IT" FOR DRACULA LAID ON THE BACK PORCH COFFIN COUNTING TO 50 AND THEN SCREAMED OUT IN THE DARK "I'M COMING ALIVE!" WHICH WOULD MAKE YOU FEEL LIKE SUDDENLY PEEING.
2
THE MOST REALISTIC DRACULA WAS MY BROTHER ARNOLD. HE WAS THE KING OF EVIL LAUGHTER AND PERFECT ACCENT ON "I VANT TO SUCK YOUR BLOOD." THE WORST WAS MARLYS WHO YELLED "YOU'RE CHEATING, YOU GUYS! I'M TELLING!" AS IF DRACULA EVER TALKED LIKE THAT.
YOU'RE SUPPOSED TO SAY "HAIL MARY 1-2-3" BEFORE YOU TOUCH THE BASE. YOU'RE OUT! AND QUIT MAKIN' THE SIGN OF THE CROSS AT ME, YA STUPE. IT'S TOO LATE. I SAID YOU ARE OUT! NOW GO TO MY COFFIN, I DON'T GOT ALL DAY.
3
ON THE NIGHT I HID THE LONGEST, THE TREES WERE COVERED WITH WHITE WHITE FLOWERS. I CLIMBED ONE BAREFOOT AND SAT WAY UP ON A HIGH BRANCH SMELLING THE AIR AND WATCHING THE SHAPE OF MY BROTHER WALKING SLOW THROUGH THE GRASS BELOW ME WITH HIS ARM ACROSS HIS FACE LIKE A CAPE, WONDERING WHERE IN THE WORLD I WAS.
4

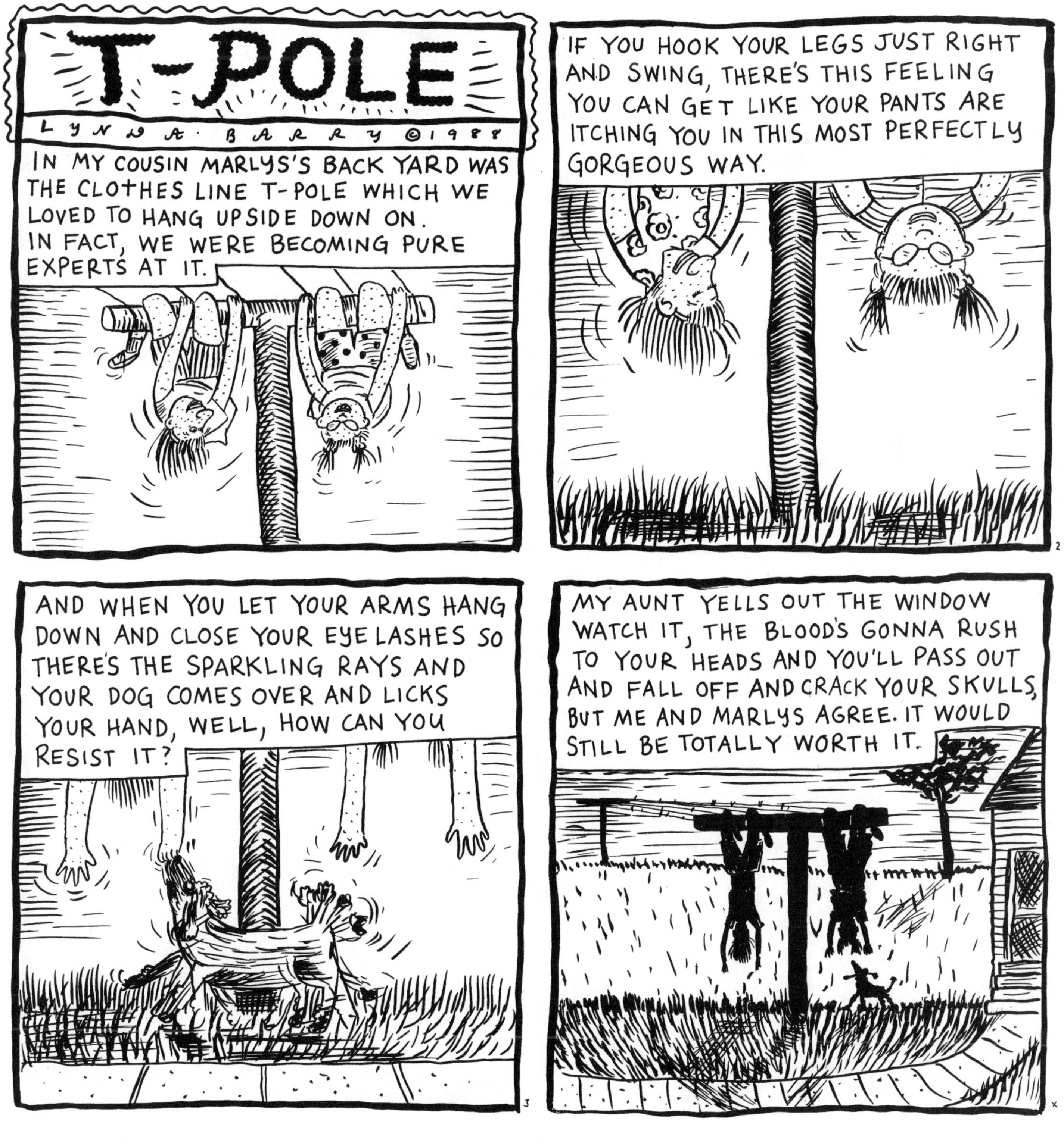
T-POLE
LYNDA BARRY ©1988
IN MY COUSIN MARLYS'S BACK YARD WAS THE CLOTHES LINE T-POLE WHICH WE LOVED TO HANG UPSIDE DOWN ON. IN FACT, WE WERE BECOMING PURE EXPERTS AT IT.
IF YOU HOOK YOUR LEGS JUST RIGHT AND SWING, THERE'S THIS FEELING YOU CAN GET LIKE YOUR PANTS ARE ITCHING YOU IN THIS MOST PERFECTLY GORGEOUS WAY.
AND WHEN YOU LET YOUR ARMS HANG DOWN AND CLOSE YOUR EYELASHES SO THERE'S THE SPARKLING RAYS AND YOUR DOG COMES OVER AND LICKS YOUR HAND, WELL, HOW CAN YOU RESIST IT?
MY AUNT YELLS OUT THE WINDOW WATCH IT, THE BLOOD'S GONNA RUSH TO YOUR HEADS AND YOU'LL PASS OUT AND FALL OFF AND CRACK YOUR SKULLS, BUT ME AND MARLYS AGREE. IT WOULD STILL BE TOTALLY WORTH IT.

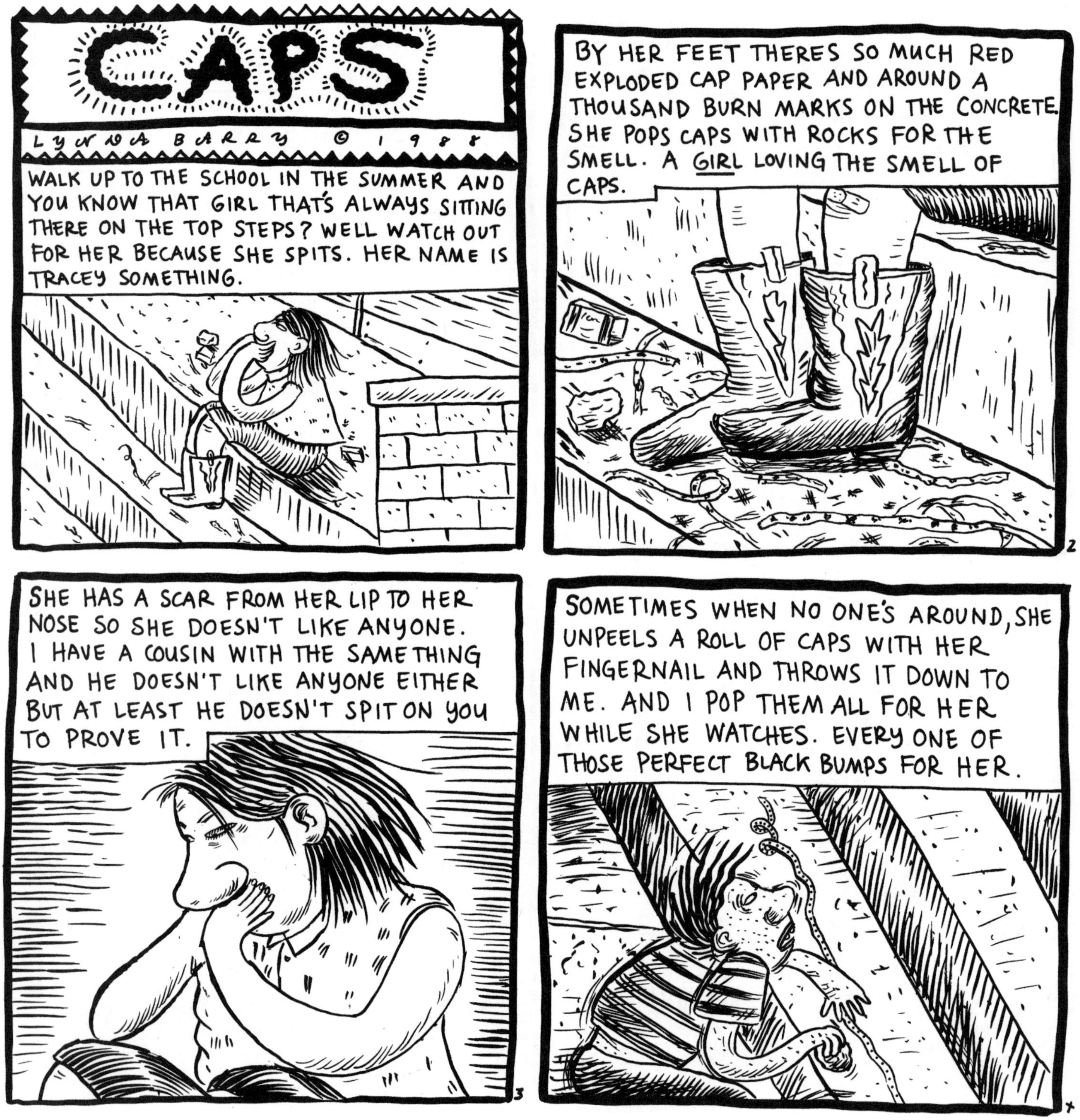
CAPS
LYNDA BARRY © 1988
WALK UP TO THE SCHOOL IN THE SUMMER AND YOU KNOW THAT GIRL THAT'S ALWAYS SITTING THERE ON THE TOP STEPS? WELL WATCH OUT FOR HER BECAUSE SHE SPITS. HER NAME IS TRACEY SOMETHING.
BY HER FEET THERES SO MUCH RED EXPLODED CAP PAPER AND AROUND A THOUSAND BURN MARKS ON THE CONCRETE. SHE POPS CAPS WITH ROCKS FOR THE SMELL. A GIRL LOVING THE SMELL OF CAPS.
2
SHE HAS A SCAR FROM HER LIP TO HER NOSE SO SHE DOESN'T LIKE ANYONE. I HAVE A COUSIN WITH THE SAME THING AND HE DOESN'T LIKE ANYONE EITHER BUT AT LEAST HE DOESN'T SPIT ON YOU TO PROVE IT.
3
SOMETIMES WHEN NO ONE'S AROUND, SHE UNPEELS A ROLL OF CAPS WITH HER FINGERNAIL AND THROWS IT DOWN TO ME. AND I POP THEM ALL FOR HER WHILE SHE WATCHES. EVERY ONE OF THOSE PERFECT BLACK BUMPS FOR HER.
4

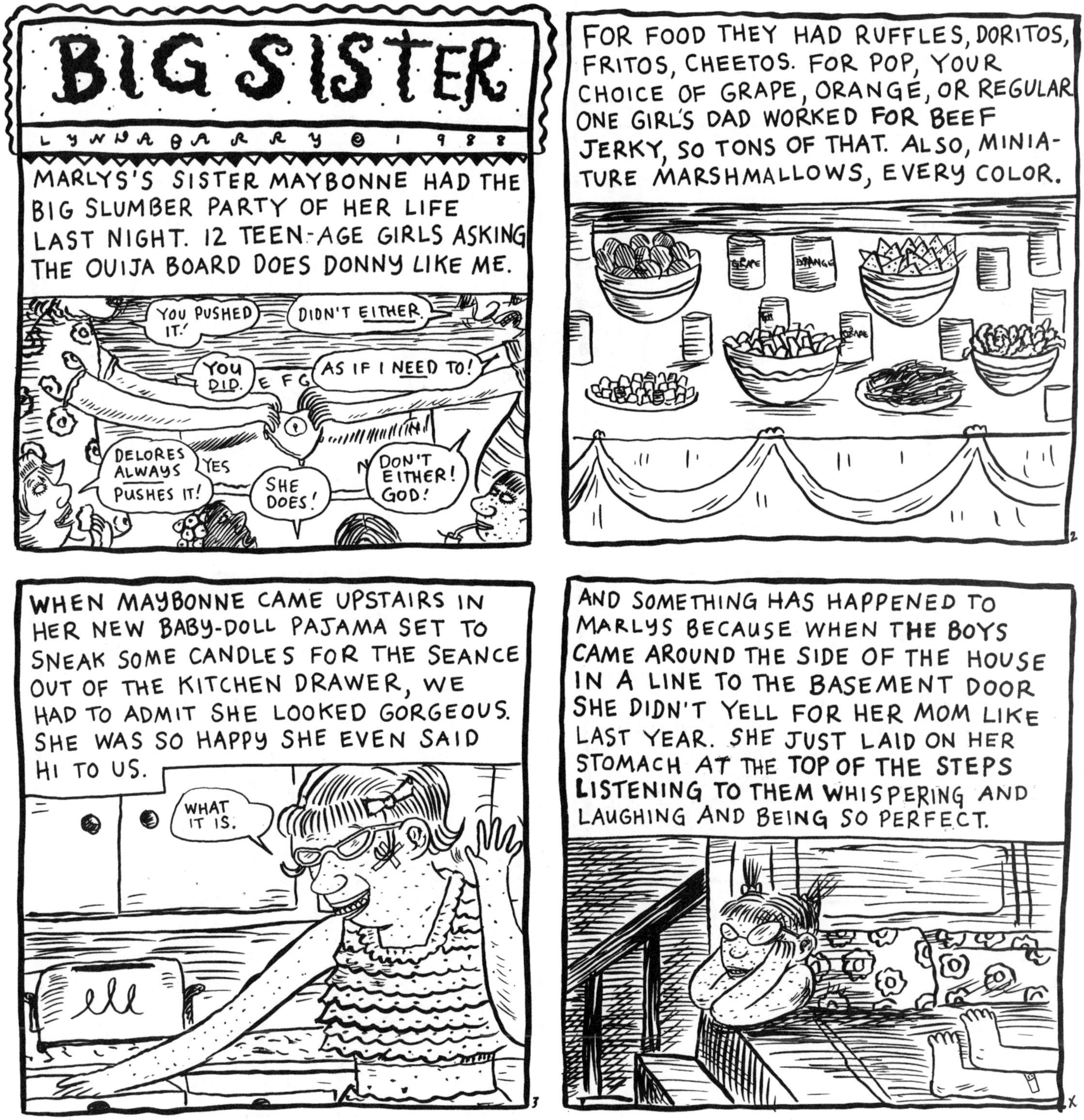
BIG SISTER
LYNDA BARRY ©1988
MARLYS'S SISTER MAYBONNE HAD THE BIG SLUMBER PARTY OF HER LIFE LAST NIGHT. 12 TEEN-AGE GIRLS ASKING THE OUIJA BOARD DOES DONNY LIKE ME.
YOU PUSHED IT!
DIDN'T EITHER.
YOU DID.
E F G
AS IF I NEED TO!
DELORES ALWAYS PUSHES IT!
YES
SHE DOES!
DON'T EITHER! GOD!
FOR FOOD THEY HAD RUFFLES, DORITOS, FRITOS, CHEETOS. FOR POP, YOUR CHOICE OF GRAPE, ORANGE, OR REGULAR. ONE GIRL'S DAD WORKED FOR BEEF JERKY, SO TONS OF THAT. ALSO, MINIATURE MARSHMALLOWS, EVERY COLOR.
GRAPE
ORANGE
GRAPE
WHEN MAYBONNE CAME UPSTAIRS IN HER NEW BABY-DOLL PAJAMA SET TO SNEAK SOME CANDLES FOR THE SEANCE OUT OF THE KITCHEN DRAWER, WE HAD TO ADMIT SHE LOOKED GORGEOUS. SHE WAS SO HAPPY SHE EVEN SAID HI TO US.
WHAT IT IS.
AND SOMETHING HAS HAPPENED TO MARLYS BECAUSE WHEN THE BOYS CAME AROUND THE SIDE OF THE HOUSE IN A LINE TO THE BASEMENT DOOR SHE DIDN'T YELL FOR HER MOM LIKE LAST YEAR. SHE JUST LAID ON HER STOMACH AT THE TOP OF THE STEPS LISTENING TO THEM WHISPERING AND LAUGHING AND BEING SO PERFECT.

DON'T BUG ME

BY LYNDA BARRY ©1988

IT STARTED BY MY COUSIN MAYBONNE SAYING DON'T BUG HER BECAUSE HER BODY WAS GOING THROUGH SPECIAL CHANGES. THEN SHE CALLS UP HER FRIEND SHARON AND WHISPERS "GUESS WHAT, GEORGE IS VISITING."

WHO'S GEORGE?

DON'T BE SO RETARDED.

1

THEN SHE GOES INTO THE FRONT ROOM AND LIES DOWN ON HER STOMACH AND LISTENS TO THE SONG "COLOR MY WORLD" OVER AND OVER WHICH MARLYS SAYS MEANS SHE HAS CRAMPS.

MIDOL

2

AND WHEN MARLYS GOES TO TURN ON THE WONDERFUL WORLD OF DISNEY, MAYBONNE STARTS YELLING NO WAY BECAUSE SHE IS TOO SENSITIVE TO WATCH ANY PROGRAMS OF HELPLESS ANIMALS IN DANGER RIGHT NOW AND MARLYS SAYS THAT'S TOO BAD, TOUGH LUCK, I'M WATCHING IT.

3

SO THEN MAYBONNE STARTS SCREAMING "MOM! MOM!" AND MARLYS OPENS THE FRONT DOOR AND YELLS OUT "MY NAME IS MAYBONNE AND I CONTROL THE WORLD BECAUSE OF OH MY UTERUS!" AND I DON'T KNOW WHAT HAPPENED AFTER THAT BECAUSE THE FIRST THING MY AUNT SAID WHEN SHE CAME IN THE ROOM WAS FOR ME TO GO HOME.

4

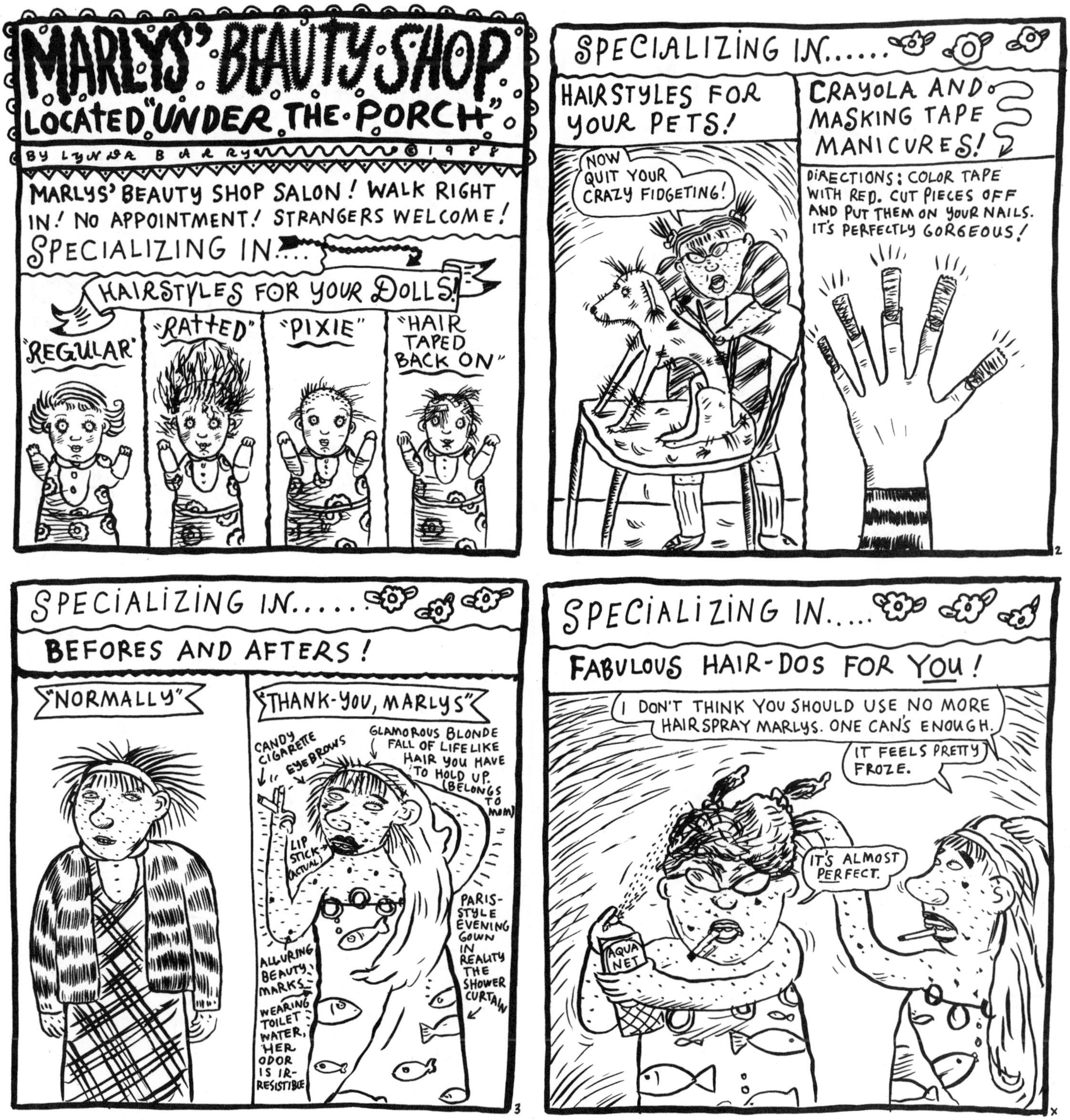

MARLYS' BEAUTY SHOP
LOCATED "UNDER THE PORCH"
BY LYNDA BARRY ©1988
MARLYS' BEAUTY SHOP SALON! WALK RIGHT IN! NO APPOINTMENT! STRANGERS WELCOME!
SPECIALIZING IN....
HAIRSTYLES FOR YOUR DOLLS!
"REGULAR"
"RATTED"
"PIXIE"
"HAIR TAPED BACK ON"
SPECIALIZING IN......
HAIRSTYLES FOR YOUR PETS!
NOW QUIT YOUR CRAZY FIDGETING!
CRAYOLA AND MASKING TAPE MANICURES!
DIRECTIONS: COLOR TAPE WITH RED. CUT PIECES OFF AND PUT THEM ON YOUR NAILS. IT'S PERFECTLY GORGEOUS!
2
SPECIALIZING IN.....
BEFORES AND AFTERS!
"NORMALLY"
"THANK-YOU, MARLYS"
CANDY CIGARETTE
EYEBROWS
GLAMOROUS BLONDE FALL OF LIFELIKE HAIR YOU HAVE TO HOLD UP. (BELONGS TO MOM)
LIP STICK (ACTUAL)
PARIS-STYLE EVENING GOWN IN REALITY THE SHOWER CURTAIN
ALLURING BEAUTY MARKS
WEARING TOILET WATER, HER ODOR IS IR-RESISTIBLE
3
SPECIALIZING IN.....
FABULOUS HAIR-DOS FOR YOU!
I DON'T THINK YOU SHOULD USE NO MORE HAIRSPRAY MARLYS. ONE CAN'S ENOUGH.
IT FEELS PRETTY FROZE.
IT'S ALMOST PERFECT.
AQUA NET

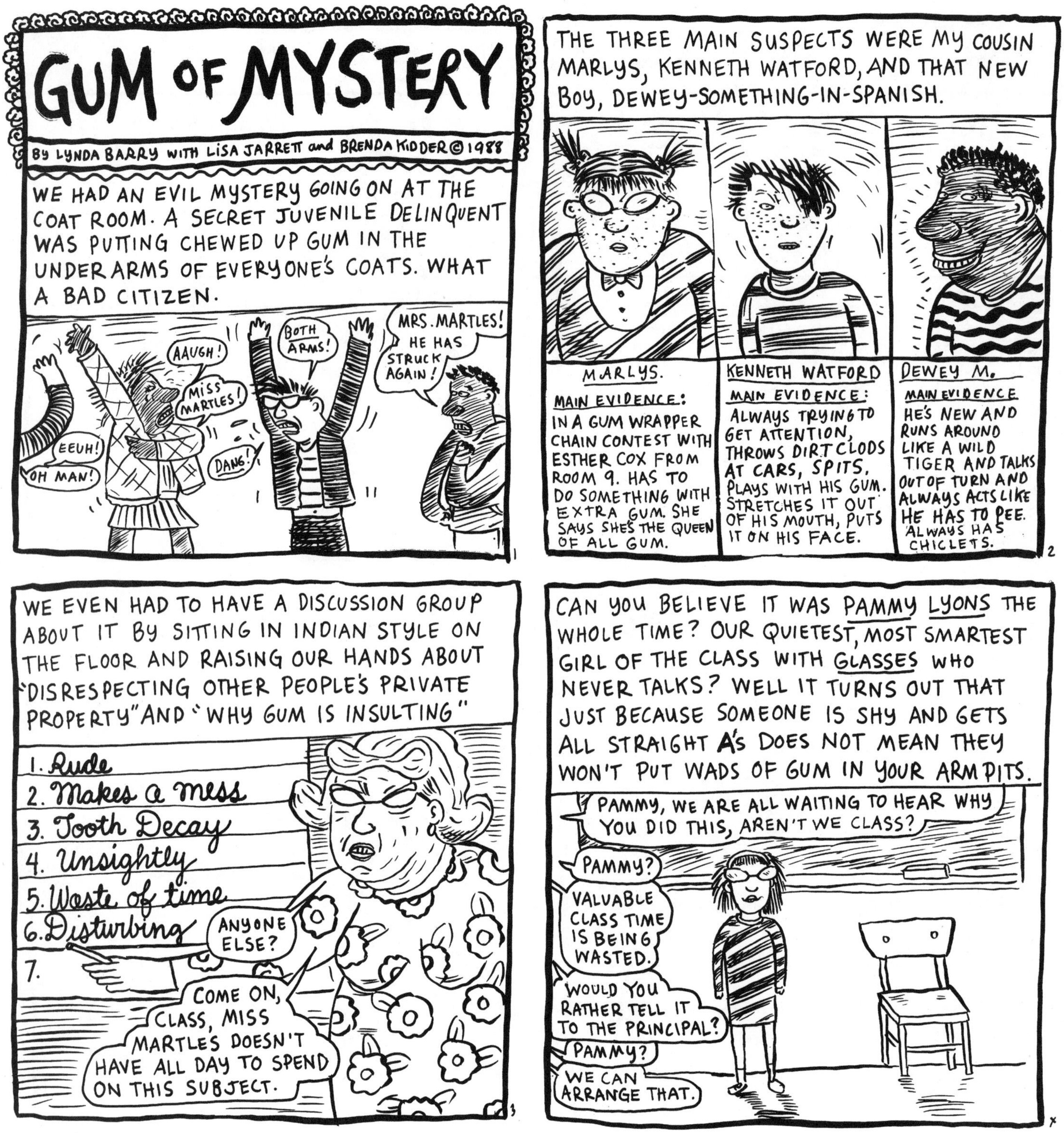
GUM OF MYSTERY
BY LYNDA BARRY WITH LISA JARRETT and BRENDA KIDDER © 1988
WE HAD AN EVIL MYSTERY GOING ON AT THE COAT ROOM. A SECRET JUVENILE DELINQUENT WAS PUTTING CHEWED UP GUM IN THE UNDERARMS OF EVERYONE'S COATS. WHAT A BAD CITIZEN.
AAUGH!
BOTH ARMS!
MRS. MARTLES! HE HAS STRUCK AGAIN!
MISS MARTLES!
EEUH!
OH MAN!
DANG!
1
THE THREE MAIN SUSPECTS WERE MY COUSIN MARLYS, KENNETH WATFORD, AND THAT NEW BOY, DEWEY-SOMETHING-IN-SPANISH.
MARLYS.
MAIN EVIDENCE:
IN A GUM WRAPPER CHAIN CONTEST WITH ESTHER COX FROM ROOM 9. HAS TO DO SOMETHING WITH EXTRA GUM. SHE SAYS SHE'S THE QUEEN OF ALL GUM.
KENNETH WATFORD
MAIN EVIDENCE:
ALWAYS TRYING TO GET ATTENTION, THROWS DIRT CLODS AT CARS, SPITS. PLAYS WITH HIS GUM. STRETCHES IT OUT OF HIS MOUTH, PUTS IT ON HIS FACE.
DEWEY M.
MAIN EVIDENCE
HE'S NEW AND RUNS AROUND LIKE A WILD TIGER AND TALKS OUT OF TURN AND ALWAYS ACTS LIKE HE HAS TO PEE. ALWAYS HAS CHICLETS.
2
WE EVEN HAD TO HAVE A DISCUSSION GROUP ABOUT IT BY SITTING IN INDIAN STYLE ON THE FLOOR AND RAISING OUR HANDS ABOUT "DISRESPECTING OTHER PEOPLE'S PRIVATE PROPERTY" AND "WHY GUM IS INSULTING"
1. Rude
2. Makes a mess
3. Tooth Decay
4. Unsightly
5. Waste of time
6. Disturbing
7.
ANYONE ELSE?
COME ON, CLASS, MISS MARTLES DOESN'T HAVE ALL DAY TO SPEND ON THIS SUBJECT.
3
CAN YOU BELIEVE IT WAS PAMMY LYONS THE WHOLE TIME? OUR QUIETEST, MOST SMARTEST GIRL OF THE CLASS WITH GLASSES WHO NEVER TALKS? WELL IT TURNS OUT THAT JUST BECAUSE SOMEONE IS SHY AND GETS ALL STRAIGHT A'S DOES NOT MEAN THEY WON'T PUT WADS OF GUM IN YOUR ARMPITS.
PAMMY, WE ARE ALL WAITING TO HEAR WHY YOU DID THIS, AREN'T WE CLASS?
PAMMY?
VALUABLE CLASS TIME IS BEING WASTED.
WOULD YOU RATHER TELL IT TO THE PRINCIPAL?
PAMMY?
WE CAN ARRANGE THAT.
x

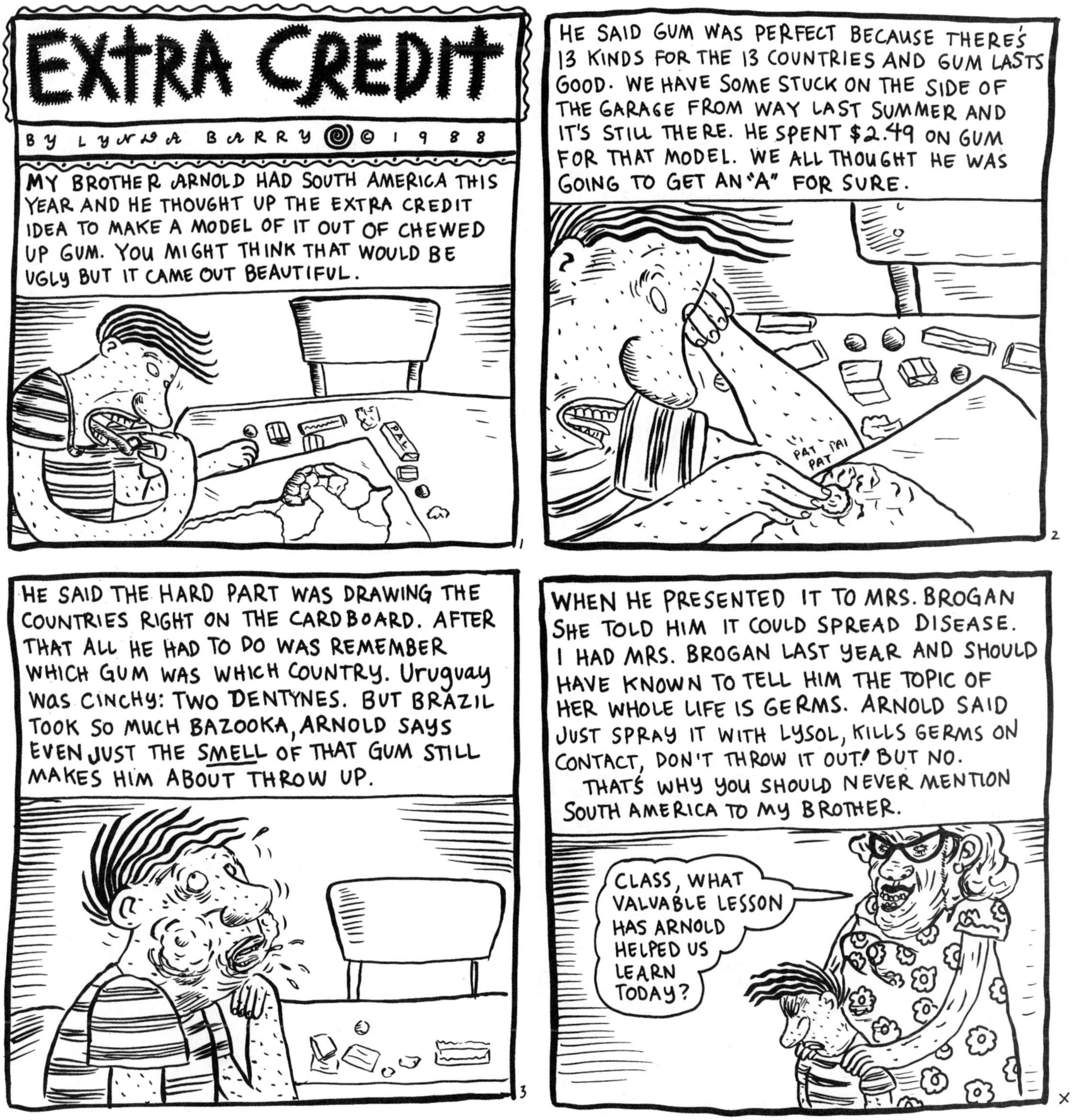
EXTRA CREDIT
BY LYNDA BARRY ©1988
MY BROTHER ARNOLD HAD SOUTH AMERICA THIS YEAR AND HE THOUGHT UP THE EXTRA CREDIT IDEA TO MAKE A MODEL OF IT OUT OF CHEWED UP GUM. YOU MIGHT THINK THAT WOULD BE UGLY BUT IT CAME OUT BEAUTIFUL.
PAL
HE SAID GUM WAS PERFECT BECAUSE THERE'S 13 KINDS FOR THE 13 COUNTRIES AND GUM LASTS GOOD. WE HAVE SOME STUCK ON THE SIDE OF THE GARAGE FROM WAY LAST SUMMER AND IT'S STILL THERE. HE SPENT $2.49 ON GUM FOR THAT MODEL. WE ALL THOUGHT HE WAS GOING TO GET AN "A" FOR SURE.
PAT PAT PAT
HE SAID THE HARD PART WAS DRAWING THE COUNTRIES RIGHT ON THE CARDBOARD. AFTER THAT ALL HE HAD TO DO WAS REMEMBER WHICH GUM WAS WHICH COUNTRY. Uruguay was CINCHY: TWO DENTYNES. BUT BRAZIL TOOK SO MUCH BAZOOKA, ARNOLD SAYS EVEN JUST THE SMELL OF THAT GUM STILL MAKES HIM ABOUT THROW UP.
WHEN HE PRESENTED IT TO MRS. BROGAN SHE TOLD HIM IT COULD SPREAD DISEASE. I HAD MRS. BROGAN LAST YEAR AND SHOULD HAVE KNOWN TO TELL HIM THE TOPIC OF HER WHOLE LIFE IS GERMS. ARNOLD SAID JUST SPRAY IT WITH LYSOL, KILLS GERMS ON CONTACT, DON'T THROW IT OUT! BUT NO.
THAT'S WHY YOU SHOULD NEVER MENTION SOUTH AMERICA TO MY BROTHER.
CLASS, WHAT VALUABLE LESSON HAS ARNOLD HELPED US LEARN TODAY?

KINGDOMS

BY LYNDA BARRY ©1988

MY BROTHER FREDDIE IS GROWING MOLD IN JARS UNDER HIS BED. I DON'T KNOW IF I SHOULD TELL ON HIM NOW, OR JUST WAIT UNTIL MOM FINDS OUT ABOUT IT NATURALLY.

I KEPT WONDERING WHY ARE HIS LEGS ALWAYS STICKING OUT FROM UNDER HIS BED EVERY TIME I GO BY FOR ABOUT FIVE DAYS NOW? THE ANSWER IS TEN JARS OF MOLD, ALL KINDS. MILK MOLD, ORANGES MOLD, DOUGHNUT MOLD, MOLD GALORE. HOW CAN ANYONE GET SPECIAL FEELINGS FROM SOMETHING LIKE THAT?

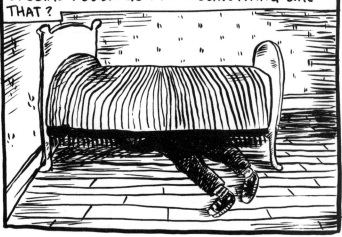

LAST NIGHT I SAW HIM SNEAK THE FLASH-LIGHT UP FROM THE BASEMENT AND I SAID "I'M TELLING" AND HE SAID "OK BUT COME LOOK FIRST." WE LAID ON OUR STOMACHS UNDER HIS BED AS HE FEATURED EACH ONE OF THE MOLDS IN THE SPOTLIGHT. HE TOLD ME THERE WAS A WHOLE MIDGET KINGDOM IN EVERY ONE OF HIS JARS.

HE TOLD ME A POLICEMAN CUT HIS FACE SHAVING ONE MORNING AND HIS WIFE PUT SOME MOLDY BREAD ON IT AND HE GOT INSTANTLY HEALED. "WHAT A DISCOVERY!" MY BROTHER SAID.
SO THAT'S WHY I GOT THIS CORN IN THE BABY FOOD JAR SAVED FROM LUNCH TO GIVE TO HIM AS A SURPRISE. SOME TIMES IT JUST KILLS ME THE THINGS HE DOES.

NEW NEIGHBORS

BY LYNDA BARRY © 1988

WHO MOVED IN NEXT DOOR WHERE NOBODY LASTED WAS THE DAWSINS. A MIXED UP COUPLE, BOTH OLD. MR. DAWSIN HAS A NAKED TATOO ON ONE ARM AND TAKES OUT HIS TEETH WHENEVER WE SAY HI. HE'S FRIENDLY.

MRS. DAWSIN IS FROM ANOTHER COUNTRY WHERE IT'S NORMAL TO SIT DOWN AND SMOKE A CIGARETTE WITH THE LIGHTED END IN YOUR MOUTH. HER MAIN ENGLISH TO US IS "NO MY DARLING" EVERY TIME WE BEG HER PLEASE PLEASE PLEASE TEACH US HER GREAT SMOKING ABILITY.

AND DON'T FORGET ABOUT THE CATS. 14, I SWEAR ON THE BIBLE. THEY BUILT A PEN ON THE BACK OF THE HOUSE AND I CAN SEE FROM MY BEDROOM THE CATS COMING OUT THE LITTLE DOOR, WALKING IN A CIRCLE AND GOING BACK IN NON STOP. MY AUNT SAYS MRS. DAWSINS PEOPLE EAT CATS BUT I COUNTED AND THERE'S STILL NONE MISSING.

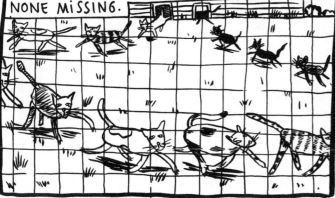

I WAS OVER ENJOYING MR. DAWSIN SINGING TO HIS FAVORITE RECORD "COUNTING FLOWERS ON THE WALL" WITH HIS FACE ABOUT ONE INCH FROM THE SPEAKER, WHEN I NOTICED A LITTLE PICTURE OF A LADY, ALMOST A HULA, NEXT TO A SAILOR MAN. CAN YOU BELIEVE IT? IT'S THEM FROM ABOUT FIFTY THOUSAND YEARS AGO.

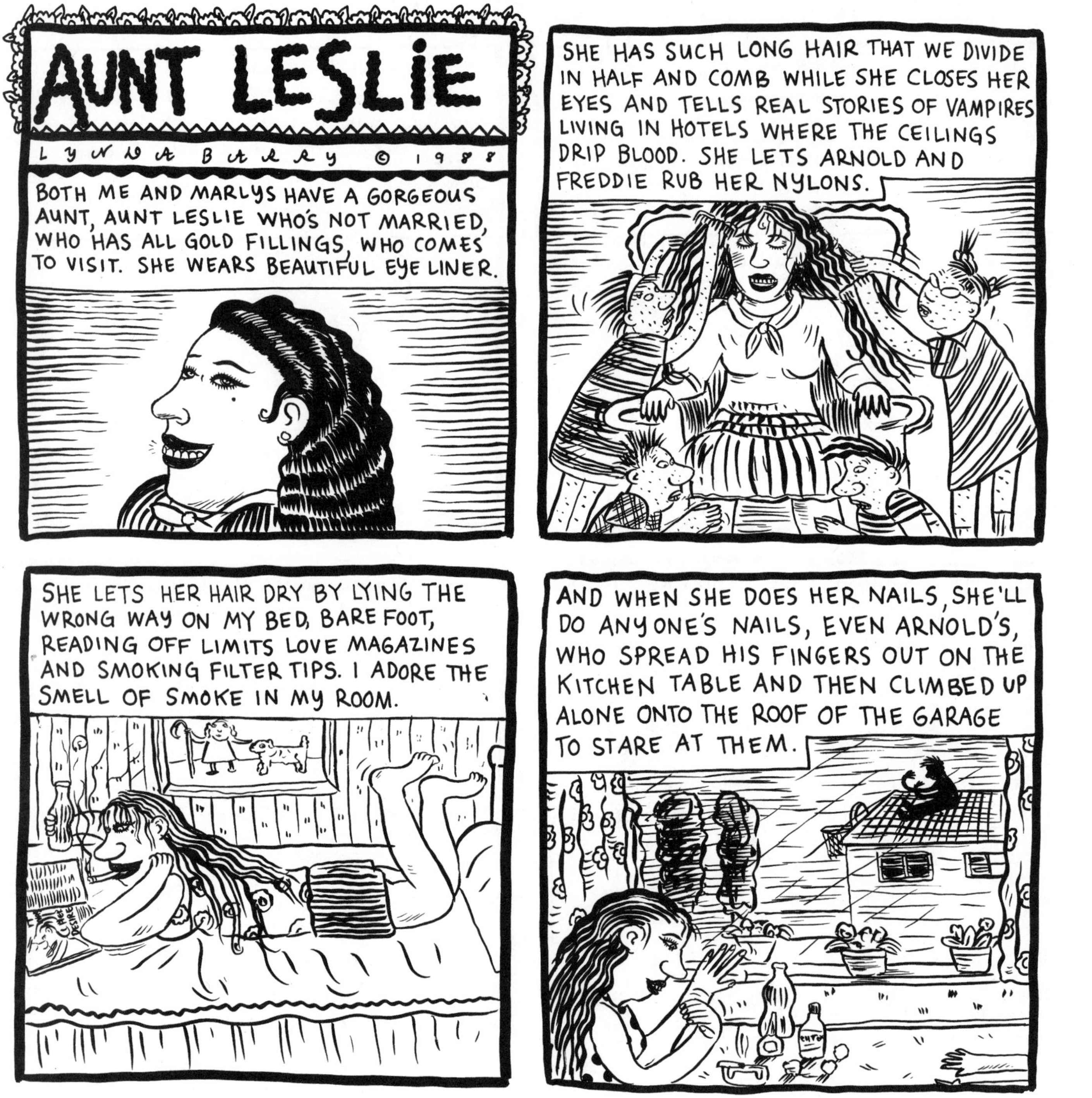
AUNT LESLIE
LYNDA BARRY © 1988
BOTH ME AND MARLYS HAVE A GORGEOUS AUNT, AUNT LESLIE WHO'S NOT MARRIED, WHO HAS ALL GOLD FILLINGS, WHO COMES TO VISIT. SHE WEARS BEAUTIFUL EYE LINER.
SHE HAS SUCH LONG HAIR THAT WE DIVIDE IN HALF AND COMB WHILE SHE CLOSES HER EYES AND TELLS REAL STORIES OF VAMPIRES LIVING IN HOTELS WHERE THE CEILINGS DRIP BLOOD. SHE LETS ARNOLD AND FREDDIE RUB HER NYLONS.
SHE LETS HER HAIR DRY BY LYING THE WRONG WAY ON MY BED, BARE FOOT, READING OFF LIMITS LOVE MAGAZINES AND SMOKING FILTER TIPS. I ADORE THE SMELL OF SMOKE IN MY ROOM.
AND WHEN SHE DOES HER NAILS, SHE'LL DO ANYONE'S NAILS, EVEN ARNOLD'S, WHO SPREAD HIS FINGERS OUT ON THE KITCHEN TABLE AND THEN CLIMBED UP ALONE ONTO THE ROOF OF THE GARAGE TO STARE AT THEM.

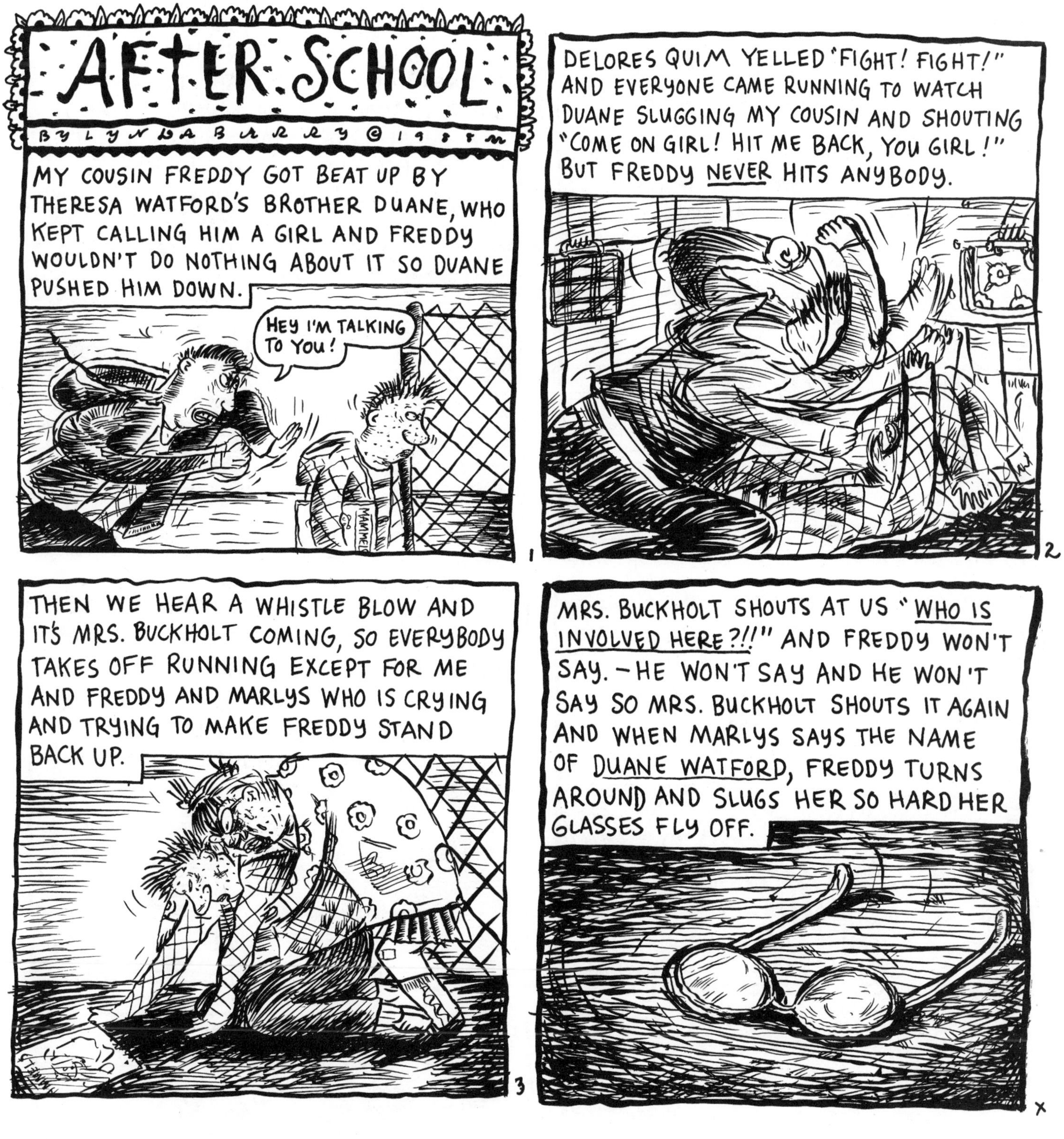
AFTER SCHOOL
BY LYNDA BARRY ©1988
MY COUSIN FREDDY GOT BEAT UP BY THERESA WATFORD'S BROTHER DUANE, WHO KEPT CALLING HIM A GIRL AND FREDDY WOULDN'T DO NOTHING ABOUT IT SO DUANE PUSHED HIM DOWN.
HEY I'M TALKING TO YOU!
DELORES QUIM YELLED "FIGHT! FIGHT!" AND EVERYONE CAME RUNNING TO WATCH DUANE SLUGGING MY COUSIN AND SHOUTING "COME ON GIRL! HIT ME BACK, YOU GIRL!" BUT FREDDY NEVER HITS ANYBODY.
THEN WE HEAR A WHISTLE BLOW AND IT'S MRS. BUCKHOLT COMING, SO EVERYBODY TAKES OFF RUNNING EXCEPT FOR ME AND FREDDY AND MARLYS WHO IS CRYING AND TRYING TO MAKE FREDDY STAND BACK UP.
MRS. BUCKHOLT SHOUTS AT US "WHO IS INVOLVED HERE?!!" AND FREDDY WON'T SAY. —HE WON'T SAY AND HE WON'T SAY SO MRS. BUCKHOLT SHOUTS IT AGAIN AND WHEN MARLYS SAYS THE NAME OF DUANE WATFORD, FREDDY TURNS AROUND AND SLUGS HER SO HARD HER GLASSES FLY OFF.

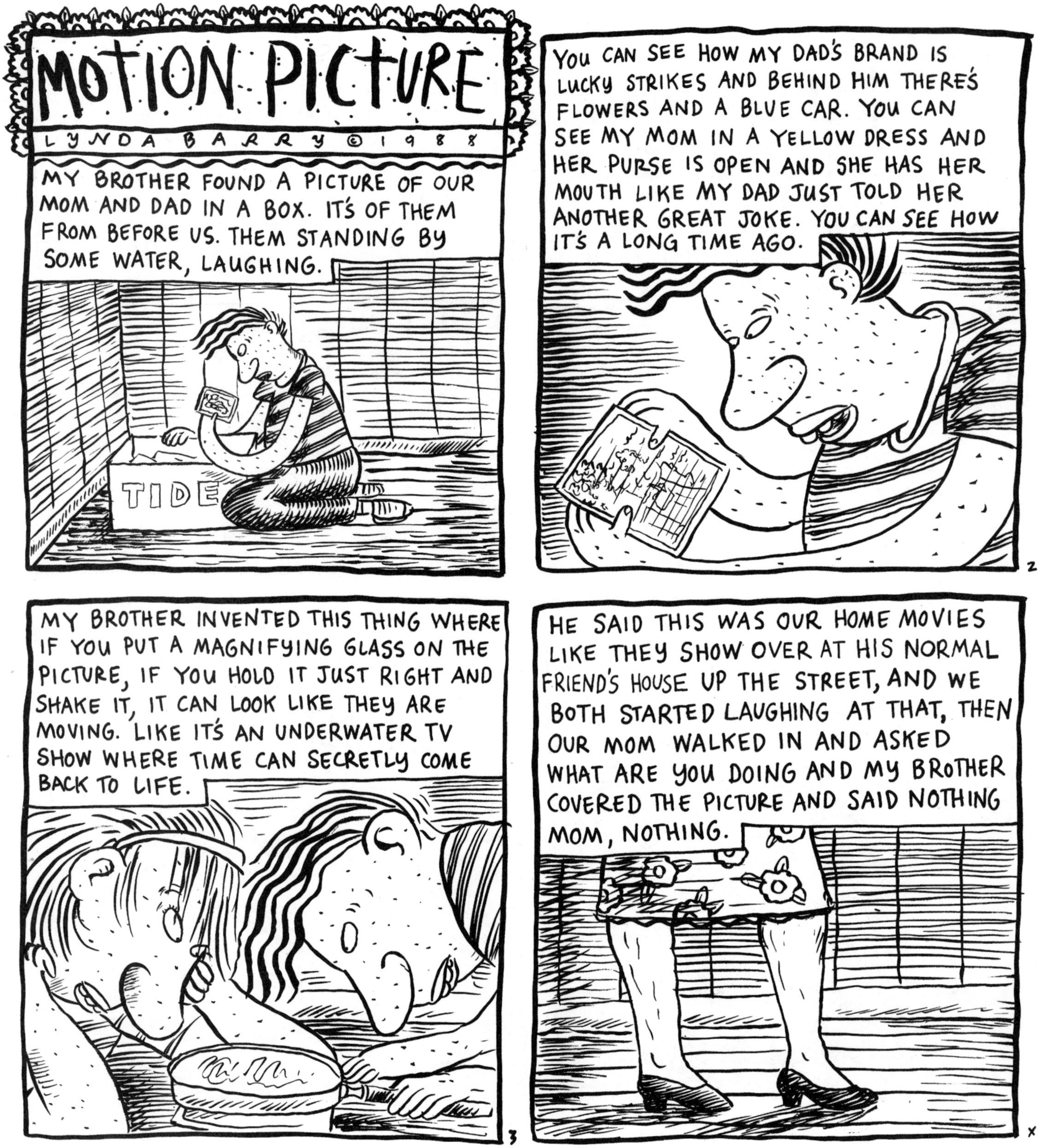
MOTION PICTURE
LYNDA BARRY ©1988
MY BROTHER FOUND A PICTURE OF OUR MOM AND DAD IN A BOX. IT'S OF THEM FROM BEFORE US. THEM STANDING BY SOME WATER, LAUGHING.
TIDE
YOU CAN SEE HOW MY DAD'S BRAND IS LUCKY STRIKES AND BEHIND HIM THERE'S FLOWERS AND A BLUE CAR. YOU CAN SEE MY MOM IN A YELLOW DRESS AND HER PURSE IS OPEN AND SHE HAS HER MOUTH LIKE MY DAD JUST TOLD HER ANOTHER GREAT JOKE. YOU CAN SEE HOW IT'S A LONG TIME AGO.
2
MY BROTHER INVENTED THIS THING WHERE IF YOU PUT A MAGNIFYING GLASS ON THE PICTURE, IF YOU HOLD IT JUST RIGHT AND SHAKE IT, IT CAN LOOK LIKE THEY ARE MOVING. LIKE IT'S AN UNDERWATER TV SHOW WHERE TIME CAN SECRETLY COME BACK TO LIFE.
3
HE SAID THIS WAS OUR HOME MOVIES LIKE THEY SHOW OVER AT HIS NORMAL FRIEND'S HOUSE UP THE STREET, AND WE BOTH STARTED LAUGHING AT THAT, THEN OUR MOM WALKED IN AND ASKED WHAT ARE YOU DOING AND MY BROTHER COVERED THE PICTURE AND SAID NOTHING MOM, NOTHING.
x

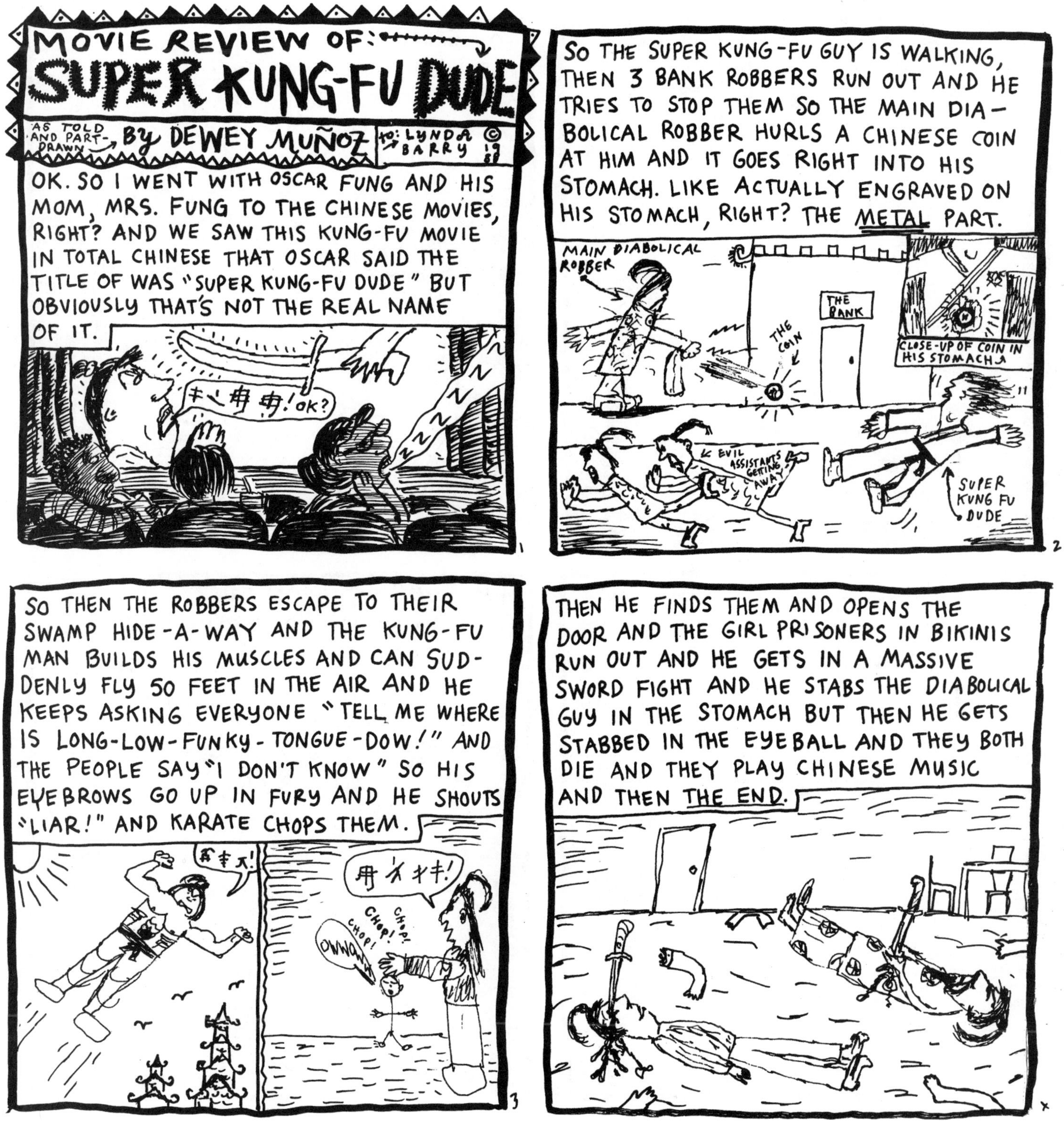
MOVIE REVIEW OF:
SUPER KUNG-FU DUDE
AS TOLD AND PART-DRAWN BY DEWEY MUÑOZ
to: LYNDA BARRY © 1988
OK. SO I WENT WITH OSCAR FUNG AND HIS MOM, MRS. FUNG TO THE CHINESE MOVIES, RIGHT? AND WE SAW THIS KUNG-FU MOVIE IN TOTAL CHINESE THAT OSCAR SAID THE TITLE OF WAS "SUPER KUNG-FU DUDE" BUT OBVIOUSLY THAT'S NOT THE REAL NAME OF IT.
OK?
1
SO THE SUPER KUNG-FU GUY IS WALKING, THEN 3 BANK ROBBERS RUN OUT AND HE TRIES TO STOP THEM SO THE MAIN DIABOLICAL ROBBER HURLS A CHINESE COIN AT HIM AND IT GOES RIGHT INTO HIS STOMACH. LIKE ACTUALLY ENGRAVED ON HIS STOMACH, RIGHT? THE METAL PART.
MAIN DIABOLICAL ROBBER
THE BANK
THE COIN
CLOSE-UP OF COIN IN HIS STOMACH
EVIL ASSISTANTS GETTING AWAY
SUPER KUNG FU DUDE
2
SO THEN THE ROBBERS ESCAPE TO THEIR SWAMP HIDE-A-WAY AND THE KUNG-FU MAN BUILDS HIS MUSCLES AND CAN SUDDENLY FLY 50 FEET IN THE AIR AND HE KEEPS ASKING EVERYONE "TELL ME WHERE IS LONG-LOW-FUNKY-TONGUE-DOW!" AND THE PEOPLE SAY "I DON'T KNOW" SO HIS EYEBROWS GO UP IN FURY AND HE SHOUTS "LIAR!" AND KARATE CHOPS THEM.
CHOP! CHOP! CHOP!
OWWW!
3
THEN HE FINDS THEM AND OPENS THE DOOR AND THE GIRL PRISONERS IN BIKINIS RUN OUT AND HE GETS IN A MASSIVE SWORD FIGHT AND HE STABS THE DIABOLICAL GUY IN THE STOMACH BUT THEN HE GETS STABBED IN THE EYEBALL AND THEY BOTH DIE AND THEY PLAY CHINESE MUSIC AND THEN THE END.
4

JUMP SHOT

BY LYNDA BOLD SOUL SISTER BARRY © 1988

THE TEENAGER NAME OF RICHARD COMES OUT LATE SOME NIGHTS TO SHOOT BASKETS ON OUR CORNER. YOU CAN WATCH HIM FROM MY BEDROOM WINDOW.

YOU CAN LIE ON THE BED AND HEAR THE BALL, THE PING PING OF IT AGAINST THE STREET BOUNCING. YOU CAN HEAR HIM WALK IT, THEN RUN IT AND DO HIS PERFECT HOOK SHOT.

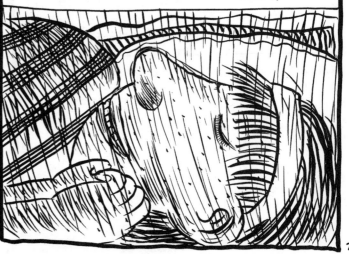

2

BOUNCE, BOUNCE, BOUNCE, STOP. THE FAST NO-SOUND OF HIS FEET IN THE AIR, THE BALL FLYING UP, PAUSE, THEN WHAM-WHAM AGAINST THE BACK BOARD, A HIGH BOUNCE OFF THE RIM, HIM WHISPERING SON OF A BITCH.

3

HIM JUMPING UP ON THE CORNER, HIM JUMPING HIGH AND TURNING IN THE AIR UNDER A STREET LIGHT WITH A THOUSAND MILLION BUGS FLYING AROUND IT GOING WILD, WILD, WILD,

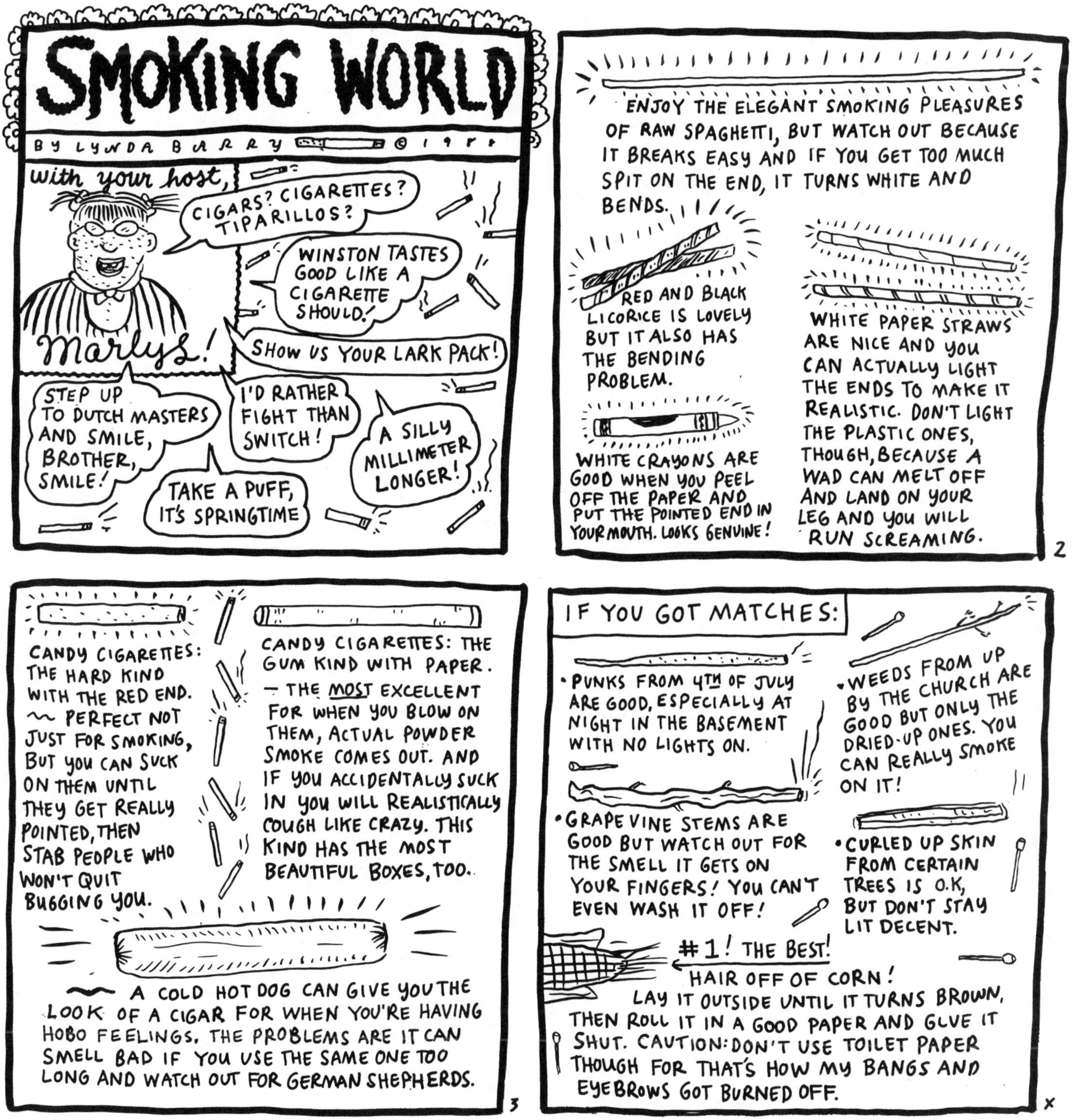

SMOKING WORLD
BY LYNDA BARRY ©198
with your host, Marlys!
CIGARS? CIGARETTES? TIPARILLOS?
WINSTON TASTES GOOD LIKE A CIGARETTE SHOULD!
SHOW US YOUR LARK PACK!
STEP UP TO DUTCH MASTERS AND SMILE, BROTHER, SMILE!
I'D RATHER FIGHT THAN SWITCH!
A SILLY MILLIMETER LONGER!
TAKE A PUFF, IT'S SPRINGTIME
ENJOY THE ELEGANT SMOKING PLEASURES OF RAW SPAGHETTI, BUT WATCH OUT BECAUSE IT BREAKS EASY AND IF YOU GET TOO MUCH SPIT ON THE END, IT TURNS WHITE AND BENDS.
RED AND BLACK LICORICE IS LOVELY BUT IT ALSO HAS THE BENDING PROBLEM.
WHITE CRAYONS ARE GOOD WHEN YOU PEEL OFF THE PAPER AND PUT THE POINTED END IN YOUR MOUTH. LOOKS GENUINE!
WHITE PAPER STRAWS ARE NICE AND YOU CAN ACTUALLY LIGHT THE ENDS TO MAKE IT REALISTIC. DON'T LIGHT THE PLASTIC ONES, THOUGH, BECAUSE A WAD CAN MELT OFF AND LAND ON YOUR LEG AND YOU WILL RUN SCREAMING.
2
CANDY CIGARETTES: THE HARD KIND WITH THE RED END. ~ PERFECT NOT JUST FOR SMOKING, BUT YOU CAN SUCK ON THEM UNTIL THEY GET REALLY POINTED, THEN STAB PEOPLE WHO WON'T QUIT BUGGING YOU.
CANDY CIGARETTES: THE GUM KIND WITH PAPER. — THE MOST EXCELLENT FOR WHEN YOU BLOW ON THEM, ACTUAL POWDER SMOKE COMES OUT. AND IF YOU ACCIDENTALLY SUCK IN YOU WILL REALISTICALLY COUGH LIKE CRAZY. THIS KIND HAS THE MOST BEAUTIFUL BOXES, TOO.
~ A COLD HOT DOG CAN GIVE YOU THE LOOK OF A CIGAR FOR WHEN YOU'RE HAVING HOBO FEELINGS. THE PROBLEMS ARE IT CAN SMELL BAD IF YOU USE THE SAME ONE TOO LONG AND WATCH OUT FOR GERMAN SHEPHERDS.
3
IF YOU GOT MATCHES:
• PUNKS FROM 4TH OF JULY ARE GOOD, ESPECIALLY AT NIGHT IN THE BASEMENT WITH NO LIGHTS ON.
• GRAPE VINE STEMS ARE GOOD BUT WATCH OUT FOR THE SMELL IT GETS ON YOUR FINGERS! YOU CAN'T EVEN WASH IT OFF!
• WEEDS FROM UP BY THE CHURCH ARE GOOD BUT ONLY THE DRIED-UP ONES. YOU CAN REALLY SMOKE ON IT!
• CURLED UP SKIN FROM CERTAIN TREES IS O.K, BUT DON'T STAY LIT DECENT.
#1! THE BEST! HAIR OFF OF CORN! LAY IT OUTSIDE UNTIL IT TURNS BROWN, THEN ROLL IT IN A GOOD PAPER AND GLUE IT SHUT. CAUTION: DON'T USE TOILET PAPER THOUGH FOR THAT'S HOW MY BANGS AND EYEBROWS GOT BURNED OFF.
x

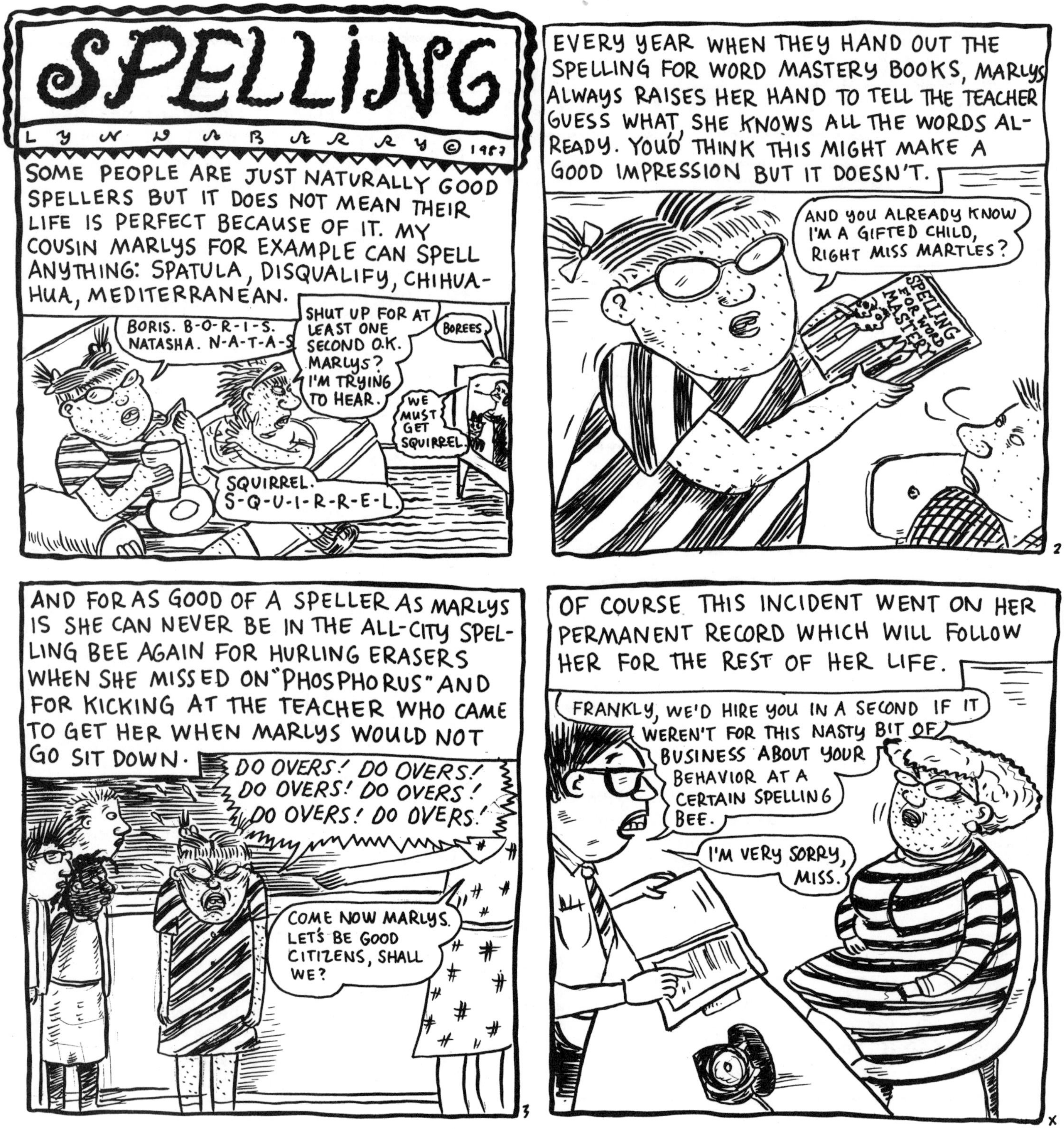
SPELLING
LYNDA BARRY © 1987
SOME PEOPLE ARE JUST NATURALLY GOOD SPELLERS BUT IT DOES NOT MEAN THEIR LIFE IS PERFECT BECAUSE OF IT. MY COUSIN MARLYS FOR EXAMPLE CAN SPELL ANYTHING: SPATULA, DISQUALIFY, CHIHUAHUA, MEDITERRANEAN.
BORIS. B-O-R-I-S. NATASHA. N-A-T-A-S
SHUT UP FOR AT LEAST ONE SECOND O.K. MARLYS? I'M TRYING TO HEAR.
BOREES.
WE MUST GET SQUIRREL.
SQUIRREL. S-Q-U-I-R-R-E-L.
EVERY YEAR WHEN THEY HAND OUT THE SPELLING FOR WORD MASTERY BOOKS, MARLYS ALWAYS RAISES HER HAND TO TELL THE TEACHER GUESS WHAT, SHE KNOWS ALL THE WORDS ALREADY. YOU'D THINK THIS MIGHT MAKE A GOOD IMPRESSION BUT IT DOESN'T.
AND YOU ALREADY KNOW I'M A GIFTED CHILD, RIGHT MISS MARTLES?
SPELLING FOR WORD MASTERY
AND FOR AS GOOD OF A SPELLER AS MARLYS IS SHE CAN NEVER BE IN THE ALL-CITY SPELLING BEE AGAIN FOR HURLING ERASERS WHEN SHE MISSED ON "PHOSPHORUS" AND FOR KICKING AT THE TEACHER WHO CAME TO GET HER WHEN MARLYS WOULD NOT GO SIT DOWN.
DO OVERS! DO OVERS! DO OVERS! DO OVERS! DO OVERS! DO OVERS!
COME NOW MARLYS. LET'S BE GOOD CITIZENS, SHALL WE?
OF COURSE THIS INCIDENT WENT ON HER PERMANENT RECORD WHICH WILL FOLLOW HER FOR THE REST OF HER LIFE.
FRANKLY, WE'D HIRE YOU IN A SECOND IF IT WEREN'T FOR THIS NASTY BIT OF BUSINESS ABOUT YOUR BEHAVIOR AT A CERTAIN SPELLING BEE.
I'M VERY SORRY, MISS.

MARLYS' LOVE

BY LYNDA BARRY © 1988

MY COUSIN MARLYS WAS BENDING OVER ONE DAY, LOOKING AT SOME ANTS, WHEN A TEENAGER NAMED RICHARD CAME THROUGH THE GATE WITH A TENNIS RACQUET LOOKING FOR MARLYS' SISTER, MAYBONNE.

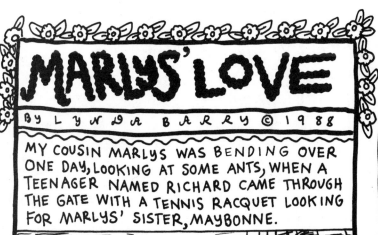

WHEN HE WALKED BY MARLYS HE SAID "HI, SQUIRT" AND TAPPED THE TENNIS RACQUET ON HER BEHIND LIKE YOU DO WHEN ANYBODY'S BENT OVER, AND WHEN MARLYS STOOD UP, SHE WAS IN LOVE.

MAYBONNE'S VOICE CAME OUT THE FRONT DOOR SAYING JUST A SEC SO RICHARD SAT DOWN ON THE TOP STEP AND MARLYS STOOD ON THE BOTTOM ONE AND SAID WANT TO SEE ME DO THE MEXICAN HAT DANCE?

IT WAS HER SPECIALTY.

THE UPSTAIRS WINDOW SHOVED OPEN AND MAYBONNE'S HEAD CAME OUT YELLING BUG OFF MARLYS, WILL YOU? BUT NO, SHE COULDN'T. SHE COULDN'T, SHE COULDN'T, SHE JUST COULDN'T.

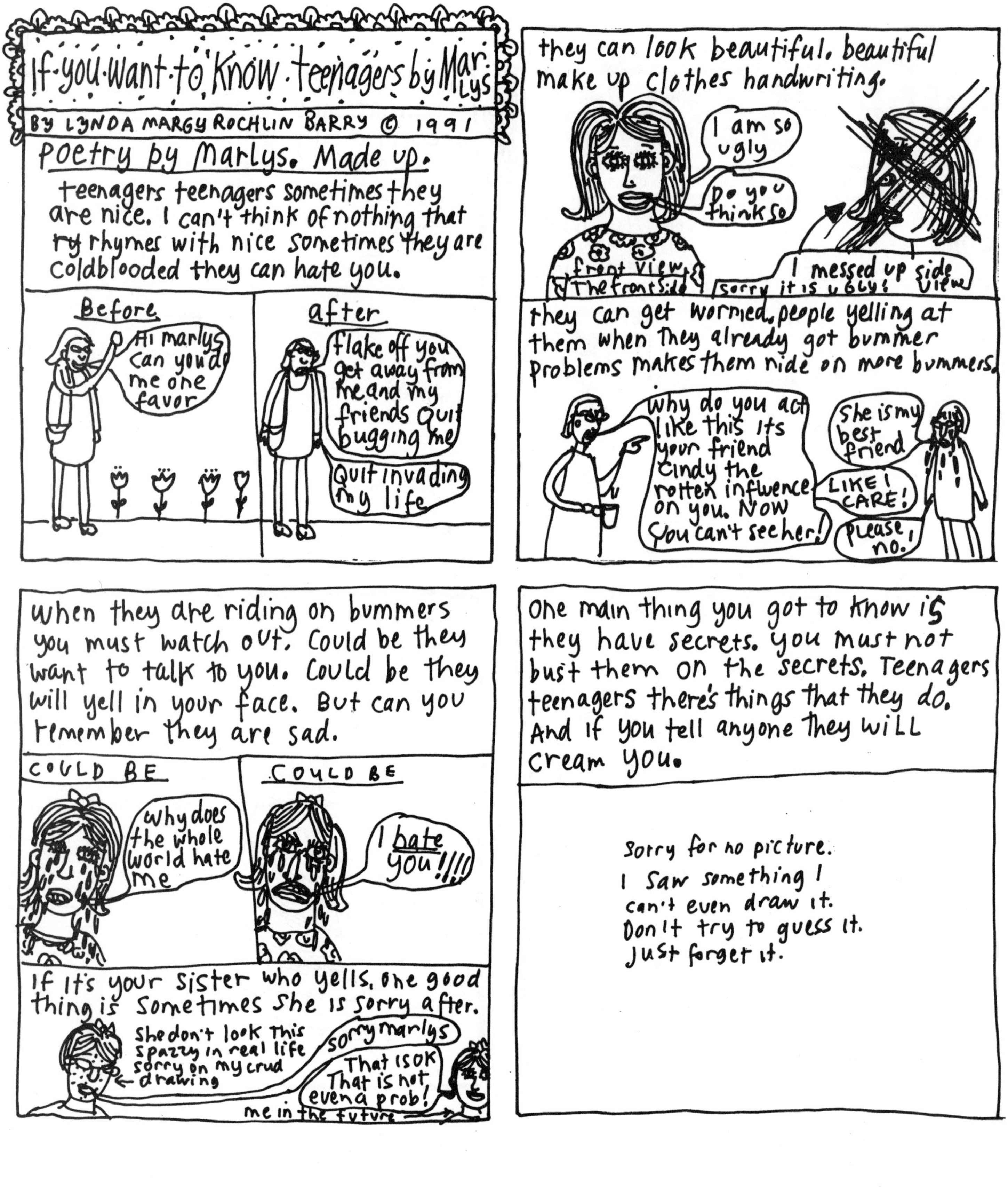
If you want to know teenagers by Marlys
BY LYNDA MARGY ROCHLIN BARRY © 1991
Poetry by Marlys. Made up.
teenagers teenagers sometimes they are nice. I can't think of nothing that ry rhymes with nice sometimes they are coldblooded they can hate you.
Before
Hi marlys can you do me one favor
after
Flake off you get away from me and my friends Quit bugging me
Quit invading my life
they can look beautiful. beautiful make up clothes handwriting.
I am so ugly
Do you think so
front view. The front side
I messed up side view sorry it is ugly!
they can get worried. people yelling at them when they already got bummer problems makes them ride on more bummers.
Why do you act like this its your friend Cindy the rotten influence on you. Now you can't see her!
She is my best friend
LIKE I CARE!
Please no!
when they are riding on bummers you must watch out. Could be they want to talk to you. Could be they will yell in your face. But can you remember they are sad.
COULD BE
why does the whole world hate me
COULD BE
I hate you!!!!
If it's your sister who yells. one good thing is Sometimes she is sorry after.
She don't look this spazzy in real life sorry on my crud drawing
sorry marlys
That is OK That is not even a prob!
me in the future
One main thing you got to know is they have secrets. you must not bust them on the secrets. Teenagers teenagers there's things that they do. And if you tell anyone they will cream you.
Sorry for no picture. I saw something I can't even draw it. Don't try to guess it. Just forget it.

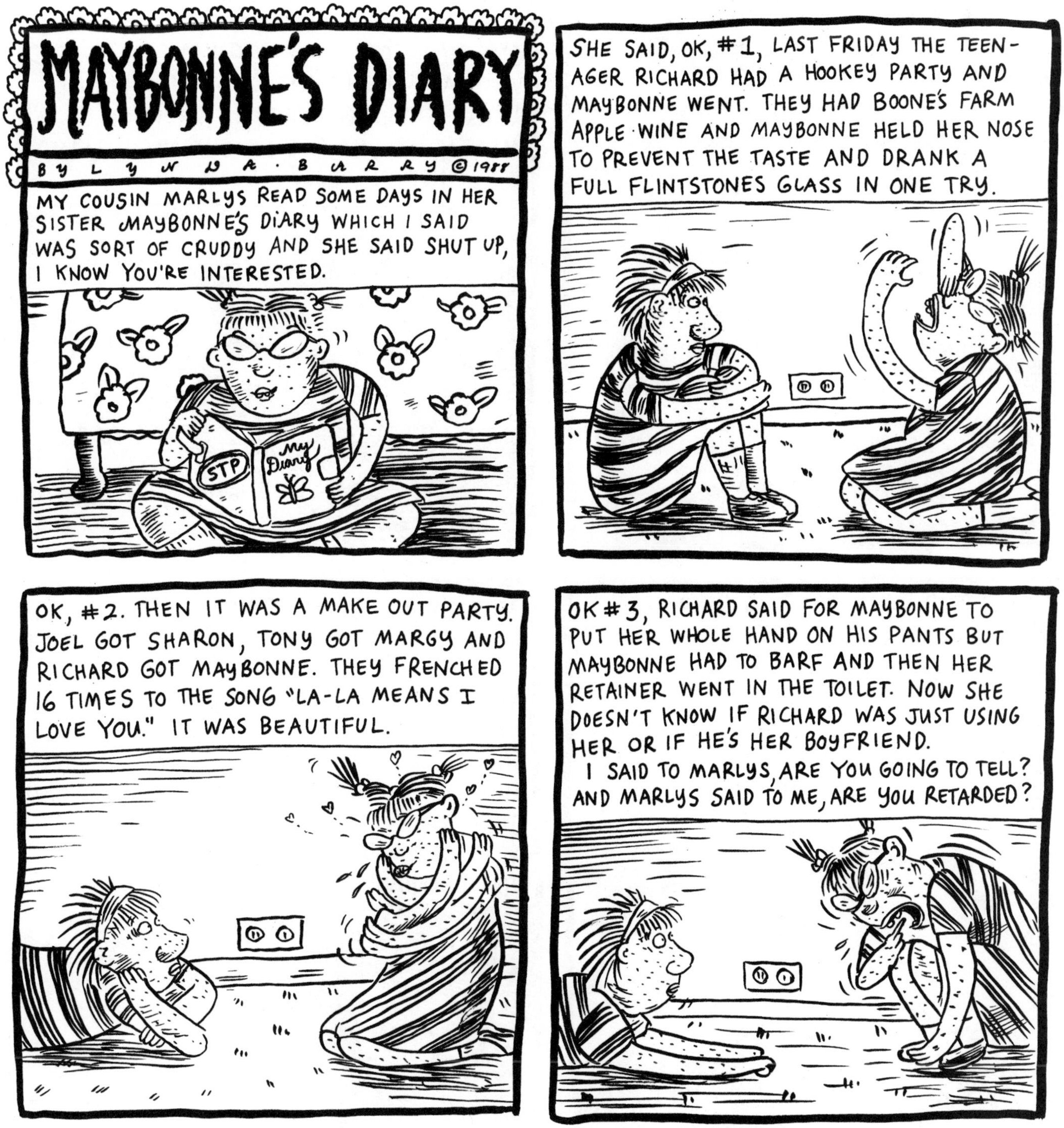
MAYBONNE'S DIARY
BY LYNDA BARRY ©1988
MY COUSIN MARLYS READ SOME DAYS IN HER SISTER MAYBONNE'S DIARY WHICH I SAID WAS SORT OF CRUDDY AND SHE SAID SHUT UP, I KNOW YOU'RE INTERESTED.
STP
My Diary
SHE SAID, OK, #1, LAST FRIDAY THE TEEN-AGER RICHARD HAD A HOOKEY PARTY AND MAYBONNE WENT. THEY HAD BOONE'S FARM APPLE·WINE AND MAYBONNE HELD HER NOSE TO PREVENT THE TASTE AND DRANK A FULL FLINTSTONES GLASS IN ONE TRY.
OK, #2. THEN IT WAS A MAKE OUT PARTY. JOEL GOT SHARON, TONY GOT MARGY AND RICHARD GOT MAYBONNE. THEY FRENCHED 16 TIMES TO THE SONG "LA-LA MEANS I LOVE YOU." IT WAS BEAUTIFUL.
OK #3, RICHARD SAID FOR MAYBONNE TO PUT HER WHOLE HAND ON HIS PANTS BUT MAYBONNE HAD TO BARF AND THEN HER RETAINER WENT IN THE TOILET. NOW SHE DOESN'T KNOW IF RICHARD WAS JUST USING HER OR IF HE'S HER BOYFRIEND.
I SAID TO MARLYS, ARE YOU GOING TO TELL? AND MARLYS SAID TO ME, ARE YOU RETARDED?

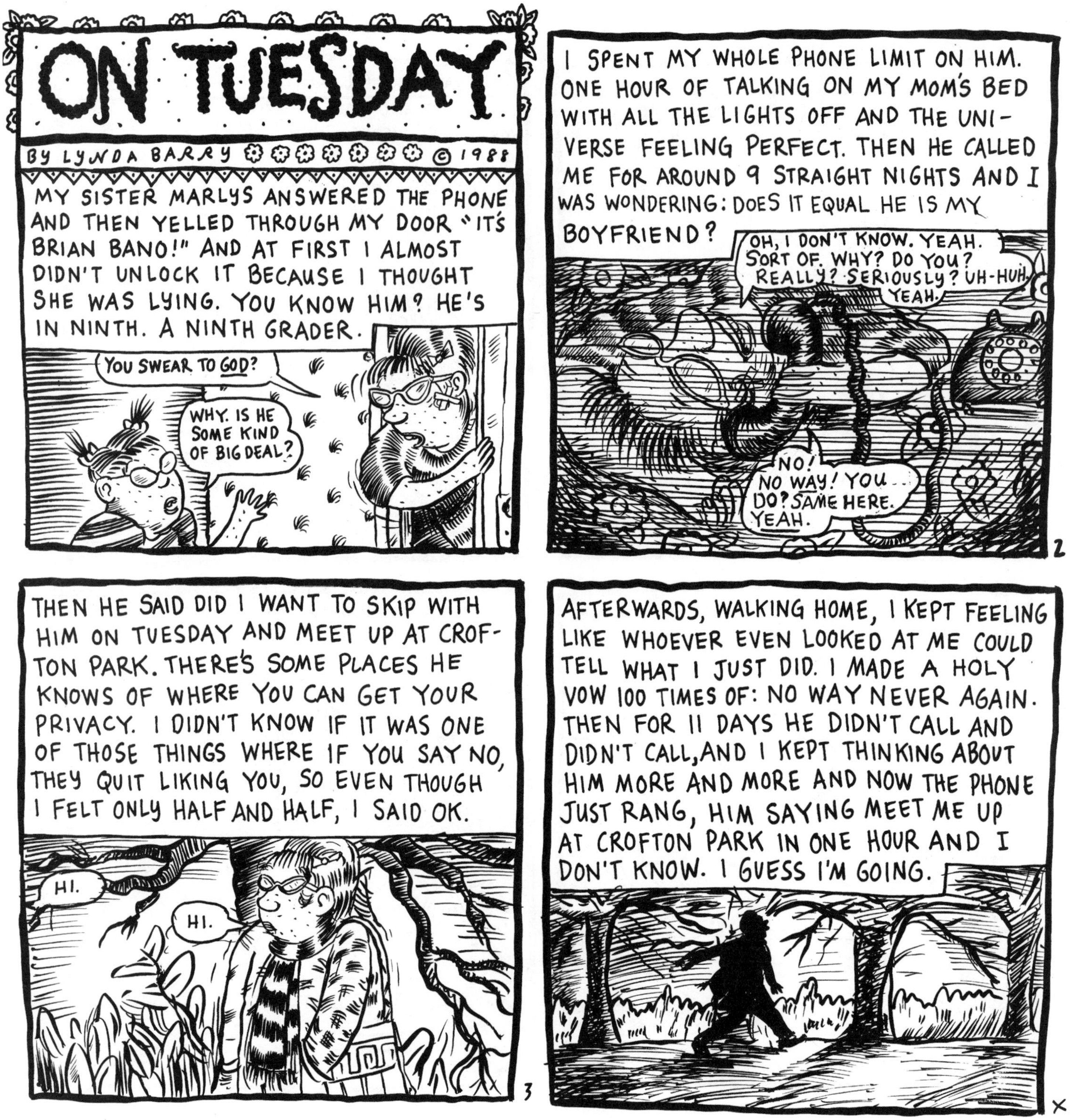
ON TUESDAY
BY LYNDA BARRY ©1988
MY SISTER MARLYS ANSWERED THE PHONE AND THEN YELLED THROUGH MY DOOR "IT'S BRIAN BANO!" AND AT FIRST I ALMOST DIDN'T UNLOCK IT BECAUSE I THOUGHT SHE WAS LYING. YOU KNOW HIM? HE'S IN NINTH. A NINTH GRADER.
YOU SWEAR TO GOD?
WHY. IS HE SOME KIND OF BIG DEAL?
I SPENT MY WHOLE PHONE LIMIT ON HIM. ONE HOUR OF TALKING ON MY MOM'S BED WITH ALL THE LIGHTS OFF AND THE UNIVERSE FEELING PERFECT. THEN HE CALLED ME FOR AROUND 9 STRAIGHT NIGHTS AND I WAS WONDERING: DOES IT EQUAL HE IS MY BOYFRIEND?
OH, I DON'T KNOW. YEAH. SORT OF. WHY? DO YOU? REALLY? SERIOUSLY? UH-HUH. YEAH.
NO! NO WAY! YOU DO? SAME HERE. YEAH.
2
THEN HE SAID DID I WANT TO SKIP WITH HIM ON TUESDAY AND MEET UP AT CROFTON PARK. THERE'S SOME PLACES HE KNOWS OF WHERE YOU CAN GET YOUR PRIVACY. I DIDN'T KNOW IF IT WAS ONE OF THOSE THINGS WHERE IF YOU SAY NO, THEY QUIT LIKING YOU, SO EVEN THOUGH I FELT ONLY HALF AND HALF, I SAID OK.
HI.
HI.
3
AFTERWARDS, WALKING HOME, I KEPT FEELING LIKE WHOEVER EVEN LOOKED AT ME COULD TELL WHAT I JUST DID. I MADE A HOLY VOW 100 TIMES OF: NO WAY NEVER AGAIN. THEN FOR 11 DAYS HE DIDN'T CALL AND DIDN'T CALL, AND I KEPT THINKING ABOUT HIM MORE AND MORE AND NOW THE PHONE JUST RANG, HIM SAYING MEET ME UP AT CROFTON PARK IN ONE HOUR AND I DON'T KNOW. I GUESS I'M GOING.
x

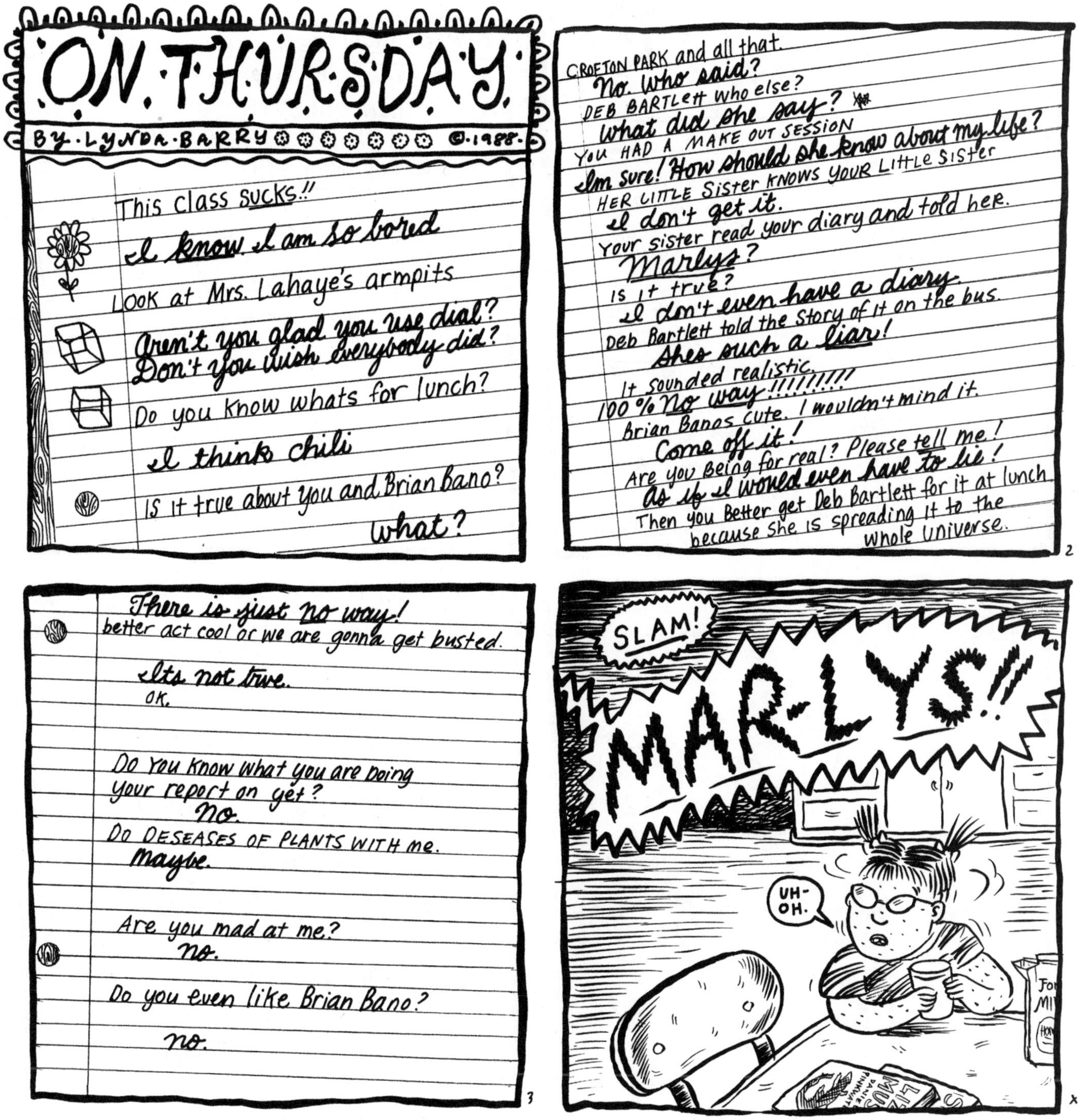

ON THURSDAY
BY LYNDA BARRY ©1988.
This class sucks!!
I know I am so bored
Look at Mrs. Lahaye's armpits
Aren't you glad you use dial? Don't you wish everybody did?
Do you know whats for lunch?
I think chili
Is it true about you and Brian Bano?
what?
CROFTON PARK and all that.
No. Who said?
DEB BARTLETT who else?
What did she say?
YOU HAD A MAKE OUT SESSION
I'm sure! How should she know about my life?
HER LITTLE SISTER KNOWS YOUR LITTLE SISTER
I don't get it.
Your sister read your diary and told her.
Marlys?
Is it true?
I don't even have a diary.
Deb Bartlett told the story of it on the bus.
Shes such a liar!
It sounded realistic.
100% No way!!!!!!!!!
Brian Banos cute. I wouldn't mind it.
Come off it!
Are you Being for real? Please tell me!
As if I would even have to lie!
Then you Better get Deb Bartlett for it at lunch because She is spreading it to the whole universe.
2
There is just no way!
better act cool or we are gonna get busted.
Its not true.
OK.
Do You know What you are Doing your report on yet?
No.
Do DESEASES OF PLANTS WITH me.
Maybe.
Are you mad at me?
no.
Do you even like Brian Bano?
no.
3
SLAM!
MAR-LYS!!
UH-OH.

HOW TO DRAW GIRLS
LYNDA 12 STITCHES BARRY © 1988
WITH YOUR HOST
MARLYS
"OK. THE FIRST NUMBER ONE THING IN DRAWING GIRLS IS PRACTICE YOUR EYES! GET THEM MATCHING OR YOUR DRAWING WILL LOOK LIKE THERE'S A MENTAL PROBLEM!"
EYEBALL GOES IN the MIDDLE.
EYEBROWS
DON'T FORGET CURLY EYELASHES.
OK NOW PUT ON THE LINES
KEEP ON DOING IT UNTIL YOU GET IT PERFECT BUT DON'T JUST WASTE PAPER!
IT MAKES THE EYES BEAUTIFUL!
NUMBER TWO: THE MOUTH AND NOSE IS EASY! FIRST DRAW THE SHAPE OF HER HEAD IN A "U". THEN YOU JUST ADD ON THE KIND OF MOUTH AND NOSE YOU WANT DEPENDING ON HER PERSONALITY!
SHY
SAD
MOVIE STAR
BEAUTIFUL VAMPIRE
FASHION MODEL
STEWARDESS
2
NUMBER THREE: WHAT ABOUT HER HAIR? THERE'S A LOT OF HAIR-DOS FOR HER TO HAVE! THERE'S A LOT OF STYLES!
PEEK-A-BOO
A BEAUTY PAGEANT
INDIAN PRINCESS
WEE! WEE!
A FRANCE LADY
A GORGEOUS FLIP
RATTED BUBBLE
3
NUMBER FOUR: THE HARDEST PART: YOU HAVE TO DRAW HER WHOLE BODY AND THIS IS WHERE YOU CAN WRECK EVERYTHING SO BE CAREFUL! MY SECRET IS: DRAW A LONG BEAUTIFUL DRESS AND HER HOLDING FLOWERS AND DON'T FORGET SOME ELEGANT ACCESSORIES!
A CROWN ALWAYS LOOKS LOVELY.
FLOWERS CAN HIDE HANDS THAT'S TOO HARD TO DRAW
PUT IN BIRDS
DRAW ON A WATCH
HER PURSE. IT'S IMPORTANT
DECORATE THE DRESS PLEASE
DRAW A TREE HERE AND SHE CAN LOOK LIKE SHES IN THE FOREST
SHOES CAN STICK OUT
THE END By MARLYS
x

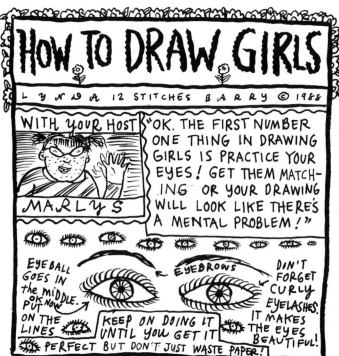

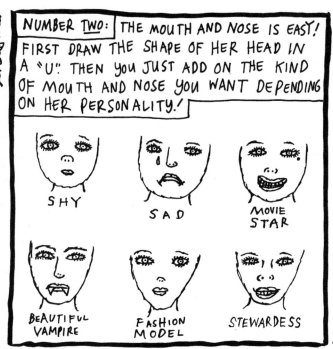

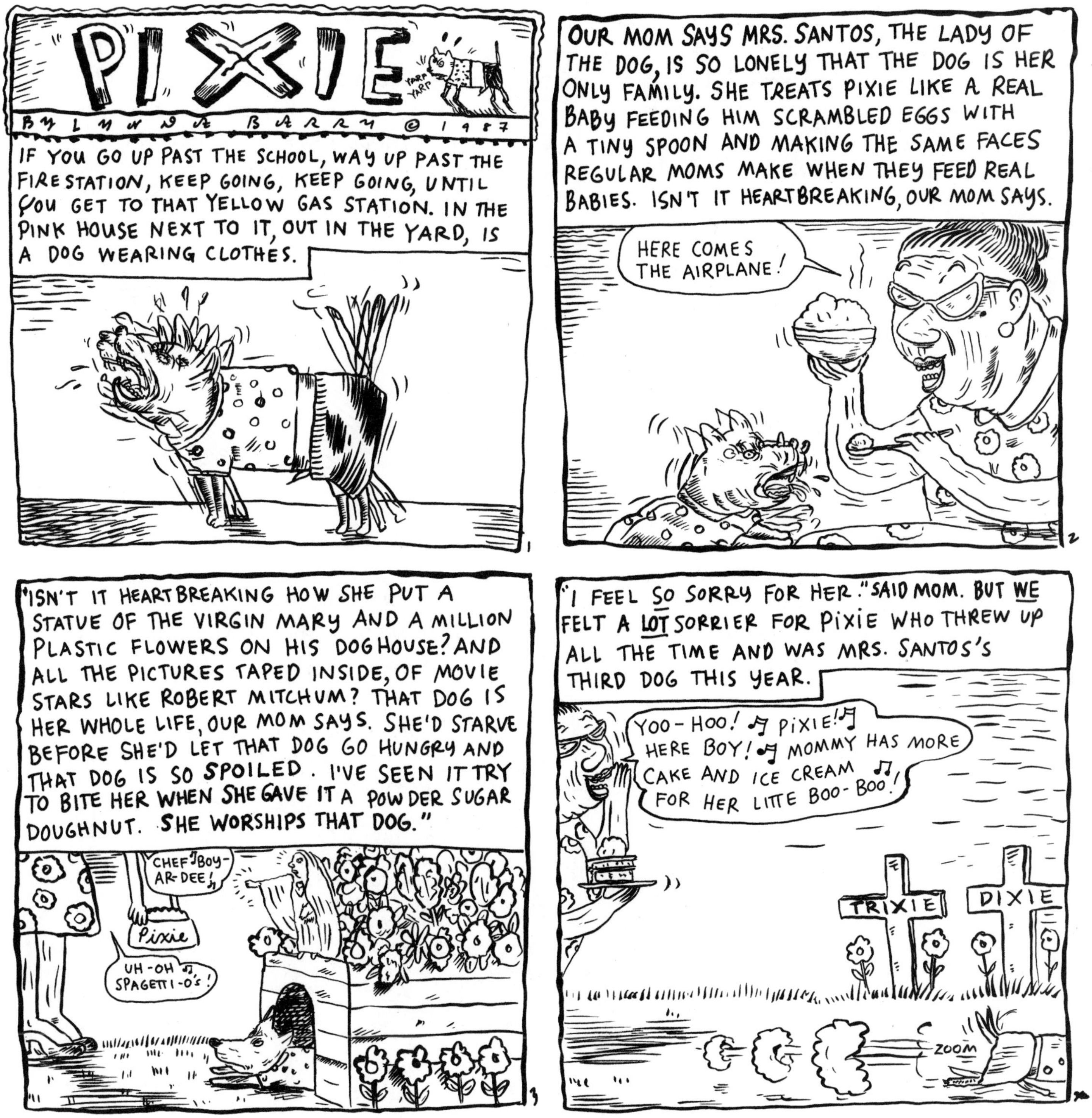
PIXIE
YARP YARP
BY LYNDA BARRY ©1987
IF YOU GO UP PAST THE SCHOOL, WAY UP PAST THE FIRESTATION, KEEP GOING, KEEP GOING, UNTIL YOU GET TO THAT YELLOW GAS STATION. IN THE PINK HOUSE NEXT TO IT, OUT IN THE YARD, IS A DOG WEARING CLOTHES.
OUR MOM SAYS MRS. SANTOS, THE LADY OF THE DOG, IS SO LONELY THAT THE DOG IS HER ONLY FAMILY. SHE TREATS PIXIE LIKE A REAL BABY FEEDING HIM SCRAMBLED EGGS WITH A TINY SPOON AND MAKING THE SAME FACES REGULAR MOMS MAKE WHEN THEY FEED REAL BABIES. ISN'T IT HEARTBREAKING, OUR MOM SAYS.
HERE COMES THE AIRPLANE!
"ISN'T IT HEARTBREAKING HOW SHE PUT A STATUE OF THE VIRGIN MARY AND A MILLION PLASTIC FLOWERS ON HIS DOGHOUSE? AND ALL THE PICTURES TAPED INSIDE, OF MOVIE STARS LIKE ROBERT MITCHUM? THAT DOG IS HER WHOLE LIFE, OUR MOM SAYS. SHE'D STARVE BEFORE SHE'D LET THAT DOG GO HUNGRY AND THAT DOG IS SO SPOILED. I'VE SEEN IT TRY TO BITE HER WHEN SHE GAVE IT A POWDER SUGAR DOUGHNUT. SHE WORSHIPS THAT DOG."
CHEF BOY-AR-DEE!
Pixie
UH-OH SPAGETTI-O'S!
"I FEEL SO SORRY FOR HER." SAID MOM. BUT WE FELT A LOT SORRIER FOR PIXIE WHO THREW UP ALL THE TIME AND WAS MRS. SANTOS'S THIRD DOG THIS YEAR.
YOO-HOO! PIXIE! HERE BOY! MOMMY HAS MORE CAKE AND ICE CREAM FOR HER LITTE BOO-BOO!
TRIXIE
DIXIE
ZOOM

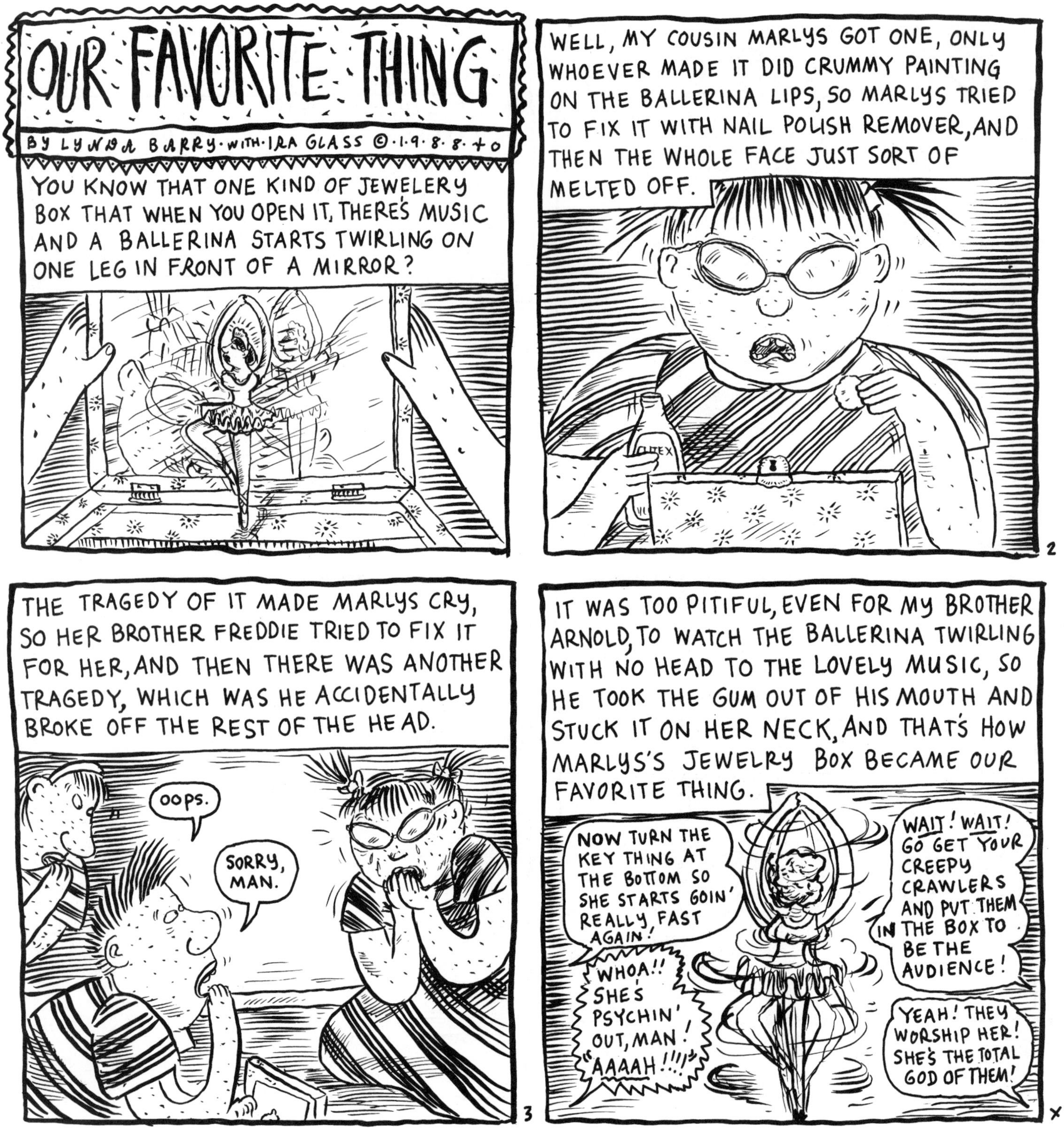
OUR FAVORITE THING
BY LYNDA BARRY · WITH · IRA GLASS ©·1·9·8·8·+0
YOU KNOW THAT ONE KIND OF JEWELERY BOX THAT WHEN YOU OPEN IT, THERE'S MUSIC AND A BALLERINA STARTS TWIRLING ON ONE LEG IN FRONT OF A MIRROR?
WELL, MY COUSIN MARLYS GOT ONE, ONLY WHOEVER MADE IT DID CRUMMY PAINTING ON THE BALLERINA LIPS, SO MARLYS TRIED TO FIX IT WITH NAIL POLISH REMOVER, AND THEN THE WHOLE FACE JUST SORT OF MELTED OFF.
2
THE TRAGEDY OF IT MADE MARLYS CRY, SO HER BROTHER FREDDIE TRIED TO FIX IT FOR HER, AND THEN THERE WAS ANOTHER TRAGEDY, WHICH WAS HE ACCIDENTALLY BROKE OFF THE REST OF THE HEAD.
OOPS.
SORRY, MAN.
3
IT WAS TOO PITIFUL, EVEN FOR MY BROTHER ARNOLD, TO WATCH THE BALLERINA TWIRLING WITH NO HEAD TO THE LOVELY MUSIC, SO HE TOOK THE GUM OUT OF HIS MOUTH AND STUCK IT ON HER NECK, AND THAT'S HOW MARLYS'S JEWELRY BOX BECAME OUR FAVORITE THING.
NOW TURN THE KEY THING AT THE BOTTOM SO SHE STARTS GOIN' REALLY FAST AGAIN!
WHOA!! SHE'S PSYCHIN' OUT, MAN! "AAAAH!!!!"
WAIT! WAIT! GO GET YOUR CREEPY CRAWLERS AND PUT THEM IN THE BOX TO BE THE AUDIENCE!
YEAH! THEY WORSHIP HER! SHE'S THE TOTAL GOD OF THEM!
X

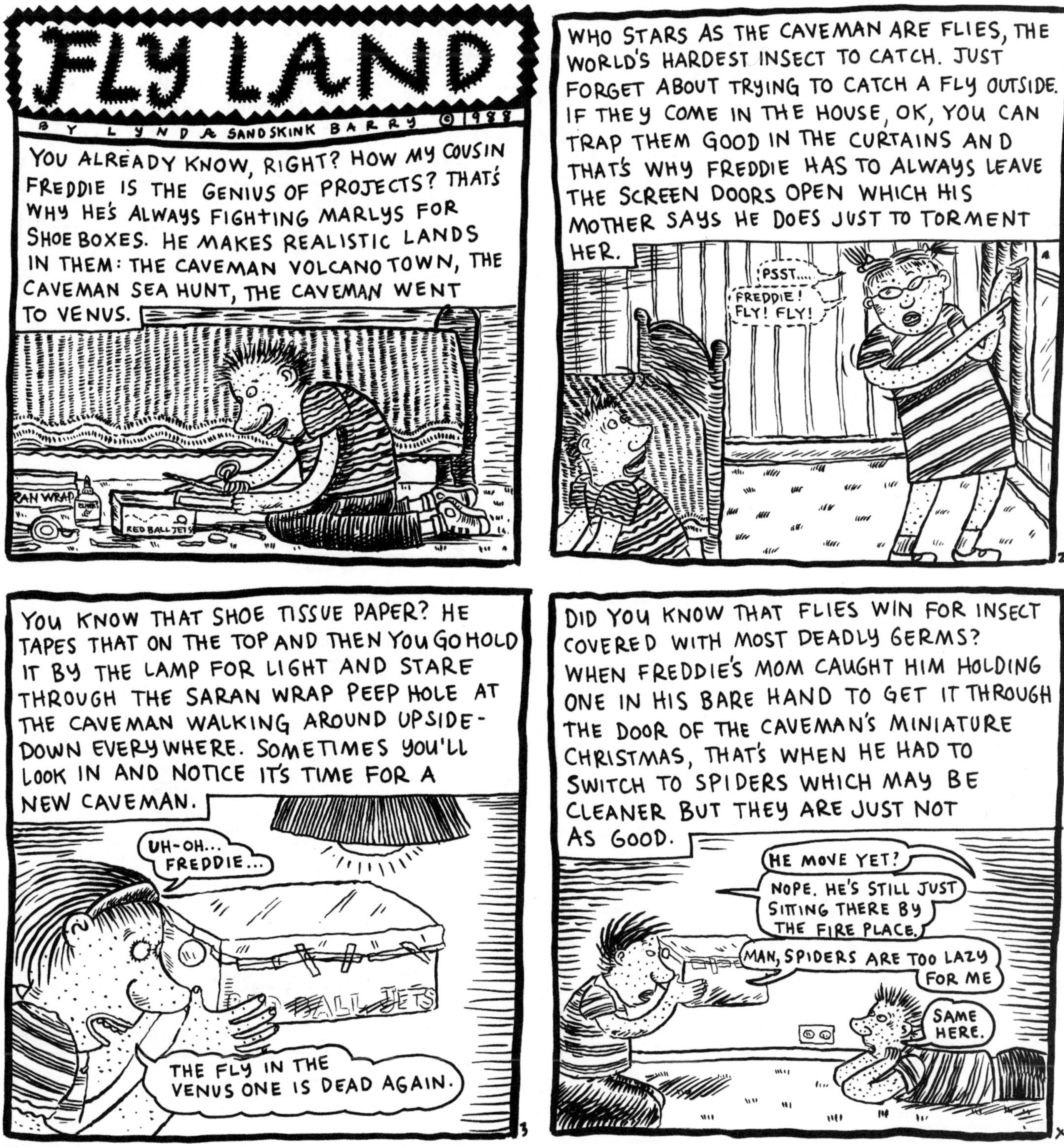
FLY LAND
BY LYNDA SANDSKINK BARRY ©1988
YOU ALREADY KNOW, RIGHT? HOW MY COUSIN FREDDIE IS THE GENIUS OF PROJECTS? THAT'S WHY HE'S ALWAYS FIGHTING MARLYS FOR SHOE BOXES. HE MAKES REALISTIC LANDS IN THEM: THE CAVEMAN VOLCANO TOWN, THE CAVEMAN SEA HUNT, THE CAVEMAN WENT TO VENUS.
RAN WRAP
RED BALL JETS
WHO STARS AS THE CAVEMAN ARE FLIES, THE WORLD'S HARDEST INSECT TO CATCH. JUST FORGET ABOUT TRYING TO CATCH A FLY OUTSIDE. IF THEY COME IN THE HOUSE, OK, YOU CAN TRAP THEM GOOD IN THE CURTAINS AND THAT'S WHY FREDDIE HAS TO ALWAYS LEAVE THE SCREEN DOORS OPEN WHICH HIS MOTHER SAYS HE DOES JUST TO TORMENT HER.
PSST.....
FREDDIE! FLY! FLY!
YOU KNOW THAT SHOE TISSUE PAPER? HE TAPES THAT ON THE TOP AND THEN YOU GO HOLD IT BY THE LAMP FOR LIGHT AND STARE THROUGH THE SARAN WRAP PEEP HOLE AT THE CAVEMAN WALKING AROUND UPSIDE-DOWN EVERYWHERE. SOMETIMES YOU'LL LOOK IN AND NOTICE IT'S TIME FOR A NEW CAVEMAN.
UH-OH... FREDDIE...
RED BALL JETS
THE FLY IN THE VENUS ONE IS DEAD AGAIN.
DID YOU KNOW THAT FLIES WIN FOR INSECT COVERED WITH MOST DEADLY GERMS? WHEN FREDDIE'S MOM CAUGHT HIM HOLDING ONE IN HIS BARE HAND TO GET IT THROUGH THE DOOR OF THE CAVEMAN'S MINIATURE CHRISTMAS, THAT'S WHEN HE HAD TO SWITCH TO SPIDERS WHICH MAY BE CLEANER BUT THEY ARE JUST NOT AS GOOD.
HE MOVE YET?
NOPE. HE'S STILL JUST SITTING THERE BY THE FIRE PLACE.
MAN, SPIDERS ARE TOO LAZY FOR ME
SAME HERE.

MY BEAUTIFUL DRESS

BY LYNDA BARRY © 1988

IT CAME FROM MY COUSIN DEBBIE'S IN THE MAIL. HER MOM WROTE A LETTER THAT DEBBIE COULDN'T FIT IT NOW BECAUSE SHE WAS SO MATURE UPSTAIRS. I ABOUT HAD AN ATTACK WHEN I SAW IT, IT WAS SO BEAUTIFUL.

"PROBABLY DIDN'T EVEN WEAR IT TEN TIMES" MY MOTHER SAID. "THE WAY MY SISTER THROWS MONEY AWAY ON THOSE KIDS, I'M TELLING YOU. MY GOD, THE IRONING THAT HAS TO GO INTO IT! THE SKIRT MUST HAVE TEN YARDS OF FABRIC. TRY IT ON." SHE SAID.

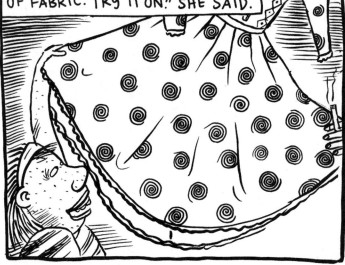

THAT NIGHT WHEN EVERYONE WAS ASLEEP, I PULLED THE DRESS OFF THE HANGER AND PUT IT ON IN THE BATHROOM. I HAD TO BALANCE MYSELF UP ON THE EDGES OF THE TUB TO SEE IN THE MIRROR HOW GORGEOUS I LOOKED. AND EVERYTHING WOULD HAVE BEEN OK IF I DIDN'T SUDDENLY GET THE IDEA TO DO SOME OF MY MODERN DANCES.

AT THE HOSPITAL THEY SAID THERE WAS NO CHOICE ABOUT CUTTING THE DRESS OFF OF ME IN ORDER TO SET MY BROKEN COLLAR-BONE. I SAID TO MY MOTHER AT LEAST SAVE THE PIECES, MAYBE WE COULD SEW IT BACK TOGETHER. "THE HELL I WILL" MY MOTHER SAID.

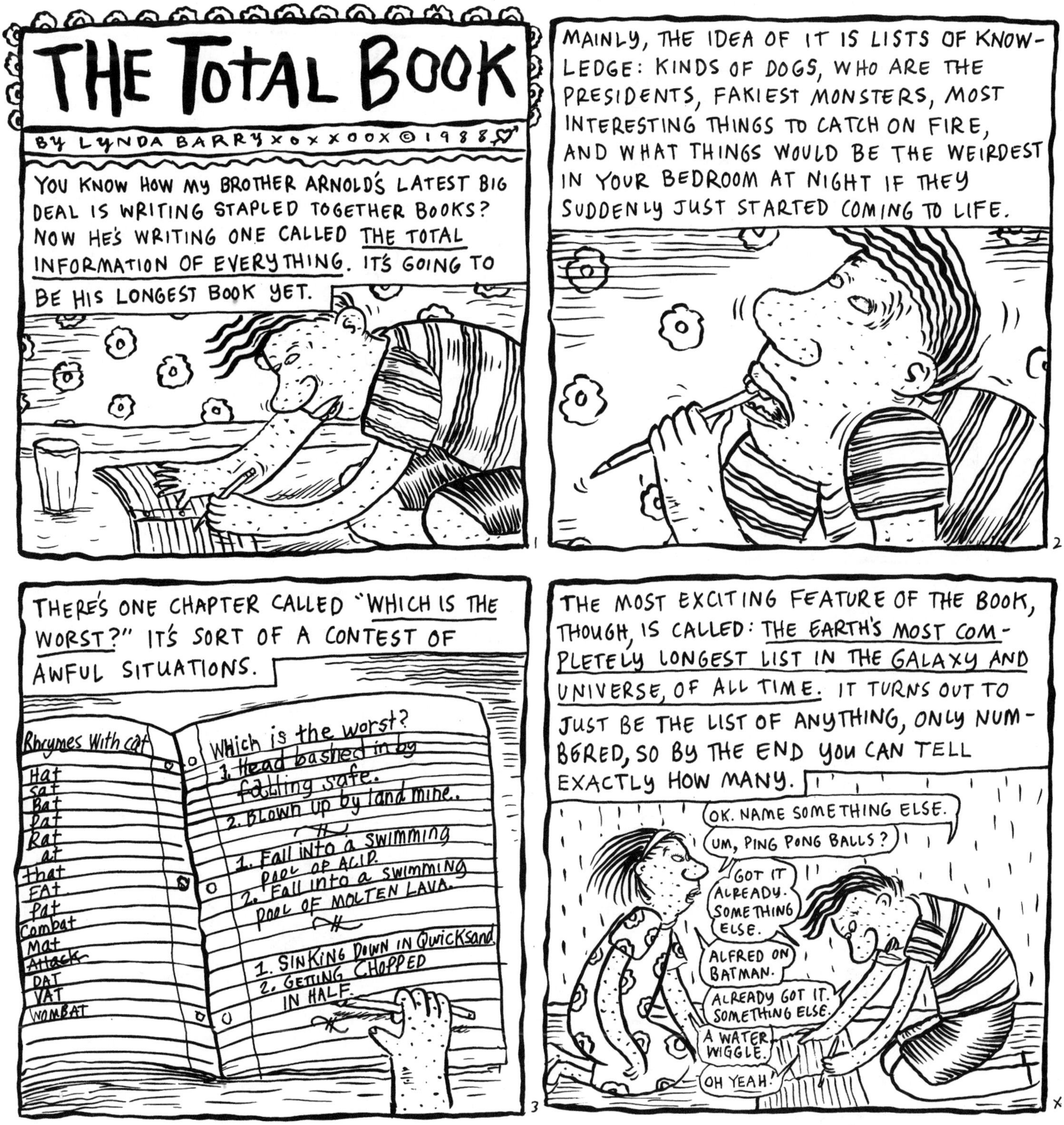
THE TOTAL BOOK
BY LYNDA BARRY xoxxoox © 1988
YOU KNOW HOW MY BROTHER ARNOLD'S LATEST BIG DEAL IS WRITING STAPLED TOGETHER BOOKS? NOW HE'S WRITING ONE CALLED THE TOTAL INFORMATION OF EVERYTHING. IT'S GOING TO BE HIS LONGEST BOOK YET.
1
MAINLY, THE IDEA OF IT IS LISTS OF KNOW-LEDGE: KINDS OF DOGS, WHO ARE THE PRESIDENTS, FAKIEST MONSTERS, MOST INTERESTING THINGS TO CATCH ON FIRE, AND WHAT THINGS WOULD BE THE WEIRDEST IN YOUR BEDROOM AT NIGHT IF THEY SUDDENLY JUST STARTED COMING TO LIFE.
2
THERE'S ONE CHAPTER CALLED "WHICH IS THE WORST?" IT'S SORT OF A CONTEST OF AWFUL SITUATIONS.
Rhymes With cat
Hat
sat
Bat
Pat
Rat
at
that
FAt
Pat
Combat
Mat
Attack
DAT
VAT
WOMBAT
Which is the worst?
1. Head bashed in by falling safe.
2. Blown up by land mine.
1. Fall into a swimming pool of ACID.
2. Fall into a swimming pool of MOLTEN LAVA.
1. SINKING DOWN IN QuicKsand.
2. GETTING CHOPPED IN HALF.
3
THE MOST EXCITING FEATURE OF THE BOOK, THOUGH, IS CALLED: THE EARTH'S MOST COM-PLETELY LONGEST LIST IN THE GALAXY AND UNIVERSE, OF ALL TIME. IT TURNS OUT TO JUST BE THE LIST OF ANYTHING, ONLY NUM-BERED, SO BY THE END YOU CAN TELL EXACTLY HOW MANY.
OK. NAME SOMETHING ELSE.
UM, PING PONG BALLS?
GOT IT ALREADY. SOMETHING ELSE.
ALFRED ON BATMAN.
ALREADY GOT IT. SOMETHING ELSE.
A WATER WIGGLE.
OH YEAH!
x

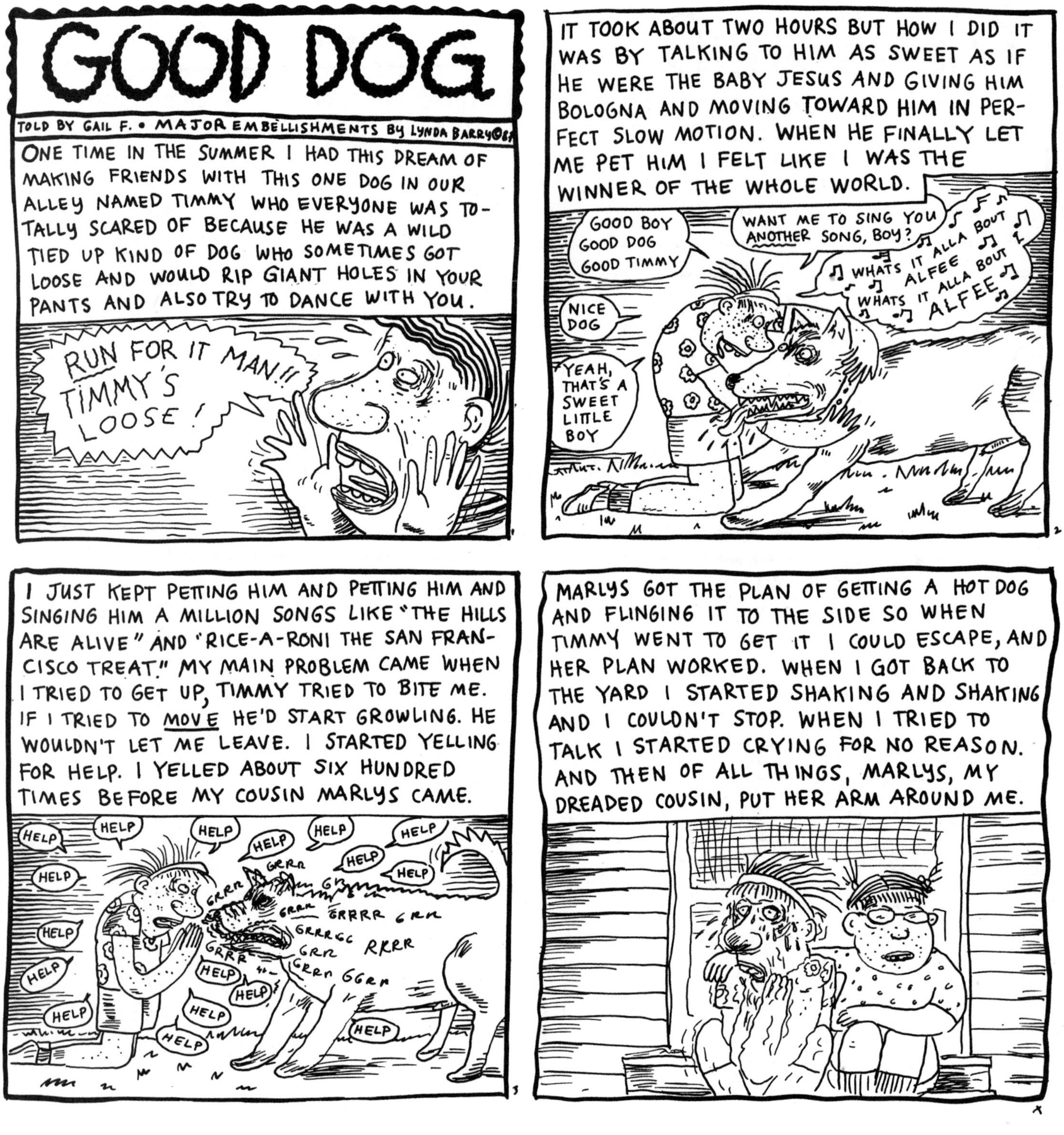
GOOD DOG
TOLD BY GAIL F. • MAJOR EMBELLISHMENTS BY LYNDA BARRY©87
ONE TIME IN THE SUMMER I HAD THIS DREAM OF MAKING FRIENDS WITH THIS ONE DOG IN OUR ALLEY NAMED TIMMY WHO EVERYONE WAS TOTALLY SCARED OF BECAUSE HE WAS A WILD TIED UP KIND OF DOG WHO SOMETIMES GOT LOOSE AND WOULD RIP GIANT HOLES IN YOUR PANTS AND ALSO TRY TO DANCE WITH YOU.
RUN FOR IT MAN!! TIMMY'S LOOSE!
IT TOOK ABOUT TWO HOURS BUT HOW I DID IT WAS BY TALKING TO HIM AS SWEET AS IF HE WERE THE BABY JESUS AND GIVING HIM BOLOGNA AND MOVING TOWARD HIM IN PERFECT SLOW MOTION. WHEN HE FINALLY LET ME PET HIM I FELT LIKE I WAS THE WINNER OF THE WHOLE WORLD.
GOOD BOY GOOD DOG GOOD TIMMY
WANT ME TO SING YOU ANOTHER SONG, BOY?
WHATS IT ALLA BOUT ALFEE WHATS IT ALLA BOUT ALFEE
NICE DOG
YEAH, THAT'S A SWEET LITTLE BOY
I JUST KEPT PETTING HIM AND PETTING HIM AND SINGING HIM A MILLION SONGS LIKE "THE HILLS ARE ALIVE" AND "RICE-A-RONI THE SAN FRANCISCO TREAT." MY MAIN PROBLEM CAME WHEN I TRIED TO GET UP, TIMMY TRIED TO BITE ME. IF I TRIED TO MOVE HE'D START GROWLING. HE WOULDN'T LET ME LEAVE. I STARTED YELLING FOR HELP. I YELLED ABOUT SIX HUNDRED TIMES BEFORE MY COUSIN MARLYS CAME.
HELP HELP HELP HELP HELP HELP HELP HELP HELP HELP HELP HELP HELP HELP HELP HELP HELP
GRRR GRRR GRRRR GRR GRRRGG GRR RRRR GRRR GRRR GGRR
MARLYS GOT THE PLAN OF GETTING A HOT DOG AND FLINGING IT TO THE SIDE SO WHEN TIMMY WENT TO GET IT I COULD ESCAPE, AND HER PLAN WORKED. WHEN I GOT BACK TO THE YARD I STARTED SHAKING AND SHAKING AND I COULDN'T STOP. WHEN I TRIED TO TALK I STARTED CRYING FOR NO REASON. AND THEN OF ALL THINGS, MARLYS, MY DREADED COUSIN, PUT HER ARM AROUND ME.

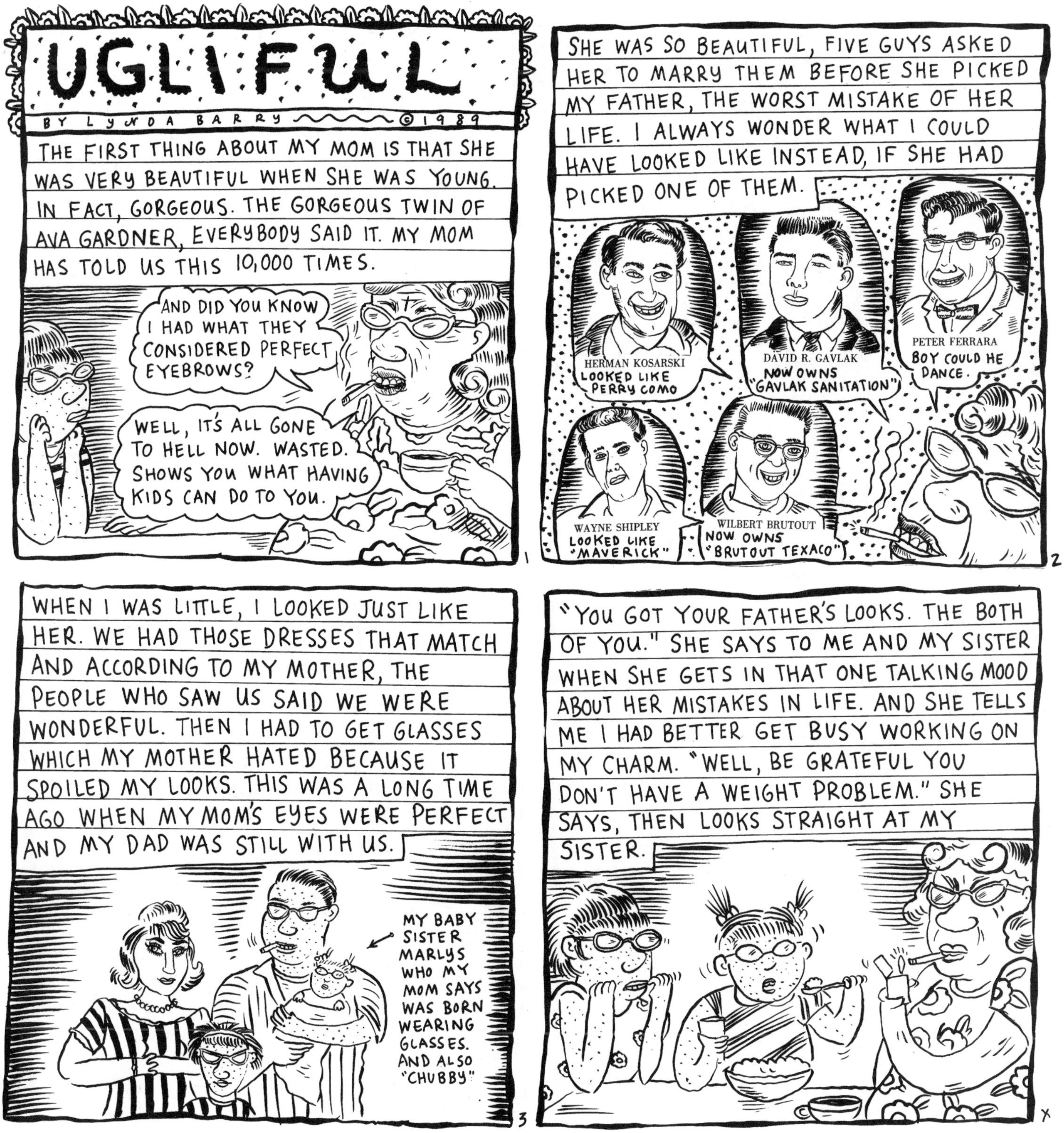
UGLIFUL
BY LYNDA BARRY ©1989
THE FIRST THING ABOUT MY MOM IS THAT SHE WAS VERY BEAUTIFUL WHEN SHE WAS YOUNG. IN FACT, GORGEOUS. THE GORGEOUS TWIN OF AVA GARDNER, EVERYBODY SAID IT. MY MOM HAS TOLD US THIS 10,000 TIMES.
AND DID YOU KNOW I HAD WHAT THEY CONSIDERED PERFECT EYEBROWS?
WELL, IT'S ALL GONE TO HELL NOW. WASTED. SHOWS YOU WHAT HAVING KIDS CAN DO TO YOU.
1
SHE WAS SO BEAUTIFUL, FIVE GUYS ASKED HER TO MARRY THEM BEFORE SHE PICKED MY FATHER, THE WORST MISTAKE OF HER LIFE. I ALWAYS WONDER WHAT I COULD HAVE LOOKED LIKE INSTEAD, IF SHE HAD PICKED ONE OF THEM.
HERMAN KOSARSKI
LOOKED LIKE PERRY COMO
DAVID R. GAVLAK
NOW OWNS "GAVLAK SANITATION"
PETER FERRARA
BOY COULD HE DANCE.
WAYNE SHIPLEY
LOOKED LIKE "MAVERICK"
WILBERT BRUTOUT
NOW OWNS "BRUTOUT TEXACO"
2
WHEN I WAS LITTLE, I LOOKED JUST LIKE HER. WE HAD THOSE DRESSES THAT MATCH AND ACCORDING TO MY MOTHER, THE PEOPLE WHO SAW US SAID WE WERE WONDERFUL. THEN I HAD TO GET GLASSES WHICH MY MOTHER HATED BECAUSE IT SPOILED MY LOOKS. THIS WAS A LONG TIME AGO WHEN MY MOM'S EYES WERE PERFECT AND MY DAD WAS STILL WITH US.
MY BABY SISTER MARLYS WHO MY MOM SAYS WAS BORN WEARING GLASSES. AND ALSO "CHUBBY"
3
"YOU GOT YOUR FATHER'S LOOKS. THE BOTH OF YOU." SHE SAYS TO ME AND MY SISTER WHEN SHE GETS IN THAT ONE TALKING MOOD ABOUT HER MISTAKES IN LIFE. AND SHE TELLS ME I HAD BETTER GET BUSY WORKING ON MY CHARM. "WELL, BE GRATEFUL YOU DON'T HAVE A WEIGHT PROBLEM." SHE SAYS, THEN LOOKS STRAIGHT AT MY SISTER.
X

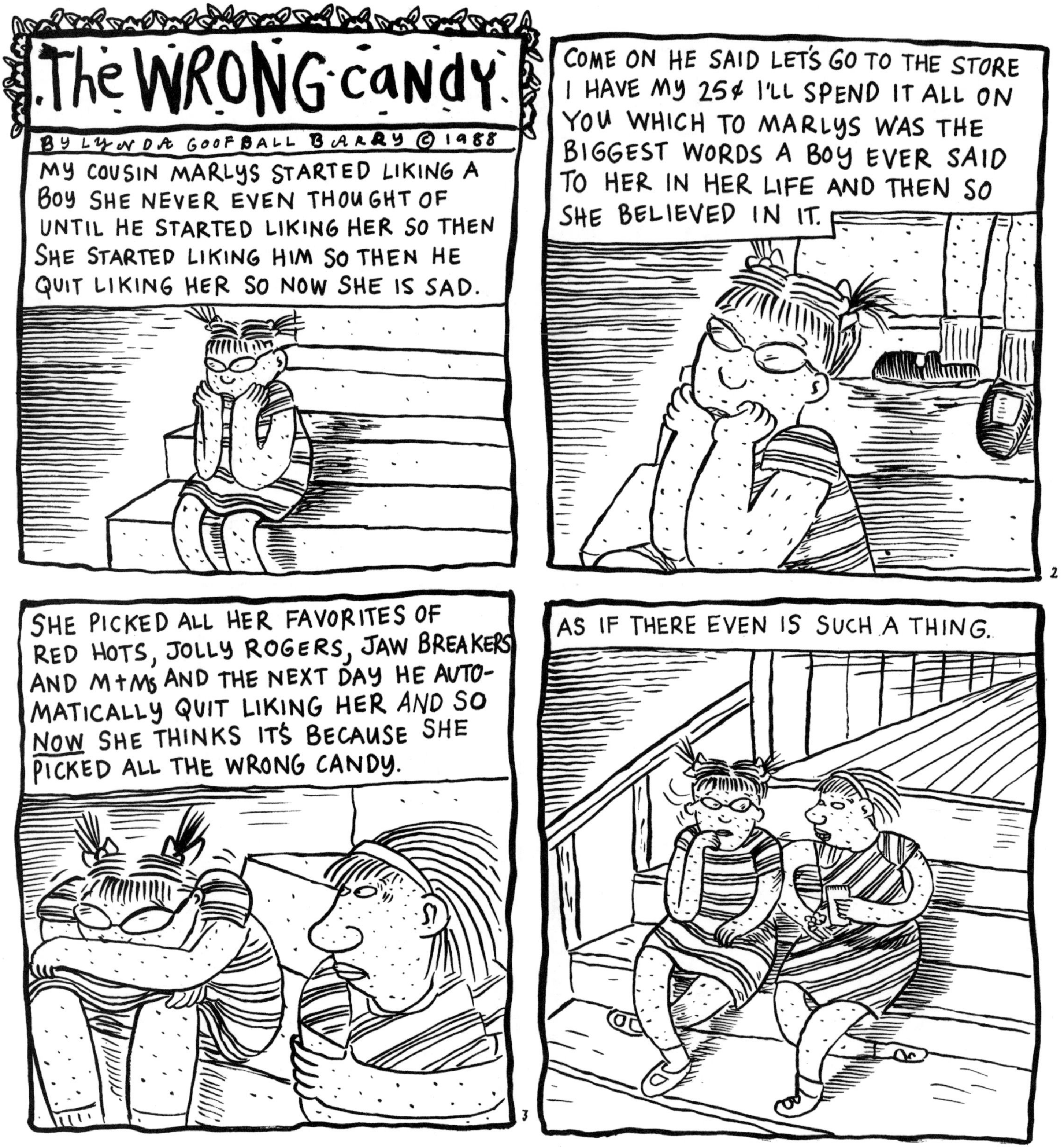
The WRONG candy
BY LYNDA GOOFBALL BARRY © 1988
MY COUSIN MARLYS STARTED LIKING A BOY SHE NEVER EVEN THOUGHT OF UNTIL HE STARTED LIKING HER SO THEN SHE STARTED LIKING HIM SO THEN HE QUIT LIKING HER SO NOW SHE IS SAD.
COME ON HE SAID LET'S GO TO THE STORE I HAVE MY 25¢ I'LL SPEND IT ALL ON YOU WHICH TO MARLYS WAS THE BIGGEST WORDS A BOY EVER SAID TO HER IN HER LIFE AND THEN SO SHE BELIEVED IN IT.
SHE PICKED ALL HER FAVORITES OF RED HOTS, JOLLY ROGERS, JAW BREAKERS AND M+Ms AND THE NEXT DAY HE AUTOMATICALLY QUIT LIKING HER AND SO NOW SHE THINKS IT'S BECAUSE SHE PICKED ALL THE WRONG CANDY.
AS IF THERE EVEN IS SUCH A THING.

WADING MARLYS

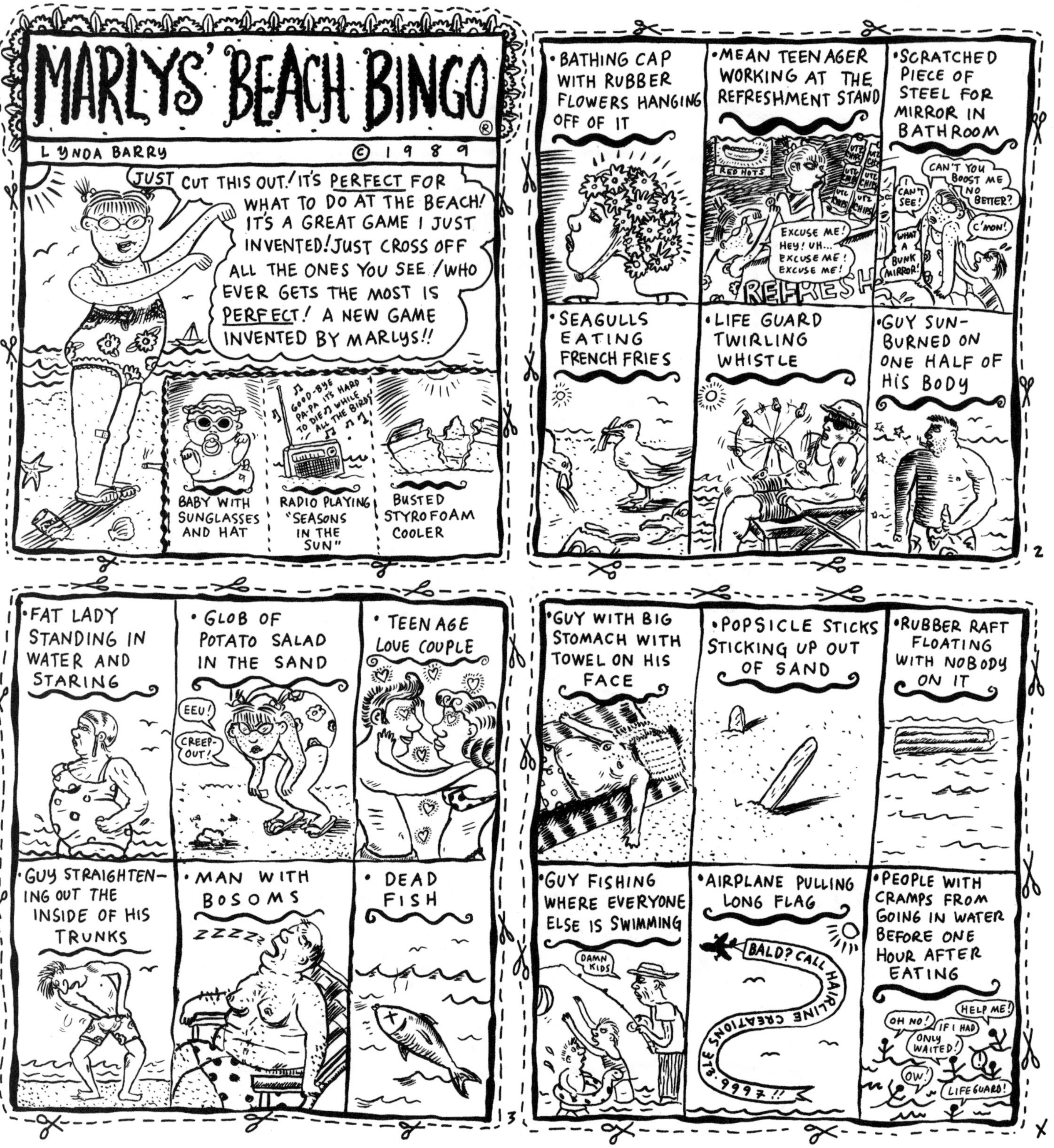
MARLYS' BEACH BINGO ®
LYNDA BARRY © 1989
JUST CUT THIS OUT! IT'S PERFECT FOR WHAT TO DO AT THE BEACH! IT'S A GREAT GAME I JUST INVENTED! JUST CROSS OFF ALL THE ONES YOU SEE! WHO EVER GETS THE MOST IS PERFECT! A NEW GAME INVENTED BY MARLYS!!
BABY WITH SUNGLASSES AND HAT
GOOD-BYE PA-PA IT'S HARD TO DIE WHILE ALL THE BIRDS
RADIO PLAYING "SEASONS IN THE SUN"
BUSTED STYROFOAM COOLER
•BATHING CAP WITH RUBBER FLOWERS HANGING OFF OF IT
•MEAN TEEN AGER WORKING AT THE REFRESHMENT STAND
RED HOTS
UTZ CHIPS
EXCUSE ME! HEY! UH... EXCUSE ME! EXCUSE ME!
REFRESH
•SCRATCHED PIECE OF STEEL FOR MIRROR IN BATHROOM
CAN'T YOU BOOST ME NO BETTER?
I CAN'T SEE!
C'MON!
WHAT A BUNK MIRROR!
•SEAGULLS EATING FRENCH FRIES
•LIFE GUARD TWIRLING WHISTLE
•GUY SUN-BURNED ON ONE HALF OF HIS BODY
2
•FAT LADY STANDING IN WATER AND STARING
•GLOB OF POTATO SALAD IN THE SAND
EEU!
CREEP-OUT!
•TEEN AGE LOVE COUPLE
•GUY STRAIGHTEN-ING OUT THE INSIDE OF HIS TRUNKS
•MAN WITH BOSOMS
ZZZZZ
•DEAD FISH
3
•GUY WITH BIG STOMACH WITH TOWEL ON HIS FACE
•POPSICLE STICKS STICKING UP OUT OF SAND
•RUBBER RAFT FLOATING WITH NOBODY ON IT
•GUY FISHING WHERE EVERYONE ELSE IS SWIMMING
DAMN KIDS
•AIRPLANE PULLING LONG FLAG
BALD? CALL HAIRLINE CREATIONS 3.8.3-9997!!
•PEOPLE WITH CRAMPS FROM GOING IN WATER BEFORE ONE HOUR AFTER EATING
HELP ME!
OH NO!
IF I HAD ONLY WAITED!
OW!
LIFEGUARD!
X

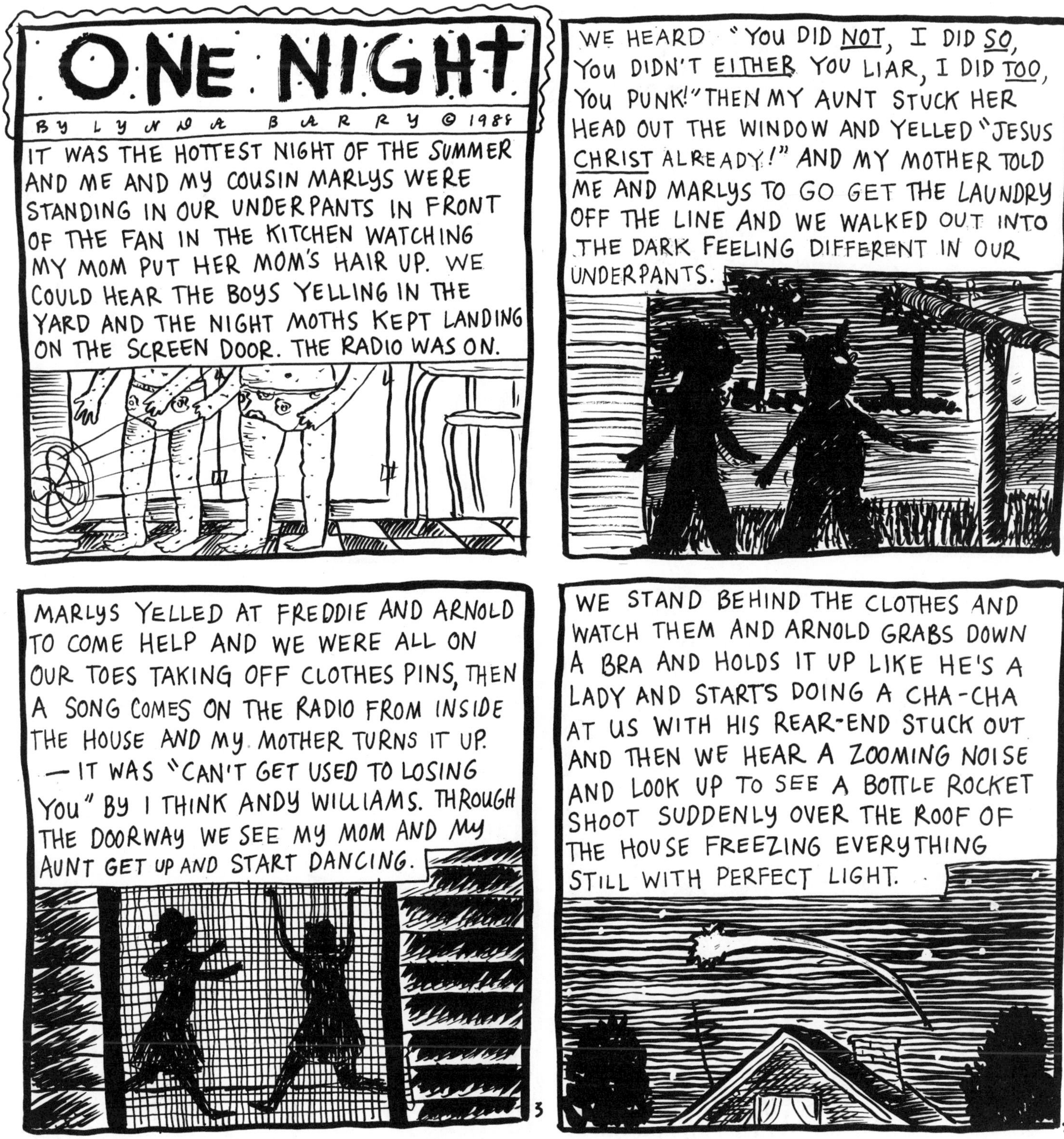
ONE NIGHT
BY LYNDA BARRY © 1988
IT WAS THE HOTTEST NIGHT OF THE SUMMER AND ME AND MY COUSIN MARLYS WERE STANDING IN OUR UNDERPANTS IN FRONT OF THE FAN IN THE KITCHEN WATCHING MY MOM PUT HER MOM'S HAIR UP. WE COULD HEAR THE BOYS YELLING IN THE YARD AND THE NIGHT MOTHS KEPT LANDING ON THE SCREEN DOOR. THE RADIO WAS ON.
WE HEARD "YOU DID NOT, I DID SO, YOU DIDN'T EITHER YOU LIAR, I DID TOO, YOU PUNK!" THEN MY AUNT STUCK HER HEAD OUT THE WINDOW AND YELLED "JESUS CHRIST ALREADY!" AND MY MOTHER TOLD ME AND MARLYS TO GO GET THE LAUNDRY OFF THE LINE AND WE WALKED OUT INTO THE DARK FEELING DIFFERENT IN OUR UNDERPANTS.
2
MARLYS YELLED AT FREDDIE AND ARNOLD TO COME HELP AND WE WERE ALL ON OUR TOES TAKING OFF CLOTHES PINS, THEN A SONG COMES ON THE RADIO FROM INSIDE THE HOUSE AND MY MOTHER TURNS IT UP. — IT WAS "CAN'T GET USED TO LOSING YOU" BY I THINK ANDY WILLIAMS. THROUGH THE DOORWAY WE SEE MY MOM AND MY AUNT GET UP AND START DANCING.
3
WE STAND BEHIND THE CLOTHES AND WATCH THEM AND ARNOLD GRABS DOWN A BRA AND HOLDS IT UP LIKE HE'S A LADY AND STARTS DOING A CHA-CHA AT US WITH HIS REAR-END STUCK OUT AND THEN WE HEAR A ZOOMING NOISE AND LOOK UP TO SEE A BOTTLE ROCKET SHOOT SUDDENLY OVER THE ROOF OF THE HOUSE FREEZING EVERYTHING STILL WITH PERFECT LIGHT.

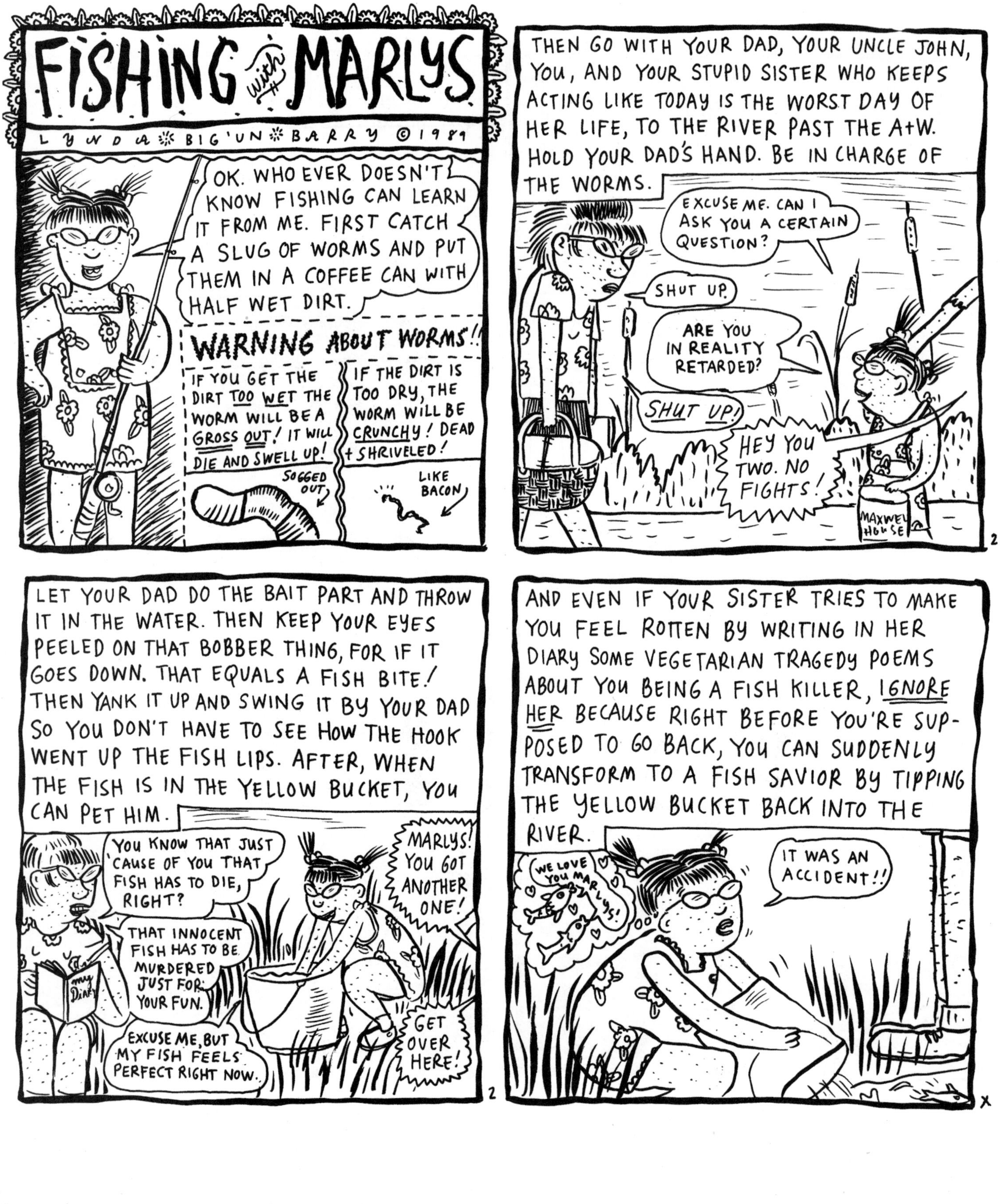
FISHING with MARLYS
LYNDA * BIG'UN * BARRY ©1989
OK. WHO EVER DOESN'T KNOW FISHING CAN LEARN IT FROM ME. FIRST CATCH A SLUG OF WORMS AND PUT THEM IN A COFFEE CAN WITH HALF WET DIRT.
WARNING ABOUT WORMS!!
IF YOU GET THE DIRT TOO WET THE WORM WILL BE A GROSS OUT! IT WILL DIE AND SWELL UP!
IF THE DIRT IS TOO DRY, THE WORM WILL BE CRUNCHY! DEAD + SHRIVELED!
SOGGED OUT
LIKE BACON
THEN GO WITH YOUR DAD, YOUR UNCLE JOHN, YOU, AND YOUR STUPID SISTER WHO KEEPS ACTING LIKE TODAY IS THE WORST DAY OF HER LIFE, TO THE RIVER PAST THE A+W. HOLD YOUR DAD'S HAND. BE IN CHARGE OF THE WORMS.
EXCUSE ME. CAN I ASK YOU A CERTAIN QUESTION?
SHUT UP.
ARE YOU IN REALITY RETARDED?
SHUT UP!
HEY YOU TWO. NO FIGHTS!
MAXWELL HOUSE
2
LET YOUR DAD DO THE BAIT PART AND THROW IT IN THE WATER. THEN KEEP YOUR EYES PEELED ON THAT BOBBER THING, FOR IF IT GOES DOWN. THAT EQUALS A FISH BITE! THEN YANK IT UP AND SWING IT BY YOUR DAD SO YOU DON'T HAVE TO SEE HOW THE HOOK WENT UP THE FISH LIPS. AFTER, WHEN THE FISH IS IN THE YELLOW BUCKET, YOU CAN PET HIM.
YOU KNOW THAT JUST CAUSE OF YOU THAT FISH HAS TO DIE, RIGHT?
MARLYS! YOU GOT ANOTHER ONE!
THAT INNOCENT FISH HAS TO BE MURDERED JUST FOR YOUR FUN.
my Diary
EXCUSE ME, BUT MY FISH FEELS PERFECT RIGHT NOW.
GET OVER HERE!
2
AND EVEN IF YOUR SISTER TRIES TO MAKE YOU FEEL ROTTEN BY WRITING IN HER DIARY SOME VEGETARIAN TRAGEDY POEMS ABOUT YOU BEING A FISH KILLER, IGNORE HER BECAUSE RIGHT BEFORE YOU'RE SUP-POSED TO GO BACK, YOU CAN SUDDENLY TRANSFORM TO A FISH SAVIOR BY TIPPING THE YELLOW BUCKET BACK INTO THE RIVER.
WE LOVE YOU MARLYS!
IT WAS AN ACCIDENT!!
X

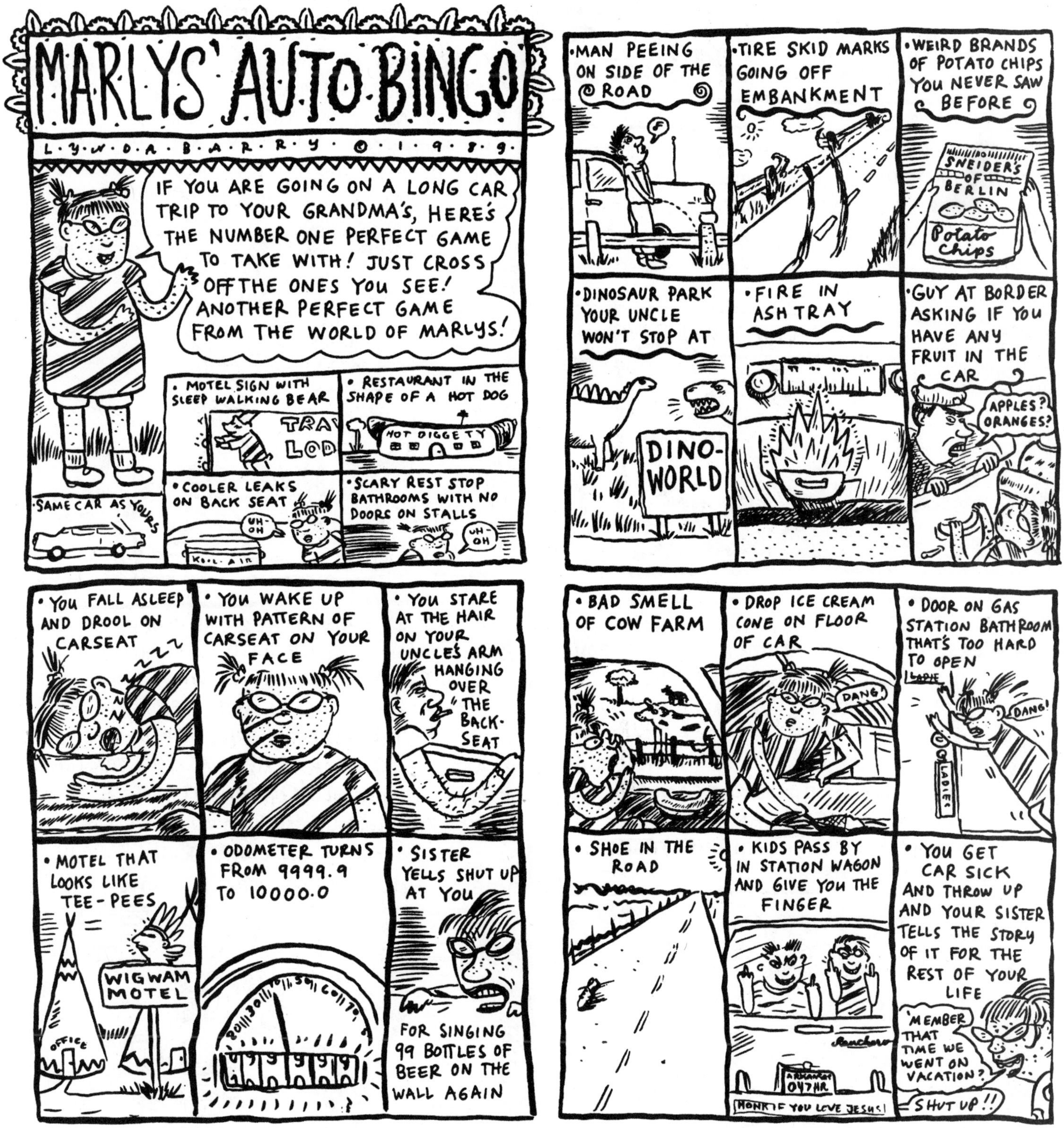

MARLYS' AUTO BINGO
L·Y·N·D·A·B·A·R·R·Y·©·1·9·8·9·
IF YOU ARE GOING ON A LONG CAR TRIP TO YOUR GRANDMA'S, HERE'S THE NUMBER ONE PERFECT GAME TO TAKE WITH! JUST CROSS OFF THE ONES YOU SEE! ANOTHER PERFECT GAME FROM THE WORLD OF MARLYS!
• MOTEL SIGN WITH SLEEP WALKING BEAR
TRAV LOD
• RESTAURANT IN THE SHAPE OF A HOT DOG
HOT DIGGETY
• SAME CAR AS YOURS
• COOLER LEAKS ON BACK SEAT
UH-OH
• SCARY REST STOP BATHROOMS WITH NO DOORS ON STALLS
UH-OH
• MAN PEEING ON SIDE OF THE ROAD
• TIRE SKID MARKS GOING OFF EMBANKMENT
• WEIRD BRANDS OF POTATO CHIPS YOU NEVER SAW BEFORE
SNEIDER'S OF BERLIN Potato Chips
• DINOSAUR PARK YOUR UNCLE WON'T STOP AT
DINO-WORLD
• FIRE IN ASH TRAY
• GUY AT BORDER ASKING IF YOU HAVE ANY FRUIT IN THE CAR
APPLES? ORANGES?
• YOU FALL ASLEEP AND DROOL ON CARSEAT
• YOU WAKE UP WITH PATTERN OF CARSEAT ON YOUR FACE
• YOU STARE AT THE HAIR ON YOUR UNCLE'S ARM HANGING OVER THE BACK-SEAT
• MOTEL THAT LOOKS LIKE TEE-PEES
WIGWAM MOTEL
OFFICE
• ODOMETER TURNS FROM 9999.9 TO 10000.0
• SISTER YELLS SHUT UP AT YOU FOR SINGING 99 BOTTLES OF BEER ON THE WALL AGAIN
• BAD SMELL OF COW FARM
• DROP ICE CREAM CONE ON FLOOR OF CAR
DANG!
• DOOR ON GAS STATION BATHROOM THAT'S TOO HARD TO OPEN
LADIES
DANG!
• SHOE IN THE ROAD
• KIDS PASS BY IN STATION WAGON AND GIVE YOU THE FINGER
Ranchero
047HR
HONK IF YOU LOVE JESUS!
• YOU GET CAR SICK AND THROW UP AND YOUR SISTER TELLS THE STORY OF IT FOR THE REST OF YOUR LIFE
'MEMBER THAT TIME WE WENT ON VACATION?
SHUT UP!!

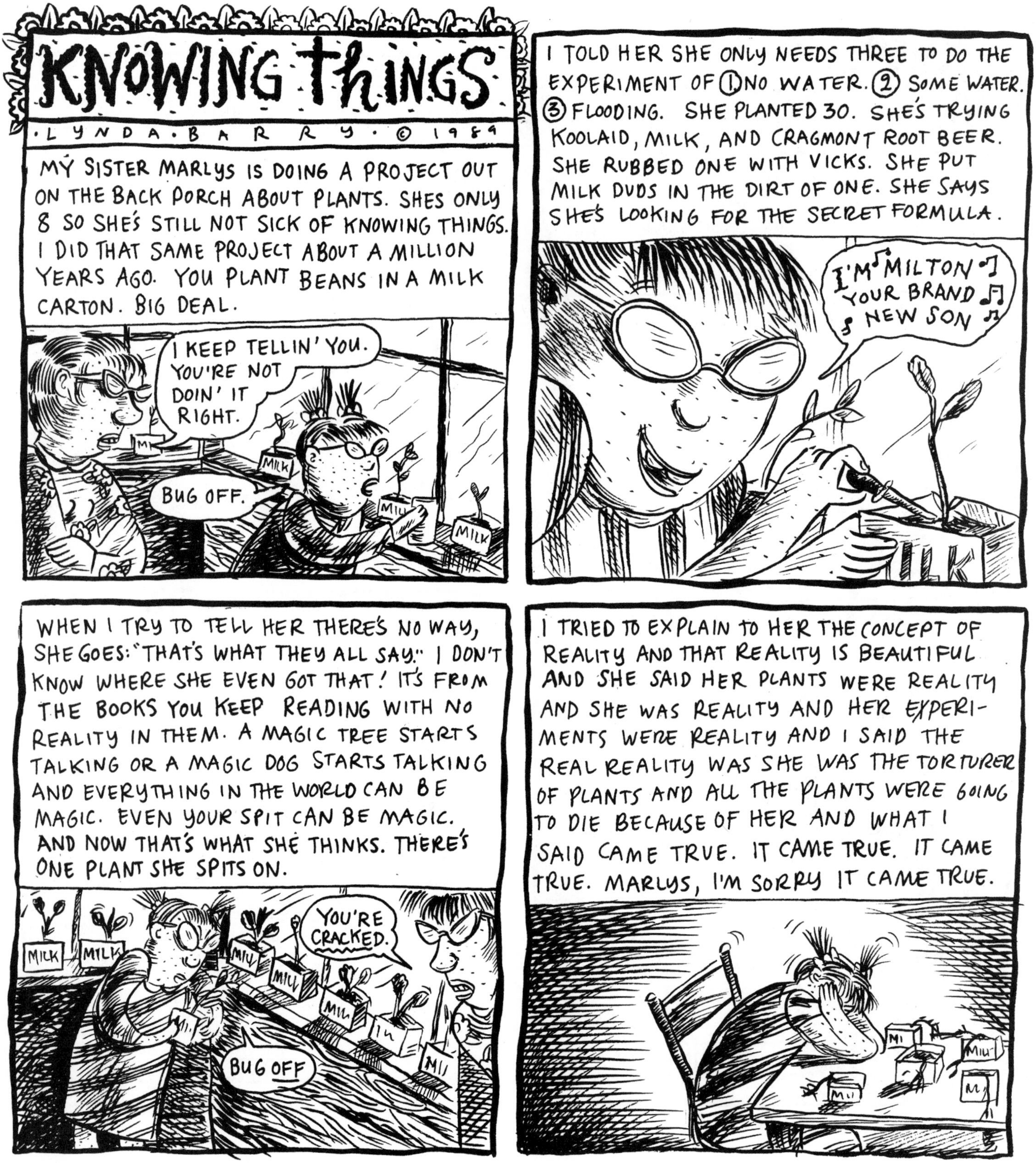
KNOWING THINGS
·LYNDA·BARRY·© 1989
MY SISTER MARLYS IS DOING A PROJECT OUT ON THE BACK PORCH ABOUT PLANTS. SHES ONLY 8 SO SHE'S STILL NOT SICK OF KNOWING THINGS. I DID THAT SAME PROJECT ABOUT A MILLION YEARS AGO. YOU PLANT BEANS IN A MILK CARTON. BIG DEAL.
I KEEP TELLIN' YOU. YOU'RE NOT DOIN' IT RIGHT.
BUG OFF.
MILK
I TOLD HER SHE ONLY NEEDS THREE TO DO THE EXPERIMENT OF ① NO WATER. ② SOME WATER. ③ FLOODING. SHE PLANTED 30. SHE'S TRYING KOOLAID, MILK, AND CRAGMONT ROOT BEER. SHE RUBBED ONE WITH VICKS. SHE PUT MILK DUDS IN THE DIRT OF ONE. SHE SAYS SHE'S LOOKING FOR THE SECRET FORMULA.
I'M MILTON YOUR BRAND NEW SON
ILK
WHEN I TRY TO TELL HER THERE'S NO WAY, SHE GOES: "THAT'S WHAT THEY ALL SAY." I DON'T KNOW WHERE SHE EVEN GOT THAT! IT'S FROM THE BOOKS YOU KEEP READING WITH NO REALITY IN THEM. A MAGIC TREE STARTS TALKING OR A MAGIC DOG STARTS TALKING AND EVERYTHING IN THE WORLD CAN BE MAGIC. EVEN YOUR SPIT CAN BE MAGIC. AND NOW THAT'S WHAT SHE THINKS. THERE'S ONE PLANT SHE SPITS ON.
YOU'RE CRACKED.
BUG OFF
I TRIED TO EXPLAIN TO HER THE CONCEPT OF REALITY AND THAT REALITY IS BEAUTIFUL AND SHE SAID HER PLANTS WERE REALITY AND SHE WAS REALITY AND HER EXPERIMENTS WERE REALITY AND I SAID THE REAL REALITY WAS SHE WAS THE TORTURER OF PLANTS AND ALL THE PLANTS WERE GOING TO DIE BECAUSE OF HER AND WHAT I SAID CAME TRUE. IT CAME TRUE. IT CAME TRUE. MARLYS, I'M SORRY IT CAME TRUE.

MARLYS the STAR

BY LYNDA 8-TRACK TAPE BARRY ©1987

WHO KNOWS HOW IT HAPPENED BUT MARLYS GOT PICKED TO RIDE ON THE <u>FLOAT</u> IN THE <u>PARADE</u> WEARING A <u>UNIFORM</u>. WHEN MOM DROPPED US OFF, SHE HAD IT ON AND SHOUTED "ATTEN-<u>HUT</u>!", "ABOUT FACE!", AND "YOU HAVE THE RIGHT TO REMAIN SILENT!" MY BROTHER SECRETLY GAVE HER THE FINGER AND SO DID I BECAUSE THE FACT IS WE WERE SO JEALOUS WE COULD DIE.

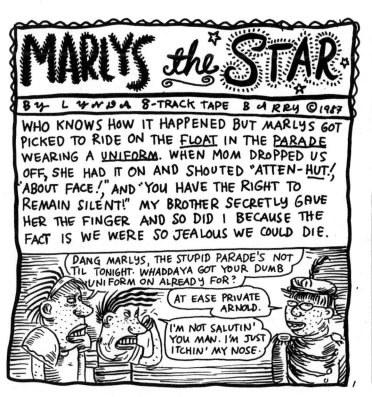

DANG MARLYS, THE STUPID PARADE'S NOT TIL TONIGHT. WHADDAYA GOT YOUR DUMB UNIFORM ON ALREADY FOR?

AT EASE PRIVATE ARNOLD.

I'M NOT SALUTIN' YOU MAN. I'M JUST ITCHIN' MY NOSE.

AFTER ABOUT A ZILLION YEARS OF WAITING, RIGHT WHEN YOUR BUTT IS DEAD FROM SITTING ON THE CURB, THE PARADE MEN COME RUNNING BY POINTING TO YOUR SHOES AND YELLING "MOVE THEM BACK! MOVE THEM OUT OF THE WAY!" AND BEFORE YOU KNOW IT A MILLION THINGS ARE GOING BY. THE BANDS ARE SO LOUD IT'S LIKE THEY'RE MARCHING ALL OVER YOU AND IF YOU SQUAT DOWN IT CAN BE PRETTY INTERESTING TO WATCH THEIR FEET.

THE HORSE RIDERS GO BY, MORE BANDS GO BY, OUR PRINCIPAL AND ONE TEACHER FROM OUR SCHOOL AND THE JANITOR GO BY IN A GROUP OF DADS WEARING THEIR OLD ARMY UNIFORMS AND HATS AND MEDALS, THE BEAUTY CONTESTS GO BY SITTING ON THE BACKS OF CONVERTIBLES WAVING THEIR GLOVES AT YOU AND THE ONE CAR WITH THE QUEEN AND TWO PRINCESSES, HAS A GUY DRIVING IT WHO MY BROTHER BET ME A MILLION DOLLARS WAS DEAN MARTIN.

THE CLOWNS THREW THE WORST CANDY IN THE WORLD AT US AND WHEN THEY CAME UP TO GRAB YOU, YOU COULD SEE THEIR MAKE-UP AND THEY SMELLED DRUNK. THEN ALL OF A SUDDEN, HERE COMES THE FLOAT WITH MARLYS ON IT— AND BEFORE ME AND MY BROTHER KNEW WHAT WE WERE DOING WE STARTED YELLING "YAY MARLYS! YAY MARLYS!" AND SCREAMING, AND MARLYS DID THAT GLOVE WAVE JUST PERFECT AT US AND SHE STARTED LAUGHING AND WE STARTED LAUGHING AND I GUESS I'LL JUST NEVER FORGET THAT FOREVER.

THE LAST UP

LYNDA BARRY © 1988

IT WAS AFTER DINNER ON THE LAST SUNDAY BEFORE THE FIRST DAY OF SCHOOL. WE WERE PLAYING OUR REGULAR KICKBALL GAME IN THE STREET AND IT WAS STARTING TO GET DARK. EVERYBODY WAS THERE.

EVEN THE TEENAGERS WHO COULD DRIVE WERE THERE. THE TEAMS GOT SO BIG, YOU HAD TO WAIT FOREVER JUST TO GET YOUR UPS. IT KEPT GETTING DARKER AND DARKER. PRETTY SOON THE MOMS STARTED TO COME OUT ON THE PORCHES TO CALL THE DIFFERENT NAMES OF US TO COME HOME.

YOUR MOM'S CALLING YA

THAT'S YOUR MOM

CAN I TAKE YOUR UPS, MAN?

EVERYONE KEPT SHOUTING JUST A SEC MOM, IN A MINUTE MOM, I'M COMING MOM, BUT NO ONE COULD STAND TO LEAVE BEFORE THEY GOT THEIR TURN. NOW IT WAS SO DARK YOU COULD HARDLY SEE THE BALL. FINALLY, IT WAS MY UPS. I WAS THE LAST ONE.

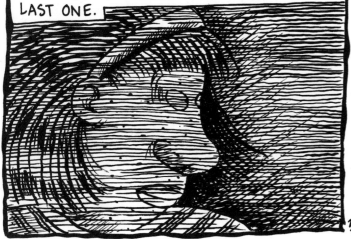

WHEN THE TEENAGER RICHARD ROLLED THE BALL TO ME, I COULD HEAR MY MOM START TO CALL MY NAME. I BACKED UP TO MAKE THE HARDEST KICK OF MY LIFE. WHEN MY FOOT TOUCHED THE BALL EVERY STREETLIGHT ON THE BLOCK SUDDENLY CAME ON AT ONCE AND MY BROTHER YELLED I GOT IT! I GOT IT! AND WE ALL STOOD STILL WATCHING HIM WITH HIS ARMS UP IN THE AIR WAITING TO MAKE THE LAST BIG CATCH.

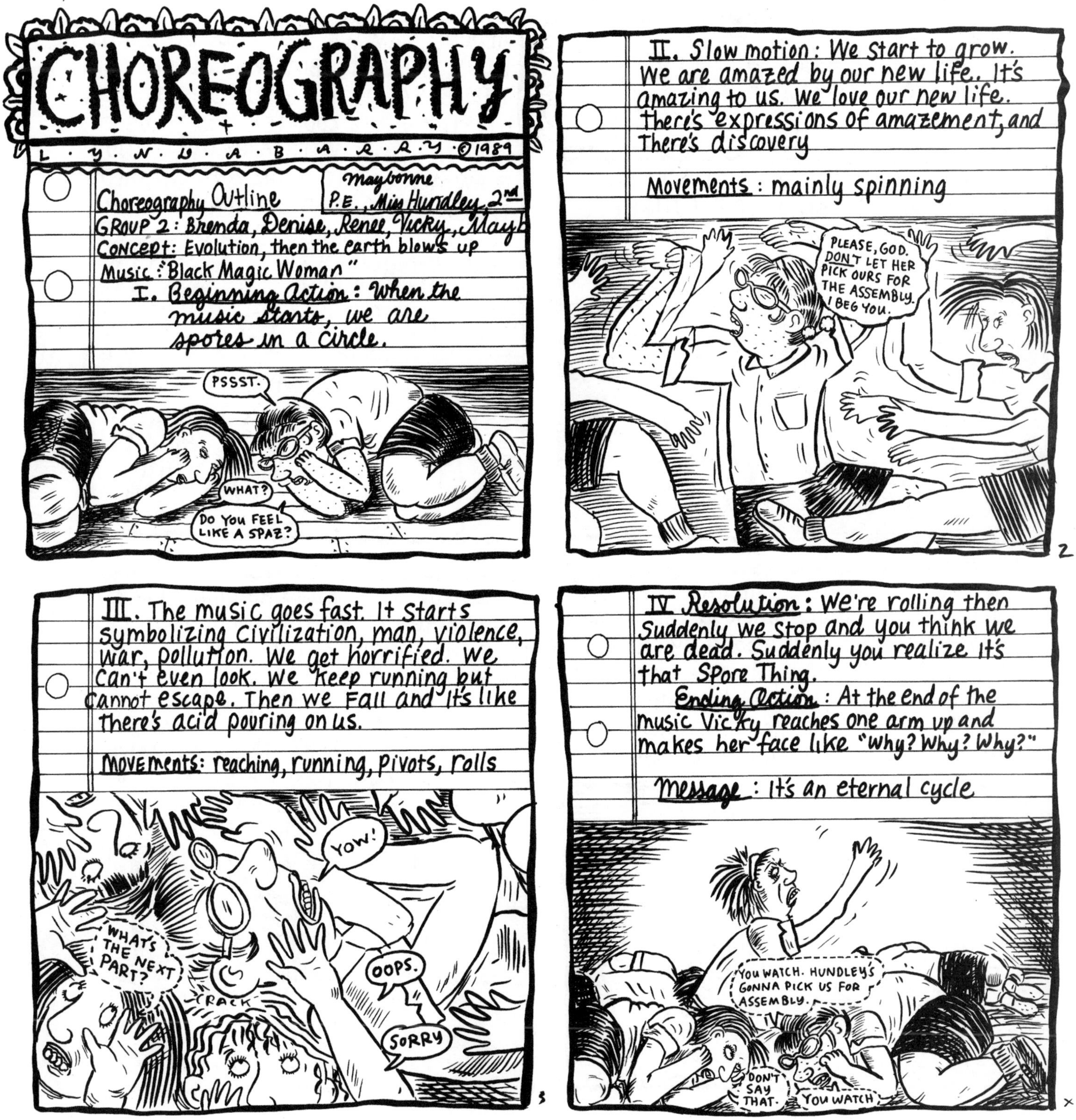

CHOREOGRAPHY
LYNDA BARRY ©1989
Maybonne
P.E., Miss Hundley, 2nd
Choreography Outline
GROUP 2: Brenda, Denise, Renee, Vicky, Mayb
Concept: Evolution, then the earth blows up
Music: "Black Magic Woman"
I. Beginning Action: When the music starts, we are spores in a circle.
PSSST.
WHAT?
DO YOU FEEL LIKE A SPAZ?
II. Slow motion: We start to grow. We are amazed by our new life. It's amazing to us. We love our new life. There's expressions of amazement, and There's discovery
Movements: mainly spinning
PLEASE, GOD, DON'T LET HER PICK OURS FOR THE ASSEMBLY. I BEG YOU.
III. The music goes fast. It starts symbolizing civilization, man, violence, war, pollution. We get horrified. We can't even look. We keep running but cannot escape. Then we Fall and it's like there's acid pouring on us.
Movements: reaching, running, pivots, rolls
YOW!
WHAT'S THE NEXT PART?
OOPS.
CRACK
SORRY
IV Resolution: We're rolling then suddenly we stop and you think we are dead. Suddenly you realize it's that Spore Thing.
Ending Action: At the end of the music Vicky reaches one arm up and makes her face like "Why? Why? Why?"
Message: It's an eternal cycle
YOU WATCH. HUNDLEY'S GONNA PICK US FOR ASSEMBLY.
DON'T SAY THAT.
YOU WATCH.

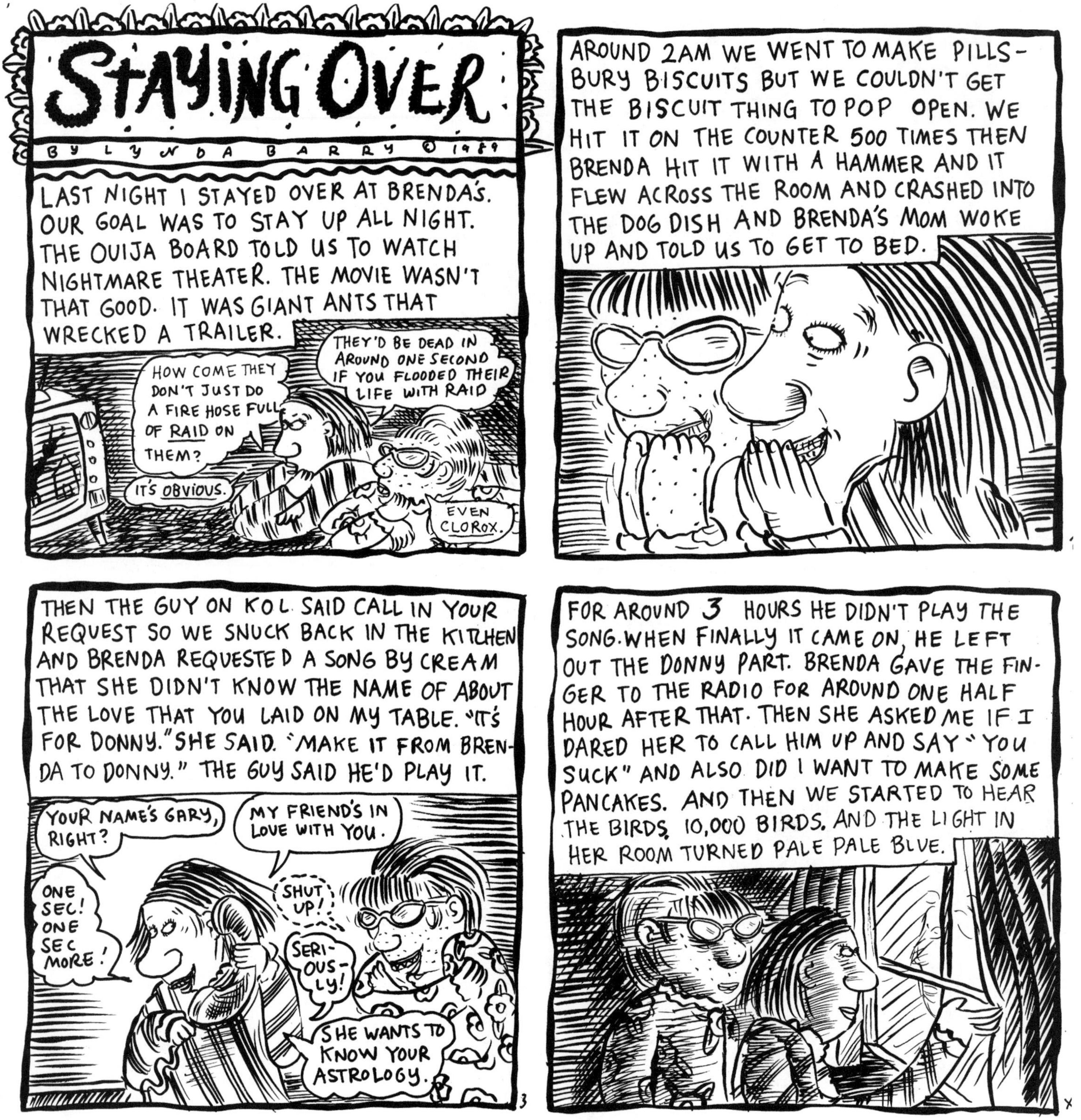
STAYING OVER
BY LYNDA BARRY ©1989
LAST NIGHT I STAYED OVER AT BRENDA'S. OUR GOAL WAS TO STAY UP ALL NIGHT. THE OUIJA BOARD TOLD US TO WATCH NIGHTMARE THEATER. THE MOVIE WASN'T THAT GOOD. IT WAS GIANT ANTS THAT WRECKED A TRAILER.
HOW COME THEY DON'T JUST DO A FIRE HOSE FULL OF RAID ON THEM?
THEY'D BE DEAD IN AROUND ONE SECOND IF YOU FLOODED THEIR LIFE WITH RAID
IT'S OBVIOUS.
EVEN CLOROX.
AROUND 2AM WE WENT TO MAKE PILLSBURY BISCUITS BUT WE COULDN'T GET THE BISCUIT THING TO POP OPEN. WE HIT IT ON THE COUNTER 500 TIMES THEN BRENDA HIT IT WITH A HAMMER AND IT FLEW ACROSS THE ROOM AND CRASHED INTO THE DOG DISH AND BRENDA'S MOM WOKE UP AND TOLD US TO GET TO BED.
THEN THE GUY ON KOL SAID CALL IN YOUR REQUEST SO WE SNUCK BACK IN THE KITCHEN AND BRENDA REQUESTED A SONG BY CREAM THAT SHE DIDN'T KNOW THE NAME OF ABOUT THE LOVE THAT YOU LAID ON MY TABLE. "IT'S FOR DONNY." SHE SAID. "MAKE IT FROM BRENDA TO DONNY." THE GUY SAID HE'D PLAY IT.
YOUR NAME'S GARY, RIGHT?
MY FRIEND'S IN LOVE WITH YOU.
ONE SEC! ONE SEC MORE!
SHUT UP!
SERIOUSLY!
SHE WANTS TO KNOW YOUR ASTROLOGY.
FOR AROUND 3 HOURS HE DIDN'T PLAY THE SONG. WHEN FINALLY IT CAME ON, HE LEFT OUT THE DONNY PART. BRENDA GAVE THE FINGER TO THE RADIO FOR AROUND ONE HALF HOUR AFTER THAT. THEN SHE ASKED ME IF I DARED HER TO CALL HIM UP AND SAY "YOU SUCK" AND ALSO DID I WANT TO MAKE SOME PANCAKES. AND THEN WE STARTED TO HEAR THE BIRDS. 10,000 BIRDS. AND THE LIGHT IN HER ROOM TURNED PALE PALE BLUE.

TOPIC: HAIR

BY LYNDA BARRY, © 1989 CHICAGO, ILL.

HAIR

✿ Maybonne
Home Ec. Period 3

Topic: Hair

1. What is hair?
Hair is a projection growing off of a mammel. A certain kind of projection. It has many uses. It grows on every Mammel.

THE HAIR

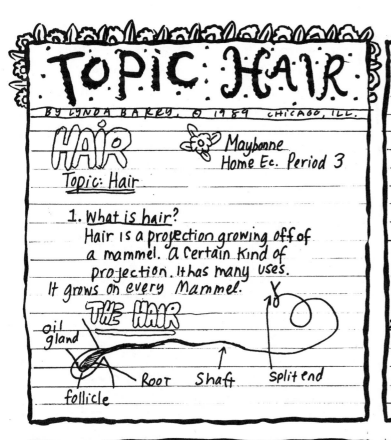

oil gland

follicle

Root

Shaft

Split end

2. What is the best hairstyle for you?
It depends on your ~~face~~ head . face head

3. Give some examples of hairstyles for the different shapes of heads.

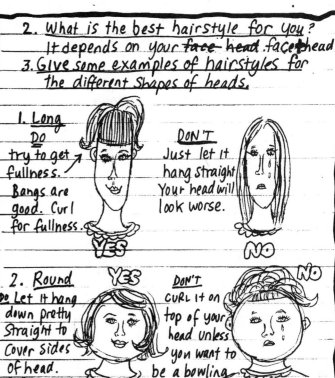

1. Long

DO try to get fullness. Bangs are good. Curl for fullness.

YES

DON'T Just let it hang straight. Your head will look worse.

NO

2. Round

YES

Do Let it hang down pretty straight to cover sides of head. Curl the ends.

DON'T Curl it on top of your head unless you want to be a bowling ball head !!

NO

3. Pearshaped.

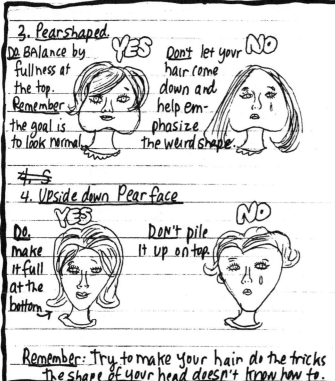

Do. Balance by fullness at the top. Remember the goal is to look normal.

YES

Don't let your hair come down and help emphasize the weird shape.

NO

4. Upside down Pear face

YES

Do. make it full at the bottom.

DON'T pile it up on top.

NO

Remember: Try to make your hair do the tricks the shape of your head doesn't know how to.

5. What is good for your hair?
Foods: milk, egg yolks, animal livers, oils eating

6. Fact or Myth? jello will make your hair grow.
Myth

7. What are good things to do to your hair?
brushing, shampoo, creme rinse, a sensible hairstyle that does not look rediculous

8. What are bad things to do to your hair?
ratting. Too much sun in. Ironing it. wearing a fall that doesn't match. letting your friend cut it. ~~think~~ thinking you are cool because it looks good.

9. What have you learned from this chapter?
I have a weird shaped head but I can correct it with hair. Also hair is dead.

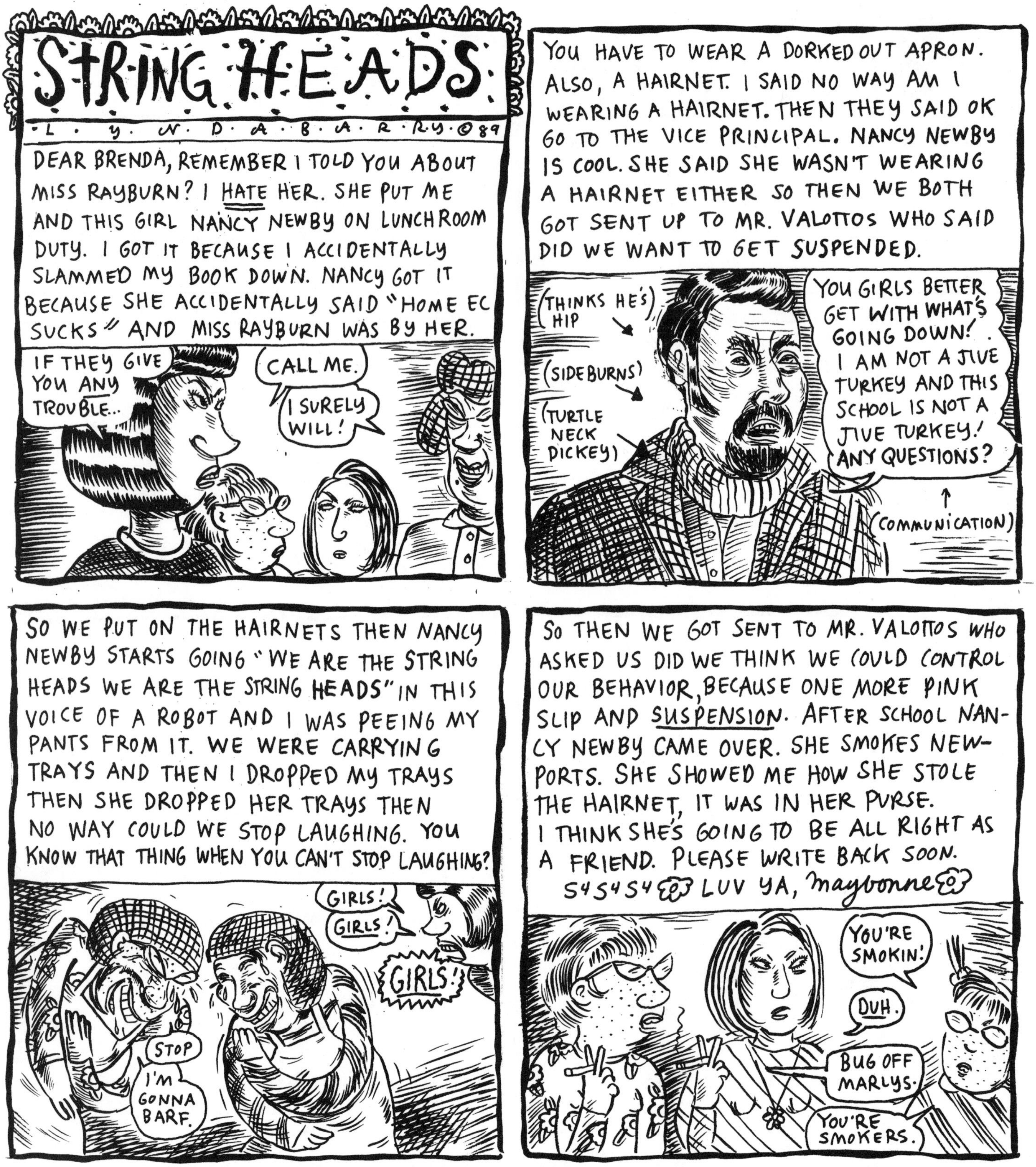
STRING HEADS
LYNDA BARRY ©89
DEAR BRENDA, REMEMBER I TOLD YOU ABOUT MISS RAYBURN? I HATE HER. SHE PUT ME AND THIS GIRL NANCY NEWBY ON LUNCHROOM DUTY. I GOT IT BECAUSE I ACCIDENTALLY SLAMMED MY BOOK DOWN. NANCY GOT IT BECAUSE SHE ACCIDENTALLY SAID "HOME EC SUCKS" AND MISS RAYBURN WAS BY HER.
IF THEY GIVE YOU ANY TROUBLE...
CALL ME.
I SURELY WILL!
YOU HAVE TO WEAR A DORKED OUT APRON. ALSO, A HAIRNET. I SAID NO WAY AM I WEARING A HAIRNET. THEN THEY SAID OK GO TO THE VICE PRINCIPAL. NANCY NEWBY IS COOL. SHE SAID SHE WASN'T WEARING A HAIRNET EITHER SO THEN WE BOTH GOT SENT UP TO MR. VALOTTOS WHO SAID DID WE WANT TO GET SUSPENDED.
(THINKS HE'S HIP)
(SIDEBURNS)
(TURTLE NECK DICKEY)
YOU GIRLS BETTER GET WITH WHAT'S GOING DOWN! I AM NOT A JIVE TURKEY AND THIS SCHOOL IS NOT A JIVE TURKEY! ANY QUESTIONS?
(COMMUNICATION)
SO WE PUT ON THE HAIRNETS THEN NANCY NEWBY STARTS GOING "WE ARE THE STRING HEADS WE ARE THE STRING HEADS" IN THIS VOICE OF A ROBOT AND I WAS PEEING MY PANTS FROM IT. WE WERE CARRYING TRAYS AND THEN I DROPPED MY TRAYS THEN SHE DROPPED HER TRAYS THEN NO WAY COULD WE STOP LAUGHING. YOU KNOW THAT THING WHEN YOU CAN'T STOP LAUGHING?
GIRLS!
GIRLS!
GIRLS!
STOP
I'M GONNA BARF.
SO THEN WE GOT SENT TO MR. VALOTTOS WHO ASKED US DID WE THINK WE COULD CONTROL OUR BEHAVIOR, BECAUSE ONE MORE PINK SLIP AND SUSPENSION. AFTER SCHOOL NANCY NEWBY CAME OVER. SHE SMOKES NEWPORTS. SHE SHOWED ME HOW SHE STOLE THE HAIRNET, IT WAS IN HER PURSE. I THINK SHE'S GOING TO BE ALL RIGHT AS A FRIEND. PLEASE WRITE BACK SOON.
S4S4S4 LUV YA, maybonne
YOU'RE SMOKIN!
DUH.
BUG OFF MARLYS.
YOU'RE SMOKERS.

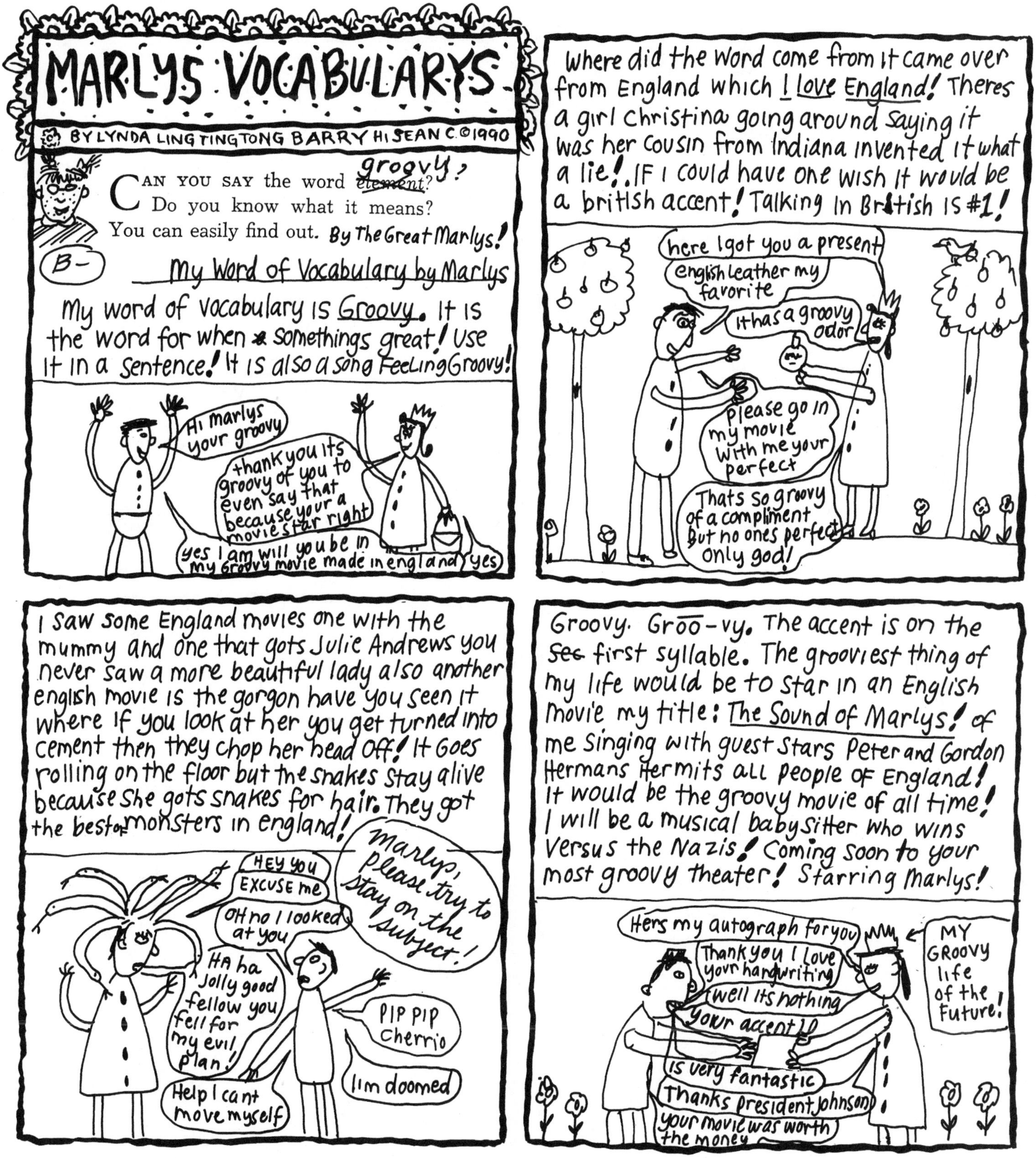
MARLYS VOCABULARYS
© BY LYNDA LING TING TONG BARRY HI SEAN C. ©1990
CAN YOU SAY the word ~~element~~ groovy? Do you know what it means? You can easily find out. By The Great Marlys!
B-
My Word of Vocabulary by Marlys
My word of vocabulary is Groovy. It is the word for when somethings great! Use it in a sentence! It is also a song Feeling Groovy!
Hi marlys your groovy
thank you its groovy of you to even say that because your a movie star right
yes I am will you be in my Groovy movie made in england
yes
Where did the word come from it came over from England which I love England! Theres a girl Christina going around saying it was her cousin from Indiana invented it what a lie!. If I could have one wish it would be a british accent! Talking in British is #1!
here I got you a present
english leather my favorite
it has a groovy odor
please go in my movie with me your perfect
Thats so groovy of a compliment But no ones perfect only god!
I saw some England movies one with the mummy and one that gots Julie Andrews you never saw a more beautiful lady also another english movie is the gorgon have you seen it where if you look at her you get turned into cement then they chop her head off! It Goes rolling on the floor but the snakes stay alive because she gots snakes for hair. They got the best of monsters in england!
Marlys, please try to stay on the subject!
HEY you
EXCUSE me
OH no I looked at you
Ha ha jolly good fellow you fell for my evil plan!
PIP PIP Cherrio
Help I cant move myself
I'm doomed
Groovy. Groo-vy. The accent is on the ~~sec~~ first syllable. The grooviest thing of my life would be to star in an English movie my title: The Sound of Marlys! of me singing with guest stars Peter and Gordon Hermans Hermits all people of England! It would be the groovy movie of all time! I will be a musical baby sitter who wins versus the Nazis! Coming soon to your most groovy theater! Starring Marlys!
Hers my autograph for you
MY GROOVY life of the Future!
Thank you I love your handwriting
well its nothing
your accent is very fantastic
Thanks President Johnson
your movie was worth the money

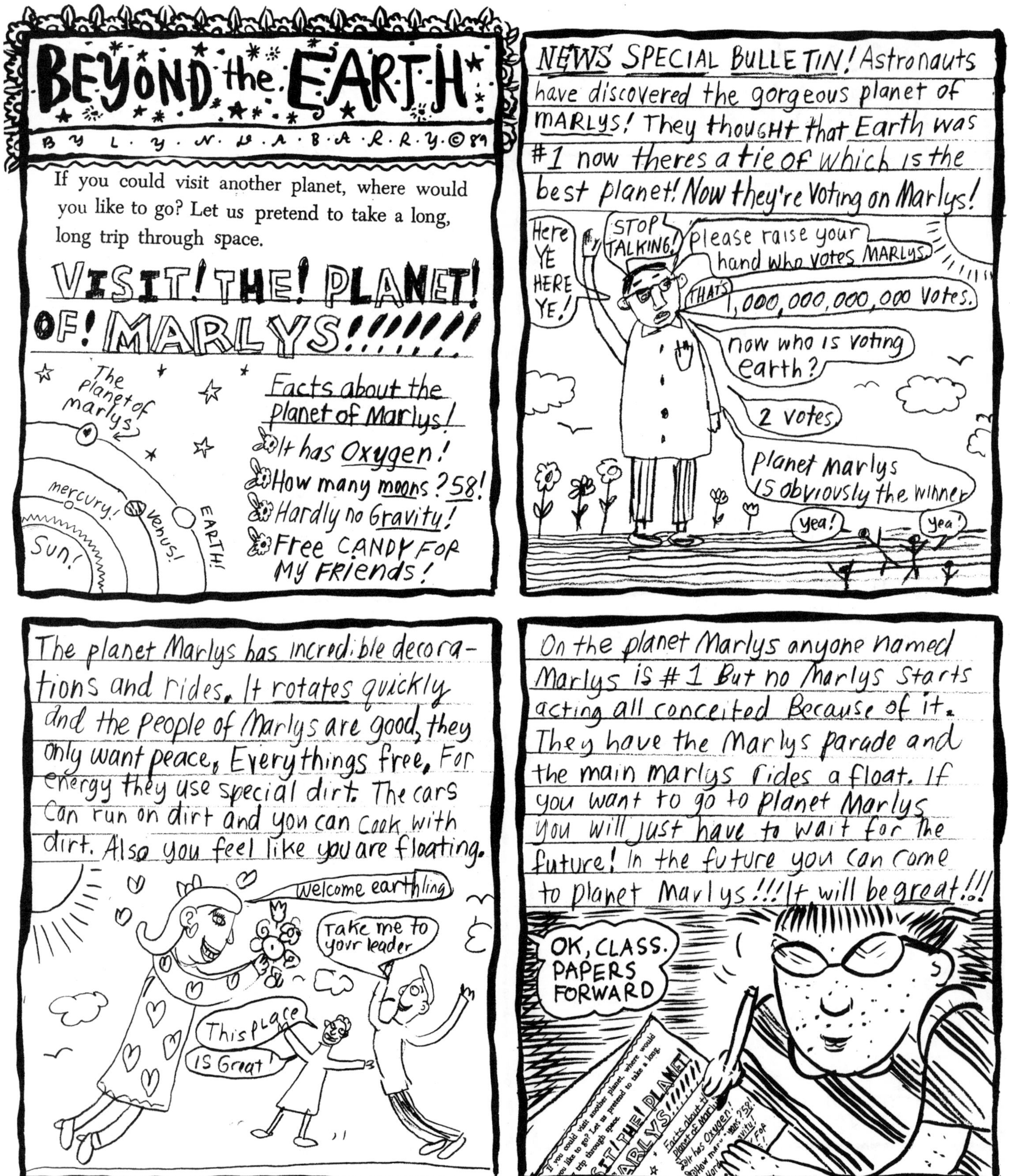

BEYOND the EARTH
BY LYNDA BARRY ©89
If you could visit another planet, where would you like to go? Let us pretend to take a long, long trip through space.
VISIT! THE! PLANET! OF! MARLYS!!!!!!!!
The planet of marlys
mercury!
Venus!
EARTH!
Sun!
Facts about the planet of Marlys!
It has Oxygen!
How many moons? 58!
Hardly no Gravity!
Free CANDY FOR MY FRIENDS!
NEWS SPECIAL BULLETIN! Astronauts have discovered the gorgeous planet of MARLYS! They thought that Earth was #1 now theres a tie of which is the best planet! Now they're voting on Marlys!
Here YE HERE YE!
STOP TALKING!
please raise your hand who votes MARLYS.
THAT'S 1,000,000,000,000 votes.
now who is voting earth?
2 votes.
planet marlys is obviously the winner
yea!
yea!
The planet Marlys has incredible decorations and rides. It rotates quickly and the people of Marlys are good, they only want peace. Everythings free. For energy they use special dirt. The cars can run on dirt and you can cook with dirt. Also you feel like you are floating.
welcome earthling
Take me to your leader
This place is Great
On the planet Marlys anyone named Marlys is #1 But no Marlys starts acting all conceited Because of it. They have the Marlys parade and the main marlys rides a float. If you want to go to planet Marlys you will just have to wait for the future! In the future you can come to planet Marlys!!! It will be great!!!
OK, CLASS. PAPERS FORWARD

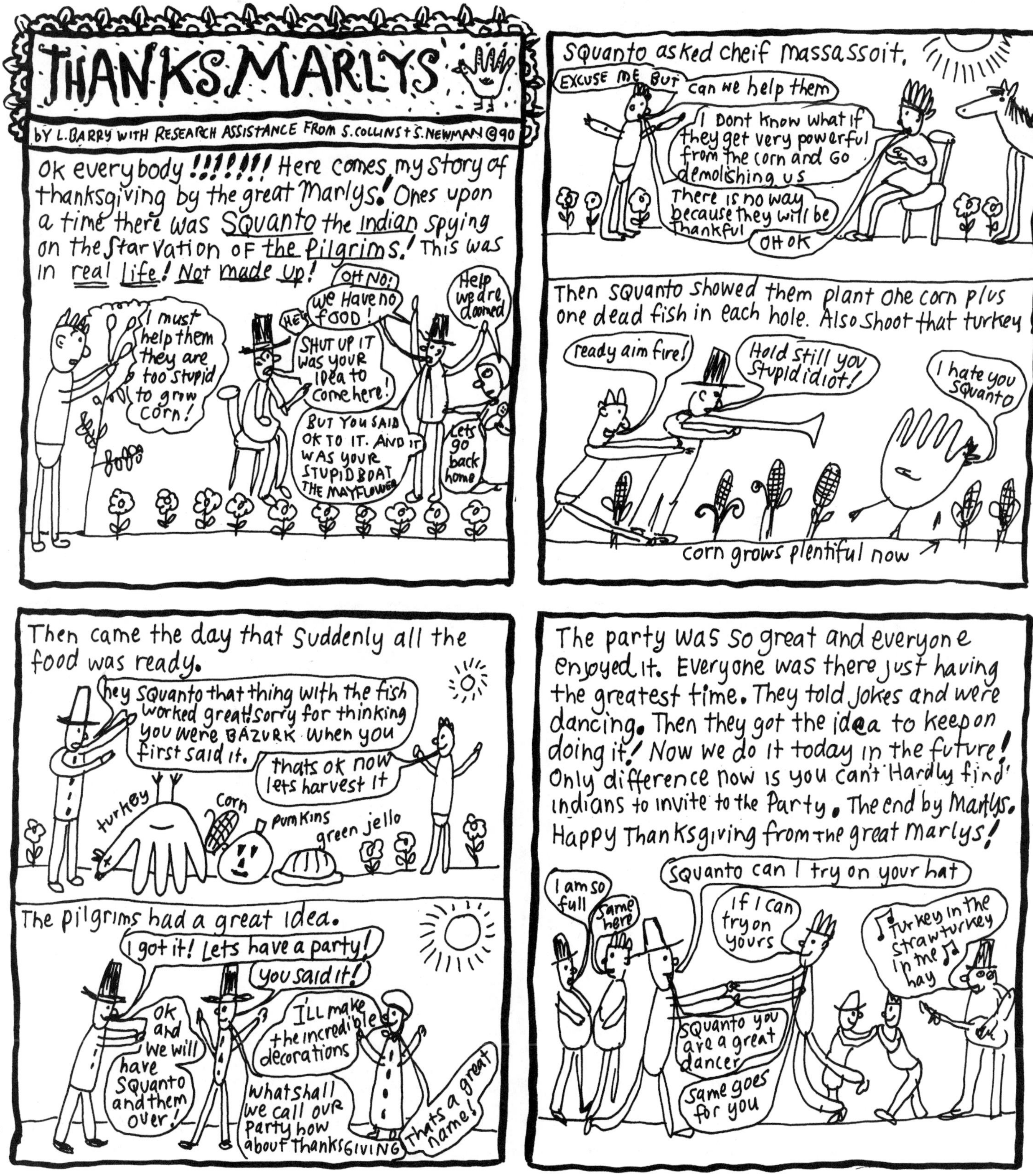
THANKSMARLYS
BY L. BARRY WITH RESEARCH ASSISTANCE FROM S. COLLINS + S. NEWMAN ©90
Ok everybody !!!!!!! Here comes my story of thanksgiving by the great Marlys! Ones upon a time there was Squanto the Indian spying on the starvation of the Pilgrims! This was in real life! Not made up!
I must help them they are too stupid to grow corn!
OH NO! We Have no food!
HEY
SHUT UP IT WAS YOUR IDEA TO COME HERE!
BUT YOU SAID OK TO IT. AND IT WAS YOUR STUPID BOAT THE MAYFLOWER
Help we're doomed
Lets go back home
Squanto asked cheif massassoit,
EXCUSE ME BUT can we help them
I Dont know what if they get very powerful from the corn and go demolishing us
There is no way because they will be Thankful
OH OK
Then squanto showed them plant one corn plus one dead fish in each hole. Also shoot that turkey
ready aim fire!
Hold still you stupid idiot!
I hate you Squanto
corn grows plentiful now
Then came the day that suddenly all the food was ready.
hey squanto that thing with the fish worked great! sorry for thinking you were BAZURK when you first said it.
thats ok now lets harvest it
turkey
corn
pumkins
green jello
The pilgrims had a great idea.
I got it! Lets have a party!
you said it!
ok and we will have Squanto and them over!
I'LL make the incredible decorations
what shall we call our party how about thanksGIVING
Thats a great name!
The party was so great and everyone enjoyed it. Everyone was there just having the greatest time. They told jokes and were dancing. Then they got the idea to keep on doing it! Now we do it today in the future! Only difference now is you can't Hardly find indians to invite to the Party. The end by Marlys. Happy Thanksgiving from the great Marlys!
I am so full
Same here
Squanto can I try on your hat
If I can try on yours
Turkey in the straw turkey in the hay
Squanto you are a great dancer
Same goes for you

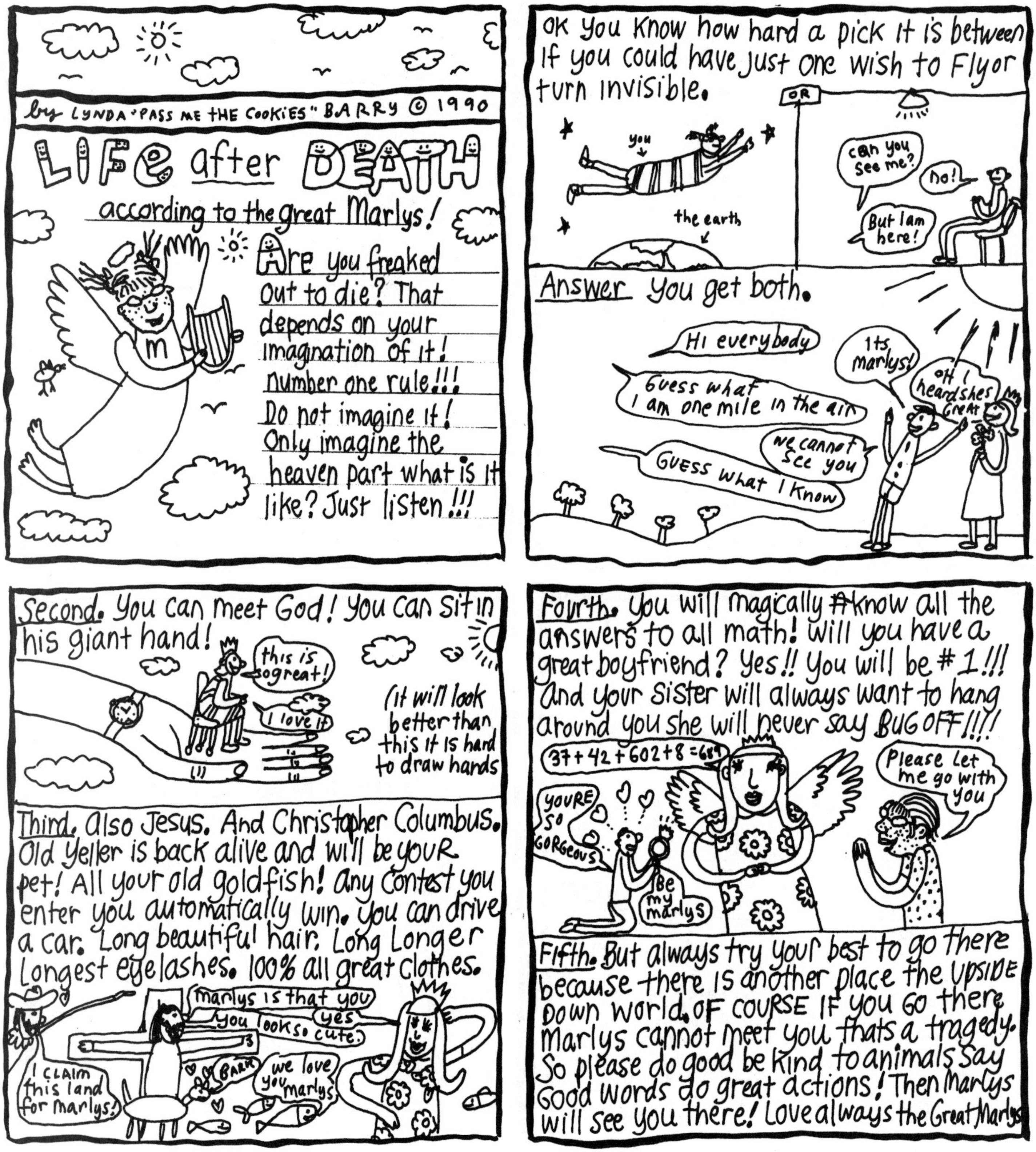
by LYNDA "PASS ME THE COOKIES" BARRY © 1990
LIFE after DEATH
according to the great Marlys!
Are you freaked out to die? That depends on your imagination of it! number one rule!!! Do not imagine it! Only imagine the heaven part what is it like? Just listen!!!
OK you know how hard a pick it is between if you could have just one wish to Fly or turn invisible.
OR
you
the earth
can you see me?
No!
But I am here!
Answer You get both.
Hi everybody
Guess what I am one mile in the air
Guess what I know
Its marlys!
Oh I heard shes great
We cannot see you
Second. You can meet God! You can sit in his giant hand!
this is so great!
I love it
(It will look better than this it is hard to draw hands
Third. Also Jesus. And Christopher Columbus. Old Yeller is back alive and will be your pet! All your old goldfish! Any contest you enter you automatically win. You can drive a car. Long beautiful hair. Long Longer Longest eyelashes. 100% all great clothes.
Marlys is that you
yes
you look so cute.
I claim this land for marlys!
Bark
we love you marlys
Fourth. You will magically ~~A~~ know all the answers to all math! Will you have a great boyfriend? Yes!! You will be #1!!! And your sister will always want to hang around you she will never say BUG OFF!!!!
37+42+602+8=689
YOURE SO GORGEOUS
Be my marlys
Please let me go with you
Fifth. But always try your best to go there because there is another place the UPSIDE DOWN world. OF COURSE IF YOU GO there Marlys cannot meet you thats a tragedy. So please do good be kind to animals say good words do great actions! Then Marlys will see you there! Love always the Great Marlys

FLOWER MARLYS

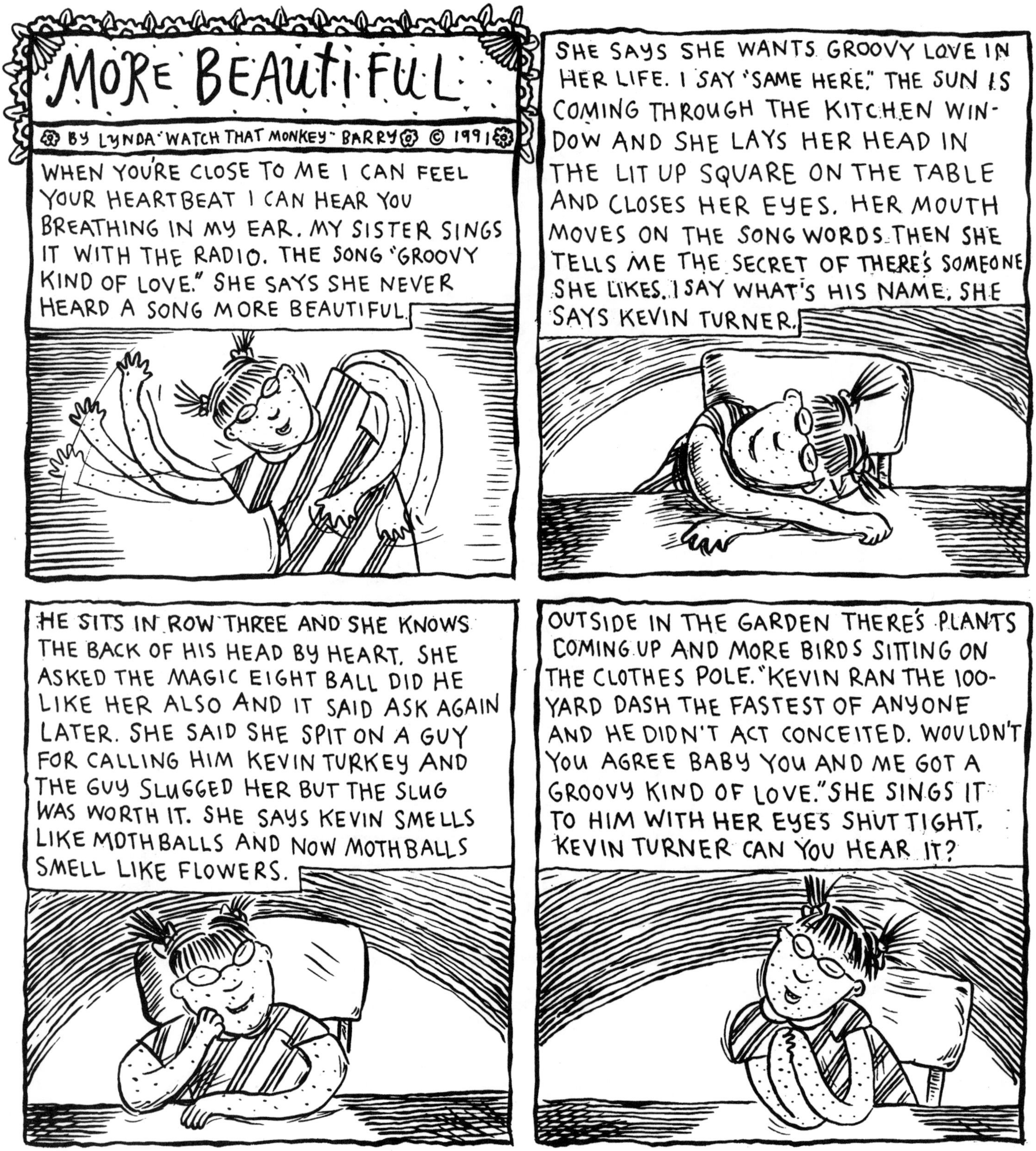

MORE BEAUTIFUL
BY LYNDA "WATCH THAT MONKEY" BARRY © 1991
WHEN YOU'RE CLOSE TO ME I CAN FEEL YOUR HEARTBEAT I CAN HEAR YOU BREATHING IN MY EAR. MY SISTER SINGS IT WITH THE RADIO. THE SONG "GROOVY KIND OF LOVE." SHE SAYS SHE NEVER HEARD A SONG MORE BEAUTIFUL.
SHE SAYS SHE WANTS GROOVY LOVE IN HER LIFE. I SAY "SAME HERE." THE SUN IS COMING THROUGH THE KITCHEN WINDOW AND SHE LAYS HER HEAD IN THE LIT UP SQUARE ON THE TABLE AND CLOSES HER EYES. HER MOUTH MOVES ON THE SONG WORDS THEN SHE TELLS ME THE SECRET OF THERE'S SOMEONE SHE LIKES. I SAY WHAT'S HIS NAME. SHE SAYS KEVIN TURNER.
HE SITS IN ROW THREE AND SHE KNOWS THE BACK OF HIS HEAD BY HEART. SHE ASKED THE MAGIC EIGHT BALL DID HE LIKE HER ALSO AND IT SAID ASK AGAIN LATER. SHE SAID SHE SPIT ON A GUY FOR CALLING HIM KEVIN TURKEY AND THE GUY SLUGGED HER BUT THE SLUG WAS WORTH IT. SHE SAYS KEVIN SMELLS LIKE MOTHBALLS AND NOW MOTHBALLS SMELL LIKE FLOWERS.
OUTSIDE IN THE GARDEN THERE'S PLANTS COMING UP AND MORE BIRDS SITTING ON THE CLOTHES POLE. "KEVIN RAN THE 100-YARD DASH THE FASTEST OF ANYONE AND HE DIDN'T ACT CONCEITED. WOULDN'T YOU AGREE BABY YOU AND ME GOT A GROOVY KIND OF LOVE." SHE SINGS IT TO HIM WITH HER EYES SHUT TIGHT. KEVIN TURNER CAN YOU HEAR IT?

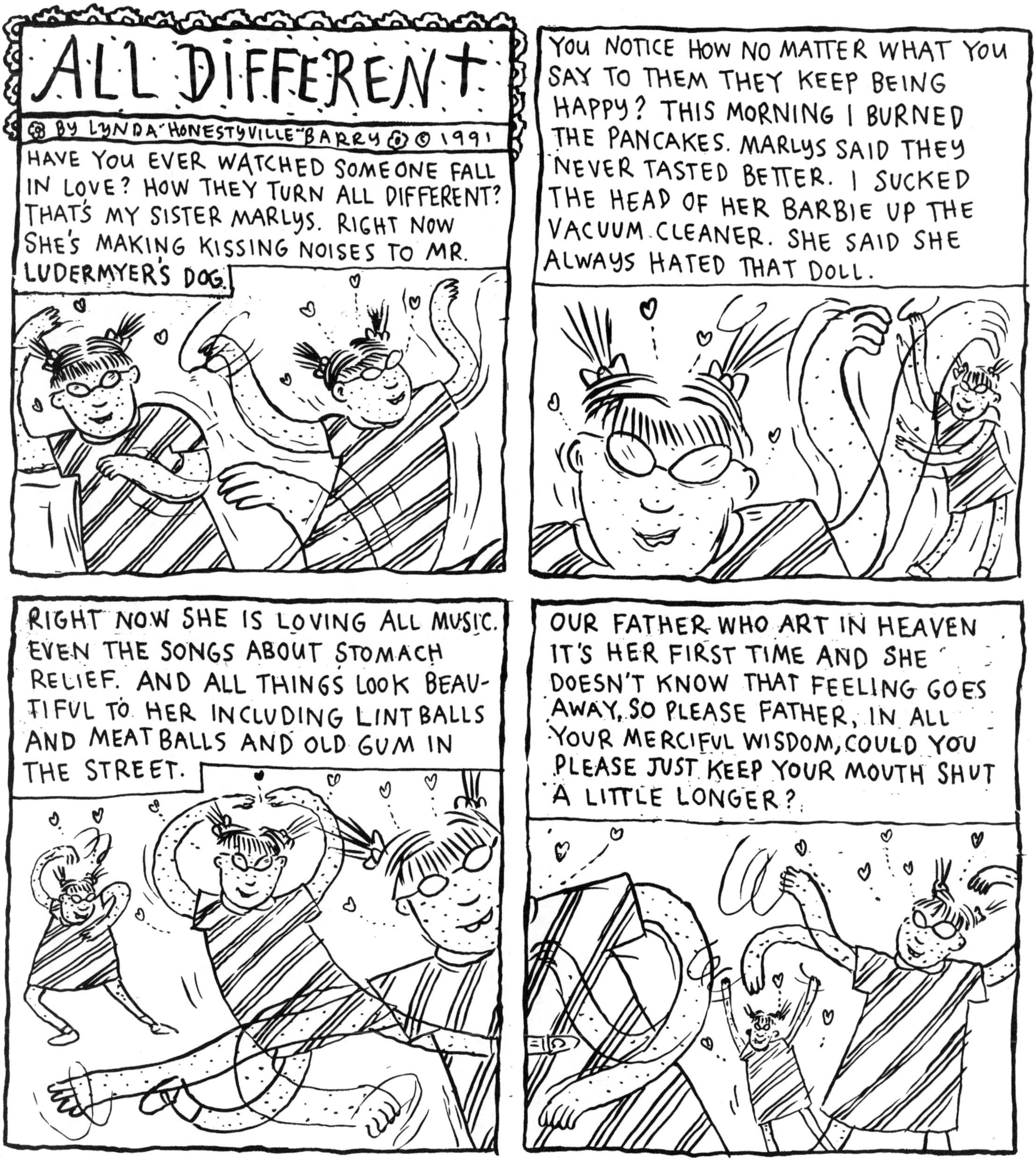
ALL DIFFERENT
BY LYNDA "HONESTYVILLE" BARRY © 1991
HAVE YOU EVER WATCHED SOMEONE FALL IN LOVE? HOW THEY TURN ALL DIFFERENT? THAT'S MY SISTER MARLYS. RIGHT NOW SHE'S MAKING KISSING NOISES TO MR. LUDERMYER'S DOG.
YOU NOTICE HOW NO MATTER WHAT YOU SAY TO THEM THEY KEEP BEING HAPPY? THIS MORNING I BURNED THE PANCAKES. MARLYS SAID THEY NEVER TASTED BETTER. I SUCKED THE HEAD OF HER BARBIE UP THE VACUUM CLEANER. SHE SAID SHE ALWAYS HATED THAT DOLL.
RIGHT NOW SHE IS LOVING ALL MUSIC. EVEN THE SONGS ABOUT STOMACH RELIEF. AND ALL THINGS LOOK BEAUTIFUL TO HER INCLUDING LINT BALLS AND MEAT BALLS AND OLD GUM IN THE STREET.
OUR FATHER WHO ART IN HEAVEN IT'S HER FIRST TIME AND SHE DOESN'T KNOW THAT FEELING GOES AWAY, SO PLEASE FATHER, IN ALL YOUR MERCIFUL WISDOM, COULD YOU PLEASE JUST KEEP YOUR MOUTH SHUT A LITTLE LONGER?

WHY DID HE?

BY LYNDA BARRY WITH LAUREN GAFFNEY © 1991

THE BOY NAMED KEVIN TURNER WHO MARLYS LOVES, LOVES HER BACK. MARLYS SAYS SHE KNOWS HE LOVES HER BACK OR ELSE WHY DID HE WAIT FOR HER EVERY DAY BY ROOM 4 SAYING "HI MARLYS. HI TWINKIE."

TWINKIE BECAUSE MARLYS ALWAYS SPLIT HER PACKAGE WITH HIM. SHE HAS WIPED OUT ALL THE MONEY IN HER ABRAHAM LINCOLN HEAD BANK BUYING TWINKIES TO SPLIT WITH KEVIN TURNER. KEVIN TURNER, KEVIN TURNER. SHE HAS SAID HIS NAME 100 TIMES FAST WITH HER EYES CLOSED TIGHT.

MARLYS SAYS SHE KNOWS HE LOVES HER BACK EVEN THOUGH AROUND HIS FRIENDS HE ACTED DIFFERENT. TODAY AROUND HIS FRIENDS HE SAID THE SAME NAME FOR HER, TWINKIE, ONLY SHOUTING IT NOW AND LAUGHING. TWINKIE AND SOME OTHER WORDS AND MARLYS SAYS IT'S NO BIG DEAL.

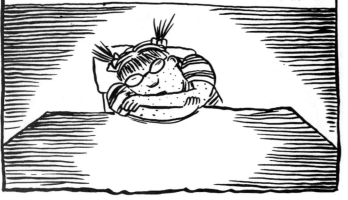

NO BIG DEAL, SHE SAYS, THEN LOOKS DOWN AND STOPS TALKING. AND FOR THE FIRST TIME I EVER SAW, SHE'S QUIET. JUST QUIET AND STARING DOWN WITHOUT MOVING.

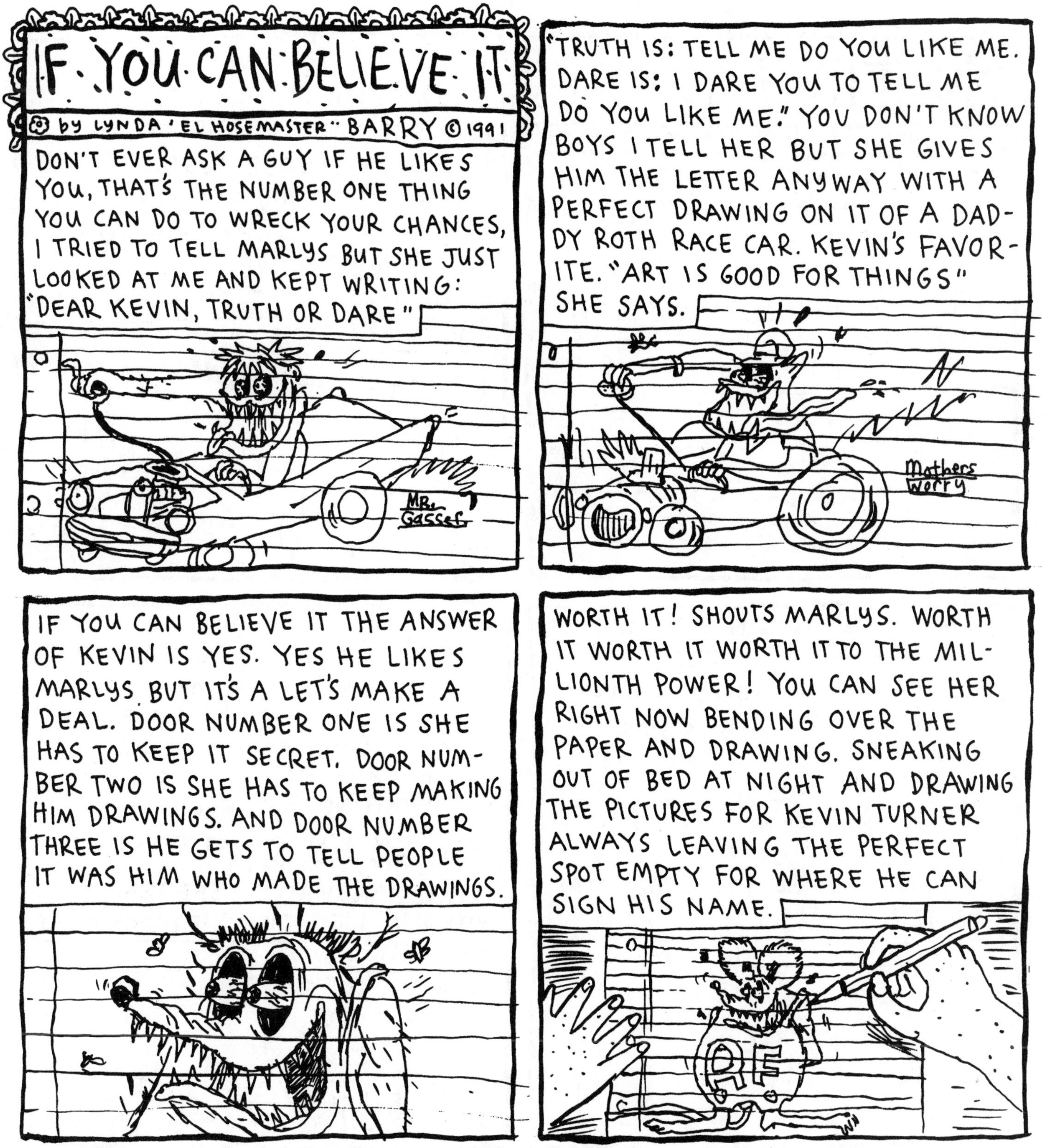
IF YOU CAN BELIEVE IT
by LYNDA "EL HOSEMASTER" BARRY ©1991
DON'T EVER ASK A GUY IF HE LIKES YOU, THAT'S THE NUMBER ONE THING YOU CAN DO TO WRECK YOUR CHANCES, I TRIED TO TELL MARLYS BUT SHE JUST LOOKED AT ME AND KEPT WRITING: "DEAR KEVIN, TRUTH OR DARE"
MR. Gasser
"TRUTH IS: TELL ME DO YOU LIKE ME. DARE IS: I DARE YOU TO TELL ME DO YOU LIKE ME." YOU DON'T KNOW BOYS I TELL HER BUT SHE GIVES HIM THE LETTER ANYWAY WITH A PERFECT DRAWING ON IT OF A DADDY ROTH RACE CAR. KEVIN'S FAVORITE. "ART IS GOOD FOR THINGS" SHE SAYS.
Mothers worry
IF YOU CAN BELIEVE IT THE ANSWER OF KEVIN IS YES. YES HE LIKES MARLYS BUT IT'S A LET'S MAKE A DEAL. DOOR NUMBER ONE IS SHE HAS TO KEEP IT SECRET. DOOR NUMBER TWO IS SHE HAS TO KEEP MAKING HIM DRAWINGS. AND DOOR NUMBER THREE IS HE GETS TO TELL PEOPLE IT WAS HIM WHO MADE THE DRAWINGS.
WORTH IT! SHOUTS MARLYS. WORTH IT WORTH IT WORTH IT TO THE MILLIONTH POWER! YOU CAN SEE HER RIGHT NOW BENDING OVER THE PAPER AND DRAWING. SNEAKING OUT OF BED AT NIGHT AND DRAWING THE PICTURES FOR KEVIN TURNER ALWAYS LEAVING THE PERFECT SPOT EMPTY FOR WHERE HE CAN SIGN HIS NAME.
RF

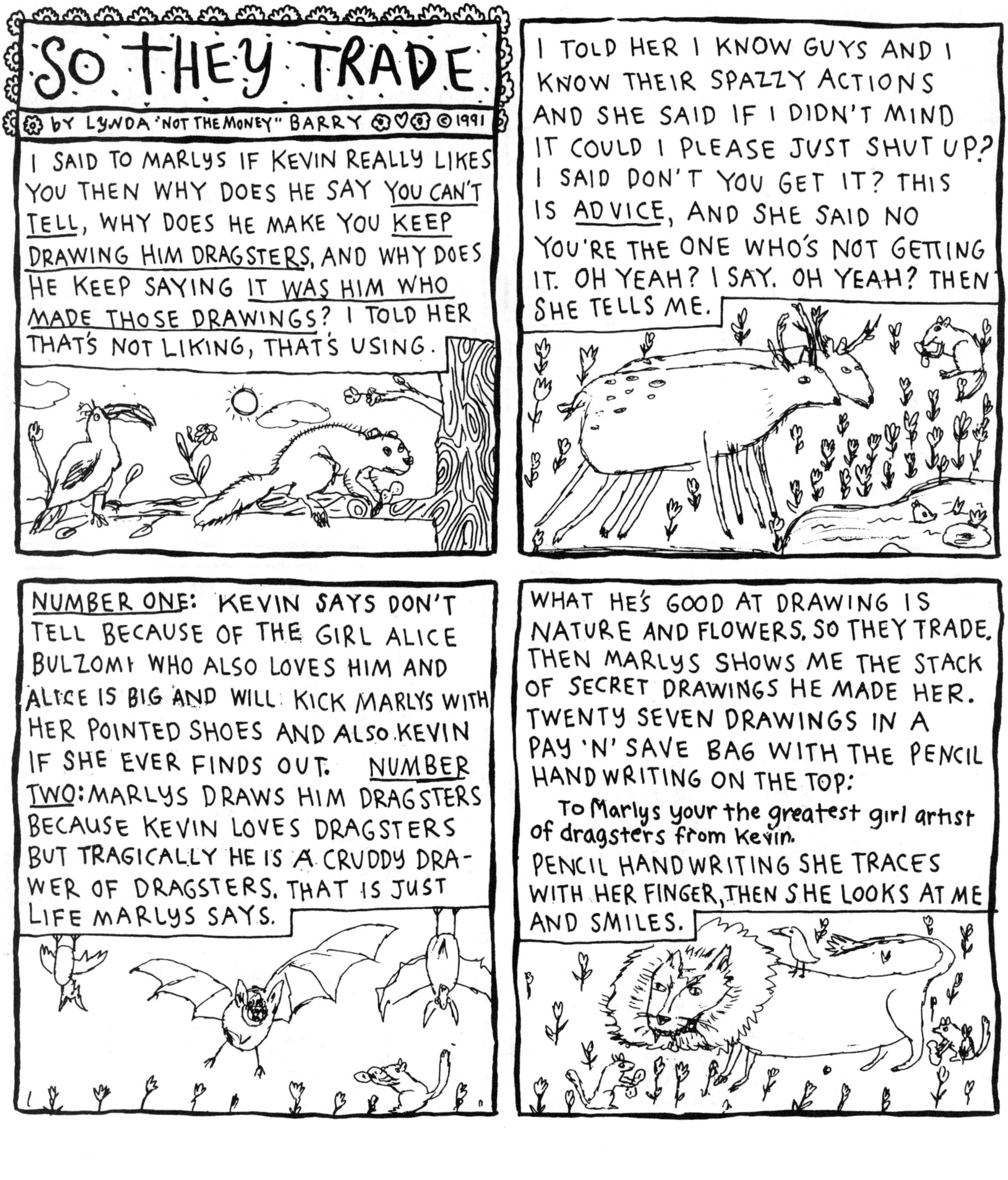
SO THEY TRADE
BY LYNDA "NOT THE MONEY" BARRY ©1991
I SAID TO MARLYS IF KEVIN REALLY LIKES YOU THEN WHY DOES HE SAY YOU CAN'T TELL, WHY DOES HE MAKE YOU KEEP DRAWING HIM DRAGSTERS, AND WHY DOES HE KEEP SAYING IT WAS HIM WHO MADE THOSE DRAWINGS? I TOLD HER THAT'S NOT LIKING, THAT'S USING.
I TOLD HER I KNOW GUYS AND I KNOW THEIR SPAZZY ACTIONS AND SHE SAID IF I DIDN'T MIND IT COULD I PLEASE JUST SHUT UP? I SAID DON'T YOU GET IT? THIS IS ADVICE, AND SHE SAID NO YOU'RE THE ONE WHO'S NOT GETTING IT. OH YEAH? I SAY. OH YEAH? THEN SHE TELLS ME.
NUMBER ONE: KEVIN SAYS DON'T TELL BECAUSE OF THE GIRL ALICE BULZOMI WHO ALSO LOVES HIM AND ALICE IS BIG AND WILL KICK MARLYS WITH HER POINTED SHOES AND ALSO KEVIN IF SHE EVER FINDS OUT. NUMBER TWO: MARLYS DRAWS HIM DRAGSTERS BECAUSE KEVIN LOVES DRAGSTERS BUT TRAGICALLY HE IS A CRUDDY DRAWER OF DRAGSTERS. THAT IS JUST LIFE MARLYS SAYS.
WHAT HE'S GOOD AT DRAWING IS NATURE AND FLOWERS. SO THEY TRADE. THEN MARLYS SHOWS ME THE STACK OF SECRET DRAWINGS HE MADE HER. TWENTY SEVEN DRAWINGS IN A PAY 'N' SAVE BAG WITH THE PENCIL HAND WRITING ON THE TOP:
To Marlys your the greatest girl artist of dragsters from Kevin.
PENCIL HANDWRITING SHE TRACES WITH HER FINGER, THEN SHE LOOKS AT ME AND SMILES.

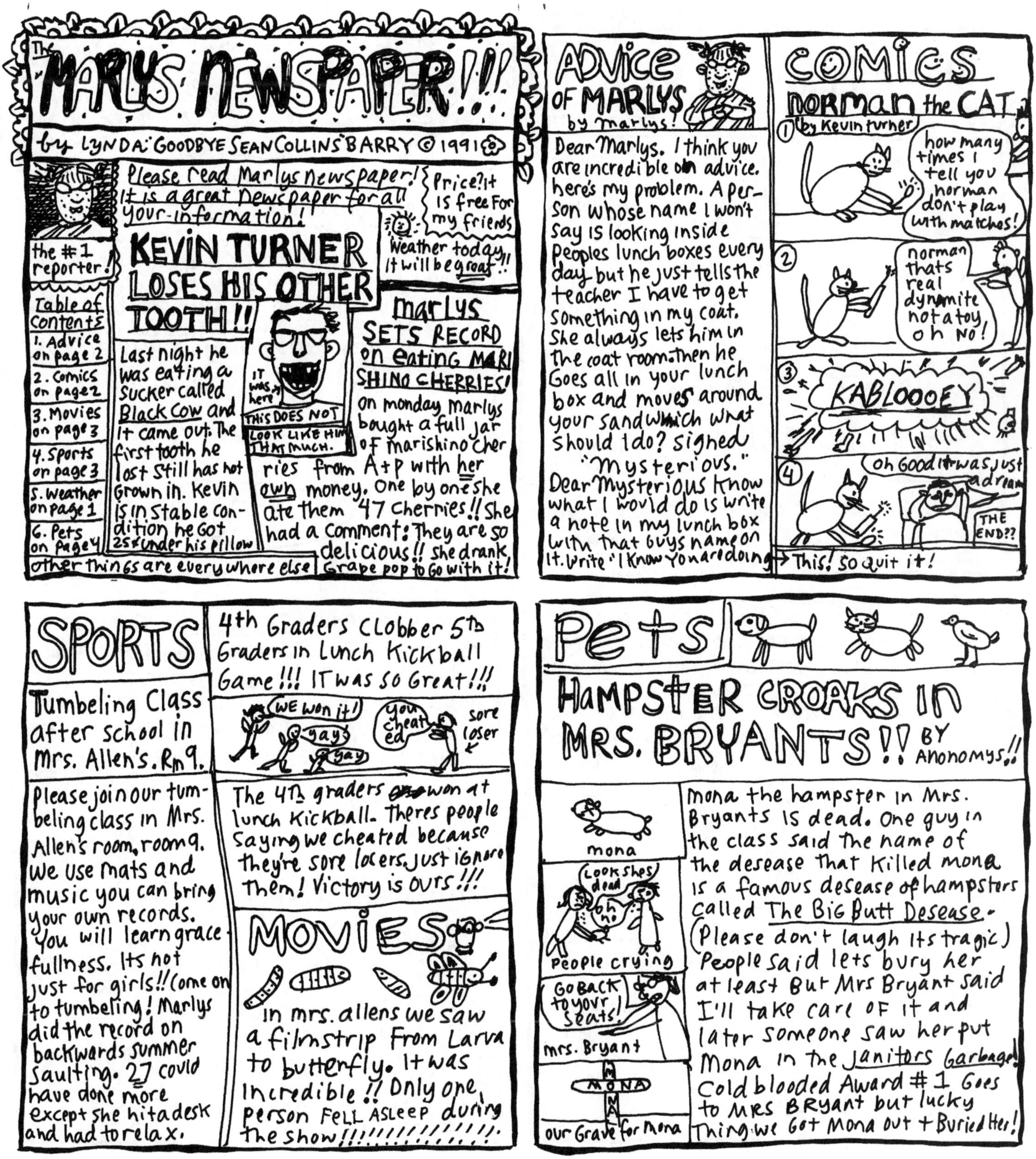
The MARLYS NEWSPAPER!!!
by LYNDA GOODBYE SEAN COLLINS BARRY © 1991
the #1 reporter!
Please read Marlys newspaper! It is a great newspaper for all your-information!
Price? It is free for my friends
Weather today it will be great!!
Table of contents
1. Advice on page 2
2. Comics on page 2
3. Movies on page 3
4. Sports on page 3
5. Weather on page 1
6. Pets on page 4
other things are everywhere else
KEVIN TURNER LOSES HIS OTHER TOOTH!!
Last night he was eating a sucker called Black Cow and it came out. The first tooth he lost still has not grown in. Kevin is in stable condition he got 25¢ under his pillow
It was here
THIS DOES NOT LOOK LIKE HIM THAT MUCH.
MARLYS SETS RECORD ON EATING MARISHINO CHERRIES!
On monday marlys bought a full jar of marishino cherries from A+P with her own money. One by one she ate them 47 cherries!! She had a comment: They are so delicious!! she drank grape pop to go with it!
ADVICE OF MARLYS by Marlys!
Dear Marlys. I think you are incredible on advice. here's my problem. A person whose name I won't say is looking inside peoples lunch boxes every day but he just tells the teacher I have to get something in my coat. She always lets him in the coat room. Then he goes all in your lunch box and moves around your sandwich what should I do? signed "Mysterious."
Dear Mysterious Know what I would do is write a note in my lunch box with that guys name on it. Write "I know you are doing → This! so quit it!
COMICS
NORMAN the CAT by Kevin Turner
1
how many times I tell you norman don't play with matches!
2
norman thats real dynamite not a toy oh no!
3
KABLOOOEY
4
oh good it was just a dream
THE END??
SPORTS
Tumbeling Class after school in Mrs. Allen's. Rm 9.
Please join our tumbeling class in Mrs. Allen's room, room 9. We use mats and music you can bring your own records. You will learn gracefullness. Its not just for girls!! Come on to tumbeling! Marlys did the record on backwards summer saulting. 27 could have done more except she hit a desk and had to relax.
4th Graders Clobber 5th Graders in Lunch Kickball Game!!! It was so Great!!!
WE won it!
yay
yay
you cheated
sore loser
The 4th graders won at lunch kickball. Theres people saying we cheated because they're sore losers. Just ignore them! Victory is ours!!!
MOVIES
In mrs. allens we saw a filmstrip from Larva to butterfly. It was incredible!! Only one person FELL ASLEEP during the show!!!!!!!!!!!!!!
Pets
HAMPSTER CROAKS IN MRS. BRYANTS!! BY ANONOMYS!!
mona
Look shes dead
oh no
People crying
Go back to your seats!
mrs. Bryant
MONA
our Grave for Mona
Mona the hampster in Mrs. Bryants is dead. One guy in the class said the name of the desease that killed mona is a famous desease of hampsters called The Big Butt Desease. (Please don't laugh its tragic) People said lets bury her at least but Mrs Bryant said I'll take care of it and later someone saw her put Mona in the Janitors Garbage! Cold blooded Award #1 goes to Mrs Bryant but lucky thing we got Mona out + Buried Her!

OUR DOMESTIC POULTRY
BY LYNDA "TAKE A LETTER MARIA" BARRY © 1991
Workbook p. 36 chap. 6
Marlys Mullen
Our Domestic Poultry
by Marlys Mullen
Chickens are old. In china there was chickens 3,000 years ago. In India. In the Indies. In Columbus. He ate them. They came to the USA on boats.
here Col. Sanders! a present
pilgrim
What is it?
The name of it is a chicken
oh thank you now I got a job!
I will call it finger licking good!
Theres 2 kinds of chickens. Useful and Fancy
Fancy ones are just for looks. To run in your yard to make it look beautiful.
Come Back!
NO ONE RUNS FROM COL. SANDERS!
Fancy
USEFUL
The useful ones make eggs and also you eat them. Theres lots of varieties But they all hate Col. Sanders. (Thats a joke, son!) People have fixed it so useful chickens cannot fly. That can be called coldblooded. They have 3 stomachs. They eat chicken-feed but they will eat Fritos.
2. proventriculus
1. crop
3. gizzard
Food in a chicken will not get chewed! so Don't give them Gum not even Dentene. It goes down to the first stomach called Crop. Then into proventriculus. then Gizzard where theres rocks (actual) grinding it. The rest is usual.
A certain chicken can lay 300 Eggs a year! It is done by breeding.
I can lay 300 eggs a year
So could my mom!
please fall in love
$ $
GIRL
BOY
farmer
The little egg grows in the chicken then goes down a tube.
Then a shell goes around it. But the work-book didn't say how. or how the chicken can lay it without Breaking it. Thats the part I don't get.
? ?
It takes about 21 DAYS for the chick to Grow in the EGG then they poke a hole in the shell with the BEAK. Some chicks will grow up to lay eggs. OTHER CHICKS will grow up to be meat or fried chicken. Except very smart fast runners.
hey you
The end?
Extra credit: Do chicken pox come from chickens?
A. NO. It comes from smelling someones breath or the scabs of the chicken pox. Chicken pox makes you feel terrible.
Chickens Do not.

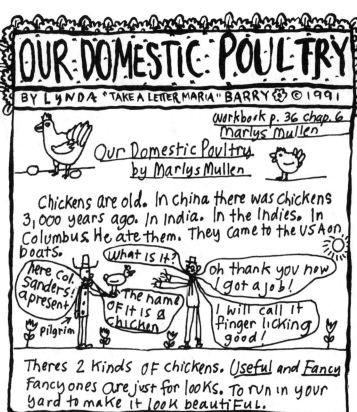

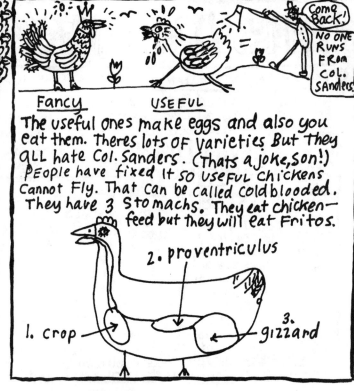

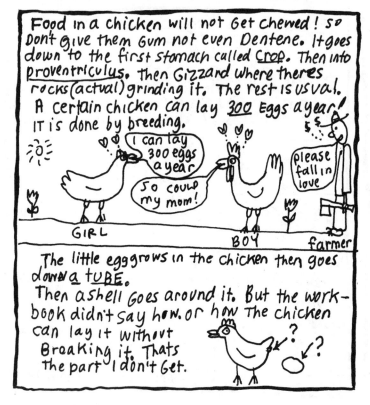

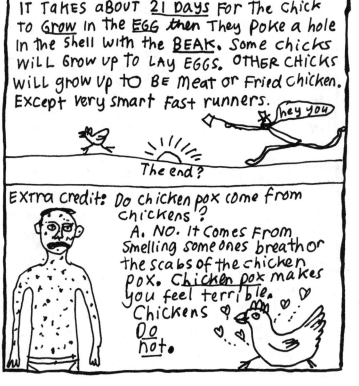

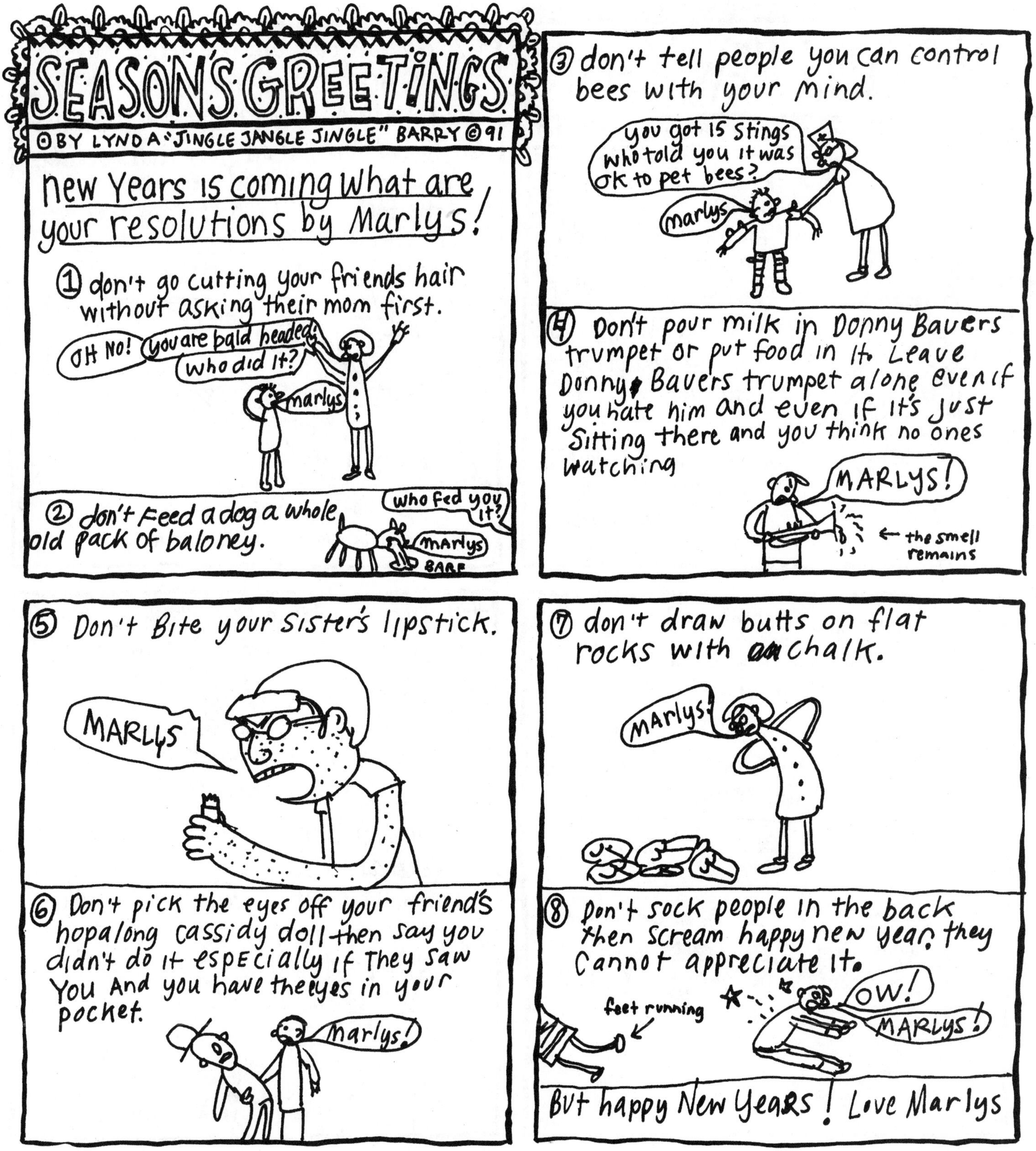
SEASON'S GREETINGS
©BY LYNDA "JINGLE JANGLE JINGLE" BARRY ©91
new Years is coming what are your resolutions by Marlys!
① don't go cutting your friends hair without asking their mom first.
OH NO! you are bald headed! who did it?
marlys
② don't feed a dog a whole old pack of baloney.
who fed you it?
marlys
BARF
③ don't tell people you can control bees with your mind.
you got 15 stings who told you it was ok to pet bees?
marlys
④ Don't pour milk in Donny Bauers trumpet or put food in it. Leave Donny Bauers trumpet alone even if you hate him and even if it's just sitting there and you think no ones watching
MARLYS!
← the smell remains
⑤ Don't Bite your sister's lipstick.
MARLYS
⑥ Don't pick the eyes off your friend's hopalong cassidy doll then say you didn't do it especially if they saw you and you have the eyes in your pocket.
marlys!
⑦ don't draw butts on flat rocks with chalk.
Marlys!
⑧ Don't sock people in the back then scream happy new year. they cannot appreciate it.
feet running
OW!
MARLYS!
But happy New Years! Love Marlys

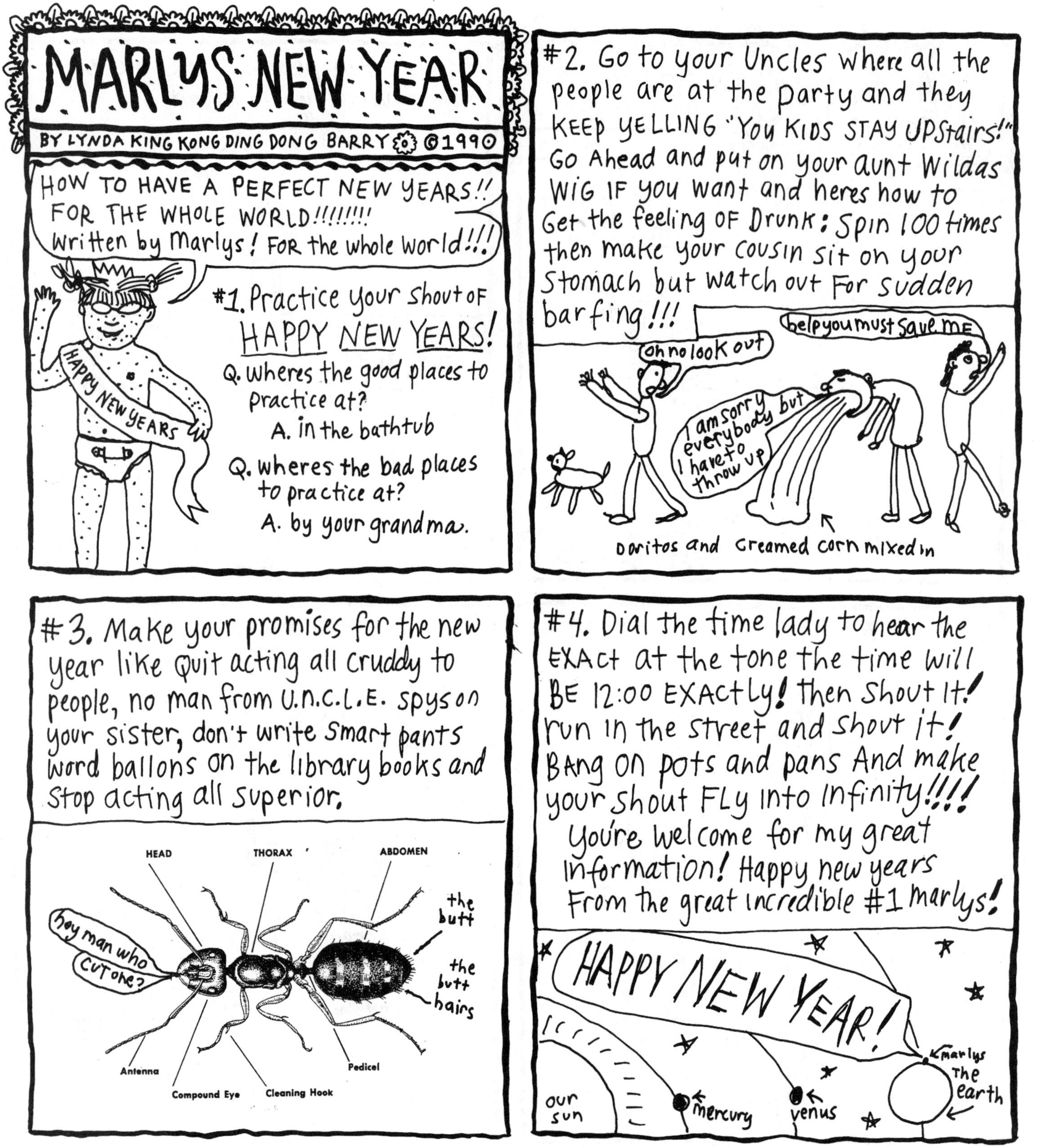
MARLYS NEW YEAR
BY LYNDA KING KONG DING DONG BARRY ©1990
HOW TO HAVE A PERFECT NEW YEARS!! FOR THE WHOLE WORLD!!!!!!!! Written by Marlys! For the whole world!!!
#1. Practice your shout of HAPPY NEW YEARS!
Q. wheres the good places to practice at?
A. in the bathtub
Q. wheres the bad places to practice at?
A. by your grandma.
HAPPY NEW YEARS
#2. Go to your Uncles where all the people are at the party and they KEEP YELLING "You KIDS STAY UPStairs!" Go Ahead and put on your aunt Wildas WIG IF you want and heres how to Get the feeling OF Drunk: Spin 100 times then make your cousin sit on your Stomach but watch out For sudden barfing!!!
oh no look out
help you must save me
I am sorry everybody but I have to throw up
Doritos and creamed corn mixed in
#3. Make your promises for the new year like quit acting all cruddy to people, no man from U.N.C.L.E. spys on your sister, don't write smart pants word ballons on the library books and Stop acting all superior.
HEAD
THORAX
ABDOMEN
hey man who cut one?
the butt
the butt hairs
Antenna
Compound Eye
Cleaning Hook
Pedicel
#4. Dial the time lady to hear the EXAct at the tone the time will BE 12:00 EXActLy! then Shout it! run in the street and Shout it! BAng on pots and pans And make your shout FLy into Infinity!!!!
You're welcome for my great information! Happy new years From the great incredible #1 marlys!
HAPPY NEW YEAR!
marlys
The earth
our sun
mercury
venus

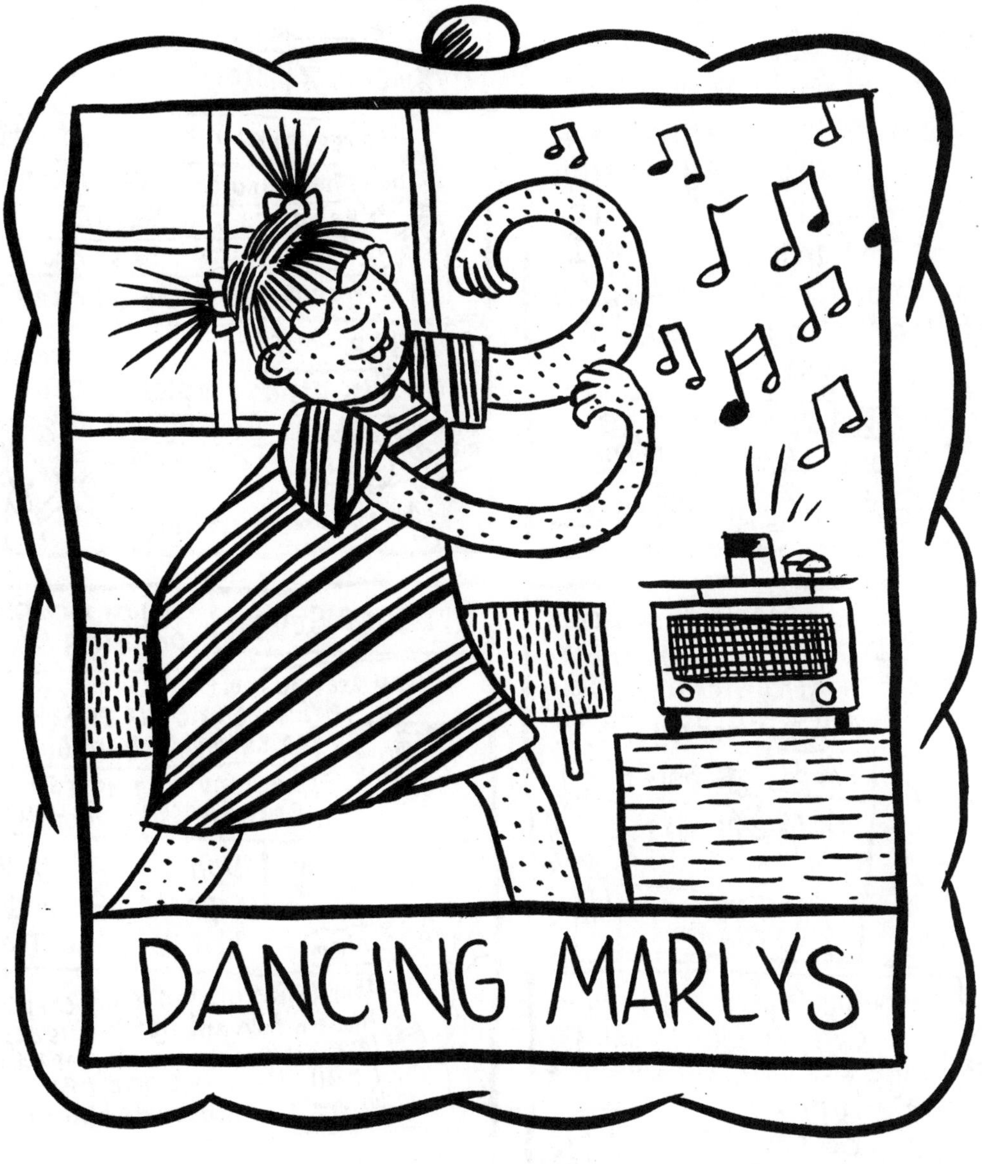
DANCING MARLYS

HOW TO GROOVE ON LIFE

BY LYNDA "DO YOU DYE YOUR HAIR?" BARRY ©1991

OF COURSE BY MARLYS!!

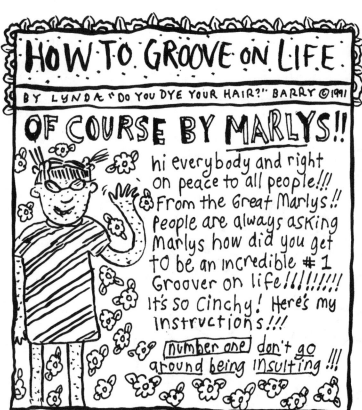

hi everybody and right on peace to all people!!! From the Great Marlys!! people are always asking Marlys how did you get to be an incredible #1 Groover on life!!!!!!!!! It's so Cinchy! Here's my Instructions!!!

number one don't go around being insulting!!!

number two Be Kind to animals for it is hard to Groove on life when they are biting you!!!

Here Boy
Have some poison baloney
Wrong
ow wait wait it was just a joke!
LATer on

NUMBER 3 Don't hog everything!!!!

Everything in the world that's decent is mine!!
Then why don't You share it!!!
Because why should I?
So You won't be so cruddy!
That is incredible advice!!

NUMBER four Fix your hair all Gorgeous! and fix other peoples hair all gorgeous!!!

EXCUSE ME
Do you like it? it is Gorgeous Created by marlys! She's incredible!
PLEASE I must have her phone number

Number Five don't tell people they are Bad singers don't you think Its nice they are even singing also you should Sing more not just happy birthday!!!!!!

Wrong
I just heard your singing it was awful!
RIGHT
one more time!
Is this a trick?
NO! my dream has come true!

Number SIX Don't make people listen to your singing for too many songs thouGH. Let everyone Get a turn!

now for my 1,000,009th number I would like to sing they call the wind MariaH!
You can sing in a minute I just got 30,000,000 more to GO.
HELP ME
Excuse me can I please sing one?

NUMBER SEVEN enjoy yourself at parties!!!

why are you inviting me to the party don't You notice something For example my one Giant ear?
I am inviting you so I CAN dance with you!

NUMBER 8 Don't copy your book reports off the back of the books. Too Fakey.

ok here's my report. Ahem
abandoning his mordant criticism of modern men and morals it is a powerful love story of incredible impact and I really liked this one part where the house gets blown up.

NUMBER 9 the Last one IF you Are in a bad mood just remember It will always Go away. This is Very bad news for people who Like their bad moods but they are NOT the #1 GROOVERS!!!!!!!!!!!!

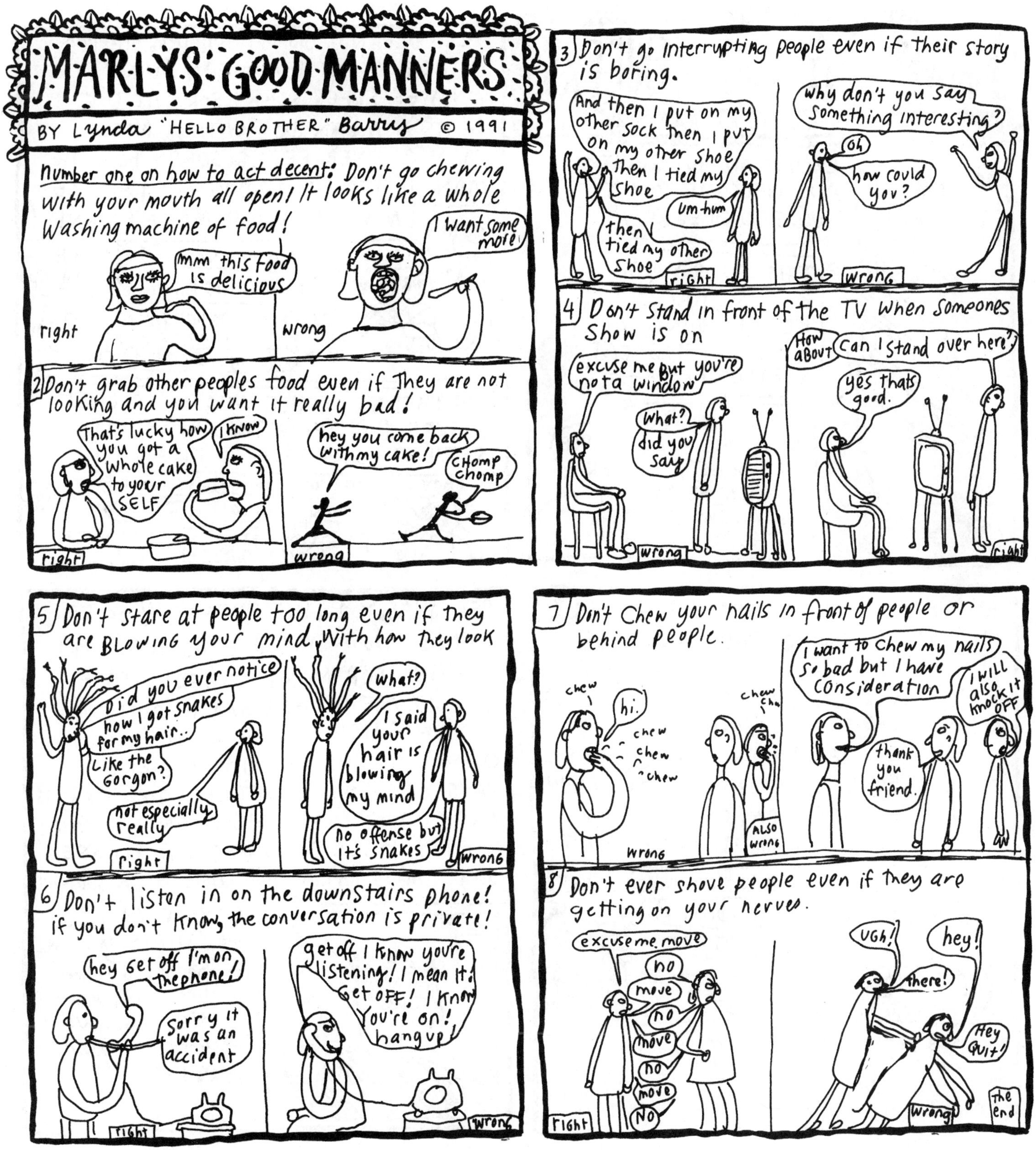

MARLYS: GOOD MANNERS
BY Lynda "HELLO BROTHER" Barry © 1991
number one on how to act decent: Don't go chewing with your mouth all open! It looks like a whole washing machine of food!
mmm this food is delicious
right
I want some more
wrong
2 Don't grab other peoples food even if they are not looking and you want it really bad!
That's lucky how you got a whole cake to your SELF
I know
right
hey you come back with my cake!
CHOMP chomp
wrong
3 Don't go interrupting people even if their story is boring.
And then I put on my other sock then I put on my other shoe then I tied my shoe
um-hum
then I tied my other shoe
right
why don't you say something interesting?
oh
how could you?
wrong
4 Don't stand in front of the TV when someones show is on
excuse me but you're not a window
What? did you say
wrong
How about
can I stand over here?
yes thats good.
right
5 Don't stare at people too long even if they are blowing your mind with how they look
Did you ever notice how I got snakes for my hair..
Like the Gorgon?
not especially really
right
what?
I said your hair is blowing my mind
no offense but it's snakes
wrong
6 Don't listen in on the downstairs phone! if you don't know, the conversation is private!
hey get off I'm on the phone!
sorry it was an accident
right
get off I know you're listening! I mean it! Get OFF! I know you're on! hang up!
wrong
7 Don't chew your nails in front of people or behind people.
chew
hi.
chew
chew
chew
wrong
chew chew
ALSO wrong
I want to chew my nails so bad but I have consideration
I WILL also knock it OFF
thank you friend.
8 Don't ever shove people even if they are getting on your nerves.
excuse me move
no
move
no
move
no
move
NO
right
UGH!
hey!
there!
Hey quit!
wrong
The end

MARLYS' GUIDE to QUEERS

by LYNDA "SEAN COLLINS" BARRY © 1991

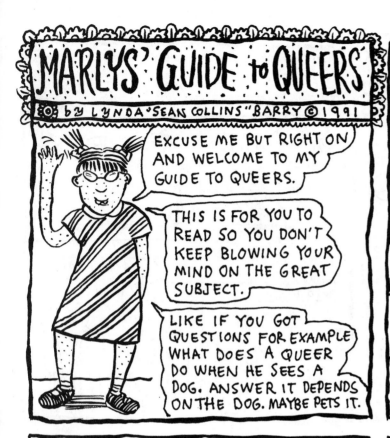

EXCUSE ME BUT RIGHT ON AND WELCOME TO MY GUIDE TO QUEERS.

THIS IS FOR YOU TO READ SO YOU DON'T KEEP BLOWING YOUR MIND ON THE GREAT SUBJECT.

LIKE IF YOU GOT QUESTIONS FOR EXAMPLE WHAT DOES A QUEER DO WHEN HE SEES A DOG. ANSWER IT DEPENDS ON THE DOG. MAYBE PETS IT.

ALSO DEPENDS ON WHOSE DOG. IF IT'S A NICE DOG WITH A MEAN MAN? ANSWER FEELS SORRY FOR THE DOG. IF IT'S A MEAN DOG WITH A NICE MAN. ANSWER FEELS SORRY FOR THE MAN. IF IT'S A NICE DOG WITH A NICE MAN. ANSWER MAKE FRIENDS!

Hi

Hi Your dog is nice also you are

THANKS

Hi what's his name

LOOK OUT HE'S A QUEER

pooky do you think that's a dumb name

noway it's great

RUN FOR IT.

ALSO THERE'S PEOPLE WHO DON'T LIKE QUEERS. ONE THING THEY'RE THINKING IS THE QUEERS GOING TO KISS THEM

hey you don't come near me

LIKE I WOULD EVER WANT TO

YOU DO SO WANT TO!

AS IF.

WHY NOT?

YOU GET ON MY NERVES

ANOTHER THING IS WHO IS A QUEER? ANSWER MY UNCLE JOHN. ANOTHER ONE IS BILL. THEY TOOK ME AND MY SISTER TO THE DRIVE IN AND MY FRIEND KEVIN TURNER. IT WAS SO GREAT BUT NOW THAT THEY ARE KNOWN QUEERS YOU CAN FORGET THAT WILL HAPPEN AGAIN UNTIL THE MIRACLE DAY OF PEOPLE QUIT BEING SO STUPID. WILL IT COME? I DON'T KNOW.

Can kevin come to the movies

I AM DOOMED

not if queers will be there

There's usually queers at movies though.

Then forget it

ok Byekevin

Sorry your moms BERSURK.

THERE'S PEOPLE WHO WILL HIT YOU IF THEY FIND OUT YOU ARE QUEER

MY UNCLE JOHN HAS A SCAR ON HIS FOREHEAD FROM IT. THE POLICE SAID "FORGET IT."

PERSONALLY I LIKE QUEERS!!! SO FAR I ONLY KNOW TWO QUEERS AND I AM LOOKING FOR MORE QUEERS!!! SO IF YOU SEE ME PLEASE SAY HI DON'T BE ALL SNOBBISH!!! ALSO IF YOU KNOW OTHER QUEERS TELL THEM "MARLYS SAYS HI." SAY "RIGHT ON FROM MARLYS" AND DO THE POWER SIGN. AND IF YOU SEE MY UNCLE JOHN AND BILL PLEASE SAY I MISS THEM AND COME BACK SOON.

Love truely,
* Marlys *
P.S. heres my school picture if you want to stick it in your billfold!!! It would be an honor!!!

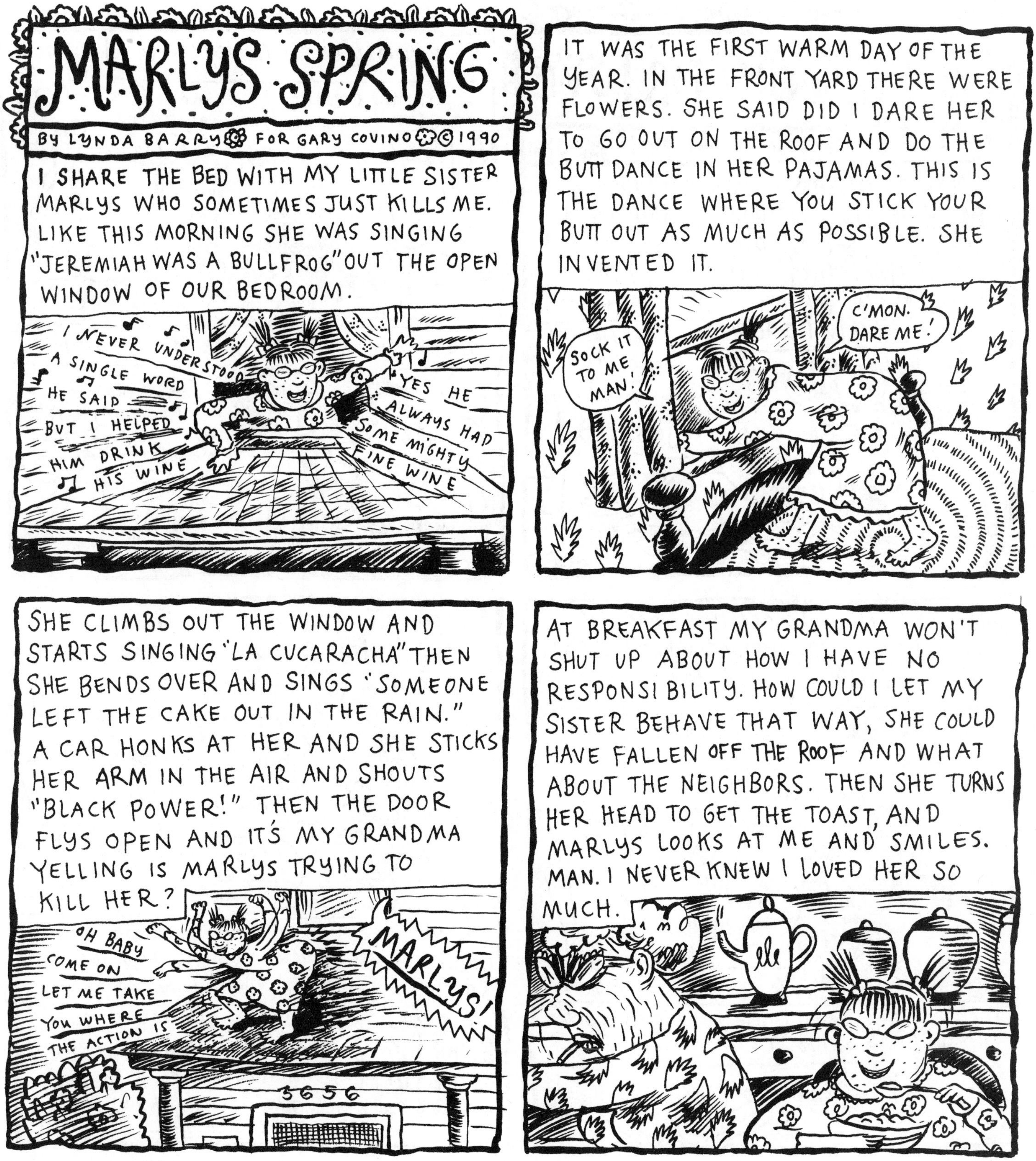
MARLYS SPRING
BY LYNDA BARRY FOR GARY COVINO ©1990
I SHARE THE BED WITH MY LITTLE SISTER MARLYS WHO SOMETIMES JUST KILLS ME. LIKE THIS MORNING SHE WAS SINGING "JEREMIAH WAS A BULLFROG" OUT THE OPEN WINDOW OF OUR BEDROOM.
I NEVER UNDERSTOOD A SINGLE WORD HE SAID BUT I HELPED HIM DRINK HIS WINE
YES HE ALWAYS HAD SOME MIGHTY FINE WINE
IT WAS THE FIRST WARM DAY OF THE YEAR. IN THE FRONT YARD THERE WERE FLOWERS. SHE SAID DID I DARE HER TO GO OUT ON THE ROOF AND DO THE BUTT DANCE IN HER PAJAMAS. THIS IS THE DANCE WHERE YOU STICK YOUR BUTT OUT AS MUCH AS POSSIBLE. SHE INVENTED IT.
SOCK IT TO ME MAN!
C'MON. DARE ME!
SHE CLIMBS OUT THE WINDOW AND STARTS SINGING "LA CUCARACHA" THEN SHE BENDS OVER AND SINGS "SOMEONE LEFT THE CAKE OUT IN THE RAIN." A CAR HONKS AT HER AND SHE STICKS HER ARM IN THE AIR AND SHOUTS "BLACK POWER!" THEN THE DOOR FLYS OPEN AND IT'S MY GRANDMA YELLING IS MARLYS TRYING TO KILL HER?
OH BABY COME ON LET ME TAKE YOU WHERE THE ACTION IS
MARLYS!
3656
AT BREAKFAST MY GRANDMA WON'T SHUT UP ABOUT HOW I HAVE NO RESPONSIBILITY. HOW COULD I LET MY SISTER BEHAVE THAT WAY, SHE COULD HAVE FALLEN OFF THE ROOF AND WHAT ABOUT THE NEIGHBORS. THEN SHE TURNS HER HEAD TO GET THE TOAST, AND MARLYS LOOKS AT ME AND SMILES. MAN. I NEVER KNEW I LOVED HER SO MUCH.

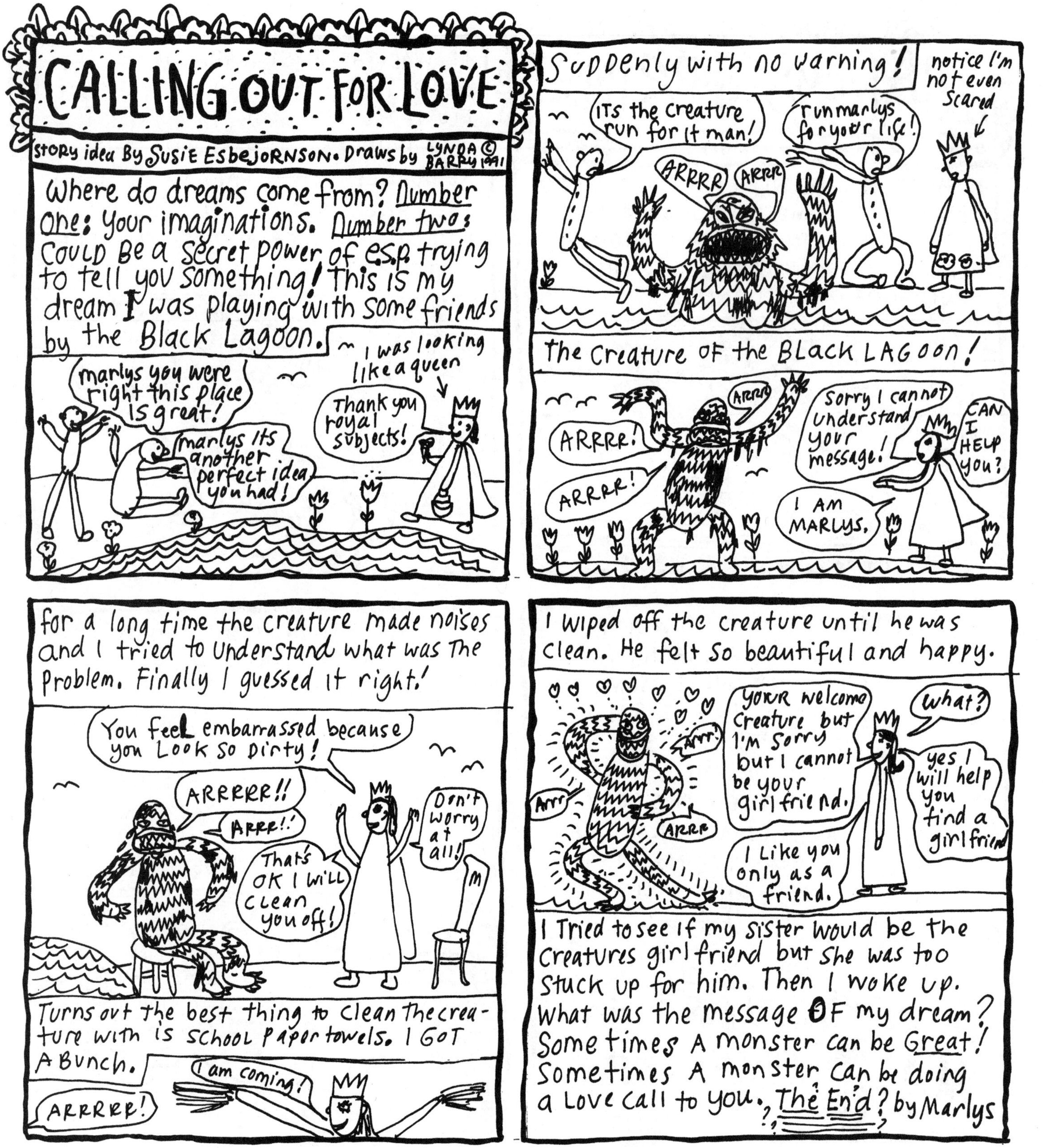
CALLING OUT FOR LOVE
story idea By Susie Esbejornson. Draws by Lynda Barry © 1991
Where do dreams come from? Number one: your imaginations. Number two: could be a secret power of e.s.p trying to tell you something! This is my dream I was playing with some friends by the Black Lagoon.
marlys you were right this place is great!
marlys its another perfect idea you had!
I was looking like a queen
Thank you royal subjects!
Suddenly with no warning!
notice I'm not even scared
Its the creature run for it man!
run marlys for your life!
ARRRR
ARRR
The creature of the Black Lagoon!
ARRRR!
ARRR
ARRRR!
Sorry I cannot understand your message!
CAN I HELP you?
I AM MARLYS.
for a long time the creature made noises and I tried to understand what was the problem. Finally I guessed it right!
You feel embarrassed because you look so dirty!
ARRRRR!!
ARRR!!
That's OK I will clean you off!
Don't worry at all!
Turns out the best thing to clean the creature with is school paper towels. I GOT A Bunch.
ARRRRR!
I am coming!
I wiped off the creature until he was clean. He felt so beautiful and happy.
Arrr
Arrr!
ARRR
Your welcome creature but I'm sorry but I cannot be your girlfriend.
I Like you only as a friend.
What?
yes I will help you find a girlfrie
I Tried to see if my sister would be the creatures girlfriend but she was too stuck up for him. Then I woke up. What was the message OF my dream? Sometimes A monster can be Great! Sometimes A monster can be doing a Love call to you. The End? by Marlys

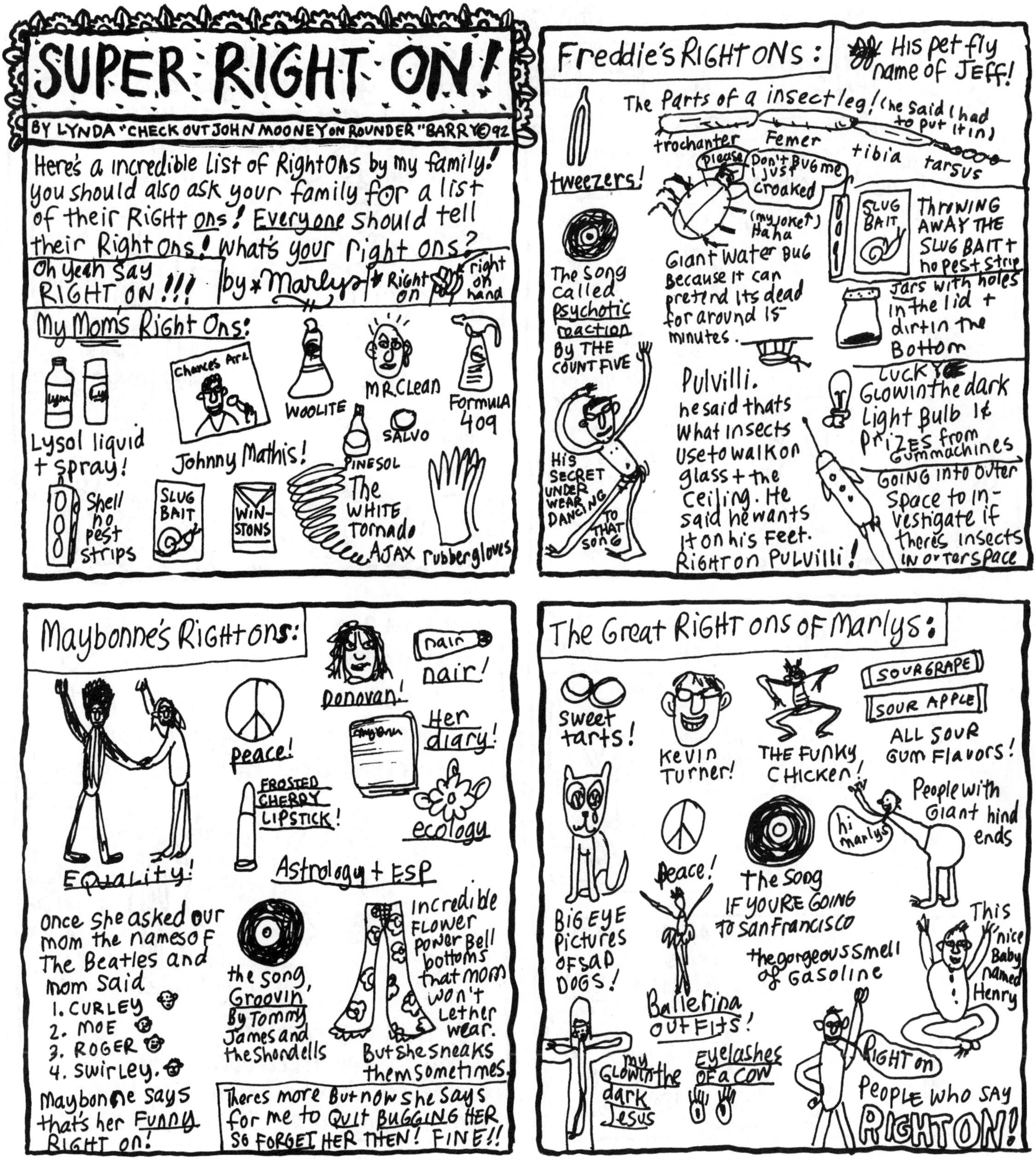
SUPER RIGHT ON!
BY LYNDA "CHECK OUT JOHN MOONEY ON ROUNDER" BARRY ©92
Here's a incredible list of Right ons by my family! you should also ask your family for a list of their RIGHT ons! Everyone should tell their Right ons! what's your right ons?
Oh yeah say RIGHT ON!!!
by * Marlys
* Right on
right on hand
My Mom's Right Ons:
Lysol
Lysol liquid + spray!
Chances Are
Johnny Mathis!
WOOLITE
MR. Clean
FORMULA 409
SALVO
PINESOL
Shell no pest strips
SLUG BAIT
WIN-STONS
The WHITE Tornado AJAX
rubbergloves
Freddie's RIGHT ONs:
His pet fly name of JEFF!
The Parts of a insect leg! (he said I had to put it in)
trochanter
Femer
tibia
tarsus
tweezers!
Please
Don't Bug me I just Croaked
(my joke!) Haha
Giant Water BUG Because it can pretend its dead for around 15 minutes.
SLUG BAIT
THROWING AWAY THE SLUG BAIT + no pest strip
The song called psychotic reaction By THE COUNT FIVE
Jars with holes in the lid + dirt in the Bottom
Pulvilli. he said thats what insects use to walk on glass + the ceiling. He said he wants it on his Feet. RIGHT ON PULVILLI!
LUCKY Glow in the dark Light Bulb 1¢ Prizes from Gum machines
His SECRET UNDER WEAR DANCING TO THAT SONG
GOING into outer Space to investigate if theres insects in orter space
Maybonne's Right ons:
Donovan!
nair
nair!
peace!
Her diary!
FROSTED CHERRY LIPSTICK!
ecology
EQUALITY!
Astrology + ESP
once she asked our mom the names of The Beatles and mom said
1. CURLEY
2. MOE
3. ROGER
4. SWIRLEY.
the song, Groovin' By Tommy James and the Shondells
incredible FLOWER power Bell bottoms that mom won't let her wear.
But she sneaks them sometimes.
Maybonne says that's her Funny RIGHT on!
Theres more But now she says for me to QUIT BUGGING HER SO FORGET HER THEN! FINE!!
The Great RIGHT ons of Marlys:
sweet tarts!
Kevin Turner!
THE FUNKY CHICKEN!
SOUR GRAPE
SOUR APPLE
ALL SOUR GUM Flavors!
People with Giant hind ends
hi marlys
BIG EYE Pictures OF SAD DOGS!
peace!
The Song IF YOU'RE GOING TO San Francisco
the gorgeous smell of Gasoline
This nice Baby named Henry
Ballerina OUTFITS!
my Glow in the dark Jesus
Eyelashes of a cow
RIGHT on
People who say RIGHT ON!

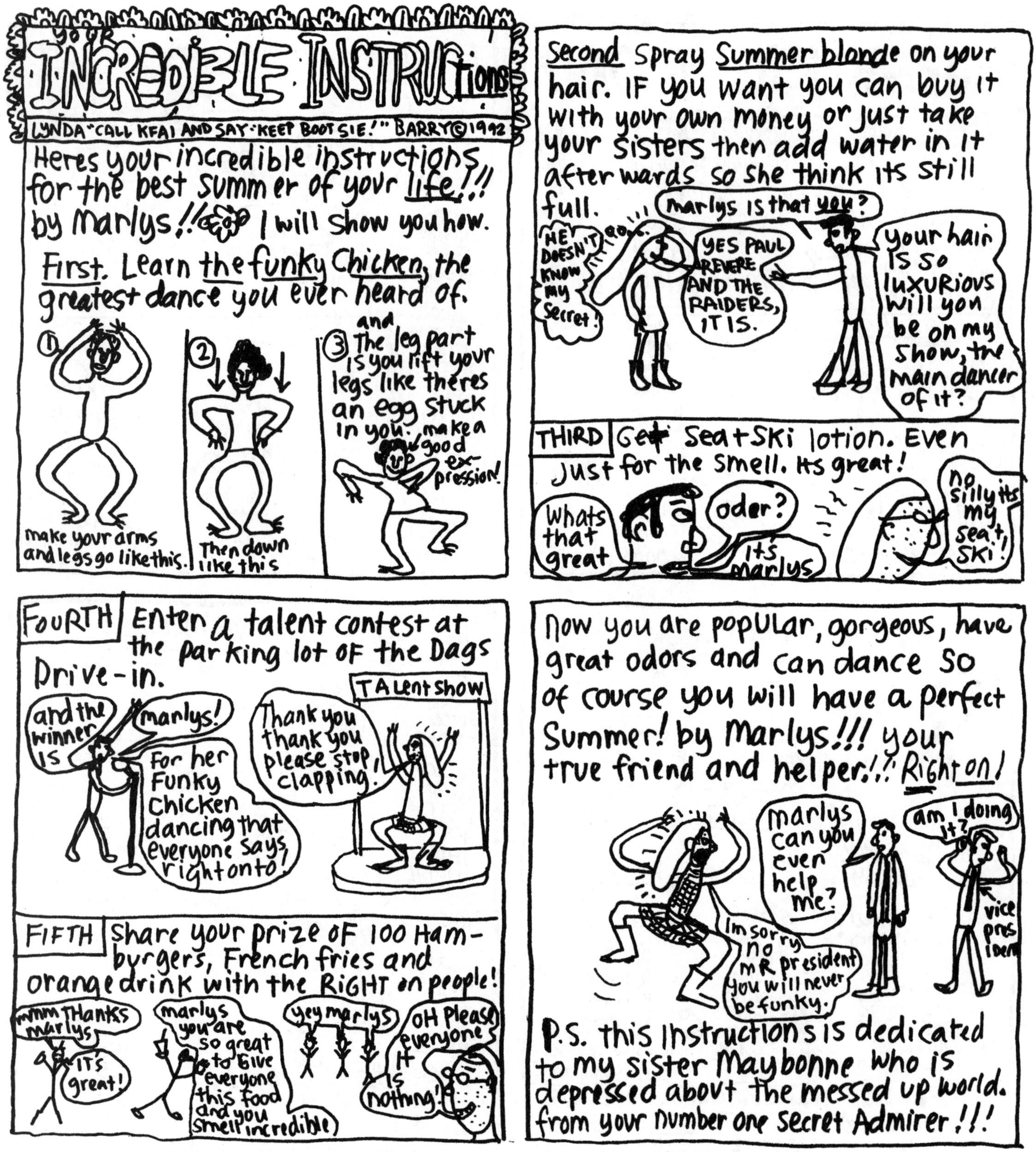
YOUR INCREDIBLE INSTRUCTIONS
LYNDA "CALL KFAI AND SAY: KEEP BOOTSIE!" BARRY © 1992
Heres your incredible instructions for the best summer of your life!!! by Marlys!! I will show you how.
First. Learn the funky Chicken, the greatest dance you ever heard of.
1
make your arms and legs go like this.
2
Then down like this
3
and The leg part is you lift your legs like theres an egg stuck in you. make a good ex-pression!
Second Spray Summer blonde on your hair. If you want you can buy it with your own money or just take your sisters then add water in it afterwards so she think its still full.
HE DOESN'T KNOW MY Secret!
Marlys is that you?
YES PAUL REVERE AND THE RAIDERS, IT IS.
Your hair is so luxurious will you be on my show, the main dancer of it?
THIRD Get Sea+Ski lotion. Even just for the smell. Its great!
Whats that great
odor?
Its Marlys
no silly its my Sea+Ski!
FOURTH Enter a talent contest at the parking lot of the Dags Drive-in.
and the winner is
Marlys!
For her Funky Chicken dancing that everyone says right on to!
TALENT SHOW
Thank you thank you please stop clapping!
FIFTH Share your prize of 100 Hamburgers, French fries and orange drink with the RIGHT on people!
mmm Thanks Marlys
It's great!
Marlys you are so great to give everyone this food and you smell incredible
yey Marlys
OH Please everyone it is nothing!
Now you are popular, gorgeous, have great odors and can dance so of course you will have a perfect Summer! by Marlys!!! your true friend and helper!!! Right on!
Marlys can you even help me?
am I doing it?
vice president
Im sorry no MR president you will never be funky.
P.S. this instructions is dedicated to my sister Maybonne who is depressed about the messed up world. from your number one Secret Admirer!!!

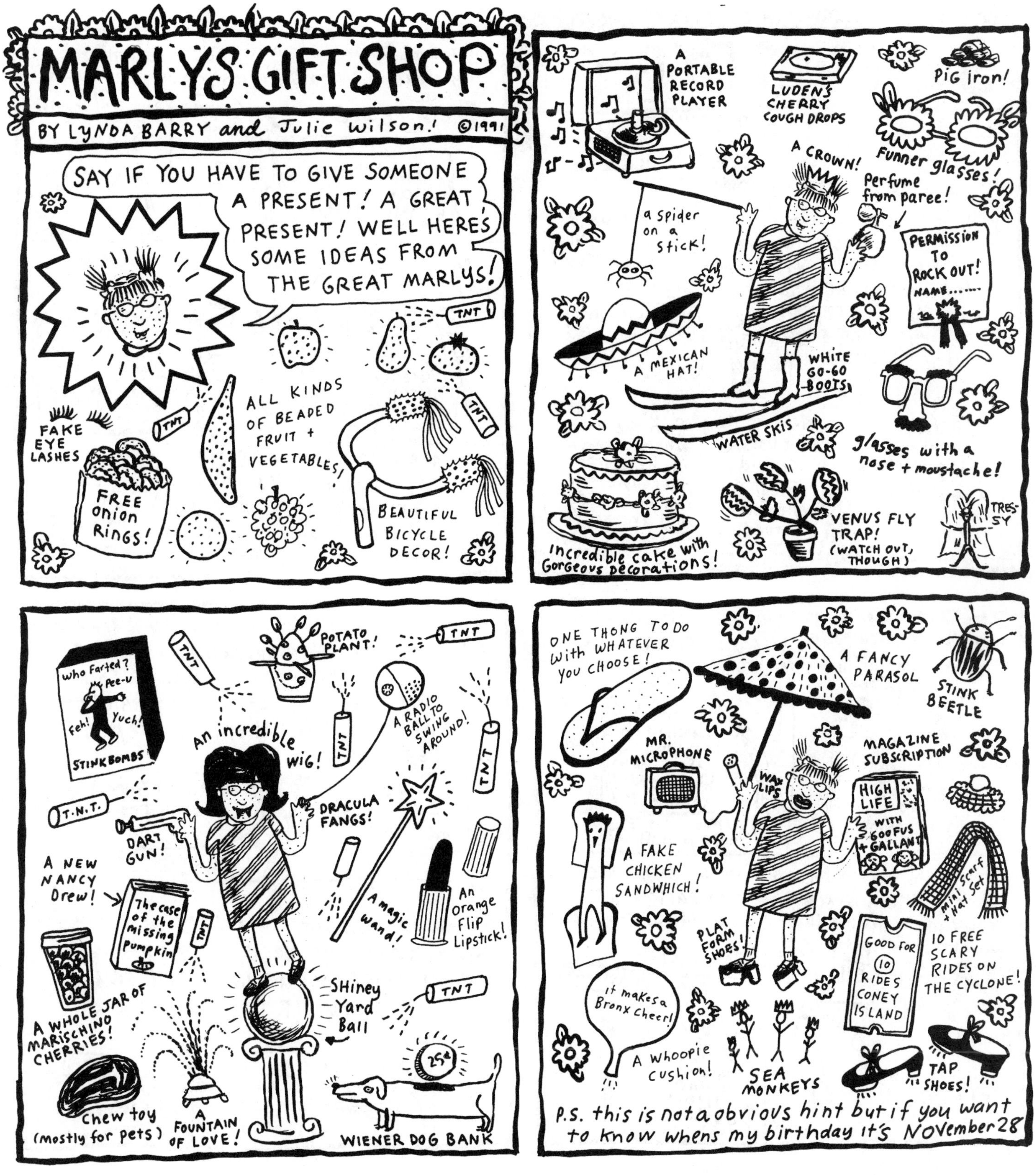
MARLYS GIFT SHOP
BY LYNDA BARRY and Julie Wilson! ©1991
SAY IF YOU HAVE TO GIVE SOMEONE A PRESENT! A GREAT PRESENT! WELL HERES SOME IDEAS FROM THE GREAT MARLYS!
TNT
FAKE EYE LASHES
TNT
ALL KINDS OF BEADED FRUIT + VEGETABLES!
TNT
FREE onion RINGS!
BEAUTIFUL BICYCLE DECOR!
A PORTABLE RECORD PLAYER
LUDENS CHERRY COUGH DROPS
PIG iron!
Funner glasses!
A CROWN!
Perfume from paree!
a spider on a stick!
PERMISSION TO ROCK OUT!
NAME.......
A MEXICAN HAT!
WHITE GO-GO BOOTS
WATER SKIS
glasses with a nose + moustache!
incredible cake with Gorgeous decorations!
VENUS FLY TRAP! (WATCH OUT, THOUGH)
TRES-SY
Who Farted? Pee-U
Feh! Yuch!
STINK BOMBS
TNT
POTATO PLANT!
TNT
A RADIO BALL TO SWING AROUND!
An incredible WIG!
TNT
TNT
T.N.T.
DRACULA FANGS!
DART GUN!
A NEW NANCY Drew!
The case of the missing pumpkin
TNT
A magic wand!
An orange Flip Lipstick!
A WHOLE JAR OF MARISCHINO CHERRIES!
SHiney Yard Ball
TNT
25¢
Chew toy (mostly for pets)
A FOUNTAIN OF LOVE!
WIENER DOG BANK
ONE THONG TO DO with WHATEVER YOU CHOOSE!
A FANCY PARASOL
STINK BEETLE
MR. MICROPHONE
MAGAZINE SUBSCRIPTION
WAX LIPS
HIGH LIFE
WITH GOOFUS + GALLANT
A FAKE CHICKEN SANDWHICH!
Mini Scarf + Hat Set
PLAT FORM SHOES!
GOOD FOR 10 RIDES CONEY ISLAND
10 FREE SCARY RIDES ON THE CYCLONE!
It makes a Bronx Cheer!
A Whoopie cushion!
SEA MONKEYS
TAP SHOES!
P.S. this is not a obvious hint but if you want to know whens my birthday it's November 28

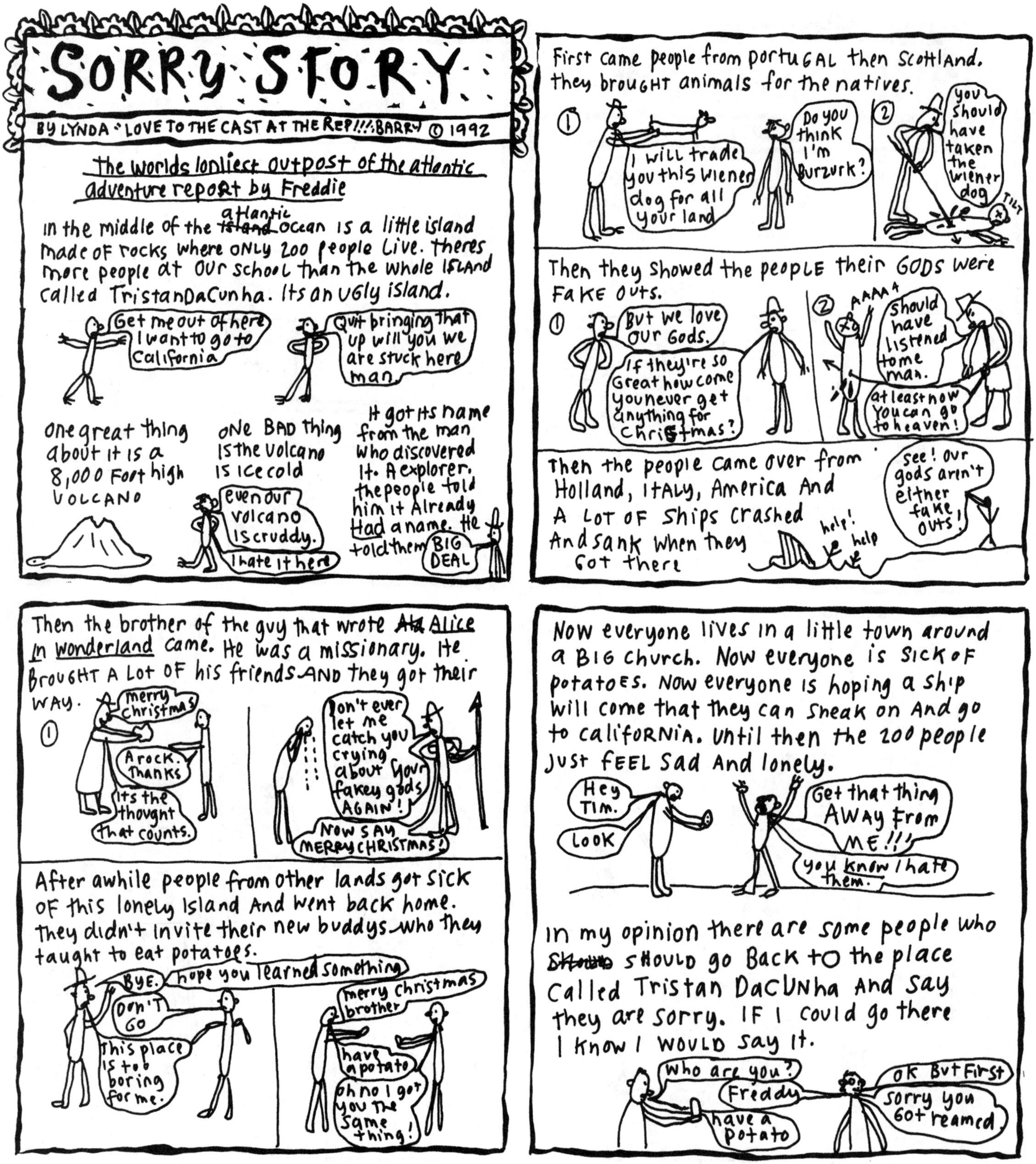

SORRY STORY
BY LYNDA • LOVE TO THE CAST AT THE REP!!! • BARRY © 1992
the worlds lonliest outpost of the atlantic adventure report by Freddie
In the middle of the ~~island~~ atlantic ocean is a little island made of rocks where ONLY 200 people Live. theres more people at OUR SchooL than the whole ISLAND called TristanDaCunha. Its an UGly island.
Get me out of here I want to go to California
Quit bringing that up will you we are stuck here man.
one great thing about it is a 8,000 Foot high VOLCANO
oNE BAD thing Is the Volcano Is Ice cold
even our volcano Is cruddy.
I hate it here
It got its name from the man who discovered It. A explorer. the people told him it Already Had a name. He told them
BIG DEAL
First came people from PORTUGAL then Scottland. they brought animals for the natives.
1
I will trade you this wiener dog for all your land
Do you think I'm Burzurk?
2
You should have taken the wiener dog
TILT
Then they showed the people their GODS were FAKE OUTS.
1
But we love our Gods.
If they're so Great how come you never get anything for Christmas?
2
AAAAA
Should have listened to me man.
at least now you can go to heaven!
Then the people came over from Holland, ITALY, America And A LOT OF Ships crashed And sank when they Got there
help!
help
See! our gods arn't either fake outs!
Then the brother of the guy that wrote ~~Ala~~ Alice In Wonderland came. He was a missionary. He BROUGHT A LOT OF his friends AND they got their WAY.
1
merry christmas
A rock. Thanks
Its the thought that counts.
Don't ever let me catch you crying about your fakey gods AGAIN!
Now SAY MERRY CHRISTMAS!
After awhile people from other lands got sick of this lonely Island And went back home. They didn't invite their new buddys who they taught to eat potatoes.
BYE.
hope you learned something
Don't Go
This place is too boring for me.
merry christmas brother
have a potato
oh no I got you the same thing!
Now everyone lives in a little town around a BIG church. Now everyone is SICK OF potatoES. Now everyone is hoping a ship will come that they can sneak on And go to california. Until then the 200 people just FEEL Sad And lonely.
Hey Tim.
Look
Get that thing AWAY from ME!!!
you know I hate them.
In my opinion there are some people who ~~Shoul~~ SHOULD go Back to the place Called Tristan DaCUnha And Say they are sorry. IF I could go there I know I WOULD Say it.
Who are you?
Freddy
have a potato
OK But First
Sorry you Got reamed.

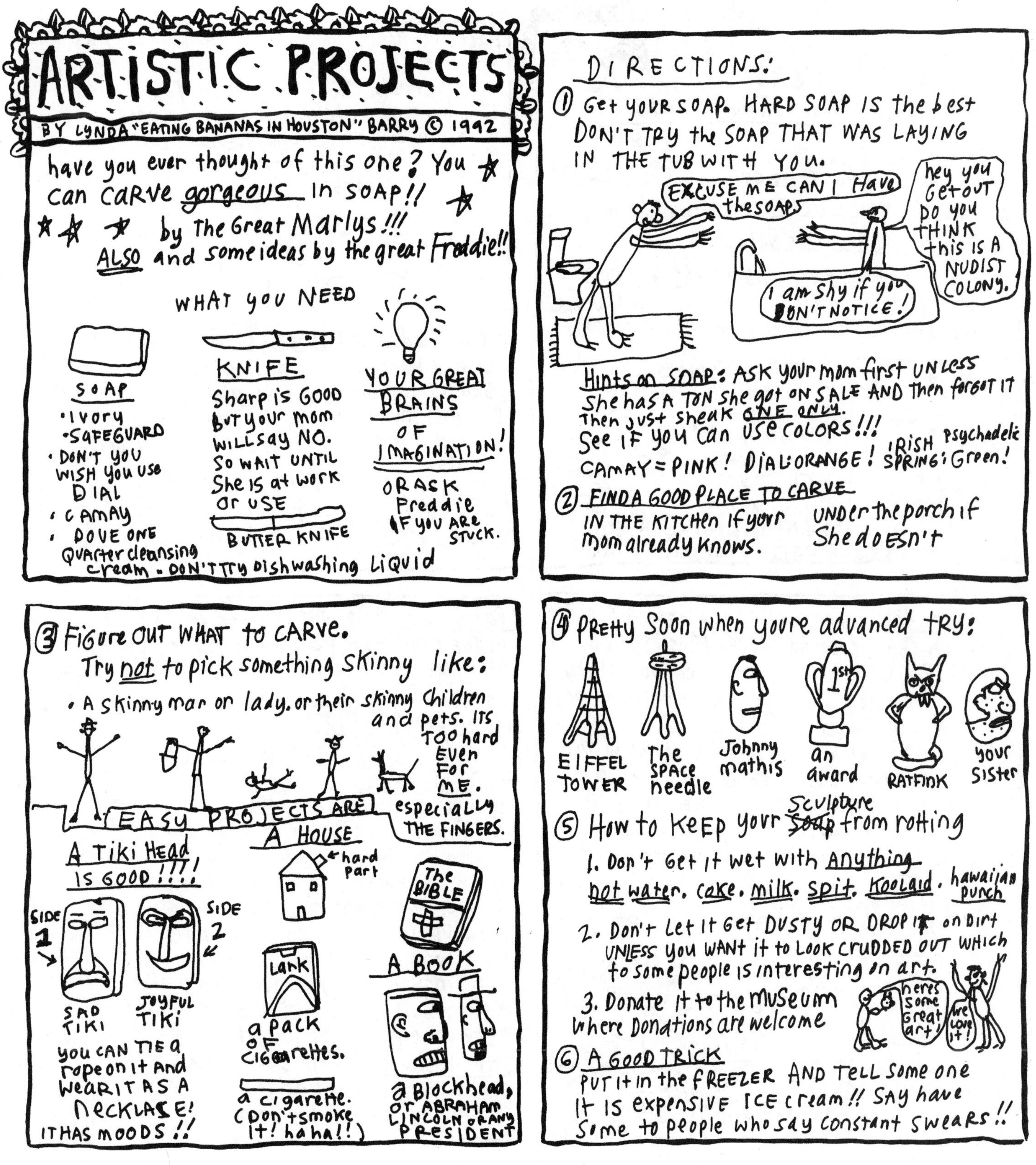
ARTISTIC PROJECTS
BY LYNDA "EATING BANANAS IN HOUSTON" BARRY © 1992
have you ever thought of this one? You can carve gorgeous in SOAP!! by the Great Marlys!!!
ALSO and some ideas by the great Freddie!!
WHAT you NEED
SOAP
•Ivory
•SAFEGUARD
•DON'T you WISH you use DIAL
•CAMAY
•DOVE ONE Quarter cleansing cream • DON'T TRY DISHWASHING LIQUID
KNIFE
Sharp is GOOD but your mom will say NO. SO WAIT UNTIL She is at work or USE
BUTTER KNIFE
YOUR GREAT BRAINS OF IMAGINATION!
OR ASK Freddie IF you ARE STUCK.
DIRECTIONS:
① Get your SOAP. HARD SOAP IS the best DON'T TRY the SOAP THAT WAS LAYING IN THE TUB WITH YOU.
EXCUSE ME CAN I Have the SOAP
hey you Get out Do you THINK this is A NUDIST COLONY.
I am Shy if you DON'T NOTICE!
Hints on SOAP: ASK your mom first UNLESS She has A TON she got ON SALE AND then forgot it Then just sneak ONE ONLY.
See IF you can use colors!!!
CAMAY = PINK! DIAL: ORANGE! IRISH SPRING: Green! Psychadelic
② FIND A GOOD PLACE TO CARVE
IN THE KITCHEN If your mom already knows.
UNDER the porch if She doesn't
③ Figure OUT WHAT to CARVE.
Try not to pick something skinny like:
• A skinny man or lady, or their skinny children and pets. ITS Too hard Even For ME. especially THE FINGERS.
EASY PROJECTS ARE
A TIKI HEAD IS GOOD!!!!
SIDE 1
SIDE 2
SAD TIKI
JOYFUL TIKI
you CAN TIE a rope on it And WEAR IT AS A NECKLASE! IT HAS MOODS!!
A HOUSE
hard part
The BIBLE
Lark
a pack of cigarettes.
a cigarette. (Don't smoke It! ha ha!!)
A BOOK
a Blockhead, or ABRAHAM LINCOLN or ANY PRESIDENT
④ Pretty Soon when youre advanced try:
EIFFEL TOWER
The SPACE needle
Johnny mathis
1st
an award
RATFINK
your Sister
⑤ How to keep your Soap Sculpture from rotting
1. Don't Get it wet with Anything not water. cake. milk. spit. Koolaid. hawaiian punch
2. Don't Let it Get DUSTY OR DROP IT on Dirt UNLESS you WANT it to LOOK CRUDDED OUT WHICH to some people is interesting on art.
3. Donate it to the museum where Donations are welcome
heres some Great art!
We Love it!
⑥ A GOOD TRICK
PUT it in the FREEZER AND TELL some one it is expensive ICE cream!! Say have some to people who say constant swears!!

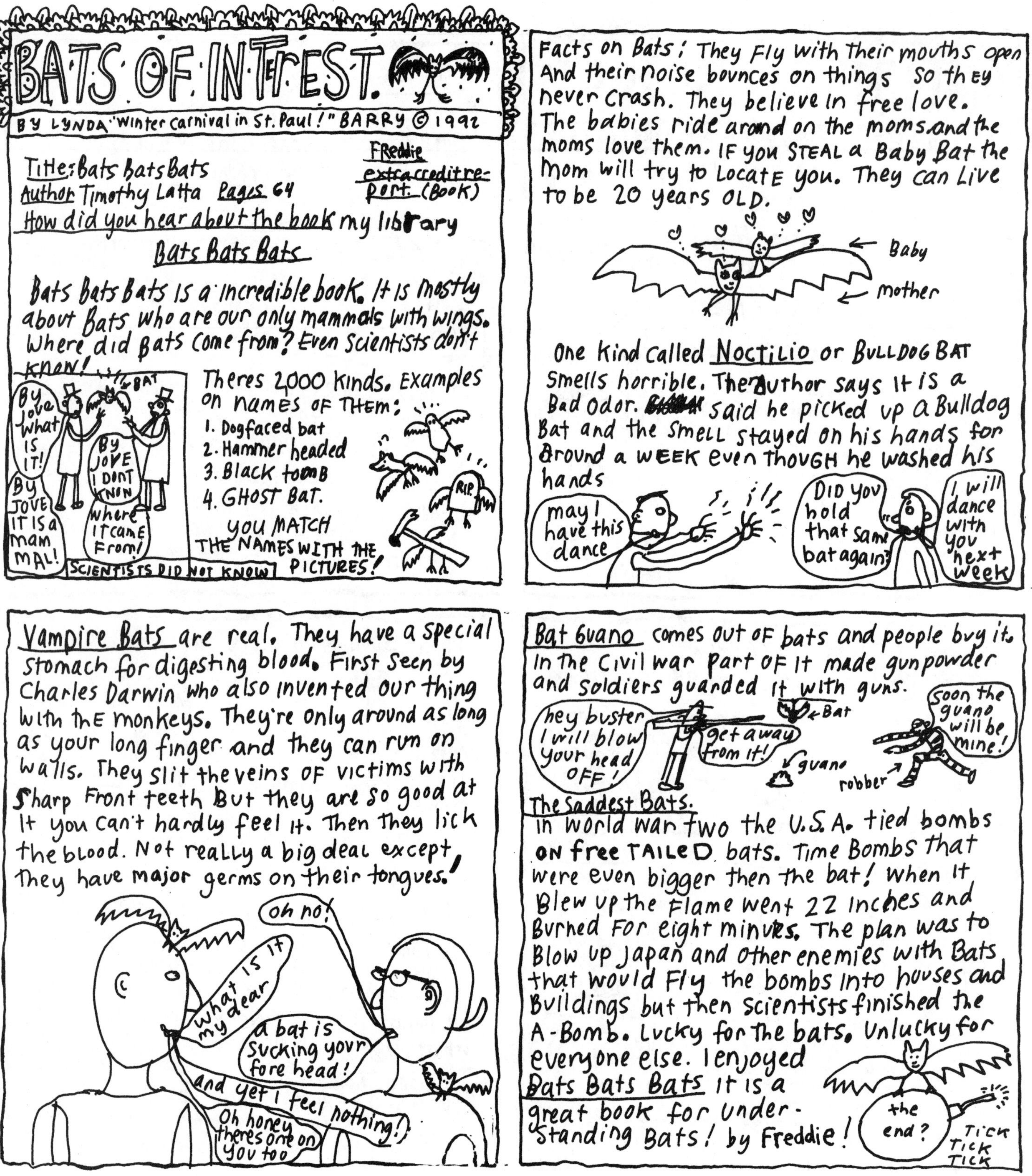
BATS OF INTEREST.
BY LYNDA "Winter carnival in St. Paul!" BARRY © 1992
Title: Bats Bats Bats
Author Timothy Latta Pages 64
Freddie extra credit report. (Book)
How did you hear about the book my library
Bats Bats Bats
Bats Bats Bats is a incredible book. It is mostly about Bats who are our only mammals with wings. Where did Bats come from? Even scientists don't know!
BAT
By Jove what is it!
By Jove I dont know where it came from!
By Jove it is a mam mal!
SCIENTISTS DID NOT KNOW
Theres 2000 kinds. Examples on names of them:
1. Dogfaced bat
2. Hammer headed
3. Black toomb
4. GHOST BAT.
YOU MATCH THE NAMES WITH THE PICTURES!
R.I.P.
Facts on Bats; They fly with their mouths open And their noise bounces on things so they never crash. They believe in free love. The babies ride around on the moms and the moms love them. If you steal a Baby Bat the mom will try to locate you. They can live to be 20 years OLD.
Baby
mother
One kind called NOCTILIO or BULLDOG BAT smells horrible. The author says it is a Bad odor. [redacted] said he picked up a Bulldog Bat and the smell stayed on his hands for around a WEEK even though he washed his hands
may I have this dance
DID you hold that same bat again?
I will dance with you next week
Vampire Bats are real. They have a special stomach for digesting blood. First seen by Charles Darwin who also invented our thing with the monkeys. They're only around as long as your long finger and they can run on walls. They slit the veins of victims with sharp front teeth But they are so good at it you can't hardly feel it. Then they lick the blood. Not really a big deal except, they have major germs on their tongues!
oh no!
what is it my dear
a bat is sucking your fore head!
and yet I feel nothing!
Oh honey theres one on you too
Bat Guano comes out of bats and people buy it. In the Civil war part of it made gunpowder and soldiers guarded it with guns.
hey buster I will blow your head OFF!
get away from it!
Bat
guano
Soon the guano will be mine!
robber
The Saddest Bats.
In World War two the U.S.A. tied bombs on free TAILED bats. Time Bombs that were even bigger then the bat! When it blew up the flame went 22 inches and burned for eight minutes. The plan was to blow up Japan and other enemies with Bats that would fly the bombs into houses and buildings but then scientists finished the A-Bomb. Lucky for the bats. Unlucky for everyone else. I enjoyed Bats Bats Bats It is a great book for under-standing Bats! by Freddie!
the end?
TICK TICK TICK

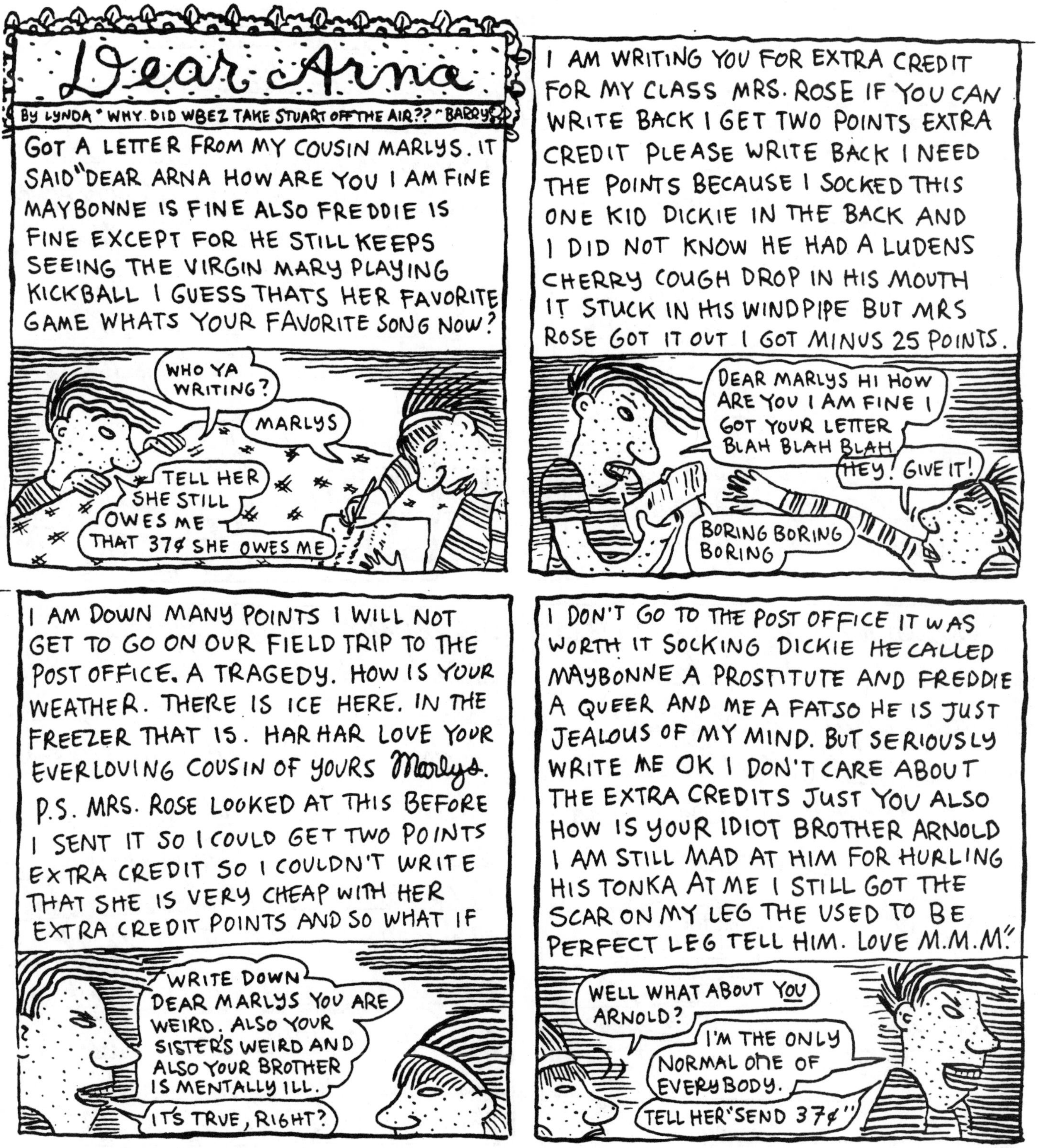

Dear Arna
BY LYNDA "WHY DID WBEZ TAKE STUART OFF THE AIR??" BARRY
GOT A LETTER FROM MY COUSIN MARLYS. IT SAID "DEAR ARNA HOW ARE YOU I AM FINE MAYBONNE IS FINE ALSO FREDDIE IS FINE EXCEPT FOR HE STILL KEEPS SEEING THE VIRGIN MARY PLAYING KICKBALL I GUESS THATS HER FAVORITE GAME WHATS YOUR FAVORITE SONG NOW?
WHO YA WRITING?
MARLYS
TELL HER SHE STILL OWES ME THAT 37¢ SHE OWES ME
I AM WRITING YOU FOR EXTRA CREDIT FOR MY CLASS MRS. ROSE IF YOU CAN WRITE BACK I GET TWO POINTS EXTRA CREDIT PLEASE WRITE BACK I NEED THE POINTS BECAUSE I SOCKED THIS ONE KID DICKIE IN THE BACK AND I DID NOT KNOW HE HAD A LUDENS CHERRY COUGH DROP IN HIS MOUTH IT STUCK IN HIS WINDPIPE BUT MRS ROSE GOT IT OUT I GOT MINUS 25 POINTS.
DEAR MARLYS HI HOW ARE YOU I AM FINE I GOT YOUR LETTER BLAH BLAH BLAH
HEY! GIVE IT!
BORING BORING BORING
I AM DOWN MANY POINTS I WILL NOT GET TO GO ON OUR FIELD TRIP TO THE POST OFFICE. A TRAGEDY. HOW IS YOUR WEATHER. THERE IS ICE HERE. IN THE FREEZER THAT IS. HAR HAR LOVE YOUR EVERLOVING COUSIN OF YOURS Marlys. P.S. MRS. ROSE LOOKED AT THIS BEFORE I SENT IT SO I COULD GET TWO POINTS EXTRA CREDIT SO I COULDN'T WRITE THAT SHE IS VERY CHEAP WITH HER EXTRA CREDIT POINTS AND SO WHAT IF
WRITE DOWN DEAR MARLYS YOU ARE WEIRD. ALSO YOUR SISTER'S WEIRD AND ALSO YOUR BROTHER IS MENTALLY ILL.
IT'S TRUE, RIGHT?
I DON'T GO TO THE POST OFFICE IT WAS WORTH IT SOCKING DICKIE HE CALLED MAYBONNE A PROSTITUTE AND FREDDIE A QUEER AND ME A FATSO HE IS JUST JEALOUS OF MY MIND. BUT SERIOUSLY WRITE ME OK I DON'T CARE ABOUT THE EXTRA CREDITS JUST YOU ALSO HOW IS YOUR IDIOT BROTHER ARNOLD I AM STILL MAD AT HIM FOR HURLING HIS TONKA AT ME I STILL GOT THE SCAR ON MY LEG THE USED TO BE PERFECT LEG TELL HIM. LOVE M.M.M."
WELL WHAT ABOUT YOU ARNOLD?
I'M THE ONLY NORMAL ONE OF EVERYBODY.
TELL HER "SEND 37¢"

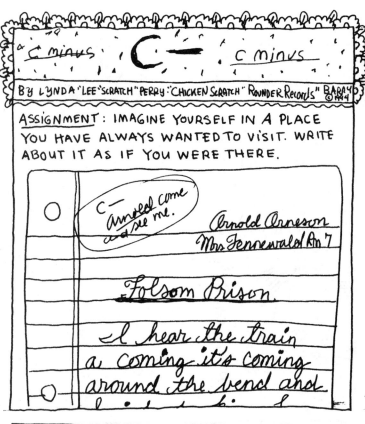

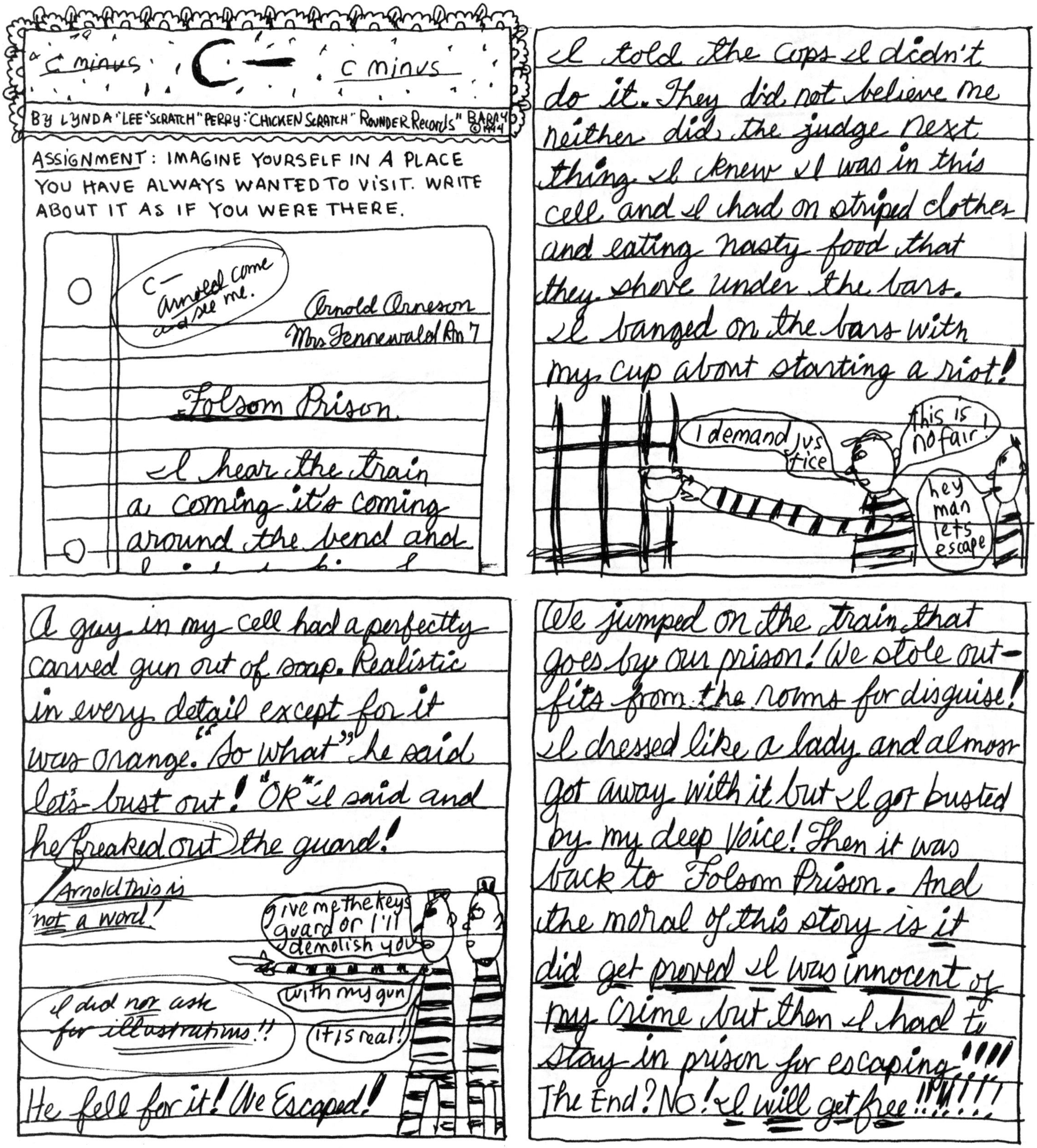

"c minus" C— c minus

BY LYNDA "LEE" "SCRATCH" PERRY "CHICKEN SCRATCH" ROUNDER RECORDS" BARRY © 1994

ASSIGNMENT: IMAGINE YOURSELF IN A PLACE YOU HAVE ALWAYS WANTED TO VISIT. WRITE ABOUT IT AS IF YOU WERE THERE.

C— Arnold come and see me.

Arnold Arneson
Mrs Fennewald Rm 7

Folsom Prison.

I hear the train a coming it's coming around the bend and

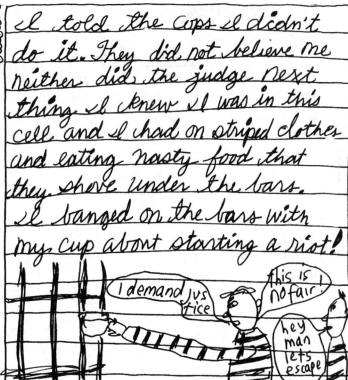

I told the cops I didn't do it. They did not believe me neither did the judge. Next thing I knew I was in this cell and I had on striped clothes and eating nasty food that they shove under the bars. I banged on the bars with my cup about starting a riot!

I demand jus tice

this is no fair!

hey man lets escape

A guy in my cell had a perfectly carved gun out of soap. Realistic in every detail except for it was orange. "So what" he said "lets bust out! "OK" I said and he freaked out the guard!

Arnold this is not a word!

Give me the keys guard or I'll demolish you

with my gun

It is real!

I did not ask for illustrations!!

He fell for it! We Escaped!

We jumped on the train that goes by our prison! We stole out-fits from the rooms for disguise! I dressed like a lady and almost got away with it but I got busted by my deep voice! Then it was back to Folsom Prison. And the moral of this story is it did get proved I was innocent of my crime but then I had to stay in prison for escaping!!! The End? No! I will get free!!!!!!

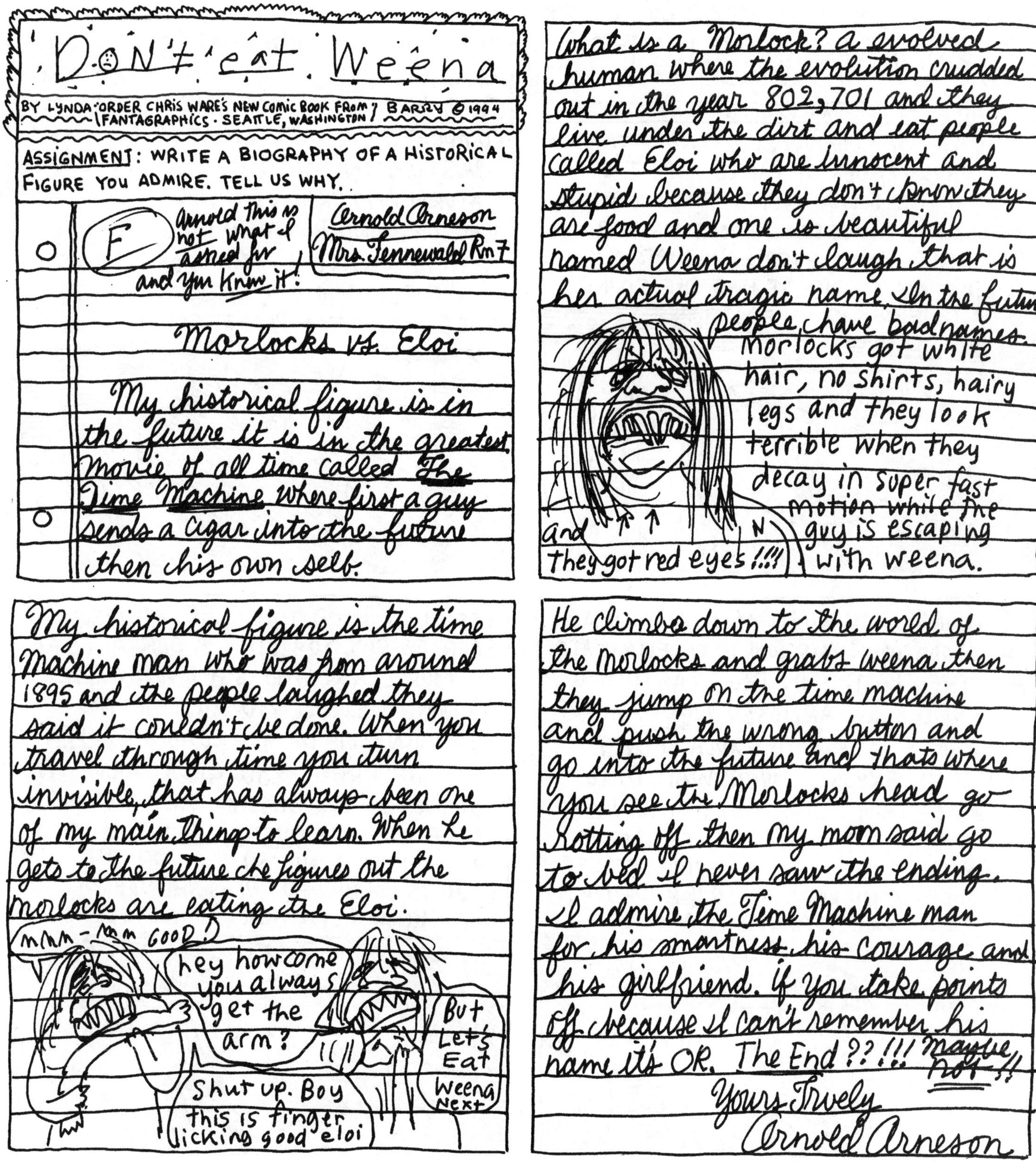

DON'T EAT WEENA

BY LYNDA ·ORDER CHRIS WARE'S NEW COMIC BOOK FROM BARRY ©1994 FANTAGRAPHICS · SEATTLE, WASHINGTON

ASSIGNMENT: WRITE A BIOGRAPHY OF A HISTORICAL FIGURE YOU ADMIRE. TELL US WHY.

F — Arnold this is not what I asked for and you know it!

Arnold Arneson
Mrs. Tennewabel Rm 7

Morlocks vs. Eloi

My historical figure is in the future it is in the greatest movie of all time called The Time Machine where first a guy sends a cigar into the future then his own self.

What is a Morlock? a evolved human where the evolution crudded out in the year 802,701 and they live under the dirt and eat people called Eloi who are innocent and stupid because they don't know they are food and one is beautiful named Weena don't laugh that is her actual tragic name. In the future people have bad names. Morlocks got white hair, no shirts, hairy legs and they look terrible when they decay in super fast motion while the guy is escaping with weena.

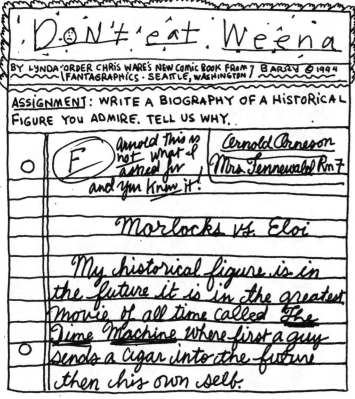

and they got red eyes!!!!

My historical figure is the time machine man who was from around 1895 and the people laughed they said it couldn't be done. When you travel through time you turn invisible, that has always been one of my main thing to learn. When he gets to the future he figures out the morlocks are eating the Eloi. (mmm-mmm GOOD!)

hey how come you always get the arm?

But Let's Eat Weena Next

Shut up. Boy this is finger licking good eloi

He climbs down to the world of the Morlocks and grabs weena then they jump on the time machine and push the wrong button and go into the future and thats where you see the Morlocks head go Rotting off. then my mom said go to bed I never saw the ending. I admire the Time Machine man for his smartness, his courage and his girlfriend. If you take points off because I can't remember his name its OK. The End ??!!! maybe not !!

Yours Truely
Arnold Arneson

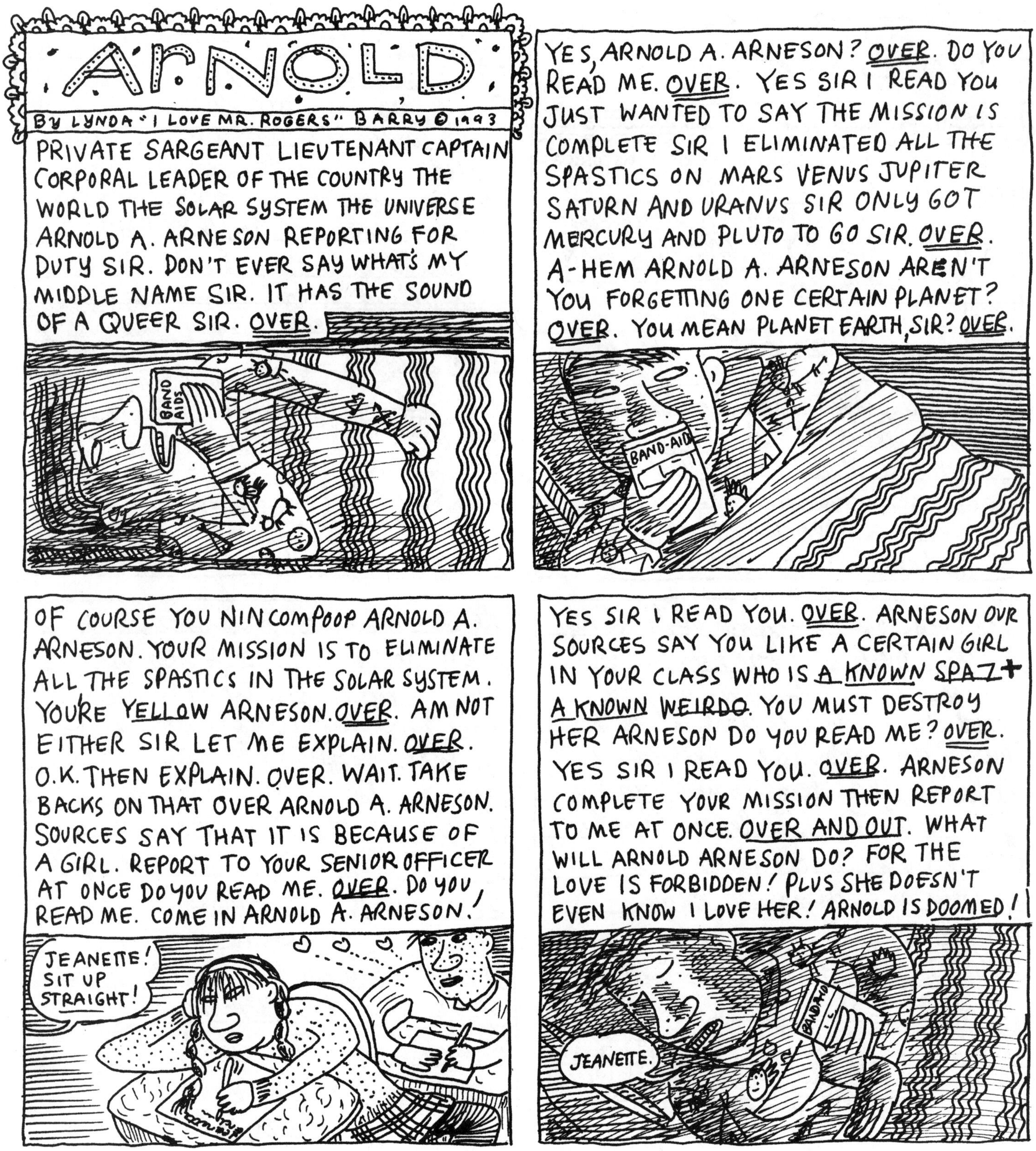

ARNOLD
BY LYNDA "I LOVE MR. ROGERS" BARRY © 1993
PRIVATE SARGEANT LIEUTENANT CAPTAIN CORPORAL LEADER OF THE COUNTRY THE WORLD THE SOLAR SYSTEM THE UNIVERSE ARNOLD A. ARNESON REPORTING FOR DUTY SIR. DON'T EVER SAY WHAT'S MY MIDDLE NAME SIR. IT HAS THE SOUND OF A QUEER SIR. OVER.
BAND AIDS
YES, ARNOLD A. ARNESON? OVER. DO YOU READ ME. OVER. YES SIR I READ YOU JUST WANTED TO SAY THE MISSION IS COMPLETE SIR I ELIMINATED ALL THE SPASTICS ON MARS VENUS JUPITER SATURN AND URANUS SIR ONLY GOT MERCURY AND PLUTO TO GO SIR. OVER. A-HEM ARNOLD A. ARNESON AREN'T YOU FORGETTING ONE CERTAIN PLANET? OVER. YOU MEAN PLANET EARTH, SIR? OVER.
BAND-AID
OF COURSE YOU NINCOMPOOP ARNOLD A. ARNESON. YOUR MISSION IS TO ELIMINATE ALL THE SPASTICS IN THE SOLAR SYSTEM. YOU'RE YELLOW ARNESON. OVER. AM NOT EITHER SIR LET ME EXPLAIN. OVER. O.K. THEN EXPLAIN. OVER. WAIT. TAKE BACKS ON THAT OVER ARNOLD A. ARNESON. SOURCES SAY THAT IT IS BECAUSE OF A GIRL. REPORT TO YOUR SENIOR OFFICER AT ONCE DO YOU READ ME. OVER. DO YOU READ ME. COME IN ARNOLD A. ARNESON!
JEANETTE! SIT UP STRAIGHT!
YES SIR I READ YOU. OVER. ARNESON OUR SOURCES SAY YOU LIKE A CERTAIN GIRL IN YOUR CLASS WHO IS A KNOWN SPAZ + A KNOWN WEIRDO. YOU MUST DESTROY HER ARNESON DO YOU READ ME? OVER. YES SIR I READ YOU. OVER. ARNESON COMPLETE YOUR MISSION THEN REPORT TO ME AT ONCE. OVER AND OUT. WHAT WILL ARNOLD ARNESON DO? FOR THE LOVE IS FORBIDDEN! PLUS SHE DOESN'T EVEN KNOW I LOVE HER! ARNOLD IS DOOMED!
JEANETTE.
BAND AID

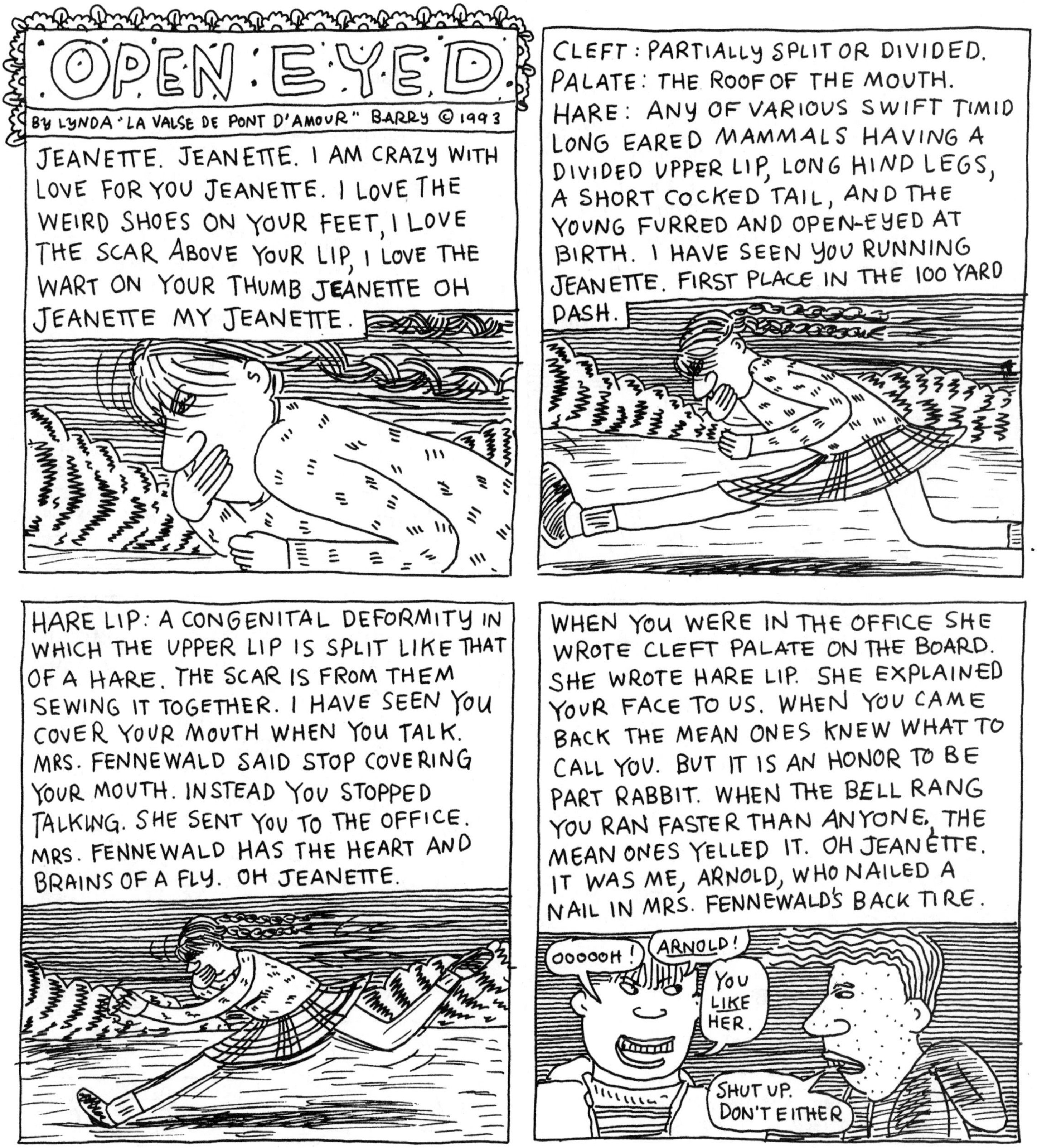
OPEN EYED
BY LYNDA "LA VALSE DE PONT D'AMOUR" BARRY © 1993
JEANETTE. JEANETTE. I AM CRAZY WITH LOVE FOR YOU JEANETTE. I LOVE THE WEIRD SHOES ON YOUR FEET, I LOVE THE SCAR ABOVE YOUR LIP, I LOVE THE WART ON YOUR THUMB JEANETTE OH JEANETTE MY JEANETTE.
CLEFT: PARTIALLY SPLIT OR DIVIDED. PALATE: THE ROOF OF THE MOUTH. HARE: ANY OF VARIOUS SWIFT TIMID LONG EARED MAMMALS HAVING A DIVIDED UPPER LIP, LONG HIND LEGS, A SHORT COCKED TAIL, AND THE YOUNG FURRED AND OPEN-EYED AT BIRTH. I HAVE SEEN YOU RUNNING JEANETTE. FIRST PLACE IN THE 100 YARD DASH.
HARE LIP: A CONGENITAL DEFORMITY IN WHICH THE UPPER LIP IS SPLIT LIKE THAT OF A HARE. THE SCAR IS FROM THEM SEWING IT TOGETHER. I HAVE SEEN YOU COVER YOUR MOUTH WHEN YOU TALK. MRS. FENNEWALD SAID STOP COVERING YOUR MOUTH. INSTEAD YOU STOPPED TALKING. SHE SENT YOU TO THE OFFICE. MRS. FENNEWALD HAS THE HEART AND BRAINS OF A FLY. OH JEANETTE.
WHEN YOU WERE IN THE OFFICE SHE WROTE CLEFT PALATE ON THE BOARD. SHE WROTE HARE LIP. SHE EXPLAINED YOUR FACE TO US. WHEN YOU CAME BACK THE MEAN ONES KNEW WHAT TO CALL YOU. BUT IT IS AN HONOR TO BE PART RABBIT. WHEN THE BELL RANG YOU RAN FASTER THAN ANYONE, THE MEAN ONES YELLED IT. OH JEANETTE. IT WAS ME, ARNOLD, WHO NAILED A NAIL IN MRS. FENNEWALD'S BACK TIRE.
OOOOOH!
ARNOLD!
YOU LIKE HER.
SHUT UP. DON'T EITHER

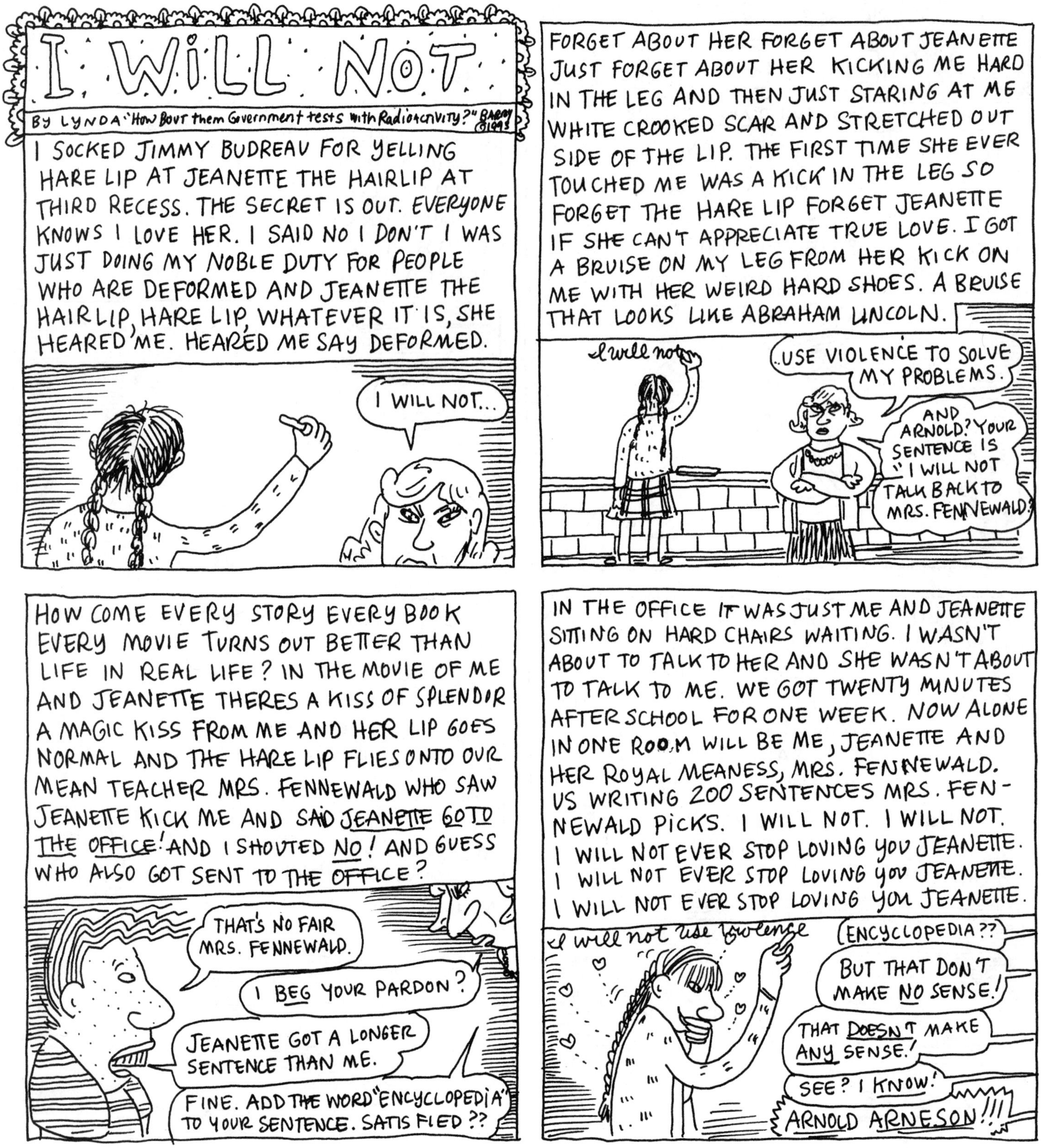
I WILL NOT
BY LYNDA "How Bout them Government tests with Radioactivity?" BARRY ©1993
I SOCKED JIMMY BUDREAU FOR YELLING HARE LIP AT JEANETTE THE HAIRLIP AT THIRD RECESS. THE SECRET IS OUT. EVERYONE KNOWS I LOVE HER. I SAID NO I DON'T I WAS JUST DOING MY NOBLE DUTY FOR PEOPLE WHO ARE DEFORMED AND JEANETTE THE HAIRLIP, HARE LIP, WHATEVER IT IS, SHE HEARED ME. HEARED ME SAY DEFORMED.
I WILL NOT...
FORGET ABOUT HER FORGET ABOUT JEANETTE JUST FORGET ABOUT HER KICKING ME HARD IN THE LEG AND THEN JUST STARING AT ME WHITE CROOKED SCAR AND STRETCHED OUT SIDE OF THE LIP. THE FIRST TIME SHE EVER TOUCHED ME WAS A KICK IN THE LEG SO FORGET THE HARE LIP FORGET JEANETTE IF SHE CAN'T APPRECIATE TRUE LOVE. I GOT A BRUISE ON MY LEG FROM HER KICK ON ME WITH HER WEIRD HARD SHOES. A BRUISE THAT LOOKS LIKE ABRAHAM LINCOLN.
I will not
..USE VIOLENCE TO SOLVE MY PROBLEMS.
AND ARNOLD? YOUR SENTENCE IS "I WILL NOT TALK BACK TO MRS. FENNEWALD."
HOW COME EVERY STORY EVERY BOOK EVERY MOVIE TURNS OUT BETTER THAN LIFE IN REAL LIFE? IN THE MOVIE OF ME AND JEANETTE THERES A KISS OF SPLENDOR A MAGIC KISS FROM ME AND HER LIP GOES NORMAL AND THE HARE LIP FLIES ONTO OUR MEAN TEACHER MRS. FENNEWALD WHO SAW JEANETTE KICK ME AND SAID JEANETTE GO TO THE OFFICE! AND I SHOUTED NO! AND GUESS WHO ALSO GOT SENT TO THE OFFICE?
THAT'S NO FAIR MRS. FENNEWALD.
I BEG YOUR PARDON?
JEANETTE GOT A LONGER SENTENCE THAN ME.
FINE. ADD THE WORD "ENCYCLOPEDIA" TO YOUR SENTENCE. SATISFIED??
IN THE OFFICE IT WAS JUST ME AND JEANETTE SITTING ON HARD CHAIRS WAITING. I WASN'T ABOUT TO TALK TO HER AND SHE WASN'T ABOUT TO TALK TO ME. WE GOT TWENTY MINUTES AFTER SCHOOL FOR ONE WEEK. NOW ALONE IN ONE ROOM WILL BE ME, JEANETTE AND HER ROYAL MEANESS, MRS. FENNEWALD. US WRITING 200 SENTENCES MRS. FENNEWALD PICKS. I WILL NOT. I WILL NOT. I WILL NOT EVER STOP LOVING YOU JEANETTE. I WILL NOT EVER STOP LOVING YOU JEANETTE. I WILL NOT EVER STOP LOVING YOU JEANETTE.
I will not use violence
(ENCYCLOPEDIA??
BUT THAT DON'T MAKE NO SENSE!
THAT DOESN'T MAKE ANY SENSE!
SEE? I KNOW!
ARNOLD ARNESON!!!

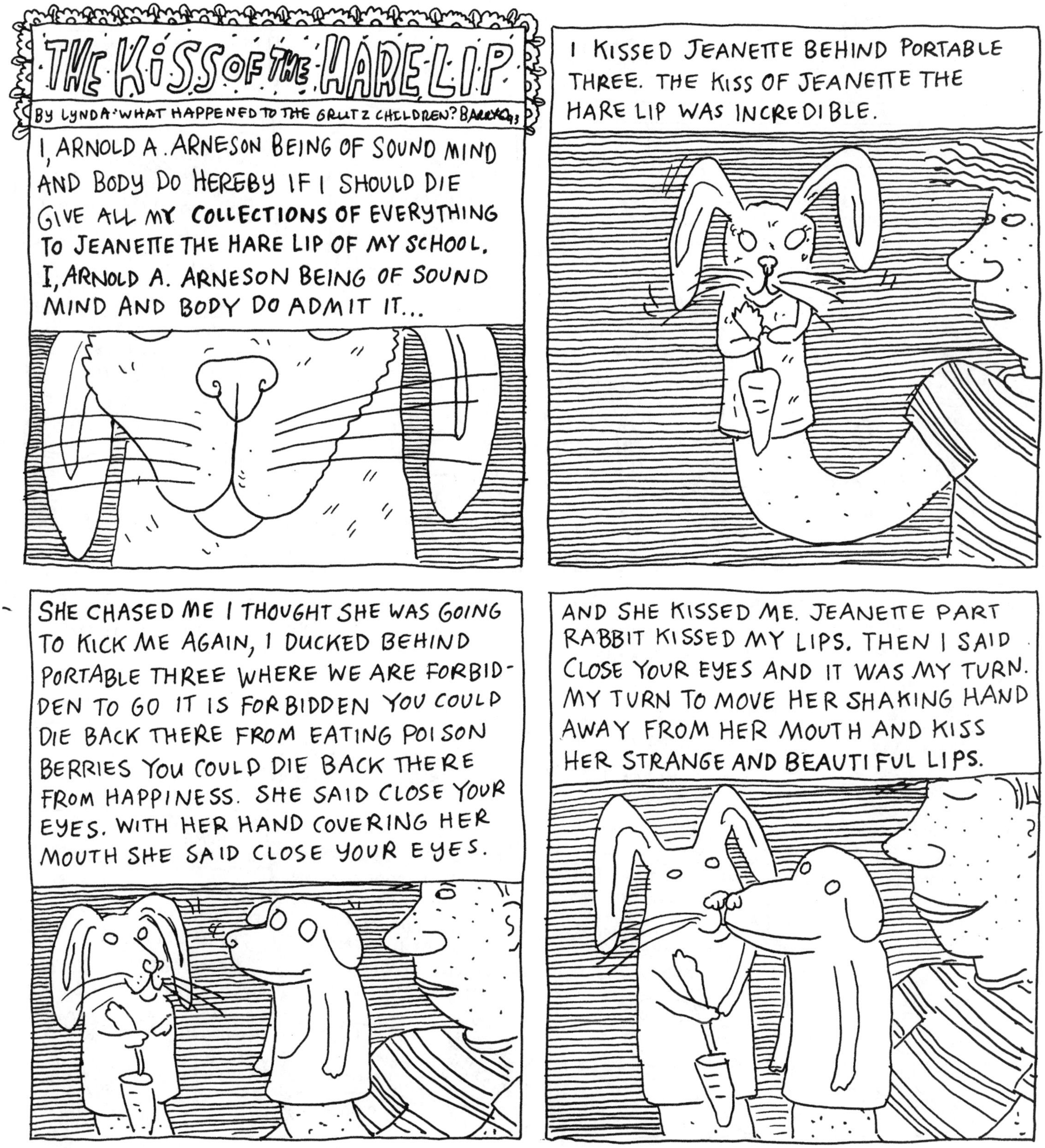
THE KISS OF THE HARE LIP
BY LYNDA 'WHAT HAPPENED TO THE GRUTZ CHILDREN?' BARRY ©93
I, ARNOLD A. ARNESON BEING OF SOUND MIND AND BODY DO HEREBY IF I SHOULD DIE GIVE ALL MY COLLECTIONS OF EVERYTHING TO JEANETTE THE HARE LIP OF MY SCHOOL. I, ARNOLD A. ARNESON BEING OF SOUND MIND AND BODY DO ADMIT IT...
I KISSED JEANETTE BEHIND PORTABLE THREE. THE KISS OF JEANETTE THE HARE LIP WAS INCREDIBLE.
SHE CHASED ME I THOUGHT SHE WAS GOING TO KICK ME AGAIN, I DUCKED BEHIND PORTABLE THREE WHERE WE ARE FORBIDDEN TO GO IT IS FORBIDDEN YOU COULD DIE BACK THERE FROM EATING POISON BERRIES YOU COULD DIE BACK THERE FROM HAPPINESS. SHE SAID CLOSE YOUR EYES. WITH HER HAND COVERING HER MOUTH SHE SAID CLOSE YOUR EYES.
AND SHE KISSED ME. JEANETTE PART RABBIT KISSED MY LIPS. THEN I SAID CLOSE YOUR EYES AND IT WAS MY TURN. MY TURN TO MOVE HER SHAKING HAND AWAY FROM HER MOUTH AND KISS HER STRANGE AND BEAUTIFUL LIPS.

VERY SUPERSTITIONS!

BY LYNDA "HANDGUN HELL" BARRY © 1993

By the Great MARLYS!! IF YOU Don't already got enough Superstitions here are some actual ones you can use!! By Marlys!

LICK A JUJUBEE AND CRAM IT AGAINST YOUR FOREHEAD UNTIL IT STICKS. SAY THE ALPABET KIND OF FAST

A B C D E F G H I J K L M N O P Q R K

THE LETTER IT FALLS OFF ON STARTS THE NAME OF YOUR TRUE LOVE

BLUE BEADS PREVENT COLDS

SPILLING THE MILK OUT OF YOUR CEREAL BOWL ONTO A SHAG CARPET MEANS

UH OH

MARLYS!

THERE WILL BE A QUARREL VERY SOON!

IT IS BAD LUCK TO EAT PASTE ON WEDNESDAYS

BUT IT'S THE MINT KIND

NOT TODAY, THANK YOU

IF A BEE COMES INTO YOUR CLASS IT MEANS PRETTY SOON YOU'LL HAVE A SUBSTITUTE TEACHER

HELLO

I'M MRS. PINK-BOTTOM

WHAT IS SO FUNNY, CLASS?

MEMORIZE THIS POEM "CATS ON ITS BRAIN IT'S GOING TO RAIN"

SAY IT WHEN YOU SEE A CAT SLEEPING LIKE THAT AND IT WILL COME TRUE!! POSSIBLY!!

FOR THE BEST LUCK FROM A CHAIN LETTER just send it to the president!

OH GOD NOT ANOTHER ONE!

MORE MAIL SIR

MORE DAMN CHAIN LETTERS

TOUCH EACH BUTTON ON A NEW DRESS SAYING "LADY, BABY, HIPPY, QUEEN, ELEPHANT, MONKEY, TANGERINE" TO FIND OUT WHICH ONE YOU ARE!

YEY!

YEY! I'M A HIPPY!

You YANKED THEM OTHER TWO BUTTONS OFF MARLYS I SAW YOU.

ALL RIGHT MAN!

SO? SHUT UP TANGERINO!

TO GET WARTS, WRITE DOWN HOW MANY YOU WANT ON A LEAF AND DROP IT DOWN THE SEWER GRATE. THEN SIT BACK AND WAIT FOR THEM TO GROW!

WHAT BEAUTIFUL WARTS

THERE'S 18

BE MY LOVE!

IF YOU WANT TO GO BALD TIE DIRTY SOCKS TO YOUR HEAD

REALLY WORKS!!

OH JIM YOU ARE BALD!

THANKS TO MARLYS

BE MY LOVE!

A DOG STARING AT A PIECE OF BALONEY MEANS

A SURPRISE PARTY !!!!

A DEAD FLY ON A WINDOW SILL MEANS

YOU WILL SOON WALK ON FOREIGN SOIL!!

TO CURE HICCUPS SUCK ON A MILKDUD. WHEN HICCUPS STOP TAKE OUT MILKDUD AND LOOK AT IT BECAUSE THAT WILL BE THE SHAPE OF YOUR FUTURE HUS-BANDS HEAD.

OH NO I CHEWED MINE!

DO OVERS!

I HOPE YOU ENJOYED MY INCREDIBLE SUPERSTITIONS!

REMEMBER: IF YOUR NOSE ITCHES IT'S A SIGN OF ME THINKING LOVING THOUGHTS OF YOU!

Love, MARLYS!

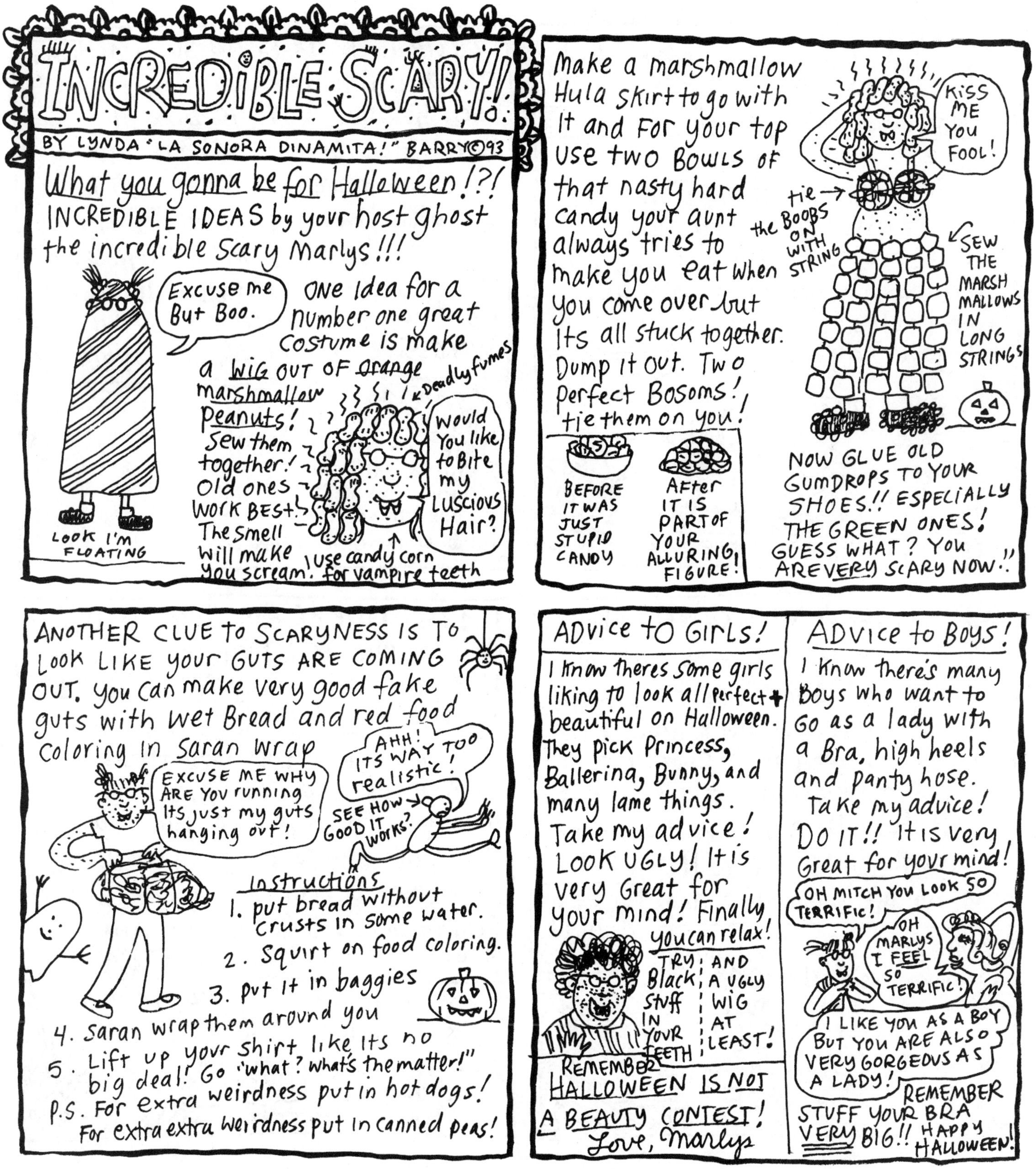
INCREDIBLE SCARY!
BY LYNDA "LA SONORA DINAMITA!" BARRY ©93
What you gonna be for Halloween!?! INCREDIBLE IDEAS by your host ghost the incredible Scary Marlys!!!
Excuse me But Boo.
LOOK I'M FLOATING
One idea for a number one great costume is make a WIG out of orange marshmallow peanuts! Sew them together! Old ones work best! The smell will make you scream!
Deadly fumes
Would you like to Bite my Luscious Hair?
Use candy corn for vampire teeth
Make a marshmallow Hula skirt to go with it and for your top use two Bowls of that nasty hard candy your aunt always tries to make you eat when you come over but its all stuck together. Dump it out. Two perfect Bosoms! tie them on you!
KISS ME YOU FOOL!
tie the BOOBS ON WITH STRING
SEW THE MARSH MALLOWS IN LONG STRINGS
BEFORE IT WAS JUST STUPID CANDY
AFTER IT IS PART OF YOUR ALLURING FIGURE!
NOW GLUE OLD GUMDROPS TO YOUR SHOES!! ESPECIALLY THE GREEN ONES! GUESS WHAT? YOU ARE VERY SCARY NOW!!
ANOTHER CLUE TO SCARYNESS IS TO LOOK LIKE YOUR GUTS ARE COMING OUT. You can make very good fake guts with wet Bread and red food coloring in Saran Wrap
EXCUSE ME WHY ARE YOU RUNNING ITS JUST MY GUTS HANGING OUT!
AHH! ITS WAY TOO realistic!
SEE HOW GOOD IT WORKS?
Instructions
1. put bread without crusts in some water.
2. Squirt on food coloring.
3. put it in baggies
4. Saran wrap them around you
5. Lift up your shirt like its no big deal! Go "what? what's the matter!"
P.S. For extra weirdness put in hot dogs! For extra extra weirdness put in canned peas!
ADVICE TO GIRLS!
I know theres some girls liking to look all perfect + beautiful on Halloween. They pick Princess, Ballerina, Bunny, and many lame things. Take my advice! LOOK UGLY! It is very Great for your mind! Finally you can relax!
TRY Black Stuff IN YOUR TEETH
AND A UGLY WIG AT LEAST!
REMEMBER HALLOWEEN IS NOT A BEAUTY CONTEST! Love, Marlys
ADVICE TO BOYS!
I know there's many Boys who want to Go as a lady with a Bra, high heels and panty hose. Take my advice! DO IT!! It is very Great for your mind!
OH MITCH YOU LOOK SO TERRIFIC!
OH MARLYS I FEEL SO TERRIFIC!
I LIKE YOU AS A BOY BUT YOU ARE ALSO VERY GORGEOUS AS A LADY!
REMEMBER STUFF YOUR BRA VERY BIG!! HAPPY HALLOWEEN!

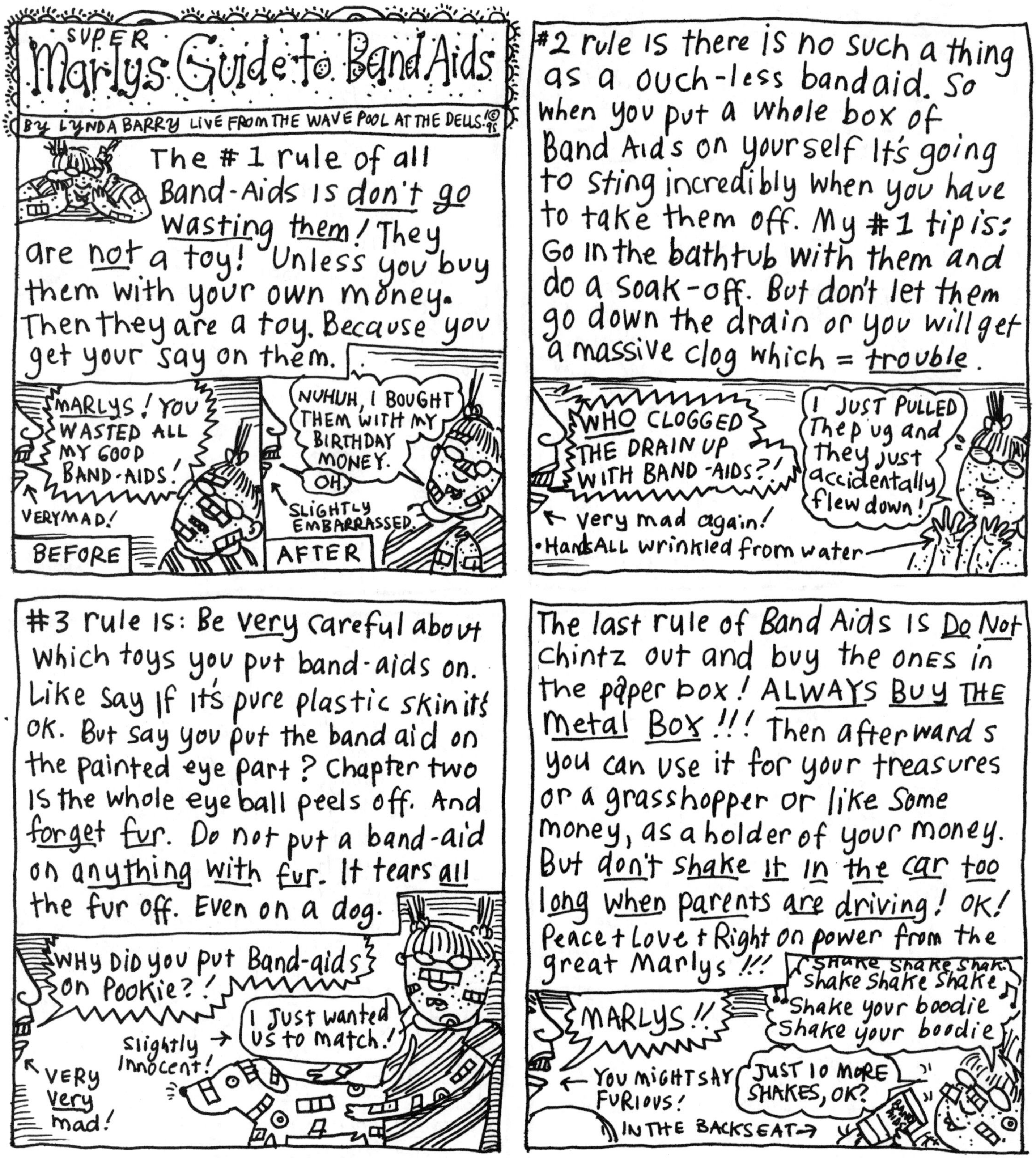
SUPER Marlys Guide to Band Aids
BY LYNDA BARRY LIVE FROM THE WAVE POOL AT THE DELLS ©95
The #1 rule of all Band-Aids is don't go wasting them! They are not a toy! Unless you buy them with your own money. Then they are a toy. Because you get your say on them.
MARLYS! YOU WASTED ALL MY GOOD BAND-AIDS!
VERY MAD!
BEFORE
NUHUH, I BOUGHT THEM WITH MY BIRTHDAY MONEY.
OH.
SLIGHTLY EMBARRASSED.
AFTER
#2 rule is there is no such a thing as a ouch-less bandaid. So when you put a whole box of Band Aids on yourself It's going to sting incredibly when you have to take them off. My #1 tip is: Go in the bathtub with them and do a soak-off. But don't let them go down the drain or you will get a massive clog which = trouble.
WHO CLOGGED THE DRAIN UP WITH BAND-AIDS?!
I JUST PULLED The plug and They just accidentally flew down!
very mad again!
•Hands ALL wrinkled from water
#3 rule is: Be very careful about which toys you put band-aids on. Like say if it's pure plastic skin it's OK. But say you put the band aid on the painted eye part? Chapter two is the whole eye ball peels off. And forget fur. Do not put a band-aid on anything with fur. It tears all the fur off. Even on a dog.
WHY DID you put Band-aids on Pookie?!
I Just wanted us to match!
slightly innocent!
VERY very mad!
The last rule of Band Aids is Do Not chintz out and buy the ones in the paper box! ALWAYS BUY THE Metal Box!!! Then afterwards you can use it for your treasures or a grasshopper or like some money, as a holder of your money. But don't shake it in the car too long when parents are driving! OK! Peace + Love + Right on power from the great Marlys!!!
Shake shake shake shake shake shake Shake your boodie Shake your boodie
MARLYS!!
YOU MIGHT SAY FURIOUS!
JUST 10 MORE SHAKES, OK?
IN THE BACKSEAT

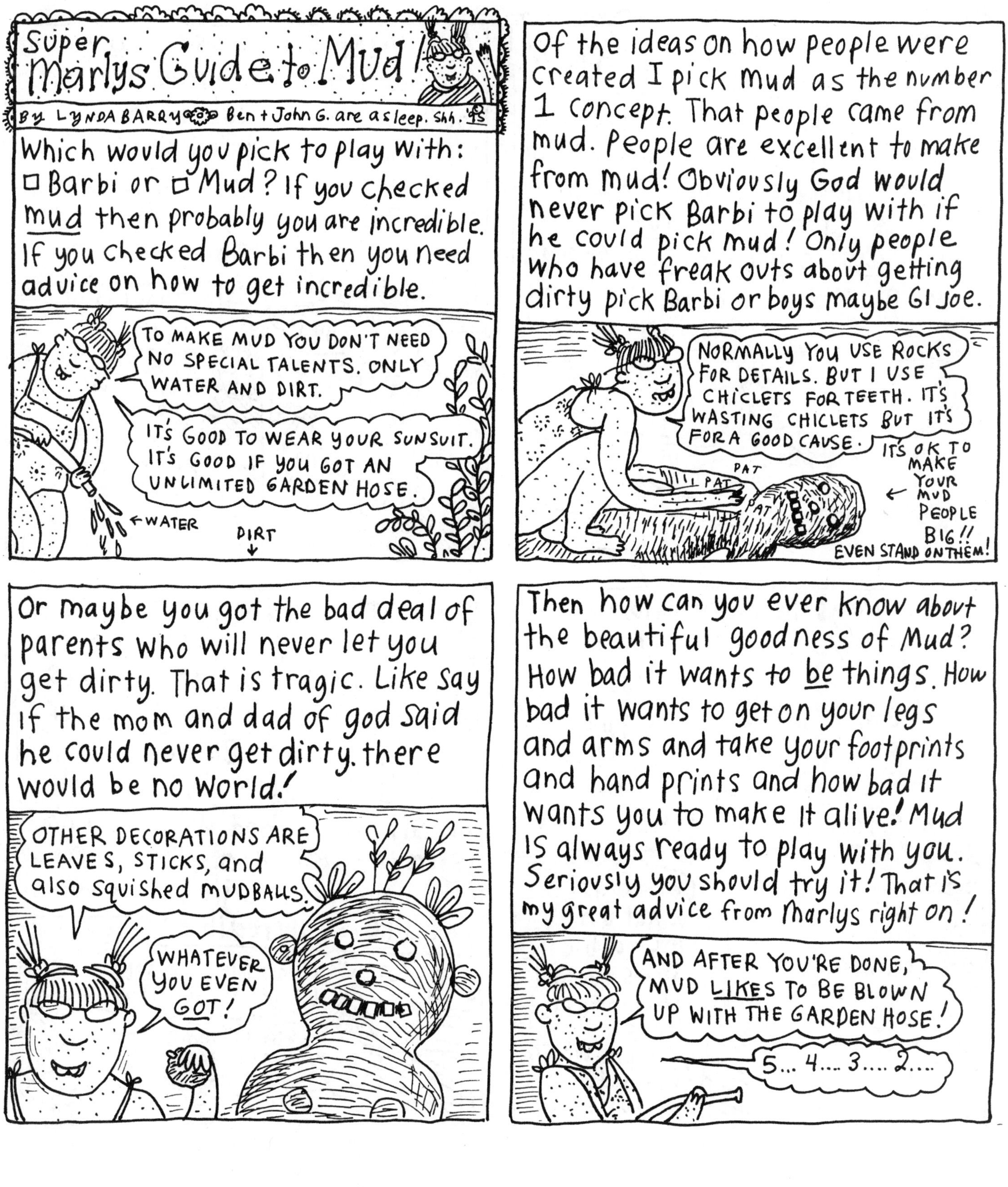

Super Marlys Guide to Mud!
By LYNDA BARRY Ben + John G. are asleep. Shh. '95
Which would you pick to play with: □ Barbi or □ Mud? If you checked mud then probably you are incredible. If you checked Barbi then you need advice on how to get incredible.
TO MAKE MUD YOU DON'T NEED NO SPECIAL TALENTS. ONLY WATER AND DIRT.
IT'S GOOD TO WEAR YOUR SUNSUIT. IT'S GOOD IF YOU GOT AN UNLIMITED GARDEN HOSE.
←WATER
DIRT ↓
Of the ideas on how people were created I pick mud as the number 1 concept. That people came from mud. People are excellent to make from mud! Obviously God would never pick Barbi to play with if he could pick mud! Only people who have freak outs about getting dirty pick Barbi or boys maybe GI Joe.
NORMALLY YOU USE ROCKS FOR DETAILS. BUT I USE CHICLETS FOR TEETH. IT'S WASTING CHICLETS BUT IT'S FOR A GOOD CAUSE.
PAT
PAT
PAT
IT'S OK TO MAKE YOUR MUD PEOPLE BIG!! ←
EVEN STAND ON THEM!
Or maybe you got the bad deal of parents who will never let you get dirty. That is tragic. Like say if the mom and dad of god said he could never get dirty. there would be no world!
OTHER DECORATIONS ARE LEAVES, STICKS, and also squished MUDBALLS.
WHATEVER YOU EVEN GOT!
Then how can you ever know about the beautiful goodness of Mud? How bad it wants to be things. How bad it wants to get on your legs and arms and take your footprints and hand prints and how bad it wants you to make it alive! Mud is always ready to play with you. Seriously you should try it! That is my great advice from Marlys right on!
AND AFTER YOU'RE DONE, MUD LIKES TO BE BLOWN UP WITH THE GARDEN HOSE!
5... 4.... 3.... 2....

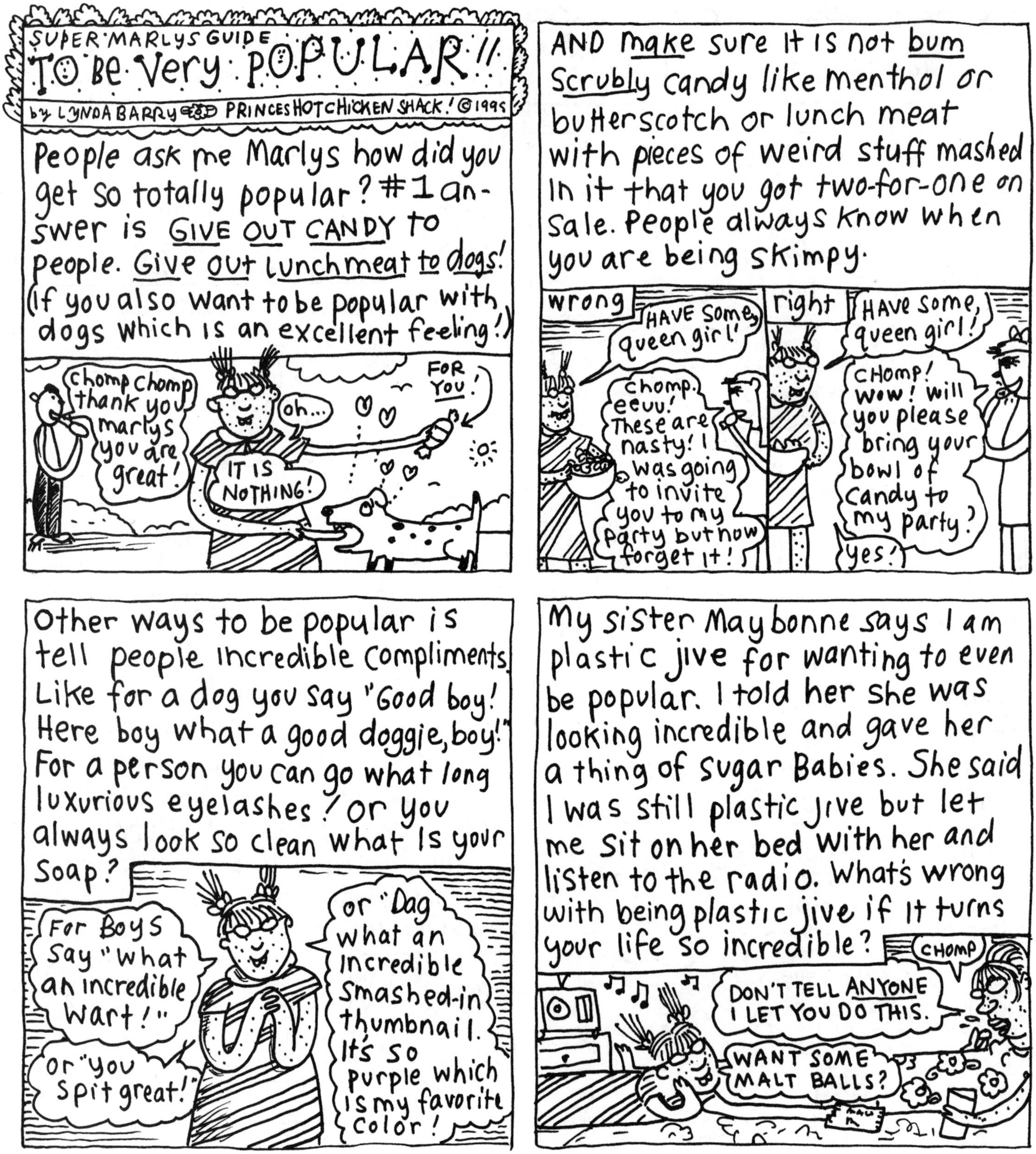
SUPER MARLYS GUIDE
TO BE VERY POPULAR!!
by LYNDA BARRY PRINCES HOT CHICKEN SHACK! ©1995
People ask me Marlys how did you get so totally popular? #1 answer is GIVE OUT CANDY to people. Give out lunchmeat to dogs! (If you also want to be popular with dogs which is an excellent feeling!)
chomp chomp thank you marlys you are great!
oh...
FOR YOU!
IT IS NOTHING!
AND make sure it is not bum Scrubly candy like menthol or butterscotch or lunch meat with pieces of weird stuff mashed in it that you got two-for-one on sale. People always know when you are being skimpy.
wrong
HAVE Some, queen girl!
chomp. eeuu! These are nasty! I was going to invite you to my party but now forget it!
right
HAVE Some, queen girl!
CHOMP! WOW! will you please bring your bowl of candy to my party?
yes!
Other ways to be popular is tell people incredible compliments. Like for a dog you say "Good boy! Here boy what a good doggie, boy!" For a person you can go what long luxurious eyelashes! or you always look so clean what is your soap?
For Boys say "what an incredible wart!"
or "you spit great!"
or "Dag what an incredible smashed-in thumbnail. It's so purple which is my favorite color!
My sister Maybonne says I am plastic jive for wanting to even be popular. I told her she was looking incredible and gave her a thing of Sugar Babies. She said I was still plastic jive but let me sit on her bed with her and listen to the radio. What's wrong with being plastic jive if it turns your life so incredible?
CHOMP
DON'T TELL ANYONE I LET YOU DO THIS.
WANT SOME MALT BALLS?

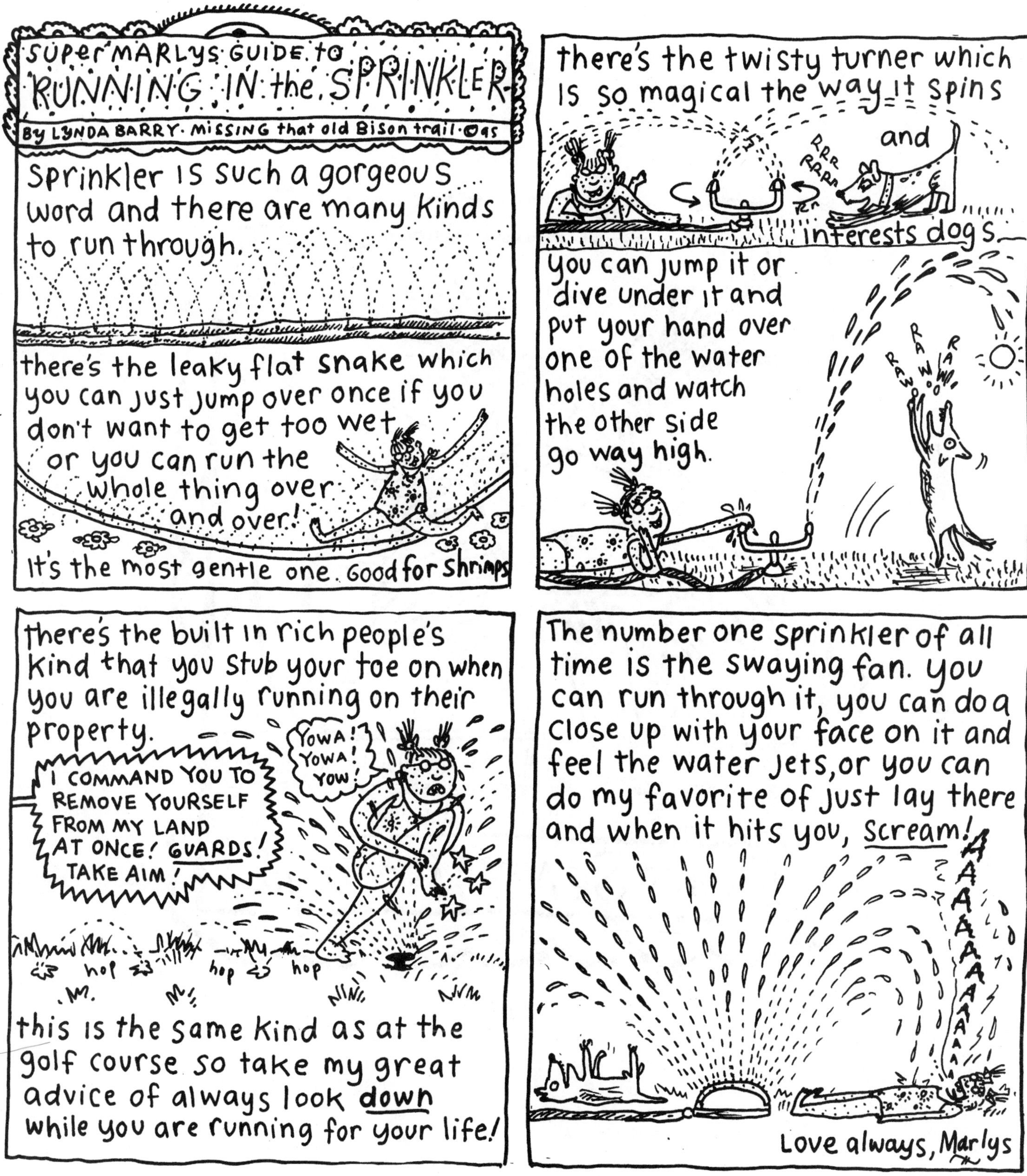
SUPER MARLYS GUIDE TO
RUNNING IN the SPRINKLER
BY LYNDA BARRY · MISSING that old Bison trail · ©95
Sprinkler is such a gorgeous word and there are many kinds to run through.
there's the leaky flat snake which you can just jump over once if you don't want to get too wet
or you can run the whole thing over and over!
It's the most gentle one. Good for Shrimps
there's the twisty turner which is so magical the way it spins
and
RRR RRRR
interests dogs.
you can jump it or dive under it and put your hand over one of the water holes and watch the other side go way high.
RAW RAW
there's the built in rich people's kind that you stub your toe on when you are illegally running on their property.
I COMMAND YOU TO REMOVE YOURSELF FROM MY LAND AT ONCE! GUARDS! TAKE AIM!
YOWA! YOWA! YOW!
hop hop hop
this is the same kind as at the golf course so take my great advice of always look down while you are running for your life!
The number one sprinkler of all time is the swaying fan. You can run through it, you can do a close up with your face on it and feel the water jets, or you can do my favorite of just lay there and when it hits you, scream!
AAAAAAAAAAAA
Love always, Marlys

FRONT SEAT Marlys !

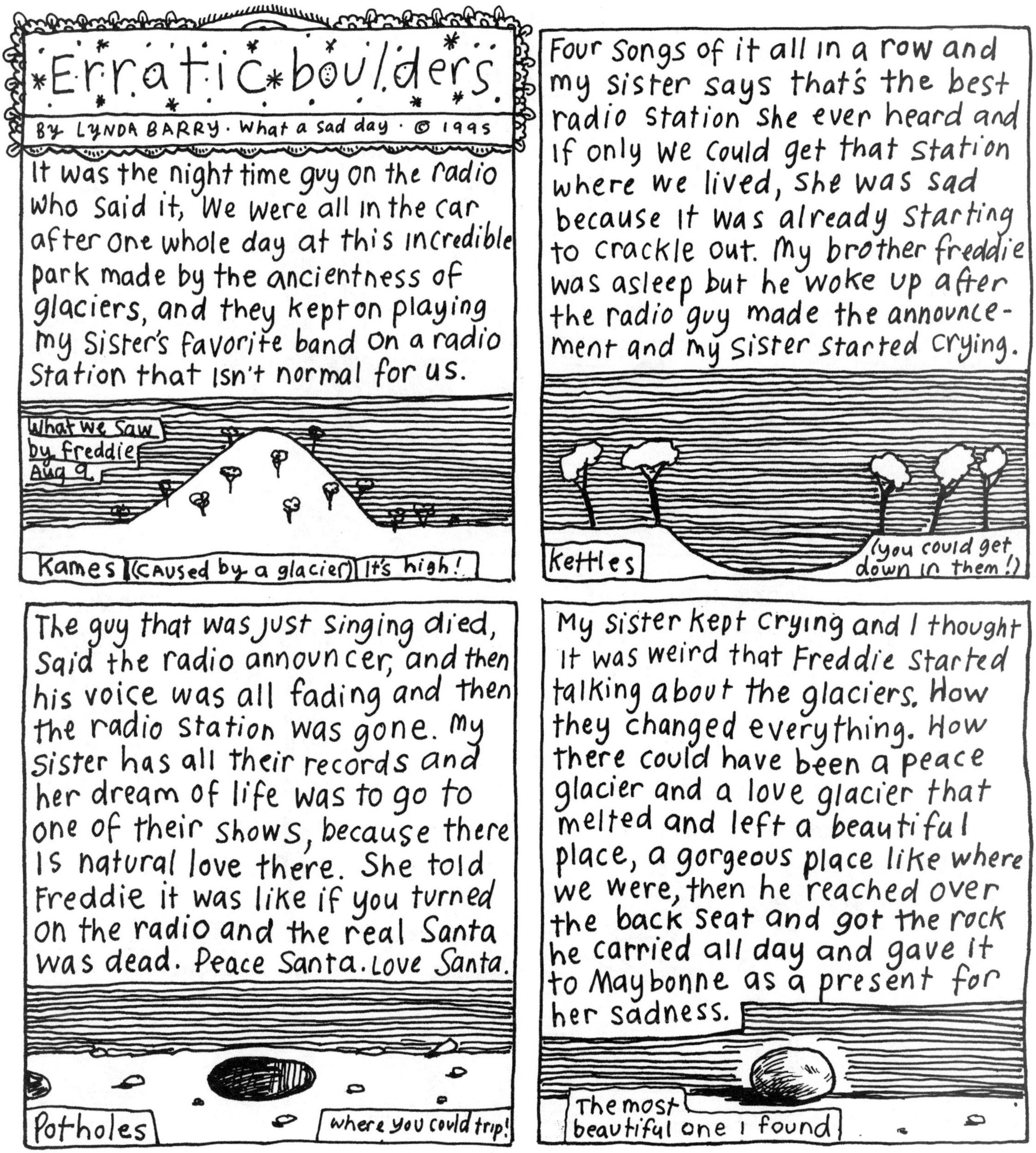
Erratic boulders
By LYNDA BARRY · What a sad day · © 1995
It was the night time guy on the radio who said it, We were all in the car after one whole day at this incredible park made by the ancientness of glaciers, and they kept on playing my sister's favorite band on a radio station that isn't normal for us.
What we saw by freddie Aug 9.
Kames
(caused by a glacier)
It's high!
Four songs of it all in a row and my sister says that's the best radio station she ever heard and if only we could get that station where we lived, she was sad because it was already starting to crackle out. My brother freddie was asleep but he woke up after the radio guy made the announcement and my sister started crying.
Kettles
(you could get down in them!)
The guy that was just singing died, said the radio announcer, and then his voice was all fading and then the radio station was gone. My sister has all their records and her dream of life was to go to one of their shows, because there is natural love there. She told Freddie it was like if you turned on the radio and the real Santa was dead. Peace Santa. Love Santa.
Potholes
where you could trip!
My sister kept crying and I thought it was weird that Freddie started talking about the glaciers. How they changed everything. How there could have been a peace glacier and a love glacier that melted and left a beautiful place, a gorgeous place like where we were, then he reached over the back seat and got the rock he carried all day and gave it to Maybonne as a present for her sadness.
The most beautiful one I found

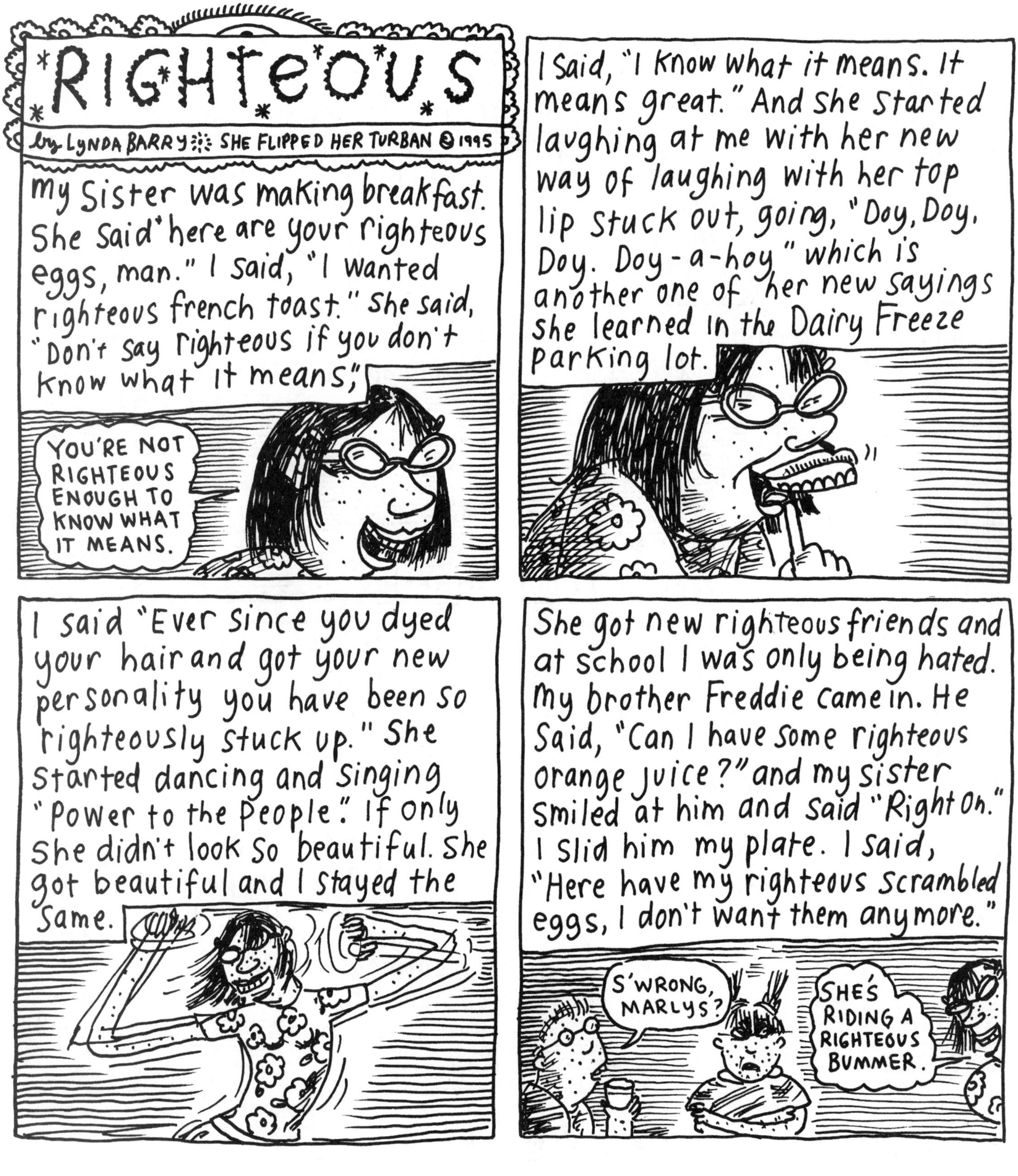
RIGHTEOUS
by LYNDA BARRY SHE FLIPPED HER TURBAN © 1995
My sister was making breakfast. She said "here are your righteous eggs, man." I said, "I wanted righteous french toast." She said, "Don't say righteous if you don't know what it means."
YOU'RE NOT RIGHTEOUS ENOUGH TO KNOW WHAT IT MEANS.
I said, "I know what it means. It means great." And she started laughing at me with her new way of laughing with her top lip stuck out, going, "Doy, Doy, Doy. Doy-a-hoy" which is another one of her new sayings she learned in the Dairy Freeze parking lot.
I said "Ever since you dyed your hair and got your new personality you have been so righteously stuck up." She started dancing and singing "Power to the People." If only she didn't look so beautiful. She got beautiful and I stayed the same.
She got new righteous friends and at school I was only being hated. My brother Freddie came in. He said, "Can I have some righteous orange juice?" and my sister smiled at him and said "Right On." I slid him my plate. I said, "Here have my righteous scrambled eggs, I don't want them anymore."
S'WRONG, MARLYS?
SHE'S RIDING A RIGHTEOUS BUMMER.

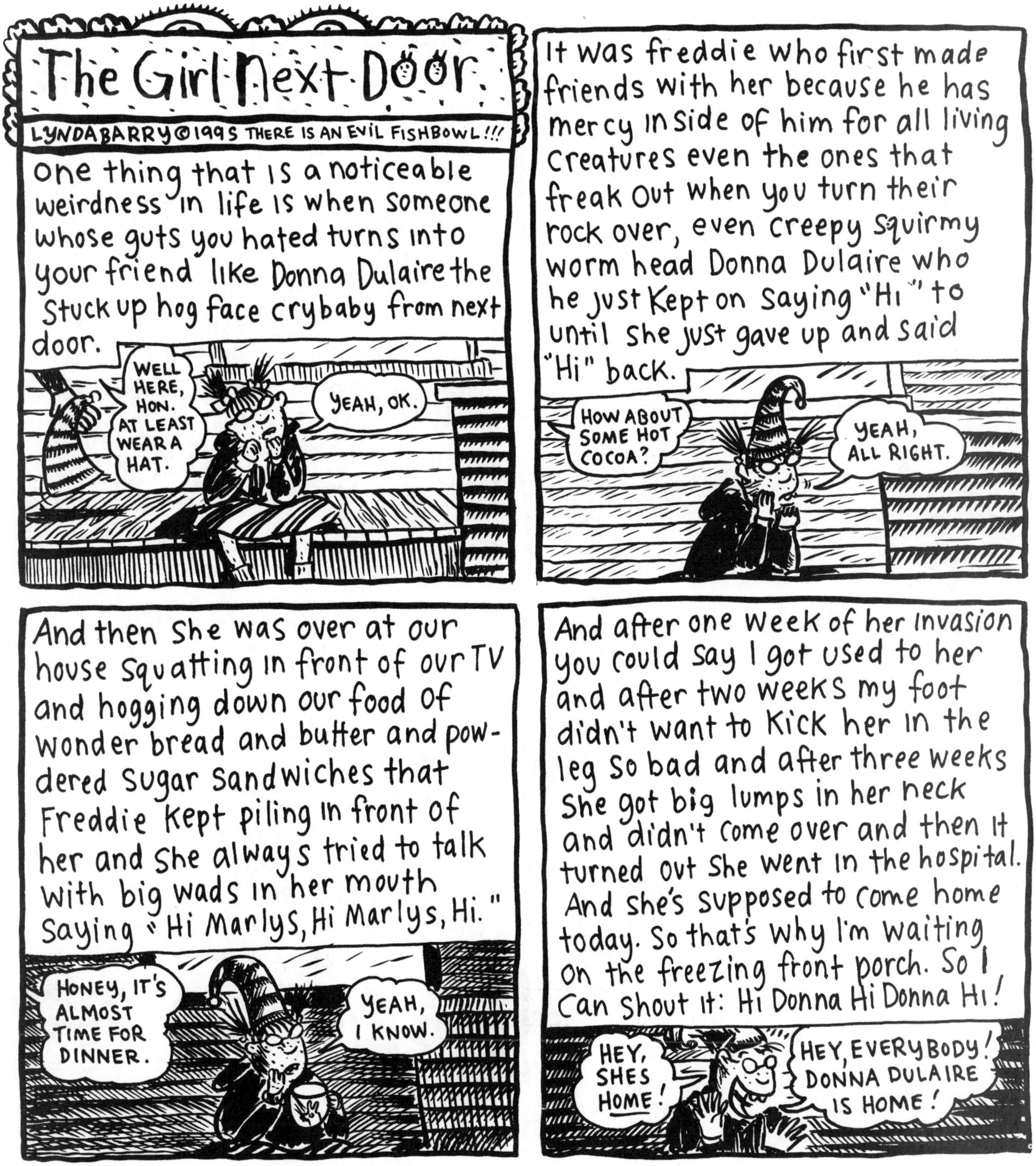
The Girl Next Door
LYNDA BARRY © 1995 THERE IS AN EVIL FISHBOWL!!!
One thing that is a noticeable weirdness in life is when someone whose guts you hated turns into your friend like Donna Dulaire the stuck up hog face crybaby from next door.
WELL HERE, HON. AT LEAST WEAR A HAT.
YEAH, OK.
It was Freddie who first made friends with her because he has mercy inside of him for all living creatures even the ones that freak out when you turn their rock over, even creepy squirmy worm head Donna Dulaire who he just kept on saying "Hi" to until she just gave up and said "Hi" back.
HOW ABOUT SOME HOT COCOA?
YEAH, ALL RIGHT.
And then she was over at our house squatting in front of our TV and hogging down our food of Wonder bread and butter and powdered sugar sandwiches that Freddie kept piling in front of her and she always tried to talk with big wads in her mouth saying "Hi Marlys, Hi Marlys, Hi."
HONEY, IT'S ALMOST TIME FOR DINNER.
YEAH, I KNOW.
And after one week of her invasion you could say I got used to her and after two weeks my foot didn't want to kick her in the leg so bad and after three weeks she got big lumps in her neck and didn't come over and then it turned out she went in the hospital. And she's supposed to come home today. So that's why I'm waiting on the freezing front porch. So I can shout it: Hi Donna Hi Donna Hi!
HEY, SHES HOME!
HEY, EVERYBODY! DONNA DULAIRE IS HOME!

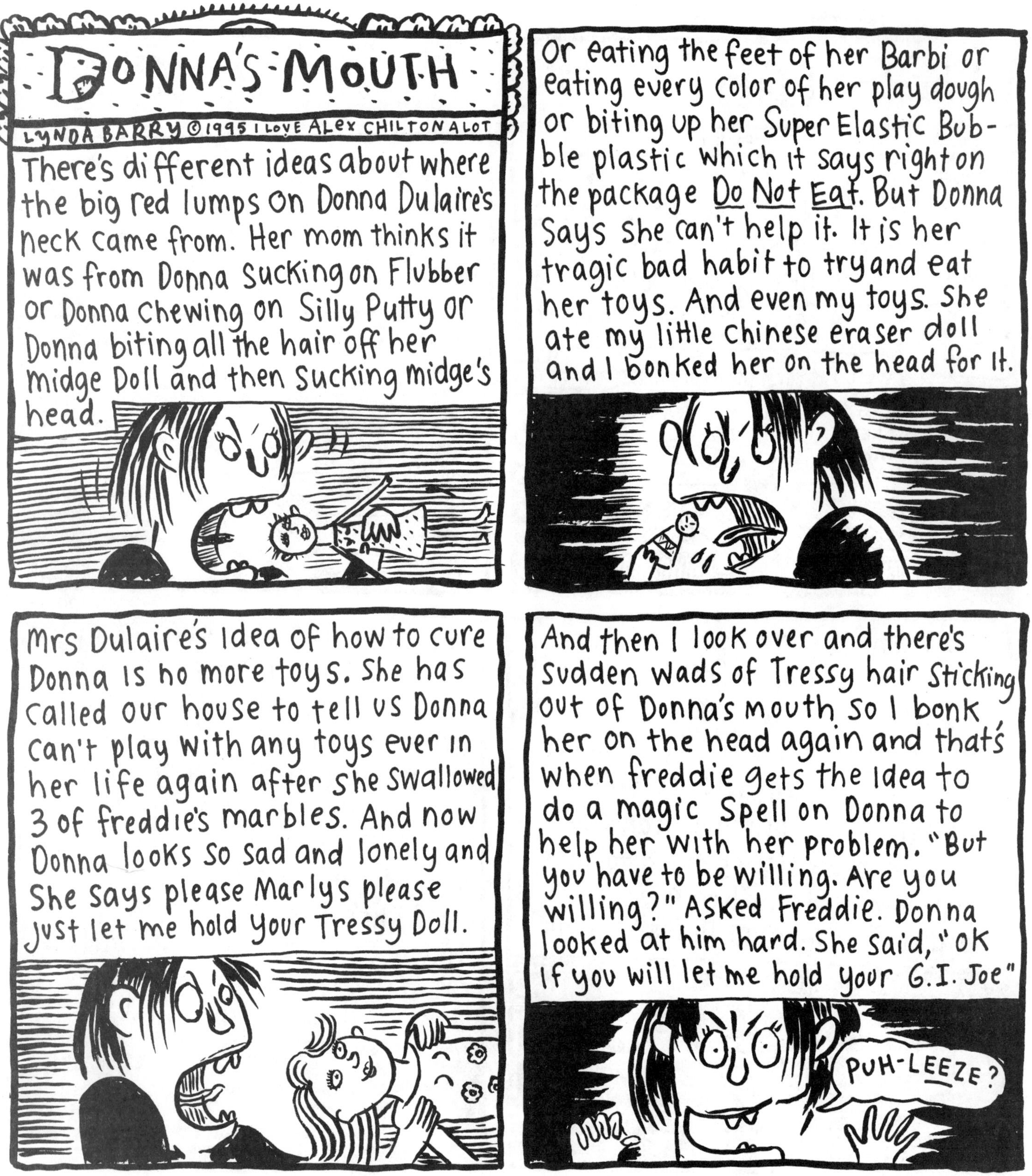
DONNA'S MOUTH
LYNDA BARRY ©1995 I LOVE ALEX CHILTON ALOT
There's different ideas about where the big red lumps on Donna Dulaire's neck came from. Her mom thinks it was from Donna sucking on Flubber or Donna chewing on Silly Putty or Donna biting all the hair off her midge Doll and then sucking midge's head.
Or eating the feet of her Barbi or eating every color of her play dough or biting up her Super Elastic Bubble plastic which it says right on the package Do Not Eat. But Donna says she can't help it. It is her tragic bad habit to try and eat her toys. And even my toys. She ate my little chinese eraser doll and I bonked her on the head for it.
Mrs Dulaire's idea of how to cure Donna is no more toys. She has called our house to tell us Donna can't play with any toys ever in her life again after she swallowed 3 of freddie's marbles. And now Donna looks so sad and lonely and she says please Marlys please just let me hold your Tressy Doll.
And then I look over and there's sudden wads of Tressy hair sticking out of Donna's mouth so I bonk her on the head again and that's when freddie gets the idea to do a magic spell on Donna to help her with her problem. "But you have to be willing. Are you willing?" Asked Freddie. Donna looked at him hard. She said, "OK if you will let me hold your G.I. Joe"
PUH-LEEZE?

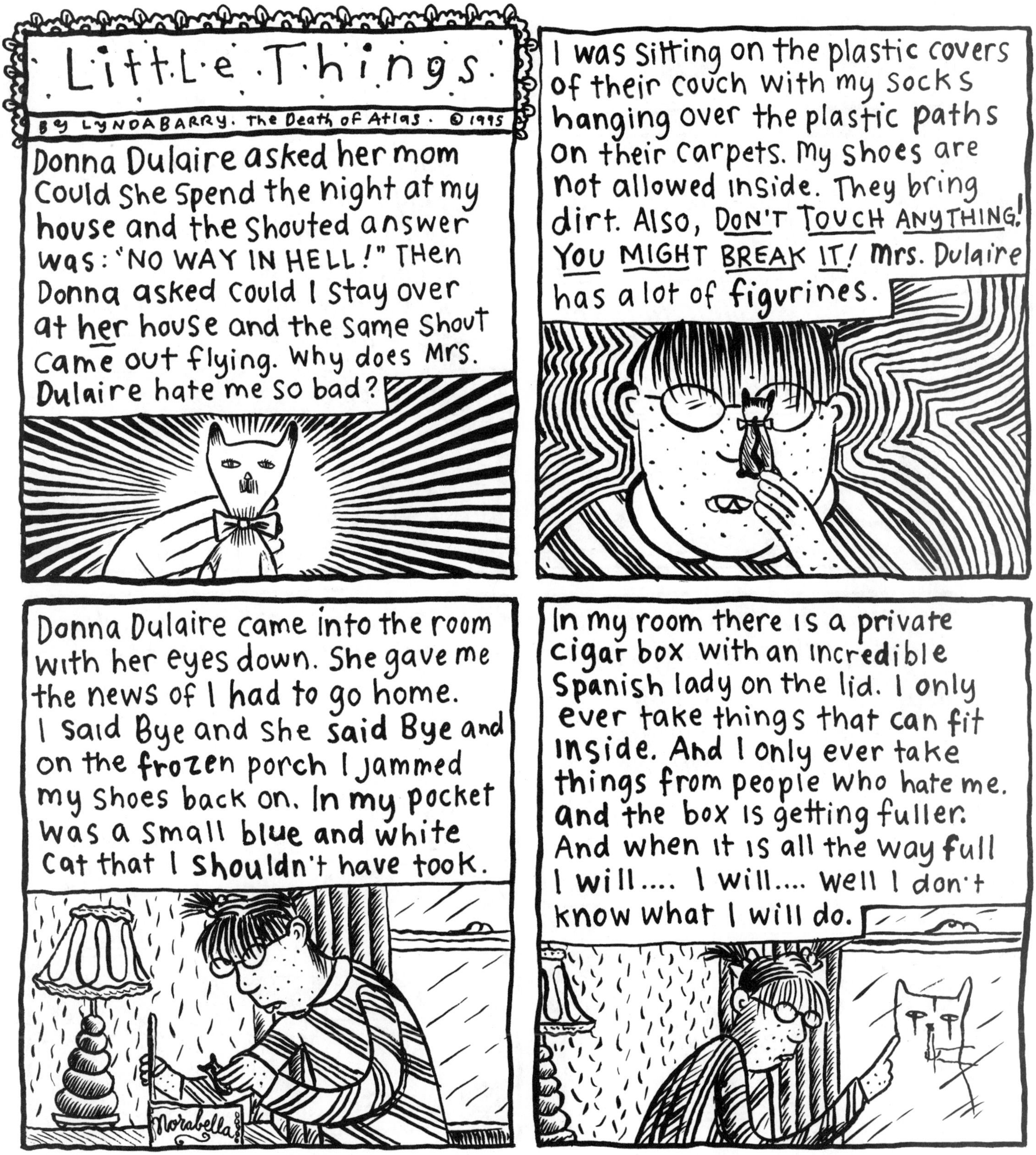
Little Things
By Lynda Barry. The Death of Atlas. © 1995
Donna Dulaire asked her mom could she spend the night at my house and the shouted answer was: "NO WAY IN HELL!" Then Donna asked could I stay over at her house and the same shout came out flying. Why does Mrs. Dulaire hate me so bad?
I was sitting on the plastic covers of their couch with my socks hanging over the plastic paths on their carpets. My shoes are not allowed inside. They bring dirt. Also, DON'T TOUCH ANYTHING! YOU MIGHT BREAK IT! Mrs. Dulaire has a lot of figurines.
Donna Dulaire came into the room with her eyes down. She gave me the news of I had to go home. I said Bye and she said Bye and on the frozen porch I jammed my shoes back on. In my pocket was a small blue and white cat that I shouldn't have took.
Morabella
In my room there is a private cigar box with an incredible Spanish lady on the lid. I only ever take things that can fit inside. And I only ever take things from people who hate me. and the box is getting fuller. And when it is all the way full I will.... I will.... well I don't know what I will do.

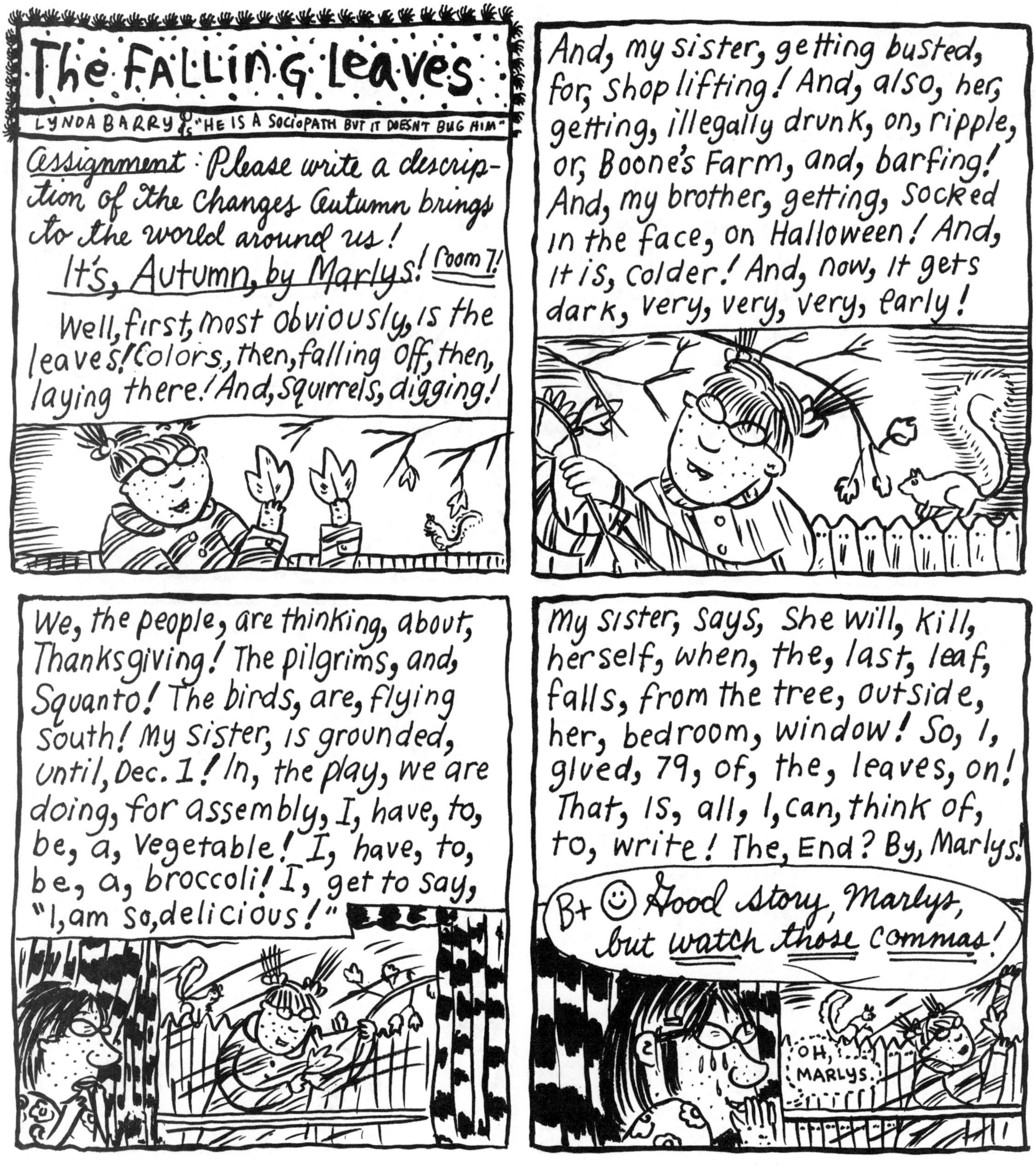
The Falling Leaves
LYNDA BARRY "HE IS A SOCIOPATH BUT IT DOESN'T BUG HIM"
Assignment: Please write a description of the changes Autumn brings to the world around us!
It's, Autumn, by Marlys! Room 7!
Well, first, most obviously, is the leaves! Colors, then, falling off, then, laying there! And, squirrels, digging!
And, my sister, getting busted, for, shop lifting! And, also, her, getting, illegally drunk, on, ripple, or, Boone's Farm, and, barfing! And, my brother, getting, socked in the face, on Halloween! And, it is, colder! And, now, it gets dark, very, very, very, early!
We, the people, are thinking, about, Thanksgiving! The pilgrims, and, Squanto! The birds, are, flying south! My sister, is grounded, until, Dec. 1! In, the play, we are doing, for assembly, I, have, to, be, a, vegetable! I, have, to, be, a, broccoli! I, get to say, "I, am so, delicious!"
My sister, says, she will, kill, herself, when, the, last, leaf, falls, from the tree, outside, her, bedroom, window! So, I, glued, 79, of, the, leaves, on! That, is, all, I, can, think of, to, write! The, End? By, Marlys!
B+ ☺ Good story, Marlys, but watch those commas!
OH, MARLYS.

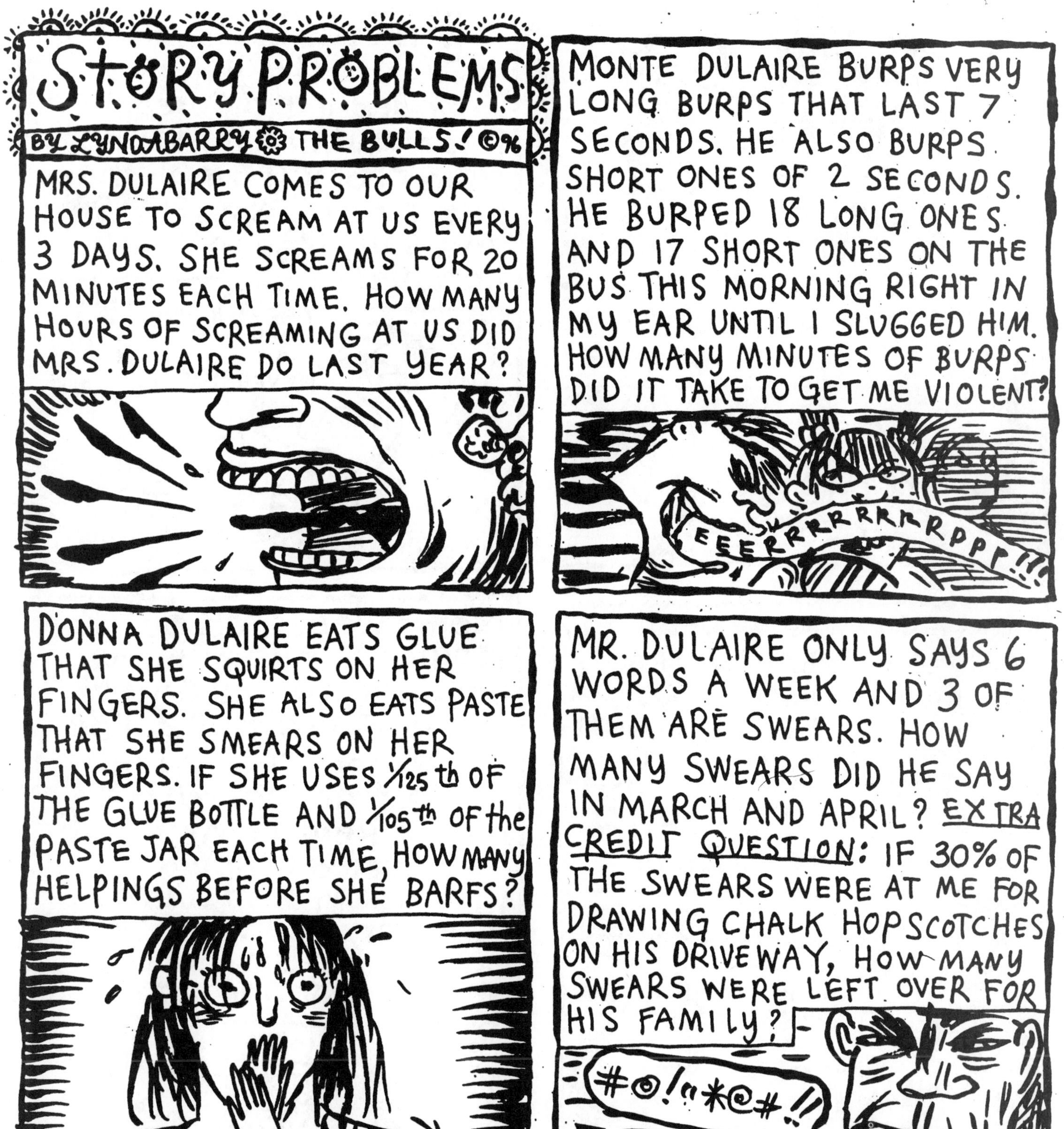
STORY PROBLEMS
BY LYNDA BARRY ✿ THE BULLS! ©96
MRS. DULAIRE COMES TO OUR HOUSE TO SCREAM AT US EVERY 3 DAYS. SHE SCREAMS FOR 20 MINUTES EACH TIME. HOW MANY HOURS OF SCREAMING AT US DID MRS. DULAIRE DO LAST YEAR?
MONTE DULAIRE BURPS VERY LONG BURPS THAT LAST 7 SECONDS. HE ALSO BURPS SHORT ONES OF 2 SECONDS. HE BURPED 18 LONG ONES AND 17 SHORT ONES ON THE BUS THIS MORNING RIGHT IN MY EAR UNTIL I SLUGGED HIM. HOW MANY MINUTES OF BURPS DID IT TAKE TO GET ME VIOLENT?
EEEERRRRRRRRRRRRPPP!!!
DONNA DULAIRE EATS GLUE THAT SHE SQUIRTS ON HER FINGERS. SHE ALSO EATS PASTE THAT SHE SMEARS ON HER FINGERS. IF SHE USES 1/125th OF THE GLUE BOTTLE AND 1/105th OF the PASTE JAR EACH TIME, HOW MANY HELPINGS BEFORE SHE BARFS?
MR. DULAIRE ONLY SAYS 6 WORDS A WEEK AND 3 OF THEM ARE SWEARS. HOW MANY SWEARS DID HE SAY IN MARCH AND APRIL? EXTRA CREDIT QUESTION: IF 30% OF THE SWEARS WERE AT ME FOR DRAWING CHALK HOPSCOTCHES ON HIS DRIVEWAY, HOW MANY SWEARS WERE LEFT OVER FOR HIS FAMILY?
#@!"*@#!!

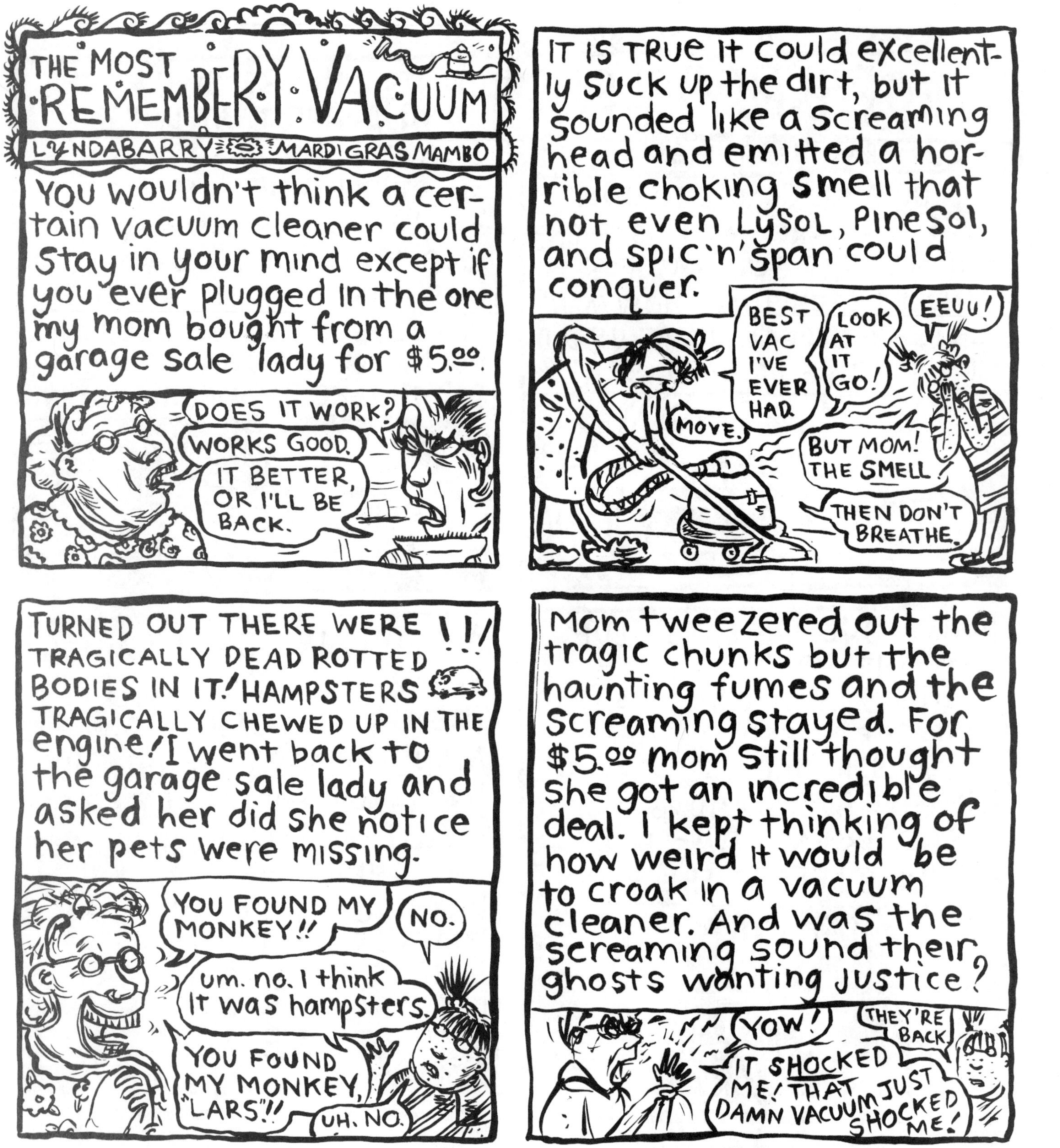
THE MOST REMEMBERY VACUUM
LYNDA BARRY MARDI GRAS MAMBO
You wouldn't think a certain vacuum cleaner could stay in your mind except if you ever plugged in the one my mom bought from a garage sale lady for $5.00.
DOES IT WORK?
WORKS GOOD.
IT BETTER, OR I'LL BE BACK.
It is true it could excellently suck up the dirt, but it sounded like a screaming head and emitted a horrible choking smell that not even Lysol, Pine Sol, and spic'n'span could conquer.
BEST VAC I'VE EVER HAD
LOOK AT IT GO!
EEUU!
MOVE.
BUT MOM! THE SMELL
THEN DON'T BREATHE.
TURNED OUT THERE WERE !!! TRAGICALLY DEAD ROTTED BODIES IN IT! HAMPSTERS TRAGICALLY CHEWED UP IN THE engine! I went back to the garage sale lady and asked her did she notice her pets were missing.
YOU FOUND MY MONKEY!!
NO.
um. no. I think it was hampsters.
YOU FOUND MY MONKEY, "LARS"!!
UH. NO.
Mom tweezered out the tragic chunks but the haunting fumes and the screaming stayed. For $5.00 mom still thought she got an incredible deal. I kept thinking of how weird it would be to croak in a vacuum cleaner. And was the screaming sound their ghosts wanting justice?
YOW!
THEY'RE BACK.
IT SHOCKED ME! THAT DAMN VACUUM JUST SHOCKED ME!

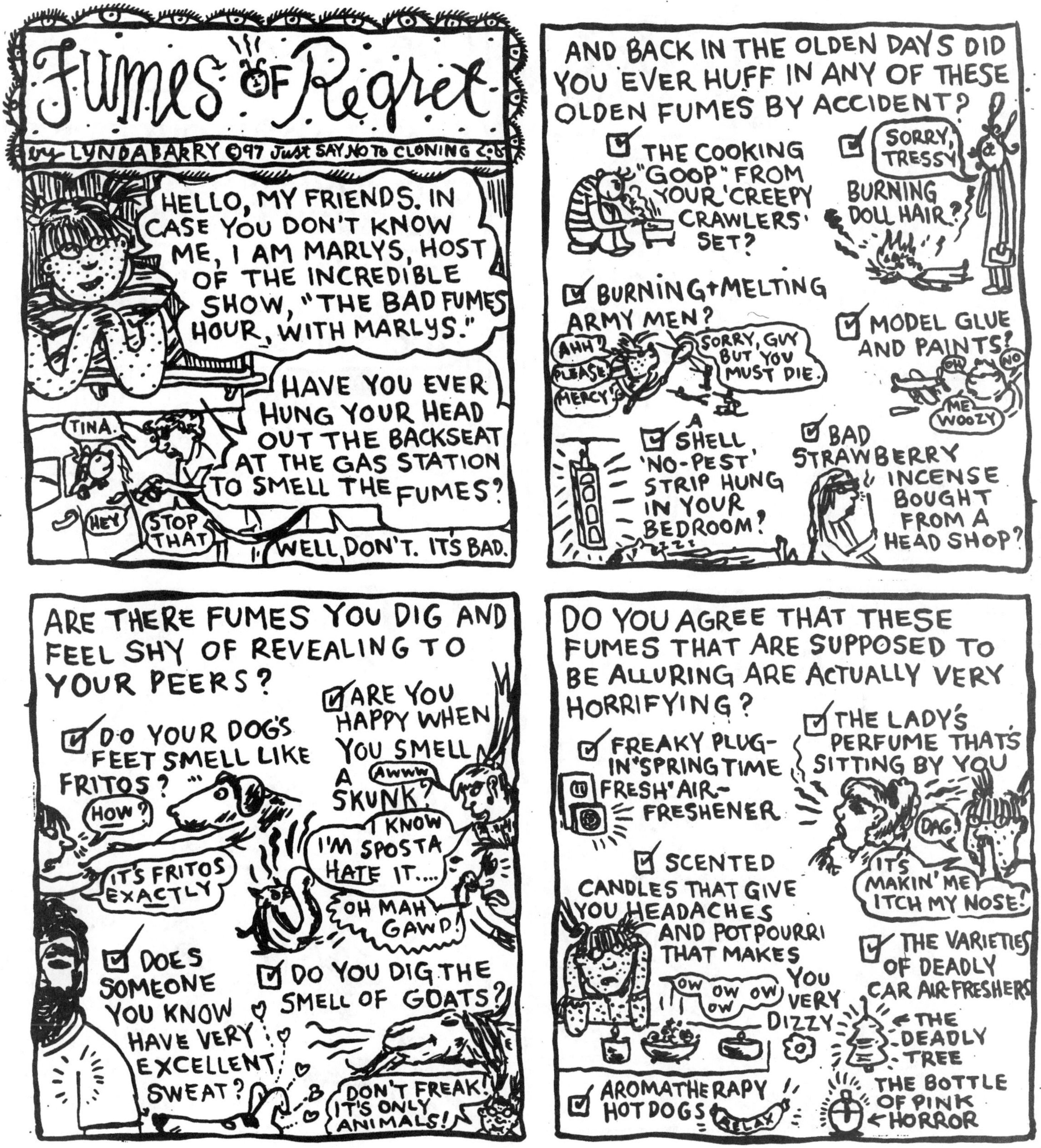
FUMES OF REGRET
BY LYNDA BARRY ©97 JUST SAY NO TO CLONING
HELLO, MY FRIENDS. IN CASE YOU DON'T KNOW ME, I AM MARLYS, HOST OF THE INCREDIBLE SHOW, "THE BAD FUMES HOUR, WITH MARLYS."
HAVE YOU EVER HUNG YOUR HEAD OUT THE BACKSEAT AT THE GAS STATION TO SMELL THE FUMES?
TINA.
HEY
STOP THAT
WELL, DON'T. IT'S BAD.
AND BACK IN THE OLDEN DAYS DID YOU EVER HUFF IN ANY OF THESE OLDEN FUMES BY ACCIDENT?
THE COOKING "GOOP" FROM YOUR 'CREEPY CRAWLERS' SET?
SORRY, TRESSY
BURNING DOLL HAIR?
BURNING + MELTING ARMY MEN?
AHH!
PLEASE
MERCY
SORRY, GUY BUT YOU MUST DIE.
MODEL GLUE AND PAINTS?
OH
NO
ME WOOZY
A SHELL 'NO-PEST' STRIP HUNG IN YOUR BEDROOM?
BAD STRAWBERRY INCENSE BOUGHT FROM A HEAD SHOP?
ARE THERE FUMES YOU DIG AND FEEL SHY OF REVEALING TO YOUR PEERS?
DO YOUR DOG'S FEET SMELL LIKE FRITOS?
HOW?
IT'S FRITOS EXACTLY
ARE YOU HAPPY WHEN YOU SMELL A SKUNK?
AWWW
I KNOW I'M SPOSTA HATE IT....
OH MAH GAWD!
DOES SOMEONE YOU KNOW HAVE VERY EXCELLENT SWEAT?
DO YOU DIG THE SMELL OF GOATS?
DON'T FREAK! IT'S ONLY ANIMALS!
DO YOU AGREE THAT THESE FUMES THAT ARE SUPPOSED TO BE ALLURING ARE ACTUALLY VERY HORRIFYING?
FREAKY PLUG-IN 'SPRING TIME FRESH' AIR-FRESHENER
THE LADY'S PERFUME THAT'S SITTING BY YOU
DAG.
IT'S MAKIN' ME ITCH MY NOSE!
SCENTED CANDLES THAT GIVE YOU HEADACHES AND POTPOURRI THAT MAKES YOU VERY DIZZY
OW OW OW OW
THE VARIETIES OF DEADLY CAR AIR-FRESHERS
THE DEADLY TREE
THE BOTTLE OF PINK HORROR
AROMATHERAPY HOT DOGS
RELAX

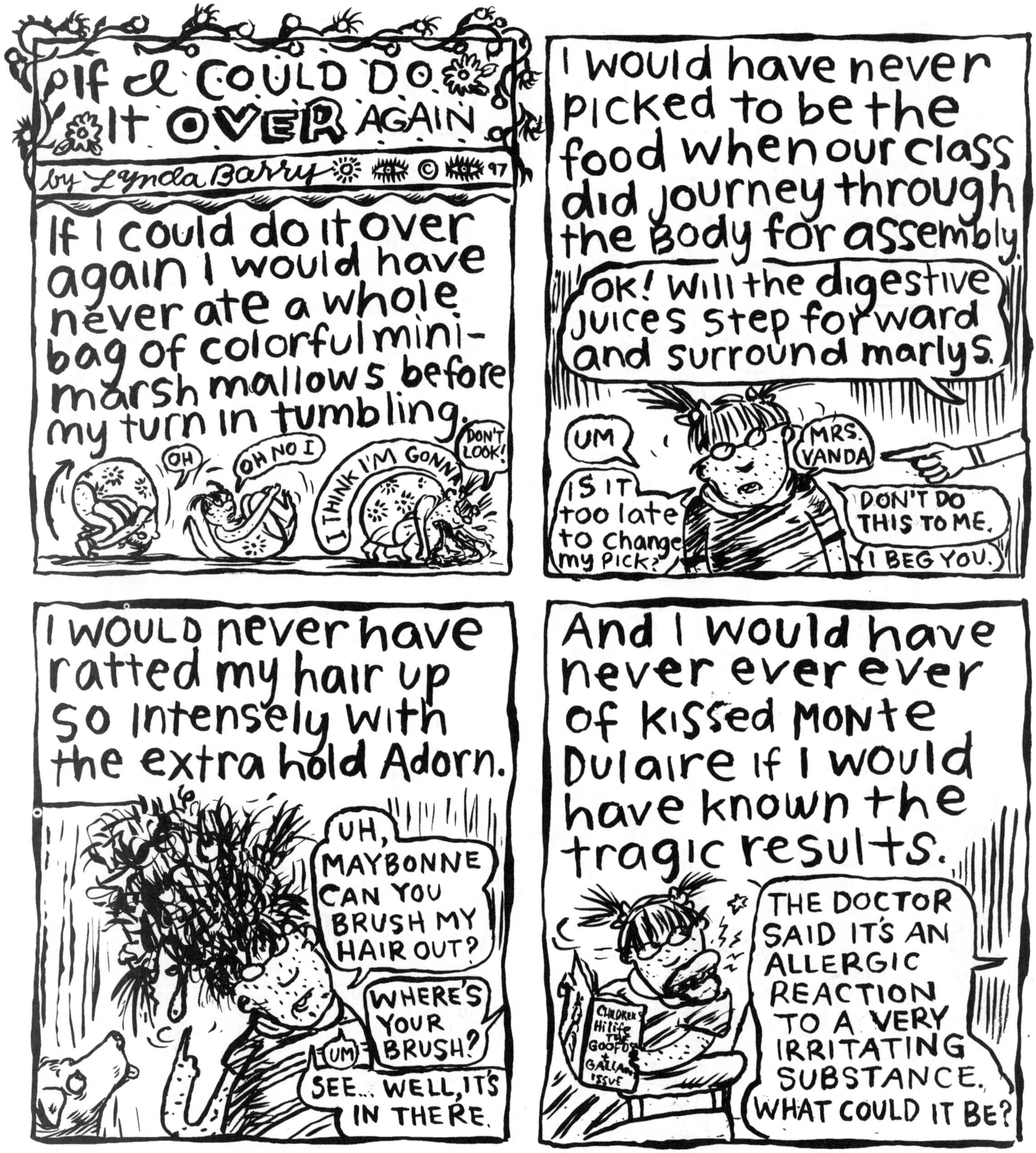

If I COULD DO IT OVER AGAIN
by Lynda Barry © 97
If I could do it over again I would have never ate a whole bag of colorful mini-marshmallows before my turn in tumbling.
OH
OH NO I
I THINK I'M GONNA
DON'T LOOK!
I would have never picked to be the food when our class did Journey through the Body for assembly.
OK! Will the digestive juices step forward and surround marlys.
UM
IS IT too late to change my pick?
MRS. VANDA
DON'T DO THIS TO ME.
I BEG YOU.
I WOULD never have ratted my hair up so intensely with the extra hold Adorn.
UH, MAYBONNE CAN YOU BRUSH MY HAIR OUT?
WHERE'S YOUR BRUSH?
UM
SEE... WELL, IT'S IN THERE.
And I would have never ever ever of kissed Monte Dulaire if I would have known the tragic results.
THE DOCTOR SAID IT'S AN ALLERGIC REACTION TO A VERY IRRITATING SUBSTANCE. WHAT COULD IT BE?
CHILDREN'S Hilife THE GOOFUS & GALLANT ISSUE

SCIENTIFIC MARLYS!

WONDERS (actual) OF the DEEP
CONVOLUTA Roscoffensis
BY Lynda Barry ©97 Happy B-DAY DON·G!

MARLYS and Skreddy 57 GO MICRO TO BRING YOU DETAILS concerning A MIND BLOWING little CREATURE.

I'M LIKING THIS WATERY WORLD!

HEY, CONVOLUTA, WHAT IT IS!

CONVOLUTA IS A DINKY FLAT WORM THAT LIVES IN THE SAND ON CERTAIN SHORES. SHE LETS TINY SEAWEED LIVE INSIDE HER. SHE DOESN'T HAVE A MOUTH OR A BRAIN BUT HER LIFE VIBRATIONS ARE SO MELLOW. WHEN THE TIDE GOES OUT, SHE RISES TO THE TOP OF THE SAND AND GETS PHOTOSYNTHESIS LOVE.

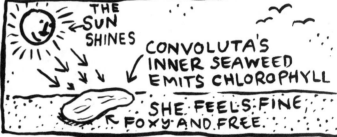

THE SUN SHINES

CONVOLUTA'S INNER SEAWEED EMITS CHLOROPHYLL

SHE FEELS FINE, FOXY AND FREE.

WHEN THE TIDE COMES IN, SHE GOES DEEP DOWN INTO THE SAND AND ACTS VERY SENSUOUS. WHEN THE TIDE GOES OUT SHE RISES AGAIN. BUT WHAT IS SO WILD ABOUT CONVOLUTA IS: SHE WILL DO THIS EVEN IN A FISHBOWL! SHE IS SO SENSITIVE, SHE CAN FEEL THE TIDE IN A MAYONNAISE JAR!

THAR SHE BLOWS

HELLMANS

DAG, CONVOLUTA!

AND THE SCIENTISTS SAY HOW? NO BRAIN, EYES OR EARS OR SUDDEN BONG HITS THAT GIVE ENLIGHTENMENT. HOW DOES CONVOLUTA DO IT? SHE DIDN'T TELL MARLYS AND SKREDDY 57 BUT SHE GAVE THEM WONDER ANYWAY AND THEY WANTED ME TO PASS IT ON TO YOU.

HEY! LET'S GO FIND THE CLOWN-FISH.

YEAH. HE OWES ME MONEY.

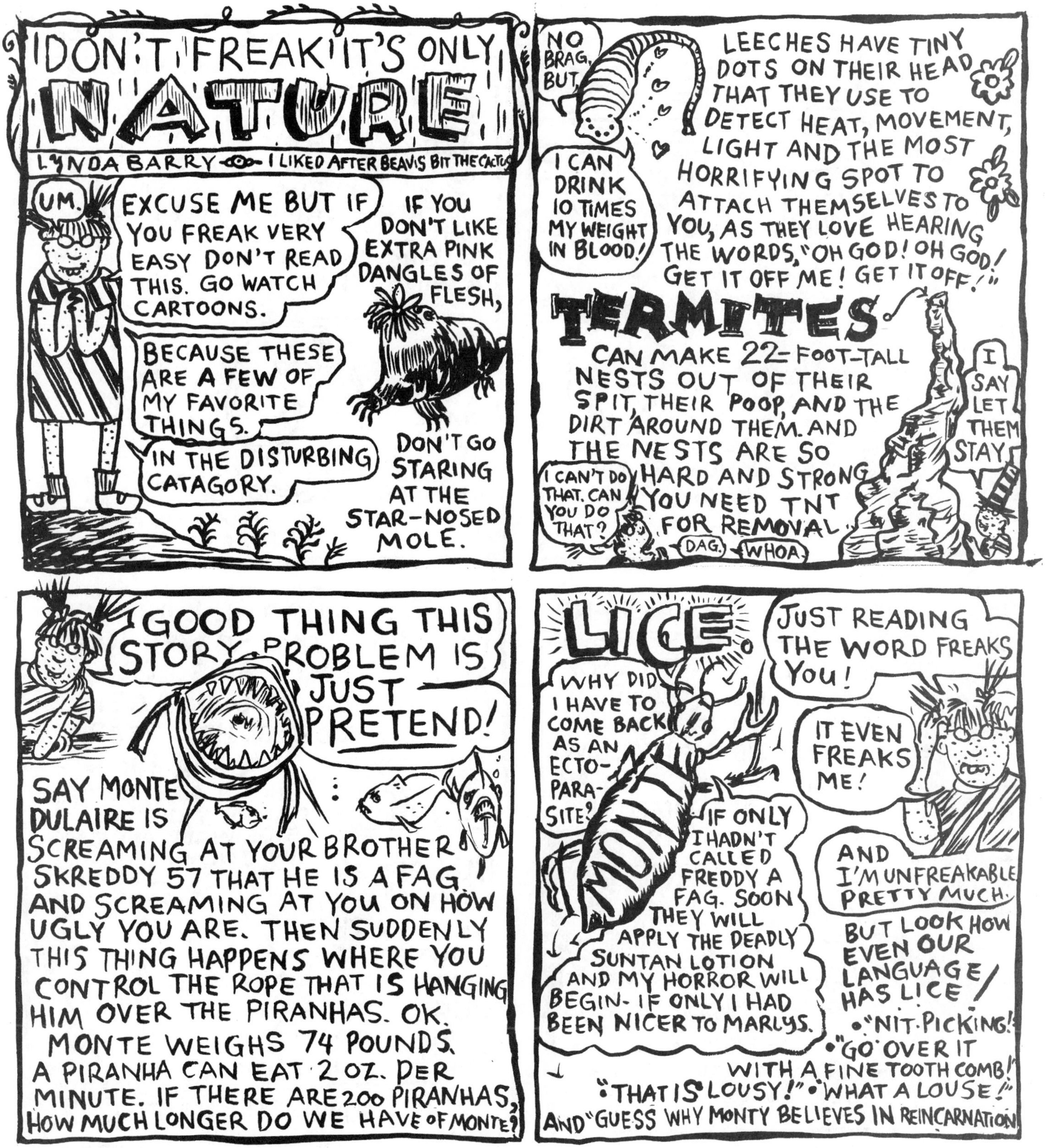

DON'T FREAK IT'S ONLY
NATURE
LYNDA BARRY I LIKED AFTER BEAVIS BIT THE CACTUS
UM.
EXCUSE ME BUT IF YOU FREAK VERY EASY DON'T READ THIS. GO WATCH CARTOONS.
BECAUSE THESE ARE A FEW OF MY FAVORITE THINGS.
IN THE DISTURBING CATAGORY.
IF YOU DON'T LIKE EXTRA PINK DANGLES OF FLESH,
DON'T GO STARING AT THE STAR-NOSED MOLE.
NO BRAG, BUT,
I CAN DRINK 10 TIMES MY WEIGHT IN BLOOD!
LEECHES HAVE TINY DOTS ON THEIR HEAD THAT THEY USE TO DETECT HEAT, MOVEMENT, LIGHT AND THE MOST HORRIFYING SPOT TO ATTACH THEMSELVES TO YOU, AS THEY LOVE HEARING THE WORDS, "OH GOD! OH GOD! GET IT OFF ME! GET IT OFF!"
TERMITES
CAN MAKE 22-FOOT-TALL NESTS OUT OF THEIR SPIT, THEIR POOP, AND THE DIRT AROUND THEM. AND THE NESTS ARE SO HARD AND STRONG YOU NEED TNT FOR REMOVAL.
I CAN'T DO THAT. CAN YOU DO THAT?
DAG.
WHOA.
I SAY LET THEM STAY.
GOOD THING THIS STORY PROBLEM IS JUST PRETEND!
SAY MONTE DULAIRE IS SCREAMING AT YOUR BROTHER SKREDDY 57 THAT HE IS A FAG AND SCREAMING AT YOU ON HOW UGLY YOU ARE. THEN SUDDENLY THIS THING HAPPENS WHERE YOU CONTROL THE ROPE THAT IS HANGING HIM OVER THE PIRANHAS. OK. MONTE WEIGHS 74 POUNDS. A PIRANHA CAN EAT 2 OZ. PER MINUTE. IF THERE ARE 200 PIRANHAS, HOW MUCH LONGER DO WE HAVE OF MONTE?
LICE
JUST READING THE WORD FREAKS YOU!
WHY DID I HAVE TO COME BACK AS AN ECTO-PARA-SITE?
MONTY
IF ONLY I HADN'T CALLED FREDDY A FAG. SOON THEY WILL APPLY THE DEADLY SUNTAN LOTION AND MY HORROR WILL BEGIN. IF ONLY I HAD BEEN NICER TO MARLYS.
IT EVEN FREAKS ME!
AND I'M UNFREAKABLE PRETTY MUCH.
BUT LOOK HOW EVEN OUR LANGUAGE HAS LICE!
• "NIT-PICKING!"
• "GO OVER IT WITH A FINE TOOTH COMB!"
• "THAT IS LOUSY!" • "WHAT A LOUSE!"
AND "GUESS WHY MONTY BELIEVES IN REINCARNATION

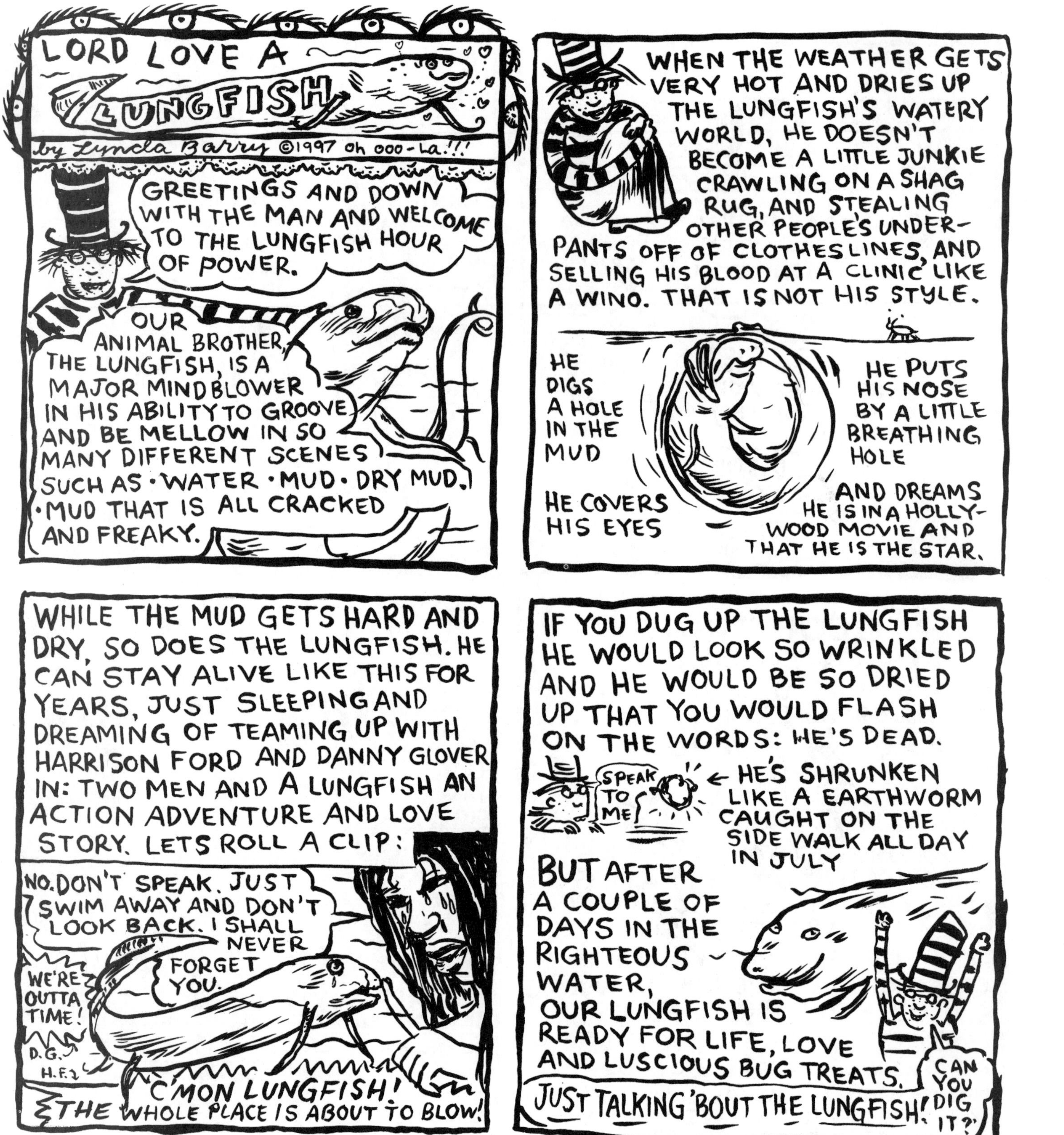
LORD LOVE A LUNGFISH
by Lynda Barry ©1997 oh ooo-La!!!
GREETINGS AND DOWN WITH THE MAN AND WELCOME TO THE LUNGFISH HOUR OF POWER.
OUR ANIMAL BROTHER, THE LUNGFISH, IS A MAJOR MIND BLOWER IN HIS ABILITY TO GROOVE AND BE MELLOW IN SO MANY DIFFERENT SCENES SUCH AS • WATER • MUD • DRY MUD. • MUD THAT IS ALL CRACKED AND FREAKY.
WHEN THE WEATHER GETS VERY HOT AND DRIES UP THE LUNGFISH'S WATERY WORLD, HE DOESN'T BECOME A LITTLE JUNKIE CRAWLING ON A SHAG RUG, AND STEALING OTHER PEOPLE'S UNDER-PANTS OFF OF CLOTHES LINES, AND SELLING HIS BLOOD AT A CLINIC LIKE A WINO. THAT IS NOT HIS STYLE.
HE DIGS A HOLE IN THE MUD
HE PUTS HIS NOSE BY A LITTLE BREATHING HOLE
HE COVERS HIS EYES
AND DREAMS HE IS IN A HOLLY-WOOD MOVIE AND THAT HE IS THE STAR.
WHILE THE MUD GETS HARD AND DRY, SO DOES THE LUNGFISH. HE CAN STAY ALIVE LIKE THIS FOR YEARS, JUST SLEEPING AND DREAMING OF TEAMING UP WITH HARRISON FORD AND DANNY GLOVER IN: TWO MEN AND A LUNGFISH AN ACTION ADVENTURE AND LOVE STORY. LETS ROLL A CLIP:
NO. DON'T SPEAK. JUST SWIM AWAY AND DON'T LOOK BACK. I SHALL NEVER FORGET YOU.
WE'RE OUTTA TIME!
D.G.
H.F.
C'MON LUNGFISH! THE WHOLE PLACE IS ABOUT TO BLOW!
IF YOU DUG UP THE LUNGFISH HE WOULD LOOK SO WRINKLED AND HE WOULD BE SO DRIED UP THAT YOU WOULD FLASH ON THE WORDS: HE'S DEAD.
SPEAK TO ME
← HE'S SHRUNKEN LIKE A EARTHWORM CAUGHT ON THE SIDE WALK ALL DAY IN JULY
BUT AFTER A COUPLE OF DAYS IN THE RIGHTEOUS WATER, OUR LUNGFISH IS READY FOR LIFE, LOVE AND LUSCIOUS BUG TREATS.
JUST TALKING 'BOUT THE LUNGFISH!
CAN YOU DIG IT?

MEDICAL CONDITIONS
NURSE MARLYS
Lynda Barry ©97 TAKE THE "EL" TRAIN!
HELLO AND WELCOME TO THE MARLYS MEDICAL MINUTE!
TODAY I'D LIKE TO TELL YOU MY FAVORITE CONDITIONS.
OW. OW. NURSE MARLYS! YOU ARE LEANING ON MY OPERATION! OW! GET OFF! OW!
THESE ARE REAL! NOT MADE UP! SO SIT BACK AND RELAX AND GET READY FOR...
TRAGIC NAME SYNDROME
WHERE THE PARENTS EITHER THINK TOO HARD OR DON'T THINK HARD ENOUGH ON WHAT TO NAME THE BABY.
SUFFERERS INCLUDE...
"WADLEY" "MELVINETTE" "TANGERINA-AMBER-GRIS
"BRAINARD" "SQUIDLEY" "PETULA"
"GNARLENE" "WEENUS" "FREEBIRD"
NURSE MARLYS Rx: USE YOUR INITIALS INSTEAD UNLESS THEY ARE B.O., P.U., R.S.V.P.
BRODMIDROSIS (STINK FOOT)
WHERE YOUR FEET ARE VERY RASTY WITH ODORS OF HORROR!
Nurse Marlys' Rx:
1. WASH YOUR FEET MORE ESPECIALLY IF YOU HAVE COMPANY
2. SOAK YOUR FEET IN ICED TEA.
3. SOAK YOUR FEET IN MELTED ORANGE POPSICLE FLUID
4. DIP YOUR FEET IN THE WATER OF GREEN FIZZIES.
5. CHECK SHOES FREQUENTLY FOR FISH CHUNKS
SOMETIMES I HAVE THIS CONDITION
ESPECIALLY WHEN MY EVIL COUSIN ARNOLD SNEAKS SMELL-O-RAMA ITEMS IN MY DRESS SHOES
PTYALISM (TOO MUCH SPIT)
TRY SPONGE CAKE!
OK
LENTIGO (FRECKLES)
ALSO KNOWN AS MELA-MARLYS
METEORISM
(IN 1934 THIS WAS THE NAME FOR IF YOU CUT ONE OR MORE)
WHOA!
KAHUTEK
UM. EXCUSE ME.
SERIOUSLY
CLOWNISM
(WHEN YOU GET YOUR FACE STUCK IN CLOWN-HEAD POSES)
WELL THAT'S ALL WE HAVE TIME FOR! SEE YOU NEXT WEEK!
WAIT! THE CURE FOR CLOWNISM!! WHAT IS IT!!?!

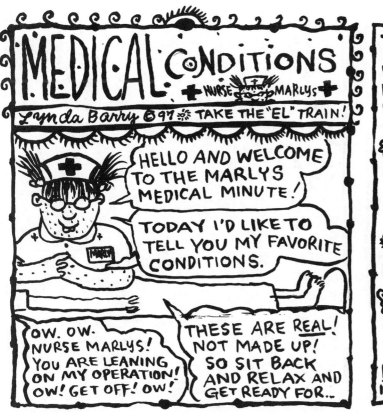

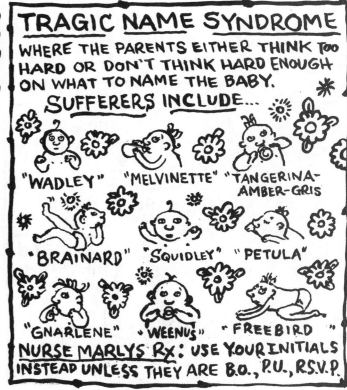

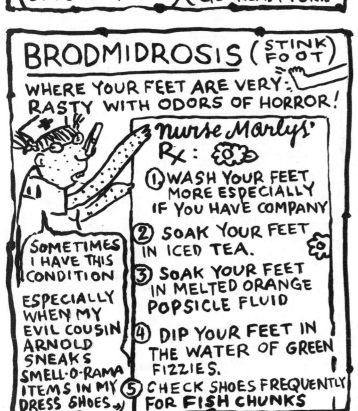

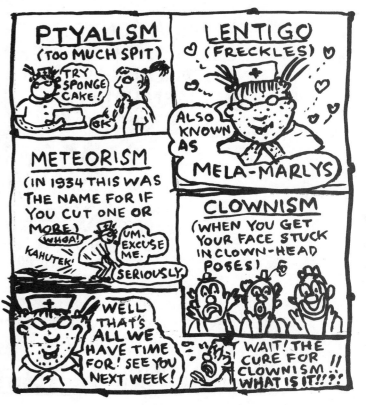

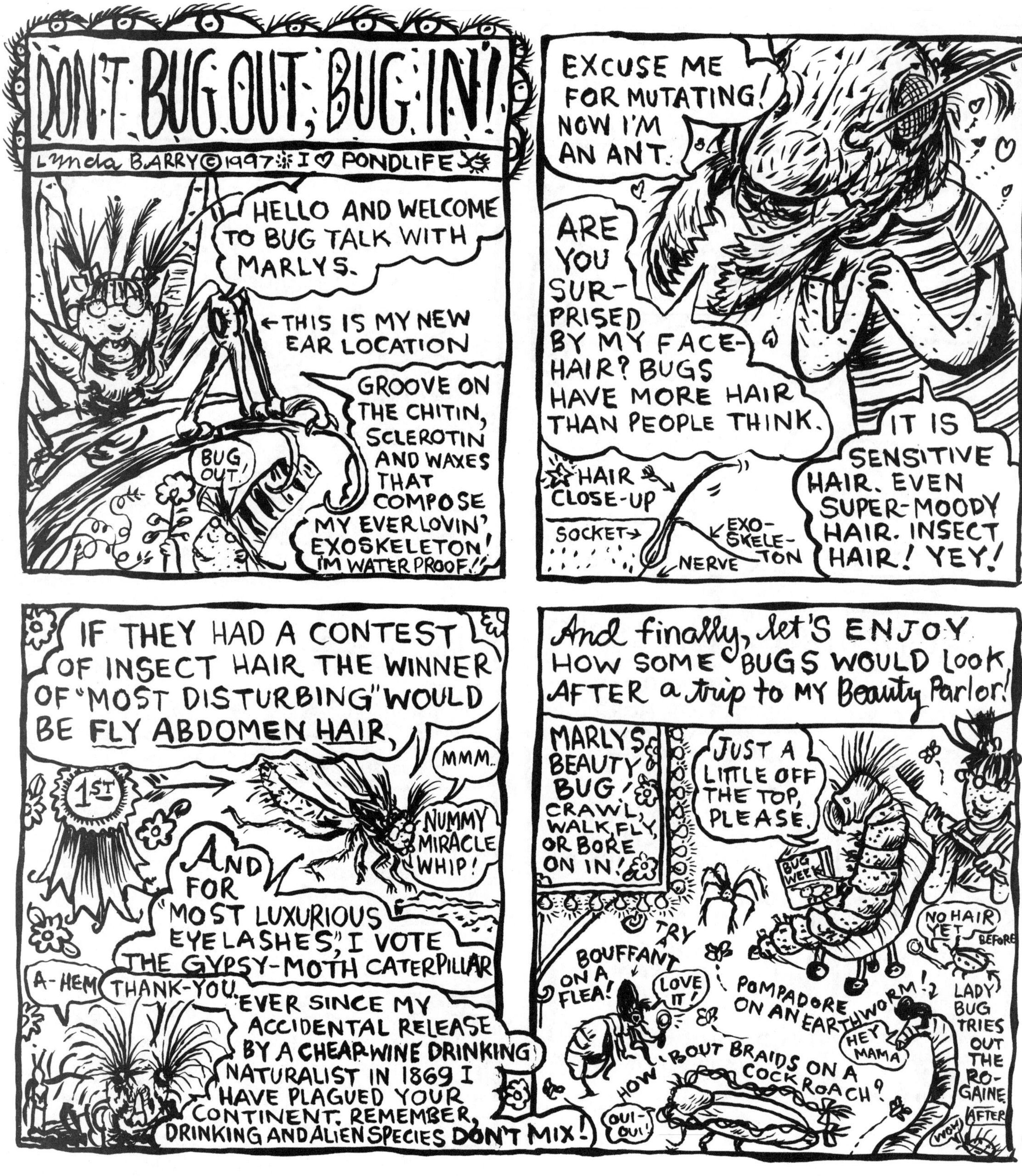
DON'T BUG OUT, BUG IN!
Lynda BARRY © 1997 I ♡ PONDLIFE
HELLO AND WELCOME TO BUG TALK WITH MARLYS.
← THIS IS MY NEW EAR LOCATION
GROOVE ON THE CHITIN, SCLEROTIN AND WAXES THAT COMPOSE MY EVERLOVIN' EXOSKELETON! I'M WATERPROOF!!
BUG OUT.
EXCUSE ME FOR MUTATING! NOW I'M AN ANT.
ARE YOU SURPRISED BY MY FACE-HAIR? BUGS HAVE MORE HAIR THAN PEOPLE THINK.
IT IS SENSITIVE HAIR. EVEN SUPER-MOODY HAIR. INSECT HAIR! YEY!
HAIR CLOSE-UP
SOCKET →
EXO-SKELE-TON
NERVE
IF THEY HAD A CONTEST OF INSECT HAIR THE WINNER OF "MOST DISTURBING" WOULD BE FLY ABDOMEN HAIR,
1ST
MMM..
NUMMY MIRACLE WHIP!
AND FOR "MOST LUXURIOUS EYELASHES," I VOTE THE GYPSY-MOTH CATERPILLAR
A-HEM
THANK-YOU. EVER SINCE MY ACCIDENTAL RELEASE BY A CHEAP-WINE DRINKING NATURALIST IN 1869 I HAVE PLAGUED YOUR CONTINENT. REMEMBER, DRINKING AND ALIEN SPECIES DON'T MIX!
And finally, let'S ENJOY HOW SOME BUGS WOULD LOOK AFTER a trip to MY Beauty Parlor!
MARLYS BEAUTY BUG, CRAWL, WALK, FLY, OR BORE ON IN!
JUST A LITTLE OFF THE TOP, PLEASE.
BUG WEEK
TRY A BOUFFANT ON A FLEA!
LOVE IT!
POMPADORE ON AN EARTHWORM!?
HEY MAMA
NO HAIR YET
BEFORE
LADY BUG TRIES OUT THE ROGAINE
AFTER
WOW
HOW 'BOUT BRAIDS ON A COCKROACH?
OUI-OUI!

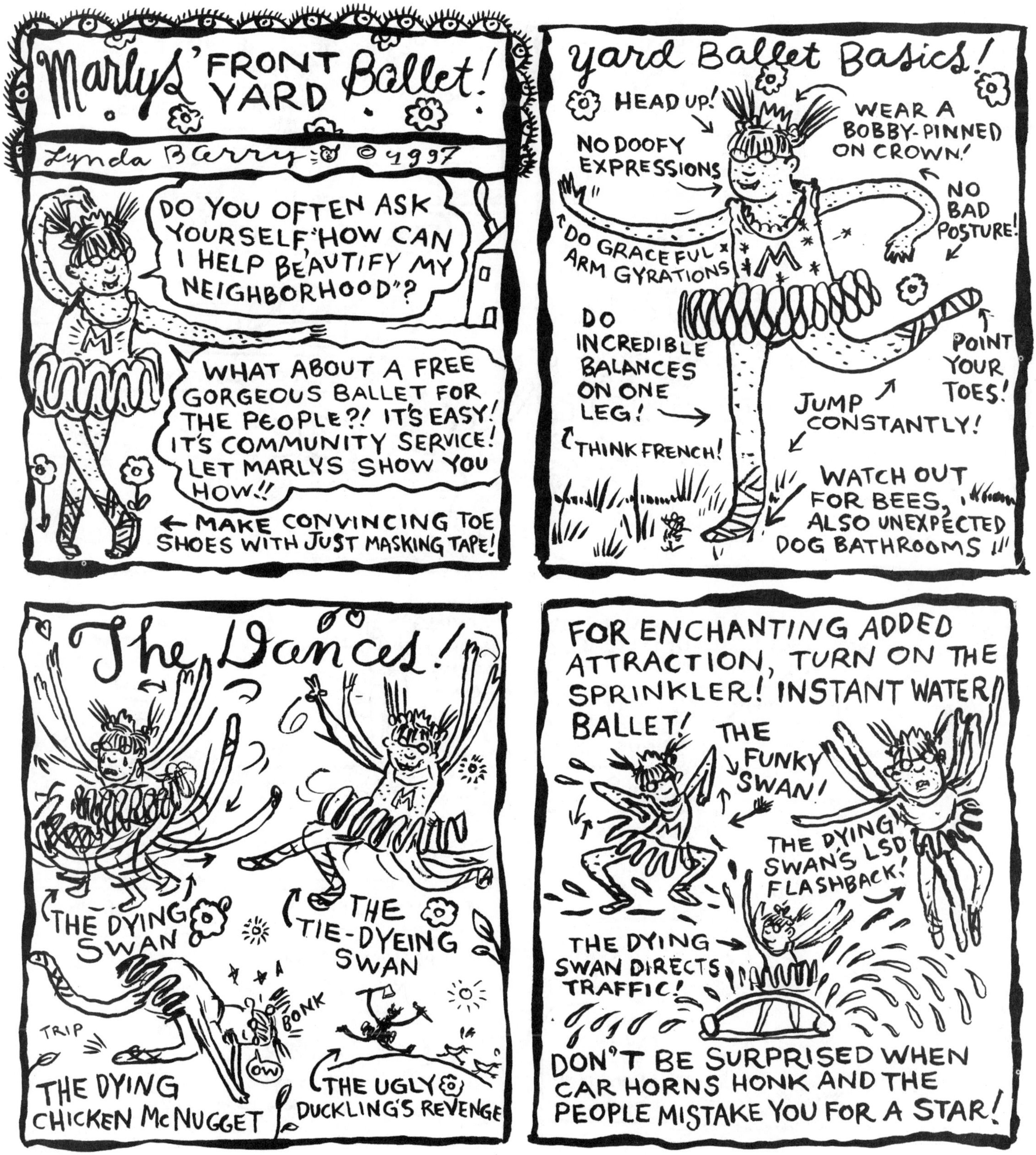
Marlys' Front Yard Ballet!
Lynda Barry © 1997
DO YOU OFTEN ASK YOURSELF "HOW CAN I HELP BEAUTIFY MY NEIGHBORHOOD"?
WHAT ABOUT A FREE GORGEOUS BALLET FOR THE PEOPLE?! IT'S EASY! IT'S COMMUNITY SERVICE! LET MARLYS SHOW YOU HOW!!
← MAKE CONVINCING TOE SHOES WITH JUST MASKING TAPE!
Yard Ballet Basics!
HEAD UP!
NO DOOFY EXPRESSIONS
WEAR A BOBBY-PINNED ON CROWN!
NO BAD POSTURE!
DO GRACEFUL ARM GYRATIONS
DO INCREDIBLE BALANCES ON ONE LEG!
THINK FRENCH!
POINT YOUR TOES!
JUMP CONSTANTLY!
WATCH OUT FOR BEES, ALSO UNEXPECTED DOG BATHROOMS!!
The Dances!
THE DYING SWAN
THE TIE-DYEING SWAN
TRIP
BONK
OW
THE DYING CHICKEN McNUGGET
THE UGLY DUCKLING'S REVENGE
FOR ENCHANTING ADDED ATTRACTION, TURN ON THE SPRINKLER! INSTANT WATER BALLET!
THE FUNKY SWAN!
THE DYING SWAN'S LSD FLASHBACK!
THE DYING SWAN DIRECTS TRAFFIC!
DON'T BE SURPRISED WHEN CAR HORNS HONK AND THE PEOPLE MISTAKE YOU FOR A STAR!

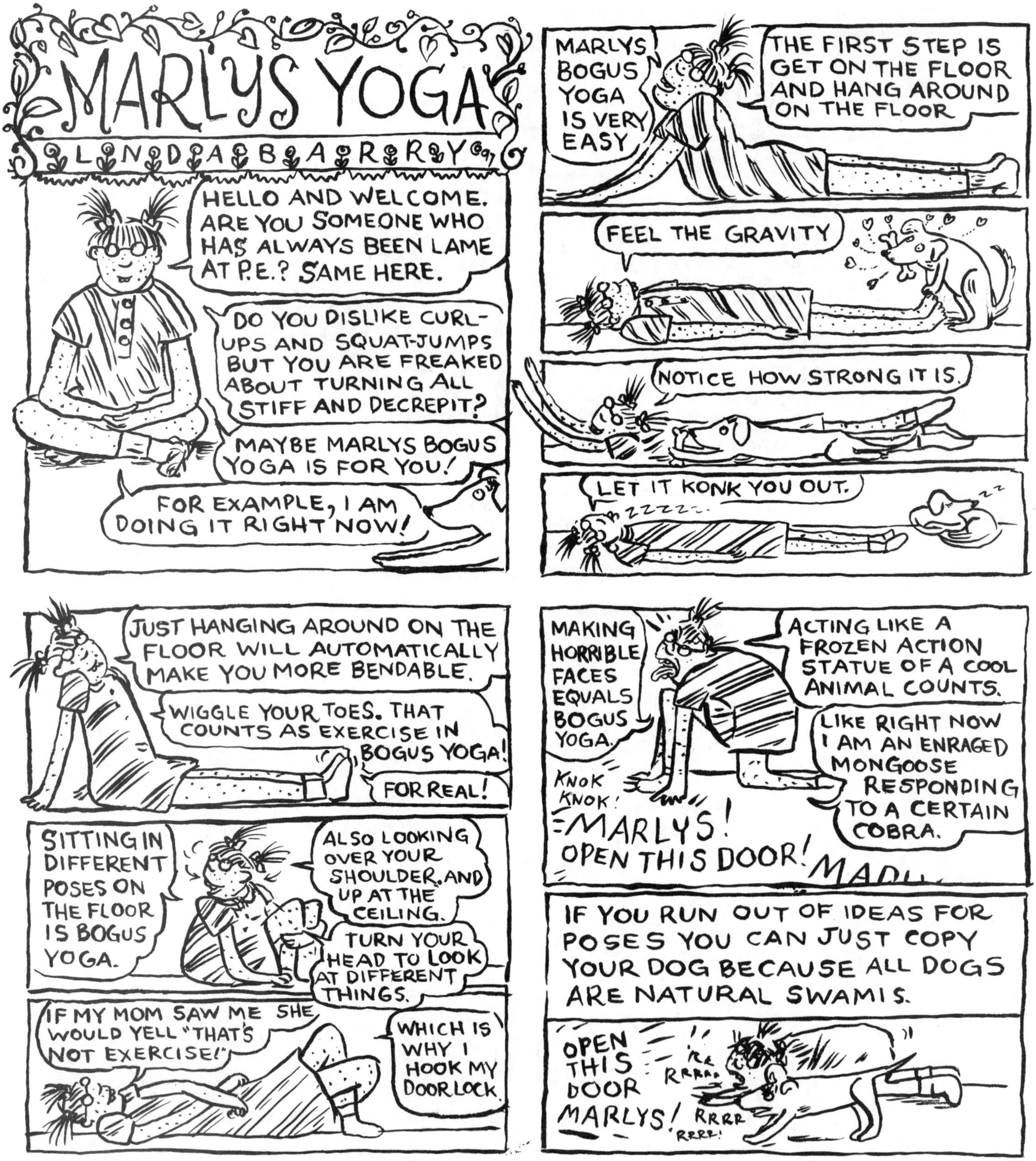
MARLYS YOGA
LYNDA BARRY ©97
HELLO AND WELCOME. ARE YOU SOMEONE WHO HAS ALWAYS BEEN LAME AT P.E.? SAME HERE.
DO YOU DISLIKE CURL-UPS AND SQUAT-JUMPS BUT YOU ARE FREAKED ABOUT TURNING ALL STIFF AND DECREPIT?
MAYBE MARLYS BOGUS YOGA IS FOR YOU!
FOR EXAMPLE, I AM DOING IT RIGHT NOW!
MARLYS BOGUS YOGA IS VERY EASY
THE FIRST STEP IS GET ON THE FLOOR AND HANG AROUND ON THE FLOOR
FEEL THE GRAVITY
NOTICE HOW STRONG IT IS.
LET IT KONK YOU OUT.
JUST HANGING AROUND ON THE FLOOR WILL AUTOMATICALLY MAKE YOU MORE BENDABLE.
WIGGLE YOUR TOES. THAT COUNTS AS EXERCISE IN BOGUS YOGA!
FOR REAL!
SITTING IN DIFFERENT POSES ON THE FLOOR IS BOGUS YOGA.
ALSO LOOKING OVER YOUR SHOULDER, AND UP AT THE CEILING.
TURN YOUR HEAD TO LOOK AT DIFFERENT THINGS.
IF MY MOM SAW ME SHE WOULD YELL "THAT'S NOT EXERCISE!"
WHICH IS WHY I HOOK MY DOOR LOCK
MAKING HORRIBLE FACES EQUALS BOGUS YOGA.
ACTING LIKE A FROZEN ACTION STATUE OF A COOL ANIMAL COUNTS.
LIKE RIGHT NOW I AM AN ENRAGED MONGOOSE RESPONDING TO A CERTAIN COBRA.
KNOK KNOK!
MARLYS! OPEN THIS DOOR! MAR...
IF YOU RUN OUT OF IDEAS FOR POSES YOU CAN JUST COPY YOUR DOG BECAUSE ALL DOGS ARE NATURAL SWAMIS.
OPEN THIS DOOR MARLYS!
RRRRR RRRR RRRR!

MARLYS YOGA · PART TWO

BY MRS. KEVIN KAWULA aka → Lynda Barry ©97

1. SIT IN QUIET CONTEMPLATION ON THE SUBJECT OF EXERCISE MACHINES.

- YES STAIR MASTER, I HEAR AND OBEY
- YES THIGH-MASTER
- YES BUTT MASTER
- YES GUT BUSTER
- YES MASTER CARD PAYMENT PLAN

2. STAND AND PONDER THE STATIONARY BICYCLE. ASK, WHERE IS THIS PERSON ACTUALLY GOING? AND COULD THE BIKE GET HOOKED TO A WASHER SO SHE COULD AT LEAST GET HER LAUNDRY CLEAN WITH HER ENERGETIC ACTIONS?

3. PLACE YOUR PALMS TOGETHER AND REFLECT ON THE CHANGES LIPOSUCTION CAN BRING.

BEFORE · AFTER

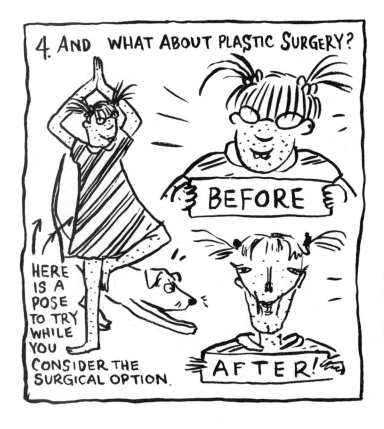

4. AND WHAT ABOUT PLASTIC SURGERY?

BEFORE

AFTER!

HERE IS A POSE TO TRY WHILE YOU CONSIDER THE SURGICAL OPTION.

5. FINALLY, MEDITATE ON WHY PEOPLE LOOK SO MEAN WHILE THEY WORK OUT.

- UM
- HI
- NICE DAY.
- SHUT THE HELL UP! CAN'T YOU SEE I'M POWER WALKING?
- YOU THINK I PAID $300ºº FOR THESE SHOES TO TALK TO YOU?
- GET YOUR UGLY DOG OUT OF MY WAY

AND THEN, GO GET A POPSICLE!

- YOW! YOU TRIPPED ME! I'M SUEING YOU!
- THE HELL YOU ARE! I'M SUEING YOU!
- MUST REACH CELL PHONE
- MUST CALL LAWYER
- WOW
- WHAT A GREAT DAY!!

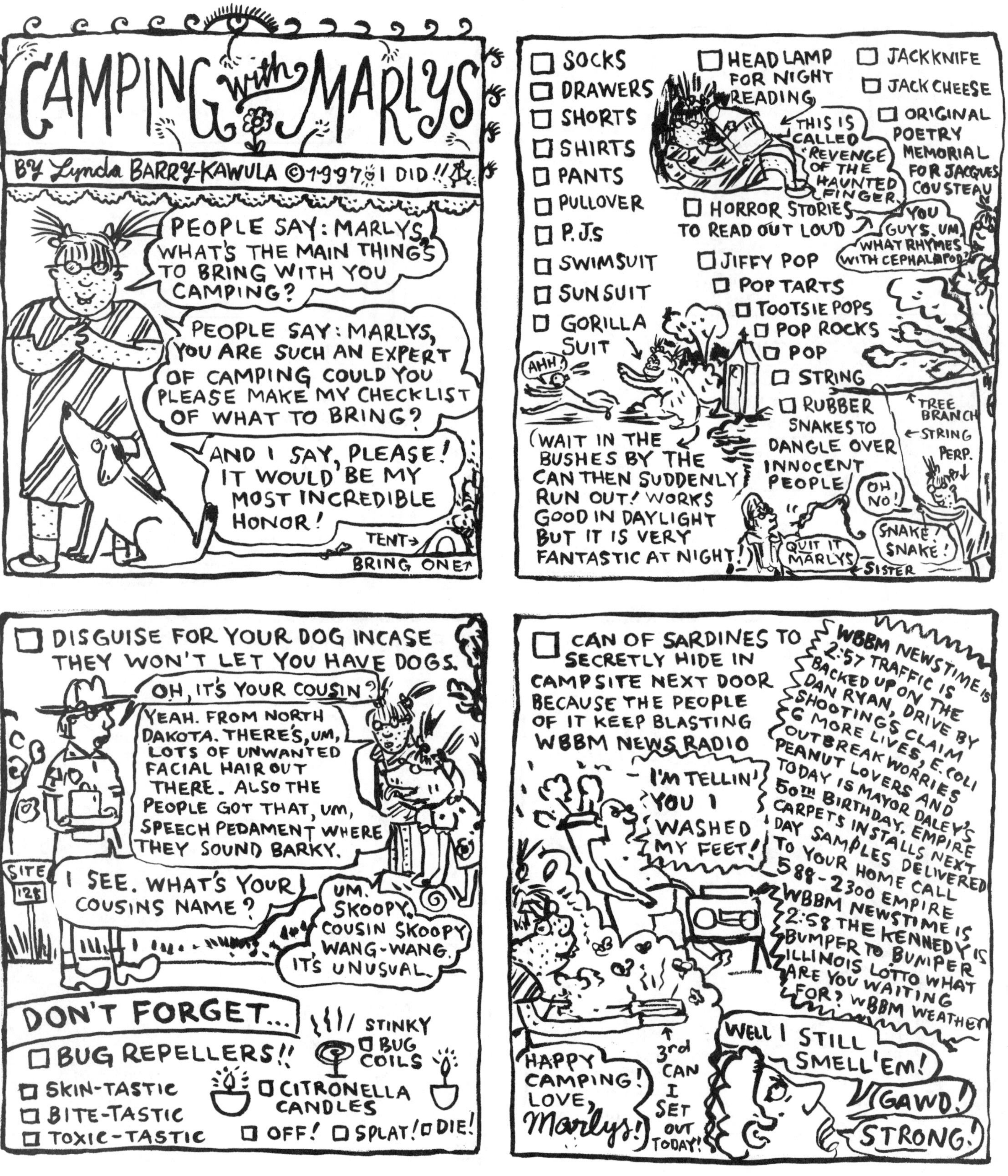
CAMPING with MARLYS
BY Lynda BARRY-KAWULA ©1997 I DID!!
PEOPLE SAY: MARLYS, WHAT'S THE MAIN THINGS TO BRING WITH YOU CAMPING?
PEOPLE SAY: MARLYS, YOU ARE SUCH AN EXPERT OF CAMPING COULD YOU PLEASE MAKE MY CHECKLIST OF WHAT TO BRING?
AND I SAY, PLEASE! IT WOULD BE MY MOST INCREDIBLE HONOR!
TENT→
BRING ONE↑
☐ SOCKS
☐ DRAWERS
☐ SHORTS
☐ SHIRTS
☐ PANTS
☐ PULLOVER
☐ P.J.s
☐ SWIMSUIT
☐ SUNSUIT
☐ GORILLA SUIT
☐ HEAD LAMP FOR NIGHT READING
THIS IS CALLED "REVENGE OF THE HAUNTED FINGER."
☐ JACKKNIFE
☐ JACK CHEESE
☐ ORIGINAL POETRY MEMORIAL FOR JACQUES COUSTEAU
YOU GUYS, UM WHAT RHYMES WITH CEPHALOPOD?
☐ HORROR STORIES TO READ OUT LOUD
☐ JIFFY POP
☐ POP TARTS
☐ TOOTSIE POPS
☐ POP ROCKS
☐ POP
☐ STRING
☐ RUBBER SNAKES TO DANGLE OVER INNOCENT PEOPLE
AHH!
(WAIT IN THE BUSHES BY THE CAN THEN SUDDENLY RUN OUT! WORKS GOOD IN DAYLIGHT BUT IT IS VERY FANTASTIC AT NIGHT!)
TREE BRANCH
←STRING
PERP.
OH NO!
SNAKE! SNAKE!
QUIT IT MARLYS
←SISTER
☐ DISGUISE FOR YOUR DOG INCASE THEY WON'T LET YOU HAVE DOGS.
OH, IT'S YOUR COUSIN?
YEAH. FROM NORTH DAKOTA. THERE'S, UM, LOTS OF UNWANTED FACIAL HAIR OUT THERE. ALSO THE PEOPLE GOT THAT, UM, SPEECH PEDAMENT WHERE THEY SOUND BARKY.
SITE 128
I SEE. WHAT'S YOUR COUSINS NAME?
UM. SKOOPY. COUSIN SKOOPY WANG-WANG. IT'S UNUSUAL.
DON'T FORGET...
☐ BUG REPELLERS!!
☐ SKIN-TASTIC
☐ BITE-TASTIC
☐ TOXIC-TASTIC
STINKY ☐ BUG COILS
☐ CITRONELLA CANDLES
☐ OFF! ☐ SPLAT! ☐ DIE!
☐ CAN OF SARDINES TO SECRETLY HIDE IN CAMPSITE NEXT DOOR BECAUSE THE PEOPLE OF IT KEEP BLASTING WBBM NEWS RADIO
WBBM NEWSTIME IS 2:57 TRAFFIC IS BACKED UP ON THE DAN RYAN, DRIVE BY SHOOTINGS CLAIM 6 MORE LIVES, E.COLI OUTBREAK WORRIES PEANUT LOVERS AND TODAY IS MAYOR DALEY'S 50TH BIRTHDAY. EMPIRE CARPETS INSTALLS NEXT DAY SAMPLES DELIVERED TO YOUR HOME CALL 588-2300 EMPIRE WBBM NEWSTIME IS 2:58 THE KENNEDY IS BUMPER TO BUMPER ILLINOIS LOTTO WHAT ARE YOU WAITING FOR? WBBM WEATHER
I'M TELLIN' YOU I WASHED MY FEET!
3rd CAN I SET OUT TODAY!
HAPPY CAMPING! LOVE, Marlys!
WELL I STILL SMELL 'EM!
GAWD!
STRONG!

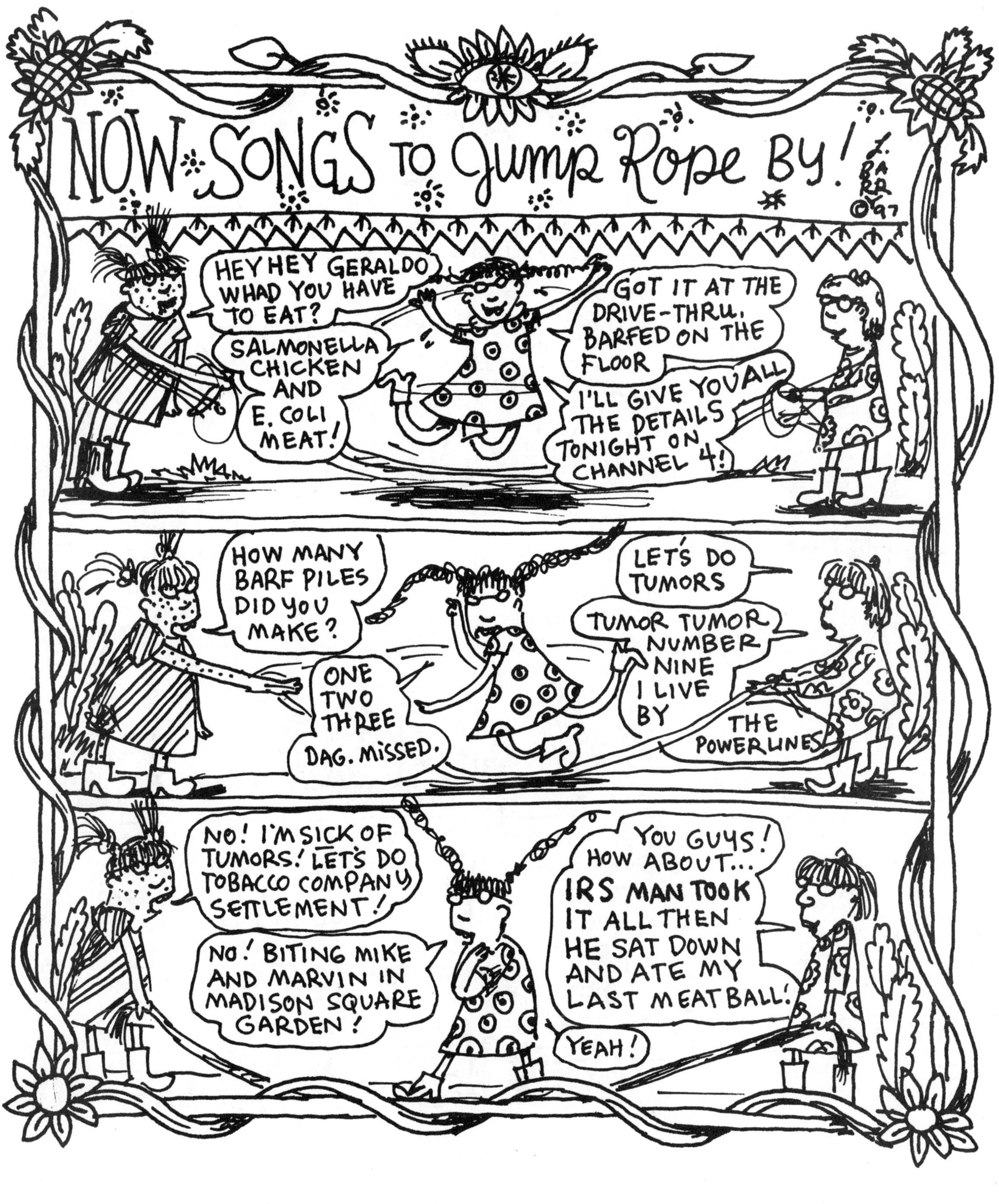
NOW SONGS TO JUMP ROPE BY!
L. BARR ©'97
HEY HEY GERALDO WHAD YOU HAVE TO EAT?
SALMONELLA CHICKEN AND E. COLI MEAT!
GOT IT AT THE DRIVE-THRU, BARFED ON THE FLOOR
I'LL GIVE YOU ALL THE DETAILS TONIGHT ON CHANNEL 4!
HOW MANY BARF PILES DID YOU MAKE?
ONE TWO THREE
DAG. MISSED.
LET'S DO TUMORS
TUMOR TUMOR NUMBER NINE I LIVE BY THE POWERLINES
NO! I'M SICK OF TUMORS! LET'S DO TOBACCO COMPANY SETTLEMENT!
NO! BITING MIKE AND MARVIN IN MADISON SQUARE GARDEN!
YOU GUYS! HOW ABOUT...
IRS MAN TOOK IT ALL THEN HE SAT DOWN AND ATE MY LAST MEATBALL!
YEAH!

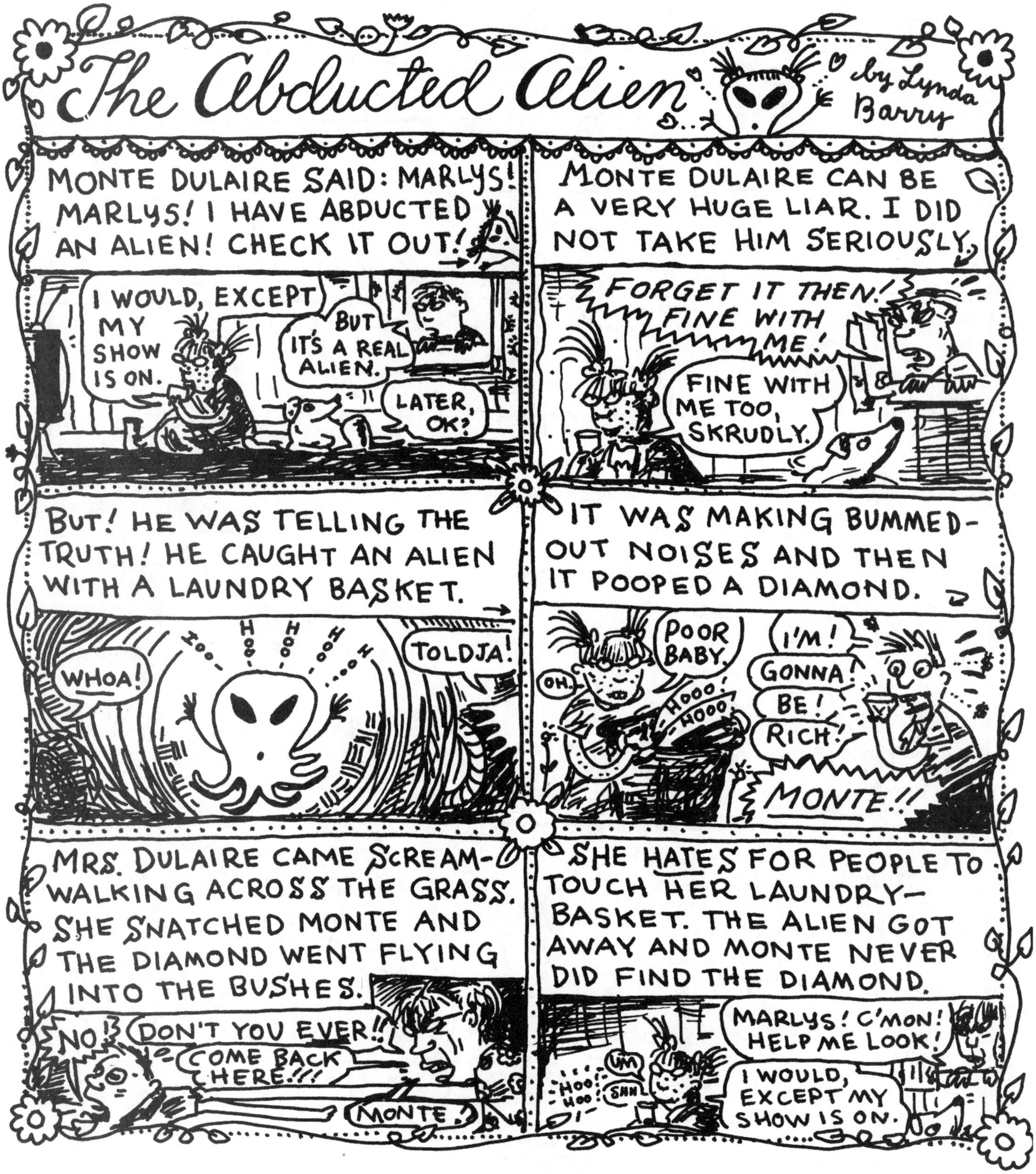
The Abducted Alien
by Lynda Barry
MONTE DULAIRE SAID: MARLYS! MARLYS! I HAVE ABDUCTED AN ALIEN! CHECK IT OUT!
I WOULD, EXCEPT MY SHOW IS ON.
BUT IT'S A REAL ALIEN.
LATER, OK?
MONTE DULAIRE CAN BE A VERY HUGE LIAR. I DID NOT TAKE HIM SERIOUSLY.
FORGET IT THEN! FINE WITH ME!
FINE WITH ME TOO, SKRUDLY.
BUT! HE WAS TELLING THE TRUTH! HE CAUGHT AN ALIEN WITH A LAUNDRY BASKET.
WHOA!
HOO... HOO HOO HOO... HOO...
TOLDJA!
IT WAS MAKING BUMMED-OUT NOISES AND THEN IT POOPED A DIAMOND.
OH.
POOR BABY.
HOOO HOOO
I'M! GONNA! BE! RICH!
MONTE!!
MRS. DULAIRE CAME SCREAM-WALKING ACROSS THE GRASS. SHE SNATCHED MONTE AND THE DIAMOND WENT FLYING INTO THE BUSHES.
NO!
DON'T YOU EVER!!
COME BACK HERE!!!
MONTE!
SHE HATES FOR PEOPLE TO TOUCH HER LAUNDRY-BASKET. THE ALIEN GOT AWAY AND MONTE NEVER DID FIND THE DIAMOND.
MARLYS! C'MON! HELP ME LOOK!
HOO HOO
UM
SHH
I WOULD, EXCEPT MY SHOW IS ON.

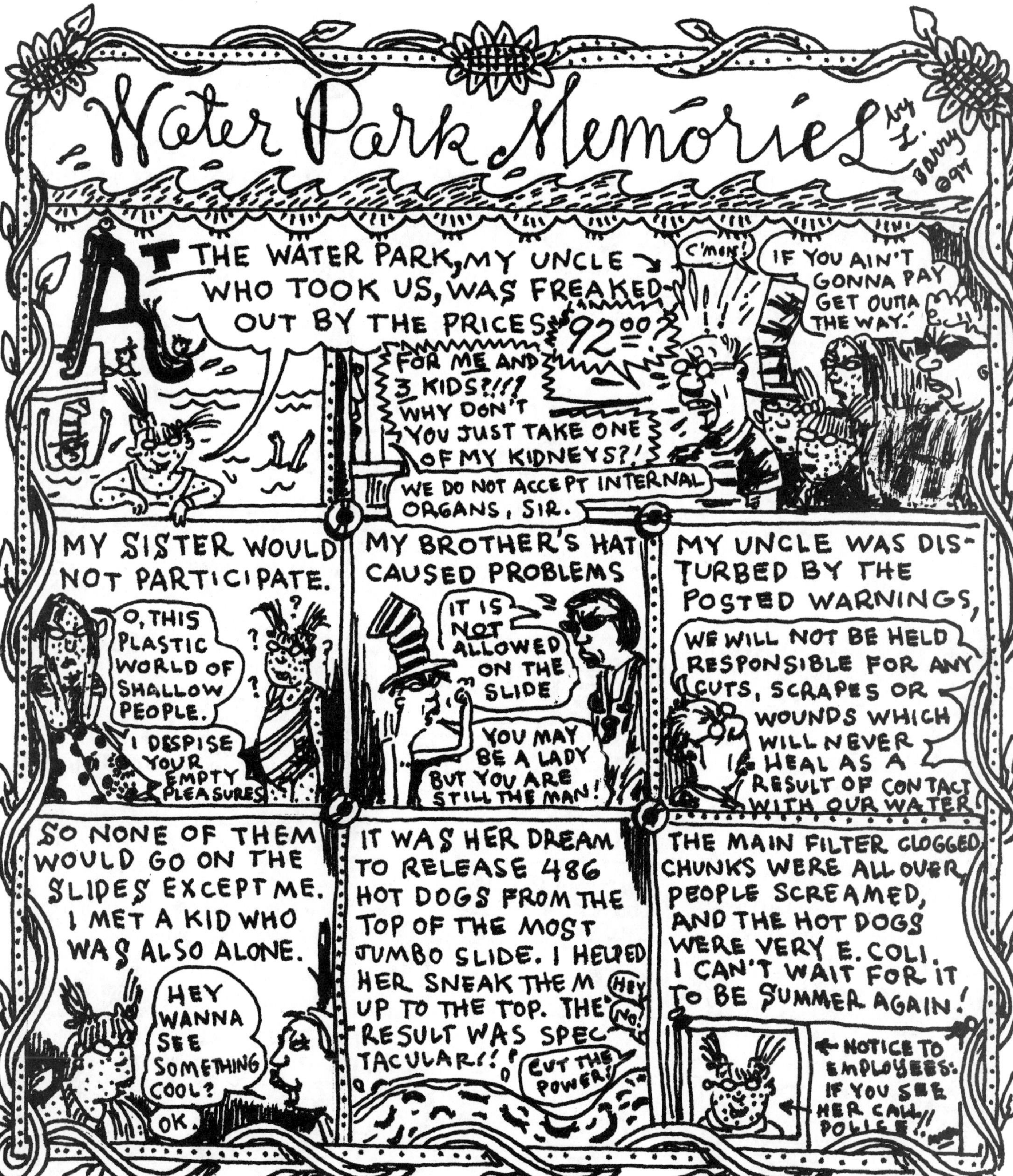
Water Park Memories
by L. Barry ©94
AT THE WATER PARK, MY UNCLE WHO TOOK US, WAS FREAKED OUT BY THE PRICES.
$92.00
FOR ME AND 3 KIDS?!!! WHY DON'T YOU JUST TAKE ONE OF MY KIDNEYS?!
WE DO NOT ACCEPT INTERNAL ORGANS, SIR.
C'MON!
IF YOU AIN'T GONNA PAY GET OUTTA THE WAY.
MY SISTER WOULD NOT PARTICIPATE.
O, THIS PLASTIC WORLD OF SHALLOW PEOPLE.
I DESPISE YOUR EMPTY PLEASURES.
MY BROTHER'S HAT CAUSED PROBLEMS
IT IS NOT ALLOWED ON THE SLIDE
YOU MAY BE A LADY BUT YOU ARE STILL THE MAN!
MY UNCLE WAS DISTURBED BY THE POSTED WARNINGS,
WE WILL NOT BE HELD RESPONSIBLE FOR ANY CUTS, SCRAPES OR WOUNDS WHICH WILL NEVER HEAL AS A RESULT OF CONTACT WITH OUR WATER
SO NONE OF THEM WOULD GO ON THE SLIDES EXCEPT ME. I MET A KID WHO WAS ALSO ALONE.
HEY WANNA SEE SOMETHING COOL?
OK.
IT WAS HER DREAM TO RELEASE 486 HOT DOGS FROM THE TOP OF THE MOST JUMBO SLIDE. I HELPED HER SNEAK THEM UP TO THE TOP. THE RESULT WAS SPECTACULAR!!
HEY NO!
CUT THE POWER!
THE MAIN FILTER CLOGGED. CHUNKS WERE ALL OVER. PEOPLE SCREAMED, AND THE HOT DOGS WERE VERY E. COLI. I CAN'T WAIT FOR IT TO BE SUMMER AGAIN!
NOTICE TO EMPLOYEES: IF YOU SEE HER CALL POLICE!!

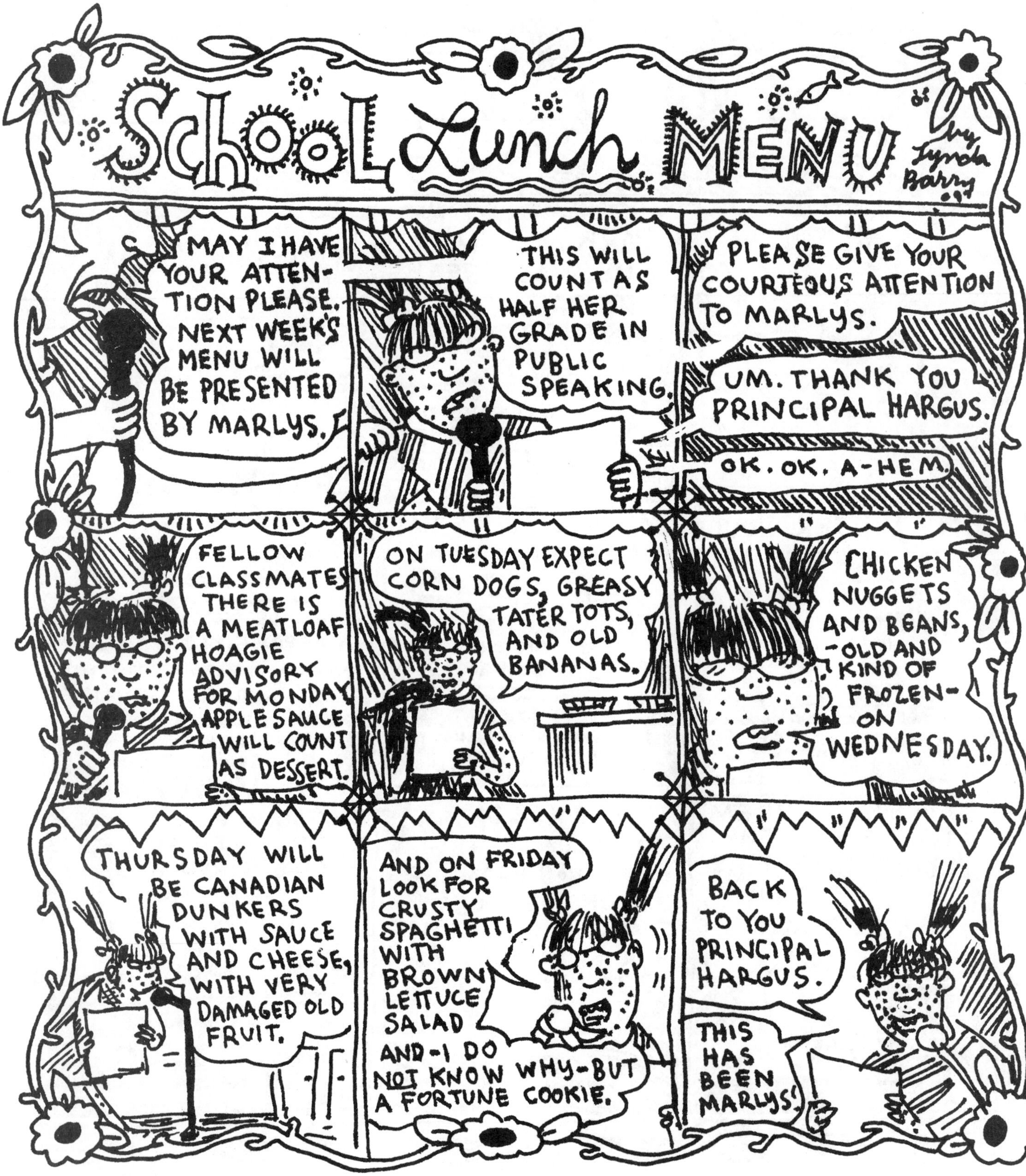
School Lunch MENU
by Lynda Barry
MAY I HAVE YOUR ATTENTION PLEASE. NEXT WEEK'S MENU WILL BE PRESENTED BY MARLYS.
THIS WILL COUNT AS HALF HER GRADE IN PUBLIC SPEAKING.
PLEASE GIVE YOUR COURTEOUS ATTENTION TO MARLYS.
UM. THANK YOU PRINCIPAL HARGUS.
OK. OK. A-HEM.
FELLOW CLASSMATES THERE IS A MEATLOAF HOAGIE ADVISORY FOR MONDAY. APPLESAUCE WILL COUNT AS DESSERT.
ON TUESDAY EXPECT CORN DOGS, GREASY TATER TOTS, AND OLD BANANAS.
CHICKEN NUGGETS AND BEANS, -OLD AND KIND OF FROZEN- ON WEDNESDAY.
THURSDAY WILL BE CANADIAN DUNKERS WITH SAUCE AND CHEESE, WITH VERY DAMAGED OLD FRUIT.
AND ON FRIDAY LOOK FOR CRUSTY SPAGHETTI WITH BROWN LETTUCE SALAD
AND-I DO NOT KNOW WHY-BUT A FORTUNE COOKIE.
BACK TO YOU PRINCIPAL HARGUS.
THIS HAS BEEN MARLYS!

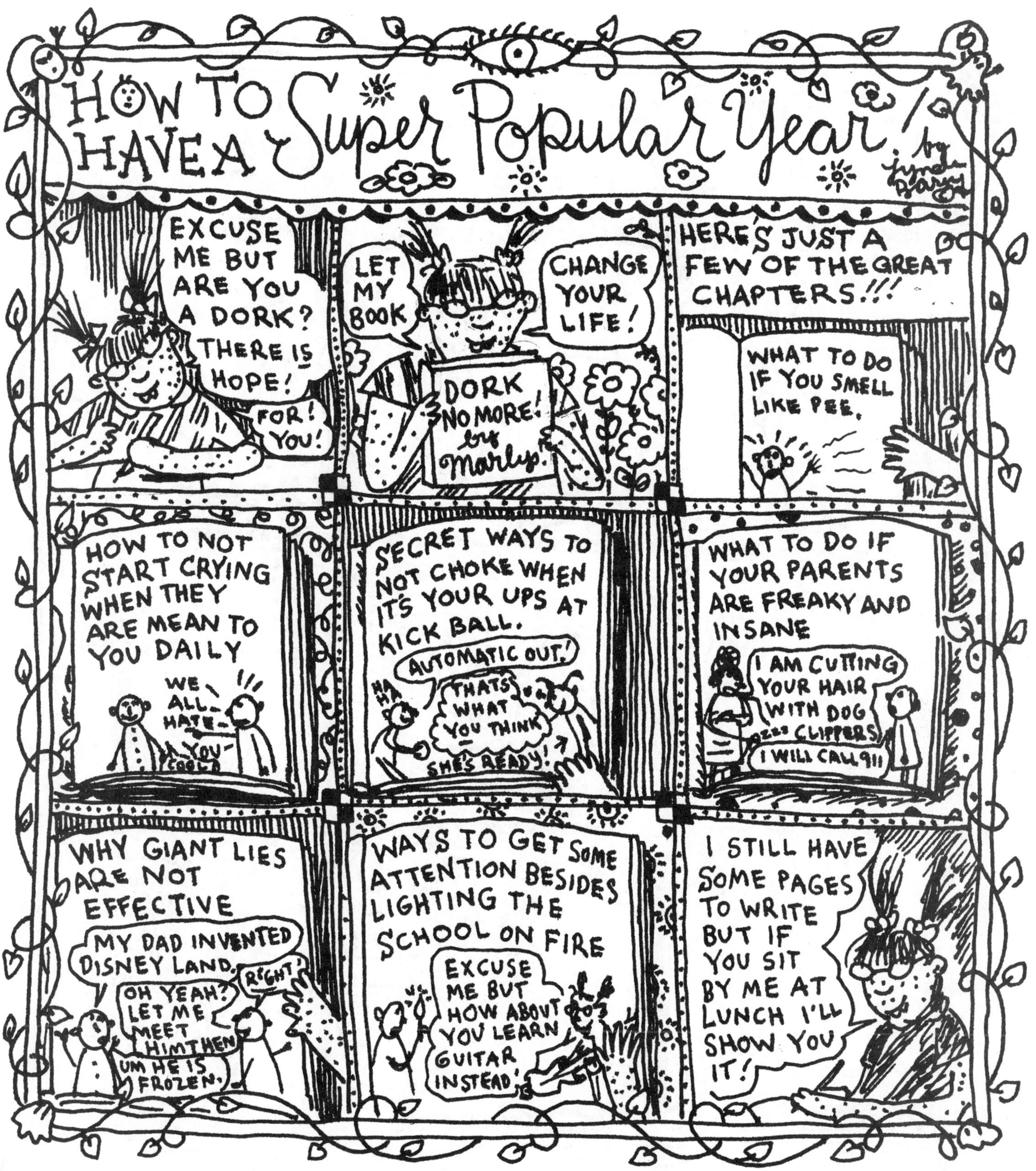
HOW TO HAVE A Super Popular Year!
by lynda barry
EXCUSE ME BUT ARE YOU A DORK? THERE IS HOPE!
FOR! YOU!
LET MY BOOK
CHANGE YOUR LIFE!
DORK NO MORE! by Marlys
HERE'S JUST A FEW OF THE GREAT CHAPTERS!!!
WHAT TO DO IF YOU SMELL LIKE PEE.
HOW TO NOT START CRYING WHEN THEY ARE MEAN TO YOU DAILY
WE ALL HATE YOU
SECRET WAYS TO NOT CHOKE WHEN IT'S YOUR UPS AT KICK BALL.
AUTOMATIC OUT!
HA HA
THATS WHAT YOU THINK
SHE'S READY!
WHAT TO DO IF YOUR PARENTS ARE FREAKY AND INSANE
I AM CUTTING YOUR HAIR WITH DOG CLIPPERS
I WILL CALL 911
WHY GIANT LIES ARE NOT EFFECTIVE
MY DAD INVENTED DISNEY LAND.
OH YEAH? LET ME MEET HIM THEN
RIGHT!
UM HE IS FROZEN.
WAYS TO GET SOME ATTENTION BESIDES LIGHTING THE SCHOOL ON FIRE
EXCUSE ME BUT HOW ABOUT YOU LEARN GUITAR INSTEAD.
I STILL HAVE SOME PAGES TO WRITE BUT IF YOU SIT BY ME AT LUNCH I'LL SHOW YOU IT!

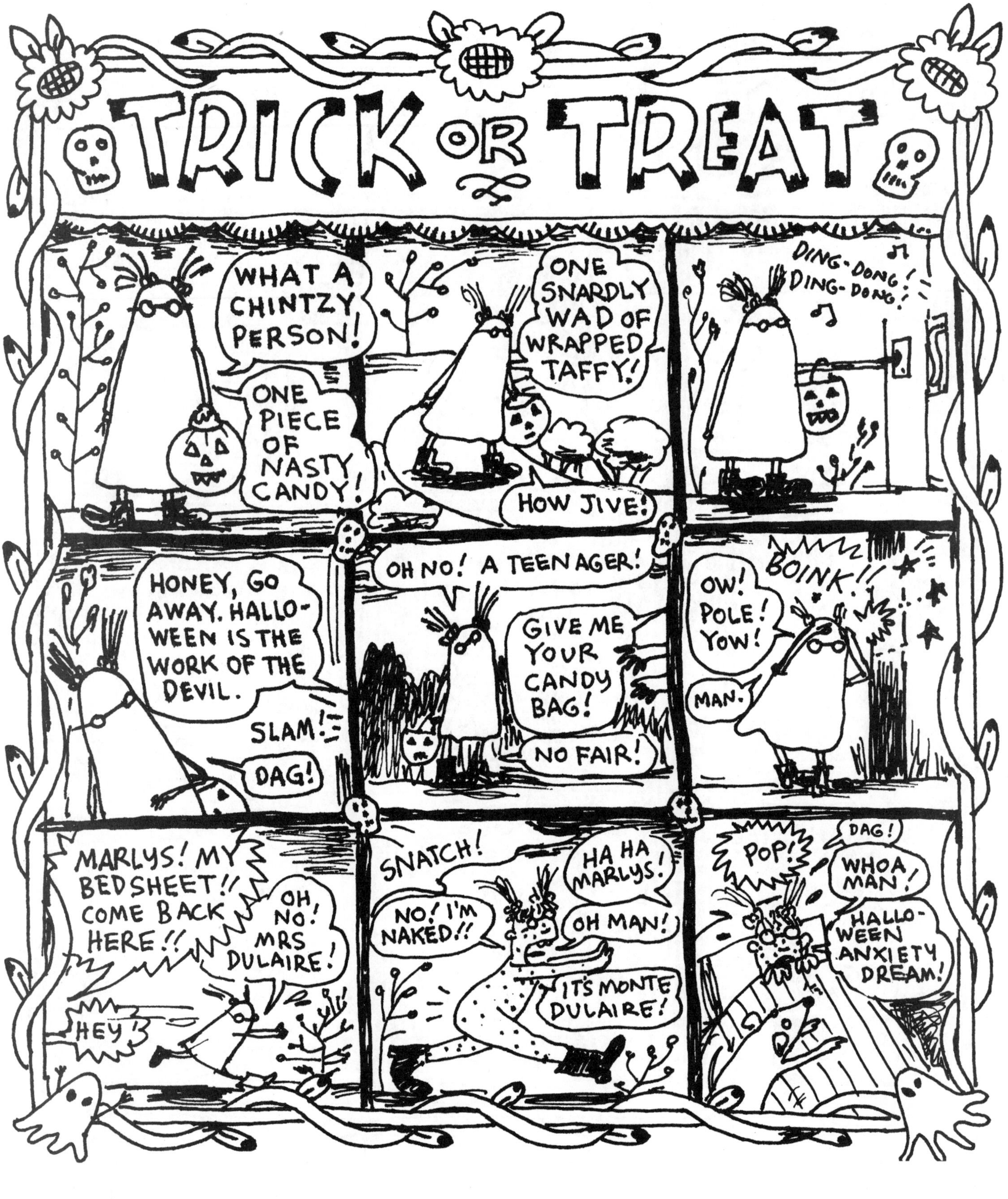
TRICK OR TREAT
WHAT A CHINTZY PERSON!
ONE PIECE OF NASTY CANDY!
ONE SNARDLY WAD OF WRAPPED TAFFY!
HOW JIVE!
DING-DONG! DING-DONG!
HONEY, GO AWAY. HALLOWEEN IS THE WORK OF THE DEVIL.
SLAM!
DAG!
OH NO! A TEENAGER!
GIVE ME YOUR CANDY BAG!
NO FAIR!
BOINK!
OW! POLE! YOW!
MAN.
MARLYS! MY BEDSHEET!! COME BACK HERE!!
OH, NO! MRS DULAIRE!
HEY!
SNATCH!
HA HA MARLYS!
NO! I'M NAKED!!
OH MAN!
IT'S MONTE DULAIRE!
POP!
DAG!
WHOA MAN!
HALLOWEEN ANXIETY DREAM!

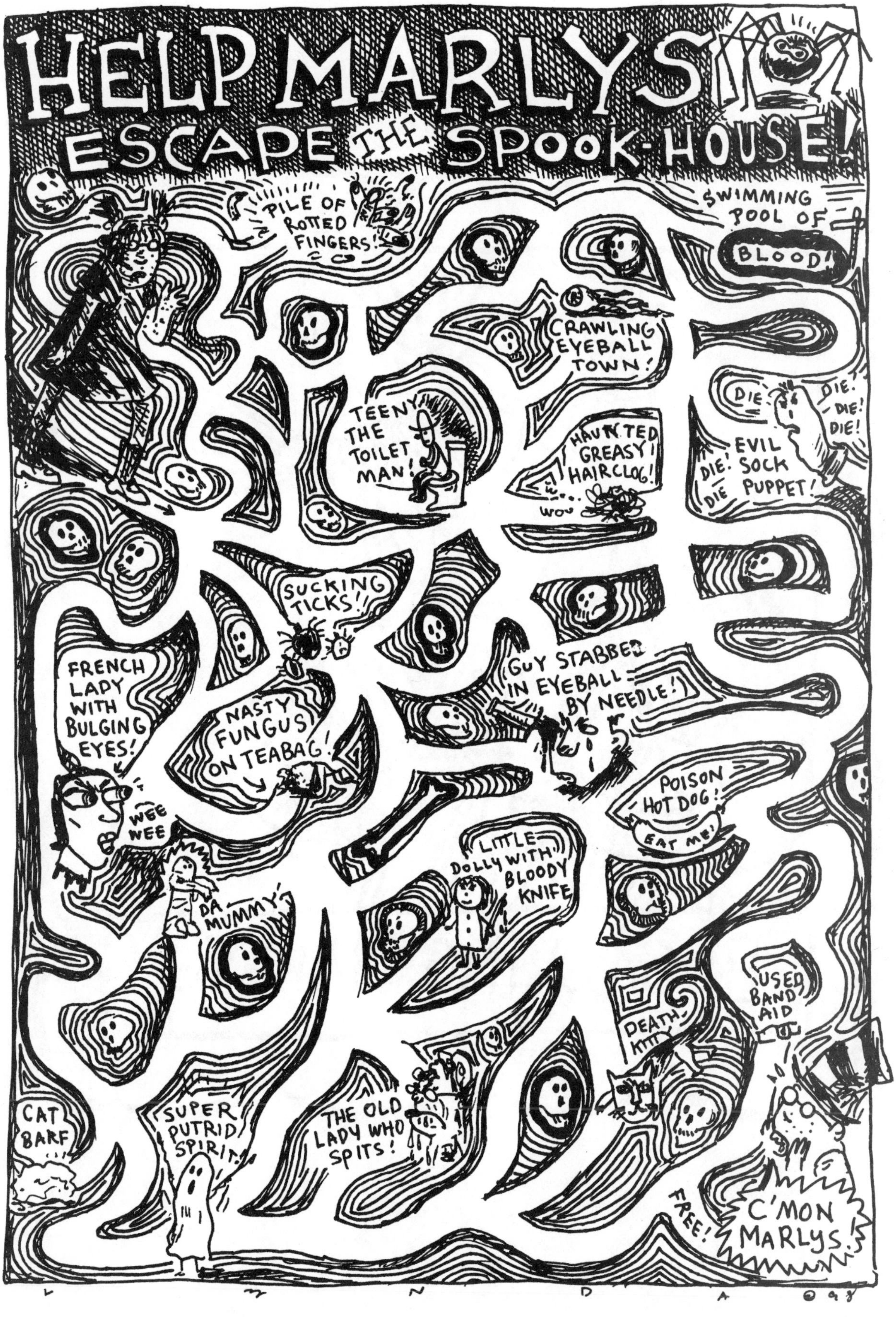
HELP MARLYS ESCAPE THE SPOOK-HOUSE!
PILE OF ROTTED FINGERS!
SWIMMING POOL OF BLOOD!
CRAWLING EYEBALL TOWN!
TEENY THE TOILET MAN!
HAUNTED GREASY HAIRCLOG!
DIE DIE! DIE! DIE! DIE! DIE
EVIL SOCK PUPPET!
SUCKING TICKS!
FRENCH LADY WITH BULGING EYES!
NASTY FUNGUS ON TEABAG!
GUY STABBED IN EYEBALL BY NEEDLE!
POISON HOT DOG!
EAT ME!
WEE WEE
LITTLE DOLLY WITH BLOODY KNIFE
DA MUMMY!
USED BAND AID
DEATH KITTY
CAT BARF
SUPER PUTRID SPIRIT!
THE OLD LADY WHO SPITS!
FREE!
C'MON MARLYS!
L Y N D A ©98

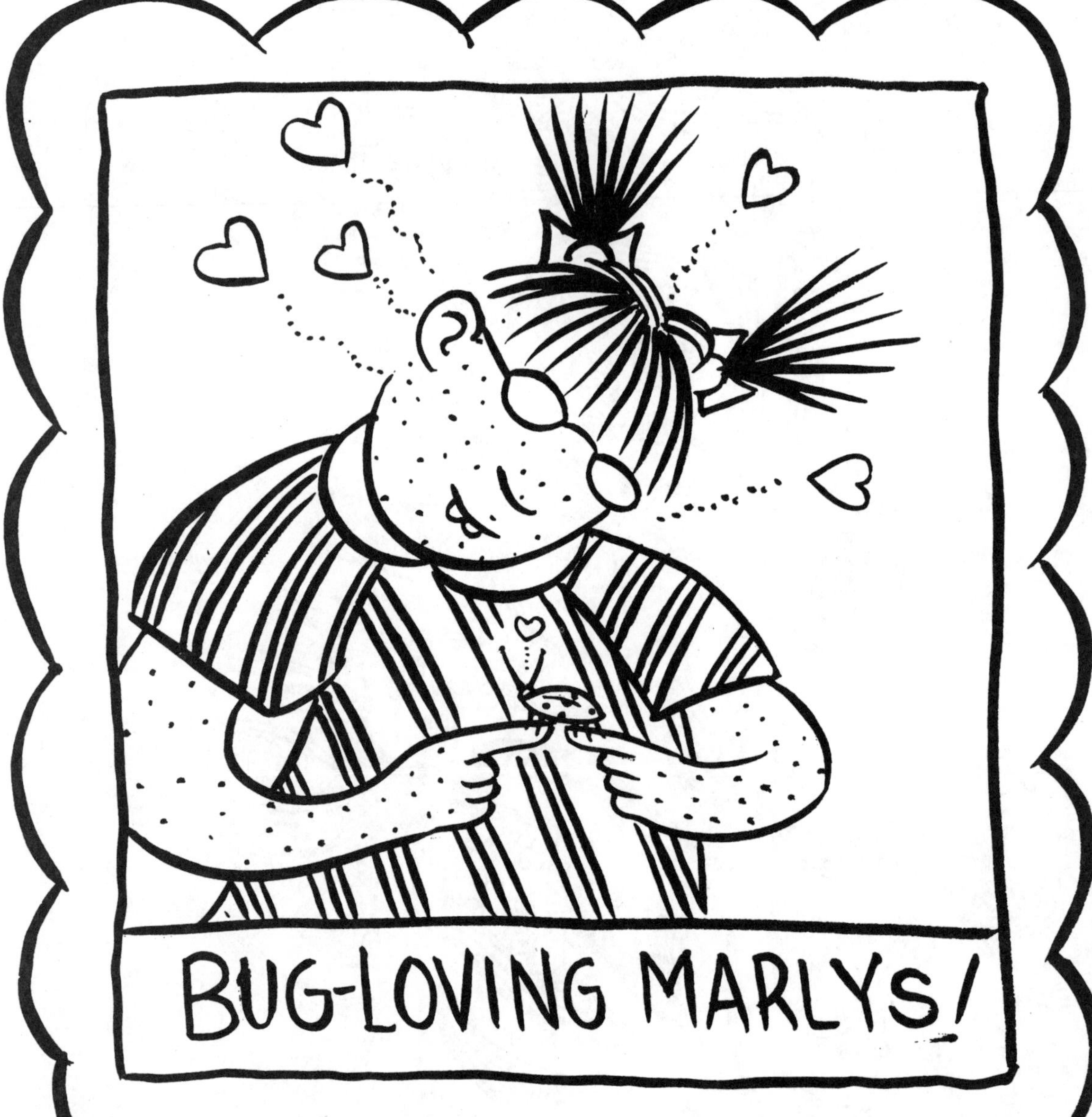
BUG-LOVING MARLYS!

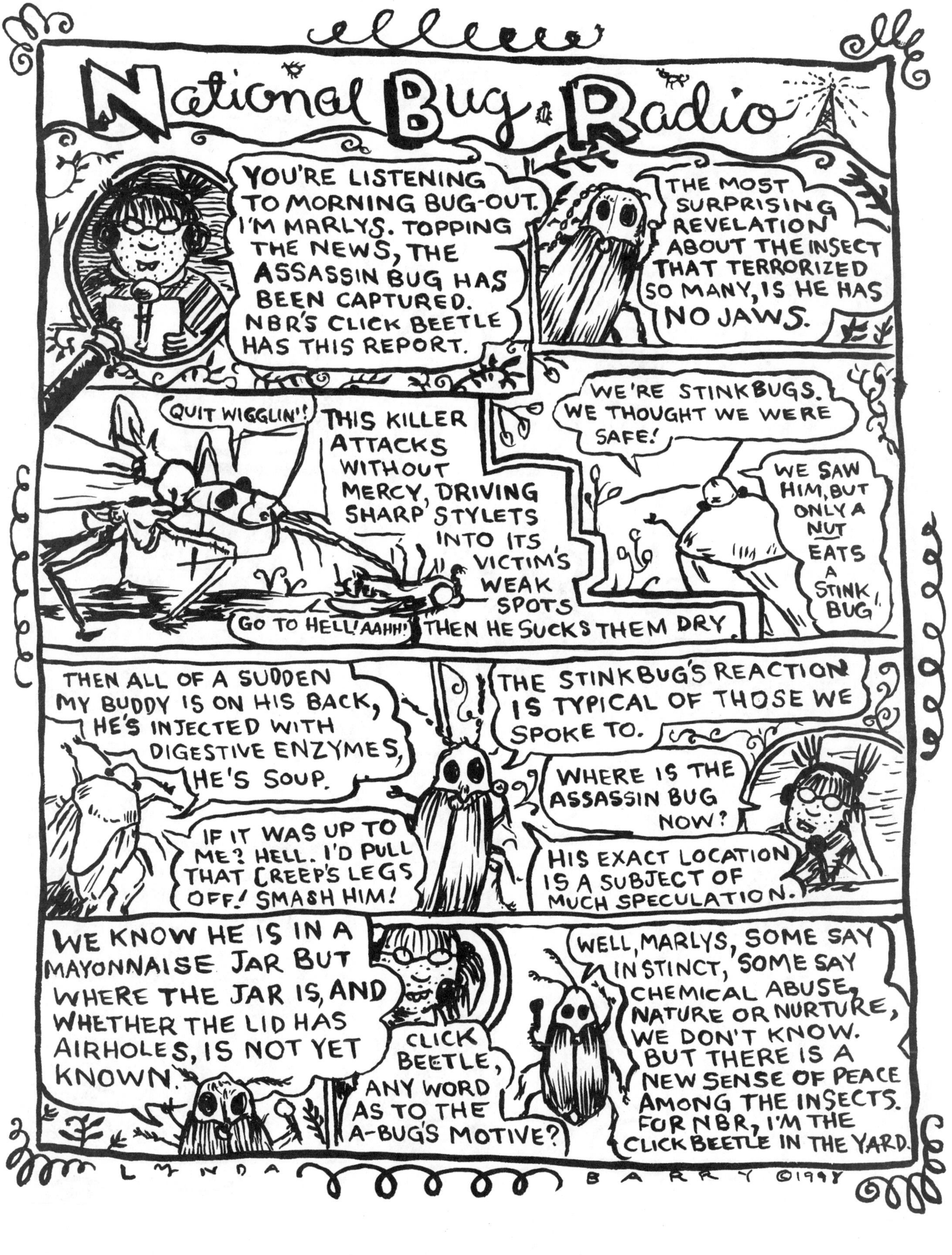

National Bug Radio
YOU'RE LISTENING TO MORNING BUG-OUT. I'M MARLYS. TOPPING THE NEWS, THE ASSASSIN BUG HAS BEEN CAPTURED. NBR'S CLICK BEETLE HAS THIS REPORT.
THE MOST SURPRISING REVELATION ABOUT THE INSECT THAT TERRORIZED SO MANY, IS HE HAS NO JAWS.
QUIT WIGGLIN'!
THIS KILLER ATTACKS WITHOUT MERCY, DRIVING SHARP STYLETS INTO ITS VICTIM'S WEAK SPOTS
GO TO HELL! AAHH!
THEN HE SUCKS THEM DRY
WE'RE STINKBUGS. WE THOUGHT WE WERE SAFE!
WE SAW HIM, BUT ONLY A NUT EATS A STINK BUG
THEN ALL OF A SUDDEN MY BUDDY IS ON HIS BACK, HE'S INJECTED WITH DIGESTIVE ENZYMES, HE'S SOUP.
IF IT WAS UP TO ME? HELL. I'D PULL THAT CREEP'S LEGS OFF! SMASH HIM!
THE STINKBUG'S REACTION IS TYPICAL OF THOSE WE SPOKE TO.
WHERE IS THE ASSASSIN BUG NOW?
HIS EXACT LOCATION IS A SUBJECT OF MUCH SPECULATION.
WE KNOW HE IS IN A MAYONNAISE JAR BUT WHERE THE JAR IS, AND WHETHER THE LID HAS AIRHOLES, IS NOT YET KNOWN.
CLICK BEETLE, ANY WORD AS TO THE A-BUG'S MOTIVE?
WELL, MARLYS, SOME SAY INSTINCT, SOME SAY CHEMICAL ABUSE, NATURE OR NURTURE, WE DON'T KNOW. BUT THERE IS A NEW SENSE OF PEACE AMONG THE INSECTS. FOR NBR, I'M THE CLICK BEETLE IN THE YARD.
LYNDA BARRY ©1998

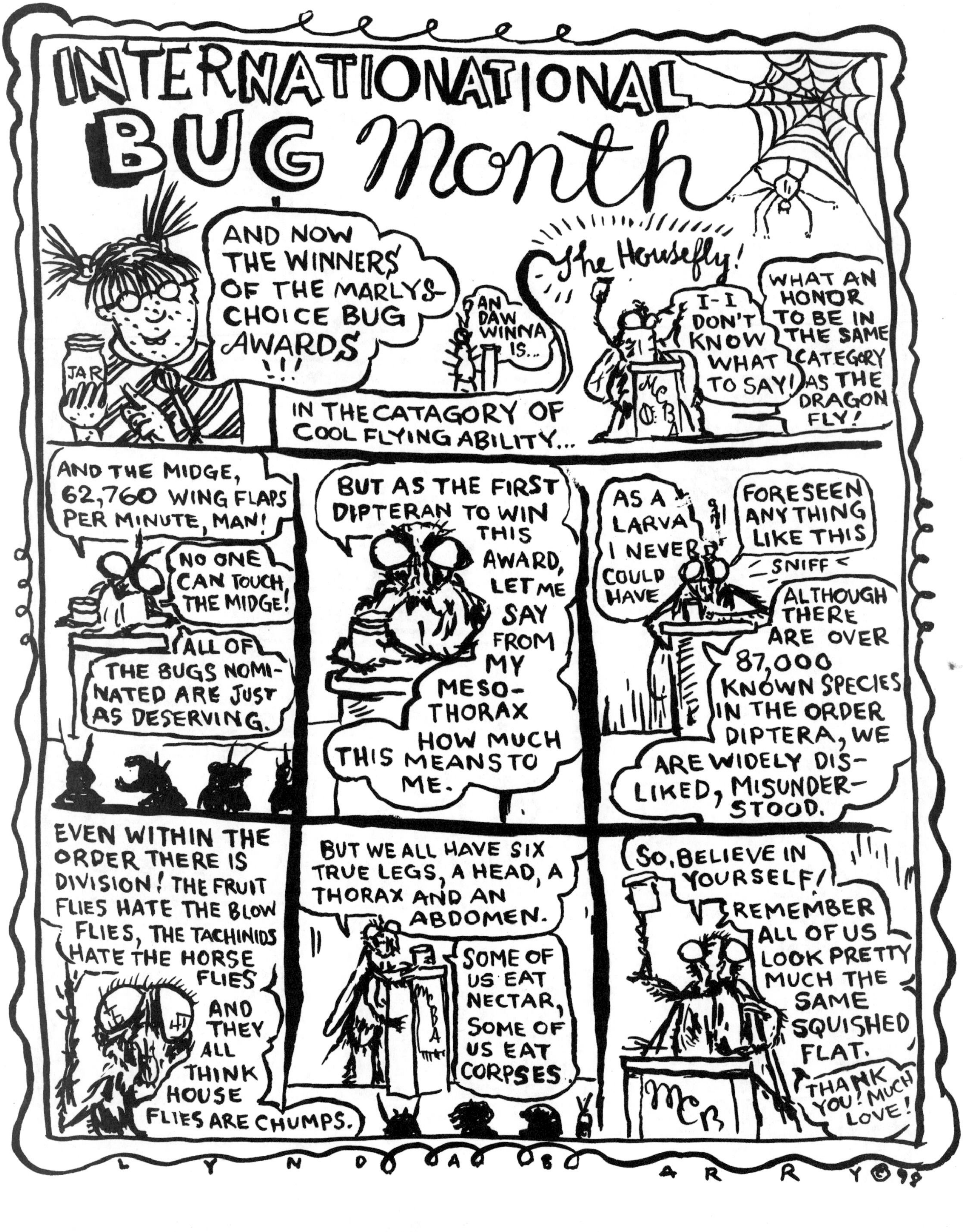
INTERNATIONATIONAL BUG Month
AND NOW THE WINNERS OF THE MARLYS CHOICE BUG AWARDS !!!
JAR
IN THE CATAGORY OF COOL FLYING ABILITY...
AN DAW WINNA IS...
The Housefly!
I-I DON'T KNOW WHAT TO SAY!
WHAT AN HONOR TO BE IN THE SAME CATEGORY AS THE DRAGON FLY!
MCB
AND THE MIDGE, 62,760 WING FLAPS PER MINUTE, MAN!
NO ONE CAN TOUCH THE MIDGE!
ALL OF THE BUGS NOMINATED ARE JUST AS DESERVING.
BUT AS THE FIRST DIPTERAN TO WIN THIS AWARD, LET ME SAY FROM MY MESOTHORAX HOW MUCH THIS MEANS TO ME.
AS A LARVA I NEVER COULD HAVE
FORESEEN ANY THING LIKE THIS
SNIFF
ALTHOUGH THERE ARE OVER 87,000 KNOWN SPECIES IN THE ORDER DIPTERA, WE ARE WIDELY DISLIKED, MISUNDERSTOOD.
EVEN WITHIN THE ORDER THERE IS DIVISION! THE FRUIT FLIES HATE THE BLOW FLIES, THE TACHINIDS HATE THE HORSE FLIES AND THEY ALL THINK HOUSE FLIES ARE CHUMPS.
BUT WE ALL HAVE SIX TRUE LEGS, A HEAD, A THORAX AND AN ABDOMEN.
SOME OF US EAT NECTAR, SOME OF US EAT CORPSES.
MCBA
SO, BELIEVE IN YOURSELF!
REMEMBER ALL OF US LOOK PRETTY MUCH THE SAME SQUISHED FLAT.
THANK YOU! MUCH LOVE!
MCB
LYNDA BARRY ©98

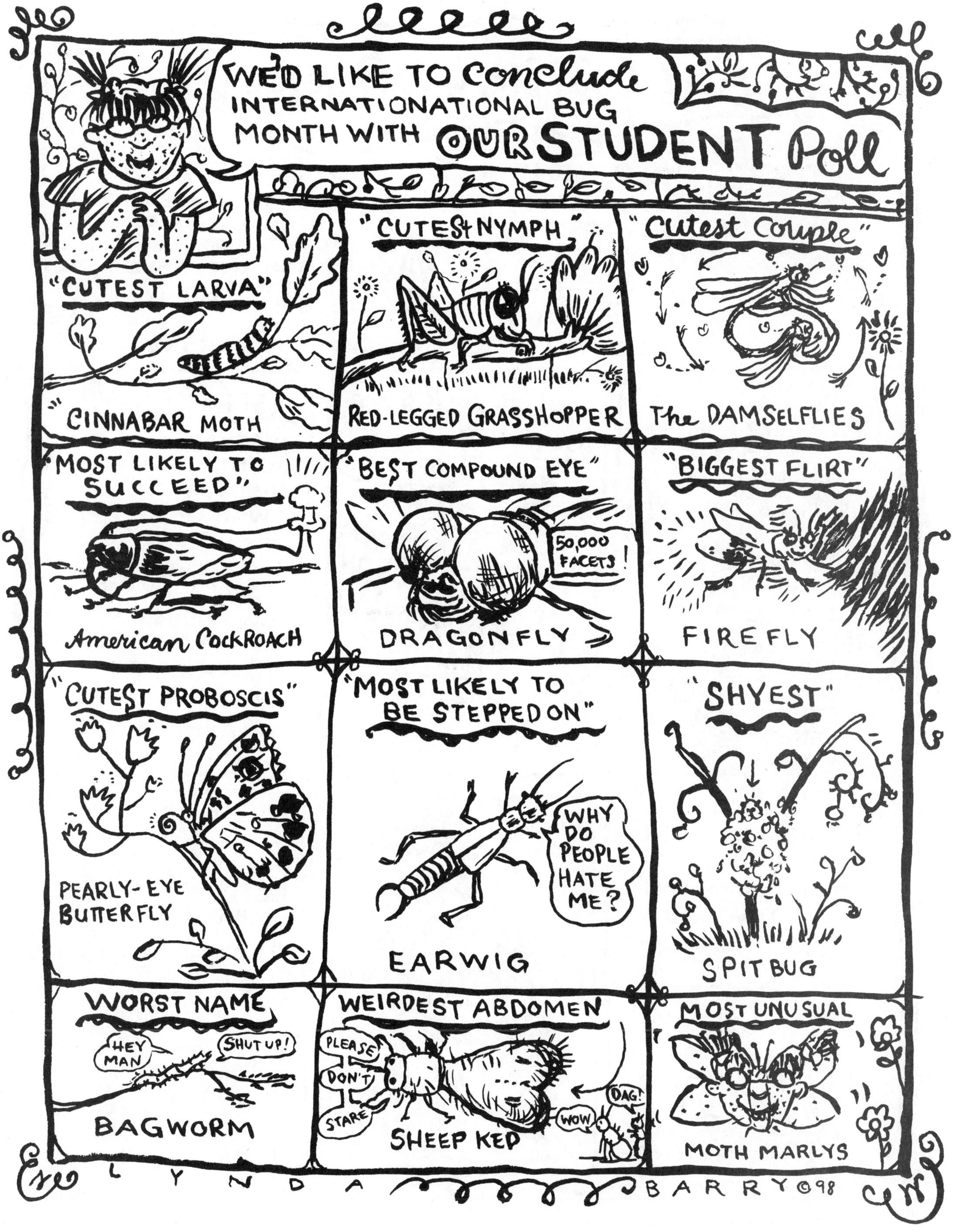
WE'D LIKE TO CONCLUDE INTERNATIONAL BUG MONTH WITH OUR STUDENT POLL
"CUTEST LARVA"
CINNABAR MOTH
"CUTEST NYMPH"
RED-LEGGED GRASSHOPPER
"Cutest Couple"
The DAMSELFLIES
"MOST LIKELY TO SUCCEED"
American COCKROACH
"BEST COMPOUND EYE"
50,000 FACETS!
DRAGONFLY
"BIGGEST FLIRT"
FIREFLY
"CUTEST PROBOSCIS"
PEARLY-EYE BUTTERFLY
"MOST LIKELY TO BE STEPPED ON"
WHY DO PEOPLE HATE ME?
EARWIG
"SHYEST"
SPITBUG
WORST NAME
HEY MAN
SHUT UP!
BAGWORM
WEIRDEST ABDOMEN
PLEASE DON'T STARE
DAG!
WOW
SHEEP KED
MOST UNUSUAL
MOTH MARLYS
LYNDA BARRY ©98

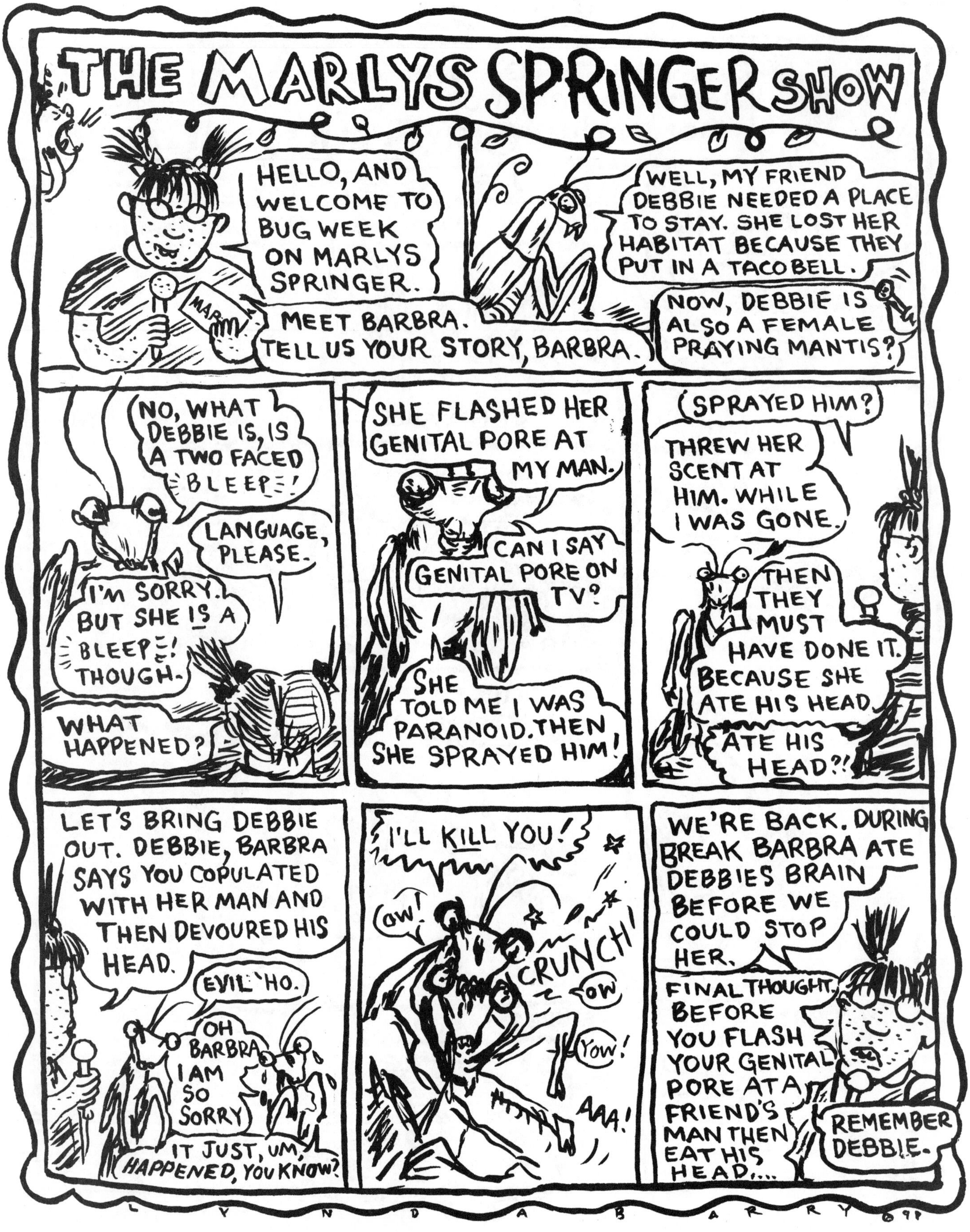
THE MARLYS SPRINGER SHOW
HELLO, AND WELCOME TO BUG WEEK ON MARLYS SPRINGER.
MARLYS
MEET BARBRA. TELL US YOUR STORY, BARBRA.
WELL, MY FRIEND DEBBIE NEEDED A PLACE TO STAY. SHE LOST HER HABITAT BECAUSE THEY PUT IN A TACO BELL.
NOW, DEBBIE IS ALSO A FEMALE PRAYING MANTIS?
NO, WHAT DEBBIE IS, IS A TWO FACED BLEEP!
LANGUAGE, PLEASE.
I'M SORRY. BUT SHE IS A BLEEP! THOUGH.
WHAT HAPPENED?
SHE FLASHED HER GENITAL PORE AT MY MAN.
CAN I SAY GENITAL PORE ON TV?
SHE TOLD ME I WAS PARANOID. THEN SHE SPRAYED HIM!
SPRAYED HIM?
THREW HER SCENT AT HIM. WHILE I WAS GONE.
THEN THEY MUST HAVE DONE IT. BECAUSE SHE ATE HIS HEAD.
ATE HIS HEAD?!
LET'S BRING DEBBIE OUT. DEBBIE, BARBRA SAYS YOU COPULATED WITH HER MAN AND THEN DEVOURED HIS HEAD.
EVIL 'HO.
OH BARBRA I AM SO SORRY
IT JUST, UM, HAPPENED, YOU KNOW?
I'LL KILL YOU!
OW!
CRUNCH!
OW
YOW!
AAA!
WE'RE BACK. DURING BREAK BARBRA ATE DEBBIES BRAIN BEFORE WE COULD STOP HER.
FINAL THOUGHT. BEFORE YOU FLASH YOUR GENITAL PORE AT A FRIEND'S MAN THEN EAT HIS HEAD....
REMEMBER DEBBIE.
LYNDA BARRY ©98

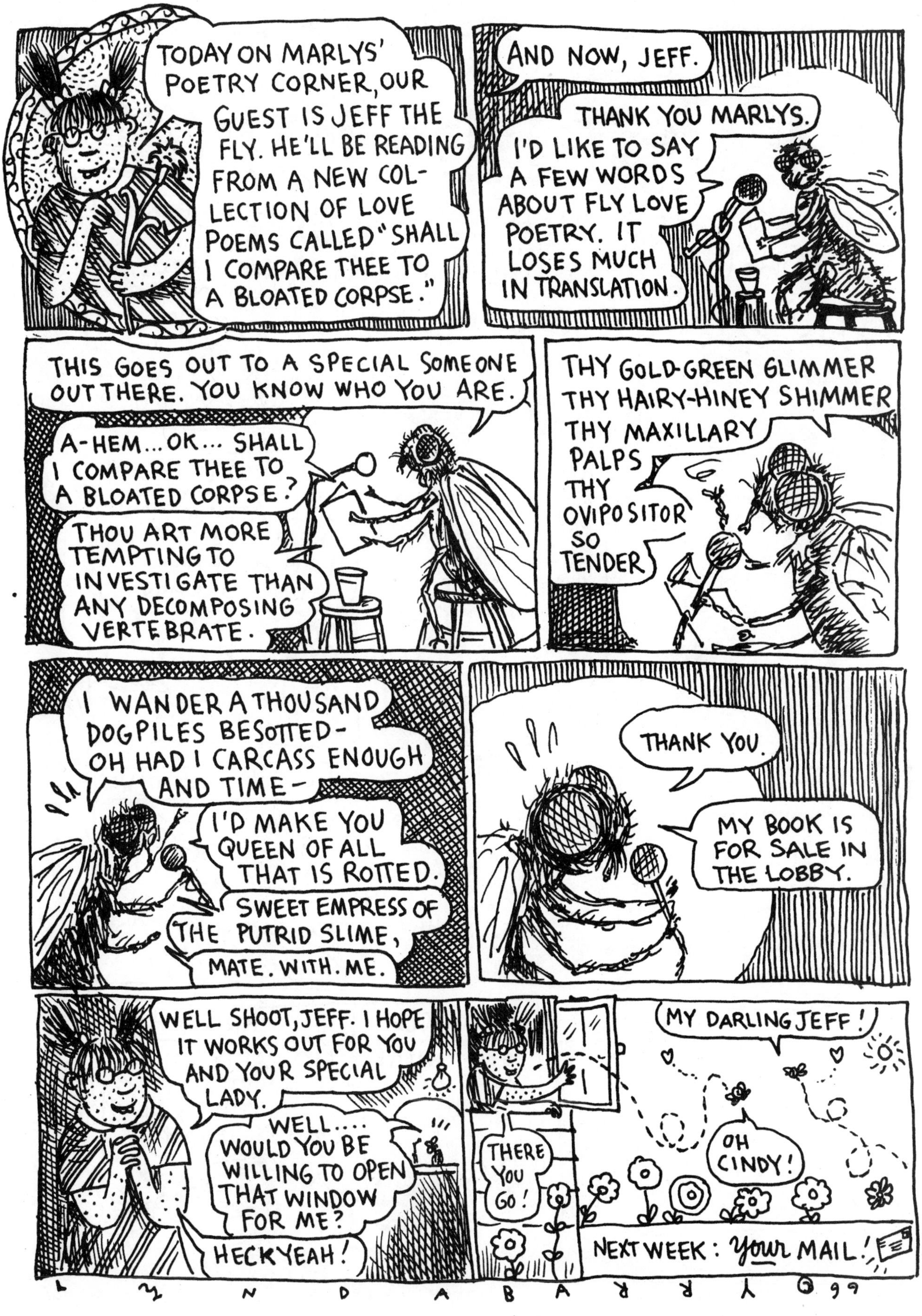
TODAY ON MARLYS' POETRY CORNER, OUR GUEST IS JEFF THE FLY. HE'LL BE READING FROM A NEW COLLECTION OF LOVE POEMS CALLED "SHALL I COMPARE THEE TO A BLOATED CORPSE."
AND NOW, JEFF.
THANK YOU MARLYS.
I'D LIKE TO SAY A FEW WORDS ABOUT FLY LOVE POETRY. IT LOSES MUCH IN TRANSLATION.
THIS GOES OUT TO A SPECIAL SOMEONE OUT THERE. YOU KNOW WHO YOU ARE.
A-HEM... OK... SHALL I COMPARE THEE TO A BLOATED CORPSE?
THOU ART MORE TEMPTING TO INVESTIGATE THAN ANY DECOMPOSING VERTEBRATE.
THY GOLD-GREEN GLIMMER THY HAIRY-HINEY SHIMMER
THY MAXILLARY PALPS
THY OVIPOSITOR SO TENDER
I WANDER A THOUSAND DOGPILES BESOTTED- OH HAD I CARCASS ENOUGH AND TIME-
I'D MAKE YOU QUEEN OF ALL THAT IS ROTTED.
SWEET EMPRESS OF THE PUTRID SLIME,
MATE. WITH. ME.
THANK YOU.
MY BOOK IS FOR SALE IN THE LOBBY.
WELL SHOOT, JEFF. I HOPE IT WORKS OUT FOR YOU AND YOUR SPECIAL LADY.
WELL.... WOULD YOU BE WILLING TO OPEN THAT WINDOW FOR ME?
HECK YEAH!
THERE YOU GO!
MY DARLING JEFF!
OH CINDY!
NEXT WEEK: YOUR MAIL!
LYNDA BARRY ©99

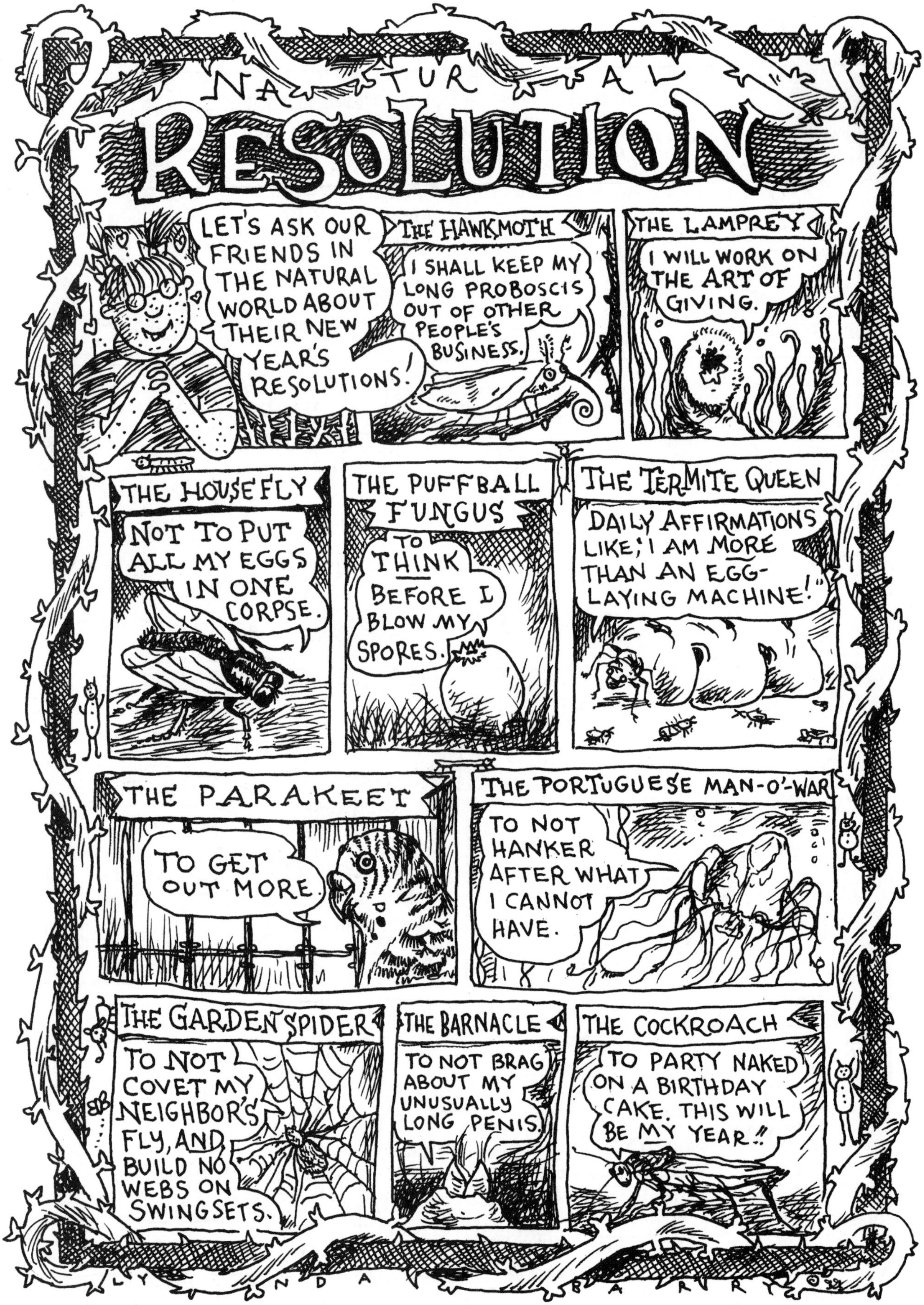
NA-TUR-AL
RESOLUTION
LET'S ASK OUR FRIENDS IN THE NATURAL WORLD ABOUT THEIR NEW YEAR'S RESOLUTIONS!
THE HAWKMOTH
I SHALL KEEP MY LONG PROBOSCIS OUT OF OTHER PEOPLE'S BUSINESS.
THE LAMPREY
I WILL WORK ON THE ART OF GIVING.
THE HOUSEFLY
NOT TO PUT ALL MY EGGS IN ONE CORPSE.
THE PUFFBALL FUNGUS
TO THINK BEFORE I BLOW MY SPORES.
THE TERMITE QUEEN
DAILY AFFIRMATIONS LIKE; I AM MORE THAN AN EGG-LAYING MACHINE!
THE PARAKEET
TO GET OUT MORE.
THE PORTUGUESE MAN-O'-WAR
TO NOT HANKER AFTER WHAT I CANNOT HAVE.
THE GARDEN SPIDER
TO NOT COVET MY NEIGHBOR'S FLY, AND BUILD NO WEBS ON SWINGSETS.
THE BARNACLE
TO NOT BRAG ABOUT MY UNUSUALLY LONG PENIS.
THE COCKROACH
TO PARTY NAKED ON A BIRTHDAY CAKE. THIS WILL BE MY YEAR!!
LYNDA BARRY

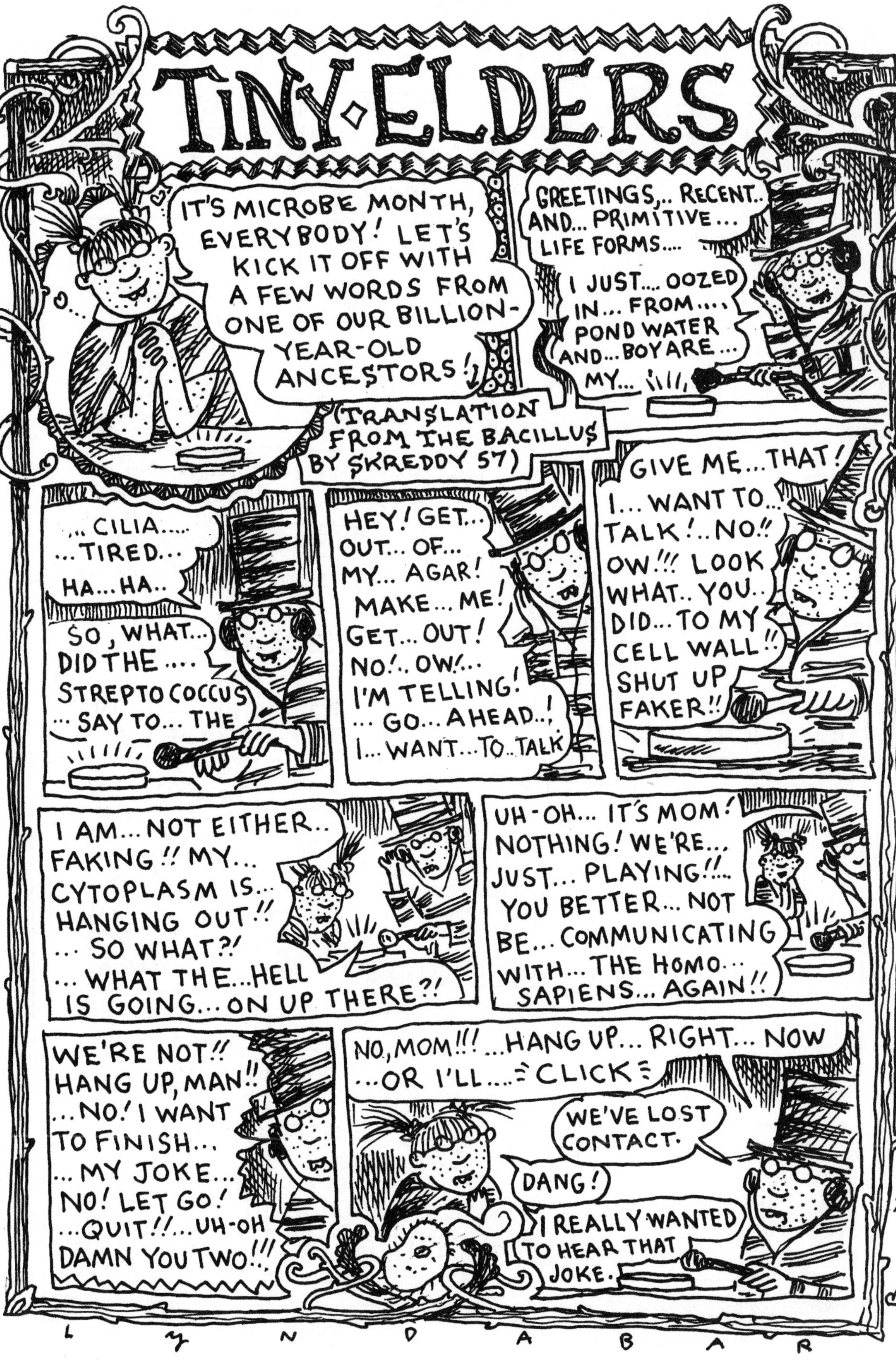
TINY ELDERS
IT'S MICROBE MONTH, EVERYBODY! LET'S KICK IT OFF WITH A FEW WORDS FROM ONE OF OUR BILLION-YEAR-OLD ANCESTORS!
(TRANSLATION FROM THE BACILLUS BY SKREDDY 57)
GREETINGS,.. RECENT.. AND... PRIMITIVE... LIFE FORMS....
I JUST.... OOZED IN... FROM..., POND WATER AND... BOY ARE... MY...
... CILIA..... ...TIRED... HA... HA..
SO, WHAT... DID THE .... STREPTOCOCCUS ... SAY TO... THE
HEY! GET... OUT... OF... MY... AGAR!
MAKE... ME! GET... OUT! NO!.. OW!...
I'M TELLING! ... GO... AHEAD..! I... WANT... TO.. TALK
GIVE ME... THAT! I... WANT TO.. TALK!.. NO!! OW!!! LOOK WHAT.. YOU.. DID... TO MY CELL WALL!!
SHUT UP FAKER!!
I AM... NOT EITHER.. FAKING!! MY... CYTOPLASM IS... HANGING OUT!! ... SO WHAT?!
... WHAT THE...HELL IS GOING... ON UP THERE?!
UH-OH... IT'S MOM! NOTHING! WE'RE... JUST... PLAYING!!...
YOU BETTER... NOT BE... COMMUNICATING WITH... THE HOMO... SAPIENS... AGAIN!!
WE'RE NOT!! HANG UP, MAN!! ...NO! I WANT TO FINISH... ...MY JOKE... NO! LET GO! ...QUIT!!... UH-OH DAMN YOU TWO!!!
NO, MOM!!! ...HANG UP... RIGHT... NOW ...OR I'LL....CLICK
WE'VE LOST CONTACT.
DANG!
I REALLY WANTED TO HEAR THAT JOKE.
LYNDA BARRY
TOODLE

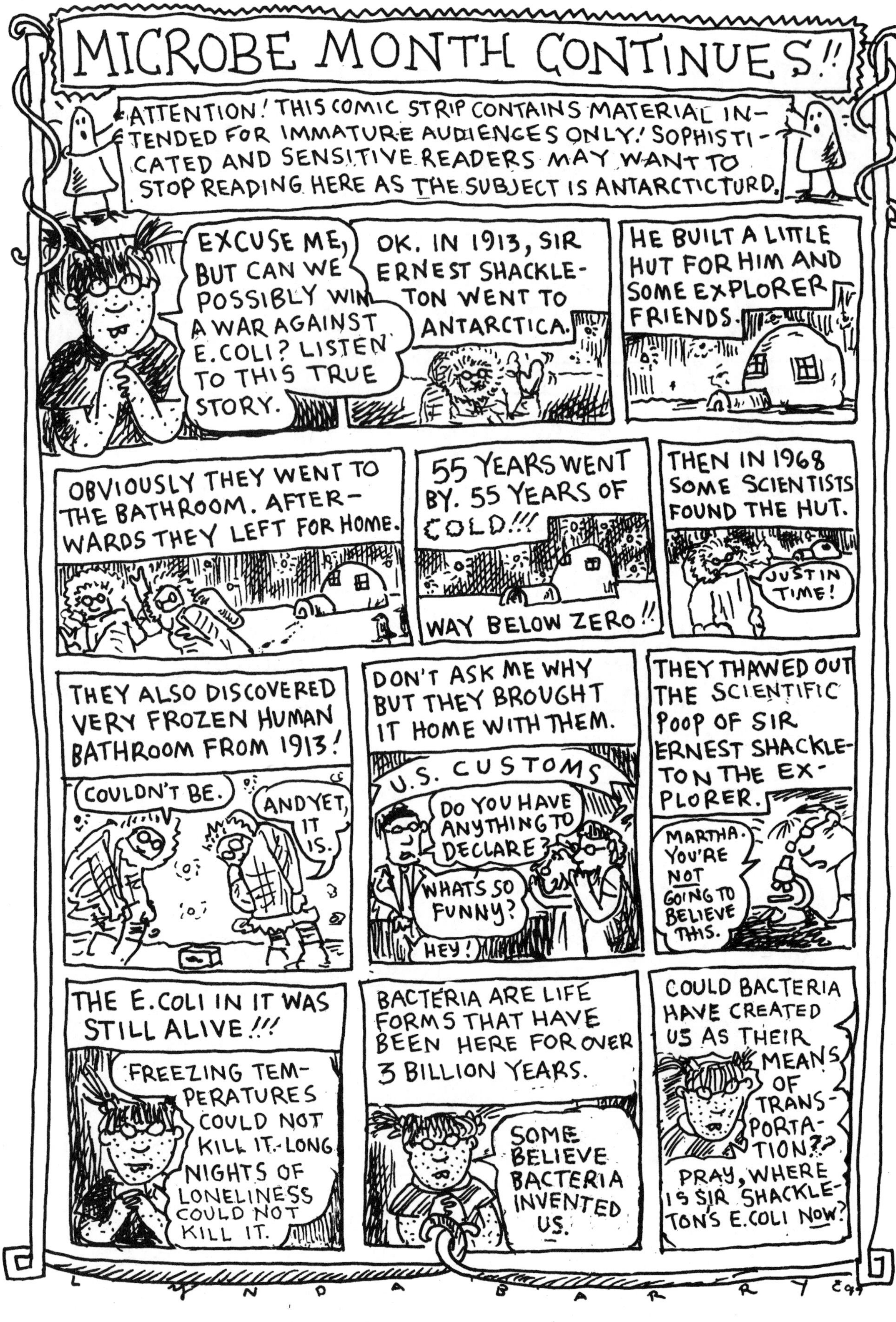
MICROBE MONTH CONTINUES!!
ATTENTION! THIS COMIC STRIP CONTAINS MATERIAL INTENDED FOR IMMATURE AUDIENCES ONLY! SOPHISTICATED AND SENSITIVE READERS MAY WANT TO STOP READING HERE AS THE SUBJECT IS ANTARCTICTURD.
EXCUSE ME, BUT CAN WE POSSIBLY WIN A WAR AGAINST E.COLI? LISTEN TO THIS TRUE STORY.
OK. IN 1913, SIR ERNEST SHACKLETON WENT TO ANTARCTICA.
HE BUILT A LITTLE HUT FOR HIM AND SOME EXPLORER FRIENDS.
OBVIOUSLY THEY WENT TO THE BATHROOM. AFTERWARDS THEY LEFT FOR HOME.
55 YEARS WENT BY. 55 YEARS OF COLD!!!
WAY BELOW ZERO!!
THEN IN 1968 SOME SCIENTISTS FOUND THE HUT.
JUST IN TIME!
THEY ALSO DISCOVERED VERY FROZEN HUMAN BATHROOM FROM 1913!
COULDN'T BE.
AND YET, IT IS.
DON'T ASK ME WHY BUT THEY BROUGHT IT HOME WITH THEM.
U.S. CUSTOMS
DO YOU HAVE ANYTHING TO DECLARE?
WHATS SO FUNNY?
HEY!
THEY THAWED OUT THE SCIENTIFIC POOP OF SIR ERNEST SHACKLETON THE EXPLORER.
MARTHA. YOU'RE NOT GOING TO BELIEVE THIS.
THE E.COLI IN IT WAS STILL ALIVE!!!
FREEZING TEMPERATURES COULD NOT KILL IT. LONG NIGHTS OF LONELINESS COULD NOT KILL IT.
BACTERIA ARE LIFE FORMS THAT HAVE BEEN HERE FOR OVER 3 BILLION YEARS.
SOME BELIEVE BACTERIA INVENTED US.
COULD BACTERIA HAVE CREATED US AS THEIR MEANS OF TRANSPORTATION??
PRAY, WHERE IS SIR SHACKLETON'S E.COLI NOW?
LYNDA BARRY ©94

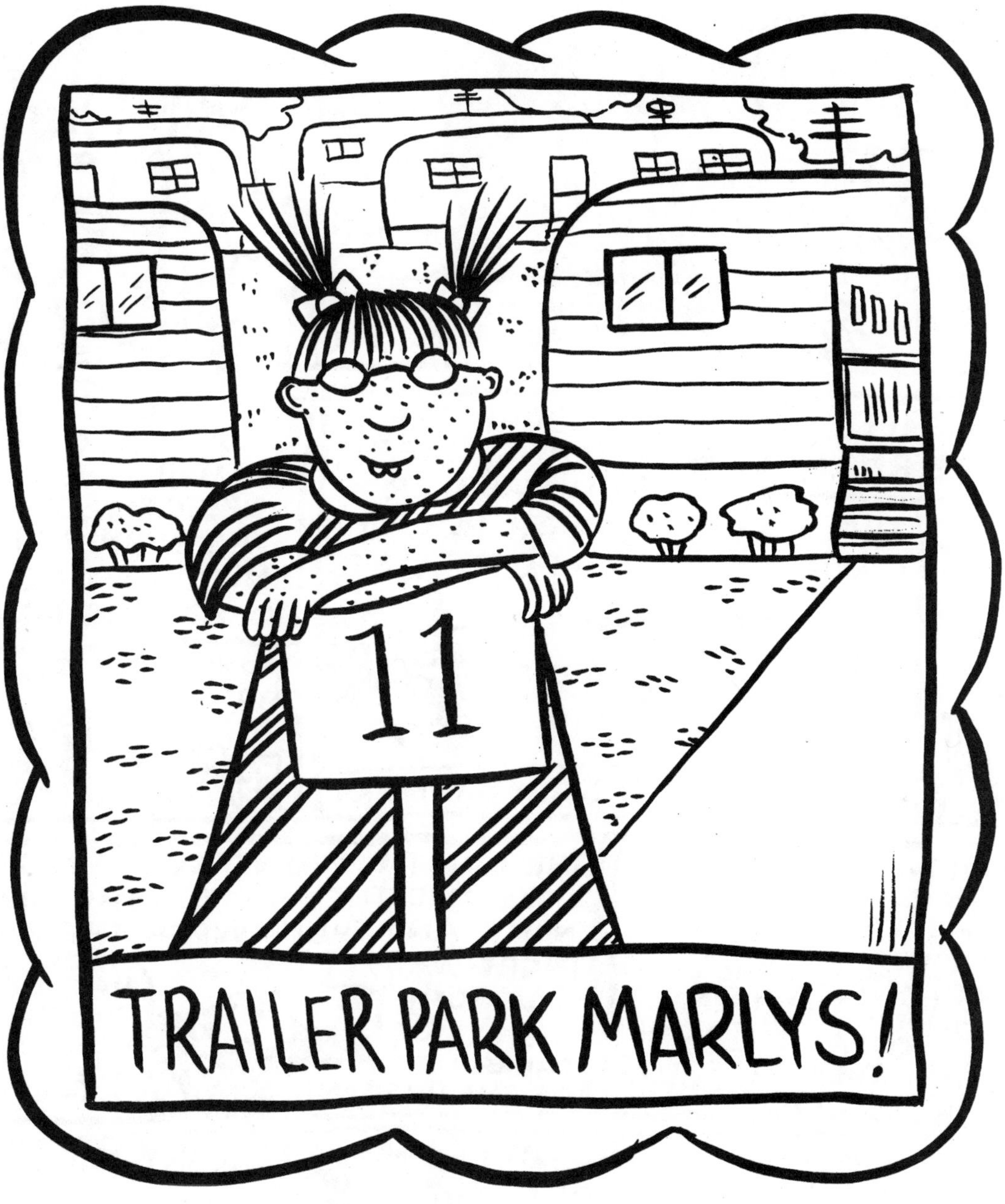
11
TRAILER PARK MARLYS!

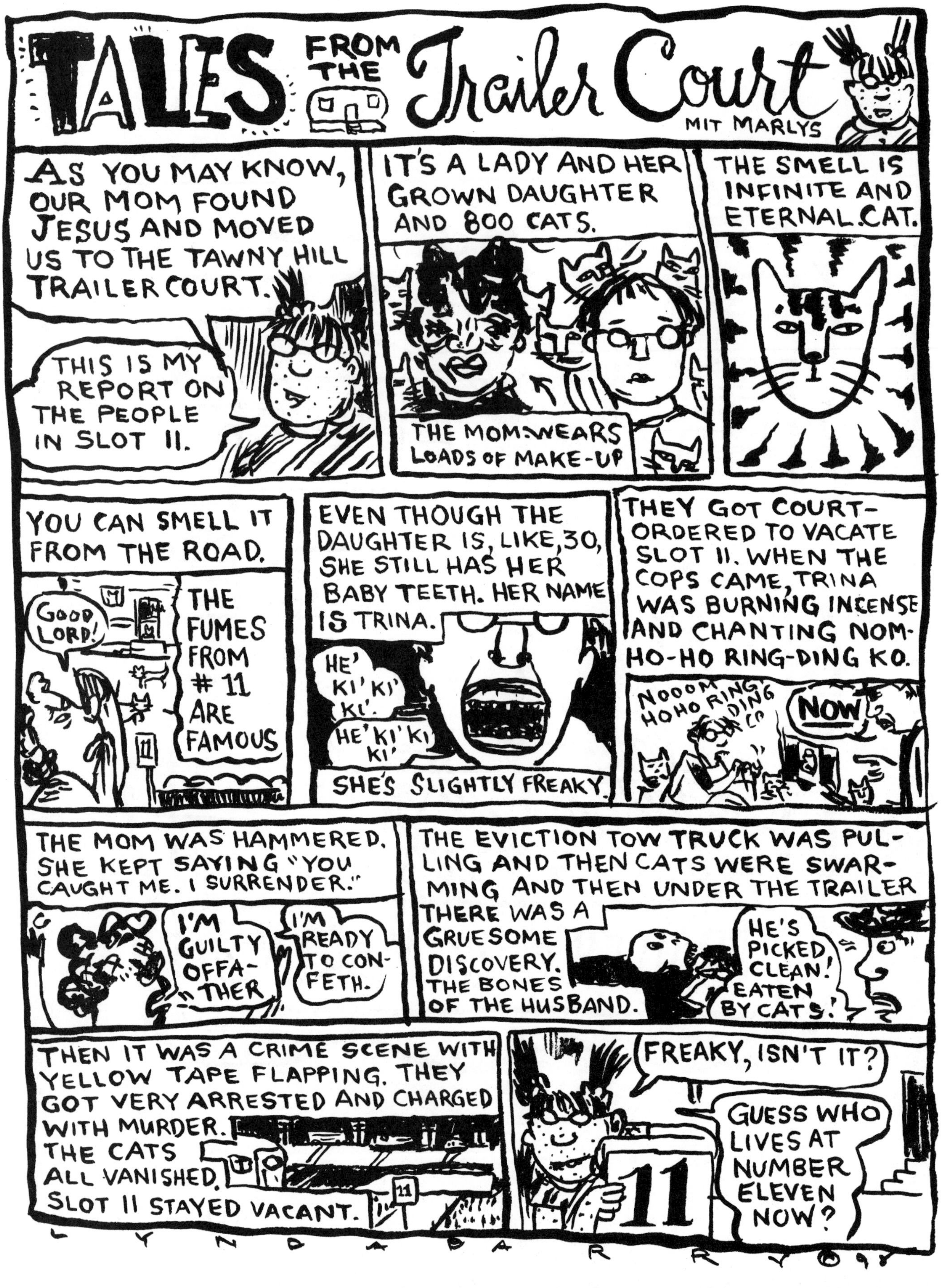
TALES FROM THE Trailer Court
MIT MARLYS
AS YOU MAY KNOW, OUR MOM FOUND JESUS AND MOVED US TO THE TAWNY HILL TRAILER COURT.
THIS IS MY REPORT ON THE PEOPLE IN SLOT 11.
IT'S A LADY AND HER GROWN DAUGHTER AND 800 CATS.
THE MOM WEARS LOADS OF MAKE-UP
THE SMELL IS INFINITE AND ETERNAL CAT.
YOU CAN SMELL IT FROM THE ROAD.
GOOD LORD!
THE FUMES FROM # 11 ARE FAMOUS
11
EVEN THOUGH THE DAUGHTER IS, LIKE, 30, SHE STILL HAS HER BABY TEETH. HER NAME IS TRINA.
HE' KI' KI' KI'.
HE' KI' KI KI'
SHE'S SLIGHTLY FREAKY.
THEY GOT COURT-ORDERED TO VACATE SLOT 11. WHEN THE COPS CAME, TRINA WAS BURNING INCENSE AND CHANTING NOM-HO-HO RING-DING KO.
NOOOM HOHO RING DING
NOW
THE MOM WAS HAMMERED. SHE KEPT SAYING "YOU CAUGHT ME. I SURRENDER."
I'M GUILTY OFFA-THER
I'M READY TO CON-FETH.
THE EVICTION TOW TRUCK WAS PULLING AND THEN CATS WERE SWARMING AND THEN UNDER THE TRAILER THERE WAS A GRUESOME DISCOVERY. THE BONES OF THE HUSBAND.
HE'S PICKED CLEAN! EATEN BY CATS!
THEN IT WAS A CRIME SCENE WITH YELLOW TAPE FLAPPING. THEY GOT VERY ARRESTED AND CHARGED WITH MURDER. THE CATS ALL VANISHED. SLOT 11 STAYED VACANT.
11
FREAKY, ISN'T IT?
GUESS WHO LIVES AT NUMBER ELEVEN NOW?
11
LYNDA BARRY ©98

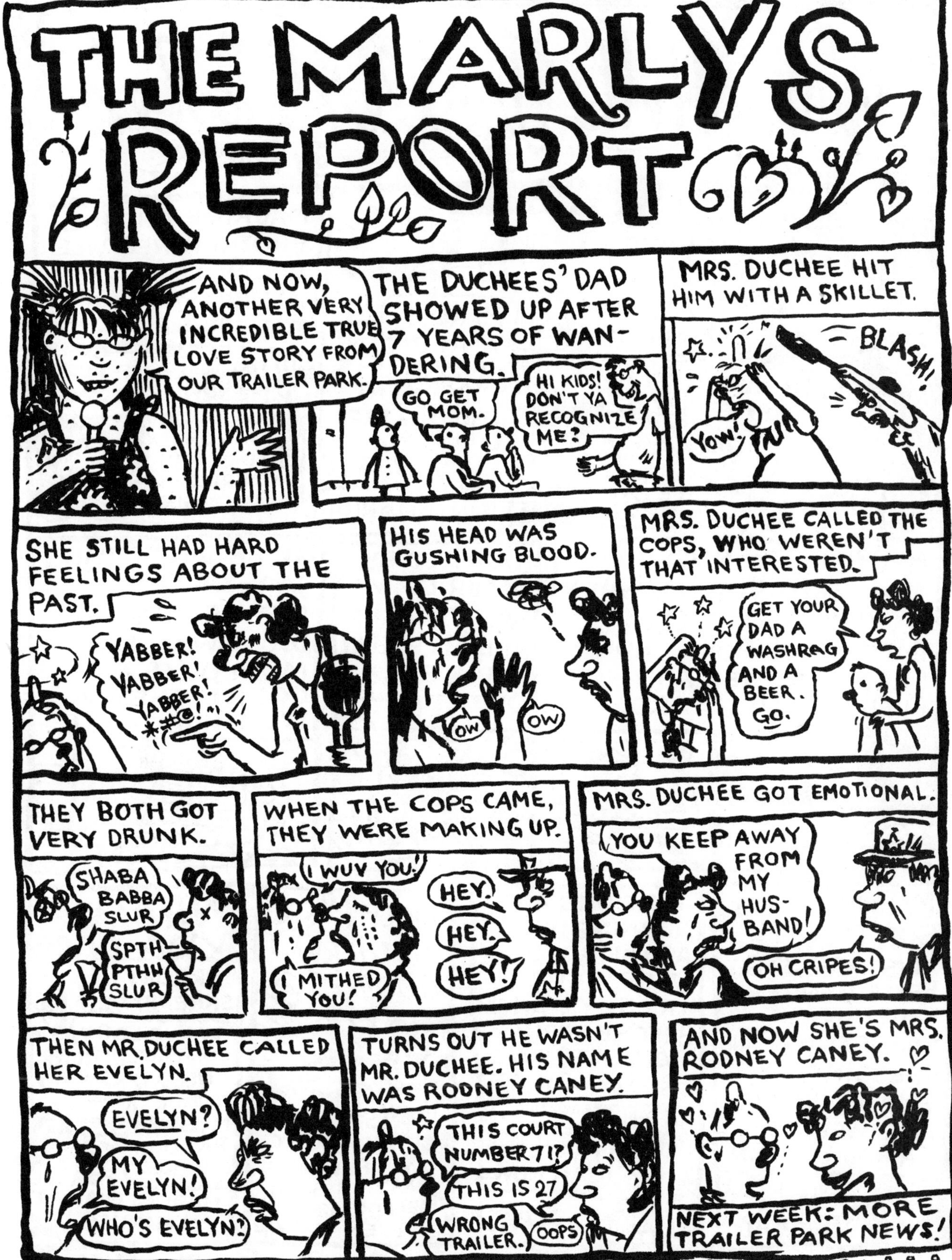
THE MARLYS REPORT
AND NOW, ANOTHER VERY INCREDIBLE TRUE LOVE STORY FROM OUR TRAILER PARK.
THE DUCHEES' DAD SHOWED UP AFTER 7 YEARS OF WANDERING.
GO GET MOM.
HI KIDS! DON'T YA RECOGNIZE ME?
MRS. DUCHEE HIT HIM WITH A SKILLET.
BLASH!
YOW!
SHE STILL HAD HARD FEELINGS ABOUT THE PAST.
YABBER! YABBER! YABBER! *#@!
HIS HEAD WAS GUSHING BLOOD.
OW
OW
MRS. DUCHEE CALLED THE COPS, WHO WEREN'T THAT INTERESTED.
GET YOUR DAD A WASHRAG AND A BEER. GO.
THEY BOTH GOT VERY DRUNK.
SHABA BABBA SLUR
SPTH PTHH SLUR
WHEN THE COPS CAME, THEY WERE MAKING UP.
I WUV YOU!
I MITHED YOU!
HEY.
HEY.
HEY!
MRS. DUCHEE GOT EMOTIONAL.
YOU KEEP AWAY FROM MY HUSBAND!
OH CRIPES!
THEN MR. DUCHEE CALLED HER EVELYN.
EVELYN?
MY EVELYN!
WHO'S EVELYN?
TURNS OUT HE WASN'T MR. DUCHEE. HIS NAME WAS RODNEY CANEY.
THIS COURT NUMBER 71?
THIS IS 27
WRONG TRAILER.
OOPS
AND NOW SHE'S MRS. RODNEY CANEY.
NEXT WEEK: MORE TRAILER PARK NEWS!
LYNDA BARRY ©1998

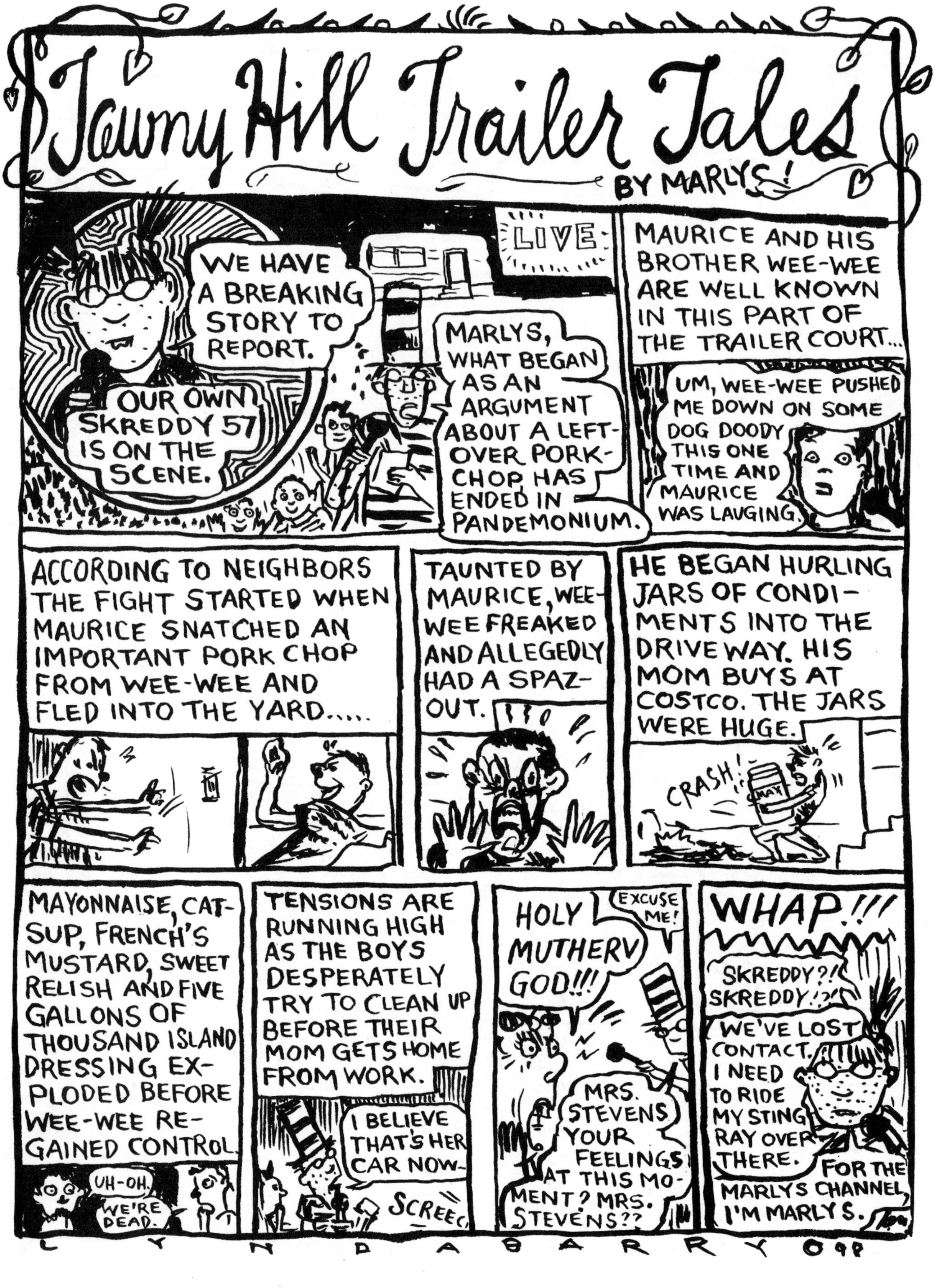
Tawny Hill Trailer Tales
BY MARLYS!
LIVE
WE HAVE A BREAKING STORY TO REPORT.
OUR OWN SKREDDY 57 IS ON THE SCENE.
MARLYS, WHAT BEGAN AS AN ARGUMENT ABOUT A LEFT-OVER PORK-CHOP HAS ENDED IN PANDEMONIUM.
MAURICE AND HIS BROTHER WEE-WEE ARE WELL KNOWN IN THIS PART OF THE TRAILER COURT...
UM, WEE-WEE PUSHED ME DOWN ON SOME DOG DOODY THIS ONE TIME AND MAURICE WAS LAUGING.
ACCORDING TO NEIGHBORS THE FIGHT STARTED WHEN MAURICE SNATCHED AN IMPORTANT PORK CHOP FROM WEE-WEE AND FLED INTO THE YARD.....
TAUNTED BY MAURICE, WEE-WEE FREAKED AND ALLEGEDLY HAD A SPAZ-OUT.
HE BEGAN HURLING JARS OF CONDI-MENTS INTO THE DRIVE WAY. HIS MOM BUYS AT COSTCO. THE JARS WERE HUGE.
CRASH!
MAY
MAYONNAISE, CAT-SUP, FRENCH'S MUSTARD, SWEET RELISH AND FIVE GALLONS OF THOUSAND ISLAND DRESSING EX-PLODED BEFORE WEE-WEE RE-GAINED CONTROL.
UH-OH.
WE'RE DEAD.
TENSIONS ARE RUNNING HIGH AS THE BOYS DESPERATELY TRY TO CLEAN UP BEFORE THEIR MOM GETS HOME FROM WORK.
I BELIEVE THAT'S HER CAR NOW-
SCREEC
HOLY MUTHERV GOD!!!
EXCUSE ME!
MRS. STEVENS YOUR FEELINGS AT THIS MO-MENT? MRS. STEVENS??
WHAP!!!
SKREDDY?!
SKREDDY!?!
WE'VE LOST CONTACT. I NEED TO RIDE MY STING RAY OVER THERE.
FOR THE MARLYS CHANNEL, I'M MARLYS.
LYNDA BARRY ©98

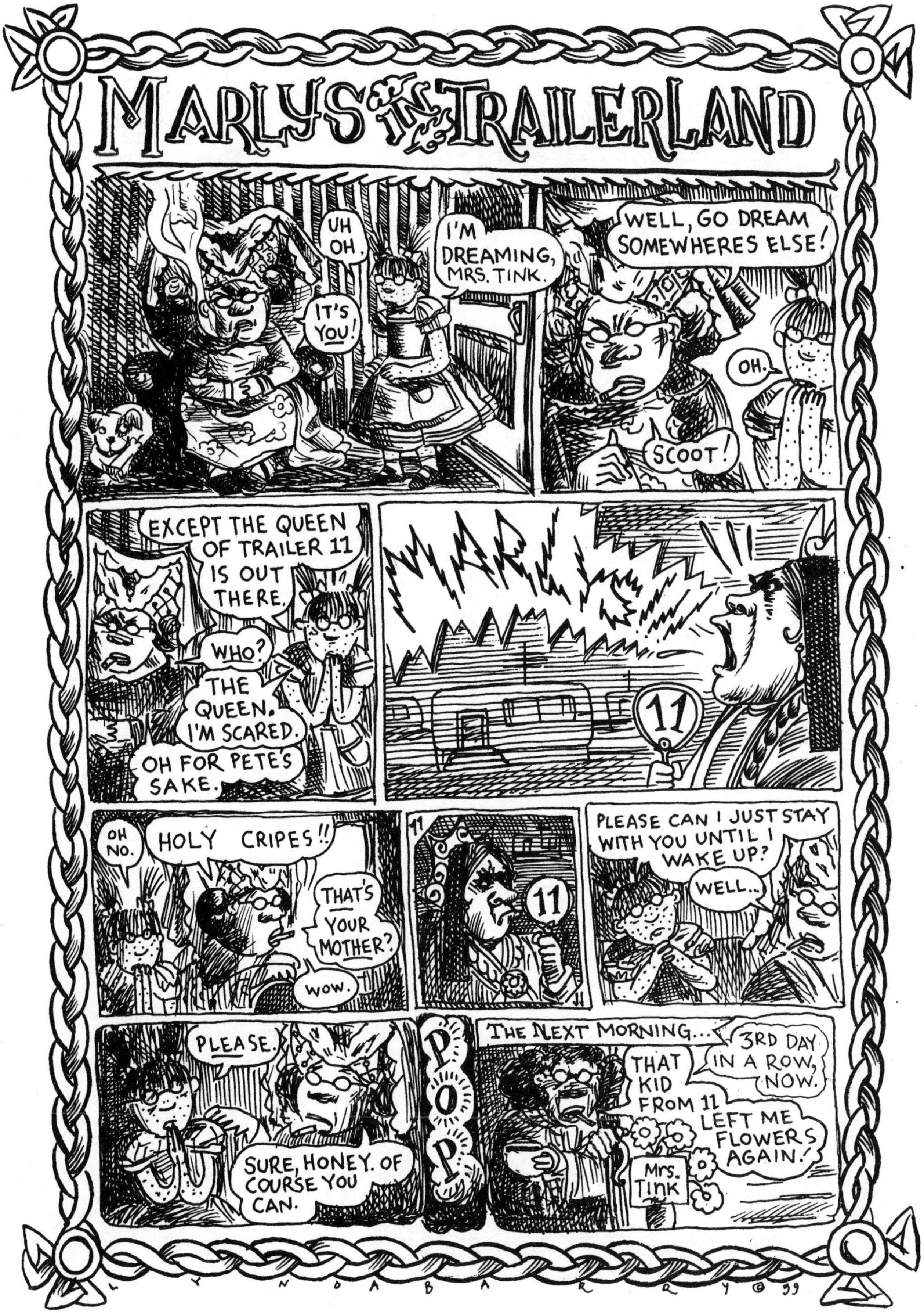

MARLYS IN TRAILERLAND
UH OH.
I'M DREAMING, MRS. TINK.
IT'S YOU!
WELL, GO DREAM SOMEWHERES ELSE!
OH.
SCOOT!
EXCEPT THE QUEEN OF TRAILER 11 IS OUT THERE.
WHO?
THE QUEEN. I'M SCARED.
OH FOR PETE'S SAKE.
MAR
11
OH NO.
HOLY CRIPES!!
THAT'S YOUR MOTHER?
WOW.
11
PLEASE CAN I JUST STAY WITH YOU UNTIL I WAKE UP?
WELL...
PLEASE.
SURE, HONEY. OF COURSE YOU CAN.
POP
THE NEXT MORNING...
THAT KID FROM 11 LEFT ME FLOWERS AGAIN!
3RD DAY IN A ROW, NOW.
Mrs. Tink
LYNDA BARRY © 99

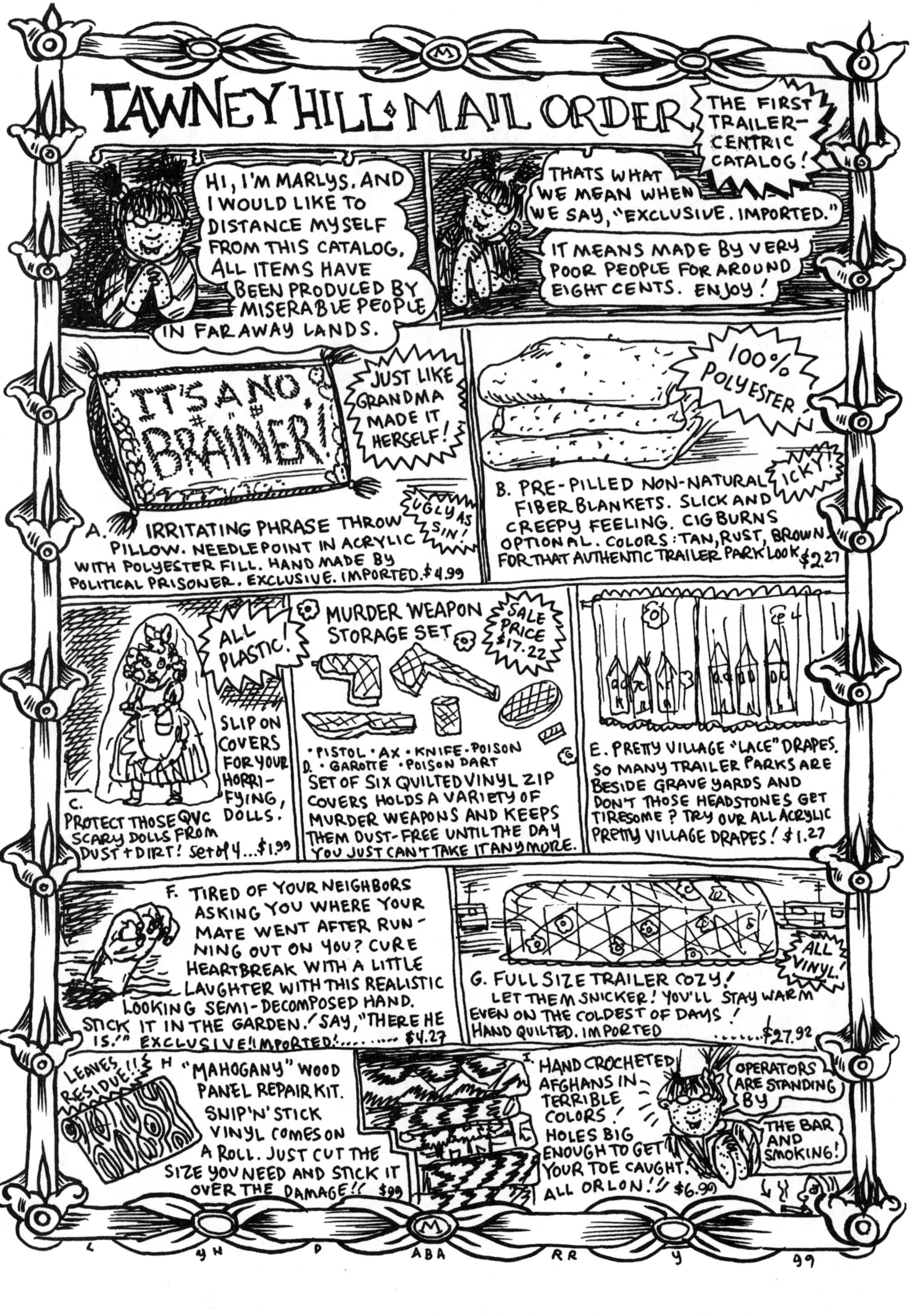
TAWNEY HILL MAIL ORDER
THE FIRST TRAILER-CENTRIC CATALOG!
HI, I'M MARLYS. AND I WOULD LIKE TO DISTANCE MYSELF FROM THIS CATALOG. ALL ITEMS HAVE BEEN PRODUCED BY MISERABLE PEOPLE IN FARAWAY LANDS.
THATS WHAT WE MEAN WHEN WE SAY, "EXCLUSIVE. IMPORTED."
IT MEANS MADE BY VERY POOR PEOPLE FOR AROUND EIGHT CENTS. ENJOY!
IT'S A NO, "#" BRAINER!
JUST LIKE GRANDMA MADE IT HERSELF!
UGLY AS SIN!
A. IRRITATING PHRASE THROW PILLOW. NEEDLEPOINT IN ACRYLIC WITH POLYESTER FILL. HAND MADE BY POLITICAL PRISONER. EXCLUSIVE. IMPORTED. $4.99
100% POLYESTER!
ICKY!
B. PRE-PILLED NON-NATURAL FIBER BLANKETS. SLICK AND CREEPY FEELING. CIG BURNS OPTIONAL. COLORS: TAN, RUST, BROWN. FOR THAT AUTHENTIC TRAILER PARK LOOK $2.27
ALL PLASTIC!
SLIP ON COVERS FOR YOUR HORRIFYING, DOLLS.
C. PROTECT THOSE QVC SCARY DOLLS FROM DUST + DIRT! Set of 4...$1.99
MURDER WEAPON STORAGE SET
SALE PRICE $17.22
• PISTOL • AX • KNIFE • POISON • GAROTTE • POISON DART
D. SET OF SIX QUILTED VINYL ZIP COVERS HOLDS A VARIETY OF MURDER WEAPONS AND KEEPS THEM DUST-FREE UNTIL THE DAY YOU JUST CAN'T TAKE IT ANYMORE.
E. PRETTY VILLAGE "LACE" DRAPES. SO MANY TRAILER PARKS ARE BESIDE GRAVE YARDS AND DON'T THOSE HEADSTONES GET TIRESOME? TRY OUR ALL ACRYLIC PRETTY VILLAGE DRAPES! $1.27
F. TIRED OF YOUR NEIGHBORS ASKING YOU WHERE YOUR MATE WENT AFTER RUNNING OUT ON YOU? CURE HEARTBREAK WITH A LITTLE LAUGHTER WITH THIS REALISTIC LOOKING SEMI-DECOMPOSED HAND. STICK IT IN THE GARDEN! SAY, "THERE HE IS!" EXCLUSIVE! IMPORTED! $4.27
ALL VINYL!
G. FULL SIZE TRAILER COZY! LET THEM SNICKER! YOU'LL STAY WARM EVEN ON THE COLDEST OF DAYS! HAND QUILTED. IMPORTED $27.92
LEAVES RESIDUE!!
H "MAHOGANY" WOOD PANEL REPAIR KIT. SNIP 'N' STICK VINYL COMES ON A ROLL. JUST CUT THE SIZE YOU NEED AND STICK IT OVER THE DAMAGE!! $99
I. HAND CROCHETED AFGHANS IN TERRIBLE COLORS! HOLES BIG ENOUGH TO GET YOUR TOE CAUGHT. ALL ORLON!! $6.99
OPERATORS ARE STANDING BY
THE BAR AND SMOKING!
LYNDA BARRY 99

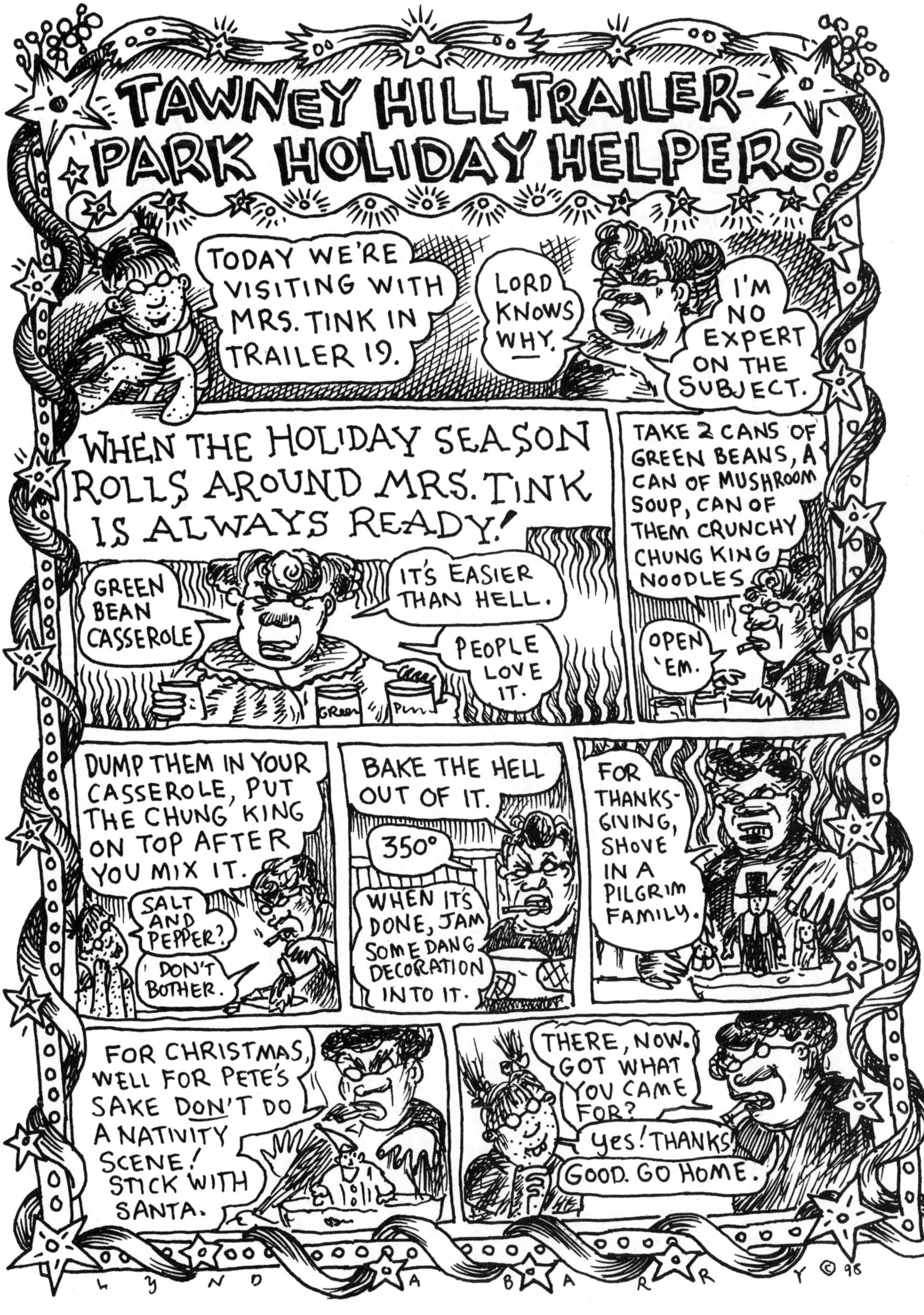

TAWNEY HILL TRAILER-PARK HOLIDAY HELPERS!
TODAY WE'RE VISITING WITH MRS. TINK IN TRAILER 19.
LORD KNOWS WHY.
I'M NO EXPERT ON THE SUBJECT.
WHEN THE HOLIDAY SEASON ROLLS AROUND MRS. TINK IS ALWAYS READY!
GREEN BEAN CASSEROLE
IT'S EASIER THAN HELL.
PEOPLE LOVE IT.
GREEN
TAKE 2 CANS OF GREEN BEANS, A CAN OF MUSHROOM SOUP, CAN OF THEM CRUNCHY CHUNG KING NOODLES
OPEN 'EM.
DUMP THEM IN YOUR CASSEROLE, PUT THE CHUNG KING ON TOP AFTER YOU MIX IT.
SALT AND PEPPER?
DON'T BOTHER.
BAKE THE HELL OUT OF IT.
350°
WHEN IT'S DONE, JAM SOME DANG DECORATION INTO IT.
FOR THANKSGIVING, SHOVE IN A PILGRIM FAMILY.
FOR CHRISTMAS, WELL FOR PETE'S SAKE DON'T DO A NATIVITY SCENE! STICK WITH SANTA.
THERE, NOW. GOT WHAT YOU CAME FOR?
YES! THANKS
GOOD. GO HOME.
LYNDA BARRY © 98

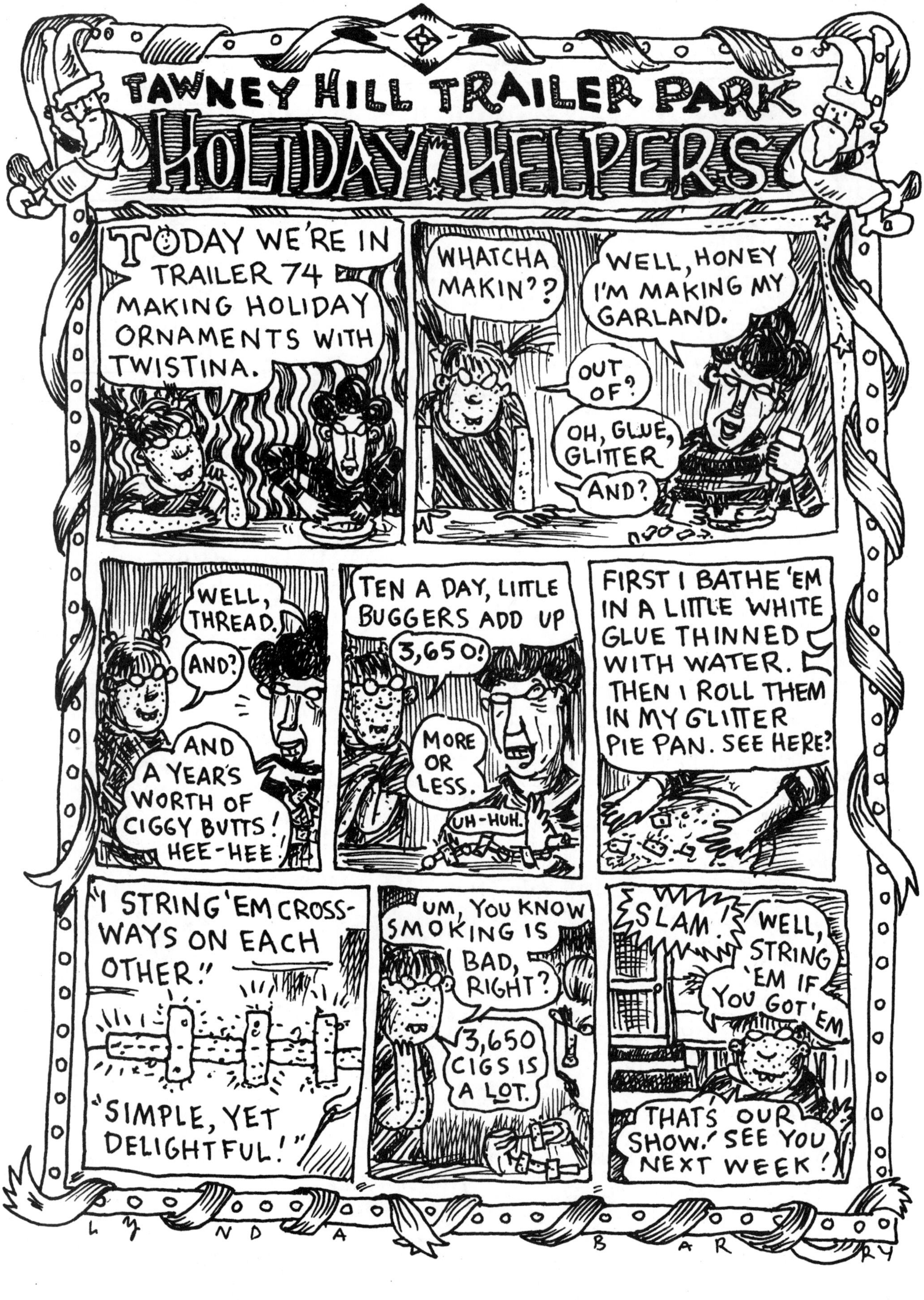
TAWNEY HILL TRAILER PARK
HOLIDAY HELPERS
TODAY WE'RE IN TRAILER 74 MAKING HOLIDAY ORNAMENTS WITH TWISTINA.
WHATCHA MAKIN'?
WELL, HONEY I'M MAKING MY GARLAND.
OUT OF?
OH, GLUE, GLITTER
AND?
WELL, THREAD.
AND?
AND A YEAR'S WORTH OF CIGGY BUTTS! HEE-HEE
TEN A DAY, LITTLE BUGGERS ADD UP
3,650!
MORE OR LESS.
UH-HUH.
FIRST I BATHE 'EM IN A LITTLE WHITE GLUE THINNED WITH WATER. THEN I ROLL THEM IN MY GLITTER PIE PAN. SEE HERE?
"I STRING 'EM CROSS-WAYS ON EACH OTHER!"
"SIMPLE, YET DELIGHTFUL!"
UM, YOU KNOW SMOKING IS BAD, RIGHT?
3,650 CIGS IS A LOT.
SLAM!
WELL, STRING 'EM IF YOU GOT 'EM
THAT'S OUR SHOW! SEE YOU NEXT WEEK!
LYNDA BARRY

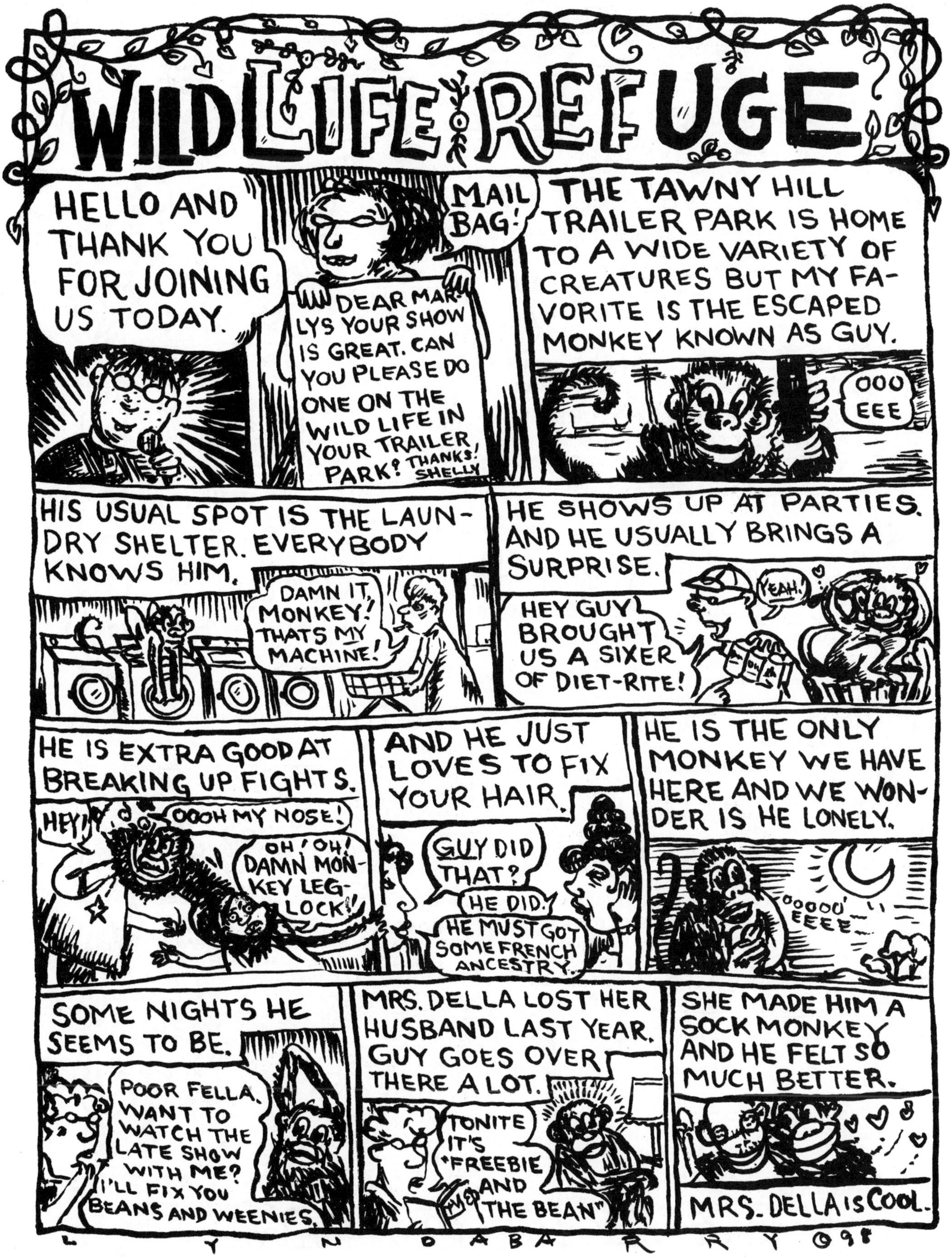
WILD LIFE REFUGE
HELLO AND THANK YOU FOR JOINING US TODAY.
MAIL BAG!
DEAR MARLYS YOUR SHOW IS GREAT. CAN YOU PLEASE DO ONE ON THE WILD LIFE IN YOUR TRAILER PARK? THANKS! SHELLY
THE TAWNY HILL TRAILER PARK IS HOME TO A WIDE VARIETY OF CREATURES BUT MY FAVORITE IS THE ESCAPED MONKEY KNOWN AS GUY.
OOO EEE
HIS USUAL SPOT IS THE LAUNDRY SHELTER. EVERYBODY KNOWS HIM.
DAMN IT, MONKEY! THATS MY MACHINE!
HE SHOWS UP AT PARTIES. AND HE USUALLY BRINGS A SURPRISE.
HEY GUY BROUGHT US A SIXER OF DIET-RITE!
YEAH!
HE IS EXTRA GOOD AT BREAKING UP FIGHTS.
HEY!
OOOH MY NOSE!
OH! OH! DAMN MONKEY LEG-LOCK!
AND HE JUST LOVES TO FIX YOUR HAIR.
GUY DID THAT?
HE DID.
HE MUST GOT SOME FRENCH ANCESTRY.
HE IS THE ONLY MONKEY WE HAVE HERE AND WE WONDER IS HE LONELY.
OOOOO EEEE
SOME NIGHTS HE SEEMS TO BE.
POOR FELLA. WANT TO WATCH THE LATE SHOW WITH ME? I'LL FIX YOU BEANS AND WEENIES.
MRS. DELLA LOST HER HUSBAND LAST YEAR. GUY GOES OVER THERE A LOT.
TONITE IT'S "FREEBIE AND THE BEAN"
SHE MADE HIM A SOCK MONKEY AND HE FELT SO MUCH BETTER.
MRS. DELLA IS COOL.
L Y N D A B A R R Y ©98

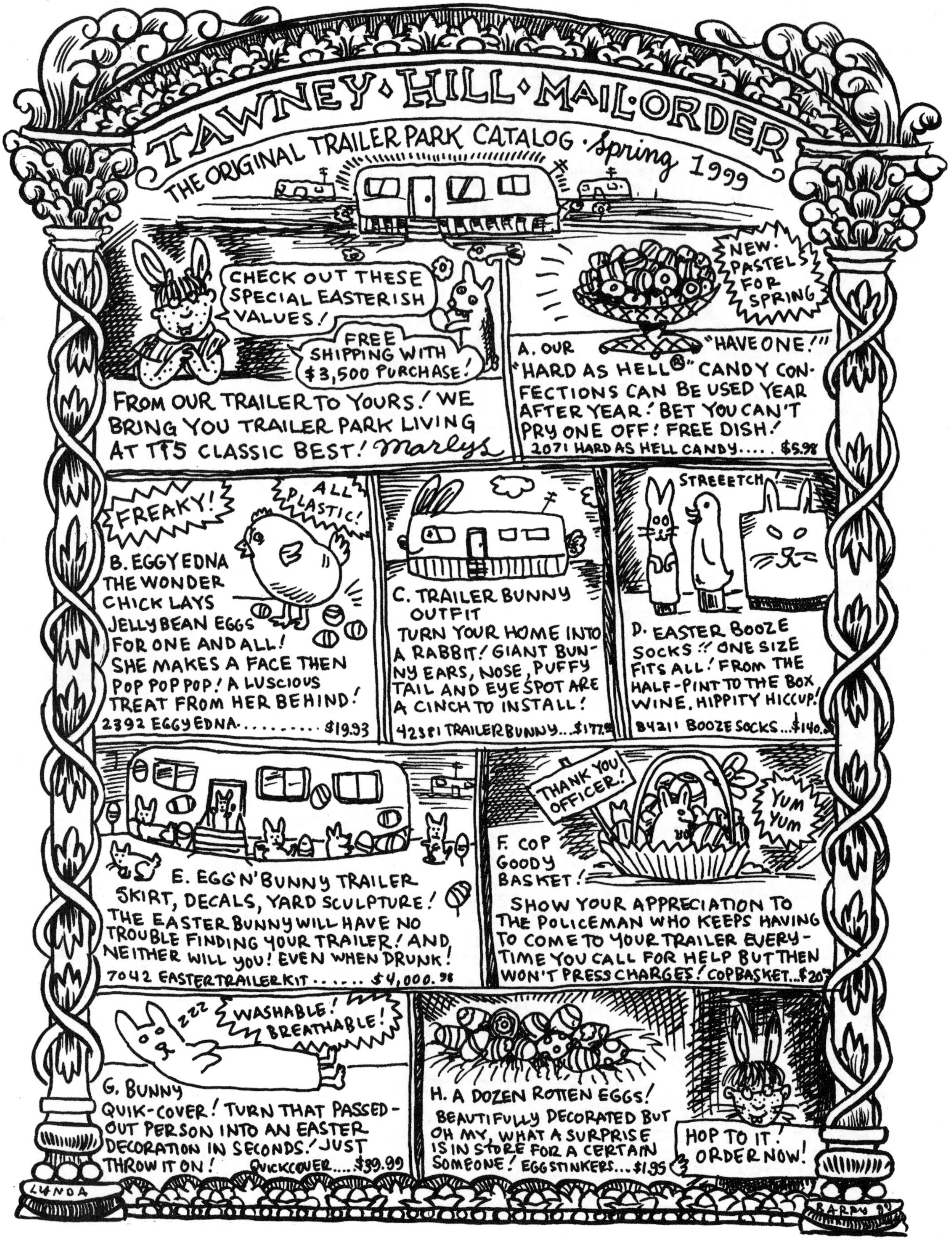
TAWNEY • HILL • MAIL • ORDER
THE ORIGINAL TRAILER PARK CATALOG • Spring 1999
CHECK OUT THESE SPECIAL EASTERISH VALUES!
FREE SHIPPING WITH $3,500 PURCHASE!
FROM OUR TRAILER TO YOURS! WE BRING YOU TRAILER PARK LIVING AT ITS CLASSIC BEST! Marlys
NEW. PASTEL FOR SPRING
A. OUR "HAVE ONE!" "HARD AS HELL®" CANDY CONFECTIONS CAN BE USED YEAR AFTER YEAR! BET YOU CAN'T PRY ONE OFF! FREE DISH!
2071 HARD AS HELL CANDY..... $5.98
FREAKY!
ALL PLASTIC!
B. EGGY EDNA THE WONDER CHICK LAYS JELLY BEAN EGGS FOR ONE AND ALL! SHE MAKES A FACE THEN POP POP POP! A LUSCIOUS TREAT FROM HER BEHIND!
2392 EGGY EDNA......... $19.93
C. TRAILER BUNNY OUTFIT
TURN YOUR HOME INTO A RABBIT! GIANT BUNNY EARS, NOSE, PUFFY TAIL AND EYE SPOT ARE A CINCH TO INSTALL!
42381 TRAILER BUNNY....$177.
STREEETCH!
D. EASTER BOOZE SOCKS!! ONE SIZE FITS ALL! FROM THE HALF-PINT TO THE BOX WINE. HIPPITY HICCUP!
B421' BOOZE SOCKS...$140.
E. EGG'N'BUNNY TRAILER SKIRT, DECALS, YARD SCULPTURE!
THE EASTER BUNNY WILL HAVE NO TROUBLE FINDING YOUR TRAILER! AND NEITHER WILL YOU! EVEN WHEN DRUNK!
7042 EASTER TRAILER KIT $4,000.98
THANK YOU OFFICER!
YUM YUM
F. COP GOODY BASKET!
SHOW YOUR APPRECIATION TO THE POLICEMAN WHO KEEPS HAVING TO COME TO YOUR TRAILER EVERYTIME YOU CALL FOR HELP BUT THEN WON'T PRESS CHARGES! COP BASKET...$20
ZZZ
WASHABLE! BREATHABLE!
G. BUNNY QUIK-COVER! TURN THAT PASSED-OUT PERSON INTO AN EASTER DECORATION IN SECONDS! JUST THROW IT ON!
QUICKCOVER....$39.99
H. A DOZEN ROTTEN EGGS!
BEAUTIFULLY DECORATED BUT OH MY, WHAT A SURPRISE IS IN STORE FOR A CERTAIN SOMEONE! EGG STINKERS....$1.95
HOP TO IT! ORDER NOW!
LYNDA
BARRY 99

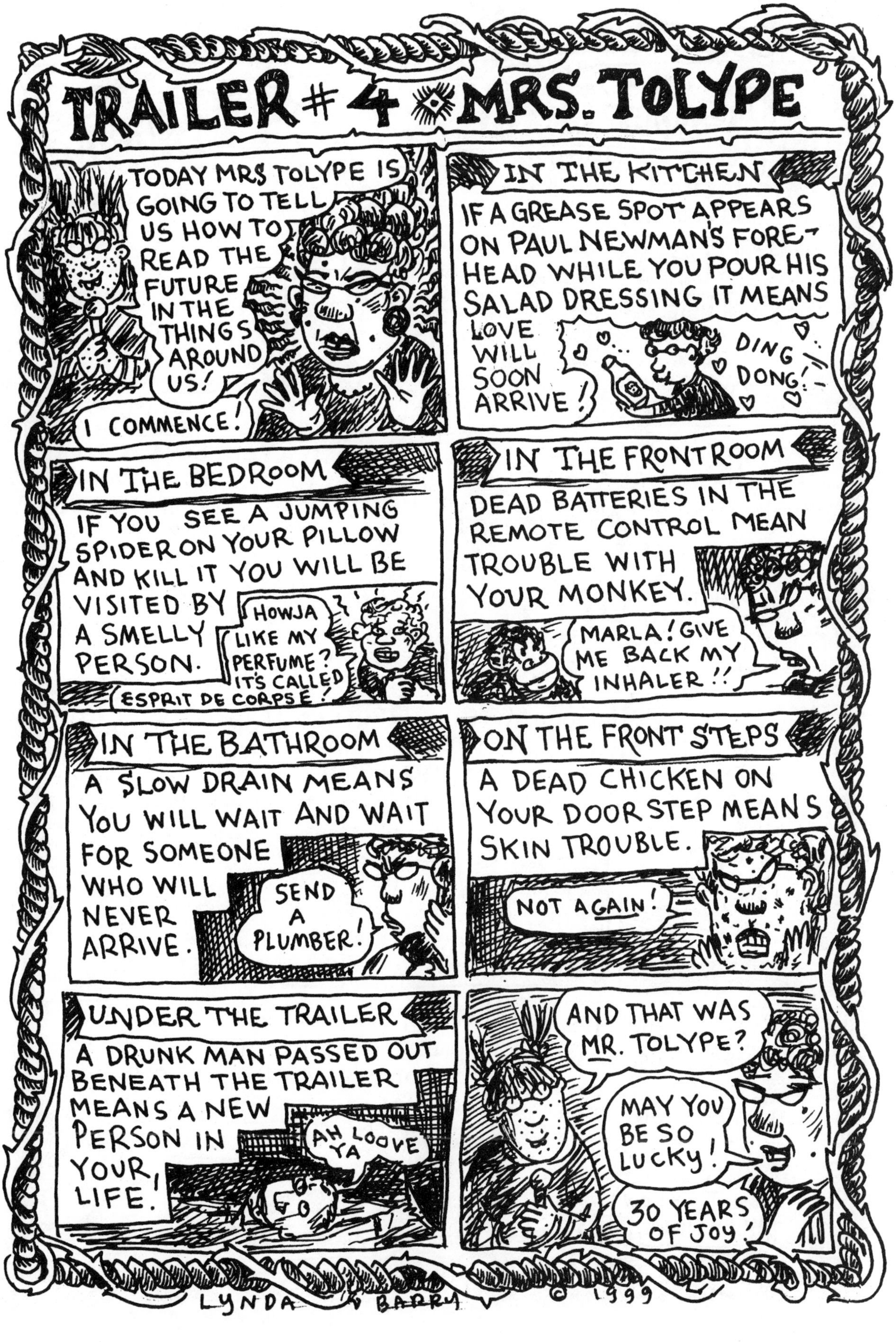
TRAILER # 4 MRS. TOLYPE
TODAY MRS TOLYPE IS GOING TO TELL US HOW TO READ THE FUTURE IN THE THINGS AROUND US!
I COMMENCE!
IN THE KITCHEN
IF A GREASE SPOT APPEARS ON PAUL NEWMAN'S FORE-HEAD WHILE YOU POUR HIS SALAD DRESSING IT MEANS
LOVE WILL SOON ARRIVE!
DING DONG!
IN THE BEDROOM
IF YOU SEE A JUMPING SPIDER ON YOUR PILLOW AND KILL IT YOU WILL BE VISITED BY A SMELLY PERSON.
HOWJA LIKE MY PERFUME? IT'S CALLED ESPRIT DE CORPSE!
IN THE FRONT ROOM
DEAD BATTERIES IN THE REMOTE CONTROL MEAN TROUBLE WITH YOUR MONKEY.
MARLA! GIVE ME BACK MY INHALER!!
IN THE BATHROOM
A SLOW DRAIN MEANS YOU WILL WAIT AND WAIT FOR SOMEONE WHO WILL NEVER ARRIVE.
SEND A PLUMBER!
ON THE FRONT STEPS
A DEAD CHICKEN ON YOUR DOOR STEP MEANS SKIN TROUBLE.
NOT AGAIN!
UNDER THE TRAILER
A DRUNK MAN PASSED OUT BENEATH THE TRAILER MEANS A NEW PERSON IN YOUR LIFE!
AH LOOOVE YA
AND THAT WAS MR. TOLYPE?
MAY YOU BE SO LUCKY!
30 YEARS OF JOY!
LYNDA BARRY © 1999

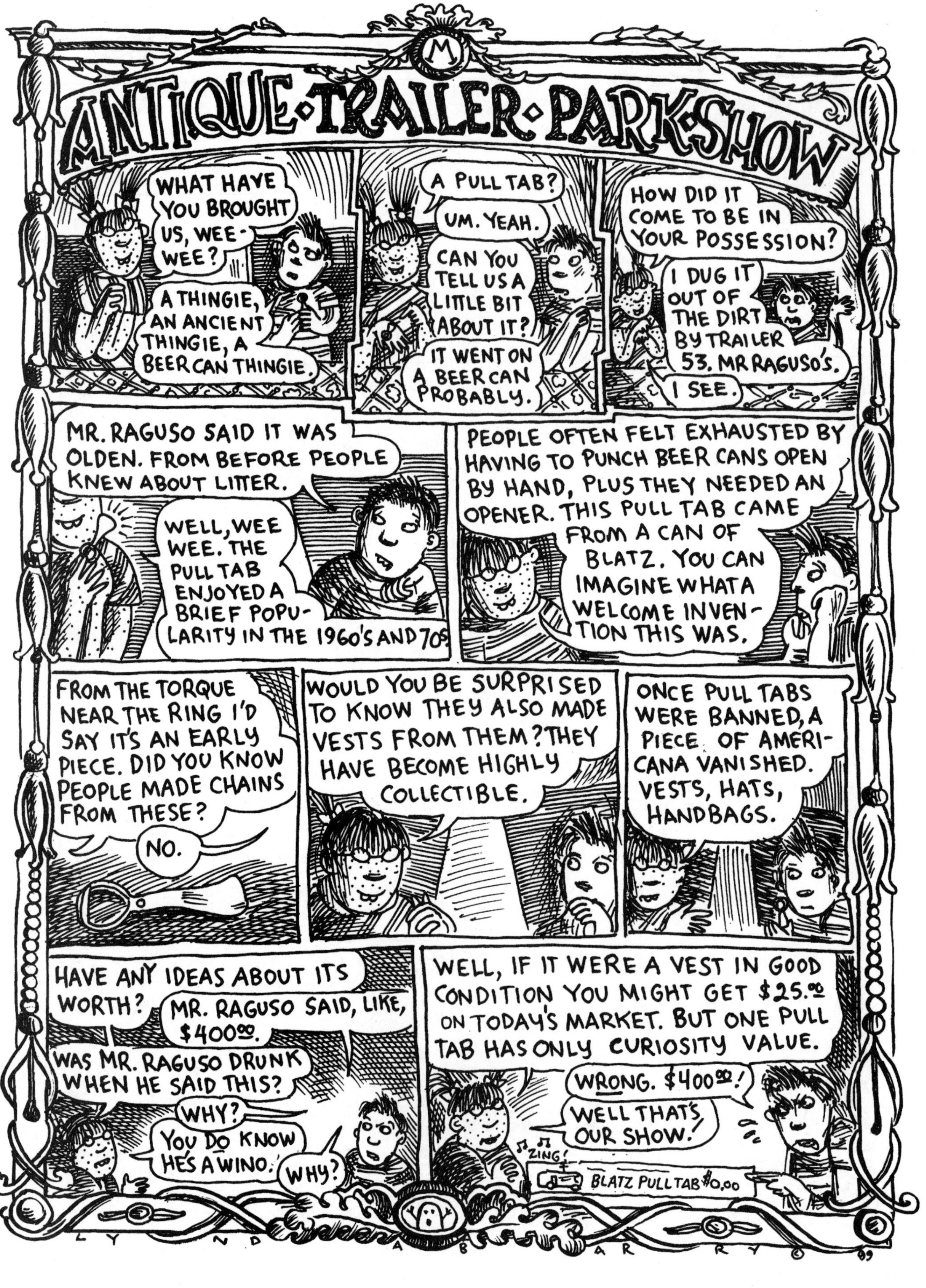

ANTIQUE • TRAILER • PARK • SHOW
WHAT HAVE YOU BROUGHT US, WEE-WEE?
A THINGIE, AN ANCIENT THINGIE, A BEER CAN THINGIE.
A PULL TAB?
UM. YEAH.
CAN YOU TELL US A LITTLE BIT ABOUT IT?
IT WENT ON A BEER CAN PROBABLY.
HOW DID IT COME TO BE IN YOUR POSSESSION?
I DUG IT OUT OF THE DIRT BY TRAILER 53. MR RAGUSO'S.
I SEE.
MR. RAGUSO SAID IT WAS OLDEN. FROM BEFORE PEOPLE KNEW ABOUT LITTER.
WELL, WEE WEE. THE PULL TAB ENJOYED A BRIEF POPULARITY IN THE 1960'S AND 70'S
PEOPLE OFTEN FELT EXHAUSTED BY HAVING TO PUNCH BEER CANS OPEN BY HAND, PLUS THEY NEEDED AN OPENER. THIS PULL TAB CAME FROM A CAN OF BLATZ. YOU CAN IMAGINE WHAT A WELCOME INVENTION THIS WAS.
FROM THE TORQUE NEAR THE RING I'D SAY IT'S AN EARLY PIECE. DID YOU KNOW PEOPLE MADE CHAINS FROM THESE?
NO.
WOULD YOU BE SURPRISED TO KNOW THEY ALSO MADE VESTS FROM THEM? THEY HAVE BECOME HIGHLY COLLECTIBLE.
ONCE PULL TABS WERE BANNED, A PIECE OF AMERICANA VANISHED. VESTS, HATS, HANDBAGS.
HAVE ANY IDEAS ABOUT ITS WORTH?
MR. RAGUSO SAID, LIKE, $400.00.
WAS MR. RAGUSO DRUNK WHEN HE SAID THIS?
WHY?
YOU DO KNOW HE'S A WINO.
WHY?
WELL, IF IT WERE A VEST IN GOOD CONDITION YOU MIGHT GET $25.00 ON TODAY'S MARKET. BUT ONE PULL TAB HAS ONLY CURIOSITY VALUE.
WRONG. $400.00!
WELL THAT'S OUR SHOW.
ZING!
BLATZ PULL TAB $0.00
LYNDA BARRY © 89

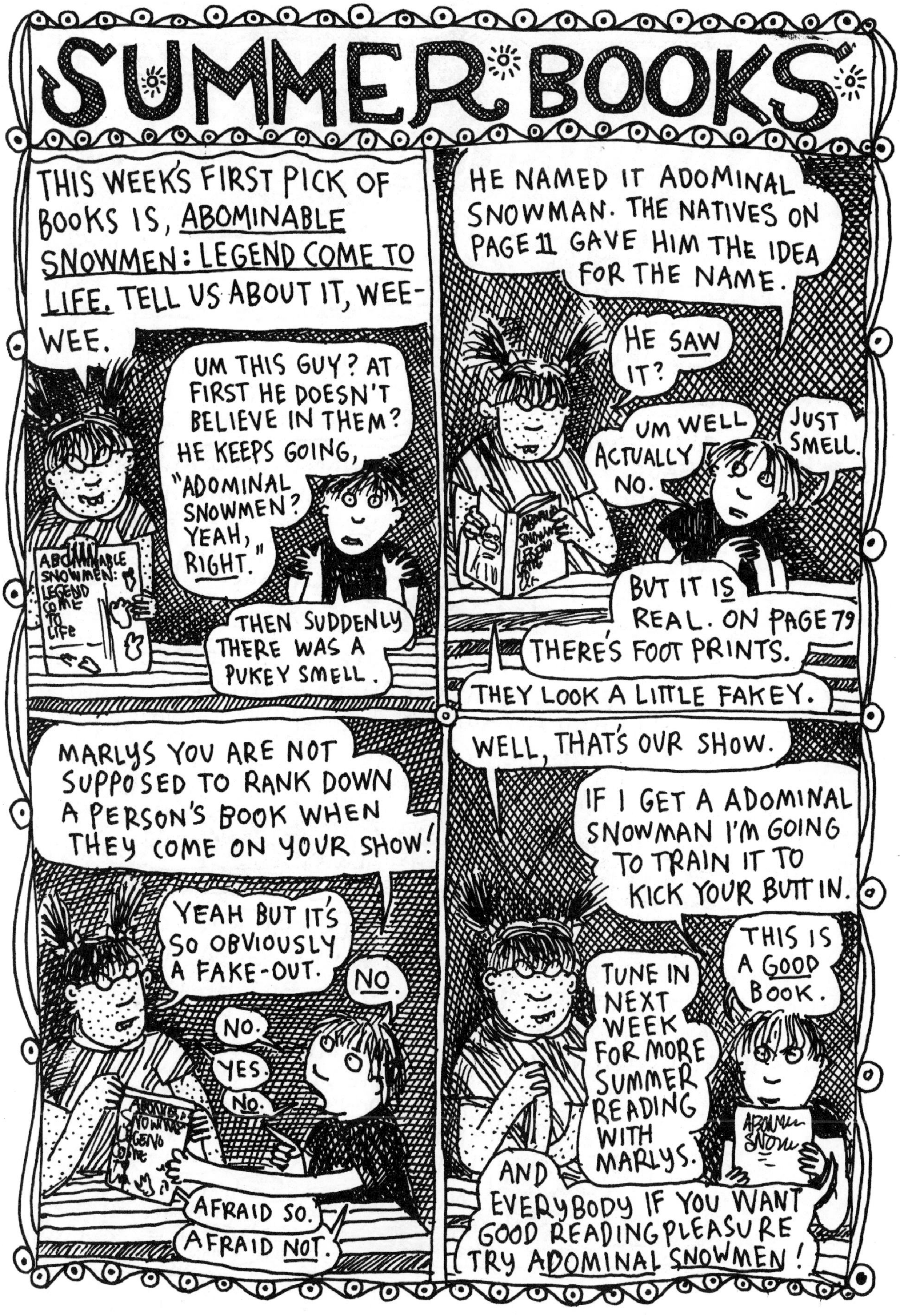
SUMMER BOOKS
THIS WEEK'S FIRST PICK OF BOOKS IS, ABOMINABLE SNOWMEN: LEGEND COME TO LIFE. TELL US ABOUT IT, WEE-WEE.
UM THIS GUY? AT FIRST HE DOESN'T BELIEVE IN THEM? HE KEEPS GOING, "ADOMINAL SNOWMEN? YEAH, RIGHT."
ABOMINABLE SNOWMEN: LEGEND COME TO LIFE
THEN SUDDENLY THERE WAS A PUKEY SMELL.
HE NAMED IT ADOMINAL SNOWMAN. THE NATIVES ON PAGE 11 GAVE HIM THE IDEA FOR THE NAME.
HE SAW IT?
UM WELL ACTUALLY NO.
JUST SMELL.
BUT IT IS REAL. ON PAGE 79 THERE'S FOOT PRINTS.
THEY LOOK A LITTLE FAKEY.
MARLYS YOU ARE NOT SUPPOSED TO RANK DOWN A PERSON'S BOOK WHEN THEY COME ON YOUR SHOW!
YEAH BUT IT'S SO OBVIOUSLY A FAKE-OUT.
NO.
NO.
YES.
NO.
AFRAID SO.
AFRAID NOT.
WELL, THAT'S OUR SHOW.
IF I GET A ADOMINAL SNOWMAN I'M GOING TO TRAIN IT TO KICK YOUR BUTT IN.
THIS IS A GOOD BOOK.
TUNE IN NEXT WEEK FOR MORE SUMMER READING WITH MARLYS.
AND EVERYBODY IF YOU WANT GOOD READING PLEASURE TRY ADOMINAL SNOWMEN!

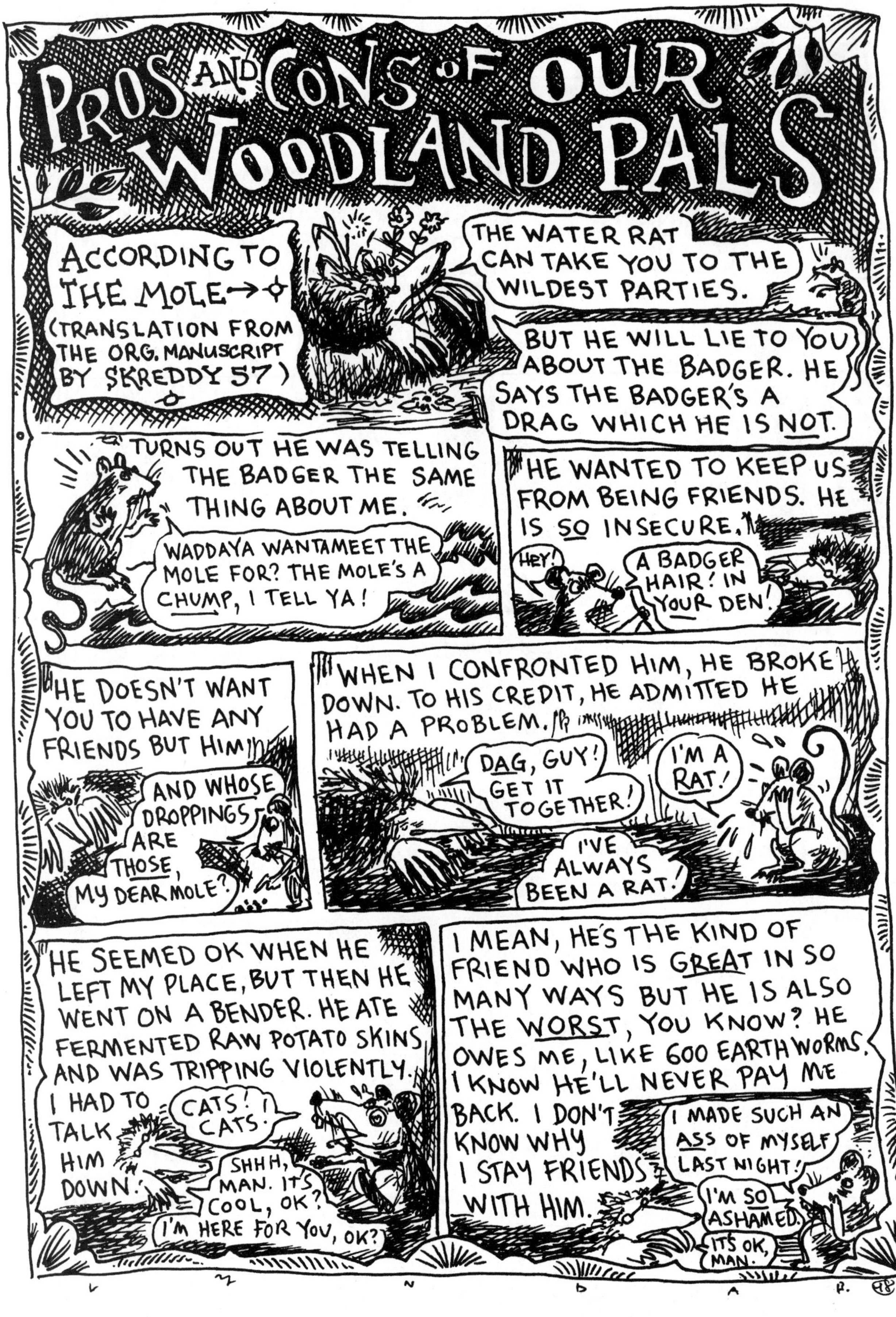
PROS AND CONS OF OUR WOODLAND PALS
ACCORDING TO THE MOLE (TRANSLATION FROM THE ORG. MANUSCRIPT BY SKREDDY 57)
THE WATER RAT CAN TAKE YOU TO THE WILDEST PARTIES.
BUT HE WILL LIE TO YOU ABOUT THE BADGER. HE SAYS THE BADGER'S A DRAG WHICH HE IS NOT.
TURNS OUT HE WAS TELLING THE BADGER THE SAME THING ABOUT ME.
WADDAYA WANTAMEET THE MOLE FOR? THE MOLE'S A CHUMP, I TELL YA!
HE WANTED TO KEEP US FROM BEING FRIENDS. HE IS SO INSECURE.
HEY!
A BADGER HAIR! IN YOUR DEN!
HE DOESN'T WANT YOU TO HAVE ANY FRIENDS BUT HIM.
AND WHOSE DROPPINGS ARE THOSE, MY DEAR MOLE?
WHEN I CONFRONTED HIM, HE BROKE DOWN. TO HIS CREDIT, HE ADMITTED HE HAD A PROBLEM.
DAG, GUY! GET IT TOGETHER!
I'M A RAT!
I'VE ALWAYS BEEN A RAT!
HE SEEMED OK WHEN HE LEFT MY PLACE, BUT THEN HE WENT ON A BENDER. HE ATE FERMENTED RAW POTATO SKINS AND WAS TRIPPING VIOLENTLY.
I HAD TO TALK HIM DOWN.
CATS! CATS!
SHHH, MAN. IT'S COOL, OK?
I'M HERE FOR YOU, OK?
I MEAN, HE'S THE KIND OF FRIEND WHO IS GREAT IN SO MANY WAYS BUT HE IS ALSO THE WORST, YOU KNOW? HE OWES ME, LIKE 600 EARTHWORMS. I KNOW HE'LL NEVER PAY ME BACK. I DON'T KNOW WHY I STAY FRIENDS WITH HIM.
I MADE SUCH AN ASS OF MYSELF LAST NIGHT!
I'M SO ASHAMED.
IT'S OK, MAN.
L Y N D A B.

MARLYS Wisdom FOR IF you are SICK

1. LET ALL THE DOGS IN THE BED! THEY HAVE MAGICAL HEALER POWERS! IF YOU DO NOT HAVE PERSONAL DOGS, JUST BORROW YOUR NEIGHBOR'S!

I FEEL THE SUPERFRAGALISTIC VIBRATIONS!

2. WHEN YOUR EXCITED FRIEND WHO TALKS REALLY LOUD INTO THE TELEPHONE WANTS TO BLAB WITH YOU, SAY PLEASE CALL BACK LATER!

IT'S FOR YOU.

IF I TALK TO HER I WILL GO BERSERK

MARLYS GUESS WHAT YOU MISSED FOR LUNCH TODAY?!!

PLEASE WILL YOU TELL HER?

3. DO NOT ASK FOR YOUR MOST FAVORITE FOOD! IF YOU BARF IT, YOU WON'T BE ABLE TO EAT IT IN THE FUTURE FOR A LONG LONG TIME!!

MARLYS ARE YOU SURE YOU WANT FRUITLOOPS AND CHOCOLATE MILK FOR DINNER?

I. AM. SURE.

4. DON'T GET FREAKED BY THE VERY WEIRD DREAMS! MOSTLY IT IS JUST THE COUGH SYRUP!

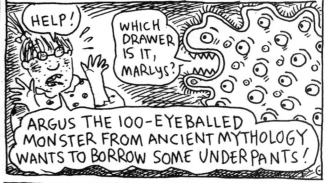

HELP!

WHICH DRAWER IS IT, MARLYS?

ARGUS THE 100-EYEBALLED MONSTER FROM ANCIENT MYTHOLOGY WANTS TO BORROW SOME UNDERPANTS!

5. IT IS IMPORTANT THAT YOU CONTROL THE ENTIRE COUCH! EVERYONE ELSE JUST SIT ON THE FLOOR! ALSO IT IS YOUR RIGHT TO HOG THE T.V.!

CHUMP.

MARLYS IS A CHUMP.

JUST BECAUSE YOU ARE SICK IT DOES NOT MEAN YOU CONTROL THE UNIVERSE!

SHUT UP!

YES IT DOES!

6. IF YOUR COUSIN SNATCHES THE REMOTE CONTROL, CALL RESCUE 911!

YES, UM, I'D LIKE TO REPORT A TRAGICAL EMERGENCY PLEASE?!

A ROBBERY!

CAN YOU PLEASE COME RIGHT AWAY? MY SHOW IS ON!

LYNDA   BARRY

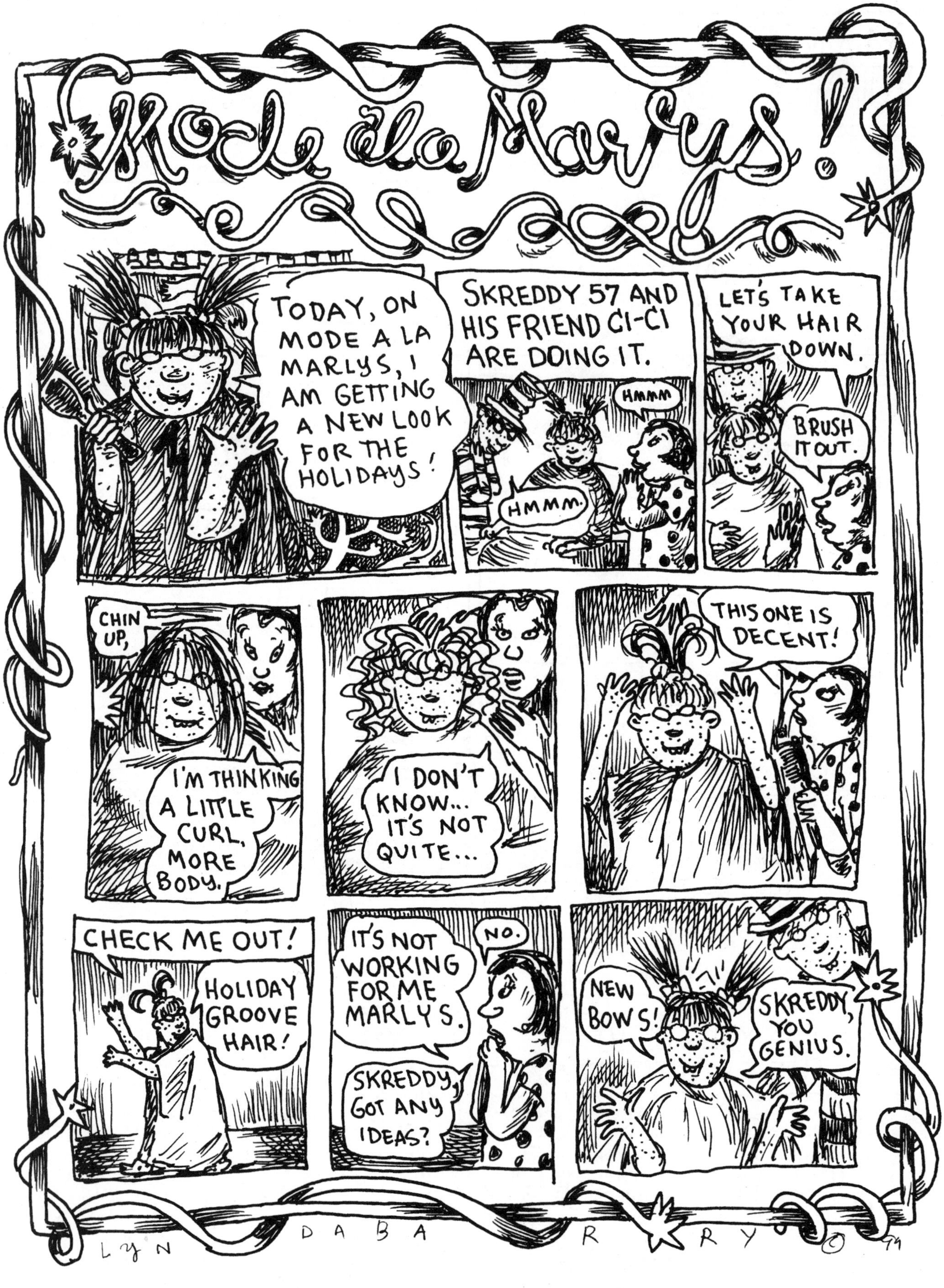
Mode à la Marlys!
TODAY, ON MODE A LA MARLYS, I AM GETTING A NEW LOOK FOR THE HOLIDAYS!
SKREDDY 57 AND HIS FRIEND CI-CI ARE DOING IT.
HMMM
HMMM.
LET'S TAKE YOUR HAIR DOWN.
BRUSH IT OUT.
CHIN UP,
I'M THINKING A LITTLE CURL, MORE BODY.
I DON'T KNOW... IT'S NOT QUITE...
THIS ONE IS DECENT!
CHECK ME OUT!
HOLIDAY GROOVE HAIR!
IT'S NOT WORKING FOR ME MARLYS.
NO.
SKREDDY, GOT ANY IDEAS?
NEW BOWS!
SKREDDY, YOU GENIUS.
LYN DA BARRY © 94

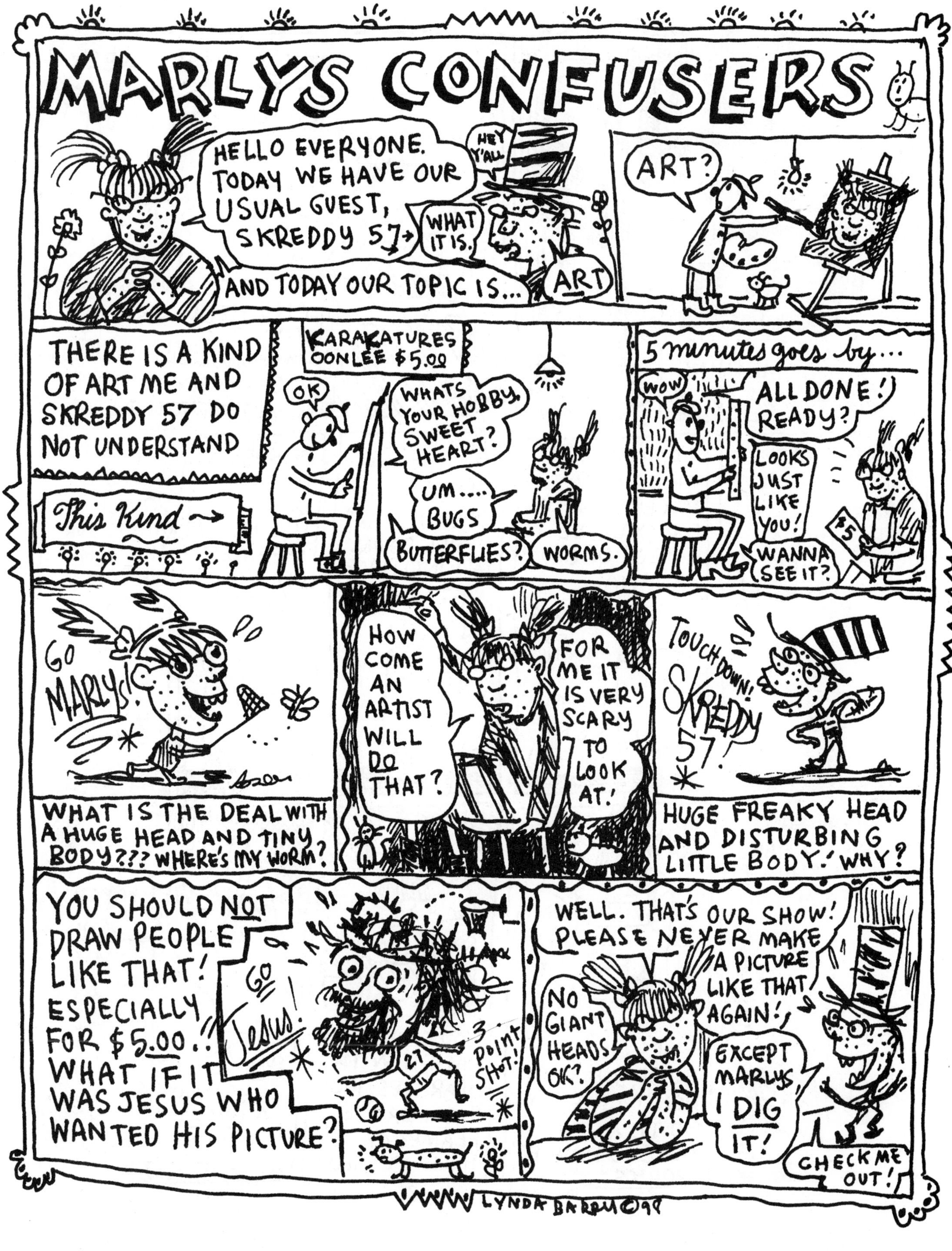
MARLYS CONFUSERS
HELLO EVERYONE. TODAY WE HAVE OUR USUAL GUEST, SKREDDY 57→
HEY Y'ALL
WHAT IT IS.
AND TODAY OUR TOPIC IS...
ART
ART?
THERE IS A KIND OF ART ME AND SKREDDY 57 DO NOT UNDERSTAND
This Kind →
KARAKATURES OONLEE $5.00
OK
WHATS YOUR HOBBY, SWEET HEART?
UM..... BUGS
BUTTERFLIES?
WORMS.
5 minutes goes by...
WOW
ALL DONE! READY?
LOOKS JUST LIKE YOU!
WANNA SEE IT?
$5
GO MARLYS!
WHAT IS THE DEAL WITH A HUGE HEAD AND TINY BODY??? WHERE'S MY WORM?
HOW COME AN ARTIST WILL DO THAT?
FOR ME IT IS VERY SCARY TO LOOK AT!
TOUCHDOWN! SKREDDY 57!
HUGE FREAKY HEAD AND DISTURBING LITTLE BODY! WHY?
YOU SHOULD NOT DRAW PEOPLE LIKE THAT! ESPECIALLY FOR $5.00.. WHAT IF IT WAS JESUS WHO WANTED HIS PICTURE?
GO Jesus!
3 POINT SHOT!
27
WELL. THAT'S OUR SHOW! PLEASE NEVER MAKE A PICTURE LIKE THAT AGAIN!
NO GIANT HEADS OK?
EXCEPT MARLYS I DIG IT!
CHECK ME OUT!
LYNDA BARRY ©98

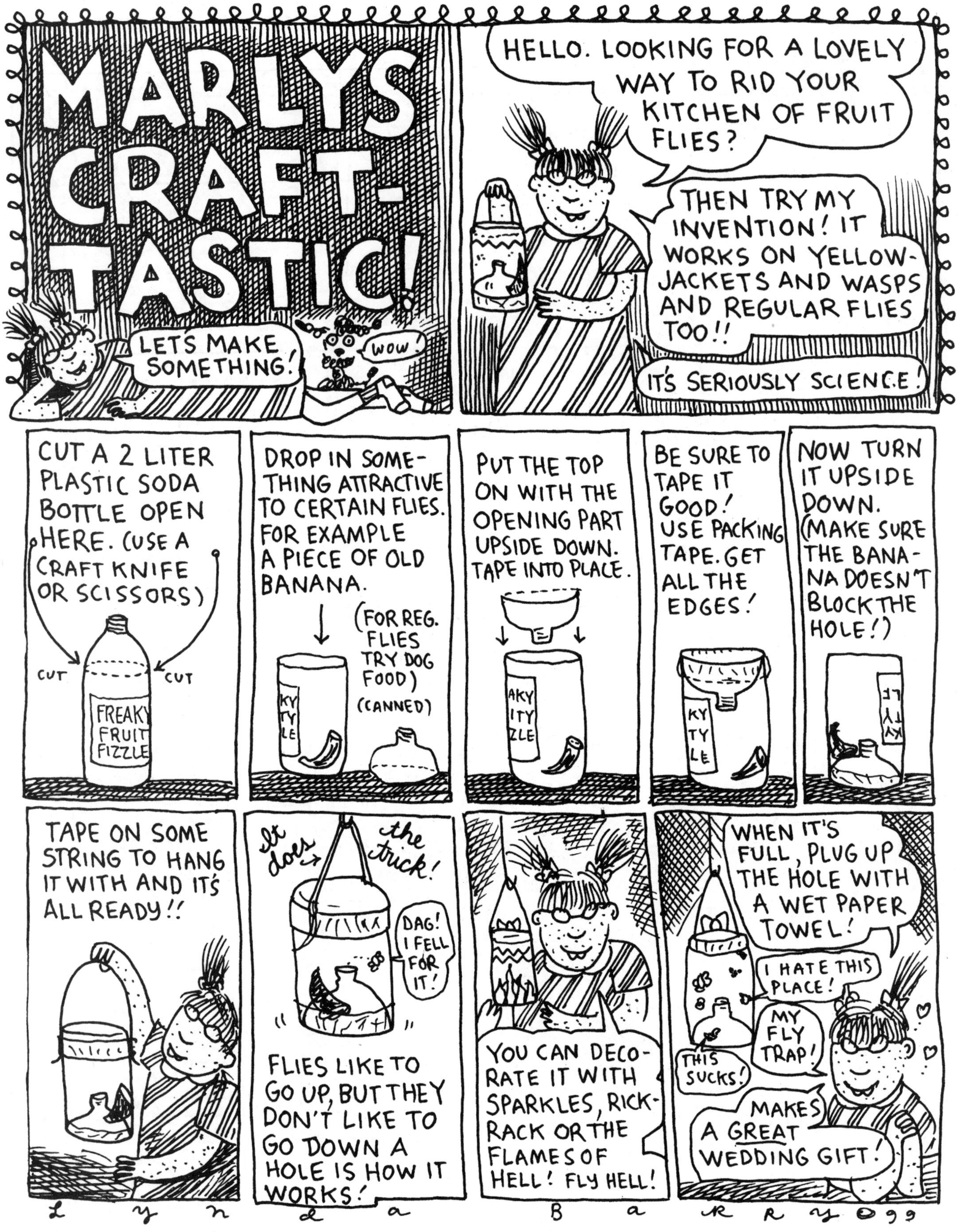
MARLYS CRAFT-TASTIC!
LETS MAKE SOMETHING!
WOW!
HELLO. LOOKING FOR A LOVELY WAY TO RID YOUR KITCHEN OF FRUIT FLIES?
THEN TRY MY INVENTION! IT WORKS ON YELLOW-JACKETS AND WASPS AND REGULAR FLIES TOO!!
IT'S SERIOUSLY SCIENCE!
CUT A 2 LITER PLASTIC SODA BOTTLE OPEN HERE. (USE A CRAFT KNIFE OR SCISSORS)
CUT
CUT
FREAKY FRUIT FIZZLE
DROP IN SOME-THING ATTRACTIVE TO CERTAIN FLIES. FOR EXAMPLE A PIECE OF OLD BANANA.
(FOR REG. FLIES TRY DOG FOOD) (CANNED)
PUT THE TOP ON WITH THE OPENING PART UPSIDE DOWN. TAPE INTO PLACE.
BE SURE TO TAPE IT GOOD! USE PACKING TAPE. GET ALL THE EDGES!
NOW TURN IT UPSIDE DOWN. (MAKE SURE THE BANA-NA DOESN'T BLOCK THE HOLE!)
TAPE ON SOME STRING TO HANG IT WITH AND IT'S ALL READY!!
It does the trick!
DAG! I FELL FOR IT!
FLIES LIKE TO GO UP, BUT THEY DON'T LIKE TO GO DOWN A HOLE IS HOW IT WORKS!
YOU CAN DECO-RATE IT WITH SPARKLES, RICK-RACK OR THE FLAMES OF HELL! FLY HELL!
WHEN IT'S FULL, PLUG UP THE HOLE WITH A WET PAPER TOWEL!
I HATE THIS PLACE!
MY FLY TRAP!
THIS SUCKS!
MAKES A GREAT WEDDING GIFT!
Lynda Barry ©99

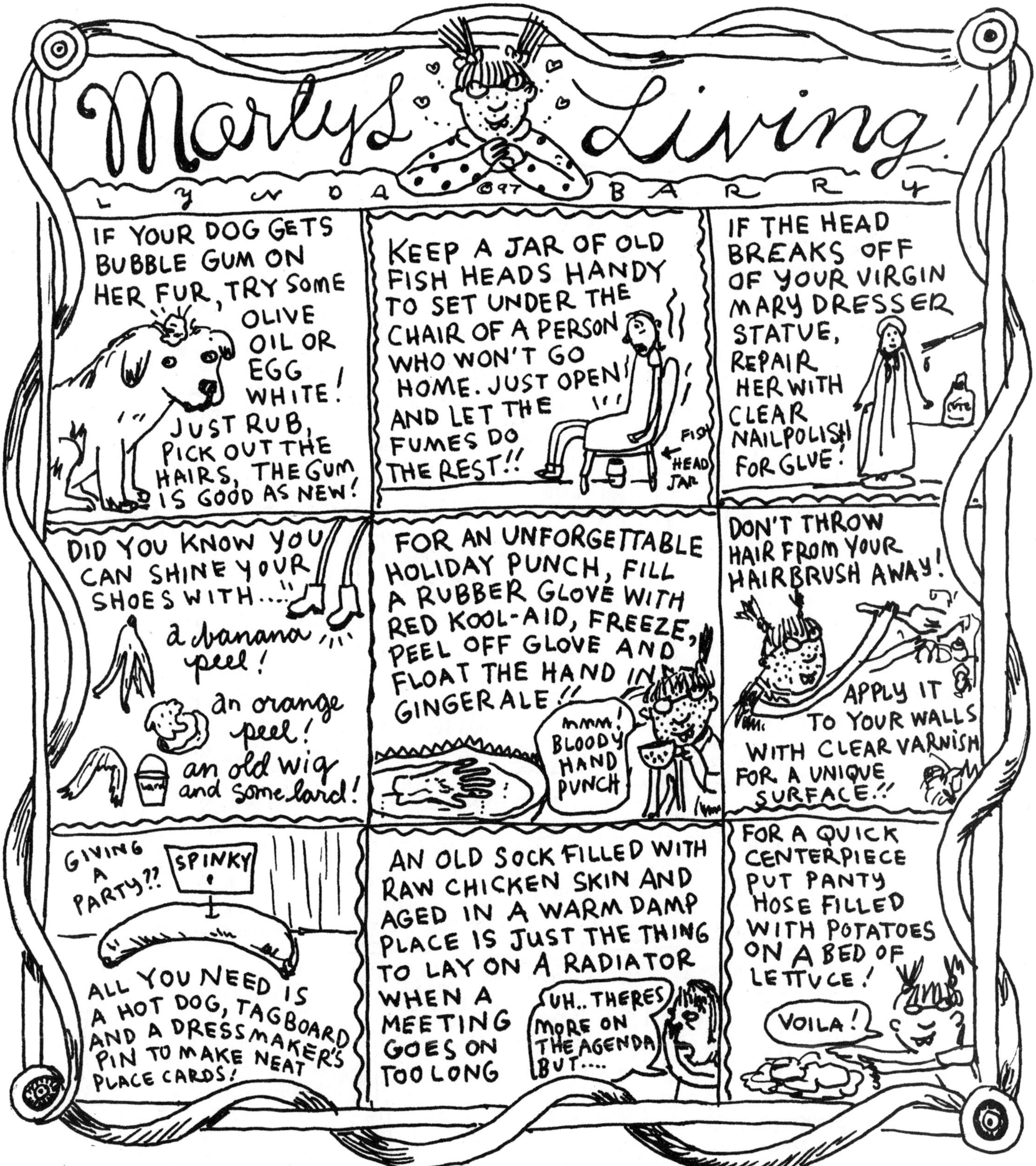
Marlys Living!
LYNDA ©97 BARRY
IF YOUR DOG GETS BUBBLE GUM ON HER FUR, TRY SOME OLIVE OIL OR EGG WHITE!
JUST RUB, PICK OUT THE HAIRS, THE GUM IS GOOD AS NEW!
KEEP A JAR OF OLD FISH HEADS HANDY TO SET UNDER THE CHAIR OF A PERSON WHO WON'T GO HOME. JUST OPEN AND LET THE FUMES DO THE REST!!
FISH HEAD JAR
IF THE HEAD BREAKS OFF OF YOUR VIRGIN MARY DRESSER STATUE, REPAIR HER WITH CLEAR NAILPOLISH FOR GLUE!
DID YOU KNOW YOU CAN SHINE YOUR SHOES WITH....!!
a banana peel!
an orange peel!
an old wig and some lard!
lard
FOR AN UNFORGETTABLE HOLIDAY PUNCH, FILL A RUBBER GLOVE WITH RED KOOL-AID, FREEZE, PEEL OFF GLOVE AND FLOAT THE HAND IN GINGERALE!!
mmm! BLOODY HAND PUNCH
DON'T THROW HAIR FROM YOUR HAIRBRUSH AWAY!
APPLY IT TO YOUR WALLS WITH CLEAR VARNISH FOR A UNIQUE SURFACE!!
GIVING A PARTY??
SPINKY
ALL YOU NEED IS A HOT DOG, TAGBOARD AND A DRESSMAKER'S PIN TO MAKE NEAT PLACE CARDS!
AN OLD SOCK FILLED WITH RAW CHICKEN SKIN AND AGED IN A WARM DAMP PLACE IS JUST THE THING TO LAY ON A RADIATOR WHEN A MEETING GOES ON TOO LONG
UH.. THERES MORE ON THE AGENDA BUT....
FOR A QUICK CENTERPIECE PUT PANTY HOSE FILLED WITH POTATOES ON A BED OF LETTUCE!
VOILA!

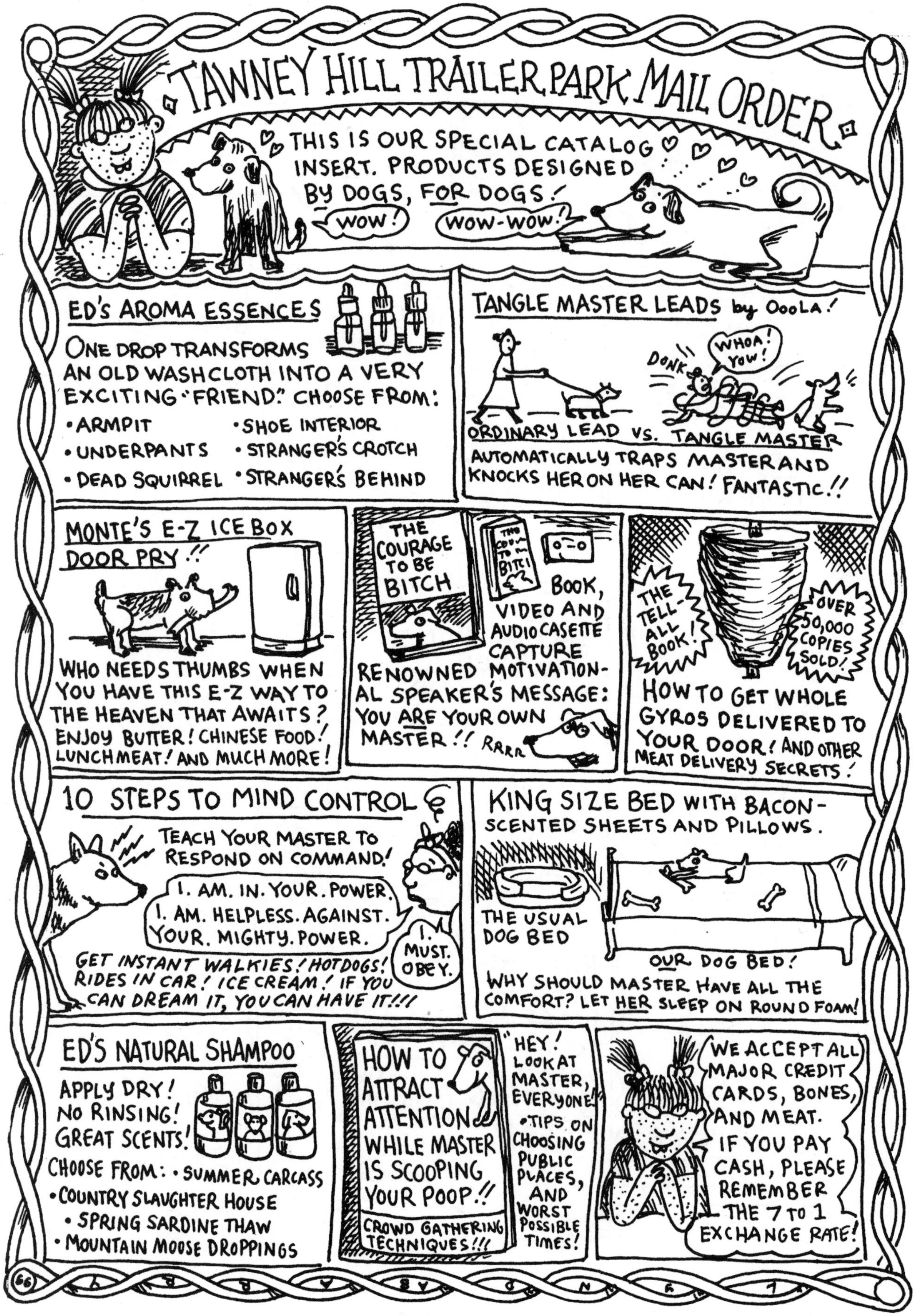
TAWNEY HILL TRAILER PARK MAIL ORDER
THIS IS OUR SPECIAL CATALOG INSERT. PRODUCTS DESIGNED BY DOGS, FOR DOGS!
WOW!
WOW-WOW!
ED'S AROMA ESSENCES
ONE DROP TRANSFORMS AN OLD WASHCLOTH INTO A VERY EXCITING "FRIEND." CHOOSE FROM:
• ARMPIT
• UNDERPANTS
• DEAD SQUIRREL
• SHOE INTERIOR
• STRANGER'S CROTCH
• STRANGER'S BEHIND
TANGLE MASTER LEADS by OooLA!
DONK
WHOA! YOW!
ORDINARY LEAD VS. TANGLE MASTER
AUTOMATICALLY TRAPS MASTER AND KNOCKS HER ON HER CAN! FANTASTIC!!
MONTE'S E-Z ICE BOX DOOR PRY!!
WHO NEEDS THUMBS WHEN YOU HAVE THIS E-Z WAY TO THE HEAVEN THAT AWAITS? ENJOY BUTTER! CHINESE FOOD! LUNCHMEAT! AND MUCH MORE!
THE COURAGE TO BE BITCH
BOOK, VIDEO AND AUDIO CASETTE CAPTURE RENOWNED MOTIVATIONAL SPEAKER'S MESSAGE: YOU ARE YOUR OWN MASTER!!
RRRR
THE TELL-ALL BOOK!
OVER 50,000 COPIES SOLD!
HOW TO GET WHOLE GYROS DELIVERED TO YOUR DOOR! AND OTHER MEAT DELIVERY SECRETS!
10 STEPS TO MIND CONTROL
TEACH YOUR MASTER TO RESPOND ON COMMAND!
I. AM. IN. YOUR. POWER. I. AM. HELPLESS. AGAINST. YOUR. MIGHTY. POWER.
I. MUST. OBEY.
GET INSTANT WALKIES! HOTDOGS! RIDES IN CAR! ICE CREAM! IF YOU CAN DREAM IT, YOU CAN HAVE IT!!!
KING SIZE BED WITH BACON-SCENTED SHEETS AND PILLOWS.
THE USUAL DOG BED
OUR DOG BED!
WHY SHOULD MASTER HAVE ALL THE COMFORT? LET HER SLEEP ON ROUND FOAM!
ED'S NATURAL SHAMPOO
APPLY DRY! NO RINSING! GREAT SCENTS!
CHOOSE FROM: • SUMMER CARCASS
• COUNTRY SLAUGHTER HOUSE
• SPRING SARDINE THAW
• MOUNTAIN MOOSE DROPPINGS
HOW TO ATTRACT ATTENTION WHILE MASTER IS SCOOPING YOUR POOP!!
CROWD GATHERING TECHNIQUES!!!
"HEY! LOOK AT MASTER, EVERYONE!"
• TIPS ON CHOOSING PUBLIC PLACES, AND WORST POSSIBLE TIMES!
WE ACCEPT ALL MAJOR CREDIT CARDS, BONES, AND MEAT.
IF YOU PAY CASH, PLEASE REMEMBER THE 7 TO 1 EXCHANGE RATE!

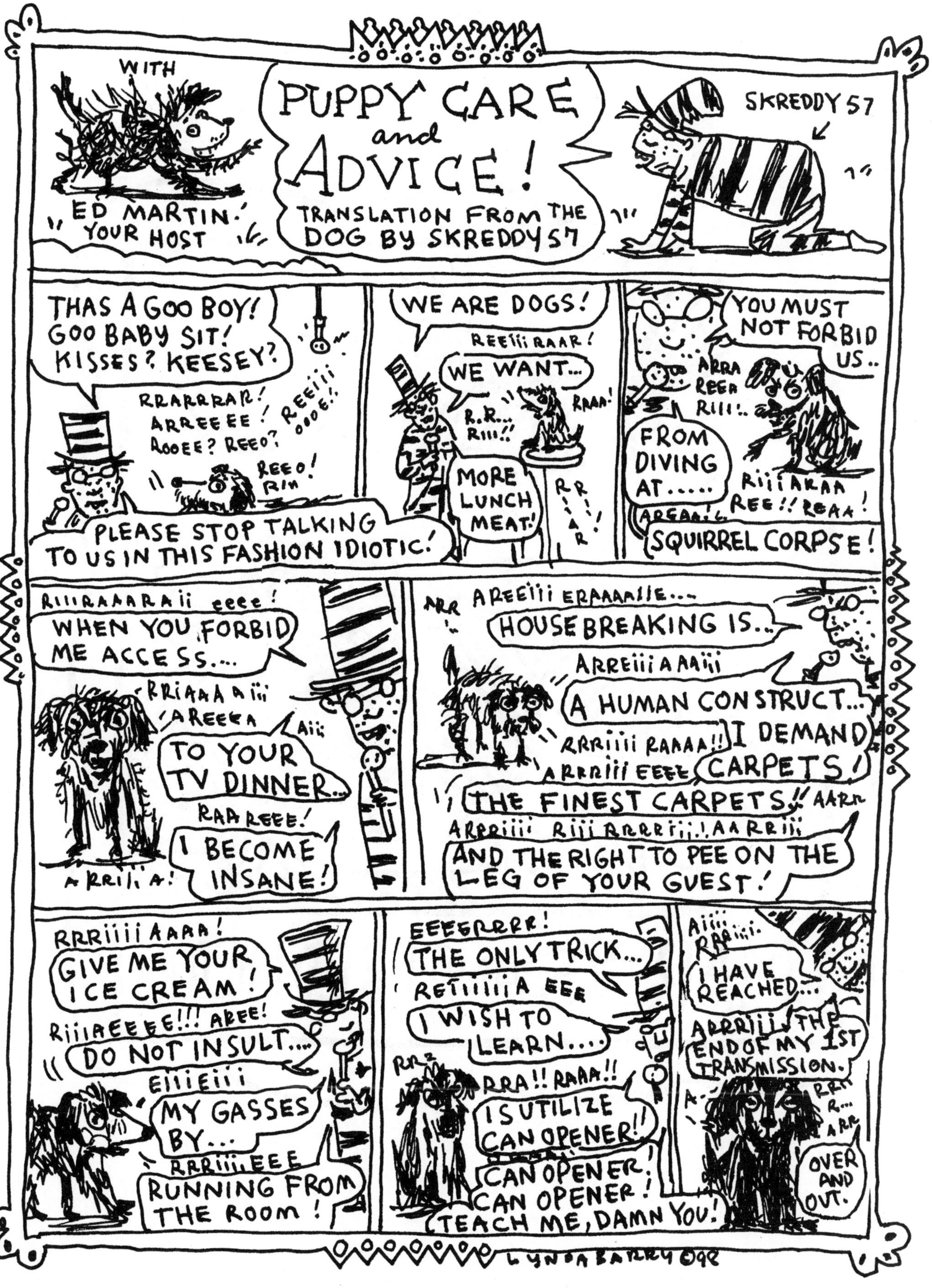

WITH
ED MARTIN! YOUR HOST
PUPPY CARE and ADVICE!
TRANSLATION FROM THE DOG BY SKREDDY 57
SKREDDY 57
THAS A GOO BOY! GOO BABY SIT! KISSES? KEESEY?
RRARRRAR! ARREEEEE! ROOEE? REEO?
REEiii OOOE!
REEO! RIM
PLEASE STOP TALKING TO US IN THIS FASHION IDIOTIC!
WE ARE DOGS!
REEiii RAAR!
WE WANT...
R.R... Riii!!
RAAA!
MORE LUNCH MEAT!
R R i A R!
YOU MUST NOT FORBID US..
ARRA REEA Riii!..
FROM DIVING AT.....
Riii ARAA REE!! REAA!
AREAA!
SQUIRREL CORPSE!
RiiiRAAARAii eeee!
WHEN YOU FORBID ME ACCESS....
RRiAAA A iii AREEEA
Aii
TO YOUR TV DINNER...
RAA REEE!
I BECOME INSANE!
ARRii A!
ARR
AREEiii ERAAAAIIE...
HOUSEBREAKING IS...
ARREiii AAAiii
A HUMAN CONSTRUCT...
RRRiiii RAAAA!!
I DEMAND CARPETS!
ARRRiii EEEE
THE FINEST CARPETS!!
AARR
ARRRiiii Riii ARRRiii AARRiii
AND THE RIGHT TO PEE ON THE LEG OF YOUR GUEST!
RRRiiii AAAA!
GIVE ME YOUR ICE CREAM!
RiiiAEEEE!!! AREE!
DO NOT INSULT....
Eiiii Eiii
MY GASSES BY...
RRRiiii EEE
RUNNING FROM THE ROOM!
EEEERRRR!
THE ONLY TRICK...
REEiiiiii A EEE
I WISH TO LEARN....
RRR
RRA!! RAAA!!
I UTILIZE CAN OPENER!!
CAN OPENER! CAN OPENER! TEACH ME, DAMN YOU!
Aiiii RRRiiii
I HAVE REACHED...
ARRRiii
THE END OF MY 1ST TRANSMISSION.
A
RRR R... ARR
OVER AND OUT.
LYNDA BARRY ©98

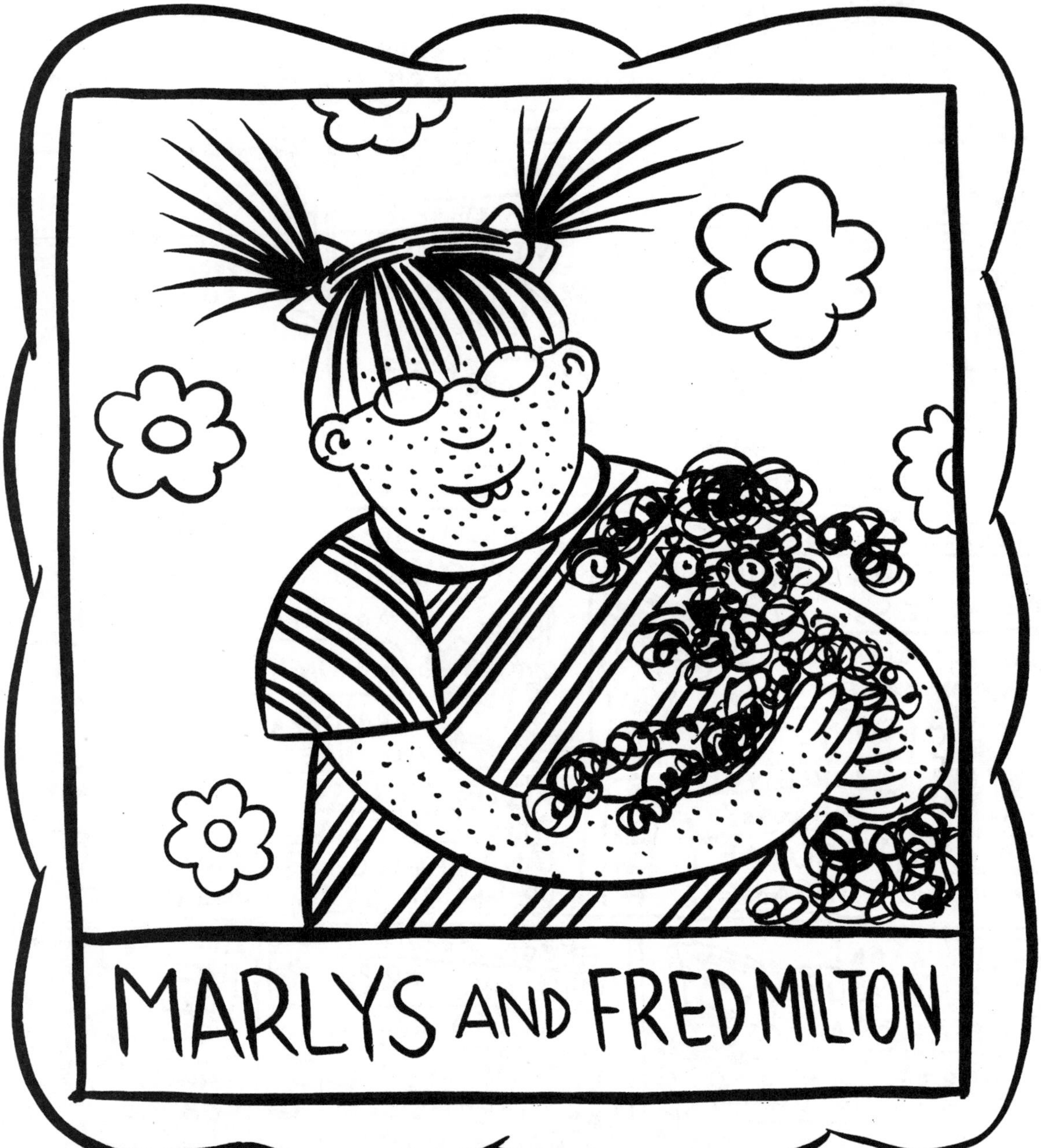
MARLYS AND FRED MILTON

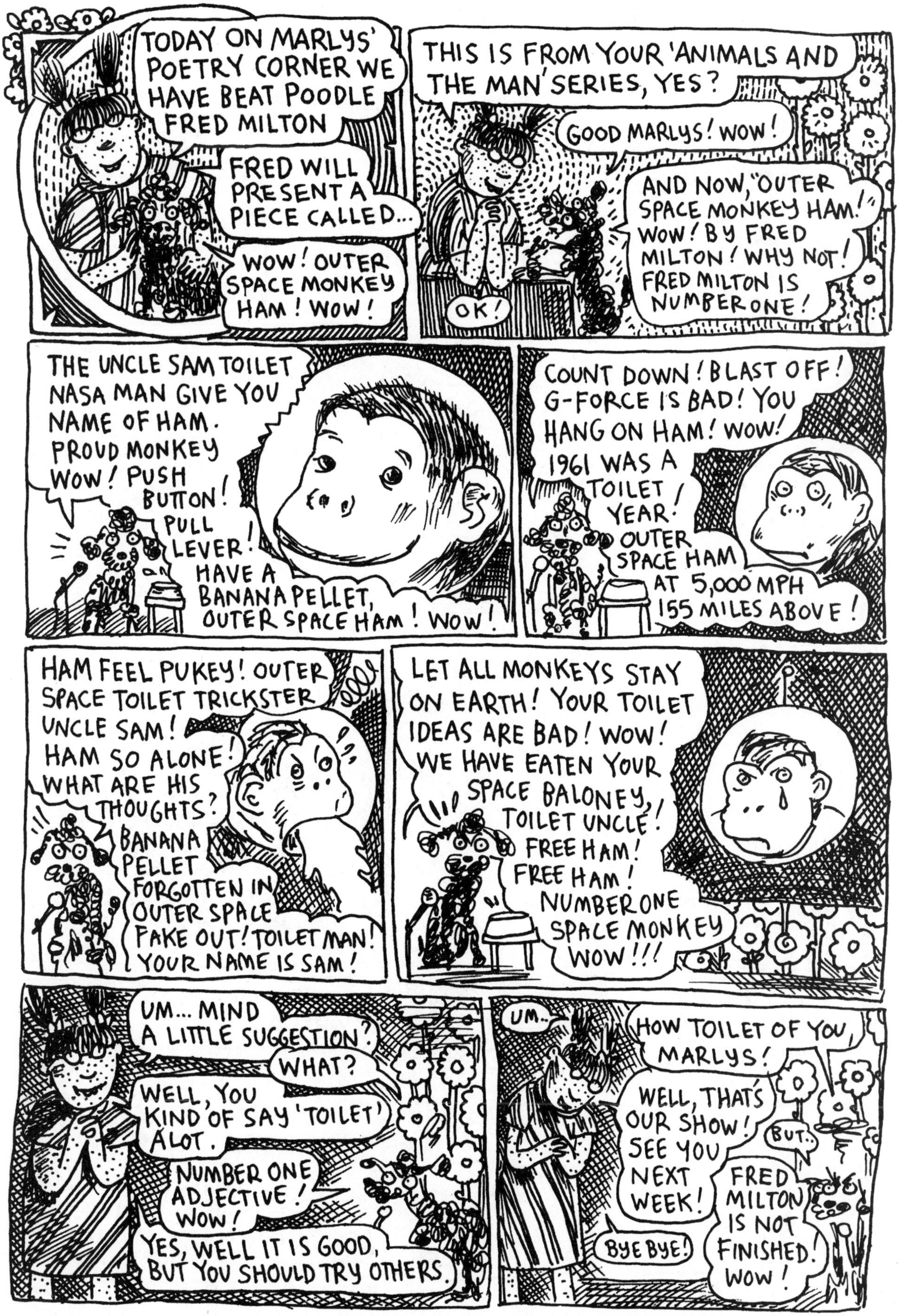
TODAY ON MARLYS' POETRY CORNER WE HAVE BEAT POODLE FRED MILTON
FRED WILL PRESENT A PIECE CALLED...
WOW! OUTER SPACE MONKEY HAM! WOW!
THIS IS FROM YOUR 'ANIMALS AND THE MAN' SERIES, YES?
GOOD MARLYS! WOW!
AND NOW, "OUTER SPACE MONKEY HAM." WOW! BY FRED MILTON! WHY NOT! FRED MILTON IS NUMBER ONE!
OK!
THE UNCLE SAM TOILET NASA MAN GIVE YOU NAME OF HAM. PROUD MONKEY WOW! PUSH BUTTON! PULL LEVER! HAVE A BANANA PELLET, OUTER SPACE HAM! WOW!
COUNT DOWN! BLAST OFF! G-FORCE IS BAD! YOU HANG ON HAM! WOW! 1961 WAS A TOILET YEAR! OUTER SPACE HAM AT 5,000 MPH 155 MILES ABOVE!
HAM FEEL PUKEY! OUTER SPACE TOILET TRICKSTER UNCLE SAM! HAM SO ALONE! WHAT ARE HIS THOUGHTS? BANANA PELLET FORGOTTEN IN OUTER SPACE FAKE OUT! TOILET MAN! YOUR NAME IS SAM!
LET ALL MONKEYS STAY ON EARTH! YOUR TOILET IDEAS ARE BAD! WOW! WE HAVE EATEN YOUR SPACE BALONEY, TOILET UNCLE! FREE HAM! FREE HAM! NUMBER ONE SPACE MONKEY WOW!!!
UM... MIND A LITTLE SUGGESTION?
WHAT?
WELL, YOU KIND OF SAY 'TOILET' ALOT.
NUMBER ONE ADJECTIVE! WOW!
YES, WELL IT IS GOOD, BUT YOU SHOULD TRY OTHERS.
UM..
HOW TOILET OF YOU, MARLYS!
WELL, THAT'S OUR SHOW! SEE YOU NEXT WEEK!
BUT..
BYE BYE!
FRED MILTON IS NOT FINISHED! WOW!

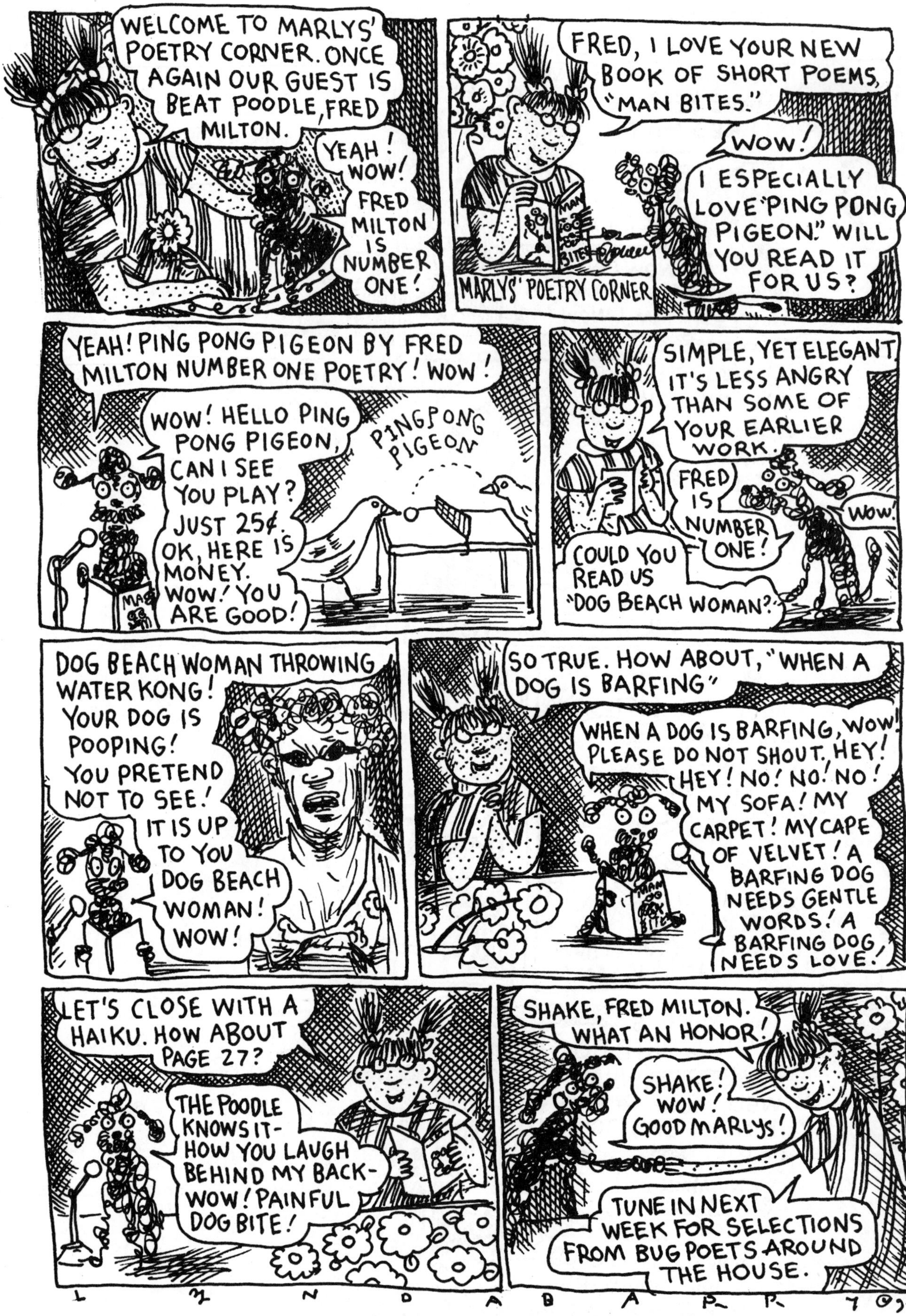
WELCOME TO MARLYS' POETRY CORNER. ONCE AGAIN OUR GUEST IS BEAT POODLE, FRED MILTON.
YEAH! WOW! FRED MILTON IS NUMBER ONE!
FRED, I LOVE YOUR NEW BOOK OF SHORT POEMS, "MAN BITES."
MARLYS' POETRY CORNER
WOW!
I ESPECIALLY LOVE "PING PONG PIGEON." WILL YOU READ IT FOR US?
YEAH! PING PONG PIGEON BY FRED MILTON NUMBER ONE POETRY! WOW!
WOW! HELLO PING PONG PIGEON, CAN I SEE YOU PLAY? JUST 25¢. OK, HERE IS MONEY. WOW! YOU ARE GOOD!
PING PONG PIGEON
SIMPLE, YET ELEGANT. IT'S LESS ANGRY THAN SOME OF YOUR EARLIER WORK.
FRED IS NUMBER ONE!
WOW!
COULD YOU READ US "DOG BEACH WOMAN?"
DOG BEACH WOMAN THROWING WATER KONG! YOUR DOG IS POOPING! YOU PRETEND NOT TO SEE! IT IS UP TO YOU DOG BEACH WOMAN! WOW!
SO TRUE. HOW ABOUT, "WHEN A DOG IS BARFING"
WHEN A DOG IS BARFING, WOW! PLEASE DO NOT SHOUT. HEY! HEY! NO! NO! NO! MY SOFA! MY CARPET! MY CAPE OF VELVET! A BARFING DOG NEEDS GENTLE WORDS! A BARFING DOG NEEDS LOVE!
LET'S CLOSE WITH A HAIKU. HOW ABOUT PAGE 27?
THE POODLE KNOWS IT- HOW YOU LAUGH BEHIND MY BACK- WOW! PAINFUL DOG BITE!
SHAKE, FRED MILTON. WHAT AN HONOR!
SHAKE! WOW! GOOD MARLYS!
TUNE IN NEXT WEEK FOR SELECTIONS FROM BUG POETS AROUND THE HOUSE.
L Y N D A B A R R Y ©99

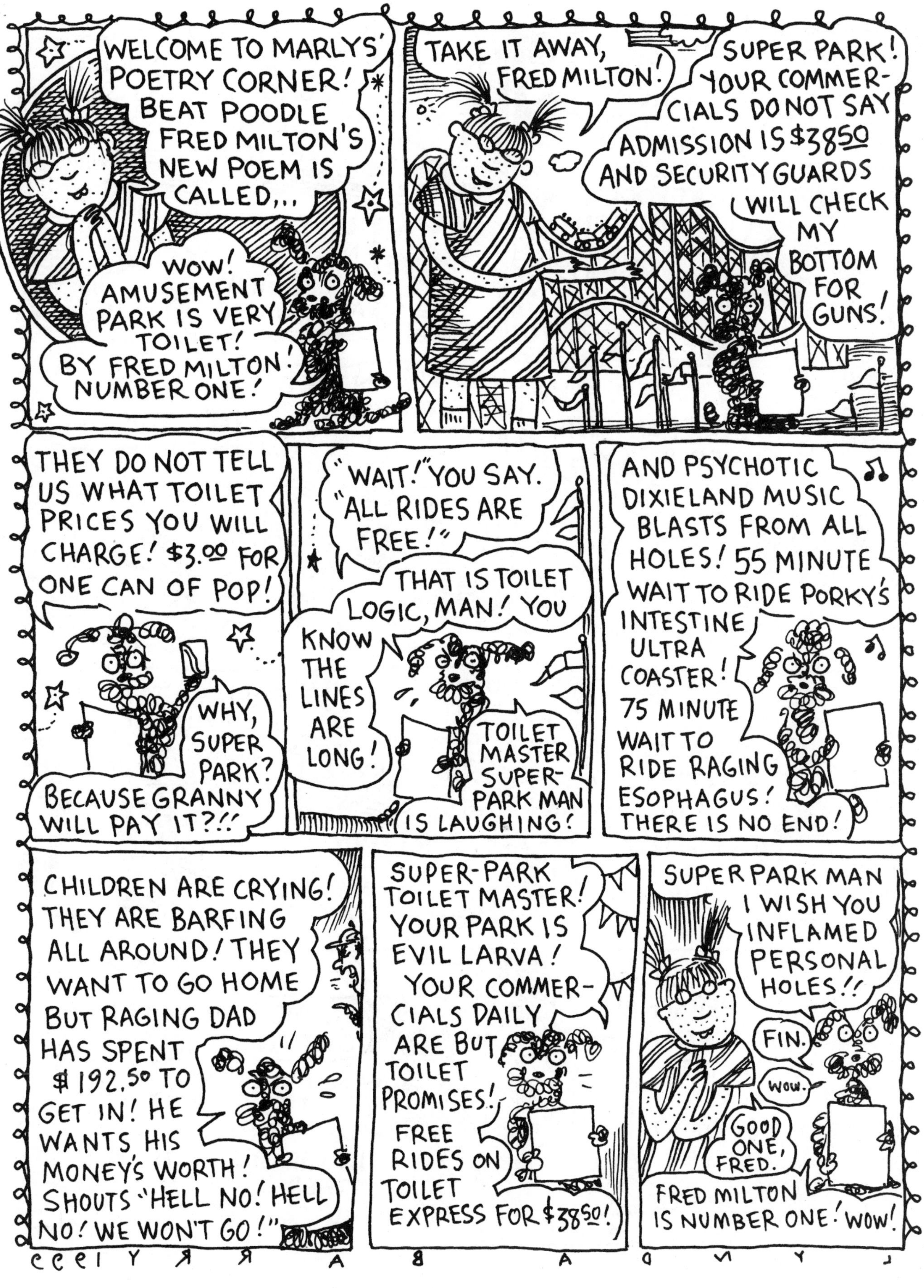
WELCOME TO MARLYS' POETRY CORNER! BEAT POODLE FRED MILTON'S NEW POEM IS CALLED,..
WOW! AMUSEMENT PARK IS VERY TOILET! BY FRED MILTON NUMBER ONE!
TAKE IT AWAY, FRED MILTON!
SUPER PARK! YOUR COMMERCIALS DO NOT SAY ADMISSION IS $38.50 AND SECURITY GUARDS WILL CHECK MY BOTTOM FOR GUNS!
THEY DO NOT TELL US WHAT TOILET PRICES YOU WILL CHARGE! $3.00 FOR ONE CAN OF POP!
WHY, SUPER PARK? BECAUSE GRANNY WILL PAY IT?!!
"WAIT!" YOU SAY. "ALL RIDES ARE FREE!"
THAT IS TOILET LOGIC, MAN! YOU KNOW THE LINES ARE LONG!
TOILET MASTER SUPER-PARK MAN IS LAUGHING!
AND PSYCHOTIC DIXIELAND MUSIC BLASTS FROM ALL HOLES! 55 MINUTE WAIT TO RIDE PORKY'S INTESTINE ULTRA COASTER! 75 MINUTE WAIT TO RIDE RAGING ESOPHAGUS! THERE IS NO END!
CHILDREN ARE CRYING! THEY ARE BARFING ALL AROUND! THEY WANT TO GO HOME BUT RAGING DAD HAS SPENT $192.50 TO GET IN! HE WANTS HIS MONEY'S WORTH! SHOUTS "HELL NO! HELL NO! WE WON'T GO!"
SUPER-PARK TOILET MASTER! YOUR PARK IS EVIL LARVA! YOUR COMMERCIALS DAILY ARE BUT TOILET PROMISES! FREE RIDES ON TOILET EXPRESS FOR $38.50!
SUPER PARK MAN I WISH YOU INFLAMED PERSONAL HOLES!!
FIN.
WOW.
GOOD ONE, FRED.
FRED MILTON IS NUMBER ONE! WOW!

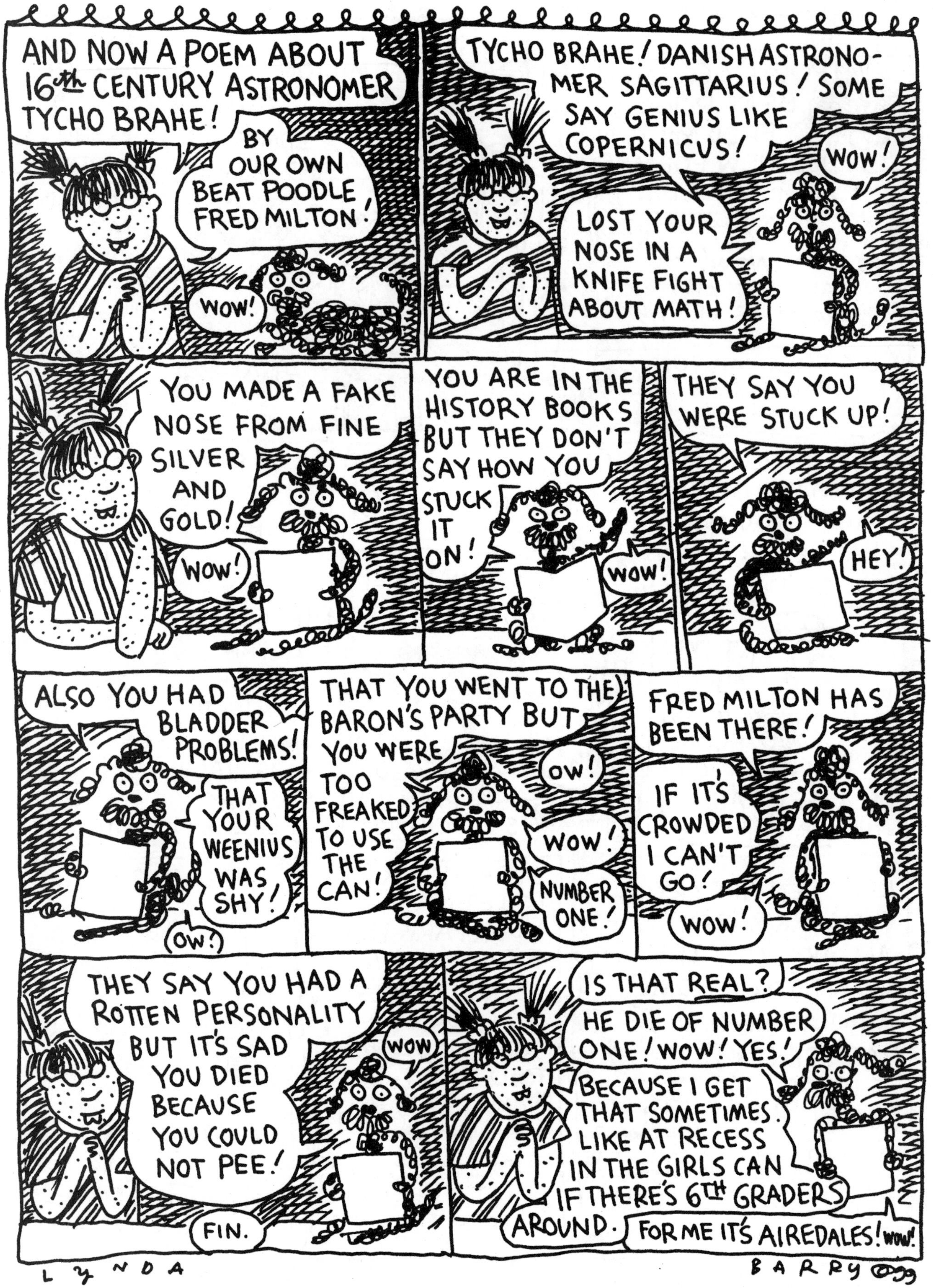
AND NOW A POEM ABOUT 16th CENTURY ASTRONOMER TYCHO BRAHE!
BY OUR OWN BEAT POODLE FRED MILTON!
WOW!
TYCHO BRAHE! DANISH ASTRONOMER SAGITTARIUS! SOME SAY GENIUS LIKE COPERNICUS!
WOW!
LOST YOUR NOSE IN A KNIFE FIGHT ABOUT MATH!
YOU MADE A FAKE NOSE FROM FINE SILVER AND GOLD!
WOW!
YOU ARE IN THE HISTORY BOOKS BUT THEY DON'T SAY HOW YOU STUCK IT ON!
WOW!
THEY SAY YOU WERE STUCK UP!
HEY!
ALSO YOU HAD BLADDER PROBLEMS!
THAT YOUR WEENIUS WAS SHY!
OW!
THAT YOU WENT TO THE BARON'S PARTY BUT YOU WERE TOO FREAKED TO USE THE CAN!
OW!
WOW!
NUMBER ONE!
FRED MILTON HAS BEEN THERE!
IF IT'S CROWDED I CAN'T GO!
WOW!
THEY SAY YOU HAD A ROTTEN PERSONALITY BUT IT'S SAD YOU DIED BECAUSE YOU COULD NOT PEE!
WOW
FIN.
IS THAT REAL?
HE DIE OF NUMBER ONE! WOW! YES!
BECAUSE I GET THAT SOMETIMES LIKE AT RECESS IN THE GIRLS CAN IF THERE'S 6TH GRADERS AROUND.
FOR ME IT'S AIREDALES!
WOW!
LYNDA BARRY ©99

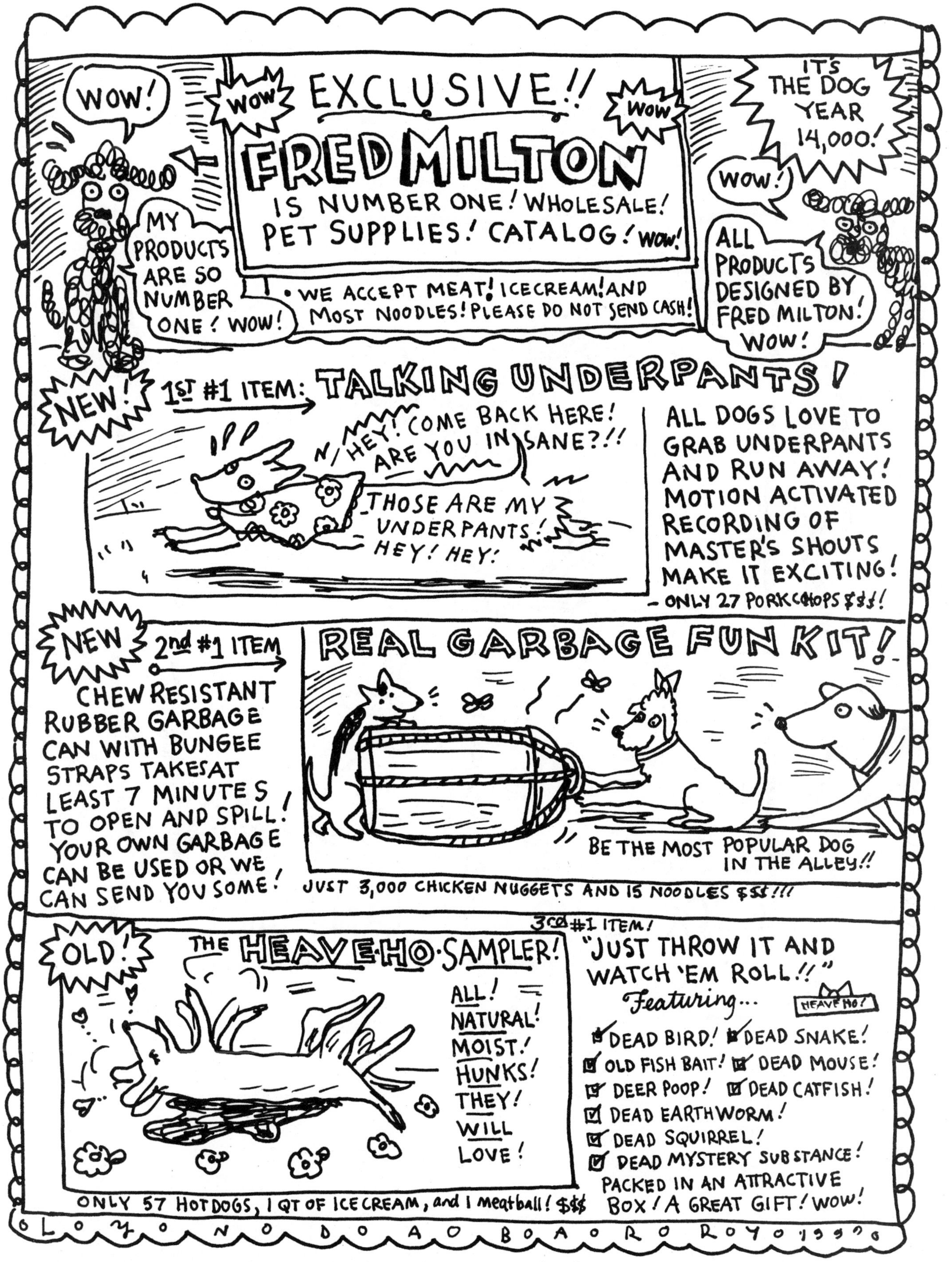

WOW!
WOW
EXCLUSIVE!!
WOW
IT'S THE DOG YEAR 14,000!
FRED MILTON
IS NUMBER ONE! WHOLESALE! PET SUPPLIES! CATALOG! WOW!
WOW!
MY PRODUCTS ARE SO NUMBER ONE! WOW!
• WE ACCEPT MEAT! ICECREAM! AND MOST NOODLES! PLEASE DO NOT SEND CASH!
ALL PRODUCTS DESIGNED BY FRED MILTON! WOW!
NEW!
1ST #1 ITEM: TALKING UNDERPANTS!
HEY! COME BACK HERE! ARE YOU INSANE?!!
THOSE ARE MY UNDERPANTS! HEY! HEY!
ALL DOGS LOVE TO GRAB UNDERPANTS AND RUN AWAY! MOTION ACTIVATED RECORDING OF MASTER'S SHOUTS MAKE IT EXCITING!
- ONLY 27 PORKCHOPS $$$!
NEW
2nd #1 ITEM
REAL GARBAGE FUN KIT!
CHEW RESISTANT RUBBER GARBAGE CAN WITH BUNGEE STRAPS TAKES AT LEAST 7 MINUTES TO OPEN AND SPILL! YOUR OWN GARBAGE CAN BE USED OR WE CAN SEND YOU SOME!
BE THE MOST POPULAR DOG IN THE ALLEY!!
JUST 3,000 CHICKEN NUGGETS AND 15 NOODLES $$$!!!
3RD #1 ITEM!
OLD!
THE HEAVE·HO·SAMPLER!
ALL! NATURAL! MOIST! HUNKS! THEY! WILL LOVE!
"JUST THROW IT AND WATCH 'EM ROLL!!"
Featuring...
HEAVE HO!
DEAD BIRD! DEAD SNAKE!
OLD FISH BAIT! DEAD MOUSE!
DEER POOP! DEAD CATFISH!
DEAD EARTHWORM!
DEAD SQUIRREL!
DEAD MYSTERY SUBSTANCE!
PACKED IN AN ATTRACTIVE BOX! A GREAT GIFT! WOW!
ONLY 57 HOTDOGS, 1 QT OF ICECREAM, and 1 meatball! $$$
LYNDA BARRY 1990

CROCHETED-AFGHAN MARLYS

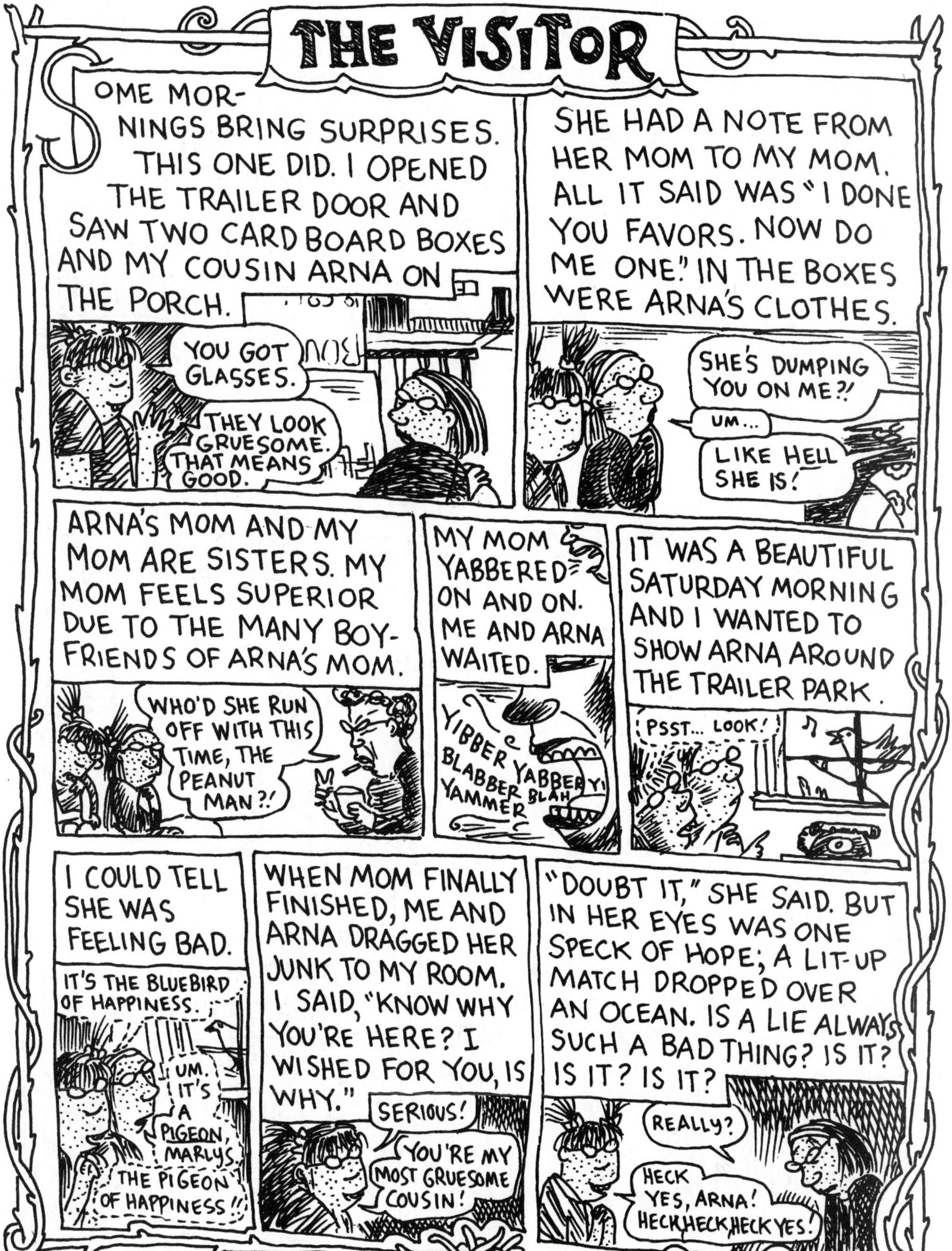
THE VISITOR
SOME MORNINGS BRING SURPRISES. THIS ONE DID. I OPENED THE TRAILER DOOR AND SAW TWO CARDBOARD BOXES AND MY COUSIN ARNA ON THE PORCH.
YOU GOT GLASSES.
THEY LOOK GRUESOME. THAT MEANS GOOD.
SHE HAD A NOTE FROM HER MOM TO MY MOM. ALL IT SAID WAS "I DONE YOU FAVORS. NOW DO ME ONE." IN THE BOXES WERE ARNA'S CLOTHES.
SHE'S DUMPING YOU ON ME?!
UM...
LIKE HELL SHE IS!
ARNA'S MOM AND MY MOM ARE SISTERS. MY MOM FEELS SUPERIOR DUE TO THE MANY BOYFRIENDS OF ARNA'S MOM.
WHO'D SHE RUN OFF WITH THIS TIME, THE PEANUT MAN?!
MY MOM YABBERED ON AND ON. ME AND ARNA WAITED.
YIBBER YABBER YI
BLABBER BLAH
YAMMER
IT WAS A BEAUTIFUL SATURDAY MORNING AND I WANTED TO SHOW ARNA AROUND THE TRAILER PARK.
PSST... LOOK!
I COULD TELL SHE WAS FEELING BAD.
IT'S THE BLUEBIRD OF HAPPINESS.
UM. IT'S A PIGEON, MARLYS.
THE PIGEON OF HAPPINESS!!
WHEN MOM FINALLY FINISHED, ME AND ARNA DRAGGED HER JUNK TO MY ROOM. I SAID, "KNOW WHY YOU'RE HERE? I WISHED FOR YOU, IS WHY."
SERIOUS!
YOU'RE MY MOST GRUESOME COUSIN!
"DOUBT IT," SHE SAID. BUT IN HER EYES WAS ONE SPECK OF HOPE; A LIT-UP MATCH DROPPED OVER AN OCEAN. IS A LIE ALWAYS SUCH A BAD THING? IS IT? IS IT? IS IT?
REALLY?
HECK YES, ARNA! HECK, HECK, HECK YES!

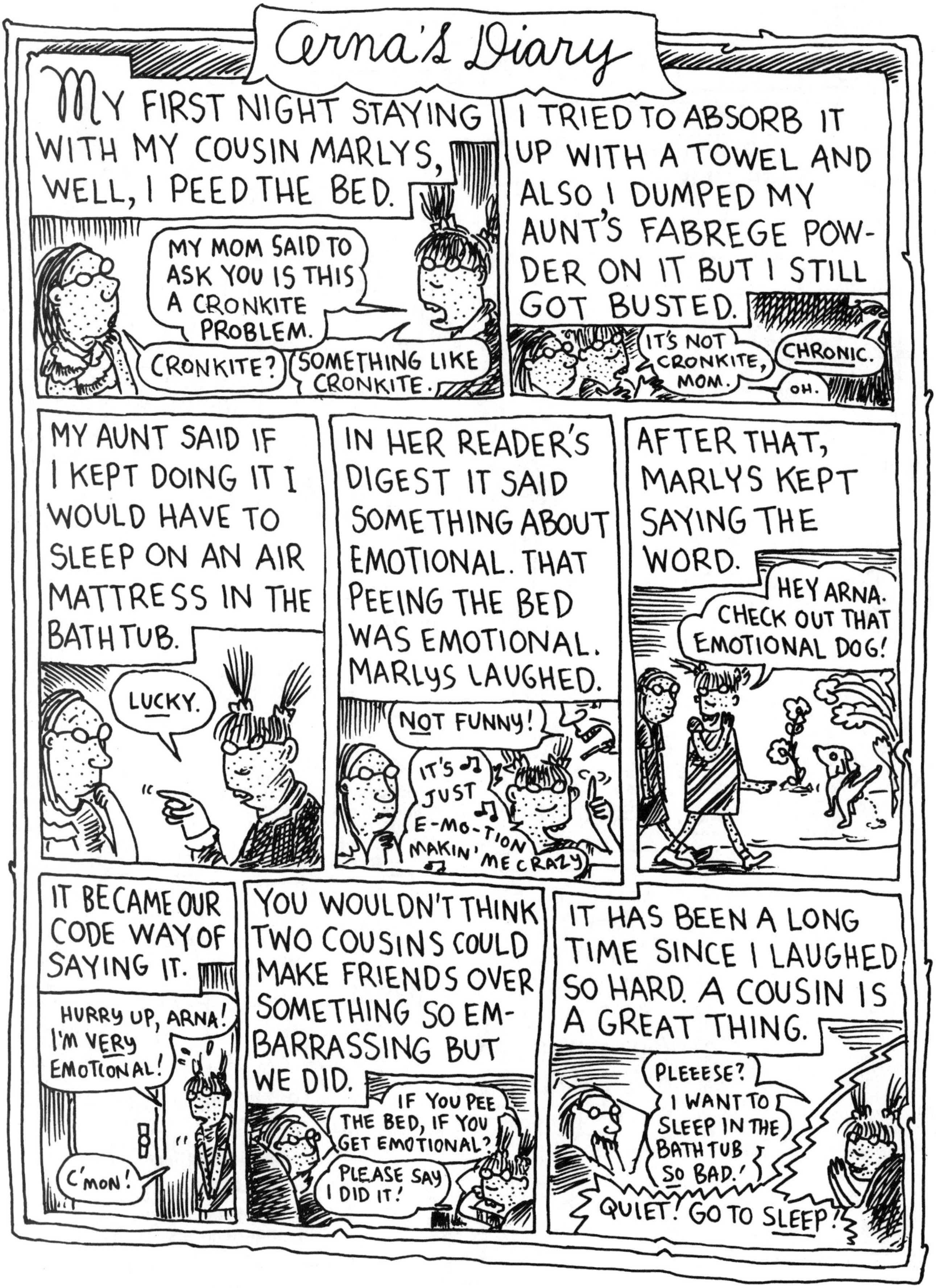
Arna's Diary
MY FIRST NIGHT STAYING WITH MY COUSIN MARLYS, WELL, I PEED THE BED.
MY MOM SAID TO ASK YOU IS THIS A CRONKITE PROBLEM.
CRONKITE?
SOMETHING LIKE CRONKITE.
I TRIED TO ABSORB IT UP WITH A TOWEL AND ALSO I DUMPED MY AUNT'S FABREGE POWDER ON IT BUT I STILL GOT BUSTED.
IT'S NOT CRONKITE, MOM.
CHRONIC.
OH.
MY AUNT SAID IF I KEPT DOING IT I WOULD HAVE TO SLEEP ON AN AIR MATTRESS IN THE BATHTUB.
LUCKY.
IN HER READER'S DIGEST IT SAID SOMETHING ABOUT EMOTIONAL. THAT PEEING THE BED WAS EMOTIONAL. MARLYS LAUGHED.
NOT FUNNY!
IT'S JUST E-MO-TION MAKIN' ME CRAZY
AFTER THAT, MARLYS KEPT SAYING THE WORD.
HEY ARNA. CHECK OUT THAT EMOTIONAL DOG!
IT BECAME OUR CODE WAY OF SAYING IT.
HURRY UP, ARNA! I'M VERY EMOTIONAL!
C'MON!
YOU WOULDN'T THINK TWO COUSINS COULD MAKE FRIENDS OVER SOMETHING SO EMBARRASSING BUT WE DID.
IF YOU PEE THE BED, IF YOU GET EMOTIONAL?
PLEASE SAY I DID IT!
IT HAS BEEN A LONG TIME SINCE I LAUGHED SO HARD. A COUSIN IS A GREAT THING.
PLEEESE? I WANT TO SLEEP IN THE BATH TUB SO BAD!
QUIET! GO TO SLEEP!

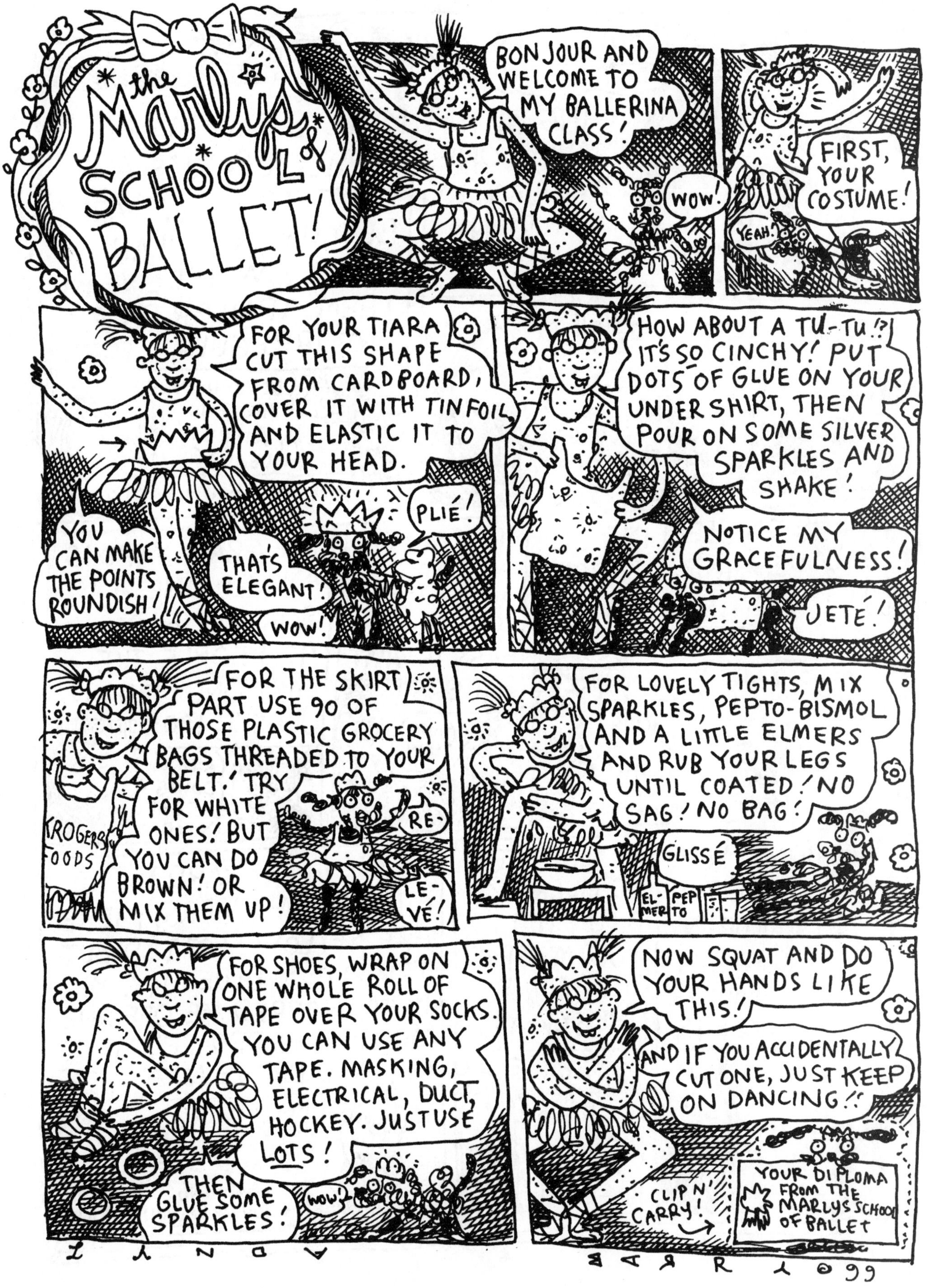
the Marlys School of BALLET!
BONJOUR AND WELCOME TO MY BALLERINA CLASS!
WOW!
FIRST, YOUR COSTUME!
YEAH!
FOR YOUR TIARA CUT THIS SHAPE FROM CARDBOARD, COVER IT WITH TINFOIL AND ELASTIC IT TO YOUR HEAD.
YOU CAN MAKE THE POINTS ROUNDISH!
THAT'S ELEGANT!
PLIÉ!
WOW!
HOW ABOUT A TU-TU!? IT'S SO CINCHY! PUT DOTS OF GLUE ON YOUR UNDERSHIRT, THEN POUR ON SOME SILVER SPARKLES AND SHAKE!
NOTICE MY GRACEFULNESS!
JETÉ!
FOR THE SKIRT PART USE 90 OF THOSE PLASTIC GROCERY BAGS THREADED TO YOUR BELT! TRY FOR WHITE ONES! BUT YOU CAN DO BROWN! OR MIX THEM UP!
KROGERS FOODS
RE-
LE-VÉ!
FOR LOVELY TIGHTS, MIX SPARKLES, PEPTO-BISMOL AND A LITTLE ELMERS AND RUB YOUR LEGS UNTIL COATED! NO SAG! NO BAG!
GLISSÉ
ELMER
PEPTO
FOR SHOES, WRAP ON ONE WHOLE ROLL OF TAPE OVER YOUR SOCKS. YOU CAN USE ANY TAPE. MASKING, ELECTRICAL, DUCT, HOCKEY. JUST USE LOTS!
THEN GLUE SOME SPARKLES!
WOW!
NOW SQUAT AND DO YOUR HANDS LIKE THIS!
AND IF YOU ACCIDENTALLY CUT ONE, JUST KEEP ON DANCING!!
CLIP N' CARRY!
YOUR DIPLOMA FROM THE MARLYS SCHOOL OF BALLET
LYNDA BARRY ©99

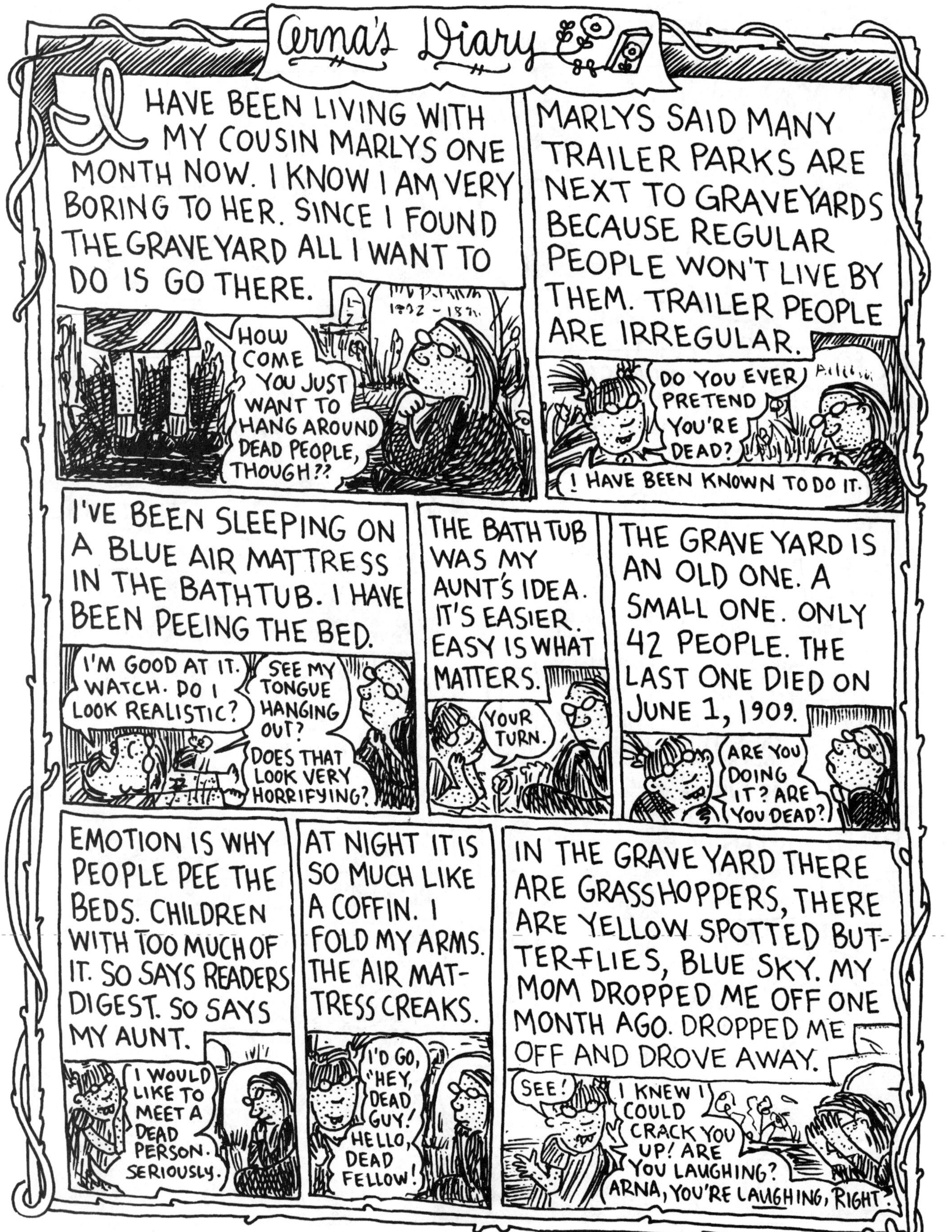
Arna's Diary
I HAVE BEEN LIVING WITH MY COUSIN MARLYS ONE MONTH NOW. I KNOW I AM VERY BORING TO HER. SINCE I FOUND THE GRAVEYARD ALL I WANT TO DO IS GO THERE.
HOW COME YOU JUST WANT TO HANG AROUND DEAD PEOPLE, THOUGH??
MARLYS SAID MANY TRAILER PARKS ARE NEXT TO GRAVEYARDS BECAUSE REGULAR PEOPLE WON'T LIVE BY THEM. TRAILER PEOPLE ARE IRREGULAR.
DO YOU EVER PRETEND YOU'RE DEAD?
I HAVE BEEN KNOWN TO DO IT.
I'VE BEEN SLEEPING ON A BLUE AIR MATTRESS IN THE BATHTUB. I HAVE BEEN PEEING THE BED.
I'M GOOD AT IT. WATCH. DO I LOOK REALISTIC?
SEE MY TONGUE HANGING OUT?
DOES THAT LOOK VERY HORRIFYING?
THE BATH TUB WAS MY AUNT'S IDEA. IT'S EASIER. EASY IS WHAT MATTERS.
YOUR TURN.
THE GRAVE YARD IS AN OLD ONE. A SMALL ONE. ONLY 42 PEOPLE. THE LAST ONE DIED ON JUNE 1, 1909.
ARE YOU DOING IT? ARE YOU DEAD?
EMOTION IS WHY PEOPLE PEE THE BEDS. CHILDREN WITH TOO MUCH OF IT. SO SAYS READERS DIGEST. SO SAYS MY AUNT.
I WOULD LIKE TO MEET A DEAD PERSON. SERIOUSLY.
AT NIGHT IT IS SO MUCH LIKE A COFFIN. I FOLD MY ARMS. THE AIR MATTRESS CREAKS.
I'D GO, "HEY, DEAD GUY! HELLO, DEAD FELLOW!
IN THE GRAVE YARD THERE ARE GRASSHOPPERS, THERE ARE YELLOW SPOTTED BUTTERFLIES, BLUE SKY. MY MOM DROPPED ME OFF ONE MONTH AGO. DROPPED ME OFF AND DROVE AWAY.
SEE!
I KNEW I COULD CRACK YOU UP! ARE YOU LAUGHING? ARNA, YOU'RE LAUGHING, RIGHT?

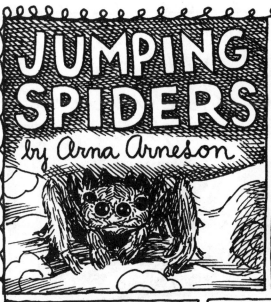

JUMPING SPIDERS

by Arna Arneson

SOMETIMES LIFE GIVES US SITUATIONS WHERE WE ARE CONFUSED AND FRIGHTENED ..... AND SOMETIMES THE JUMPING SPIDER COMES TO HELP.

DOINK! DOINK! DOINK!

WITH HIS BRIGHT FRONT EYES HE SEES ME LONELY.

ARTHROPOD ARACHNID SALTICIDAE ON MY PILLOW LOOKING.

PANORAMIC EIGHT EYED VISION TAKES IN MY SCENE: MY AUNT SHOUTING. I WET THE BED AGAIN.

THE DOOR SLAMS. I MUST SLEEP IN THE WET BED TO LEARN MY LESSON. THE JUMPING SPIDER WAVES AT ME AND BOBS. BE A SPIDER.

BE A SPIDER-GIRL WITH ME. I WILL TEACH YOU ALL CAMOUFLAGE AND TURNABOUT DEFENSE. MIMIC ME. BE A JUMPING SPIDER-GIRL.

IN THE MORNING MY AUNT SHOUTS AT ME FOR CROUCHING ON MY PILLOW. I SAY NOTHING. JUMPING SPIDERS NEVER TALK TO HER.

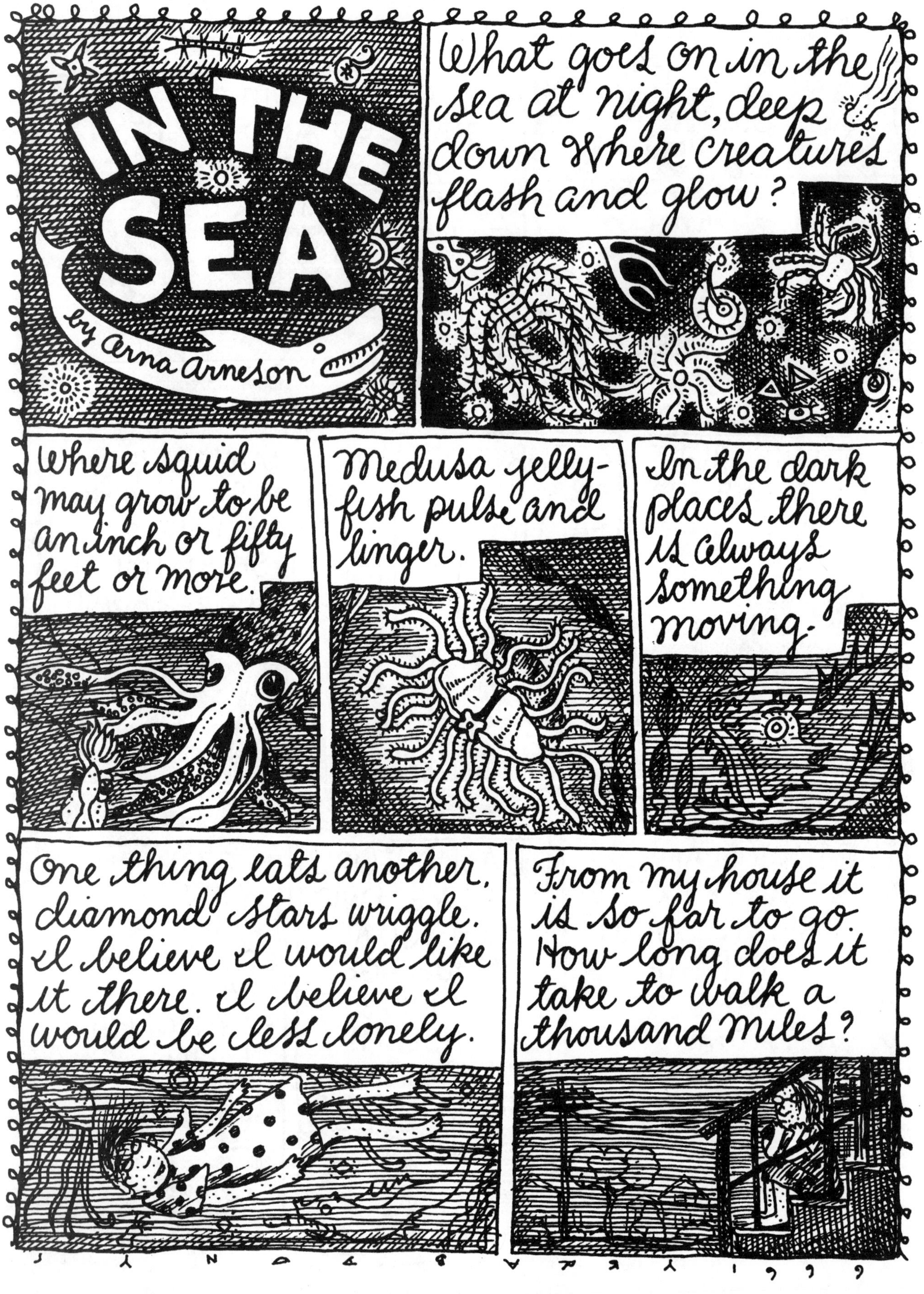
IN THE SEA
by Arna Arneson
What goes on in the sea at night, deep down where creatures flash and glow?
Where squid may grow to be an inch or fifty feet or more.
Medusa jelly-fish pulse and linger.
In the dark places there is always something moving.
One thing eats another, diamond stars wriggle. I believe I would like it there. I believe I would be less lonely.
From my house it is so far to go. How long does it take to walk a thousand miles?

MER-MONSTER MARLYS

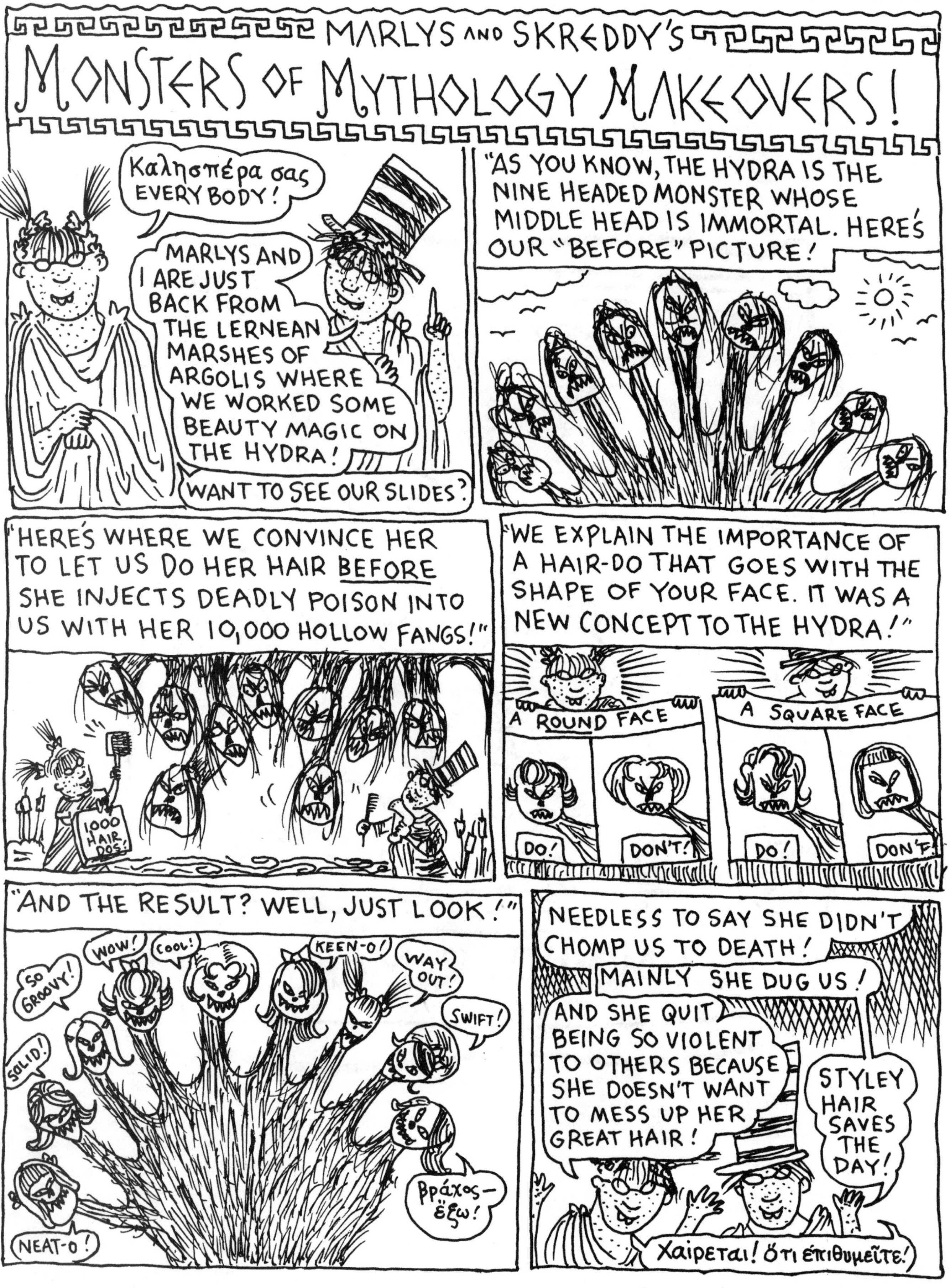
MARLYS AND SKREDDY'S
MONSTERS OF MYTHOLOGY MAKEOVERS!
Καλησπέρα σας EVERYBODY!
MARLYS AND I ARE JUST BACK FROM THE LERNEAN MARSHES OF ARGOLIS WHERE WE WORKED SOME BEAUTY MAGIC ON THE HYDRA!
WANT TO SEE OUR SLIDES?
"AS YOU KNOW, THE HYDRA IS THE NINE HEADED MONSTER WHOSE MIDDLE HEAD IS IMMORTAL. HERE'S OUR "BEFORE" PICTURE!
"HERE'S WHERE WE CONVINCE HER TO LET US DO HER HAIR BEFORE SHE INJECTS DEADLY POISON INTO US WITH HER 10,000 HOLLOW FANGS!"
1000 HAIR DOS!
"WE EXPLAIN THE IMPORTANCE OF A HAIR-DO THAT GOES WITH THE SHAPE OF YOUR FACE. IT WAS A NEW CONCEPT TO THE HYDRA!"
A ROUND FACE
DO!
DON'T!
A SQUARE FACE
DO!
DON'T!
"AND THE RESULT? WELL, JUST LOOK!"
SO GROOVY!
WOW!
COOL!
KEEN-O!
WAY OUT!
SWIFT!
SOLID!
Βράχος-έξω!
NEAT-O!
NEEDLESS TO SAY SHE DIDN'T CHOMP US TO DEATH!
MAINLY SHE DUG US!
AND SHE QUIT BEING SO VIOLENT TO OTHERS BECAUSE SHE DOESN'T WANT TO MESS UP HER GREAT HAIR!
STYLEY HAIR SAVES THE DAY!
Χαιρεται! Ότι επιθυμείτε!

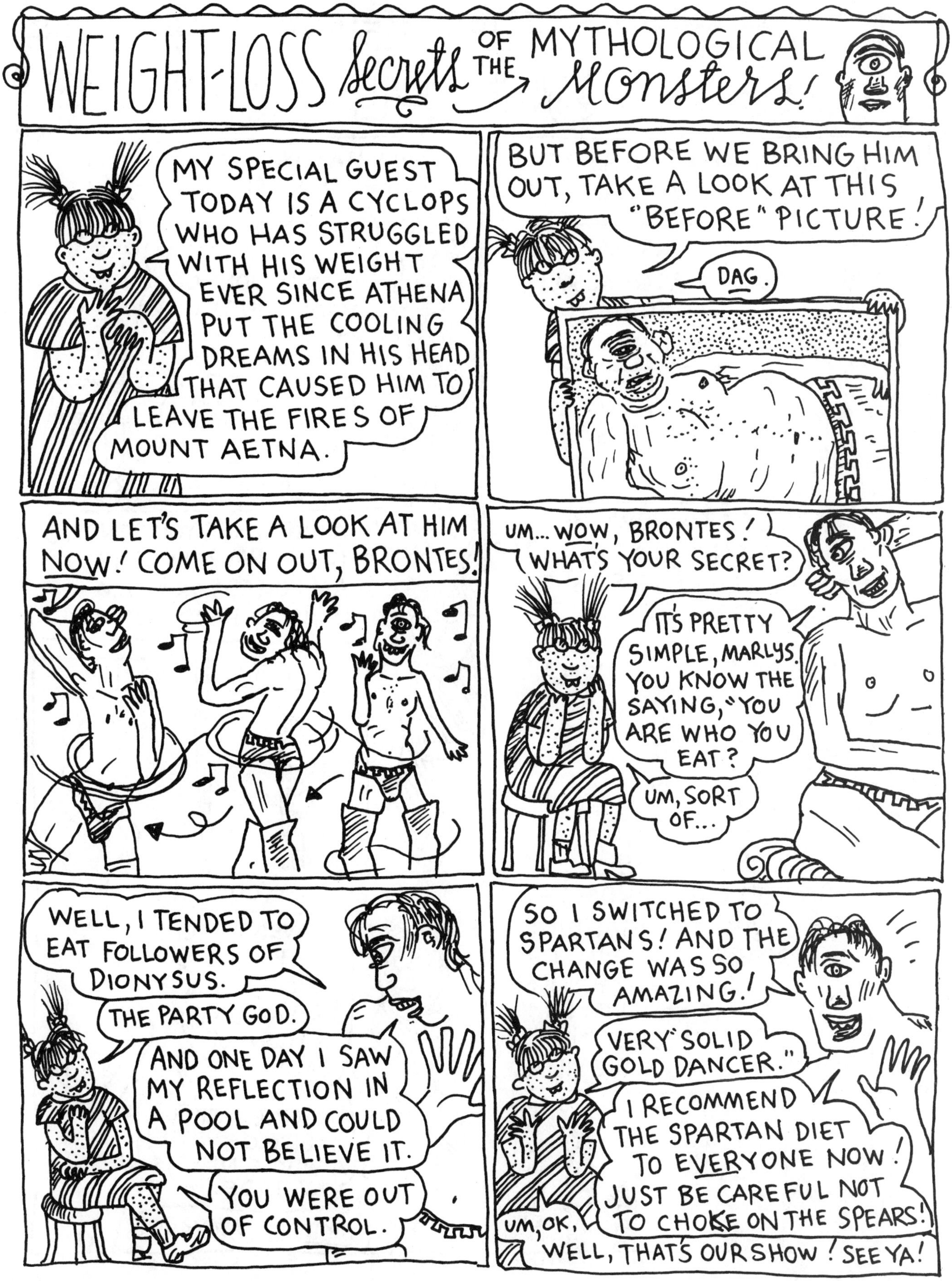
WEIGHT-LOSS Secrets OF THE MYTHOLOGICAL Monsters!
MY SPECIAL GUEST TODAY IS A CYCLOPS WHO HAS STRUGGLED WITH HIS WEIGHT EVER SINCE ATHENA PUT THE COOLING DREAMS IN HIS HEAD THAT CAUSED HIM TO LEAVE THE FIRES OF MOUNT AETNA.
BUT BEFORE WE BRING HIM OUT, TAKE A LOOK AT THIS "BEFORE" PICTURE!
DAG.
AND LET'S TAKE A LOOK AT HIM NOW! COME ON OUT, BRONTES!
UM... WOW, BRONTES! WHAT'S YOUR SECRET?
IT'S PRETTY SIMPLE, MARLYS. YOU KNOW THE SAYING, "YOU ARE WHO YOU EAT?
UM, SORT OF...
WELL, I TENDED TO EAT FOLLOWERS OF DIONYSUS.
THE PARTY GOD.
AND ONE DAY I SAW MY REFLECTION IN A POOL AND COULD NOT BELIEVE IT.
YOU WERE OUT OF CONTROL.
SO I SWITCHED TO SPARTANS! AND THE CHANGE WAS SO AMAZING!
VERY "SOLID GOLD DANCER."
I RECOMMEND THE SPARTAN DIET TO EVERYONE NOW! JUST BE CAREFUL NOT TO CHOKE ON THE SPEARS!
UM, OK,
WELL, THAT'S OUR SHOW! SEE YA!

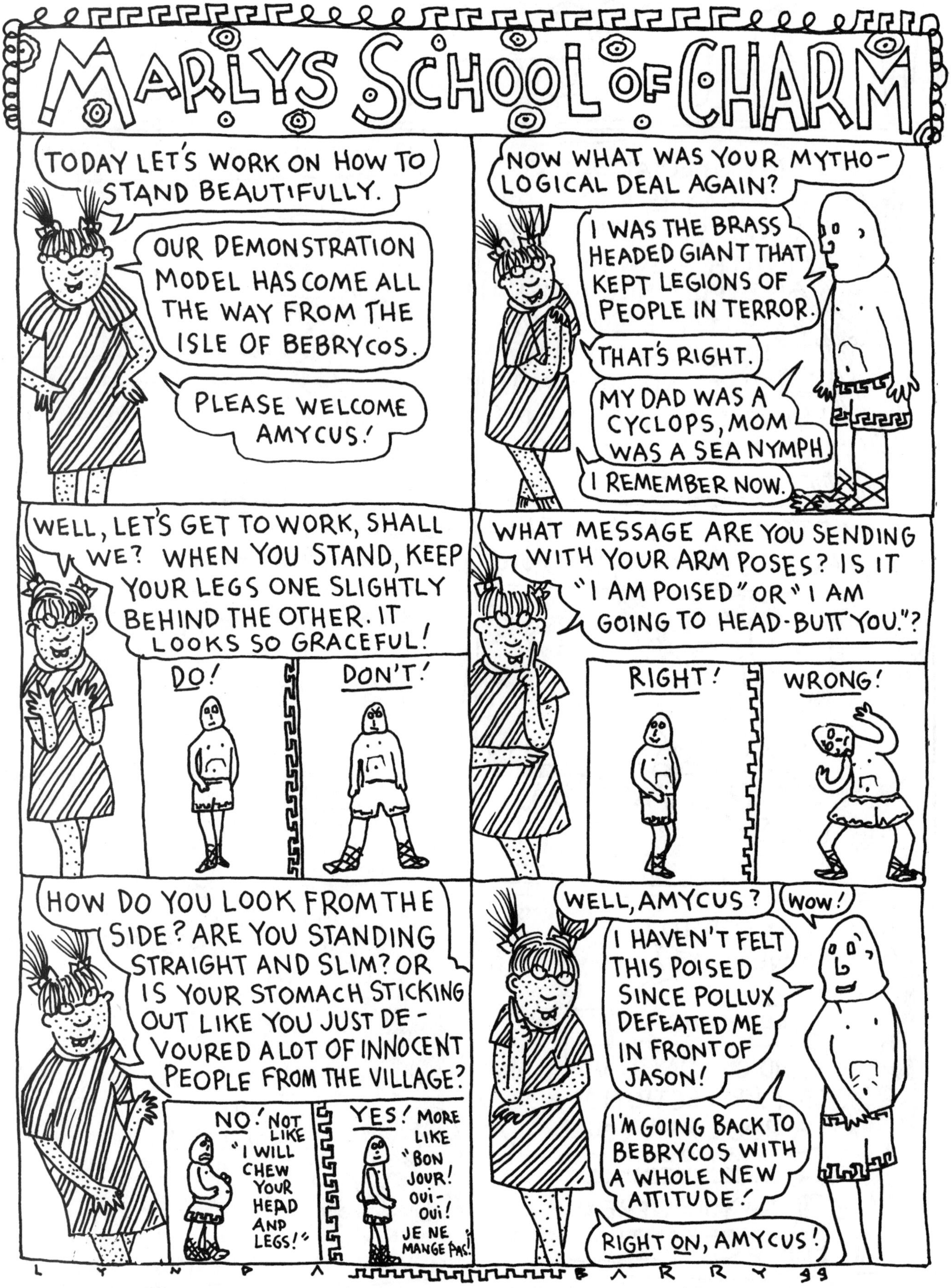
MARLYS SCHOOL OF CHARM
TODAY LET'S WORK ON HOW TO STAND BEAUTIFULLY.
OUR DEMONSTRATION MODEL HAS COME ALL THE WAY FROM THE ISLE OF BEBRYCOS.
PLEASE WELCOME AMYCUS!
NOW WHAT WAS YOUR MYTHO-LOGICAL DEAL AGAIN?
I WAS THE BRASS HEADED GIANT THAT KEPT LEGIONS OF PEOPLE IN TERROR.
THAT'S RIGHT.
MY DAD WAS A CYCLOPS, MOM WAS A SEA NYMPH
I REMEMBER NOW.
WELL, LET'S GET TO WORK, SHALL WE? WHEN YOU STAND, KEEP YOUR LEGS ONE SLIGHTLY BEHIND THE OTHER. IT LOOKS SO GRACEFUL!
DO!
DON'T!
WHAT MESSAGE ARE YOU SENDING WITH YOUR ARM POSES? IS IT "I AM POISED" OR "I AM GOING TO HEAD-BUTT YOU."?
RIGHT!
WRONG!
HOW DO YOU LOOK FROM THE SIDE? ARE YOU STANDING STRAIGHT AND SLIM? OR IS YOUR STOMACH STICKING OUT LIKE YOU JUST DE-VOURED A LOT OF INNOCENT PEOPLE FROM THE VILLAGE?
NO! NOT LIKE "I WILL CHEW YOUR HEAD AND LEGS!"
YES! MORE LIKE "BON JOUR! OUI-OUI! JE NE MANGE PAS!
WELL, AMYCUS?
WOW!
I HAVEN'T FELT THIS POISED SINCE POLLUX DEFEATED ME IN FRONT OF JASON!
I'M GOING BACK TO BEBRYCOS WITH A WHOLE NEW ATTITUDE!
RIGHT ON, AMYCUS!
LYNDA BARRY 99

THE MARLYS SCHOOL OF CHARM!

LET'S DO "HOW TO SIT IN A CHAIR".

OH. MY GUEST TODAY IS THE HAIRY BEING. HE WILL HELP ON THE DEMONSTRATION PARTS.

WELCOME, HAIRY BEING. NOW, ARE YOU MYTHOLOGICAL OR WHAT?

I'D SAY I WAS MORE PRIMITIVE.

WELL THAT'S LOVELY. LET'S GET STARTED!

NOW, OK, WHAT YOU HAVE TO DO FIRST IS SIT DOWN ON THE CHAIR GRACEFULLY. DON'T STICK YOUR REAR END OUT! LOWER IT DOWN!

WRONG!

RIGHT!

OK. NOW SIT WITH YOUR WEIGHT ON THE FRONT OF THE CHAIR, PUT YOUR HANDS ON THE CHAIR AND SLIDE YOUR HAIRY BEHIND BACKWARDS.

SLIDE IT!

DON'T TWITCH IT!

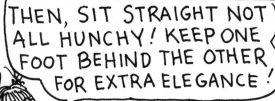

THEN, SIT STRAIGHT NOT ALL HUNCHY! KEEP ONE FOOT BEHIND THE OTHER FOR EXTRA ELEGANCE!

WRONG! THIS WAY SHOWS FAT WADS!

FANTASTIC! IT'S SLENDERIZING! NO WADS!

WELL DONE, HAIRY BEING!

I REALLY ENJOYED IT.

ME TOO.

WELL THAT'S OUR SHOW! HAPPY AND BEAUTIFUL SITTING, EVERYBODY!

LYNDA BARRY '99

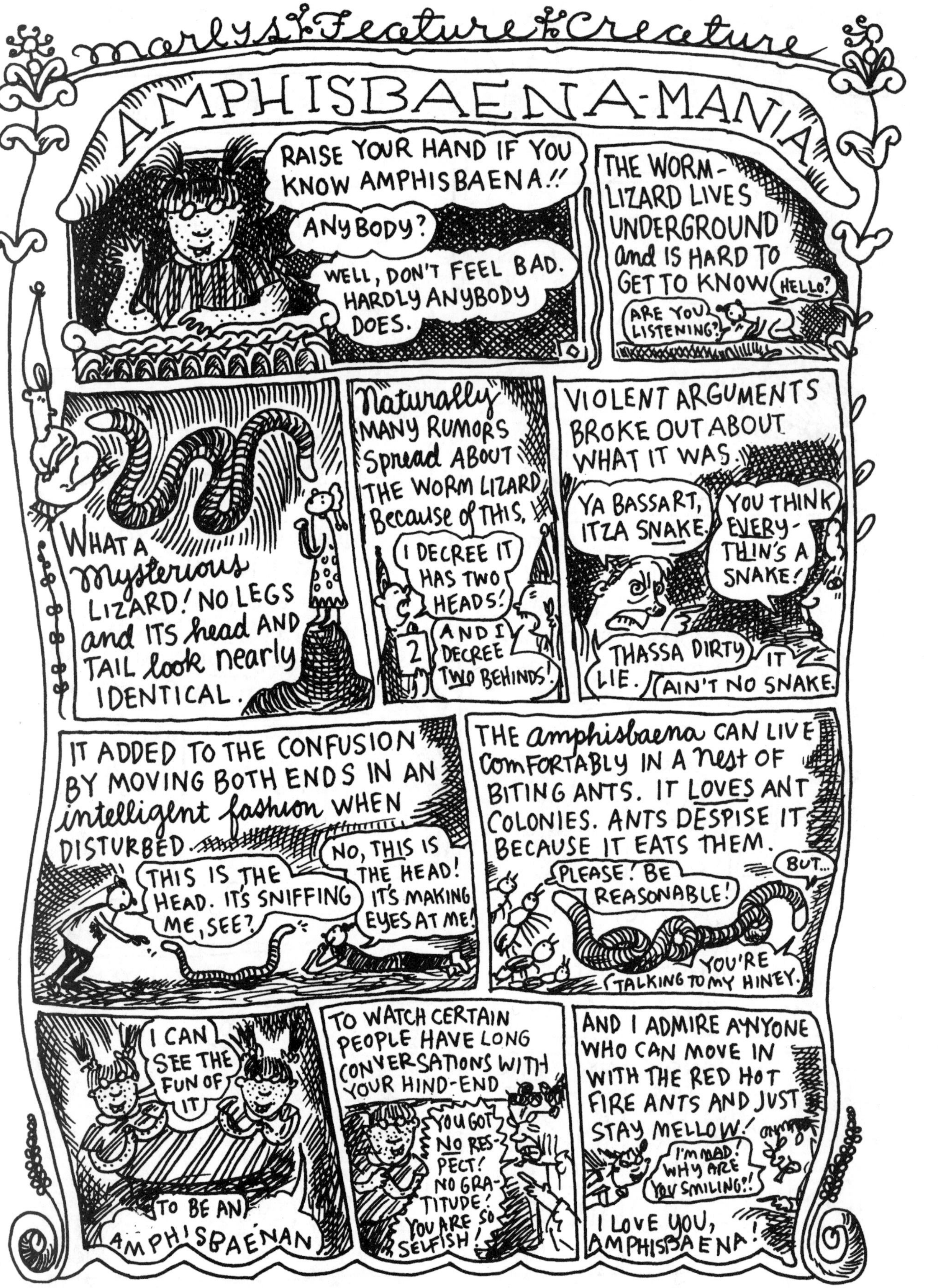
marlys's Feature Creature
AMPHISBAENA-MANIA
RAISE YOUR HAND IF YOU KNOW AMPHISBAENA!!
ANYBODY?
WELL, DON'T FEEL BAD. HARDLY ANYBODY DOES.
THE WORM-LIZARD LIVES UNDERGROUND and IS HARD TO GET TO KNOW
HELLO?
ARE YOU LISTENING?
WHAT A mysterious LIZARD! NO LEGS and ITS head AND TAIL look nearly IDENTICAL.
Naturally MANY RUMORS Spread ABOUT THE WORM LIZARD Because of THIS.
I DECREE IT HAS TWO HEADS!
2
AND I DECREE TWO BEHINDS!
VIOLENT ARGUMENTS BROKE OUT ABOUT WHAT IT WAS.
YA BASSART, ITZA SNAKE.
YOU THINK EVERYTHIN'S A SNAKE!
THASSA DIRTY LIE.
IT AIN'T NO SNAKE.
IT ADDED TO THE CONFUSION BY MOVING BOTH ENDS IN AN intelligent fashion WHEN DISTURBED.
THIS IS THE HEAD. IT'S SNIFFING ME, SEE?
NO, THIS IS THE HEAD! IT'S MAKING EYES AT ME!
THE amphisbaena CAN LIVE COMFORTABLY IN A nest OF BITING ANTS. IT LOVES ANT COLONIES. ANTS DESPISE IT BECAUSE IT EATS THEM.
PLEASE! BE REASONABLE!
BUT...
YOU'RE TALKING TO MY HINEY.
I CAN SEE THE FUN OF IT
TO BE AN AMPHISBAENAN
TO WATCH CERTAIN PEOPLE HAVE LONG CONVERSATIONS WITH YOUR HIND-END
YOU GOT NO RESPECT! NO GRATITUDE! YOU ARE SO SELFISH!
AND I ADMIRE ANYONE WHO CAN MOVE IN WITH THE RED HOT FIRE ANTS AND JUST STAY MELLOW!
I'M MAD! WHY ARE YOU SMILING?!
I LOVE YOU, AMPHISBAENA!

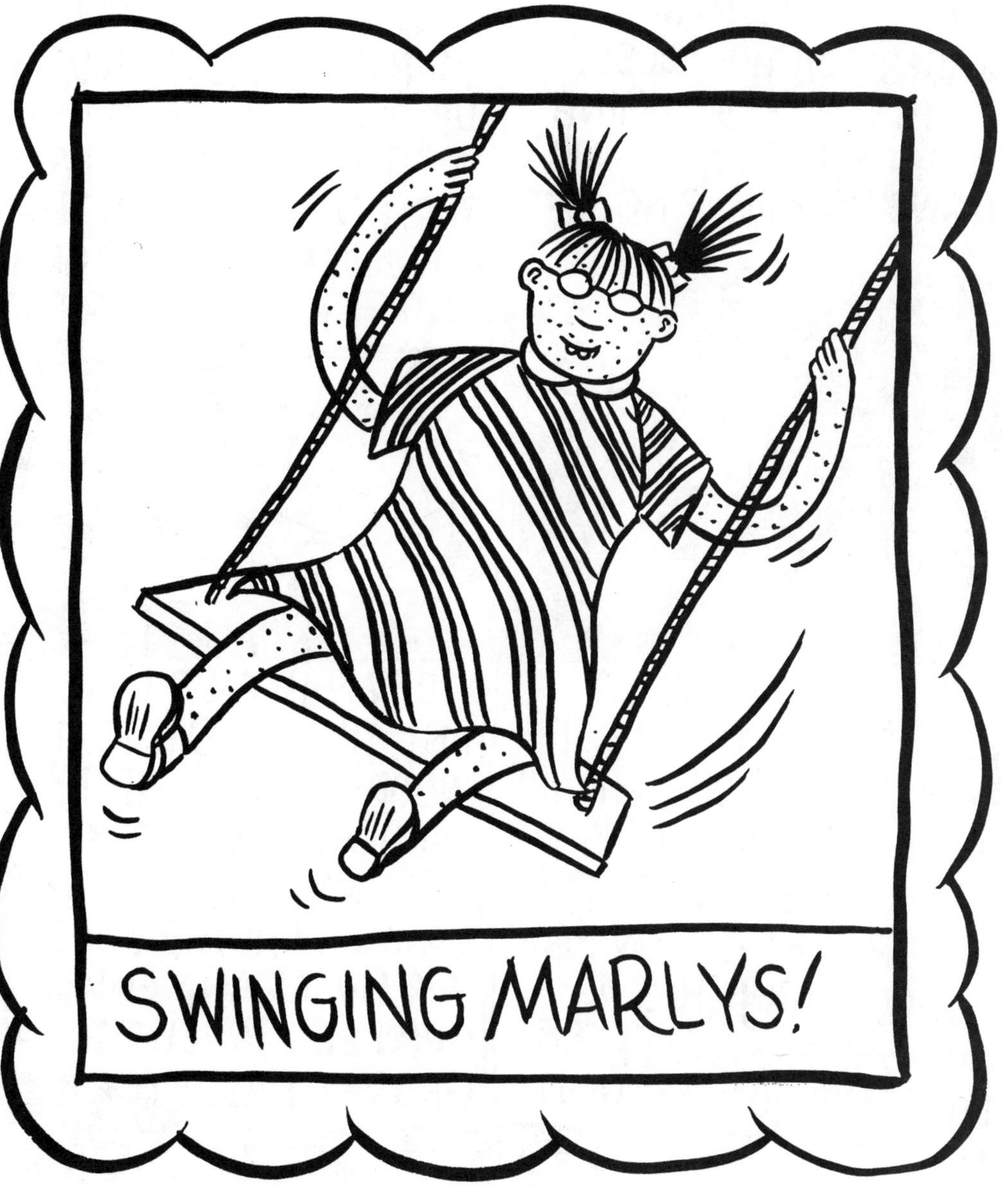
SWINGING MARLYS!

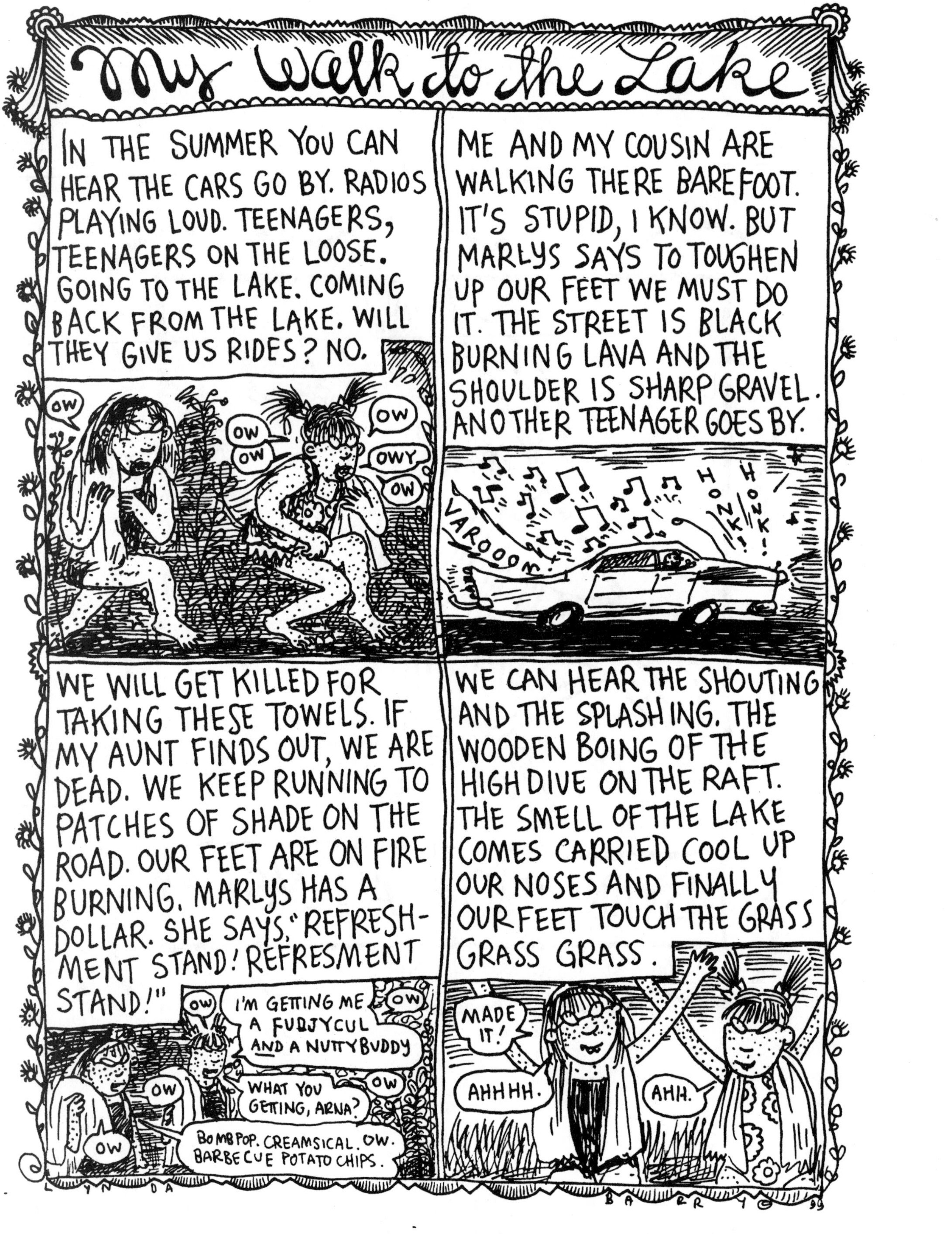
My Walk to the Lake
IN THE SUMMER YOU CAN HEAR THE CARS GO BY. RADIOS PLAYING LOUD. TEENAGERS, TEENAGERS ON THE LOOSE. GOING TO THE LAKE. COMING BACK FROM THE LAKE. WILL THEY GIVE US RIDES? NO.
OW
OW
OW
OW
OWY
OW
ME AND MY COUSIN ARE WALKING THERE BAREFOOT. IT'S STUPID, I KNOW. BUT MARLYS SAYS TO TOUGHEN UP OUR FEET WE MUST DO IT. THE STREET IS BLACK BURNING LAVA AND THE SHOULDER IS SHARP GRAVEL. ANOTHER TEENAGER GOES BY.
VAROOOM
HONK!
HONK!
WE WILL GET KILLED FOR TAKING THESE TOWELS. IF MY AUNT FINDS OUT, WE ARE DEAD. WE KEEP RUNNING TO PATCHES OF SHADE ON THE ROAD. OUR FEET ARE ON FIRE BURNING. MARLYS HAS A DOLLAR. SHE SAYS, "REFRESH-MENT STAND! REFRESMENT STAND!"
OW
I'M GETTING ME A FUDJYCUL AND A NUTTYBUDDY
OW
OW
WHAT YOU GETTING, ARNA?
OW
OW
BOMBPOP. CREAMSICAL. OW. BARBECUE POTATO CHIPS.
WE CAN HEAR THE SHOUTING AND THE SPLASHING. THE WOODEN BOING OF THE HIGHDIVE ON THE RAFT. THE SMELL OF THE LAKE COMES CARRIED COOL UP OUR NOSES AND FINALLY OUR FEET TOUCH THE GRASS GRASS GRASS.
MADE IT!
AHHHH.
AHH.
LYNDA
BARRY

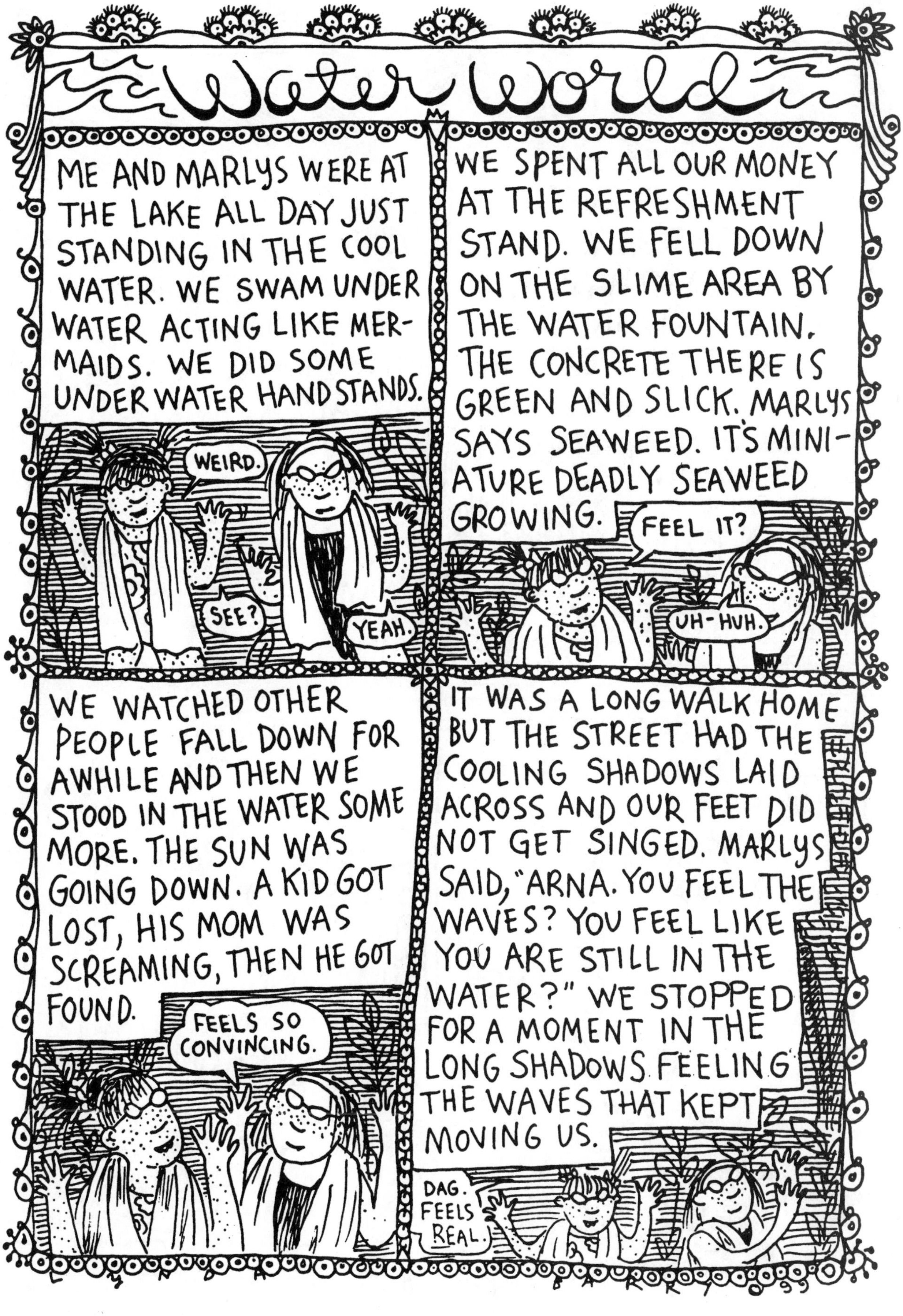
Water World
ME AND MARLYS WERE AT THE LAKE ALL DAY JUST STANDING IN THE COOL WATER. WE SWAM UNDER WATER ACTING LIKE MER-MAIDS. WE DID SOME UNDER WATER HAND STANDS.
WEIRD.
SEE?
YEAH.
WE SPENT ALL OUR MONEY AT THE REFRESHMENT STAND. WE FELL DOWN ON THE SLIME AREA BY THE WATER FOUNTAIN. THE CONCRETE THERE IS GREEN AND SLICK. MARLYS SAYS SEAWEED. IT'S MINI-ATURE DEADLY SEAWEED GROWING.
FEEL IT?
UH-HUH.
WE WATCHED OTHER PEOPLE FALL DOWN FOR AWHILE AND THEN WE STOOD IN THE WATER SOME MORE. THE SUN WAS GOING DOWN. A KID GOT LOST, HIS MOM WAS SCREAMING, THEN HE GOT FOUND.
FEELS SO CONVINCING.
IT WAS A LONG WALK HOME BUT THE STREET HAD THE COOLING SHADOWS LAID ACROSS AND OUR FEET DID NOT GET SINGED. MARLYS SAID, "ARNA. YOU FEEL THE WAVES? YOU FEEL LIKE YOU ARE STILL IN THE WATER?" WE STOPPED FOR A MOMENT IN THE LONG SHADOWS FEELING THE WAVES THAT KEPT MOVING US.
DAG. FEELS REAL.
LYNDA BARRY '99

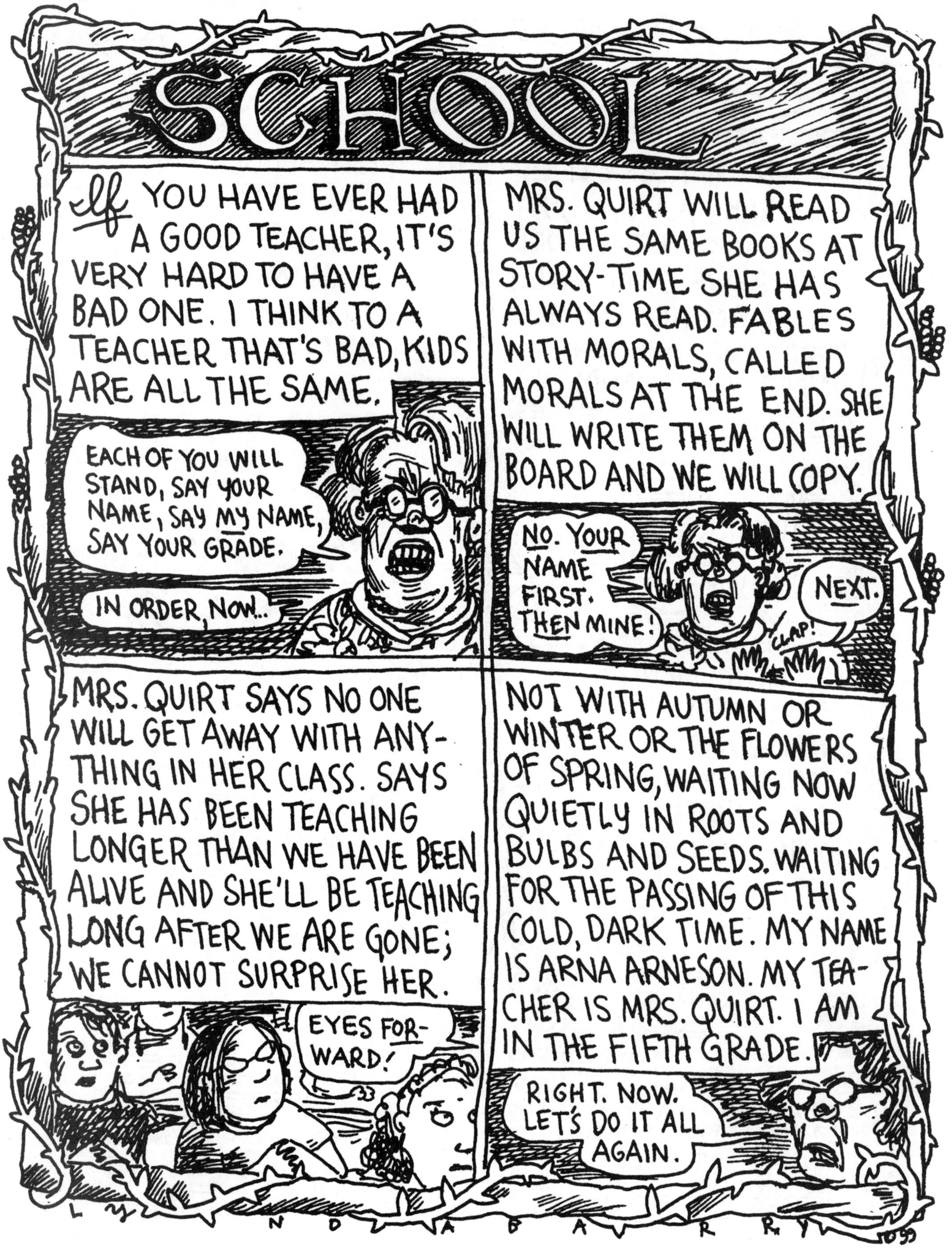
SCHOOL
IF YOU HAVE EVER HAD A GOOD TEACHER, IT'S VERY HARD TO HAVE A BAD ONE. I THINK TO A TEACHER THAT'S BAD, KIDS ARE ALL THE SAME.
EACH OF YOU WILL STAND, SAY YOUR NAME, SAY MY NAME, SAY YOUR GRADE.
IN ORDER, NOW...
MRS. QUIRT WILL READ US THE SAME BOOKS AT STORY-TIME SHE HAS ALWAYS READ. FABLES WITH MORALS, CALLED MORALS AT THE END. SHE WILL WRITE THEM ON THE BOARD AND WE WILL COPY.
NO. YOUR NAME FIRST. THEN MINE!
NEXT.
CLAP!
MRS. QUIRT SAYS NO ONE WILL GET AWAY WITH ANY-THING IN HER CLASS. SAYS SHE HAS BEEN TEACHING LONGER THAN WE HAVE BEEN ALIVE AND SHE'LL BE TEACHING LONG AFTER WE ARE GONE; WE CANNOT SURPRISE HER.
EYES FOR-WARD!
NOT WITH AUTUMN OR WINTER OR THE FLOWERS OF SPRING, WAITING NOW QUIETLY IN ROOTS AND BULBS AND SEEDS. WAITING FOR THE PASSING OF THIS COLD, DARK TIME. MY NAME IS ARNA ARNESON. MY TEA-CHER IS MRS. QUIRT. I AM IN THE FIFTH GRADE.
RIGHT. NOW. LET'S DO IT ALL AGAIN.
LYNDA BARRY

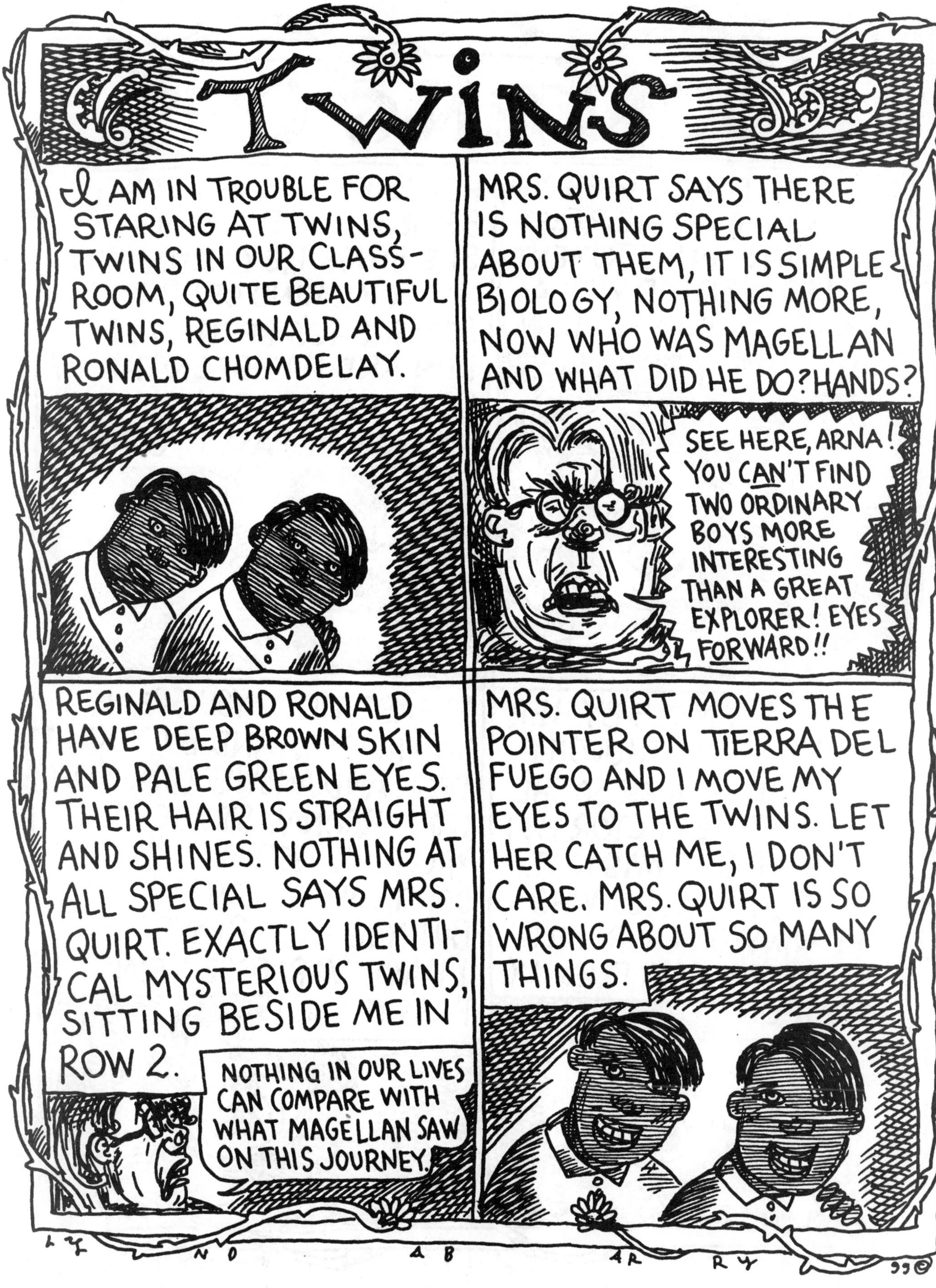
TWINS
I AM IN TROUBLE FOR STARING AT TWINS, TWINS IN OUR CLASS-ROOM, QUITE BEAUTIFUL TWINS, REGINALD AND RONALD CHOMDELAY.
MRS. QUIRT SAYS THERE IS NOTHING SPECIAL ABOUT THEM, IT IS SIMPLE BIOLOGY, NOTHING MORE, NOW WHO WAS MAGELLAN AND WHAT DID HE DO? HANDS?
SEE HERE, ARNA! YOU CAN'T FIND TWO ORDINARY BOYS MORE INTERESTING THAN A GREAT EXPLORER! EYES FORWARD!!
REGINALD AND RONALD HAVE DEEP BROWN SKIN AND PALE GREEN EYES. THEIR HAIR IS STRAIGHT AND SHINES. NOTHING AT ALL SPECIAL SAYS MRS. QUIRT. EXACTLY IDENTI-CAL MYSTERIOUS TWINS, SITTING BESIDE ME IN ROW 2.
NOTHING IN OUR LIVES CAN COMPARE WITH WHAT MAGELLAN SAW ON THIS JOURNEY.
MRS. QUIRT MOVES THE POINTER ON TIERRA DEL FUEGO AND I MOVE MY EYES TO THE TWINS. LET HER CATCH ME, I DON'T CARE. MRS. QUIRT IS SO WRONG ABOUT SO MANY THINGS.
LYNDA BARRY 99©

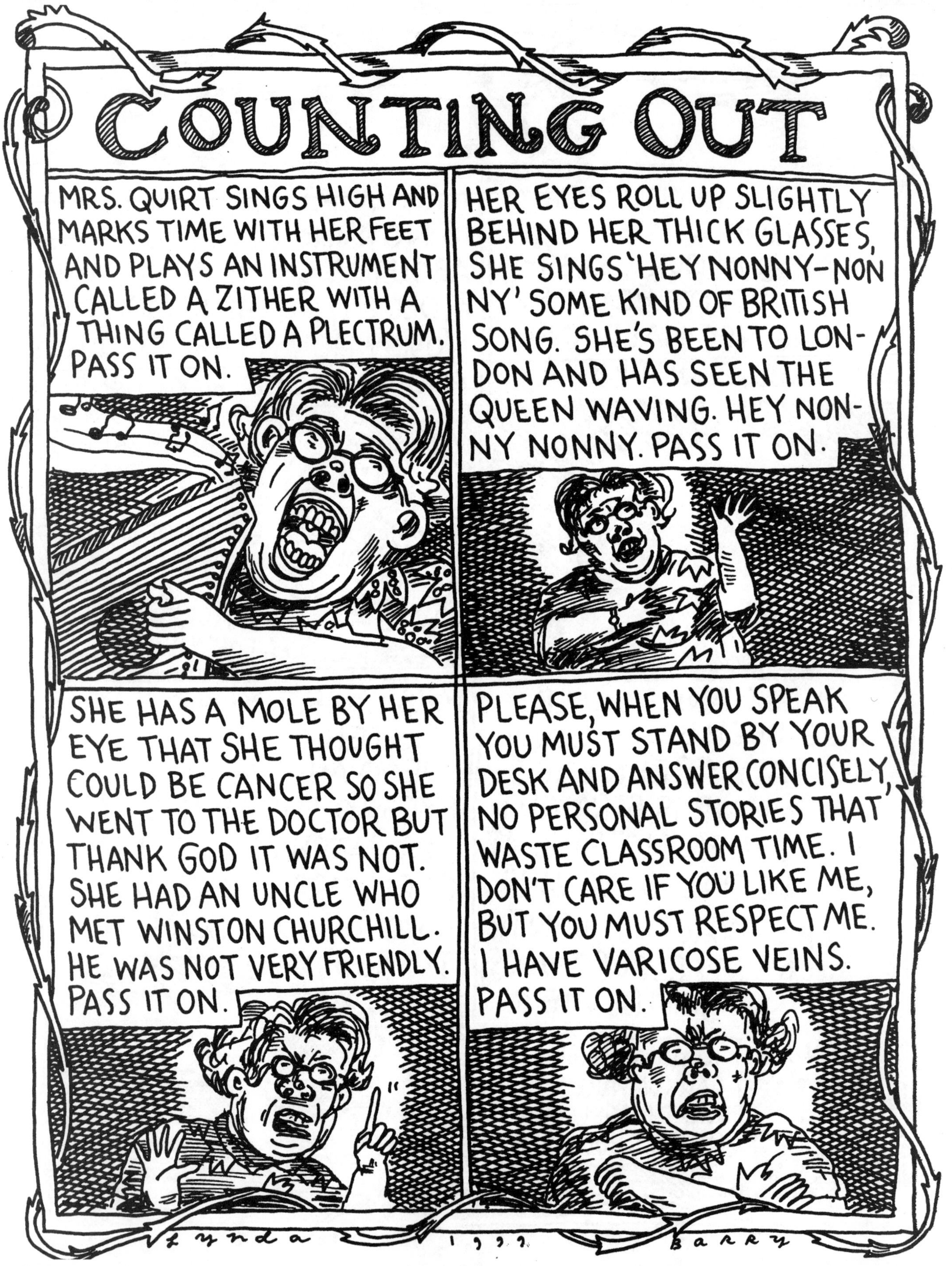
COUNTING OUT
MRS. QUIRT SINGS HIGH AND MARKS TIME WITH HER FEET AND PLAYS AN INSTRUMENT CALLED A ZITHER WITH A THING CALLED A PLECTRUM. PASS IT ON.
HER EYES ROLL UP SLIGHTLY BEHIND HER THICK GLASSES, SHE SINGS 'HEY NONNY-NONNY' SOME KIND OF BRITISH SONG. SHE'S BEEN TO LONDON AND HAS SEEN THE QUEEN WAVING. HEY NONNY NONNY. PASS IT ON.
SHE HAS A MOLE BY HER EYE THAT SHE THOUGHT COULD BE CANCER SO SHE WENT TO THE DOCTOR BUT THANK GOD IT WAS NOT. SHE HAD AN UNCLE WHO MET WINSTON CHURCHILL. HE WAS NOT VERY FRIENDLY. PASS IT ON.
PLEASE, WHEN YOU SPEAK YOU MUST STAND BY YOUR DESK AND ANSWER CONCISELY, NO PERSONAL STORIES THAT WASTE CLASSROOM TIME. I DON'T CARE IF YOU LIKE ME, BUT YOU MUST RESPECT ME. I HAVE VARICOSE VEINS. PASS IT ON.
LYNDA 1999 BARRY

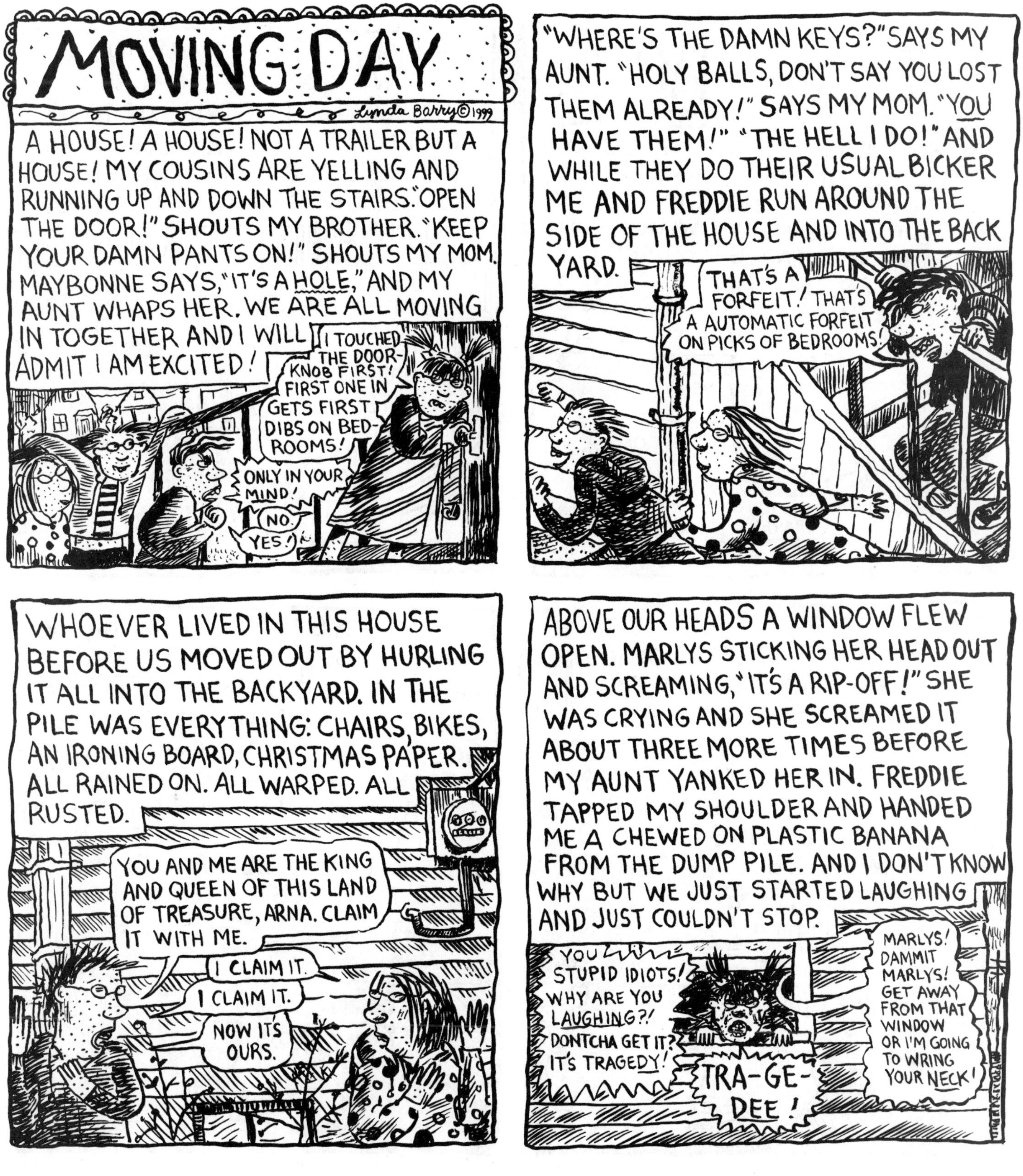
MOVING DAY
Lynda Barry © 1999
A HOUSE! A HOUSE! NOT A TRAILER BUT A HOUSE! MY COUSINS ARE YELLING AND RUNNING UP AND DOWN THE STAIRS. "OPEN THE DOOR!" SHOUTS MY BROTHER. "KEEP YOUR DAMN PANTS ON!" SHOUTS MY MOM. MAYBONNE SAYS, "IT'S A HOLE," AND MY AUNT WHAPS HER. WE ARE ALL MOVING IN TOGETHER AND I WILL ADMIT I AM EXCITED!
I TOUCHED THE DOOR-KNOB FIRST! FIRST ONE IN GETS FIRST DIBS ON BED-ROOMS!
ONLY IN YOUR MIND!
NO.
YES!
"WHERE'S THE DAMN KEYS?" SAYS MY AUNT. "HOLY BALLS, DON'T SAY YOU LOST THEM ALREADY!" SAYS MY MOM. "YOU HAVE THEM!" "THE HELL I DO!" AND WHILE THEY DO THEIR USUAL BICKER ME AND FREDDIE RUN AROUND THE SIDE OF THE HOUSE AND INTO THE BACK YARD.
THAT'S A FORFEIT! THAT'S A AUTOMATIC FORFEIT ON PICKS OF BEDROOMS!
WHOEVER LIVED IN THIS HOUSE BEFORE US MOVED OUT BY HURLING IT ALL INTO THE BACKYARD. IN THE PILE WAS EVERYTHING: CHAIRS, BIKES, AN IRONING BOARD, CHRISTMAS PAPER. ALL RAINED ON. ALL WARPED. ALL RUSTED.
YOU AND ME ARE THE KING AND QUEEN OF THIS LAND OF TREASURE, ARNA. CLAIM IT WITH ME.
I CLAIM IT.
I CLAIM IT.
NOW IT'S OURS.
ABOVE OUR HEADS A WINDOW FLEW OPEN. MARLYS STICKING HER HEAD OUT AND SCREAMING, "IT'S A RIP-OFF!" SHE WAS CRYING AND SHE SCREAMED IT ABOUT THREE MORE TIMES BEFORE MY AUNT YANKED HER IN. FREDDIE TAPPED MY SHOULDER AND HANDED ME A CHEWED ON PLASTIC BANANA FROM THE DUMP PILE. AND I DON'T KNOW WHY BUT WE JUST STARTED LAUGHING AND JUST COULDN'T STOP.
YOU STUPID IDIOTS! WHY ARE YOU LAUGHING?! DONTCHA GET IT? IT'S TRAGEDY!
TRA-GE-DEE!
MARLYS! DAMMIT MARLYS! GET AWAY FROM THAT WINDOW OR I'M GOING TO WRING YOUR NECK!

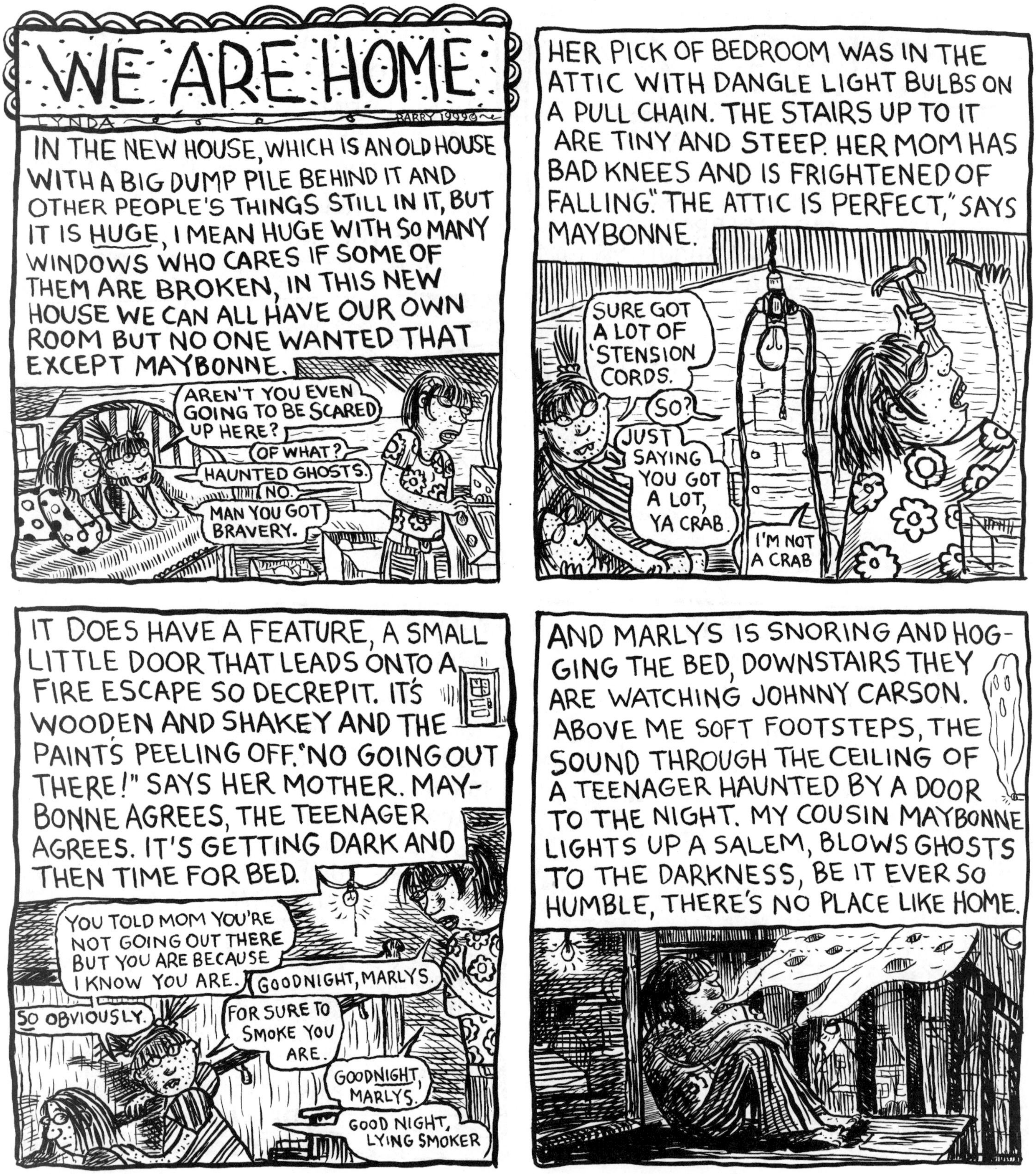
WE ARE HOME
LYNDA BARRY 1999©
IN THE NEW HOUSE, WHICH IS AN OLD HOUSE WITH A BIG DUMP PILE BEHIND IT AND OTHER PEOPLE'S THINGS STILL IN IT, BUT IT IS HUGE, I MEAN HUGE WITH SO MANY WINDOWS WHO CARES IF SOME OF THEM ARE BROKEN, IN THIS NEW HOUSE WE CAN ALL HAVE OUR OWN ROOM BUT NO ONE WANTED THAT EXCEPT MAYBONNE.
AREN'T YOU EVEN GOING TO BE SCARED UP HERE?
OF WHAT?
HAUNTED GHOSTS.
NO.
MAN YOU GOT BRAVERY.
HER PICK OF BEDROOM WAS IN THE ATTIC WITH DANGLE LIGHT BULBS ON A PULL CHAIN. THE STAIRS UP TO IT ARE TINY AND STEEP. HER MOM HAS BAD KNEES AND IS FRIGHTENED OF FALLING. "THE ATTIC IS PERFECT," SAYS MAYBONNE.
SURE GOT A LOT OF 'STENSION CORDS.
SO?
JUST SAYING YOU GOT A LOT, YA CRAB
I'M NOT A CRAB
IT DOES HAVE A FEATURE, A SMALL LITTLE DOOR THAT LEADS ONTO A FIRE ESCAPE SO DECREPIT. IT'S WOODEN AND SHAKEY AND THE PAINT'S PEELING OFF. "NO GOING OUT THERE!" SAYS HER MOTHER. MAY-BONNE AGREES, THE TEENAGER AGREES. IT'S GETTING DARK AND THEN TIME FOR BED.
YOU TOLD MOM YOU'RE NOT GOING OUT THERE BUT YOU ARE BECAUSE I KNOW YOU ARE.
GOODNIGHT, MARLYS.
SO OBVIOUSLY.
FOR SURE TO SMOKE YOU ARE.
GOODNIGHT, MARLYS.
GOOD NIGHT, LYING SMOKER
AND MARLYS IS SNORING AND HOG-GING THE BED, DOWNSTAIRS THEY ARE WATCHING JOHNNY CARSON. ABOVE ME SOFT FOOTSTEPS, THE SOUND THROUGH THE CEILING OF A TEENAGER HAUNTED BY A DOOR TO THE NIGHT. MY COUSIN MAYBONNE LIGHTS UP A SALEM, BLOWS GHOSTS TO THE DARKNESS, BE IT EVER SO HUMBLE, THERE'S NO PLACE LIKE HOME.

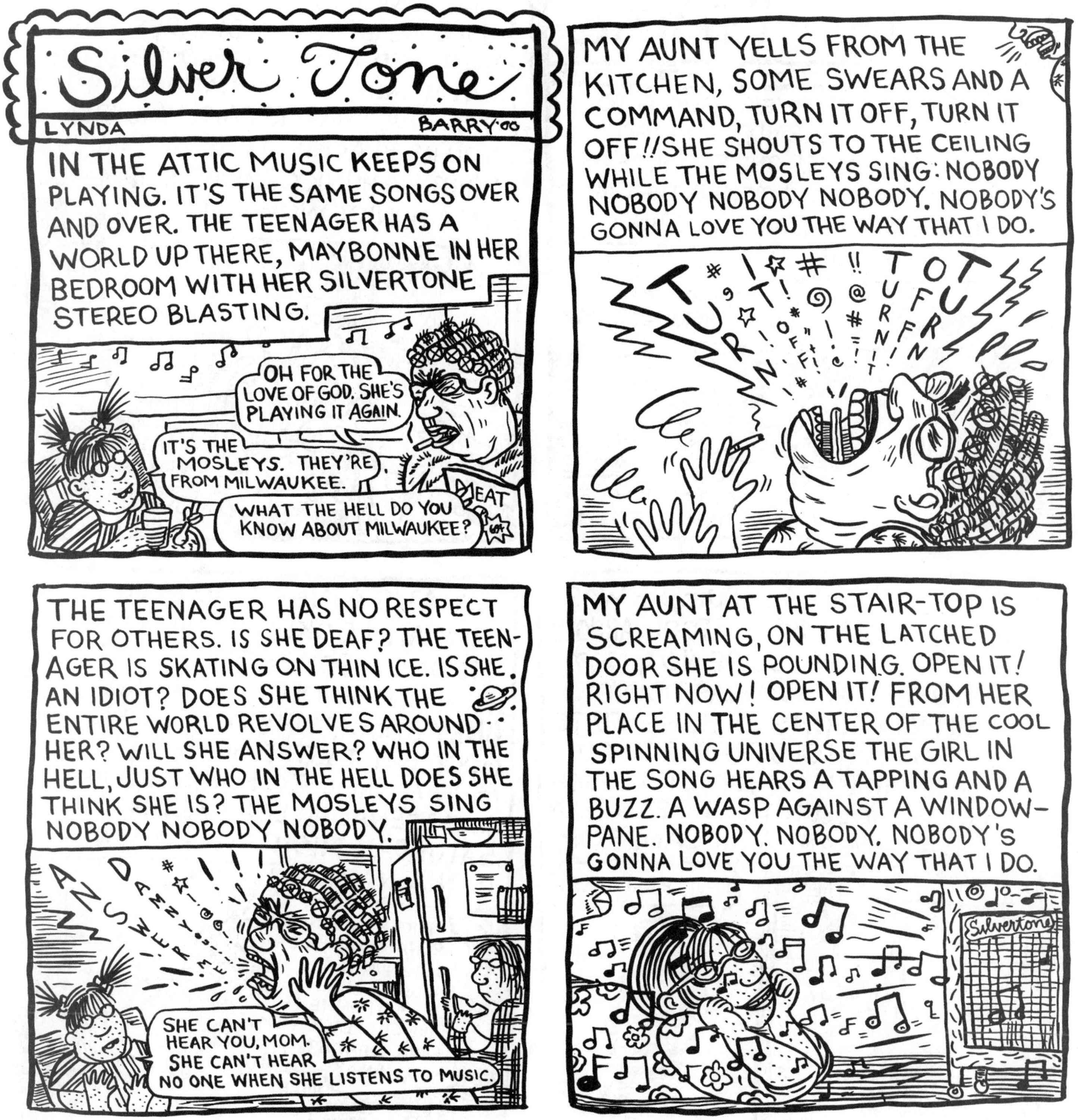
Silver Tone
LYNDA BARRY '00
IN THE ATTIC MUSIC KEEPS ON PLAYING. IT'S THE SAME SONGS OVER AND OVER. THE TEENAGER HAS A WORLD UP THERE, MAYBONNE IN HER BEDROOM WITH HER SILVERTONE STEREO BLASTING.
OH FOR THE LOVE OF GOD. SHE'S PLAYING IT AGAIN.
IT'S THE MOSLEYS. THEY'RE FROM MILWAUKEE.
WHAT THE HELL DO YOU KNOW ABOUT MILWAUKEE?
MEAT
MY AUNT YELLS FROM THE KITCHEN, SOME SWEARS AND A COMMAND, TURN IT OFF, TURN IT OFF!! SHE SHOUTS TO THE CEILING WHILE THE MOSLEYS SING: NOBODY NOBODY NOBODY NOBODY. NOBODY'S GONNA LOVE YOU THE WAY THAT I DO.
THE TEENAGER HAS NO RESPECT FOR OTHERS. IS SHE DEAF? THE TEENAGER IS SKATING ON THIN ICE. IS SHE AN IDIOT? DOES SHE THINK THE ENTIRE WORLD REVOLVES AROUND HER? WILL SHE ANSWER? WHO IN THE HELL, JUST WHO IN THE HELL DOES SHE THINK SHE IS? THE MOSLEYS SING NOBODY NOBODY NOBODY.
ANSWER ME
DAMN YOU
SHE CAN'T HEAR YOU, MOM. SHE CAN'T HEAR NO ONE WHEN SHE LISTENS TO MUSIC.
MY AUNT AT THE STAIR-TOP IS SCREAMING, ON THE LATCHED DOOR SHE IS POUNDING. OPEN IT! RIGHT NOW! OPEN IT! FROM HER PLACE IN THE CENTER OF THE COOL SPINNING UNIVERSE THE GIRL IN THE SONG HEARS A TAPPING AND A BUZZ. A WASP AGAINST A WINDOW-PANE. NOBODY. NOBODY. NOBODY'S GONNA LOVE YOU THE WAY THAT I DO.
Silvertone

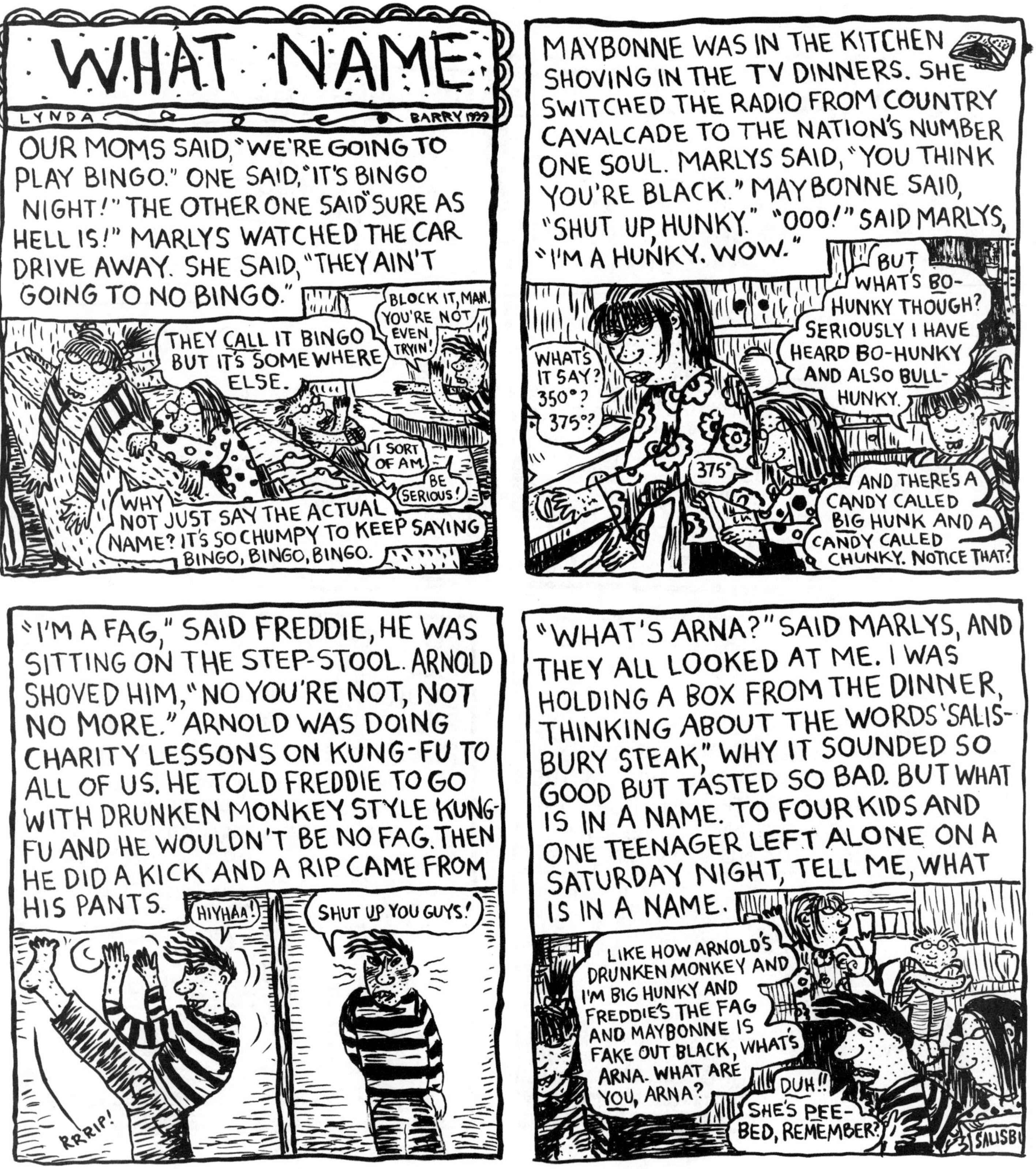

WHAT NAME
LYNDA BARRY 1999
OUR MOMS SAID, "WE'RE GOING TO PLAY BINGO." ONE SAID, "IT'S BINGO NIGHT!" THE OTHER ONE SAID "SURE AS HELL IS!" MARLYS WATCHED THE CAR DRIVE AWAY. SHE SAID, "THEY AIN'T GOING TO NO BINGO."
THEY CALL IT BINGO BUT IT'S SOMEWHERE ELSE.
BLOCK IT, MAN. YOU'RE NOT EVEN TRYIN'!
I SORT OF AM.
BE SERIOUS!
WHY NOT JUST SAY THE ACTUAL NAME? IT'S SO CHUMPY TO KEEP SAYING BINGO, BINGO, BINGO.
MAYBONNE WAS IN THE KITCHEN SHOVING IN THE TV DINNERS. SHE SWITCHED THE RADIO FROM COUNTRY CAVALCADE TO THE NATION'S NUMBER ONE SOUL. MARLYS SAID, "YOU THINK YOU'RE BLACK." MAYBONNE SAID, "SHUT UP, HUNKY." "OOO!" SAID MARLYS, "I'M A HUNKY. WOW."
WHAT'S IT SAY? 350°? 375°?
375°
BUT WHAT'S BO-HUNKY THOUGH? SERIOUSLY I HAVE HEARD BO-HUNKY AND ALSO BULL-HUNKY.
AND THERE'S A CANDY CALLED BIG HUNK AND A CANDY CALLED CHUNKY. NOTICE THAT?
"I'M A FAG," SAID FREDDIE, HE WAS SITTING ON THE STEP-STOOL. ARNOLD SHOVED HIM, "NO YOU'RE NOT, NOT NO MORE." ARNOLD WAS DOING CHARITY LESSONS ON KUNG-FU TO ALL OF US. HE TOLD FREDDIE TO GO WITH DRUNKEN MONKEY STYLE KUNG-FU AND HE WOULDN'T BE NO FAG. THEN HE DID A KICK AND A RIP CAME FROM HIS PANTS.
HIYHAA!
RRRIP!
SHUT UP YOU GUYS!
"WHAT'S ARNA?" SAID MARLYS, AND THEY ALL LOOKED AT ME. I WAS HOLDING A BOX FROM THE DINNER, THINKING ABOUT THE WORDS 'SALISBURY STEAK," WHY IT SOUNDED SO GOOD BUT TASTED SO BAD. BUT WHAT IS IN A NAME. TO FOUR KIDS AND ONE TEENAGER LEFT ALONE ON A SATURDAY NIGHT, TELL ME, WHAT IS IN A NAME.
LIKE HOW ARNOLD'S DRUNKEN MONKEY AND I'M BIG HUNKY AND FREDDIE'S THE FAG AND MAYBONNE IS FAKE OUT BLACK, WHAT'S ARNA. WHAT ARE YOU, ARNA?
DUH!! SHE'S PEE-BED, REMEMBER?
SALISBU

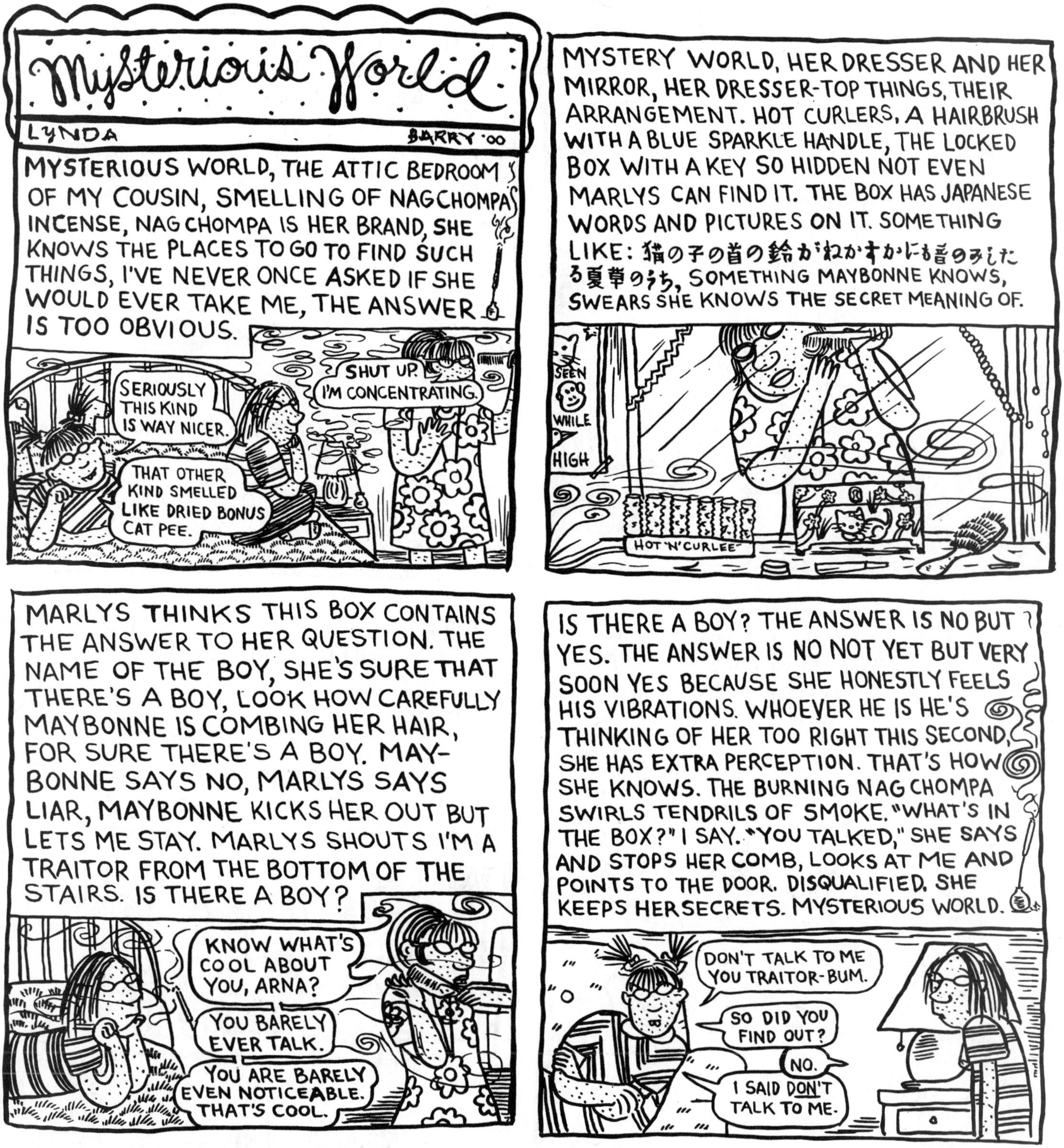
Mysterious World
LYNDA BARRY '00
MYSTERIOUS WORLD, THE ATTIC BEDROOM OF MY COUSIN, SMELLING OF NAG CHOMPA INCENSE, NAG CHOMPA IS HER BRAND, SHE KNOWS THE PLACES TO GO TO FIND SUCH THINGS, I'VE NEVER ONCE ASKED IF SHE WOULD EVER TAKE ME, THE ANSWER IS TOO OBVIOUS.
SERIOUSLY THIS KIND IS WAY NICER.
THAT OTHER KIND SMELLED LIKE DRIED BONUS CAT PEE.
SHUT UP. I'M CONCENTRATING.
MYSTERY WORLD, HER DRESSER AND HER MIRROR, HER DRESSER-TOP THINGS, THEIR ARRANGEMENT. HOT CURLERS, A HAIRBRUSH WITH A BLUE SPARKLE HANDLE, THE LOCKED BOX WITH A KEY SO HIDDEN NOT EVEN MARLYS CAN FIND IT. THE BOX HAS JAPANESE WORDS AND PICTURES ON IT. SOMETHING LIKE: 猫の子の首の鈴がねかすかにも音のみしたる夏草のうち, SOMETHING MAYBONNE KNOWS, SWEARS SHE KNOWS THE SECRET MEANING OF.
SEEN
WHILE
HIGH
HOT 'N' CURLEE
MARLYS THINKS THIS BOX CONTAINS THE ANSWER TO HER QUESTION. THE NAME OF THE BOY, SHE'S SURE THAT THERE'S A BOY, LOOK HOW CAREFULLY MAYBONNE IS COMBING HER HAIR, FOR SURE THERE'S A BOY. MAY-BONNE SAYS NO, MARLYS SAYS LIAR, MAYBONNE KICKS HER OUT BUT LETS ME STAY. MARLYS SHOUTS I'M A TRAITOR FROM THE BOTTOM OF THE STAIRS. IS THERE A BOY?
KNOW WHAT'S COOL ABOUT YOU, ARNA?
YOU BARELY EVER TALK.
YOU ARE BARELY EVEN NOTICEABLE. THAT'S COOL.
IS THERE A BOY? THE ANSWER IS NO BUT YES. THE ANSWER IS NO NOT YET BUT VERY SOON YES BECAUSE SHE HONESTLY FEELS HIS VIBRATIONS. WHOEVER HE IS HE'S THINKING OF HER TOO RIGHT THIS SECOND, SHE HAS EXTRA PERCEPTION. THAT'S HOW SHE KNOWS. THE BURNING NAG CHOMPA SWIRLS TENDRILS OF SMOKE. "WHAT'S IN THE BOX?" I SAY. "YOU TALKED," SHE SAYS AND STOPS HER COMB, LOOKS AT ME AND POINTS TO THE DOOR. DISQUALIFIED. SHE KEEPS HER SECRETS. MYSTERIOUS WORLD.
DON'T TALK TO ME YOU TRAITOR-BUM.
SO DID YOU FIND OUT?
NO.
I SAID DON'T TALK TO ME.

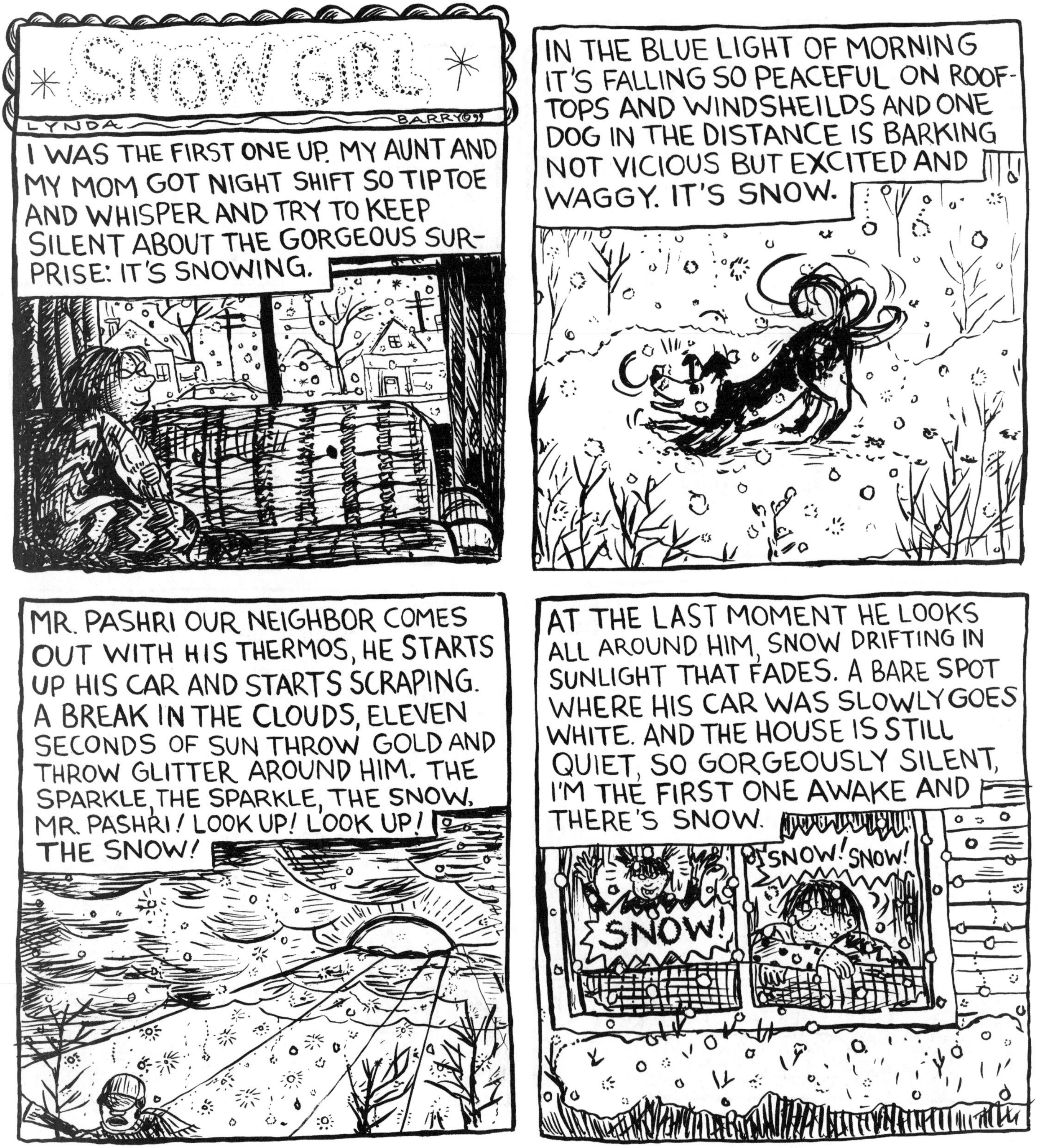
SNOW GIRL
LYNDA BARRY ©99
I WAS THE FIRST ONE UP. MY AUNT AND MY MOM GOT NIGHT SHIFT SO TIPTOE AND WHISPER AND TRY TO KEEP SILENT ABOUT THE GORGEOUS SURPRISE: IT'S SNOWING.
IN THE BLUE LIGHT OF MORNING IT'S FALLING SO PEACEFUL ON ROOFTOPS AND WINDSHEILDS AND ONE DOG IN THE DISTANCE IS BARKING NOT VICIOUS BUT EXCITED AND WAGGY. IT'S SNOW.
MR. PASHRI OUR NEIGHBOR COMES OUT WITH HIS THERMOS, HE STARTS UP HIS CAR AND STARTS SCRAPING. A BREAK IN THE CLOUDS, ELEVEN SECONDS OF SUN THROW GOLD AND THROW GLITTER AROUND HIM. THE SPARKLE, THE SPARKLE, THE SNOW, MR. PASHRI! LOOK UP! LOOK UP! THE SNOW!
AT THE LAST MOMENT HE LOOKS ALL AROUND HIM, SNOW DRIFTING IN SUNLIGHT THAT FADES. A BARE SPOT WHERE HIS CAR WAS SLOWLY GOES WHITE. AND THE HOUSE IS STILL QUIET, SO GORGEOUSLY SILENT, I'M THE FIRST ONE AWAKE AND THERE'S SNOW.
SNOW!
SNOW! SNOW!

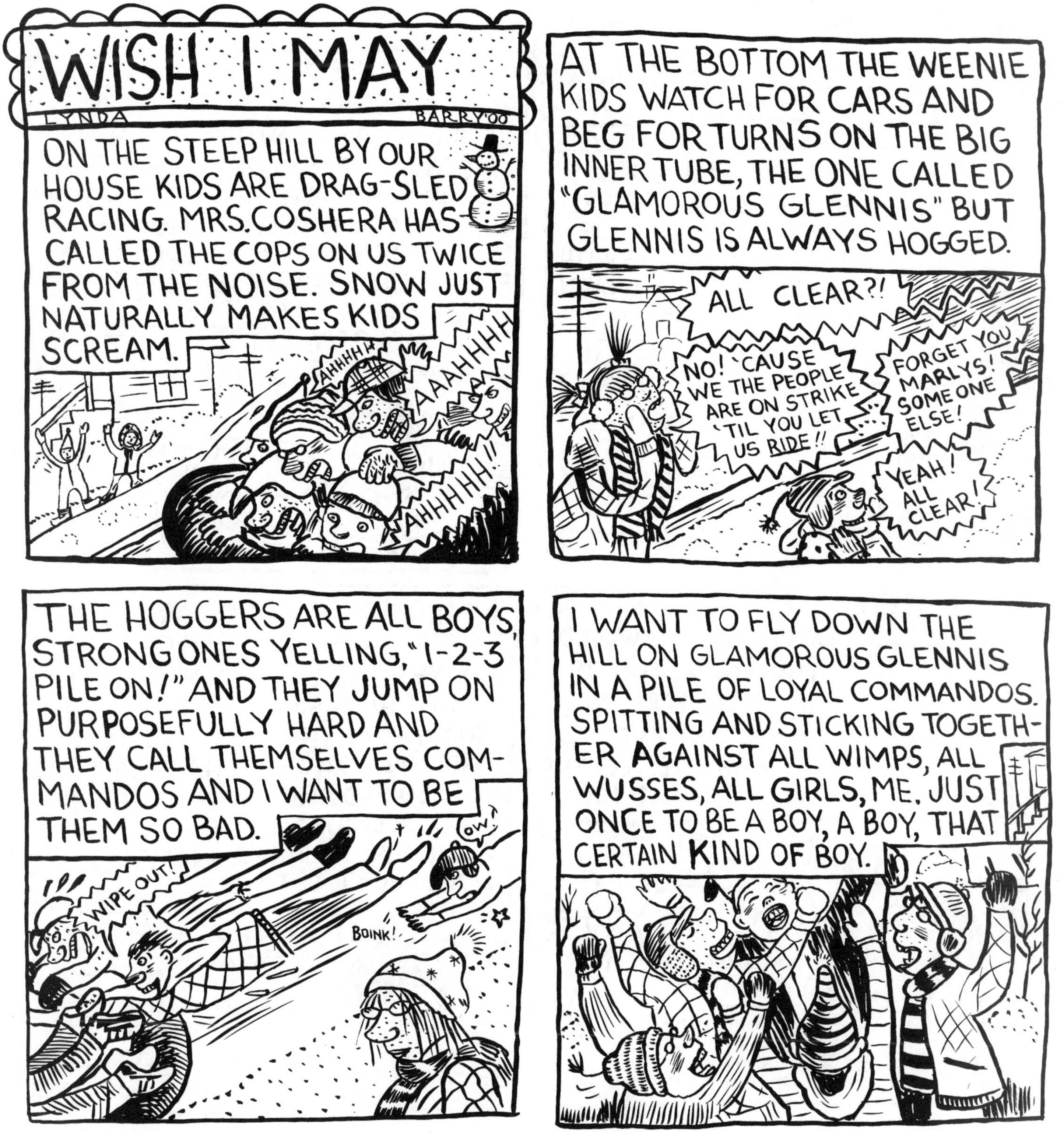
WISH I MAY
LYNDA BARRY '00
ON THE STEEP HILL BY OUR HOUSE KIDS ARE DRAG-SLED RACING. MRS. COSHERA HAS CALLED THE COPS ON US TWICE FROM THE NOISE. SNOW JUST NATURALLY MAKES KIDS SCREAM.
AHHHHH
AAAHHHH
AHHHHH!!
AT THE BOTTOM THE WEENIE KIDS WATCH FOR CARS AND BEG FOR TURNS ON THE BIG INNER TUBE, THE ONE CALLED "GLAMOROUS GLENNIS" BUT GLENNIS IS ALWAYS HOGGED.
ALL CLEAR?!
NO! 'CAUSE WE THE PEOPLE ARE ON STRIKE 'TIL YOU LET US RIDE!!
FORGET YOU MARLYS! SOME ONE ELSE!
YEAH! ALL CLEAR!
THE HOGGERS ARE ALL BOYS, STRONG ONES YELLING, "1-2-3 PILE ON!" AND THEY JUMP ON PURPOSEFULLY HARD AND THEY CALL THEMSELVES COMMANDOS AND I WANT TO BE THEM SO BAD.
OW!
WIPE OUT!
BOINK!
I WANT TO FLY DOWN THE HILL ON GLAMOROUS GLENNIS IN A PILE OF LOYAL COMMANDOS. SPITTING AND STICKING TOGETHER AGAINST ALL WIMPS, ALL WUSSES, ALL GIRLS, ME. JUST ONCE TO BE A BOY, A BOY, THAT CERTAIN KIND OF BOY.

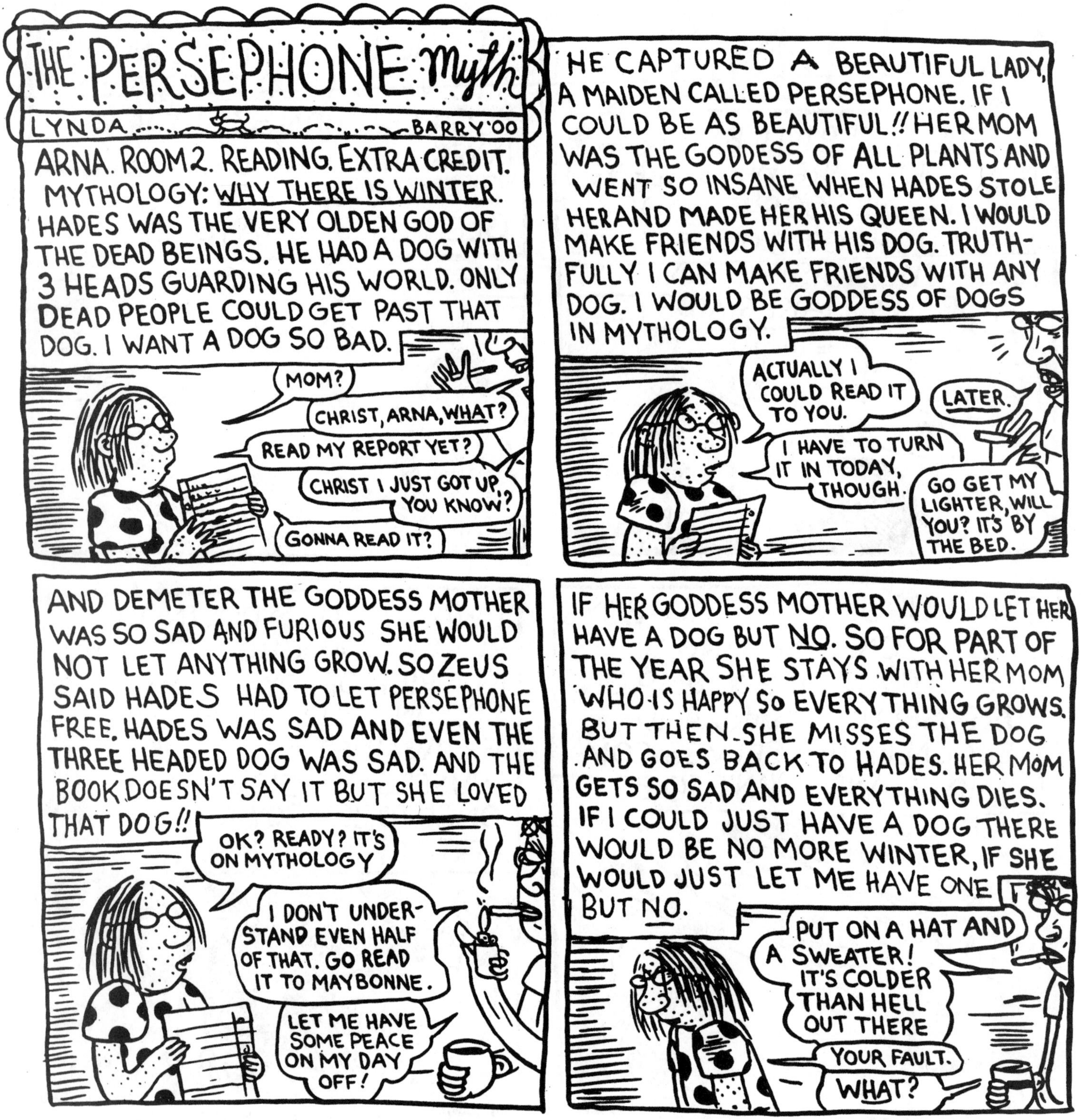
THE PERSEPHONE myth
LYNDA BARRY '00
ARNA. ROOM 2. READING. EXTRA CREDIT. MYTHOLOGY: WHY THERE IS WINTER. HADES WAS THE VERY OLDEN GOD OF THE DEAD BEINGS. HE HAD A DOG WITH 3 HEADS GUARDING HIS WORLD. ONLY DEAD PEOPLE COULD GET PAST THAT DOG. I WANT A DOG SO BAD.
MOM?
CHRIST, ARNA, WHAT?
READ MY REPORT YET?
CHRIST I JUST GOT UP, YOU KNOW?
GONNA READ IT?
HE CAPTURED A BEAUTIFUL LADY, A MAIDEN CALLED PERSEPHONE. IF I COULD BE AS BEAUTIFUL!! HER MOM WAS THE GODDESS OF ALL PLANTS AND WENT SO INSANE WHEN HADES STOLE HER AND MADE HER HIS QUEEN. I WOULD MAKE FRIENDS WITH HIS DOG. TRUTHFULLY I CAN MAKE FRIENDS WITH ANY DOG. I WOULD BE GODDESS OF DOGS IN MYTHOLOGY.
ACTUALLY I COULD READ IT TO YOU.
LATER.
I HAVE TO TURN IT IN TODAY, THOUGH.
GO GET MY LIGHTER, WILL YOU? IT'S BY THE BED.
AND DEMETER THE GODDESS MOTHER WAS SO SAD AND FURIOUS SHE WOULD NOT LET ANYTHING GROW. SO ZEUS SAID HADES HAD TO LET PERSEPHONE FREE. HADES WAS SAD AND EVEN THE THREE HEADED DOG WAS SAD. AND THE BOOK DOESN'T SAY IT BUT SHE LOVED THAT DOG!!
OK? READY? IT'S ON MYTHOLOGY
I DON'T UNDERSTAND EVEN HALF OF THAT. GO READ IT TO MAYBONNE.
LET ME HAVE SOME PEACE ON MY DAY OFF!
IF HER GODDESS MOTHER WOULD LET HER HAVE A DOG BUT NO. SO FOR PART OF THE YEAR SHE STAYS WITH HER MOM WHO IS HAPPY SO EVERYTHING GROWS. BUT THEN SHE MISSES THE DOG AND GOES BACK TO HADES. HER MOM GETS SO SAD AND EVERYTHING DIES. IF I COULD JUST HAVE A DOG THERE WOULD BE NO MORE WINTER, IF SHE WOULD JUST LET ME HAVE ONE BUT NO.
PUT ON A HAT AND A SWEATER! IT'S COLDER THAN HELL OUT THERE
YOUR FAULT.
WHAT?

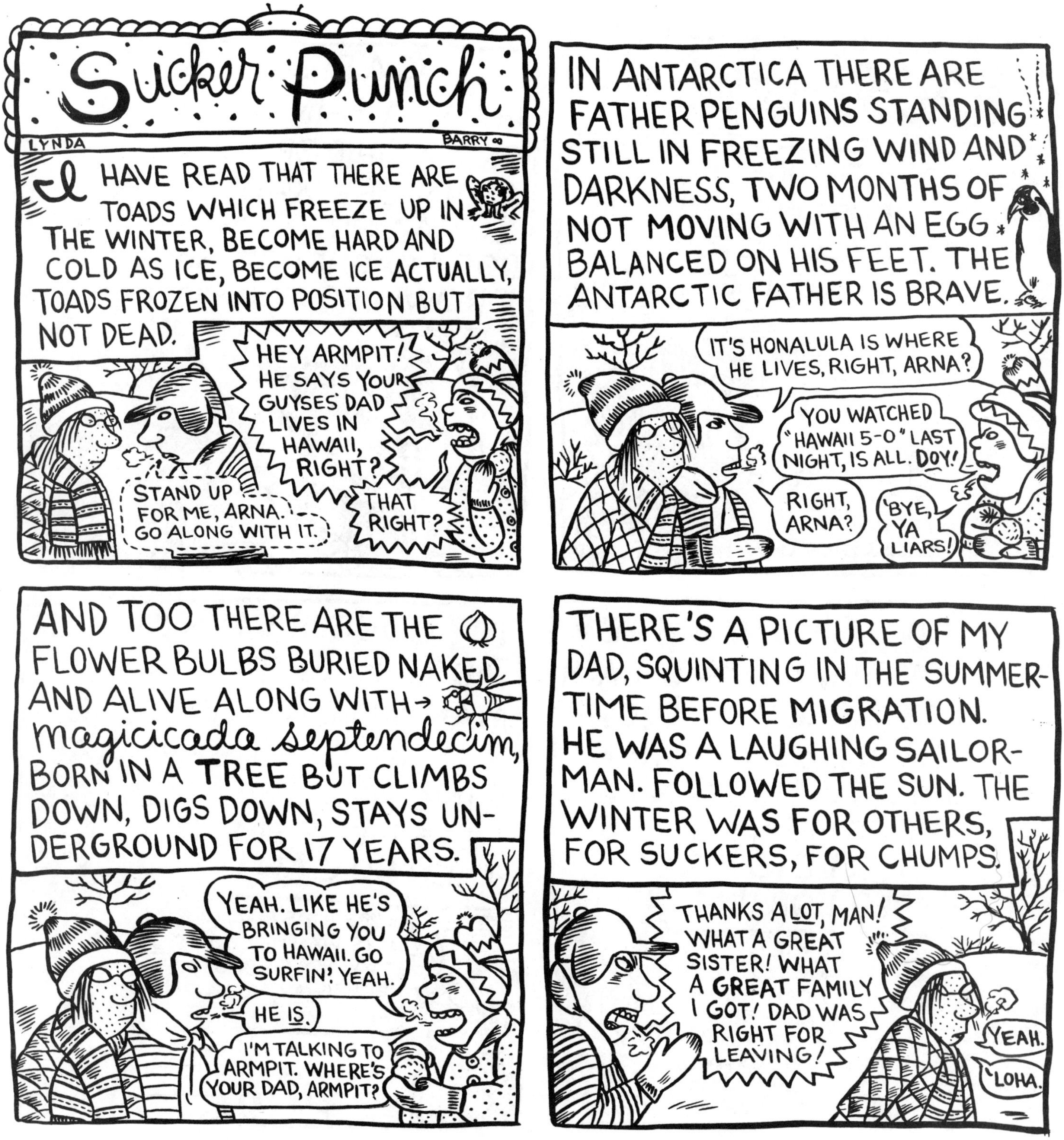
Sucker Punch
LYNDA
BARRY
I HAVE READ THAT THERE ARE TOADS WHICH FREEZE UP IN THE WINTER, BECOME HARD AND COLD AS ICE, BECOME ICE ACTUALLY, TOADS FROZEN INTO POSITION BUT NOT DEAD.
HEY ARMPIT! HE SAYS YOUR GUYSES' DAD LIVES IN HAWAII, RIGHT?
STAND UP FOR ME, ARNA. GO ALONG WITH IT.
THAT RIGHT?
IN ANTARCTICA THERE ARE FATHER PENGUINS STANDING STILL IN FREEZING WIND AND DARKNESS, TWO MONTHS OF NOT MOVING WITH AN EGG BALANCED ON HIS FEET. THE ANTARCTIC FATHER IS BRAVE.
IT'S HONALULA IS WHERE HE LIVES, RIGHT, ARNA?
YOU WATCHED "HAWAII 5-0" LAST NIGHT, IS ALL. DOY!
RIGHT, ARNA?
BYE, YA LIARS!
AND TOO THERE ARE THE FLOWER BULBS BURIED NAKED AND ALIVE ALONG WITH→ magicicada septendecim, BORN IN A TREE BUT CLIMBS DOWN, DIGS DOWN, STAYS UNDERGROUND FOR 17 YEARS.
YEAH. LIKE HE'S BRINGING YOU TO HAWAII. GO SURFIN'. YEAH.
HE IS.
I'M TALKING TO ARMPIT. WHERE'S YOUR DAD, ARMPIT?
THERE'S A PICTURE OF MY DAD, SQUINTING IN THE SUMMERTIME BEFORE MIGRATION. HE WAS A LAUGHING SAILORMAN. FOLLOWED THE SUN. THE WINTER WAS FOR OTHERS, FOR SUCKERS, FOR CHUMPS.
THANKS A LOT, MAN! WHAT A GREAT SISTER! WHAT A GREAT FAMILY I GOT! DAD WAS RIGHT FOR LEAVING!
YEAH.
'LOHA.

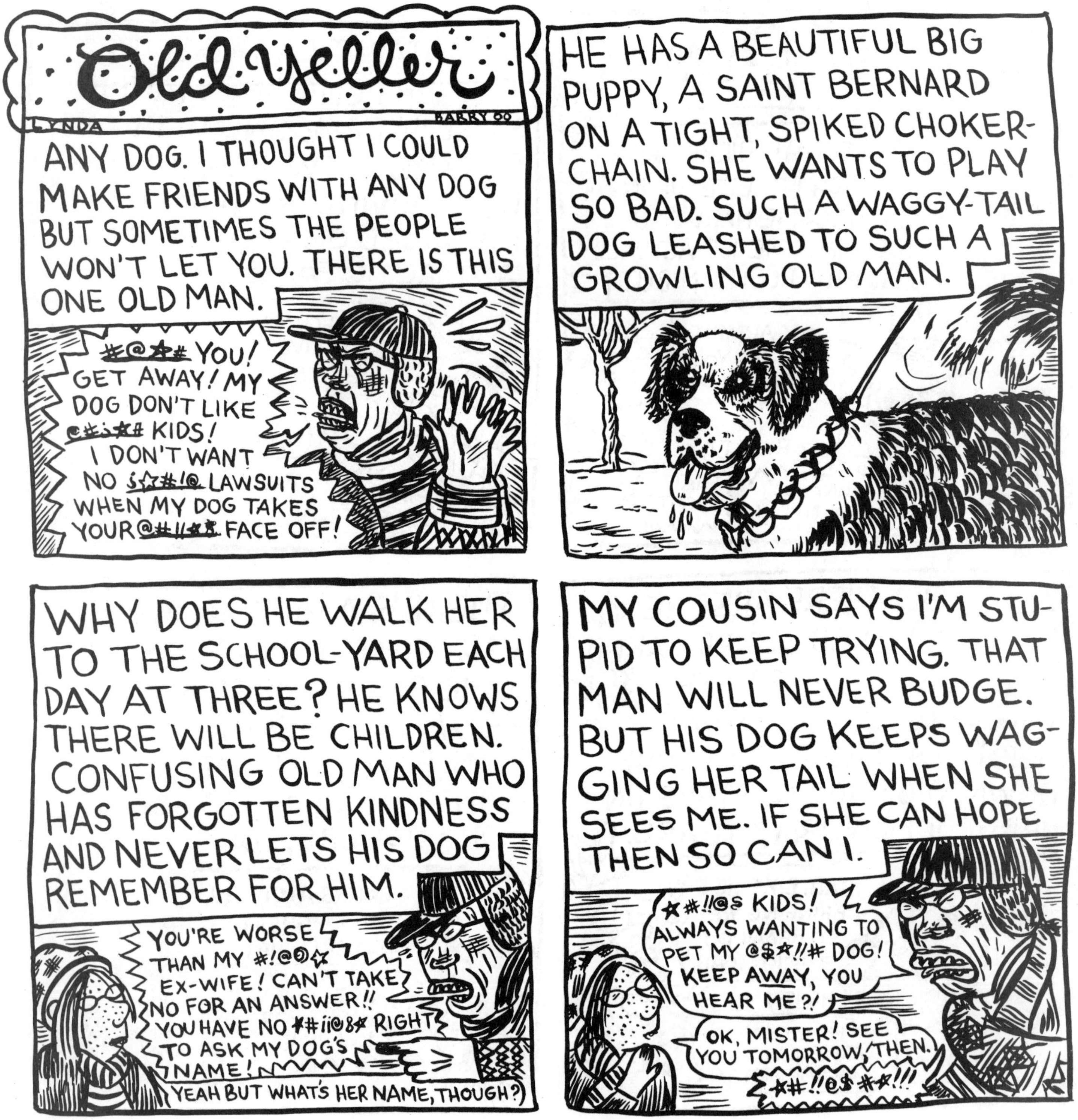

Old Yeller
LYNDA BARRY 99
ANY DOG. I THOUGHT I COULD MAKE FRIENDS WITH ANY DOG BUT SOMETIMES THE PEOPLE WON'T LET YOU. THERE IS THIS ONE OLD MAN.
#@☆# YOU! GET AWAY! MY DOG DON'T LIKE @#¡☆# KIDS! I DON'T WANT NO $☆#!@ LAWSUITS WHEN MY DOG TAKES YOUR @#!!☆$ FACE OFF!
HE HAS A BEAUTIFUL BIG PUPPY, A SAINT BERNARD ON A TIGHT, SPIKED CHOKER-CHAIN. SHE WANTS TO PLAY SO BAD. SUCH A WAGGY-TAIL DOG LEASHED TO SUCH A GROWLING OLD MAN.
WHY DOES HE WALK HER TO THE SCHOOL-YARD EACH DAY AT THREE? HE KNOWS THERE WILL BE CHILDREN. CONFUSING OLD MAN WHO HAS FORGOTTEN KINDNESS AND NEVER LETS HIS DOG REMEMBER FOR HIM.
YOU'RE WORSE THAN MY #!@@☆ EX-WIFE! CAN'T TAKE NO FOR AN ANSWER!! YOU HAVE NO #¡¡@$☆ RIGHT TO ASK MY DOG'S NAME!
YEAH BUT WHAT'S HER NAME, THOUGH?
MY COUSIN SAYS I'M STUPID TO KEEP TRYING. THAT MAN WILL NEVER BUDGE. BUT HIS DOG KEEPS WAGGING HER TAIL WHEN SHE SEES ME. IF SHE CAN HOPE THEN SO CAN I.
☆#!!@$ KIDS! ALWAYS WANTING TO PET MY @$☆!!# DOG! KEEP AWAY, YOU HEAR ME?!
OK, MISTER! SEE YOU TOMORROW, THEN.
☆#!!@$#☆!!!

See-Through

LYNDA BARRY '00

SOME PEOPLE ARE JUST NATURAL JUVENILE DELINQUENTS. LIKE MY BROTHER ARNOLD WHO GETS CONSTANT URGES TO BREAK THINGS.

DEAR LORD THAT WAS SO KEEN OF YOU TO GET JEFF KRILL BLAMED FOR THOSE WINDOWS I BUSTED.

ALSO THANK YOU FOR NO ONE KNOWING IT WAS ME THAT CLOGGED ALL THE TOILETS IN THE BOYS' CAN. AMEN.

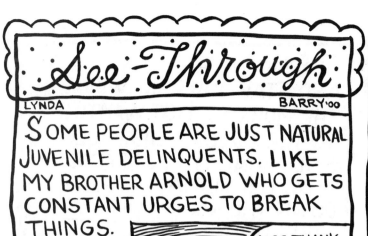

OTHER PEOPLE ARE JUST NATURALLY SMART, LIKE → MARLYS, GETTING ALL A's IN EVERY BOX ON HER REPORT CARD EXCEPT CONDUCT AND RESPONSE TO CRITICISM.

EXCUSE ME LORD FOR KICKING THAT ONE GIRL LOUISE IN THE LEG FOR HER ALWAYS RANKING ME DOWN AND FORGIVE HOW MUCH I ENJOYED IT.

ALSO THANK YOU FOR MY 100% IN EXTRA-CREDIT SPELLING ESPECIALLY ON THE WORD TONSILLECTOMY. AMEN.

AND THEN THERE ARE GENTLE PEOPLE LIKE FREDDIE WHO GETS PUSHED AROUND, LOVES NATURE, ALL NATURE, EVEN GREENISH MOLD ON WHITE BREAD.

DEAR OUR FATHER PLEASE REVEAL TO ME THE SECRETS OF FUNGI ESPECIALLY WHERE I MAY FIND SPECIMENS OF STINKHORN, WITCHES BUTTER AND CRAMP BALLS. IT'S FOR A PROJECT.

AMEN. OH. P.S. ALSO THAT GIRL LOUISE IS STILL SOCKING ME IN THE STOMACH WHEN NO ONE IS LOOKING REMEMBER I MENTIONED HER?

AND TOO THERE ARE THE BACKGROUND PEOPLE. THE ONES LIKE ME WHO ARE JUST NATURALLY SEE-THROUGH EXCEPT SOMETIMES TO DOGS. MAINLY I THANK GOD FOR DOGS.

ALL OF THEM. INCLUDING BIG FEROCIOUS, TINY YAPPY, MIXED, PURE, OLD, SMELLY, SLOW, FAST, ANY, ALL, EVERY.

THANK YOU! YOU KNOW WHY FROM YOU KNOW WHO.

AMEN.

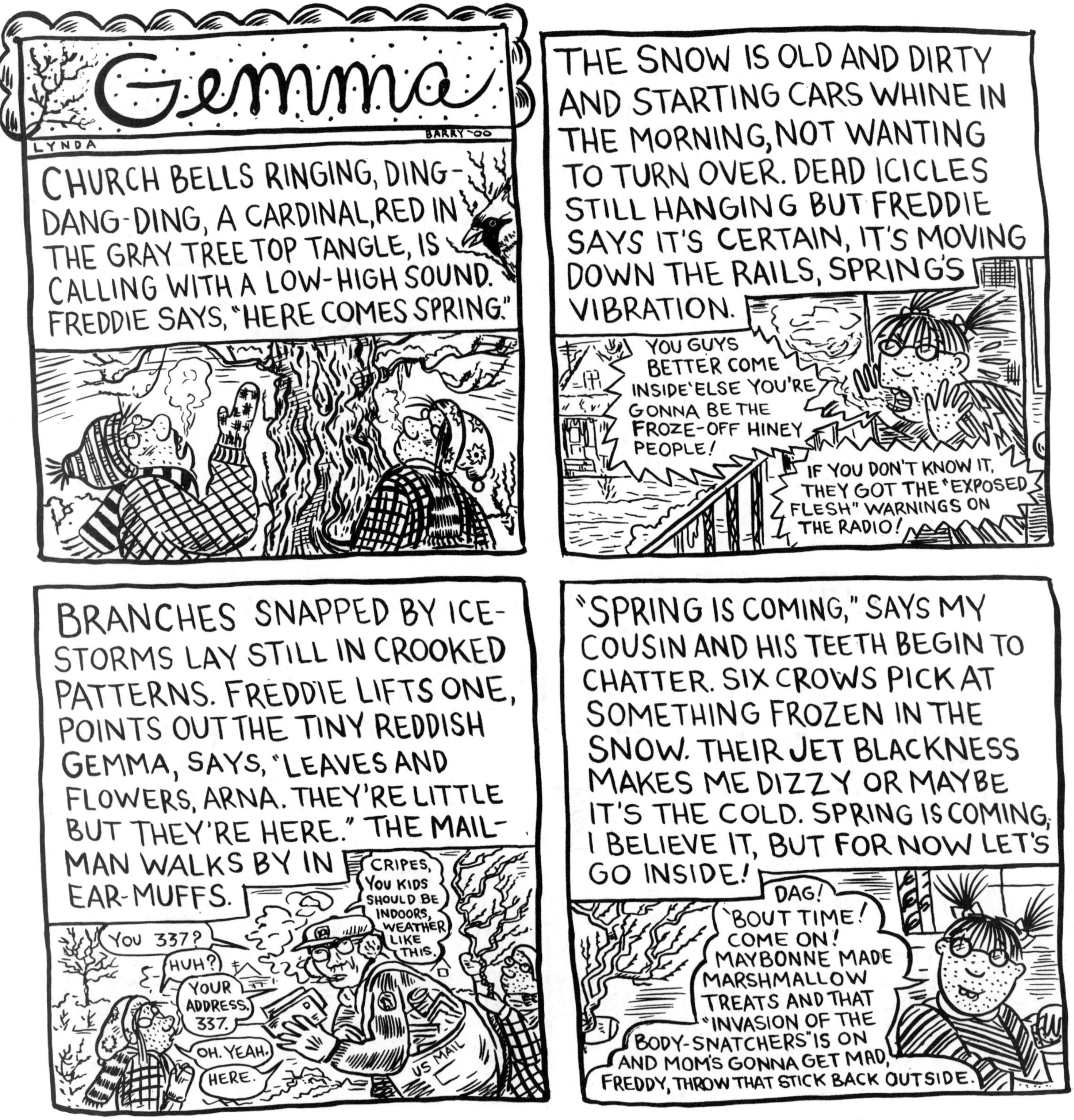

Gemma
LYNDA BARRY '00
CHURCH BELLS RINGING, DING-DANG-DING, A CARDINAL, RED IN THE GRAY TREE TOP TANGLE, IS CALLING WITH A LOW-HIGH SOUND. FREDDIE SAYS, "HERE COMES SPRING."
THE SNOW IS OLD AND DIRTY AND STARTING CARS WHINE IN THE MORNING, NOT WANTING TO TURN OVER. DEAD ICICLES STILL HANGING BUT FREDDIE SAYS IT'S CERTAIN, IT'S MOVING DOWN THE RAILS, SPRING'S VIBRATION.
YOU GUYS BETTER COME INSIDE 'ELSE YOU'RE GONNA BE THE FROZE-OFF HINEY PEOPLE!
IF YOU DON'T KNOW IT, THEY GOT THE "EXPOSED FLESH" WARNINGS ON THE RADIO!
BRANCHES SNAPPED BY ICE-STORMS LAY STILL IN CROOKED PATTERNS. FREDDIE LIFTS ONE, POINTS OUT THE TINY REDDISH GEMMA, SAYS, "LEAVES AND FLOWERS, ARNA. THEY'RE LITTLE BUT THEY'RE HERE." THE MAIL-MAN WALKS BY IN EAR-MUFFS.
CRIPES, YOU KIDS SHOULD BE INDOORS, WEATHER LIKE THIS.
YOU 337?
HUH?
YOUR ADDRESS. 337.
OH. YEAH.
HERE.
US MAIL
"SPRING IS COMING," SAYS MY COUSIN AND HIS TEETH BEGIN TO CHATTER. SIX CROWS PICK AT SOMETHING FROZEN IN THE SNOW. THEIR JET BLACKNESS MAKES ME DIZZY OR MAYBE IT'S THE COLD. SPRING IS COMING, I BELIEVE IT, BUT FOR NOW LET'S GO INSIDE!
DAG! 'BOUT TIME! COME ON! MAYBONNE MADE MARSHMALLOW TREATS AND THAT "INVASION OF THE BODY-SNATCHERS" IS ON AND MOM'S GONNA GET MAD, FREDDY, THROW THAT STICK BACK OUTSIDE.

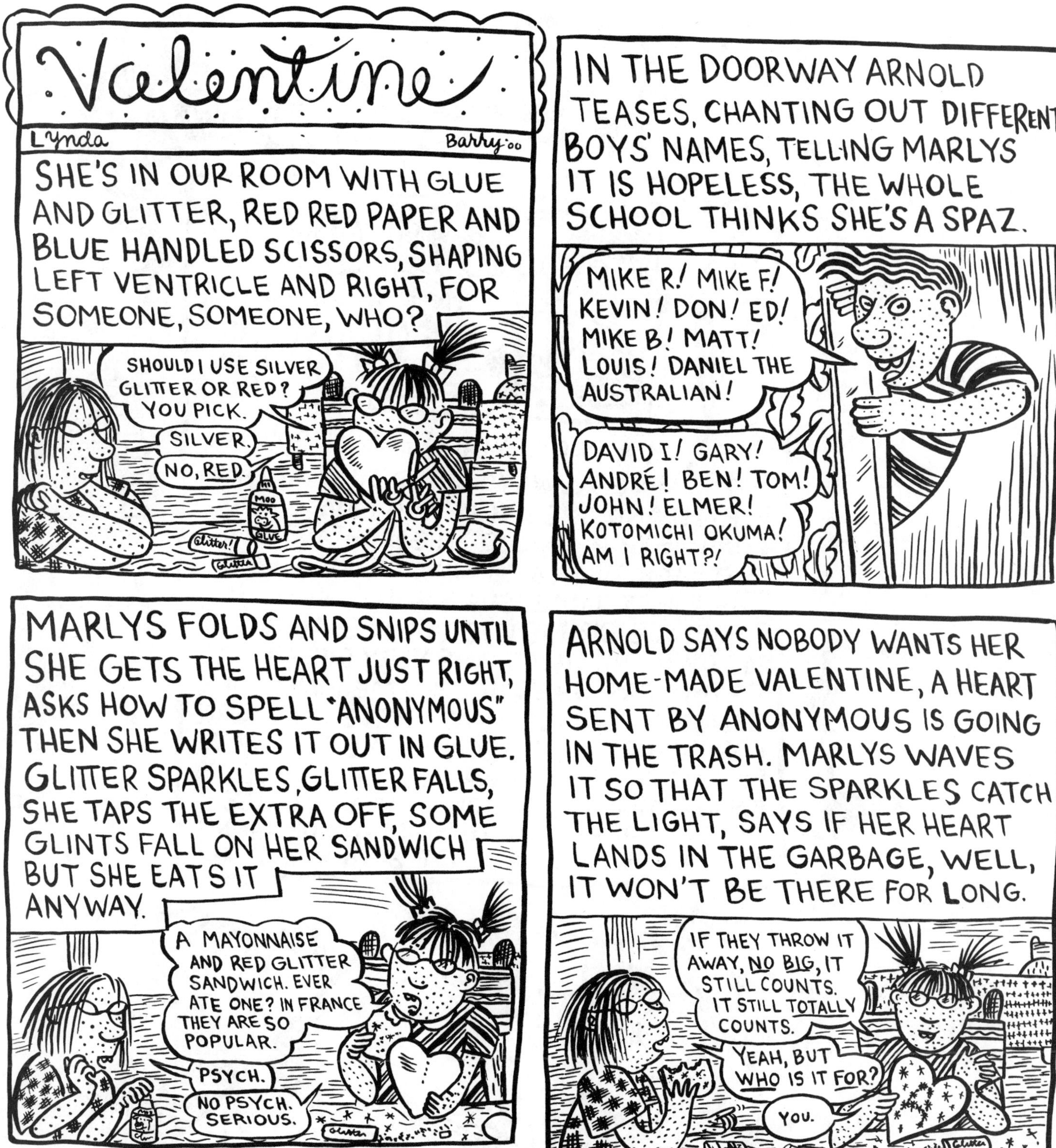
Valentine
Lynda Barry '00
SHE'S IN OUR ROOM WITH GLUE AND GLITTER, RED RED PAPER AND BLUE HANDLED SCISSORS, SHAPING LEFT VENTRICLE AND RIGHT, FOR SOMEONE, SOMEONE, WHO?
SHOULD I USE SILVER GLITTER OR RED? YOU PICK.
SILVER.
NO, RED.
IN THE DOORWAY ARNOLD TEASES, CHANTING OUT DIFFERENT BOYS' NAMES, TELLING MARLYS IT IS HOPELESS, THE WHOLE SCHOOL THINKS SHE'S A SPAZ.
MIKE R.! MIKE F! KEVIN! DON! ED! MIKE B! MATT! LOUIS! DANIEL THE AUSTRALIAN!
DAVID I! GARY! ANDRÉ! BEN! TOM! JOHN! ELMER! KOTOMICHI OKUMA! AM I RIGHT?!
MARLYS FOLDS AND SNIPS UNTIL SHE GETS THE HEART JUST RIGHT, ASKS HOW TO SPELL "ANONYMOUS" THEN SHE WRITES IT OUT IN GLUE. GLITTER SPARKLES, GLITTER FALLS, SHE TAPS THE EXTRA OFF, SOME GLINTS FALL ON HER SANDWICH BUT SHE EATS IT ANYWAY.
A MAYONNAISE AND RED GLITTER SANDWICH. EVER ATE ONE? IN FRANCE THEY ARE SO POPULAR.
PSYCH.
NO PSYCH. SERIOUS.
ARNOLD SAYS NOBODY WANTS HER HOME-MADE VALENTINE, A HEART SENT BY ANONYMOUS IS GOING IN THE TRASH. MARLYS WAVES IT SO THAT THE SPARKLES CATCH THE LIGHT, SAYS IF HER HEART LANDS IN THE GARBAGE, WELL, IT WON'T BE THERE FOR LONG.
IF THEY THROW IT AWAY, NO BIG, IT STILL COUNTS. IT STILL TOTALLY COUNTS.
YEAH, BUT WHO IS IT FOR?
YOU.

ABOUT the AUTHOR

I'M A DOG LOVING PERSON, BORN IN 1956. I'VE ALWAYS LIKED TO DRAW AND WRITE, AND ONE DAY IN 1986 I MADE THE COMIC STRIP CALLED "THE NIGHT WE ALL GOT SICK" WHERE I SAW MARLYS FOR THE FIRST TIME. SHE'S HAD A HUGE INFLUENCE ON ME EVER SINCE. ALTHOUGH MY OWN CHILDHOOD WAS VERY DIFFERENT FROM HERS, SHE'S HELPED ME MAKE SOME SENSE OF THINGS THAT I NEVER HAD WORDS FOR BEFORE. SHE BECAME THE IMAGINARY FRIEND I'D ALWAYS WANTED. I HOPE YOU ENJOY THIS COLLECTION OF HER STORIES. I'M SO HAPPY TO HAVE SO MANY OF THEM ALL IN ONE PLACE AT LAST. Lynda Barry